Pro Windows Phone App Development

Rob Cameron

Apress®

Pro Windows Phone App Development

ISBN-13 (pbk): 978-1-4302-3936-9

ISBN-13 (electronic): 978-1-4302-3937-6

President and Publisher: Paul Manning
Lead Editor: Jonathan Hassell
Development Editor: Matthew Moodie
Technical Reviewer: Robert Garrett
Editorial Board: Steve Anglin, Mark Beckner, Ewan Buckingham, Gary Cornell, Morgan Ertel, Jonathan Gennick, Jonathan Hassell, Robert Hutchinson, Michelle Lowman, James Markham, Matthew Moodie, Jeff Olson, Jeffrey Pepper, Douglas Pundick, Ben Renow-Clarke, Dominic Shakeshaft, Gwenan Spearing, Matt Wade, Tom Welsh
Coordinating Editors: Debra Kelly and Jennifer L. Blackwell
Copy Editor: Jim Compton
Compositor: Apress Production (Christine Ricketts)
Indexer: SPI Global
Artist: SPI Global
Cover Designer: Anna Ishchenko

Distributed to the book trade worldwide by Springer Science+Business Media New York, 233 Spring Street, 6th Floor, New York, NY 10013. Phone 1-800-SPRINGER, fax (201) 348-4505, e-mail orders-ny@springer-sbm.com, or visit www.springeronline.com.

For information on translations, please e-mail rights@apress.com, or visit www.apress.com.

Apress and friends of ED books may be purchased in bulk for academic, corporate, or promotional use. eBook versions and licenses are also available for most titles. For more information, reference our Special Bulk Sales–eBook Licensing web page at www.apress.com/bulk-sales.

Any source code or other supplementary materials referenced by the author in this text is available to readers at www.apress.com. For detailed information about how to locate your book's source code, go to www.apress.com/source-code/.

To my beautiful wife, Ally, whose love and patience is unending,
and to my lovely daughters Amanda and Anna, who make me so proud every day.

—Rob

Contents at a Glance

Contents

About the Author

 Rob Cameron Employed by Microsoft since 2001, Rob Cameron is an Architect Evangelist with Microsoft Corporation based out of Atlanta, Georgia. As part of Microsoft's Developer & Platform Evangelism team, Rob focuses on development tools and technologies targeting mobile devices, gaming, and embedded devices for telecommunications, cable, and media & entertainment companies. Rob has also worked on six books for Apress including authoring the latest *Pro Windows Phone App Development*. He has a master's degree in information technology management and a bachelor's degree in computer science. Visit Rob's blog at http://blogs.msdn.com/RobCamer.

About the Technical Reviewer

 Rob Garrett has worked with SharePoint since the early beta version of MOSS 2007 and has leveraged his talents for SharePoint architecture and design with Portal Solutions—a SharePoint consultant company in Rockville, MD. Rob has extensive background in .NET technologies and has developed software for Microsoft Frameworks since the early days of C++ and MFC. In pursuit of his career dreams, Rob left his birthplace in England for a journey to the United States on Thanksgiving Day 1999. Upon arrival, he enjoyed his first American meal from a gas station.

Acknowledgments

I would like to acknowledge the incredible support provided by the Apress team who patiently waited as I struggled to balance all the demands in my life the past year. Jonathan Hassell has been there with me through all of my books with Apress, and I sincerely appreciate his support. Debra Kelly has been a trooper prodding me along to keep this book on track with the help of Jennifer Blackwell through the final push.

Introduction

Authoring a book on mobile development with a title that starts with "Pro" is a daunting task. Put in too much introductory material, and you lose the knowledgeable developer looking to take his application to the next level. Breeze through key concepts, and the cross-platform professional mobile developer may struggle learning how to work with targeting a relatively new platform in Windows Phone.

Another challenge is culling down what to cover between Silverlight and the XNA Framework. Both are fabulous and interesting technologies so I strived to cover both in a single text, though this book is more geared toward Silverlight developers who are interesting in learning about the XNA Framework as well.

However, with the combination of Silverlight and XNA Framework rendering available in Windows Phone 7.5 and the Windows Phone OS 7.1 SDK, understanding XNA Framework development becomes even more relevant to Silverlight developers, and vice versa. Consider the airlines demo Microsoft showed off at MIX 11, where you can navigate a 3D rendering of the airplane to pick your seat, and you can see the amazing possibilities available with Shared Graphics Rendering.

This book provides a comprehensive overview of XAML and Silverlight since it is a critical aspect of Windows Phone development. It also focuses on many of the more challenging topics such as correctly architecting Silverlight for Windows Phone applications using the Model-View-ViewModel architecture as well as working with services, encryption, and gestures.

There are many tidbits throughout this book extracted from many long hours of working with top media brands to bring their content and applications to Windows Phone. I hope that sharing this knowledge of memory and CPU optimization gleaned from these experiences helps to bring your applications to the top of the rankings in the Windows Phone marketplace.

This update includes extensive coverage of new features available to developers on Windows Phone, including programming new sensors such as the Compass, Gyroscope, Camera, and Motion sensors. I also cover the new API enhancements available with Silverlight 4 compatibility as well as the extensive improvements in phone integration such as contacts and calendar integration.

Who This Book Is For

If you are an existing Silverlight developer, this book will provide details on how to leverage your Silverlight skills for Windows Phone. If you are a mobile developer looking to port an existing application to Windows Phone, then this book will give you the information you need, covering the core concepts and techniques fundamental for Silverlight for Windows Phone development.

Having an understanding of the .NET Framework will help, but if you are an experienced developer new to the .NET Framework, you will still be able to learn Windows Phone development using this book because much of the development is in the XAML markup language as well as in code.

■ **Note** You still may want to grab a C# programming text, such as Adam Freeman's *Introducing Visual C# 2010* (Apress, 2010) if you are not confident with C#.

The example code in this book is written in C#. However, much of the development is in XAML, not in C#, so if you are a VB.NET developer, the markup is almost exactly the same. For the examples that do include C# code in the code-behind, the code translates pretty easily, as the .NET Framework for Silverlight for Windows Phone is language agnostic.

How This Book Is Structured

This book consists of chapters that focus on individual topic areas of Windows Phone and is intended to be read in the order in which it is written; however, I strive to point to related sections in other chapters so if you need to skip ahead to a specific topic feel free to do so.

I spend a bit more time on Silverlight than the XNA Framework, but both are covered throughout the book. Chapter 1 starts with an introduction to the Windows Phone Platform, the AppHub marketplace, and Silverlight, and it concludes with a detailed introductory sample on the XNA Framework. Chapter 2 focuses exclusively on Silverlight UX development. Chapter 3 covers input, leveraging examples both for Silverlight and the XNA Framework. With the fundamentals for professional development on Windows Phone out of the way, Chapter 4 covers data persistence and the network programming model with Silverlight. It covers the new and exciting features available such as local database as well as Fast Application Switching, which end-users will love.

Chapter 5 covers integration with the Windows Phone platform, starting with coverage of how to obtain device and network information. It also covers launchers and chooser Tasks, including the new BingMapsDirectionsTask and BingSearchTask objects, which enables amazing functionality with just a few lines of code in your applications. Chapter 5 also includes coverage of the new alarm and reminder APIs as well as contacts and calendar integration. Chapter 6 covers advanced UI development, including extensive coverage of MVVM development, the Silverlight toolkit for Windows Phone, and the new RichTextBox control available in Windows Phone OS 7.1.

Chapter 7 builds on the MVVM coverage in Chapter 6, adding coverage for typical scenarios that you can extend to enable well-architected Windows Phone apps. Chapter 7 also covers App Connect, which enables integration with the pictures hub, music+video hub, and Bing Search integration.

Chapter 8 dives in deep on XNA Framework development for 2D applications, building on the introductory sample from Chapter 1. It includes coverage of how to leverage the Game Management sample from AppHub to create a professional-looking application. Chapter 8 also includes coverage of the new Shared Graphics Programming model where Silverlight and XNA Framework can render together. Chapter 9 starts off with adding polish to the Chapter 8 2D game development sample, covering saving and load as well supporting tombstoning in XNA. A simple particle system is added to the 2D game to add explosions. The game is also migrated to take advantage of shared graphics for menus. Chapter 9 then delves into the world of 3D game development, covering working with primitives and models in 3D. It also shows how to use the new Camera and Motion sensor to render a 3D object in space, which can enable interesting 3D Augmented Reality experiences.

Chapter 10 rounds out the book with additional coverage of MVVM and how to integrate globalization and localization so that you can expand the market for your applications. Chapter 10 also covers the Tile API, background processing, and push notifications.

Prerequisites

You will need a version of Visual Studio 2010, with Service Pack 1 of Visual Studio 2010 applied. You will also need to install Windows Phone Developer Tools, available here:

http://create.msdn.com/en-us/home/getting_started

You will want to download the Silverlight Toolkit for WP7, available here:

http://silverlight.codeplex.com

I also highly recommend that you review the Design Resources for Windows Phone, available here:

http://msdn.microsoft.com/en-us/library/hh202915(v=VS.92).aspx

Downloading the Code

The code is available in zip file format in the Source Code/Download section of the Apress web site. Please review the readme.txt for setup instructions.

Contacting the Author

To reach the author, please go to his blog and click the Email link to send him an email:

http://blogs.msdn.com/RobCamer

CHAPTER 1

■ ■ ■

Introduction to Windows Phone and Marketplace

Windows Phone, updated in Windows Phone 7.5, presents an exciting opportunity for developers to build and monetize mobile applications. It represents a major new investment into mobile computing by Microsoft, and in many ways is a major break from the past. To build applications for Windows Phone, it is important to understand its target consumer audience and design philosophy.

Up until roughly 2007, Windows Mobile was a growing, well-received platform targeting primarily enterprise users. Windows Mobile was taking share from competitors such as Palm and going head-to-head with RIM Blackberry, but overall it was considered fairly successful. The release of the iPhone and its consumer focus and applications store it turned the mobile device market on its head, and was a major wake-up call for Microsoft. Tack on the surge by Google's Android operating system, and the Smartphone market became hyper-competitive.

Windows Phone represents a sea change in approach by Microsoft toward mobile computing. Although Windows Mobile 6.x and earlier resembles a miniaturized version of desktop Windows, with its iconic Start screen, Windows Phone is very different with a user interface that is more similar to the ZuneHD interface – on steroids.

When the ZuneHD was introduced, it received positive feedback from critics, but it wasn't highly marketed toward consumers. It also did not have a third-party application Marketplace. Still, it was an opportunity for Microsoft to try out new mobile computing concepts on a mass audience of a few million users.

Learning from its own stumbles, taking what works from Zune, and then looking at the existing mobile landscape, Microsoft came up with Windows Phone with a dramatically different user experience from Windows Mobile, a new mobile development paradigm, and a completely different approach in the market.

With Windows Phone, Microsoft makes the end-user consumer the top priority, whereas in the past, with Windows Mobile, the original equipment manufacturer (OEM) was Microsoft's primary customer. This does not mean that Microsoft is OEMing the device directly. Instead, Microsoft spec'd out the hardware and software for the platform such that OEMs can take that specification as a basis for further innovation. OEMs can build devices with or without a keyboard, or with slightly different physical sizes, different screen types, and additional features like a camera and more storage, to name a few options.

Windows Phone devised have an 800 • 480 screen resolution, the exact same user interface and APIs, and the same range of sensors no matter what the OEM or Mobile Operator. This means that developers can build an application and be confident that it will run on all available devices.

1

> ■ **Note** Microsoft has stated that it may add a new screen resolution in the future and will provide guidance and tooling to ease development and ensure applications can run on all screens.

New Windows Phone 7.5 devices can include a Gyroscope sensor and s compass sensor available via APIs. I cover hardware in more detail later in the chapter. This may make you nervous as a developer, but the Windows Phone product team provides a software layer in the "Motion Sensor" that abstracts out the lack of Gyroscope hardware in Windows Phone RTM devices. I cover the Motion Sensor in more detail in Chapter 3 and Chapter 9.

From a software standpoint, the programming model for Windows Phone is very different from Windows Mobile. With Windows Mobile, developers created applications with either C++ or .NET Windows Forms via the .NET Compact Framework. For Windows Phone, the available programming models are Silverlight and the XNA Framework. In Windows Phone 7, Silverlight and the XNA Framework could call non-visual APIs. Windows Phone 7.5 includes "Shared Graphics," which allows Silverlight and XNA Framework graphics, which is covered in Chapter 9.

I cover the new software and capabilities in more detail in the following sections, but first let's answer the question of why develop for Windows Phone.

Why Should I Care?

As a developer, you may wonder whether you should invest in building applications for Windows Phone. The answer is "yes!" Windows Phone offers unique application features and integration to developers, allowing you to build amazing user experiences. I cover more on that in the next section as well as Marketplace, but let's first discuss market potential.

Smartphone Growth and the Nokia Partnership

The mobile phone has become a major computing platform, experiencing incredible growth. As I write this, Smartphone shipments make up approximately 10% of the mobile phone market worldwide, which includes feature phones, etc. It is expected that the share of Smartphone devices will grow to 70% of the market over the next three or four years.

Much of the growth potential is still ahead. A new or remade player in the market, such as Android and Windows Phone, can come on to the scene and capture the imagination of both developers and consumers with the right level of marketing and engineering commitment. Android has become a major player in the market along with iOS. Windows Phone is set to become a major player as well with the partnership with Nokia, a worldwide leader in the Smartphone market. The partnership demonstrates Microsoft's commitment to move into the market.

With the Nokia partnership, Nokia has committed to building phones based on the Windows Phone operating system. Nokia brings a world-class organization, a worldwide retail presence, and amazing hardware engineering to Windows Phone.

Nokia announced that it will launch its Windows Phone in six European nations in 2011, increasing the worldwide development opportunity for Windows Phone developers, given Nokia's strong presence worldwide.

In March of 2011, IDC predicted that Windows Phone will overtake iPhone and BlackBerry by 2015 (`http://seattletimes.nwsource.com/html/technologybrierdudleysblog/2014627927_idc_windows_phone_to_overtake.html`).

In April 0f 2011, Gartner predicted Windows Phone will overtake Blackberry in 2013 and will overtake iPhone in 2015 (`http://wmpoweruser.com/gartner-predicts-windows-phone-7-will-overtake-blackberry-in-2013-overtake-iphone-in-2015/?utm_source=twitterfeed&utm_medium=twitter`).

While these are third-party predictions, it is a decisive break from previous predictions regarding Windows Mobile. Time will tell how this story unfolds, but there is no doubt that the Nokia partnership is a major upheaval of the Smartphone marketplace in favor of Windows Phone. As a developer you do not want to miss out on this worldwide opportunity and market.

The Mobile Market

The Smartphone segment of the mobile device market is expected to continue significant double-digit growth in the foreseeable future. This growth stems from new users purchasing devices as well as existing function phone and feature phone users moving to Smartphones. Despite the hype, it is way too early to suggest that one platform or another has "won" the Smartphone war. There is plenty of new growth to be had in the market before competing platforms will need to focus on taking share from one another.

Take Android as an example. It has stormed onto the market and has outsold iOS devices so far in 2011. Regarding Windows Phone, Microsoft CEO Steve Ballmer claims that his company is "all-in" with respect to commitment to the mobile market and Windows Phone. The partnership with Nokia announced in early 2011 demonstrates the high-level of commitment and desire needed to bring a robust third ecosystem to market.

In describing my perspective on what Windows Phone means to Microsoft, I like to use an analogy. When Microsoft first introduced the Xbox game console, the general consensus in the market was that the Sony PlayStation had "won" the market and there was no way the Xbox could catch up. Today, I don't think anyone would question Microsoft's investment or commitment with respect to the Xbox 360. Likewise, who would have guessed that Nintendo would have made a comeback like it did with the Wii? Competition is a wonderful thing for consumers. Expect even more competition and dynamism in the mobile device market!

Current Microsoft Developers

If you are an existing .NET Framework, Silverlight, or XNA Game Studio developer, you are well on your way to having the skills needed to create great Windows Phone applications. However, there are many unique aspects to mobile device development, as well as features that are specific to Windows Phone, that require new skills. This book will present to you the information you need to bring your existing skills to bear on this new and exciting platform and to build great mobile application experiences.

▓ **Note** Windows Phone development initially supported C# only at launch. Since launch, Microsoft has added support for Visual Basic .NET development for both Silverlight applications and XNA Framework game development.

If you are new to Silverlight and XNA Game Studio, I spend time in this chapter introducing you to the basic concepts in these technologies to get you started. Combine this chapter with the online references available, and you will have the necessary foundation to proceed with the rest of this text. If you are an experienced Silverlight developer, you can skip Chapter 2 and parts of Chapters 4 and 5 that cover topics familiar to Silverlight developers.

If you are an existing Windows Mobile developer, you have a great depth of understanding of .NET and deep knowledge of mobile development considerations as well. This book will help you bring your existing knowledge to Silverlight and XNA Game Studio so that you can port your existing applications to Windows Phone.

Non-Microsoft Developers

If you are an existing mobile developer on another platform, this book will help you bring your mobile development skills to bear on Windows Phone. Windows Phone applications are written in C#, which is similar to the Java language and has roots in C, so many of the language constructs will be straightforward. For additional information on C# in general, check out the Apress title *Beginning C# 2010: From Novice to Professional*, Second Edition, by Adam Freeman.

It is challenging to write a "Pro" book and not cover some of the fundamentals. It is for this reason that I spend an entire chapter on Silverlight development to quickly help experienced mobile developers who are new to Silverlight to get started. Don't worry, though, there are plenty of advanced topics to help you build a world-class application.

Windows Phone Platform Overview

In this section, I provide an overview of the design philosophy behind Windows Phone. I also cover the available development model to familiarize you with underlying platform architecture and developer capabilities.

Phone Design Philosophy

When Microsoft introduced Windows Phone, its executives spoke about "integrated experiences" and "smart design." Without a doubt, Windows Phone presents a unique user interface as compared to other current Smartphone operating systems, as shown in Figure 1–1.

Figure 1–1. *Windows Phone Start screens*

The Windows Phone Start screen presents a lot of information in a clear fashion. Information and content is presented in a straightforward, easy to navigate manner without distraction. Controls have a minimalistic feel, allowing the user to focus on the content. Your applications should take the same approach.

Also shown in Figure 1–1 are several top-level tile icons pointing to the built-in "hubs," such as the People, Office, Pictures, Zune, Marketplace, and Xbox LIVE hubs. The hubs are the built-in, top-level panoramic experiences, meaning they scroll left and right to present content in a rich fashion. Figure 1–2 shows the pictures hub. Notice that the focus is on the content, not "chrome."

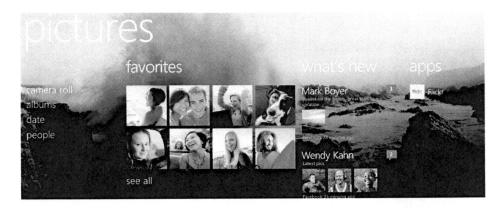

Figure 1–2. *Windows Phone pictures hub Panorama experience*

Figure 1–2 shows a wide view of the full user interface width of the Panorama experience. A user swipes left and right to view content in addition to scrolling up and down on each viewable section. Hubs provide an integrated view on data. For example, if you register an Exchange, Facebook, Twitter, LinkedIN, and Windows Live account, photos from social networks are pulled together into a single integrated view under "what's new" in the pictures hub. Photos from the camera roll are shown as well as applications that work with the pictures hub such as Flickr and Photobucket. This allows the user to explore images from all sources as well as know which applications can enhance the picture hub experience.

The Panorama control is a single page for all Panorama panes. There is a little bit of "peek" on the right that shows the next Panorama pane to indicate that you should swipe left or right with only a single heading visible at any time. In addition to Panorama, the other major navigation paradigm is called Pivot Outlook on Windows Phone, and it uses a *Pivot* control as the main landing page. The Pivot control is virtualized, designed to display large amounts of data. The Pivot shows multiple headers to indicate that you should swipe left and right, and it does not have the "peek" like the Panorama. Figure 1–3 shows an example Pivot interface running in the Emulator.

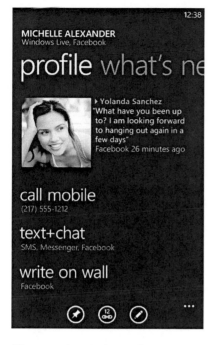

Figure 1–3. *Windows Phone Pivot experience*

In the application shown in Figure 1–3, the users touches the categories at the top, such as profile, what's new, and so on, to switch between lists of data. Selecting an item displays the details. The Pivot experience provides a great navigation experience for displaying large amounts of categorized or filtered data.

The Panorama and Pivot experiences are all part of the Metro UI design language, which is the underlying design approach for all of the Windows Phone built-in experiences. The controls available when developing for Windows Phone are skinned for Metro by default. You will see more of this in the "Silverlight Framework" section of this chapter.

Of course, you are not limited to Panorama or Pivot for application design and navigation. Windows Phone supports Pages as well for a details view of content. Most applications will support just one Panorama at most and then navigate to either a Pivot for a full list of content and then on to a Page to view content details. The key is to present a nice, clean information architecture to users.

I cover application user interface design in more detail in Chapter 3, but it is important to have an understanding of the platform philosophy up front in order to help you start to think about your application in terms of what it means to be a Windows Phone application. For more information on Windows Phone design philosophy, please check out the design resources available at `http://msdn.microsoft.com/en-us/library/ff637515%28VS.92%29.aspx,` or simply search for "design resources for Windows Phone" in your favorite Web search engine.

Hardware Capabilities

Unlike the iPhone or Blackberry, Microsoft does not produce the phone directly. Instead, Microsoft has chosen to continue to partner with mobile device OEMs in order to scale production and to promote differentiation. However, unlike with Windows Mobile 6.x and its predecessors, Microsoft has taken a more hands-on approach in specifying the underlying hardware such as chipset, CPU, GPU, Camera, Sensors, minimum memory, and so on, in addition to authoring many of the drivers.

■ **Note** Microsoft announced a major Windows Phone partnership with Nokia to produce Windows Phone devices. Predications are that this partnership will propel Windows Phone market share to 2nd or 3rd worldwide over the next couple of years.

OEMs are still free to innovate in terms of providing additional capabilities such as a physical keyboard, additional memory, and storage, but the underlying consistency ensures that applications work well across device manufactures, which greatly simplifies the efforts required of developers.

Every Windows Phone device has the following capabilities:

- Capacitive 4-point multi-touch screen
- DirectX 9 hardware acceleration
- Digital camera
- Accelerometer
- Assisted GPS
- Compass sensor (optional)
- Light sensor
- Proximity Sensor
- Gyroscope Sensor (optional for new Windows Phone 7.5 devices)

Windows Phone hardware includes a powerful ARM v7 "Cortex/Scorpion" CPU at launch and a Qualcomm MSM8655 in Windows Phone codename "Mango," a powerful NVidia Tegra GPU, a minimum of 256 MB of RAM, and 8 GB or more of flash storage. Windows Phone includes a large WVGA (800 × 480) display at launch.

At some point in the future Windows Phone will also be available with an HVGA (480 × 320) display to provide for additional hardware differentiation. Microsoft will provide tools and guidance to assist developers with creating applications that support both resolutions. However, as you learn more about Silverlight (XAML + .NET), you will be well on your way to correctly writing applications that work well on both resolutions.

For XNA Framework-based games, the Windows Phone's powerful hardware scaler can assist with scaling assets as needed, whether to allow sharing of assets with Xbox and PC versions of a game or to assist with scaling assets for the HVGA version of Windows Phone when it becomes available at some point after initial launch.

Software Capabilities

Windows Phone includes two programming models: the Silverlight and XNA Frameworks. With Windows Phone 7.5 Silverlight for Windows Phone jumps up to match the Silverlight 4 framework. Figure 1–4 illustrates the iconic breakdown shown by Microsoft when discussing the Windows Phone Application Platform at Mix, TechReady, and pretty much any other setting.

Figure 1–4. Windows Phone application platform

The upper left-hand corner of Figure 1–4 lists the two major programming models, Silverlight and XNA Framework, with the various integration points developers can take advantage of. Note that all of the underlying capabilities are accessible from either Silverlight or XNA Framework. All of these capabilities run inside the .NET Framework common language runtime in a sandboxed environment.

■ **Tip** The consumer brand name for Windows Phone codename 'Mango' is Windows Phone 7.5. The operating system name is Windows Phone OS 7.1, and the tools are Windows Phone OS 7.1 Developer Tools. I will refer to all three throughout the book, but they are the same platform/tools set.

The upper right-hand corner of Figure 1–4 lists the two primary tools you use to create Windows Phone applications, Visual Studio 2010 and Expression Blend 4. Visual Studio 2010 is the development tool most developers are familiar with already. XNA Game Studio sits inside of Visual Studio 2010 via a plug-in for game development.

A critically important tool listed in the upper right-hand corner is the Windows Phone Emulator. The Windows Phone Emulator is a virtual machine that allows developers to create applications and games without having a physical device. If you have a touch-enabled monitor, the emulator will pick up touch interactions as if running on a device.

With Windows Phone 7.5, the emulator now includes built-in location and accelerometer, which I cover in the next section

> ■ **Tip** Microsoft limits the Phone Emulator to a single processor and injects sleep events to better simulate actual device performance, but generally performance will be better in the emulator than on a device, because there are far more resources available on a desktop PC. It is therefore important to periodically test your application on a real device.

In Figure 1–4, the lower left-hand corner of the diagram represents code that you access in the cloud, such as notification services and location services that Microsoft provides, as well as custom-code you write to support your application such as web services, REST data, and so on.

The lower right-hand corner of in Figure 1–4 contains a reference to the tools that help you ship and promote your applications, primarily the Windows Marketplace for Mobile, or Marketplace for short.

Now that I covered a high-level overview of the application platform, let's dive into the programming models, Silverlight and XNA Framework. You build user experiences in Silverlight via Xml Application Markup Language (XAML) with a C# code-behind model with the .NET Framework. XAML is the serialization format of the UI elements added to the form. Since XAML is well-formed XML, it provides excellent tooling and validation support. It is also a namespace-based human-editable serialization format, allowing developers to easily modify XAML by hand.

The UI for Silverlight can be created in both Visual Studio and Expression Blend 4 for Windows Phone, though Expression Blend 4 can make some design operations such as animations and data binding much easier to code visually.

XNA Framework applications, on the other hand, are developed purely in C# or VB.NET code in Visual Studio, though there are third-party frameworks that can assist with game development through visually designing levels and the like Figure 1–5 provides a high-level breakdown of Silverlight vs. XNA Framework.

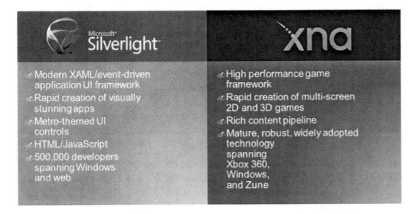

Figure 1–5. Windows Phone application programming frameworks

Both Silverlight and XNA Framework share the same application model built on top of the .NET Common Language Runtime (CLR) allowing access to libraries across frameworks. So, a Silverlight application can access the audio APIs available in XNA Framework. Likewise, an XNA Framework application can access remote server access APIs available Silverlight.

With Windows Phone 7.5 developers can also draw Silverlight and XNA to the same canvas, enabling 3D visualization in Silverlight applications as well as enabling XAML-based menus for XNA games. I cover the shared programming model in Chapter 9.

Windows Phone 7.5

The Windows Phone 7.5 update, previously codenamed "Mango," brings to Windows Phone 500 new features for consumers and more than 1,500 new APIs, new hardware with new sensors, and new tools for developers. The next couple of sections provide more detail on these features.

Consumer Features

Windows Phone 7.5 adds many new features for consumers to Windows Phone such as Threaded conversations called Threads. Threads allow a consumer to switch between texting, Facebook chat, and Windows Live Messenger all within the same conversation. Groups allow you to group contacts into personalized Live Tiles to see the latest status update and quickly send a text, email, or IM to the group right from the start screen.

In addition to Facebook, Windows Phone 7.5 now includes Twitter and LinkedIn social networks integrated into the people hub. Email now allows you to view multiple email accounts in one linked inbox. Also, all Office applications can now save data to SkyDrive. There are many other UI and feature improvements for end users, but I wanted to highlight some of the key features in the Windows Phone 7.5 update. In the next section, I highlight key developer features.

Developer Features

Windows Phone OS 7.1 and the Windows Phone OS 7.1 SDK include many new features that greatly increase the options a developer has to build unique and differentiated applications. Windows Phone OS 7.1 now includes multitasking that allows applications to run in the background while preserving battery life and performance. Fast app switching allows end users to quickly switch between apps without a full tombstone. I cover multitasking in Chapter 10.

App Connect allows applications to integrate with search results and hubs such as the music+videos hub and pictures hub. An example of search integration is if a user searches for movies, an application that shows movie times can register and be shown as part of the search results, offering unique opportunities to promote applications. App Connect is covered in Chapter 7. Here is a short list of additional features available for developers:

- *Background Agents*: Timed or on idle, live agents that update tiles, Background audio, and Background file transfer

- *Enhanced Phone Framework*: Allows access to phone data such as calendar and contacts

- Silverlight 4 compatibility including sockets

- More tasks and choosers, deeper access to user data, create alarms and reminders, etc.

- Performance improvements and new tools such as the improved emulator and the new profiler

- Local Database support

- Improved Push Notification and Live Tile experience with deep linking to application content

- Internet Explorer 9 for mobile with full support for HTML5

Windows Phone Developer Tools

The Windows Phone Developer Tools are a free download available from App Hub at http://create.msdn.com. The tools include Visual Studio 2010 Express for Windows Phone, XNA Game Studio 4, and Expression Blend 4 for Windows Phone – all you need in a single free download.

If you are currently a Visual Studio 2010 Professional or later developer, fear not – you will not lose access to all of your favorite features available in the Professional or later products. When you install the Windows Phone Developer Tools over Visual Studio 2010 Professional or later, the tool simply folds into the existing installation with no loss of functionality.

Download the tools from http://create.msdn.com and install the tools to prepare for the next two sections. The next section provides an overview of the Silverlight Tools and Framework. This book primarily focuses on building applications in Silverlight, but with Windows Phone 7.5 and "Shared Graphics," the lines are blurred between the frameworks. This is because Shared Graphics allows the Silverlight and XNA UI to be composited together on screen providing unique capabilities to Windows Phone. Therefore, the section following that one covers XNA Game Studio in detail to introduce Silverlight developers to the XNA Framework programming model.

Silverlight Tools and Framework Overview

In general, Silverlight is Microsoft's cross-web browser, cross-platform, and cross-device plug-in for delivering.NET Framework-based rich interactive applications for the Web and the Windows desktop. Silverlight has developed into a powerful programming model that consists of XAML + .NET capable of building everything from rich media applications like the NBC Olympics and CBS March Madness a few years ago to building mission-critical Line-Of-Business applications in corporations.

Silverlight for Windows Phone

Windows Phone brings the Silverlight programming model, XAML + .NET, to Windows Phone. Silverlight on Windows Phone 7.5 is based on Silverlight 4. There are some notable differences between Silverlight for the desktop and Silverlight for Windows Phone:

- Silverlight for Windows Phone applications are deployed via Marketplace on the device and via the Zune client. Silverlight applications are not deployed from the Web or side-loaded from a PC to Windows Phone.

- Silverlight for Windows Phone applications do not run in IE Mobile. Silverlight applications run directly on the phone via a host process in isolation from one another. If you are a Silverlight developer, you can think of it as a Silverlight out-of-browser application only – applications do not run in a browser.

- Some Silverlight Framework APIs are not applicable to Windows Phone. One example is the APIs that enable Silverlight in the web browser to communicate with the host browser. Because Silverlight does not run in the browser on Windows Phone, these APIs are not applicable.

- Silverlight for Windows Phone includes additional functionality to make underlying device capabilities available to developers such as the built-in sensors, tasks, and choosers to enable selecting a contact, send an SMS or email, and so on.

Despite these differences, the vast majority of the.NET Framework for Silverlight is compatible between Silverlight for the Web/desktop and Silverlight for Windows Phone.

Hello for Windows Phone

Now that you have a high-level overview of the application platform and programming model, let's dive a little bit deeper into Silverlight development with the Windows Phone Developer Tools. We start first with an overview of Visual Studio 2010.

Silverlight development was available in Visual Studio 2005 and 2008; however, support for Silverlight really shines in Visual Studio 2010, making it a first-class citizen development technology with great tooling support. I also provide a very high-level overview of Expression Blend, now in its fourth version and included as a free download for Windows Phone development as part of the Windows Phone Developer Tools.

Visual Studio 2010 Tour

Once you have the Windows Phone Developer Tools installed, fire up Visual Studio 2010 and select File New Project… to bring up the New Project dialog. Select Silverlight for Windows Phone on the left of the dialog and then select Windows Phone Application. Enter a name and location and then click OK to create it.

After the project is created, double-click on MainPage.xaml in the Solution Explorer tool window on the right to bring up the main application form or page. Figure 1–6 shows the UI with key items highlighted.

13

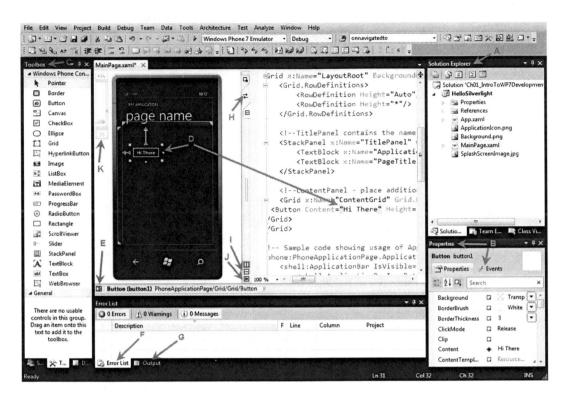

Figure 1–6. *Windows Phone Silverlight for Windows Phone design-time*

Table 1–1 explains the identified items in the figure. If you are an experienced .NET developer, some of these may be obvious to you, but other items may not be so familiar.

Table 1–1. *Visual Studio Silverlight Developer Tools*

Letter	Description
A	Solution Explorer tool window: Lists the projects and project files for the entire solution. Right-clicked enabled for those new Visual Studio, so you will want to explore. The toggle buttons at the top show/hide hidden files, refresh file lists, and provide short cuts so show the code or designer for a particular file.
B	Properties tool window: Lists the properties for the selected item in the designer or the item where the cursor is in the XAML markup file. Click the lightning bolt to switch to view the events for the selected object.
C	Toolbox tool window: Lists the controls available for drag-and-drop on to the designer.
D	The main area where designer and code files are viewed and edited. On the left is the Windows Phone designer view of the XAML code on the right. Notice the button that was dropped onto the designer. The areas point to both the design-time visualization of the button, as well as the XAML markup that actually defines the button. You can edit in either view and the changes are reflected in both views.
E	Document Outline tool window: Actually the button that displays the Document Outline as shown in Figure 1–7. It may not look like much but it presents the XAML markup, an XML tree, in a hierarchical view. As you design and develop your application, the nesting can be deep. When you select an item in the Document Outline, the focus shifts to that item for the Properties tool window. The Document Outline is an important part of your workflow to quickly find controls, modify properties, and so on.
F	When you build your project, errors show up in this tool window. Many times you can double-click on an error and it takes you to the correct line of code.
G	The Output tool window will show you what's going on during a build. It is also the window where Debug.WriteLine messages appear if you have them in your code.
H	Click this button to swap the sides where the Windows Phone designer view and the XAML view appear.
I	This arrow points to two buttons that position the Windows Phone design view and XAML view either side-by-side-or vertically.
J	Click this button to expand the Windows Phone designer to full screen.
K	Use this slider to Zoom the designer in size to fit your screen best or to drill in for more exact positioning of controls.

Figure 1–7 shows the Document Outline tool window. Once you start using it as part of your development workflow, you will find it invaluable for anything but the most trivial projects.

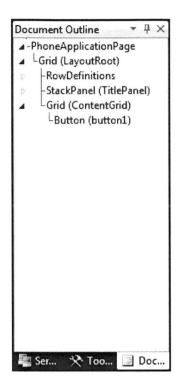

Figure 1-7. Document Outline tool window

Now that I have provided a quick tour of Visual Studio 2010 for Windows Phone development, let's dive in with some code. Add a button toward the top middle portion of the form. Double-click on the button to create the default event handler for the control, which is the Click event for a Button control. Doing so creates the following event handler that is edited to adjust the content for the button:

```
private void button1_Click(object sender, RoutedEventArgs e)
{
  (sender as Button).Content = "Hi There Reader";
}
```

We can reference the button by name, button1, created by default. In the above code, since the button1 is also the sender, we simply cast sender to button and set the Content property. A question you may be asking is how is the event handler associated with the Button object? The answer is via the XAML markup for button1, shown here:

```
<Button Content="Hi There" Height="72" HorizontalAlignment="Left" Margin="47,101,0,0"
Name="button1" VerticalAlignment="Top" Width="160" Click="button1_Click" />
```

All of the XAML was automatically generated when the control was dropped onto the designer surface except for the value configured in Content property and this line of code that associates the event handler in the MainPage.xaml.cs code-behind with the Click event for the control:

```
  Click="button1_Click"
```

You can also generate event handlers by editing XAML directly. Drag another button on to the design-surface below the first. Change the `Width` property to Auto for this button, more on that later. Next go to the markup and type `Click=` inside of the `<Button ...>` markup for the second `Button` control. Figure 1–8 shows the IntelliSense pop-up.

```
<!--ContentPanel - place additional content here-->
<Grid x:Name="ContentGrid" Grid.Row="1">
    <Button Content="Hi There" Height="72" HorizontalAlignment="L
    <Button Content="Button" Click=   Height="72" HorizontalAlign
</Grid>
</Grid>
```
`<New Event Handler>`
`button1_Click`

Figure 1–8. *XAML IntelliSense*

You can arrow up or down in the pop-up window shown in Figure 1–8 to select an existing event handler, or simply type **Tab** to generate a new event handler into the code-behind file named `button2_Click` by default. We copy the same code from the first event handler into the second event handler and click F5 or the green arrow in the toolbar in Visual Studio to run the application the emulator as shown in Figure 1–9.

Figure 1–9. *HelloSilverlight application in the emulator*

In Figure 1–9, the image on the left shows the initial state, and the image on the right shows the state after clicking both buttons. Notice that the text is clipped on the top button while the bottom button automatically expanded. Remember that when I added the second button the `Width` was set to `Auto`. By setting the `Width` to `Auto`, we rely on the Silverlight layout system to determine the appropriate width for the control. I cover the layout system in more detail in Chapter 2.

Expression Blend 4 for Windows Phone Tour

Expression Blend is a relatively new tool available from Microsoft. It was first introduced with Windows Presentation Foundation as the user experience design tool. I discussed XAML as part of the overview in this section and a little bit during the walkthrough in the previous section, but to reiterate, the UI Markup language for WPF and Silverlight is Xml Application Markup Language XAML, It has great tooling support provided in both Visual Studio and Expression Blend, which I cover here.

Expression Blend is positioned as a designer tool, more for a technical designer who takes mock-ups from Adobe Photoshop or another drawing tool and turns it into XAML. Expression Blend 4 can import from Adobe Photoshop as well as Adobe Illustrator files to help jumpstart from mock-up to XAML. Figure 1–10 shows the Expression Blend 4 UI with the `Ch01_IntroToWPDevelopment` solution open.

■ **Tip** If you are a designer, please check out the Windows Phone Design Resources available at `http://msdn.microsoft.com/en-us/library/ff637515(VS.92).aspx`. It includes design guidance as well as templates for Adobe Photoshop to help jumpstart Windows Phone design efforts.

Figure 1–10. *HelloSilverlight application in Expression Blend*

Figure 1–10 shows Expression Blend 4 with a simple project opened in order to provide an overview of the tool's major features. Table 1–2 provides a quick description of the lettered arrows.

Table 1–2. Expression Blend 4 Features

Annotation	Description
A	This is the designer surface, also known as the Artboard, which supports drag-and-drop editing.
B	Use this to zoom in or out of the designer surface as needed. Zoom out to see the entire application, or zoom in close to perform precise visual editing.
C	Tabs allow you to switch between the design surface, the XAML markup, or split view to see both the design surface and XAML.
D	These represent grid lines for laying out controls in the UI. When you move the mouse over the edge of the Grid control, the UI provides a visual cue that you can add a grid line.
E	This is the Properties window; here, several sections are collapsed so that they fit in the view.
F	The Resources window lists available resources such as styles and templates. I cover these resources throughout this book, particularly in Chapters 2, 4, and 6.
G	Clicking this chevron brings up the Asset Library, where you can search for a control if you are not sure what the icon is or whether it is visible. The Asset Library is similar to the Visual Studio toolbar area where controls are listed.
H	The little arrow in the lower right-hand corner under some of the controls shown in the Asset Library is a visual cue that related controls are available for quick access. Clicking and holding the arrow brings up a small window listing the related controls. Click a control and it becomes the visual control for that section of the Asset Library.
I	Clicking this button creates a new `Storyboard` object. You use storyboards to design animations. We talk more about storyboards later in this chapter.
J	This is the extremely useful Search text box. Type a property name, and Expression Blend 4 will search the list of properties available for the control and bring the property into view for easy access. Be sure to clear the Search text box when you've finished. Otherwise, it can be confusing when you switch objects and the filter entered in the Search text box does not apply, resulting in a blank properties window.
K	The XAML visual tree is listed in this area of Expression Blend 4. The yellow frame around the LayoutRoot control indicates that the LayoutRoot control is the active element. This means that double-clicking a control in the Asset Library will insert that control as a child to the LayoutRoot control. Double-clicking another control, such as the StackPanel, would make that one the active element and the insertion point for child controls dragged on the visual design surface.

Annotation	Description
L	New in Expression Blend 4, this extremely useful Search text box allows you to find project files quickly.
M	The Visual State Manager has an improved user interface in Expression Blend 4. More states for controls are displayed with a warning indicator when a property has been changed in more than one state group.
N	New in Expression Blend 4, the Assets tab provides fast access to project, controls, styles, behaviors, and effects assets in a nicely organized list.
O	The Data tab provides designers with the ability to create either a sample or live data source that makes it easier to design a data binding UI.

Expression Blend has many features that developers and designers will want to take advantage of, such as design-time data, animations, visual states, UI templates, and control templates.

This completes the quick overview of the Silverlight tools and programming model. I will cover user interface development in both Visual Studio and Expression Blend in more detail in Chapters 2 and 5.

As mentioned previously, with Windows Phone 7.5 developers can render a Silverlight and XNA Framework UI to create unique application experiences. To help introduce Silverlight developers to XNA Framework development, I spend a bit more time on XNA Game Studio development as part of this chapter to cover the fundamentals. I also cover the XNA Framework in Chapter 3 related to input and in Chapter 4 related to the programming model. Chapters 8 and 9 cover 2D game development, XNA Shared Graphics capabilities, and 3D game development to help professional developers understand how to get started with this great capability.

XNA Game Studio and Framework Overview

XNA Game Studio and game development with the Xbox LIVE Hub are major features of Windows Phone. The XNA Framework for Windows Phone is part of XNA Game Studio 4.0, which is a plug-in for Visual Studio 2010 that enables developers to create games for Windows, Xbox and Windows Phone.

The XNA Framework enables developers to write applications, primarily games, using managed .NET Framework code. The XNA Framework is consistent across the target platforms mentioned previously, allowing the developer to account for differences between input and display for the target platform.

Applications targeting a specific platform will have unique user input capabilities, such as the mouse and keyboard for the desktop, Xbox controller for Xbox and on the desktop if a USB controller is connected. For Windows Phone, the primary input is the touch screen and sensors. Otherwise, much of the code for a cross-platform game would be exactly the same.

Although Chapter 3 focuses on user input that applies to both Silverlight and the XNA Framework, this book has more chapters focused on Silverlight overall. Therefore, I would be remiss to not cover XNA Game Studio in this chapter to introduce you to XNA Framework development, especially with the ability to integrate Silverlight and XNA rendering now available in Windows Phone 7.5. To that end, this section will provide an XNA Game Studio overview to help provide background on the tools and a little bit on the platform. Chapters 9 and 10 are dedicated to XNA Game Studio, covering both 2D and 3D game development.

> ■ **Note** This book does not go into game development theory in heavy detail, because it is an incredibly broad topic that would consist of several courses at a university. You could easily purchase multiple books that cover an individual aspect of game development theory such as books completely focused on 3D math, game physics, artificial intelligence, game engine design, and so on. Instead I focus on providing an introduction to XNA Framework concepts including a game object model for game development in addition to advanced application development with shared graphics rendering in Windows Phone 7.5

What this book does provide you with is an understanding of the mechanics of game development so that you could port an existing game that you developed for another platform to Windows Phone, incorporate existing XNA Game Studio samples located at `http://create.msdn.com`, as well as apply game development theory obtained through additional reading into your own Windows Phone games.

Hello XNA for Windows Phone

When you install the Windows Phone Developer Tools it includes XNA Game Studio, with a dedicated template folder XNA Game Studio 4.0 in the Visual Studio 2010 New Project dialog to create either a Windows Phone game or a Windows Phone game library assembly.

All game development is done non-visually through code. You do not use Expression Blend to create games unless building the game experience in Silverlight. This makes the Emulator that much more important for XNA Framework game development. The good news is that the Windows Phone Emulator is hardware accelerated on the Windows Vista or Windows 7 development machine, enabling a great game development experience with the emulator to visually see the game in action without having to always deploy to a device. In the Windows Phone 7.5 tools update, the emulator now includes visual accelerometer simulation, which I demonstrate in Chapter 3.

> ■ **Tip** Several third-party game engines have ported their visual tools and frameworks to XNA Game Studio with support for Windows Phone. The App Hub partner link has more information here: `http://create.msdn.com/en-us/resources/partners`

In Visual Studio, let's create a new project and call it HelloXNA in our existing Chapter 1 code solution. Right-click on the solution explorer and select Add… New Project, select Windows Phone Game (4.0), and then type **HelloXNA** as the project name. Be sure to right-click on the new HelloXNA project and set it to the startup project for the solution if is not already.

After the project is created, you can see that the project layout is very different from a Silverlight project, as shown in Figure 1–11.

Figure 1–11. XNA Game Studio default project layout

Notice in Figure 1–11 there are actually two projects listed, `HelloXNA` and `HelloXNAContent`. The primary project with the output remains the HelloXNA project. The `HelloXNAContent` project is the content project for the `HelloXNA` project, which I cover in the next section.

Game Content

As noted in the previous paragraph, the content project is where the content is located – the sprites, textures, 3D models, and so on for the game. Sprites and textures generally refer to 2d images you move around the screen (sprites) and the background or surface image (textures). In our sample we create three simple .tga files to represent a background texture for the simple game, a spaceship sprite, and a hero ship sprite that the user controls and a missile sprite that is fired from the hero ship. Figure 1–12 shows the content project layout, as well as the properties for the hero ship sprite.

Figure 1–12. HelloXNAContent project files

Notice in Figure 1–12 that the heroship.tga image file has an AssetName, a `Content Importer` and `Content Processor` properties. The `Content Importer` and `Content Processor` property automatically selected when the content is added. Internally, the XNA Framework stores content assets in a custom compressed format so it uses content importers and processors to import external content into the internal format. XNA Game Studio ships with several built-in converters for common content listed here, with explanations for the less than obvious converters:

- Effect: DirectX High Level Shader Language (HLSL) .fx file (not supported on Windows Phone)
- AutoDesk FBX: .AutoDesk file format for three dimensional models
- Sprite Font Description
- MP3 Audio File
- Texture: Essentially a bitmap
- WAV Audio File
- WMA Audio File
- WMV Video File
- XACT Project: XACT is a DirectX audio tool for building rich game audio
- X File: DirectX 3D model file
- XML Content

You can create custom content importers as well as purchase third-party converters for file formats not available out of the box. However, in most cases the previous list supports the vast majority of content and content creation tools available.

The other property for content is the `AssetName`, which is based on the filename without the extension. When you load content into your game you load it via the `AssetName` property shortly.

Tip Make friends with a graphic artist if you are not very artistic. Content is just as important, if not more so then the coding in a game. There are third-party content providers that sell content you can tweak as well as higher graphic artist talent on a contractual basis. Programmer art won't cut it.

The Game Loop

Let's continue to explore the code and functionality in the `HelloXNA` project by exploring the default game loop code. When learning to build games, development centers on the game loop summarized here:

1. Load the game content and related objects.
2. Update the object's state.
3. Draw the object to the screen.

The XNA Framework provides a typical game loop development model consisting of initial content load, followed by repeated calls to the update, and draw methods. By default the XNA Framework game loop is fixed-step game loop at 30 frames per second with each frame represented by calls to draw and update. It is set to 30 frames per second (fps) to be aligned with the refresh rate of the hardware. You can change the frame rate to 60 fps using the following code:

```
GraphicsDeviceManager.SynchronizeWithVerticalRetrace = false;
game.TargetElapsedTime = FromSeconds (1/60f);
```

However, if you increase the frame rate, it will impact battery performance with possibly minimal tangible benefit. One way around this is to call update twice per each draw call by creating a custom game loop. This would be the recommended course of action over adjusting the frame rate above 30 frames per second.

Now let's dive in to the code. When we created the **HelloXNA** game project, it generates a code file Game1.cs, which is the main code file and includes the game loop logic. Listing 1–1 has the full code listing for reference.

Listing 1–1. *Generated Game1.cs*

```
using System;
using System.Collections.Generic;
using System.Linq;
using Microsoft.Xna.Framework;
using Microsoft.Xna.Framework.Audio;
using Microsoft.Xna.Framework.Content;
using Microsoft.Xna.Framework.GamerServices;
using Microsoft.Xna.Framework.Graphics;
using Microsoft.Xna.Framework.Input;
using Microsoft.Xna.Framework.Input.Touch;
using Microsoft.Xna.Framework.Media;

namespace HelloXNA
{
    /// <summary>
    /// This is the main type for your game
    /// </summary>
    public class Game1 : Microsoft.Xna.Framework.Game
    {
        GraphicsDeviceManager graphics;
        SpriteBatch spriteBatch;

        public Game1()
        {
            graphics = new GraphicsDeviceManager(this);
            Content.RootDirectory = "Content";

            // Frame rate is 30 fps by default for Windows Phone.
            TargetElapsedTime = TimeSpan.FromTicks(333333);
        }

        /// <summary>
        /// Allows the game to perform any initialization it needs to before starting to run.
```

```
/// This is where it can query for any required services and load any non-graphic
/// related content.  Calling base.Initialize will enumerate through any components
/// and initialize them as well.
/// </summary>
protected override void Initialize()
{
  // TODO: Add your initialization logic here

  base.Initialize();
}

/// <summary>
/// LoadContent will be called once per game and is the place to load
/// all of your content.
/// </summary>
protected override void LoadContent()
{
  // Create a new SpriteBatch, which can be used to draw textures.
  spriteBatch = new SpriteBatch(GraphicsDevice);

  // TODO: use this.Content to load your game content here
}

/// <summary>
/// UnloadContent will be called once per game and is the place to unload
/// all content.
/// </summary>
protected override void UnloadContent()
{
  // TODO: Unload any non ContentManager content here
}

/// <summary>
/// Allows the game to run logic such as updating the world,
/// checking for collisions, gathering input, and playing audio.
/// </summary>
/// <param name="gameTime">Provides a snapshot of timing values.</param>
protected override void Update(GameTime gameTime)
{
  // Allows the game to exit
  if (GamePad.GetState(PlayerIndex.One).Buttons.Back == ButtonState.Pressed)
    this.Exit();

  // TODO: Add your update logic here

  base.Update(gameTime);
}

/// <summary>
/// This is called when the game should draw itself.
/// </summary>
/// <param name="gameTime">Provides a snapshot of timing values.</param>
```

```
    protected override void Draw(GameTime gameTime)
    {
      GraphicsDevice.Clear(Color.CornflowerBlue);

      // TODO: Add your drawing code here

      base.Draw(gameTime);
    }
  }
}
```

Listing 1–1 is insightful reading to help you understand the game loop implementation in XNA Game Studio. The comments help you understand what to do where in the game loop code but we briefly cover the methods here starting with the constructor for `Game1` in Listing 1–1. The constructor initializes a reference to the `GraphicsDeviceManager`, which represents the graphics device. It also sets the content root directory to the `Content` folder, which is where all of our content will reside. Finally it sets the frame rate to 30 fps.

The `Initialize()` method is where developers query for required game services. Game services are objects defined by a custom Interface you create that you want to access for the entire life of the game. It is a way to expose an object, such as a 3D camera object, to many other objects. I demonstrate game services in Chapters 8 and 9.

I'm sure you can guess what the `LoadContent()` method does. It is called once per game with the idea that you load all of your content upfront so as to not impact the game loop timing by loading content on the fly in the middle of a frame.

For a game with a lot of content, this may not make the best use of resources. In this case, the game can be broken up into levels and a developer can dynamically load content at the start of each level. Users won't mind waiting a few seconds up front as the level loads, as long as the return is better game play during the level by pre-loading the content.

After loading the content in the `LoadContent` method, the next method in Listing 1–1 is the `UnLoad` method. While you have to explicitly load content in `LoadContent`, the opposite is not required. Any content that you load in the `LoadContent` method is automatically managed by XNA Framework. However, for any content that you load dynamically and that is not explicitly managed by a `ContentManager` object. An example object is a `DynamicVertexBuffer` that requires the `Dispose()` method to be called. Otherwise, content that is loaded by `ContentManager` will automatically be unloaded either when the game exits or if a developer manually removes a `GameComponent` object. A `GameComponent` is an XNA Framework feature that allows a developer to encapsulate a complex game object into the game loop in an object oriented way. I cover `GameComponents` in Chapter 9.

As mentioned, the `Update` and `Draw()` methods are the heart of the game loop. The default `Update` method checks to see if the user pushes the hard key Back button on the Windows Phone device. If so, the game exits. The other code calls `base.Update(gameTime` to allow the minimum game loop logic to occur. The `Update` method takes one parameter of type `GameTime`. The `GameTime` type contains a snapshot of game timing state that can be used by variable step (real time) or fixed-step (game time) games. The `GameTime` object has three properties all of type `TimeSpan`:

- `ElapsedGameTime`: The amount of time since the last call to the `Update` method.

- `IsRunningSlowly`: A Boolean value. If it has a value of `true`, this indicates that the `ElapsedGameTime` is running longer than the `TargetElapsedTime` for the game loop. The game should do something to speed up processing in the Update method such as reducing calculations; otherwise the game frame rate will potentially decrease by skipping calls to the `Draw` method.

- `TotalGameTime`: The amount of time since the start of the game.

Developers can use these values to perform game-related calculations, such as when a grenade object should explode after it was initially tossed, as an example.

When developing a game, always keep in mind that games, videos, movies, and so on all depend on tricking the human eye into believing that it is watching continue motion. In general, 30 fps is the minimum before the human eye starts to perceive that it is not watching continuous motion. I mentioned the two types of game loops, fixed-step and variable step. The type of game loop affects how a developer manages the user perception of motion, which we dig into in the next two sections.

Fixed-Step Game Loop

A fixed-step game loop tries to call its Update method at a regular interval, providing a fixed chunk of time for the developer to perform calculations in Update before drawing the scene. The fixed-step game loop is the default for XNA Framework. For the Xbox and Windows, the default frame rate is 60 fps in a fixed-step game loop, which means that Update is called every 1/60 of a second.

For Windows Phone, the default frame rate for a fixed-step game is 1/30 of a second, which aligns with the hardware screen refresh rate. Visually, a higher frame rate does not provide significant benefit, but it would impact battery life more.s

Based on this information, the value `TargetElapsedTime` from the `gameTime` parameter for `Update` (and `Draw`) will have a value of 1/30 of a second for the value of its `TimeSpan`. The `Update` and `Draw` methods are called every 1/30 of a second, unless `IsRunningSlowly` returns `true`. In that case, the call to `Draw` is skipped so that `Update` catches up, resulting in a reduced frame rate.

▦ **Note** When the game pauses in the debugger, the Update method is not called until the debugger resumes the game.

Variable-Step Game Loop

In this type of game, `Update` and `Draw` are called continuously without regard for the value set to the `TargetEllapsedTime` property resulting in a variable frame rate. With the fixed refresh rate for the screen of 30 fps, there may not be much gained by a viable-step loop without potentially negatively impacting battery performance.

Now that you have background on XNA Game Studio development, how content is loaded, and the game loop, let's dive in and create a simple game.

Implement the Game

In this section we start with the default game loop code generated when we created the HelloXNA project to create a simple space ship shooter game. Our game will be a simple top-down shooter where alien space ships attempt to strike the hero ship. The hero ship can shoot missiles at the alien ships to cause them to explode. Score is based on the number of alien ships blown up.

Now that we have an understanding of the game play, let's get started. We alternate between coding and background detail as we develop the game to explain key concepts. In the `Game1.cs` code file we declare four variables of type `Texture2D` named `HeroShip`, `SpaceShip`, `Missile`, and `BackgroundImage` that are initialized in the `LoadContent` method:

```
HeroShip = this.Content.Load<Texture2D>("Sprites/heroship");
SpaceShip = this.Content.Load<Texture2D>("Sprites/spaceship");
Missile = this.Content.Load<Texture2D>("Sprites/missile");
BackgroundImage = this.Content.Load<Texture2D>("Textures/background");
```

Since these assets are loaded by a `ContentManager` object, we do not need to worry about releasing the objects in the `UnloadContent` method. The `ContentManager` will take care of that for us when it goes out of scope.

Now that we loaded the content, we next cover modifications to the `Update()` and `Draw()` methods. We cover `Draw` first because we want to draw the background on the screen. To actually do the drawing to the graphics device you use a `SpriteBatch` object.

By default, the XNA Game Studio project template creates a member named `spritePatch` of type `SpriteBatch`. Within the `Draw` method, you first call `spriteBatch.Begin` then `spriteBatch.Draw` any number of times, and then `spriteBatch.End`. It is more efficient for the graphics hardware to draw to the back buffer as a batch and then draw to the back buffer to the device as opposed to drawing items one at a time directly to the graphics device. `SpriteBatch.Begin` method sets up the back buffer and the call to `SpriteBatch.End` indicates that the batch is ready to be drawn to the device.

```
spriteBatch.Begin();
spriteBatch.Draw(BackgroundImage,graphics.GraphicsDevice.Viewport.Bounds, Color.White);
spriteBatch.End();
```

Figure 1–13 shows the background image in the Emulator.

Figure 1–13. *Drawing the background in the Emulator*

The background is static for our simple game so we are finished with it. We covered `Begin` and `End` for the `SpriteBatch` class but not the `Draw` method, which has several overloads that look intimidating at first, taking rectangle objects, rotation, scale, etc.

All overloads of the `Draw` method have a couple of parameters in common in that all of the overloads take a `Texture2D` (the image to draw) and a position to draw it either in the form of a `Vector2` or a `Rectangle` object. I cover `SpriteBatch.Draw` in detail in Chapter 8, but we will cover the specific overloads we use to build the game as we go along. For the background image shown in Figure 1–13, we draw with this overload:

```
spriteBatch.Draw(BackgroundImage,graphics.GraphicsDevice.Viewport.Bounds, Color.White);
```

`BackgroundImage` is the `Texture2D` to be drawn. For the place to draw the texture, we pass in the Rectangle size of the entire screen, which is defined by `graphics.GraphicsDevice.Viewport.Bounds`. We could hard-code the values to be the shipping screen resolution of 800 × 480. However, we do not want to hardcode this value, because at some point in the future an additional screen resolution will be introduced that is 480 × 320. The last parameter in this `Draw` method overload allows you to tint `Texture2D` in a particular color. `Color.White` represents no tint at all.

Now let's shift over to the `Update` method. It is in the Update method where calculations are performed to determine where the alien ship, space ship, and missile should be drawn. In addition to the variable representing the sprite image, we also need variables to track the position and speed of the objects as well. First let's have a quick discussion on vectors.

When Windows Phone initially hits the market, the screen resolution is 800 pixels in height and 480 pixels in width. In XNA Framework, the 2D coordinate system puts 0,0 in the upper left hand corner of the screen with the positive X direction flowing to the right and positive Y direction flowing down the screen, as shown in Figure 1–14.

Figure 1–14. *The Windows Phone Portrait 2D Cartisian Plane*

■ **Note** The XNA Framework expects your game to appear in wide-screen or landscape mode by default. It is possible to build a game that runs vertically as well—I cover how in Chapter 8.

A Vector2 consists of an X and Y component that represents a direction and magnitude from the origin. As an example, since the screen is 480 pixels wide, the X axis represented as a Vector2 would have zero for the Y component, and 480 for the X component like this (480,0). Likewise, a Vector2 that represents the Y axis would have zero for the X component and 800 for the Y component like this (0,800).

A Vector2 can represent either a position or a speed. As a position, you set the X and Y component to be the values you want to place an object on the Cartesian plane. As an example, to place the upper left-hand corner of a sprite or image in the middle of the screen, you would set the sprites position to this value (240,400), which is half the screen width and height respectively.

■ **Tip** When you position a sprite, it is always relative to the upper left-hand corner of the sprite, which is considered (0,0) in terms of height and width for the sprite. If you don't take this into account and think you are positioning the center of a sprite, it will be off by half the height of the sprite toward the bottom and half the width of the sprite to the right.

Position is pretty straightforward in a 2D plane. Representing Speed as a Vector2 is similar except that the Vector2 is interpreted by its magnitude or length and direction. Imagine an arrow with its tail at position (0,0) and its head at (X,Y) such as (10,10) on a 2D plane, as illustrated in Figure 1–15.

Figure 1–15. *Vectors in a 2D plane*

If the imaginary Vector2 (0,10) represents a speed, it means that the object is moving straight down at 10 pixels per frame. If the Vector2 (10,10) represents a speed, it means that for each frame, the object is moving 10 pixels to the right and 10 pixels down. Figure 1–16 depicts a ball that has a position of (300, 160). A speed Vectors2 (50,50) is applied to the ball in a given frame.

31

Figure 1–16. *Applying speed to an object via vector addition*

Applying a speed of (50,50) redirects the ball to a southeastern direction in the plane, giving a new position of (350, 210) for the ball. We know this intuitively because X is positive to the right and Y is positive in the down position, so the Vector2 (50,50) moves the ball 50 pixels to the right and 50 pixels down. Note that we could just as easily have a speed of (-50, 50), which would intuitively move the ball to the southwest direction.

Now that you have a basic understanding of position and speed as **Vector2** objects, let's go back to the XNA Game Studio project. We will perform speed and position calculations in the **Update** method. We also need to check to see if an object has either collided with another object/sprite, or if the object collided with an edge of the screen.

If it an object collides with an object we can do several things. If the object is a golf club and the other object represents a golf ball, a developer would want to simulate the club connecting with the ball and send it flying in the opposite direction based on the ball and club **Vector2** position, the angle of impact. Another example action upon a collision is that if the collision is between an alien space ship and a missile fired from the player's space ship, the game could simulate an explosion and the alien space ship disappears from the screen.

Speaking of the player space ship, the other key component handed in the **Update** method is user input, which is also calculated using Vector2 objects. For Windows Phone user input can be in the form of a screen tap, a gesture, or the accelerometer as the major game input methods.

With the background on the screen coordinate system and Vector2D objects out of the way, you should have a pretty good idea of what the code will look like in the Update method in pseudo code:

- Handle User Input

- Apply User Input to objects

- Update Position of objects

- Detect Object and Edge Collisions

- Determine the final state and position of all objects

A key point to consider is that if the **Update** method takes too long the Game loop will decide to skip a call to the **Draw** method, resulting in dropped frames. Keep this in mind when writing code in the **Update** method.

▨ **Note** Performance considerations in game development are covered in more detail in Chapters 8 and 9.

Armed with an understanding of what we need to do in the Update method in general, let's dive into coding the game logic. We need to add a couple of member variables to represent the position and speed for our game objects, which include the hero ship, the enemy space ship, and the missile. We need to track each object's position, and speed so we declare six additional variables:

```
//Define Speed and Position vectors for objects that move
Vector2 HeroShipPosition;
Vector2 HeroShipSpeed;
Vector2 SpaceShipPosition;
Vector2 SpaceShipSpeed;
Vector2 MissilePosition;
Vector2 MissileSpeed;
```

We initialize these values in a separate method named InitializeObjects executed in LoadContent just after we load the related sprite images.

```
private void InitializeObjects()
{
  //Initialize Positon and Speed
  SpaceShipPosition = new Vector2(
    graphics.GraphicsDevice.Viewport.Width / 2 - SpaceShip.Width / 2, -SpaceShip.Height);
  SpaceShipSpeed = new Vector2(0, 2); // 2 pixels / frame "down"

  //Center hero ship width wise along the X axis
  //Place hero ship with 20 pixels underneath it in the Y axis
  HeroShipPosition = new Vector2(
    graphics.GraphicsDevice.Viewport.Width / 2 - HeroShip.Width / 2,
    graphics.GraphicsDevice.Viewport.Height - HeroShip.Height - 20f);
  HeroShipSpeed = Vector2.Zero;

  //Center Missile on Space Ship and put it 50 pixels further down
  //off screen "below" heroship
  MissilePosition = HeroShipPosition +
    new Vector2(HeroShip.Width / 2 - Missile.Width / 2, HeroShip.Height + 20f);
  MissileSpeed = new Vector2(0, -6); // 6 pixels / frame "up"

}
```

I mentioned this earlier but it is worth restating: when you draw a sprite, the position provided to the Draw method is the origin of the sprite when drawn meaning that the provided position becomes the upper left-hand corner of the sprite. In order to draw the alien spaceship and hero spaceship centered width-wise on the screen, we subtract half of the sprite's width from the position so that the middle of the sprite is centered on the screen.

I already covered how to draw in the Draw method, and we are already drawing the background, which was easy to position since it fills the entire screen. We haven't written the code to draw the hero ship, the alien spaceship, or the missile. Since we now have position information for these objects to reference in the form of the initialized variables, let's update the Draw method. We add these three lines of code to the Draw method right after we draw the background image:

```
spriteBatch.Draw(SpaceShip, SpaceShipPosition, Color.White);
spriteBatch.Draw(Missile, MissilePosition, Color.White);
spriteBatch.Draw(HeroShip, HeroShipPosition, Color.White);
```

Figure 1–17 shows the results.

Figure 1–17. *Sprite Initial Position*

We are pretty much down with the `Draw` method for our simple game and will focus on the `Update` method to make the game interactive. The first thing we do is add the basic update formula for all three objects to the `Update` method:

```
HeroShipPosition += HeroShipSpeed;
SpaceShipPosition += SpaceShipSpeed;
MissilePosition += MissileSpeed;
```

If you run the game right now, you will see the enemy spaceship move down the screen and the missile move up the screen at a slightly faster rate. Figure 1–18 shows a snapshot of the movement.

Figure 1–18. *Moving Sprites*

While pretty cool, it doesn't do much. The sprites pass through each other and then fly off to infinity in the up direction for the missile and the down direction for the alien spaceship. We can make a couple of modifications to make it somewhat more interesting as well as explain a couple of concepts.

The first modification that we make is edge detection. In the Update Method we type CheckScreenBoundaryCollision(gameTime); and then right-click on it and select Generate Method Stub.

In the newly generated method, we check to see if the missile, which has a default speed of -4 pixels / frame in the Y direction, has flown off the top of the screen, which would be a negative Y value. Since the alien space ship drops straight down at 2 pixels per frame, we check to see if it has a Y value greater than the screen height. Here is the method:

```
private void CheckScreenBoundaryCollision(GameTime gameTime)
{
  //Reset Missile if off the screen
  if (MissilePosition.Y < 0)
  {
    MissilePosition.Y = graphics.GraphicsDevice.Viewport.Height -
                        HeroShip.Height;
  }

  //Reset enemy spaceship if off the screen
  //to random drop point
  if (SpaceShipPosition.Y >
          graphics.GraphicsDevice.Viewport.Height)
  {
    SpaceShipPosition.Y = -2*SpaceShip.Height;
  }
}
```

Notice that we avoid using actual number values. As an example, we could use 480 instead of graphics.GraphicsDevice.Viewport.Height, but when the second screen resolution becomes available the game will break, because screen height in landscape mode will be 320.

The second modification to the game is to detect collisions between the alien spaceship and the missile. We create a new method, CheckForCollisions(gameTime; as before and edit the generated stub. There are many different algorithms available to detect for collisions with different levels of accuracy. The most accurate method is to compare for equality each point of the first image with every possible point in the other image. While most accurate, it is also the most CPU intensive and time consuming.

A simple method to check for collisions is to use bounding boxes. The idea is to wrap an object in a rectangle and check for collisions. The rectangle is based on the maximum length and width of the object. This can be inaccurate for irregular shapes, but costs much less in terms of CPU and time. In our simple game we generate two Rectangle objects that wrap the alien spaceship and the missile and then call the Intersects method to detect a collision. Here is the code:

```
private void CheckForCollisions(GameTime gameTime)
{
  //Alien and Missile
  Rectangle AlienRec = new Rectangle((int)SpaceShipPosition.X,
            (int)SpaceShipPosition.Y,SpaceShip.Width, SpaceShip.Height);
  Rectangle MissileRec = new Rectangle((int)MissilePosition.X,
            (int)MissilePosition.Y,Missile.Width, Missile.Height);

  if (AlienRec.Intersects(MissileRec))
  {
    SpaceShipPosition.Y = -2*SpaceShip.Height;
```

```
      MissilePosition.Y = graphics.GraphicsDevice.Viewport.Height - HeroShip.Height;
    }
  }
```

We create the two `Rectangle` objects and then check for collision by calling `if (AlienRec.Intersects(MissileRec))` and then update position similar to when there is a screen edge collision.

We now have an application that shows a dropping alien spaceship intersected by a missile over and over again. While not the most functional game, specifically because it doesn't incorporate user input or interactivity at all, it allows us to demonstrate key concepts for XNA Game Studio without inundating you with new concepts. Listing 1–2 shows the full code for our incomplete game.

Listing 1–2. Modified Game1.cs

```csharp
using System;
using System.Collections.Generic;
using System.Linq;
using Microsoft.Xna.Framework;
using Microsoft.Xna.Framework.Audio;
using Microsoft.Xna.Framework.Content;
using Microsoft.Xna.Framework.GamerServices;
using Microsoft.Xna.Framework.Graphics;
using Microsoft.Xna.Framework.Input;
using Microsoft.Xna.Framework.Input.Touch;
using Microsoft.Xna.Framework.Media;

namespace HelloXNA
{
    /// <summary>
    /// This is the main type for your game
    /// </summary>
    public class Game1 : Microsoft.Xna.Framework.Game
    {
        GraphicsDeviceManager graphics;
        SpriteBatch spriteBatch;

        //Define Texture2D objects to hold game content
        Texture2D HeroShip;
        Texture2D SpaceShip;
        Texture2D BackgroundImage;
        Texture2D Missile;

        //Define Speed and Position vectors for objects that move
        Vector2 HeroShipPosition;
        Vector2 HeroShipSpeed;
        Vector2 SpaceShipPosition;
        Vector2 SpaceShipSpeed;
        Vector2 MissilePosition;
        Vector2 MissileSpeed;

        public Game1()
        {
            graphics = new GraphicsDeviceManager(this);
```

```csharp
    Content.RootDirectory = "Content";

    // Frame rate is 30 fps by default for Windows Phone.
    TargetElapsedTime = TimeSpan.FromTicks(333333);

}

/// <summary>
/// Allows the game to perform any initialization it needs to before starting to run.
/// This is where it can query for any required services and load any non-graphic
/// related content.  Calling base.Initialize will enumerate through any components
/// and initialize them as well.
/// </summary>
protected override void Initialize()
{
    // TODO: Add your initialization logic here

    base.Initialize();
}

/// <summary>
/// LoadContent will be called once per game and is the place to load
/// all of your content.
/// </summary>
protected override void LoadContent()
{
    // Create a new SpriteBatch, which can be used to draw textures.
    spriteBatch = new SpriteBatch(GraphicsDevice);

    HeroShip = this.Content.Load<Texture2D>("Sprites/heroship");
    SpaceShip = this.Content.Load<Texture2D>("Sprites/spaceship");
    Missile = this.Content.Load<Texture2D>("Sprites/missile");
    BackgroundImage = this.Content.Load<Texture2D>("Textures/background");

    InitializeObjects();
}

private void InitializeObjects()
{
    //Initialize Positon and Speed
    SpaceShipPosition = new Vector2(
        graphics.GraphicsDevice.Viewport.Width / 2 - SpaceShip.Width / 2, -SpaceShip.Height);
    SpaceShipSpeed = new Vector2(0, 2); // 2 pixels / frame "down"

    //Center hero ship width wise along the X axis
    //Place hero ship with 20 pixels underneath it in the Y axis
    HeroShipPosition = new Vector2(
        graphics.GraphicsDevice.Viewport.Width / 2 - HeroShip.Width / 2,
        graphics.GraphicsDevice.Viewport.Height - HeroShip.Height - 20f);
    HeroShipSpeed = Vector2.Zero;

    //Center Missile on Space Ship and put it 50 pixels further down
```

```csharp
    //off screen "below" hereoship
    MissilePosition = HeroShipPosition +
      new Vector2(HeroShip.Width / 2 - Missile.Width / 2, HeroShip.Height + 20f);
    MissileSpeed = new Vector2(0, -6); // 6 pixels / frame "up"

}

/// <summary>
/// UnloadContent will be called once per game and is the place to unload
/// all content.
/// </summary>
protected override void UnloadContent()
{
    // TODO: Unload any non ContentManager content here
}

/// <summary>
/// Allows the game to run logic such as updating the world,
/// checking for collisions, gathering input, and playing audio.
/// </summary>
/// <param name="gameTime">Provides a snapshot of timing values.</param>
protected override void Update(GameTime gameTime)
{
    // Allows the game to exit
    if (GamePad.GetState(PlayerIndex.One).Buttons.Back == ButtonState.Pressed)
      this.Exit();

    // TODO: Add your update logic here
    CheckScreenBoundaryCollision(gameTime);
    CheckForCollisions(gameTime);

    HeroShipPosition += HeroShipSpeed;
    SpaceShipPosition += SpaceShipSpeed;
    MissilePosition += MissileSpeed;

    base.Update(gameTime);
}

private void CheckForCollisions(GameTime gameTime)
{
    //Alien and Missile
    Rectangle AlienRec = new Rectangle((int)SpaceShipPosition.X,
              (int)SpaceShipPosition.Y, SpaceShip.Width, SpaceShip.Height);
    Rectangle MissileRec = new Rectangle((int)MissilePosition.X,
              (int)MissilePosition.Y, Missile.Width, Missile.Height);

    if (AlienRec.Intersects(MissileRec))
    {
      SpaceShipPosition.Y = -2 * SpaceShip.Height;
      MissilePosition.Y = graphics.GraphicsDevice.Viewport.Height - HeroShip.Height;
    }
}
```

```
private void CheckScreenBoundaryCollision(GameTime gameTime)
{
  //Reset Missile if off the screen
  if (MissilePosition.Y < 0)
  {
    MissilePosition.Y = graphics.GraphicsDevice.Viewport.Height -
                        HeroShip.Height;
  }

  //Reset enemy spaceship if off the screen
  //to random drop point
  if (SpaceShipPosition.Y >
         graphics.GraphicsDevice.Viewport.Height)
  {
    SpaceShipPosition.Y = -2 * SpaceShip.Height;
  }
}



/// <summary>
/// This is called when the game should draw itself.
/// </summary>
/// <param name="gameTime">Provides a snapshot of timing values.</param>
protected override void Draw(GameTime gameTime)
{
  GraphicsDevice.Clear(Color.CornflowerBlue);

  // TODO: Add your drawing code here
  spriteBatch.Begin();
  spriteBatch.Draw(BackgroundImage, graphics.GraphicsDevice.Viewport.Bounds, Color.White);
  spriteBatch.Draw(SpaceShip, SpaceShipPosition, Color.White);
  spriteBatch.Draw(Missile, MissilePosition, Color.White);
  spriteBatch.Draw(HeroShip, HeroShipPosition, Color.White);
  spriteBatch.End();

  base.Draw(gameTime);
  }
 }
}
```

In this section I provided an introduction to the XNA Framework. I cover programming in XNA Game Studio in detail in Chapters 9 and 10, including adding much more interactivity to what we started here in Chapter 1. The next section provides a high-level overview of the Windows Marketplace for Mobile.

The Windows Phone Marketplace

There are many reasons a developer like you wants to build an application for Windows Phone, create a unique user experience, port an existing application to Windows Phone, etc. To make your creation available to customers, you submit it to App Hub at `http://create.msdn.com`.

App Hub Registration

Registering for the App Hub is a straightforward process, which you can do at `http://create.msdn.com`. For a company, registration can take a couple of weeks to fully complete because Microsoft vets the identity for companies via GeoTrust. The timeline is partially dependent on actions by you, such as clicking the email link to validate your email address and providing the necessary documentation to GeoTrust in a timely manner. GeoTrust validation is not required if registering as an individual, greatly simplifying and speeding registration for independent developers.

■**Tip** Once you register with a Windows Live ID, you cannot change it. If registering for a company, you probably don't want to lose your personal Windows Live ID so register with a new Live ID, such as `ContosoWP7@contoso.com`, that is not tied to an individual.

For companies, publisher verification ensures that consumers can feel confident that the publisher is who they say they are. This protects the consumer from a nefarious publisher impersonating their bank as a way to obtain a user's account information.

Registration costs $99 as of this writing, but check App Hub for the latest at `http://create.msdn.com`. As an example, students can register for free via the DreamSpark Program. Once registered, it allows you as the publisher to submit an unlimited number of for pay applications and 100 certification events for free applications. As of this writing, each additional certification event is $20 per application. Updates to free applications are no-charge certification events unless the application fails certification during the update.

■ **Tip** If you are a member of one of Microsoft's "Spark" programs such as BizSpark for startup business or DreamSpark for the academic community, you may be eligible for a reduced or possibly free Marketplace registration.

Microsoft is continuously updating policies to better serve its developer community. The App Hub FAQ is a great place to start for the most recent updates: `http://create.msdn.com/en-US/home/faq`.

Submitting Applications to Marketplace

When you submit an application to Marketplace, the estimated average time for an application to be approved is five days, though it is usually quicker. Microsoft validates the application against the criteria set forth in the MSDN documentation "Windows Phone Application Certification Requirements" available for review at http://create.msdn.com. The documentation covers application policy guidelines, content policy guidelines, and application certification requirements.

Windows Phone Marketplace Test Kit

The Windows Phone OS 7.1 Developer Tools includes the new Windows Phone Marketplace Test Kit. You can run the same exact tests and evaluate against the same criteria that the Microsoft certification team does. This can help ensure a smooth transition to publishing. If you work at a company publishing mobile apps, point your QA and test team to this tool.

The Marketplace Test Kit is integrated with Visual Studio. Open or create a Windows Phone project that targets Windows Phone OS 7.1 or later. Select the project you want to test in the Solution Explorer, right-click, and select Open Marketplace Test Kit. The test kit opens a new tab in Visual Studio named Marketplace Test Kit. The kit includes Automated Tests, Monitored Tests, and Manual Tests. Explore the Marketplace Test Kit in Visual Studio to understand how this wonderful tool works and can help you build high-quality applications.

Beta Testing Your Application

New in Windows Phone OS 7.1, developers can now conduct a beta test with their applications prior to releasing in Marketplace. This allows you to make your application available to a set of end users to try and test your app before making your application generally available. It is free to submit your application for beta distribution. This is a great way to get "real world" feedback.

Users can install and test your application via a "hidden link" to the application. This is also a great way to get reviewers excited about your application by inviting them to participate in the beta test.

Submitting your application for beta distribution does not put your app through the full certification process. Instead, it goes through an automated certification process resulting in quicker publication for beta distribution.

You decide who can participate in your application beta by submitting up to 100 beta tester email addresses. Once the application goes through automated publication, beta testers receive an email with a link to install the application via Marketplace.

The submission process for beta testing is via App Hub at http://create.msdn.com. Select the Private Beta Test option to get started.

Targeted Application Distribution

Targeted Application Distribution is the process of releasing your application through App Hub while keeping it hidden in the Windows Phone Marketplace. You can send the link to your application to a targeted set of users. Only those users who have the link to the application can install it; however, nothing can prevent them from sharing the link with others. Anyone who has the link can install the application.

With targeted application submission, the application will not show up in Marketplace or Marketplace search. You submit to App Hub just like you would for a normal distribution. At the end of submission there are multiple publication options including an option titled "As soon as it is certified, but make it hidden." Select this option for targeted application distribution.

Making Money

The application publisher sets the price of the application. As the publisher you collect 70% of the revenue and Microsoft keeps 30% for paid applications, which is in line with other application store revenue models. The 30% primarily covers the costs of marketplace, certification costs, and so on.

Microsoft also provides an advertising-based revenue model offering for Windows Phone. You are not required to use Microsoft's advertising offering but it does provide a very easy way to take advantage of advertising revenue.

■ **Note** Currently the advertising control and pubCenter are only supported in the United States. Microsoft will add support to the following 18 countries by the end of 2011: Australia, Belgium, Canada, Denmark, Finland, France, Germany, Hong Kong, India, Italy, Japan, Mexico, Netherlands, Norway, Spain, Sweden, Switzerland, and the United Kingdom.

The Microsoft Advertising SDK is discussed in detail as part of Chapter 6.

An important component to getting paid is potential application reach. At initial availability, Windows Phone currently support 5 languages; English, French, Italian, German and Spanish, otherwise known as EFIGS. App Hub supports application purchases in 16 countries at launch with payout to developers in 30 countries listed here:

- Australia
- Austria
- Belgium
- Brazil
- Canada
- Denmark
- Finland
- France
- Germany
- Greece
- Hong Kong
- India
- Ireland
- Italy
- Japan
- Luxembourg
- Mexico
- Netherlands
- New Zealand
- Norway
- Poland
- Portugal
- Russia
- Singapore
- Spain
- Sweden
- Switzerland
- Taiwan
- United Kingdom
- United States

In order to participate and sell your applications and get paid, you must be registered in Marketplace and have a bank account for one of these countries. With Windows Phone 7.5, App Hub supports 19 new countries: Brazil, Chile, Colombia, Czech Republic, Denmark, Finland, Greece, Hungary, India, Japan, Netherlands, Norway, Poland, Portugal, Russia, South Africa, South Korea, Sweden, and Taiwan. With Windows Phone 7.5 you can build apps for the world!

App Hub adds seven new developer markets that can submit apps: Chile, Colombia, Czech Republic, Hungary, Israel, South Africa, and South Korea. In addition, App Hub is localized for Korean and Simplified Chinese in addition to English and Japanese. As you can see, Microsoft is investing in the platform and marketplace to maximize your investment.

Marketing Matters

Making money is more than setting a price. As part of the submission process, the developer supplies the detailed description, screen shots, and marketing art for items like the background panorama for the Marketplace hub. Your tile icon is determined by the background.png file that is part of your Visual Studio Windows Phone project so be sure to update it so that it looks good on the Windows Phone Start screen. The applicationicon.png file is the smaller icon displayed in the App List. Figure 1–19 shows the App List in the emulator.

Figure 1–19. App list

The marketing art for Marketplace is incredibly important because that is what the end-user sees when viewing your application in Marketplace on the device. Also, if you study successful applications on other platforms, the mobile ISV generally includes four people or roles, a business person, a marketing person, and a couple of developers. Someone has to wear the marketing hat to promote the application beyond App Hub, such as via Social Networking channels, outreach to application review web sites, and so on. The most successful applications are those with a great business plan and great marketing behind them.

Windows Phone Web Marketplace

New in Windows Phone 7.5, users can go to the Windows Phone Web Marketplace at WindowsPhone.com to explore and purchase applications. You can now have a direct link to the web marketplace on your application web site as well. Figure 1–20 shows the new Web Marketplace's home page.

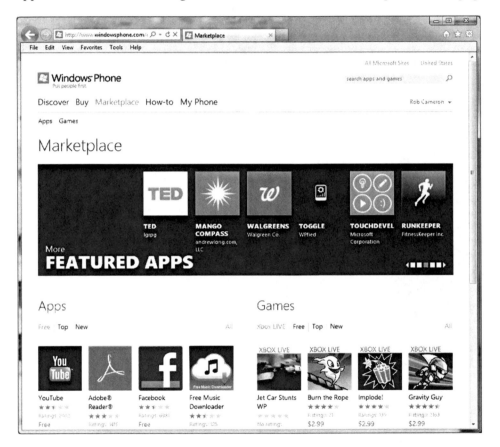

Figure 1–20. *Windows Phone Web-based Marketplace*

You can filter the search by category on the left as well as filter using the headers across the top such as 100 Newest paid apps, and so on. Clicking on an application or game provides additional details on the application as well as a deep link for the Windows Phone desktop marketplace, which is covered in the next section.

Windows Phone Marketplace on the PC

Windows Phone does not connect to your PC via Microsoft's ActiveSync or Windows Mobile Device Center. If you happen to own a Microsoft Zune media player, then you are already familiar with the Windows Phone Marketplace on the PC, which is the Zune client software available at `http://Zune.net`. Figure 1–21 shows a game found using the built-in Search functionality.

Figure 1–21. *Windows Phone Application in the Zune client*

The Zune client provides the full Microsoft Zune experience for Windows Phone, including ZunePass if you are a subscriber. In addition to the media content such as music, videos, TV, and movies, end-users can browse and select applications for download using the Zune client for their Windows Phone device. If the device is tethered either via USB or connected over a wireless network, the application will download via PC. Otherwise, if the device is not connected to the PC the application will download the next time the user launches Marketplace on his or her device.

The Windows Phone Marketplace is the only mechanism available to install an application on Windows Phone. It is not possible to "side load" an application on to a Windows Phone device outside of the Windows Phone Marketplace mechanisms unless registered in App Hub and using the Windows Phone Developer Registration tool.

▓ **Note** Applications greater than 20 MB must be installed via Zune client or over Wi-Fi.

An important function provided by the Zune client is that it allows a developer to deploy code to a connected device from Visual Studio 2010 or Expression Blend 4 for Windows Phone. I cover how to do that in the section titled "Limited Distribution of Applications" later in this chapter.

Marketplace on the Device

Marketplace on the device is a top-level hub experience that provides a one-stop shop location to find applications and games that are not managed Xbox LIVE titles.

▓ **Note** Premium Xbox LIVE games can be found in Xbox LIVE Hub. We cover Windows Phone game development in Chapters 9 and 10.

Figure 1–22 shows a mockup of the Marketplace panorama where you can see the featured app, which in this example is the eBay application. You also see categories, popular apps, what's new, and all of the featured applications. Selecting a featured app places its panoramic image as the background for the marketplace hub. In this example the eBay application is selected and its corresponding image is what is shown in the background. As a developer you can provide the panoramic art when you submit your application to Marketplace.

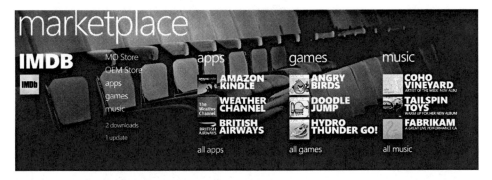

Figure 1–22. *Windows Phone Marketplace hub*

When you select an application, the application details page is displayed. An example is shown in Figure 1–23. (AP Mobile is a free application as of this writing. This image is just representative of the Marketplace details page.)

Figure 1–23. Example Marketplace application details page

The application details view provides the following information to the consumer:

- Publisher and detailed product information
- Price and Try Before You Buy
- Application screenshots
- Access to user ratings and application reviews
- Size and available options for downloading (PC or Wi-Fi only for apps greater than 20 MB vs. Over-The-Air)
- List of related applications if any
- Optionally, game content ratings for games
- More apps by the developer publisher

This information allows consumers to make an informed decision on whether to download and purchase an application. Purchasing is enabled two-ways that are self-explanatory:

- Associate a credit card with their Windows Live ID

- Mobile Operator Billing for applications

Users can make a purchase with just two taps, Buy and then a Confirm Download dialog. Mobile Operator billing provides a great user experience to end-users as the application purchase simply shows up on their monthly bill. Microsoft has found that mobile operator billing increases the likelihood of a purchase transaction by 300%.

Once purchased and downloaded, the application is available in the application list or App List to the right of the Start screen. End-users can choose to pin your application to the bottom of the Start screen by clicking and holding the application icon in the app listing selecting "Add to Quick Launch." When you download a game, it will appear in the Xbox LIVE Hub.

Note Applications cannot pin themselves automatically to the Start screen quick launch area. Only users can pin an application to the Start screen.

Supported Business Models

This is a very important and common question asked of Microsoft: what are the supported business models? Microsoft supports four business models in the App Hub:

- Paid
- Try Before Buy
- Ad-Funded
- Free

A Paid business model is very straightforward. You set a price and get paid. Try Before Buy is the concept of end users trying a free version and then purchasing the full version of the application. To take advantage of Trial mode, it is a very simple API call:

```
using Microsoft.Phone.Marketplace;
```

Instantiate a LicenseInformation object to gain access to the IsTrial() method call:

```
if (licenseInfo.IsTrial())
{
    ….//Only show level one
}
```

As the developer, you determine how the trial application functions relative to the fully paid application.

Ad-funded is where you plug your application into your own or a third-party advertising network. As users download and use your application, they view the advertisements as they go and you get paid for views, clicks-throughs, and the like, similar to on the Web. "Free" isn't really a business model per se, but it can be if the free application enables access to an existing subscription available via the web. As an example, if a newspaper or music services offers a paid Web-based subscription, they can extend that subscription to Windows Phone for free to their existing subscribers enabling anytime access via the phone.

Search, Browse, and Discover Applications

The Windows Phone Marketplace provides several types of content that users can select from such as Applications, Games, Premium Xbox LIVE Games, music, and special applications from either the Mobile Operator or the OEM who manufactured the device that a user can download.

When a user selects a category such as Featured, the panorama jumps to a Pivot experience to let a user navigate through the different categories available to make it easy for the user to filter, search, and discover applications.

When in the Marketplace app on the phone, click the Search hardware button to search within Marketplace. You can also search within the Zune marketplace windows client.

Application and Game Updates

Within the on-device marketplace in the content area of the hub users can find a list available application updates. If consumer purchases and downloads your application and you as the publisher provide an updated version in marketplace, you can make the update available automatically to your end-user installed-base and it will be listed on the Marketplace hub as an application update.

As the developer you can provide details on the update to the end-user such as bug fixes, improved performance, additional game levels, and so on, so that your installed base understands what the update provides them.

Connecting with Your End Users

When a user purchases and installs your application, it appears in the App List or Xbox LIVE Hub. The end-user can choose to make your app a favorite and pin it to the Start screen. It initially appears at the bottom of the list but end users can move it up towards the top by tap and holding the tile, then dragging it to the desired location.

Stay Connected to Users via Live Tiles

Developers can enable Live Tiles in your application so that when your end-users pin the application to the Start screen, they can receive notifications and updates dynamically directly on the application for a richer, more connected, experience. These updates include changing the background image, a count value, and a title. The update is delivered via the Windows Phone Push Notification Services, covered in Chapter 10.

Temp Users to Purchase with Try Before You Buy

The Windows Phone Developer tools and the Windows Phone application framework provides a trial API that allows developers to call `IsTrial` within the application to find out if the user has actually purchased the application or whether the application is still in trial mode. This API connects to marketplace under the covers to make this determination. This means that the trial version is the same application as the full version.

You as the publisher/developer get to determine what type of trial as well as how long the trial period lasts. For type of trial, you can determine if it is time based, based on levels, and so on. Trial applications are a powerful way to let users try the app and then convert them to paying customers.

Limiting Distribution of Applications

Once an application is published on Marketplace, it can be downloaded by any Windows Phone user. A common question is how to make an application available to a limited number of users. The next sections answer that.

Deploy an Application to Your Phone for Testing

Probably the most limited distribution for an application is deploying an application to your phone, whether a pre-production developer device or a retail phone purchased after launch. The process to developer unlock a device requires three steps:

1. Register at `http://create.msdn.com`.

2. Install the Zune Client and connect your device.

3. Launch the Windows Phone Developer Registration tool in the Windows Start screen.

I covered registration at create.msdn.com and the Zune client already. The last step is achieved by installing the Windows Phone Developer Tools download. Once installed, a Windows Start Menu folder titled Windows Phone Developer Tools is created. Navigate there to launch the Windows Phone Developer Registration tool shown in Figure 1–24 for a device that has already been registered.

Figure 1–24. The Windows Phone Developer Registration tool

Ensure that the Zune client is open and your Windows Phone device is connected before proceeding. Next enter your Windows Live ID and Password you used when you registered in marketplace at `http://create.msdn.com` and click Register. Upon success, you can now deploy code to your device.

Table 1–3 shows a list of possible error codes and related cause when deploying applications to a device either via Visual Studio or the Developer Registration tool.

Table 1–3. *Device Connectivity Error Codes*

Error Code	Explanation
0x8973180E	Zune software is not installed. Please install the latest version of Zune software.
0x8973180F	Incorrect version of the Zune software installed. Please download the latest version.
0x89731810	Corrupted device configuration. To correct this problem, reinstall Visual Studio 2010 Express for Windows Phone.
0x89731811	Zune software is not started. Please try again from the Zune to ensure that the software is running.
0x89731812	Connection to device failed. Please ensure the phone is connected and the not on the lock screen.
0x89731813	Application failed to start. Please ensure that the device has been registered and unlocked. Explanation on how to register can be found here: `http://go.microsoft.com/fwlink/?LinkId=195284`.
0x81030110	Failed to install the application. Runtime error has occurred. Capabilities WMAppManifest.xml file located in the attribute content is incorrect. (This link might help)
0x81030118	Installation of the application failed. Device is developer locked. Register for the developer unlock program before deploying the application.
0x81030119	You cannot install the application. You have reached the maximum number of applications being developed for the device can be installed on this development. Please uninstall a previous developer application.

Limit Availability to Beta Testers

With Windows Phone 7.5, App Hub now supports beta distribution, which enables developers to distribute pre-certified applications to a group of up to 100 access controlled beta testers for up to 90 days. This distribution method gives you the opportunity to test apps with a hand-picked set of beta testers more quickly and build high-quality apps before publishing them in Marketplace.

Enterprise Applications in Marketplace

Initially at launch, the App Hub does not provide a way for an enterprise to create and distribute a custom Line of Business (LOB) type application to only its employees. Microsoft has publically stated that they will enable this capability at some point in the future after Windows Phone launch.

Windows Phone 7.5 offers targeted distribution, which enables you to distribute applications through Marketplace in a hidden state, where they are not discoverable via browsing or searching Marketplace. To enable targeted users to access your hidden app you simply share the deep-link to the app with the users you want to have access via email, text, or other mechanism. Unlike beta distribution, you may distribute your app to as many users as desired and publish publicly in Marketplace at any time.

■ **Note** Targeted distribution links are not DRM'd, meaning anyone who has the link can access the application.

With that said, an enterprise can choose to publish an application to Marketplace via targeted distribution but have the application require a password to enable functionality. Perhaps a retail store enterprise wants to create an application for its in-store employees. The retail store enterprise could create and submit the application to the Marketplace, making it available to download for anyone.

If a non-employee gains access to the link, they would not have a username and password to log in. The application could be written in such a way to allow a non-employee to browse the retailer's catalog or even make in-store pickup purchases. While this scenario may not be an option for enterprise, it may be workable for many enterprises as an interim step.

Conclusion

In this chapter I provided an overview of Windows Phone, the platform. I introduced the application platform and the two major programming models: Silverlight and XNA Framework. I then dove deeper into XNA Framework programming model to balance out technology coverage as we dive into Silverlight development over the next several chapters. Finally, I covered the Marketplace so that you have a solid understanding of how to publish and monetize applications that you create. In the next chapter I will cover user interface development for Windows Phone using XAML and .NET.

CHAPTER 2

■ ■ ■

User Interface Development

Since all client applications require some sort of end-user experience, user interface development is the first topic I will dive into after the introduction provided in Chapter 1. Also, for client-application development, it is usually the first aspect of the application that developers start to experiment with in learning a new technology.

The user interface is usually the hallmark of a great application proposal or application prototype. It helps communicate what an application will look like, as well as what it will actually do. How an application looks and feels is just as important as what the application actually does. It is understandable, as users expect more from client-applications, especially non-Web-based client applications such as mobile applications.

First up is an overview of the Windows Phone application design language and design resources. The Windows Phone product team is incredibly passionate about the user interface they created for Windows Phone. In an effort to help jumpstart great user experience (UX) design and development for Windows Phone developers, the Windows Phone design team created detailed resources and guidance, which I cover in this chapter.

In this second edition of the book, I have expanded this section covering design to include a description of what makes a well-designed application. In addition, I provide coverage of Expression Blend 4 SketchFlow, which can help you create design documentation and a working prototype that you can share without having to require a Windows Phone device.

After covering design, the chapter dives into developing UX in Visual Studio 2010, with a quick background on the underlying architecture of the Silverlight programming model and the .NET Framework for Silverlight for mobile developers new to the platform. This book is not an introductory one, but this section provides hopefully enough background to fill in the major blanks as well as help understand the important namespaces and classes if you are new to Silverlight development.

The markup language for Windows Phone UX is Xml Application Markup Language (XAML). XAML development started out in Visual Studio 2005 with a basic design surface for Windows Presentation Foundation. Expression Blend was created to provide a design tool to make it easier for designers to work in XAML, but in a visual way. Both Visual Studio 2010 and Expression Blend XAML tooling has improved greatly, with unique support for phone development with Silverlight. I cover the built-in controls and capabilities using Visual Studio 2010 as the backdrop.

After covering Visual Studio 2010, UX development with Expression Blend 4 is next. As a developer, you need to learn Expression Blend 4 – it is definitely not just a tool for designers, and you will find some tasks are much easier to do in Expression Blend, such as visual data binding and creating sample data. The section covers laying out controls in Blend, sample data, data binding, and animations in Expression Blend as well.

The chapter concludes with an overview of what's new in Windows Phone OS 7.1 (Mango) as it relates to user interface development, where the biggest change in the update is moving from Silverlight 3 compatibility to Silverlight 4.

UX Performance Improvements

Developers with experience in Windows Phone have probably experienced challenges with UI performance for `ListBox` scrolling. There were a set of tips and tricks that developers leveraged to improve scroll performance for `ListBox` controls, data virtualization, etc. With Windows Phone OS 7.1 (Mango), the product team made significant improvements in controls so that developers do not have to do this work themselves. There are two major areas of improvement:

- An input thread has been added to improve performance for things such as `ListBox` scrolling.

- Images are now decoded on a background thread, which means text and other elements will appear quickly and the images will load when they are available.

`WebClient` has also been improved to return on the calling thread. I cover `WebClient` in Chapter 4. In the next section I provide an expanded overview on designing for Windows Phone.

Designing for Windows Phone

This section covers design-oriented content that a developer will find very useful. I phrase it that way because this book in general is not geared toward designers; however, just as end-users were no longer satisfied with character-based UI when graphical UI came into vogue, today's end-users expect even more from client-based mobile applications when compared to the rich UX available via the desktop. Developers are an integral part to the design/development cycle, which is why it is strongly encouraged that developers embrace design concepts as much as possible to help create better UX beyond design wireframes and visual comps.

Design Approach

The design team at Microsoft refers to the "design language" of Windows Phone, codenamed "Metro," when describing the approach they took when designing the Windows Phone UI. The Metro codename is inspired by the graphics found in transportation systems worldwide, which rely on big, bold, beautiful graphics and text to communicate to the "end-user" or traveler where they need to go. It is inspired by other sources as well, such as Zune, video games, product packaging, and the like, which focus on these key principles:

- **Light and simple:** Focus on primary tasks, achieving a lot with very little (little user effort and few phone resources, steps, and so on). Use whitespace to its full advantage.

- **Typography:** Focus on beautiful, not just legible, with sensitivity to font weight, balance, and scale to communicate a sense of hierarchy for the content.

- **Motion:** Responsive and alive UI. Transition between UI is just as important as the design of the UI. Create an animation system, not just transitions.

- **Content, not chrome:** Reduce visuals that are not content. Navigate via content itself.

- **Honest:** Design for the form factor, keeping things simple and direct. Be authentic. Content makes the UI beautiful.

Probably the most important design approach *not to take* is to simply port an iPhone or Android application to Windows Phone without modifying the user interface to match the platform. This statement is not meant to be negative toward iOS or Android user interfaces at all. Rather, the point is that you need to design for the platform. Many iOS and Android user interfaces consist of swiping left/right for the majority of the application. Windows Phone is more hierarchical with a physical Back key.

Windows Phone users are familiar with the navigation model and UX design intrinsic to the platform. Porting over an iOS/Android UX to Windows Phone without refactoring will look odd and out of place if it does not at least use the default templates for the built-in controls and font styles for text.

An excellent way to examine this further is to take a look at applications that Microsoft promotes as "showcase" examples and then compare them to their iOS or Android counterparts. Again, I am not saying one is better than the other. The key point is that the application design and information architecture is very different, yet each version, whether iOS, Android, or Windows Phone, "fits" into the platform it targets. Check-out a couple of popular applications on both platforms to see the differences.

In the next section I cover the design resources available to help you build an authentic Windows Phone user interface, whether you are creating a new application or porting an existing one.

Design Resources

The Windows Phone documentation includes several designer-oriented resources to help generate a beautiful user experience. If you are new to Windows Phone design or development, you will want to review these resources.

Windows Phone Design System – Codename Metro

The Windows Phone Design System – Codename Metro is available here:

```
http://go.microsoft.com/fwlink/?LinkID=189338
```

This document describes what the product team calls its design language: seven areas of differentiation, and "red threads," or guiding principles. The user experience of Windows Phone is partly inspired by the image of the simple and effective communication style provided by metropolitan public transportation system signage as shown in Figure 2–1.

Figure 2–1. Metropolitan signage as inspiration

The product team describes Metro as

"…our code name for our design language. We call it metro because it it's modern and clean. It's fast and in motion. It's about content and typography. And it's entirely authentic."

There are key points to take notice of in this description. "Modern and clean" means an application should provide just what is needed to get the task done, whether that task is to provide a movie, the news, or a weather forecast.

"Fast and in motion" means anything other than snappy performance is unsatisfactory. While this may seem obvious, the key here is that a user's perception is what's important. No doubt some tasks take time, so the key is to provide animation and indicators that help shape the user's perception that the application is responsive.

"Content and typography" means that the focus of the application is on the content, not application chrome. Navigate via the content with touch instead of a scroll bar is one example. Typography is incredibly important, so much so that the design team created a special font type for Windows Phone called Segoe WP that looks great onscreen and is pleasing to the eye. Finally, "authentic" means that the application does not try to do more than what it is.

UI Design and Interaction Guide for Windows Phone

The UI Design and Interaction Guide for Windows Phone is important for developers to review closely. You will find a few items in the guide that are different from other platforms:

- No "Home" button

- No "Exit" button

- Dialogs do not have a "Close" button

- Close dialogs with the "Back" button

- Do not navigate applications with buttons

- Navigate applications via content

These are just a few examples of items that developers need to think about in a different way. Here is a link to the UI Design and Interaction Guide for Windows Phone:

`http://msdn.microsoft.com/en-us/library/hh202915(v=VS.92).aspx`

It cannot be overstated: this document is a must-read for both designers and developers. It covers all of the user experience customizations, input methods, and controls to help developers and designers understand how to build a great looking Windows Phone user interface.

Reviewing this document will help you combine Metro with your company's brand in the best way, resulting in an authentic user experience that is true to your brand and Windows Phone. Figure 2–2 is a page from the document with annotations.

Figure 2–2. *UI Design and Interaction Guide format*

The UI Design and Interaction Guide for Windows Phone v2.0.pdf document prints out in a large format and is best viewed on a large monitor. Each section provides a topic item, such as "Application settings" (as shown in Figure 2–2). It displays an image and textual context for the topic item, along with guidance for designers and developers with do's and don'ts. As far as I am concerned, this document is required reading for anyone who designs or develops a Silverlight-based Windows Phone application.

Application Icons

Windows Phone design resources includes a zip of icons to use directly in your application or as a model for custom application icons you build. The application icons come in .png and XAML vector format. The .png format comes in both a light and dark variant to support the light and dark themes in Windows Phone. Figure 2–3 shows the included icons, as well as other sample icons. The image is taken from the Windows Phone Design System – Codename Metro.pdf document.

Figure 2–3. *Collage of application icons for Windows Phone*

The icons are included with the Windows Phone design resources, as well as installed by the Windows Phone Developer Tools, at C:\Program Files (x86)\Microsoft SDKs\Windows Phone\v7.1\Icons on an x64 Windows machine. The icons come in black and white to match the built-in application themes available in Windows Phone.

The most common place to use the icons is for the Application bar if included in your application; however, they be incorporated into the main UI as well.

Design Templates for Windows Phone

The design templates for Windows Phone.zip file includes 28 Adobe Photoshop files that designers can use to create pixel-perfect UX. Share this download with your Windows Phone designer friends and they will be forever grateful. It takes the guesswork out of how to size the design. It will also save rework for developers, as the templates will be ready to go when imported – more on this in the next section.

One little gem you will not want to ignore is the Design Templates for Windows Phone.pdf document that is included in the template download zip located here:

```
http://go.microsoft.com/fwlink/?LinkId=196225
```

This document details how to use the templates, which is especially important for controls that are not shipped as part of the Windows Phone Developer Tools. A great time to use this document is when you need to build UI, like a notification, where there isn't an existing control. The guidance is provided to help designers and developers match both visually and in interaction the built-in version of the control that appears in Windows Phone OS 7.0.

■ **Tip** Many additional controls are shipped in the Silverlight Toolkit for Windows Phone, which is available for download at CodePlex: `http://silverilght.codeplex.com`.

This section concludes the overview of the design resources for Windows Phone. Please do checkout these resources as it will save you rework later. The next section covers the mechanics of how designers and developers can work together to build a Silverlight for Windows Phone user interface.

Designer and Developer Mechanics

As with most client application development, Windows Phone applications begin as a sketch. If you have the full version of Expression Blend you can download and install the Expression Blend SketchFlow Template for Windows Phone, available here at `http://wp7sketchflow.codeplex.com`.

SketchFlow lets you quickly create a UI "sketch" to build out your user interface concepts without coding using Expression Blend. To get started, launch Expression Blend 4 and click File ➤ New Project, select Windows Phone, choose Windows Phone SketchFlow Application, provide a name, and click OK. The new project is created with one screen initially. You can add a control such as a `Panorama` to the screen by clicking the chevron on the toolbar on the left in Expression Blend to search for it and then double-clicking to add. Configure it to fill the area by right-clicking on the `Panorama` control in the Objects and Timeline window and select Auto Size ➤ Fill. Figure 2-4 shows the SketchFlow UI with a `ListBox` on `Panorama` Item 1 with some sample data.

Figure 2–4. *Expression Blend 4 SketchFlow interface*

I will cover how to work with sample data later in this chapter, but you can work in SketchFlow just like you normally would in Expression Blend with some enhanced capabilities for developing a design without coding. You can visually connect screens to create application navigation with the SketchFlow Map window as shown at the bottom of Figure 2-4. You can test and distribute a SketchFlow demo application for review using the SketchFlow runtime, which runs in the browser. Figure 2-5 shows an example of the SketchFlow Player.

Figure 2–5. Expression Blend 4 SketchFlow Player in the browser

Once you have a sketch of your application you can next build-out wireframes mapping the sketches to an information architecture diagram and eventually an interaction diagram. While SketchFlow allows you to interactively create and build both of these diagrams in a working prototype, you will want to create a large image mapping out these diagrams for review in addition to the SketchFlow implementation. Figure 2-6 shows an example information architecture diagram.

Figure 2–6. *Sample information architecture diagram*

The information architecture maps out the wireframes into a hierarchy. There will be interactions that are specific to a page (e.g., Search) as well as interactions between pages. Essentially any user click or possible interaction should be mapped out. This is where the interaction diagram comes into play. An example is shown in Figure 2-7.

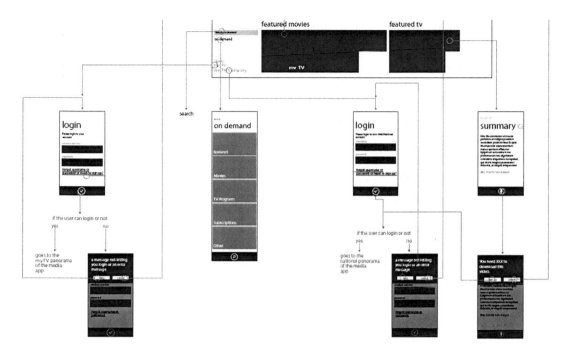

Figure 2–7. *Sample interaction diagram*

Creating an information architecture and user interaction diagram are very effective steps to help you successfully map an existing iOS or Android UI over to Windows Phone, resulting in a better, more usable application.

The next and generally last piece of design documentation is comprehensive artwork, or "visual comps" for short, that consists of a refined full user interface mock-up of what the final user interface should look like. Quite often the actual development results in a far less stunning UI when compared to original comps. This is a result of a mismatch of the output from the design process, usually a vector drawing flattened into an image format and the input of the development process, which is a development language.

Starting with Windows Presentation Foundation, XAML was introduced as a language to describe UX that is both user- and tool-consumable, meaning a developer can author XAML directly or tools vendors can build applications that allow a designer and developer to visually create UX that generates the appropriate XAML. Silverlight was introduced after XAML as a lightweight version of WPF that fits into a small (approximately 5 MB) cross-platform, cross-browser desktop plug-in. Initially Silverlight included a subset of the most commonly used features of WPF. Since its introduction, Silverlight has steadily added additional capabilities to match more closely the full capabilities available in WPF. Examples include more support for triggers, Commanding, and COM Interop, making offline desktop Silverlight a capable alternative to WPF for many desktop application scenarios.

Silverlight for Windows Phone is based on Silverlight 4, putting XAML-based development front and center in mobile application development. Also, since Silverlight for Windows Phone does not run in a browser, some features, like browser-interoperability available in Silverlight for the desktop, are removed from Silverlight for Windows Phone. Fundamentally, however, they share core capabilities.

The reason XAML is so important and useful is that the output of visual design tools can be directly consumed by developers, since the output of the visual design is human-readable XAML. Designers can use Expression Design to create rich visual designs for application control templates as well as general application UX. Expression Design supports exporting XAML.

While Expression Design is a great tool, the world of designers is dominated by the Adobe toolset. What may not be well-known by many designers is that Expression Blend 4 has excellent import capabilities to pull in the vector output from the Adobe toolset directly into Expression Blend as XAML. The Expression Blend 4 import capabilities are shown in Figure 2–8.

Figure 2–8. Expression Blend 4 file menu import capabilities

The menu offers import capabilities for three Adobe file formats: .fxg, .psd (Photoshop), and .ai (Illustrator). The .fxg file is the new file interchange format introduced in Adobe Creative Suite 5 that provides a common interchange format for the Adobe toolset. The format is very similar to .svg format. The other two file formats are the native format of Adobe's well known Photoshop and Illustrator tools. Figure 2–9 shows one of the Windows Phone design templates opened in Photoshop.

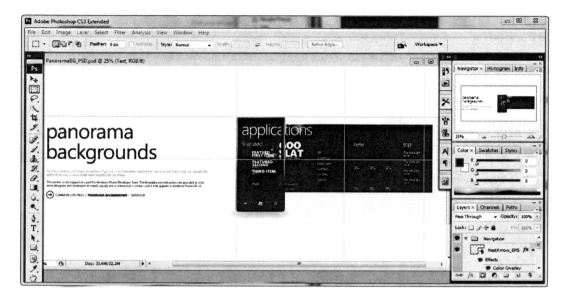

Figure 2–9. *Windows Phone design template in Photoshop*

Let's say the example in Figure 2–9 is part of a real application that you are building. In Expression Blend, you can import the background using the File ➤ Import Photoshop File … menu item and then selecting the desired layer as shown in Figure 2–10.

Figure 2–10. *Import a layer from a sample Photoshop file*

When you click OK in the dialog shown in Figure 2–10, a `Canvas` object is added to the currently opened XAML file and the image assets are brought into the project in a new folder named with the same name as the imported asset but with the suffix _images appended. At the bottom on the right of Figure 2–10 there's an option to generate a "Compatibility image" instead of attempting to import the vector components of the image as XAML. What this option does is take the selected layers and "flatten" it to a .png image. This is a handy option when you just need a flattened image instead of the layers, which in many cases has better performance than having to calculate vector-based layout.

This section provided an overview of how designers and developers can work in their preferred tools while allowing for the smoothest work stream possible with Expression Blend 4 as the bridge between a pure designer and developer.

The technical designer or developer who works in Expression Blend will also build out the interaction model for the user experience using the built-in animation capabilities, which I cover later in this chapter. Before I jump into Expression Blend 4, I next cover Visual Studio 2010 with an introduction to the .NET Framework for Silverlight for Windows Phone and an overview of the available controls.

User Interface Development in Visual Studio 2010

Visual Studio 2010 Windows Phone Developer Tools 7.1 includes several additional controls and project templates to help developers get started building their mobile application. Figure 2–11 shows the available templates.

Figure 2–11. *Visual Studio 2010 File ➤ New Project – Silverlight for Windows Phone dialog*

In Windows Phone Developer Tools 7.1, several new project templates are added including the Windows Phone Silverlight and XNA Application as well as the three background agent projects. I cover the Panorama and Pivot controls later on in this chapter, since they define unique application UI navigation architectures. In Chapter 8 I cover XNA Framework Shared Graphics, where you can render Silverlight and XNA Framework on the same surface. Background agent processing is covered in Chapter 10.

The first thing you will notice when reviewing a Silverlight for Windows Phone application is that the control templates follow the Windows Phone theme style, defaulting to the Dark theme. The other available theme is the Light theme.

■ **Note** The built-in controls will automatically adjust to application theme changes by the user; however, the developer may need to adjust the rest of the UI such as images, backgrounds, and so on, if the end-user changes the phone theme to light or vice versa. This is a certification requirement.

We create the BuiltInControls project by selecting File ➤ New ➤ Project… and select the Windows Phone Application template. Figure 2–12 shows the Solution Explorer tool window for the BuiltInControls project.

Figure 2–12. *Initial project file layout in the Solution Explorer tool window*

A typical Windows Phone project consists of an App.xaml and App.xaml.cs file that represents the non-visual Application object that is the root of the project and application structure. MainPage.xaml with the MainPage.xaml.cs code-behind file is the default initial UI for the application. There are three graphic files associated with the project structure:

- Background.png: This is a 173 × 173-pixel image that represents the application's "tile" when pinned to the Start screen. The user has to pin your tile. Applications cannot pin themselves.

- ApplicationIcon.png: This is a 62 × 62–pixel image that is the icon in the application list when installed on a device.

- SplashScreenImage.jpg: This is a 480 × 800-pixel image displayed when an application first launches. Developers do not have to do anything to show the image or hide the image. The framework handles it.

■ **Tip** From the certification requirements applications must show UI within 5 seconds and be functional within 20 seconds after launch. The splash screen image is displayed until the UI is shown.

The next section covers the Windows Phone manifest file in more detail.

WMAppManifest.xml File

A file unique to the Windows Phone Visual Studio project templates is the WMAppManifest.xml file under the properties folder. Listing 2–1 shows the default WMAppManifest.xml file for the BuiltInControls project.

Listing 2–1. WMAppManifest.xml Configuration File

```xml
<?xml version="1.0" encoding="utf-8"?>

<Deployment xmlns="http://schemas.microsoft.com/windowsphone/2009/deployment"
AppPlatformVersion="7.1">
  <App xmlns="" ProductID="{7694daf6-c945-4213-b480-c358c9ea0d2b}" Title="PhoneApp10"
RuntimeType="Silverlight" Version="1.0.0.0" Genre="apps.normal" Author="PhoneApp10 author"
Description="Sample description" Publisher="PhoneApp10">
    <IconPath IsRelative="true" IsResource="false">ApplicationIcon.png</IconPath>
    <Capabilities>
      <Capability Name="ID_CAP_GAMERSERVICES"/>
      <Capability Name="ID_CAP_IDENTITY_DEVICE"/>
      <Capability Name="ID_CAP_IDENTITY_USER"/>
      <Capability Name="ID_CAP_LOCATION"/>
      <Capability Name="ID_CAP_MEDIALIB"/>
      <Capability Name="ID_CAP_MICROPHONE"/>
      <Capability Name="ID_CAP_NETWORKING"/>
      <Capability Name="ID_CAP_PHONEDIALER"/>
      <Capability Name="ID_CAP_PUSH_NOTIFICATION"/>
      <Capability Name="ID_CAP_SENSORS"/>
      <Capability Name="ID_CAP_WEBBROWSERCOMPONENT"/>
      <Capability Name="ID_CAP_ISV_CAMERA"/>
      <Capability Name="ID_CAP_CONTACTS"/>
      <Capability Name="ID_CAP_APPOINTMENTS"/>
    </Capabilities>
    <Tasks>
      <DefaultTask  Name ="_default" NavigationPage="MainPage.xaml"/>
    </Tasks>
    <Tokens>
      <PrimaryToken TokenID="PhoneApp10Token" TaskName="_default">
        <TemplateType5>
          <BackgroundImageURI IsRelative="true"
IsResource="false">Background.png</BackgroundImageURI>
          <Count>0</Count>
          <Title>PhoneApp10</Title>
        </TemplateType5>
      </PrimaryToken>
    </Tokens>
  </App>
</Deployment>
```

When you configure project settings by right-clicking the BuiltInControls project node in the Solution Explorer and select Properties, the values are updated in AssemblyInfo.cs just like for every other .NET Framework project, but it also updates values in WMAppManifest.xml. The WMAppManifest.xml is rewritten when you submit your application to marketplace based on capabilities detection and based on the metadata provided to marketplace when submitting the application.

You can carefully edit the WMAppManifest.xml during development to help identify certification requirements. As an example, if you do not believe your application needs location information, you can remove ID_CAP_LOCATION from the Capabilities XML element. When you run your application, you will discover errors indicating that your application needs that capability. Using location means that certain certification requirements need to be met such as asking for permission as well as having a setting to disable location. Capabilities are an important part of certification.

▨ **Note** You can use the Marketplace Test Kit available in Visual Studio by right-clicking on a project and selecting the "Open Marketplace Test Kit" option.

Continuing to explore WMAppManifest.xml, the App element contains several key pieces of information. You should not change the ProductID once the application is published in Marketplace. If you change the ProductID when submitting an update, Marketplace will infer it to be a new product and not an update to an existing product. Existing users will never see the update in this case.

The Genre is configured based on user selection in the marketplace metadata. The default for Silverlight and XNA Framework is apps.normal. You can change it to Apps.Games to force the application to appear in the Games Hub on a device.

One item to be aware of is that if you rename MainPage.xaml, you should also update the DefaultTask element under the Tasks element to match the first UI Xaml page that should be displayed. If you do not, the application will fail to launch. For more information on the WMAppManifest.xml file, go to:

http://msdn.microsoft.com/en-us/library/ff769509(VS.92).aspx

If your application has a background agent, you add it to the <Tasks> section in WMManifest.xml. I'll cover more on background processing in Chapter 10. In the next section I will cover the anatomy of a Windows Phone application.

Anatomy of a Windows Phone Application

As mentioned, App.xaml and App.xaml.cs are the code files for the application object that hosts the individual pages. Listings 2–2 and 2–3 contain a default App.xaml file and its code behind file.

Listing 2–2. App.xaml File

```
<Application
    x:Class="BuiltInControls.App"
    xmlns="http://schemas.microsoft.com/winfx/2006/xaml/presentation"
    xmlns:x="http://schemas.microsoft.com/winfx/2006/xaml"
    xmlns:phone="clr-namespace:Microsoft.Phone.Controls;assembly=Microsoft.Phone"
    xmlns:shell="clr-namespace:Microsoft.Phone.Shell;assembly=Microsoft.Phone">

    <!--Application Resources-->
    <Application.Resources>
    </Application.Resources>
```

```
    <Application.ApplicationLifetimeObjects>
        <!--Required object that handles lifetime events for the application-->
        <shell:PhoneApplicationService
            Launching="Application_Launching" Closing="Application_Closing"
            Activated="Application_Activated" Deactivated="Application_Deactivated"/>
    </Application.ApplicationLifetimeObjects>
</Application>
```

Listing 2–3. App.xaml.cs Code File

```
using System;
using System.Collections.Generic;
using System.Linq;
using System.Net;
using System.Windows;
using System.Windows.Controls;
using System.Windows.Documents;
using System.Windows.Input;
using System.Windows.Media;
using System.Windows.Media.Animation;
using System.Windows.Navigation;
using System.Windows.Shapes;
using Microsoft.Phone.Controls;
using Microsoft.Phone.Shell;

namespace BuiltInControls
{
  public partial class App : Application
  {
    /// <summary>
    /// Provides easy access to the root frame of the Phone Application.
    /// </summary>
    /// <returns>The root frame of the Phone Application.</returns>
    public PhoneApplicationFrame RootFrame { get; private set; }

    /// <summary>
    /// Constructor for the Application object.
    /// </summary>
    public App()
    {
      // Global handler for uncaught exceptions.
      UnhandledException += Application_UnhandledException;

      // Show graphics profiling information while debugging.
      if (System.Diagnostics.Debugger.IsAttached)
      {
        // Display the current frame rate counters.
        Application.Current.Host.Settings.EnableFrameRateCounter = true;

        // Show the areas of the app that are being redrawn in each frame.
        //Application.Current.Host.Settings.EnableRedrawRegions = true;
```

```
        // Enable non-production analysis visualization mode,
        // which shows areas of a page that are being GPU accelerated with a colored overlay.
        //Application.Current.Host.Settings.EnableCacheVisualization = true;
    }

    // Standard Silverlight initialization
    InitializeComponent();

    // Phone-specific initialization
    InitializePhoneApplication();
}

// Code to execute when the application is launching (eg, from Start)
// This code will not execute when the application is reactivated
private void Application_Launching(object sender, LaunchingEventArgs e)
{
}

// Code to execute when the application is activated (brought to foreground)
// This code will not execute when the application is first launched
private void Application_Activated(object sender, ActivatedEventArgs e)
{
}

// Code to execute when the application is deactivated (sent to background)
// This code will not execute when the application is closing
private void Application_Deactivated(object sender, DeactivatedEventArgs e)
{
}

// Code to execute when the application is closing (eg, user hit Back)
// This code will not execute when the application is deactivated
private void Application_Closing(object sender, ClosingEventArgs e)
{
}

// Code to execute if a navigation fails
private void RootFrame_NavigationFailed(object sender, NavigationFailedEventArgs e)
{
    if (System.Diagnostics.Debugger.IsAttached)
    {
        // A navigation has failed; break into the debugger
        System.Diagnostics.Debugger.Break();
    }
}

// Code to execute on Unhandled Exceptions
private void Application_UnhandledException(object sender, ↵
ApplicationUnhandledExceptionEventArgs e)
{
    if (System.Diagnostics.Debugger.IsAttached)
```

```csharp
    {
      // An unhandled exception has occurred; break into the debugger
      System.Diagnostics.Debugger.Break();
    }
  }

  #region Phone application initialization

  // Avoid double-initialization
  private bool phoneApplicationInitialized = false;

  // Do not add any additional code to this method
  private void InitializePhoneApplication()
  {
    if (phoneApplicationInitialized)
      return;

    // Create the frame but don't set it as RootVisual yet; this allows the splash
    // screen to remain active until the application is ready to render.
    RootFrame = new PhoneApplicationFrame();
    RootFrame.Navigated += CompleteInitializePhoneApplication;

    // Handle navigation failures
    RootFrame.NavigationFailed += RootFrame_NavigationFailed;

    // Ensure we don't initialize again
    phoneApplicationInitialized = true;
  }

  // Do not add any additional code to this method
  private void CompleteInitializePhoneApplication(object sender, NavigationEventArgs e)
  {
    // Set the root visual to allow the application to render
    if (RootVisual != RootFrame)
      RootVisual = RootFrame;

    // Remove this handler since it is no longer needed
    RootFrame.Navigated -= CompleteInitializePhoneApplication;
  }

  #endregion
  }
}
```

Applications can locate application-wide resources such as data sources, styles, and templates in the Application.Resources element of App.xaml. The ApplicationLifetimeObjects element in App.xaml can contain references to classes that extend application services without having to subclass the Application class. The order of the services listed dictates the order that they are initialized and the order that lifetime event notifications are received. A class must implement the IApplicationService interface and optionally the IApplicationLifetimeAware interface in order to be an ApplicationLifetimeObject service.

The default extension that is configured in the `ApplicationLifetimeObjects` is the `Microsoft.Phone.Shell.PhoneApplicationService` extension that manages lifetime events such as `Launching`, `Closing`, `Activated`, and `Deactivated` for tombstoning, which I cover in Chapter 4. In the next section we create a Configuration Settings service that you can use to manage your application's configuration.

■**Note**　Windows Phone has a limit of 10 side-loaded applications for developers, so the source code is broken up into two solutions; therefore, if you cannot find a project, open the other Chapter 2 solution.

Configuration Settings Service

As part of user interface development, customizable settings are an important component to the user experience. In the sample source code is the `ConfigSettingsDemo` project that demonstrates how to create an application service for managing settings beyond the UI. The project contains an application lifetime service named `ConfigurationSettingsService`, which implements the `IApplicationService` interface. The project includes a Services folder containing the `ConfigurationSettingsService.cs` code file as shown in Listing 2–4.

Listing 2–4. *ConfigurationSettingsService.cs Code File*

```
using System;
using System.Collections.Generic;
using System.IO;
using System.Linq;
using System.Net;
using System.Windows;
using System.Xml.Linq;
using ConfigSettingsDemo;

namespace ConfigSettingsDemo.Services
{
  public class ConfigurationSettingsService : IApplicationService
  {
    private string _configSettingsPath = @"\Settings\";
    private string _configSettingsFileName = " ConfigurationSettings.xml";

    //Event to allow the Application object know it is safe to
    //access the settings
    public event EventHandler ConfigurationSettingsLoaded;

    #region IApplicationService Members
    void IApplicationService.StartService(ApplicationServiceContext context)
    {
      LoadConfigSettings();
    }

    private void LoadConfigSettings()
```

```
    {
      //TODO - Load ConfigSettings from isolated storage

      //Check to see if the event has any handler's attached
      //Fire event if that is the case
      if (ConfigurationSettingsLoaded != null)
        ConfigurationSettingsLoaded(this, EventArgs.Empty);
    }

    private void SaveConfigSettings()
    {
      //TODO - Save ConfigSettings to isolated storage
    }

    void IApplicationService.StopService()
    {
      SaveConfigSettings();
    }
    #endregion

    //Stores configuraiton settings in
    public Dictionary<string, string> ConfigSettings { get; set; }
  }
}
```

The sample doesn't implement the actual loading or saving of the data until I cover Isolated Storage later in Chapter 4; however, the service is fully wired up within the application. First we have to list the `ConfigurationSettingsService` in the `App.xaml` `Application.ApplicationLifetimeObjects` element. To do so, we have to make the class available in Xaml by adding an xml namespace:

```
xmlns:services="clr-namespace:ConfigSettingsDemo.Services"
```

The service can now be added to the `ApplicationLifetimeObjects` using the `services` namespace:

```
<services:ConfigurationSettingsService />
```

Adding that line of code completes the changes in `App.xaml`. In `App.xaml.cs` the `ConfigSettingsDemo.Services` is added via a `using` clause. The `App()` constructor is modified to get a reference to the `ConfigurationSettingsService` and to add an anonymous event handler that allows the configuration settings to load before launching the main user interface:

```
ConfigurationSettingsService service =
  App.Current.ApplicationLifetimeObjects[1]
  as ConfigurationSettingsService;

service.ConfigurationSettingsLoaded += new EventHandler((s, args) =>
{
  // Phone-specific initialization
  InitializePhoneApplication();
});
```

The splash screen will display until this event fires. As a test, modify `ConfigurationSettingsService`. `LoadConfigSettings` and add this line of code:

```
 System.Threading.Thread.Sleep(10000);
```

The splash screen will display for about 10 seconds. This demonstrates the effect of the anonymous event handler in allowing the configuration settings to fully load.

This completes our overview of how to create a lifetime service. I will now shift gears to a quick discussion of the events present in `App.xaml.cs`. The `App.xaml.cs` code-behind file contains the events and methods associated with the Application object. There are several important methods and events available to applications that we cover in the next few sections.

The Default App() Constructor

Besides wiring up the `Application_UnhandledException` event, the default constructor enables the `Application.Current.Host.Settings.EnableFrameRateCounter` if the debugger is attached as shown in code Listing 2–3. The frame rate counter is much more valuable on the device than in the emulator and it is something to monitor throughout development as features are added. Figure 2–13 shows the counters:

Figure 2–13. Frame rate counters

Table 2–1 explains the counters identified by letters in Figure 2–13.

Table 2–1. Frame Rate Counters

Letter	Counter	Description
A	Render Thread FPS	This is the frame rate for the render thread where animations, etc., run. Applications should try to push as much render processing as possible to the render thread from the UI thread.
B	UI Thread FPS	This is the frame rate for the UI thread where application runs. Application code execution directly affects this frame rate.
C	Texture Memory Usage	Indicates the video memory used for storing application textures.
D	Surface Counter	A count of the number of surfaces that are passed to the graphics chip.
E	Intermediate Texture Count	The number of intermediate textures created for compositing.
F	Screen Fill Rate	A metric representing the number of complete phone screens being painted each frame.

Jeff Wilcox, a senior software development engineer on the Silverlight phone and devices team at Microsoft, provides some target frame rates for good performance on his blog: www.jeff.wilcox.name/2010/07/counters/, but here is a summary:

- **Render Thread FPS:** 60 fps is great performance. 30 fps or below will show a poor experience. Turns red below 30 fps.

- **UI Thread:** This is the busiest thread. Applications must try to take as much work as possible off of the UI thread by leveraging the Render Thread or a background thread. Turns red below 15 fps.

- **Screen Fill Rate:** Below 2.0 is ideal. Above 2.5 indicates overdraw.

The frame rate counters can be zero when there isn't an animation playing on the thread at the moment and then spike during an animation or transition. Applications can play a simple continually playing animation to always show a frame rate.

The best way to leverage the frame rate counters and the screen fill rate counter is to continuously monitor them when testing on an actual device. The best time to address frame rate issues is after making a change and it results in a drop in performance. Check out the Creating High Performing Silverlight Applications for Windows Phone Samples for more information on UX performance:

www.microsoft.com/downloads/en/details.aspx?displaylang=en&FamilyID=3a8636bf-185f-↵
449a-a0ce-83502b9ec0ec

Application UnhandledException Event

The Application_UnhandledException event is where you can log, report, and display an error message to a user when something unexpected happens in your application that causes an unhandled exception. Applications should customize this event to present a friendly message to the user. Many users welcome the ability to enter feedback regarding a failure so displaying a simple UI to collect information on what the user was doing at the time and recording to a local error log for review can help increase application quality.

In the Chapter 2 Solution's ConfigSettingsDemo project's App.xaml.cs, the Application_UnhandledException event handler is modified to show an error message to the user when an exception is encountered.

```
private void Application_UnhandledException(object sender,↵
 ApplicationUnhandledExceptionEventArgs e)
{
  MessageBox.Show(
    "Error!  We logged the error.  Click OK to turn on logging mode.",
    "Error Diagnostics", MessageBoxButton.OKCancel);
  //TODO - Add logging service
  //Log error to logging service here
  //Turn on logging mode for logging service if OK clicked by user
  //Use the Microsoft.Phone.Tasks.EmailComposeTask
  //to collect exception information and offer to the user
  //to send in the exeception info.
  //Set e.Handled to true if recoverable  e.Handled = true ;

  if (System.Diagnostics.Debugger.IsAttached)
  {
```

```
    // An unhandled exception has occurred; break into the debugger
    System.Diagnostics.Debugger.Break();
  }
}
```

You can intentionally cause an error to display the error message by clicking the `DivideByZero` button at the bottom of the main page. Run the application without the debugger connected by deploying the project and running the app manually in the emulator or on a device. You will notice that the error message displays and then the application exits.

The `Application_UnhandledException` event handler arguments include the familiar sender object and an instance of the `ApplicationUnhandledExceptionEventArgs`. The `ApplicationUnhandledExceptionEventArgs` class contains the following properties:

- `ExceptionObject property`: A reference to the original exception that was thrown.

- `Handled` **property:** Set to true to if the application can recover from the error.

In the previous code, uncomment the line `e.Handled = true;` and the application will continue to run after the error is thrown. This property gives the application a chance to recover without kicking the user completely out of the application, providing a much better experience.

The comments hint at creating a logging service and adding logging to the application with the implication that the user can choose to upload the logs. Such a logging service could implement `IApplicationService,` and therefore be available anywhere in the application via the `Application.ApplicationLifetimeObjects` collection along with the Configuration Service discussed above.

Consider that, in a consumer-oriented application, you may not have a direct relationship to your customer, so you simply cannot ask them what they saw just before the crash. One option is to prompt the user if they would like to send more info. If the user agrees, display the `Microsoft.Phone.Tasks.EmailComposeTask` to send the `Exception` object's `Message` and `StackTrace` values to the support email alias. I cover the `EmailComposeTask` in Chapter 4.

Part of the overall user experience is to build applications that can recover as well as give the user an opportunity to provide additional information. Most users will be happy to do so if they like your application and want to help make it better.

Anatomy of a PhoneApplicationPage

I covered the Application object and related `PhoneApplicationFrame` object that hosts the application. You can get access to the `PhoneApplicationFrame` with code like this:

```
PhoneApplicationFrame frame = App.Current.RootVisual as PhoneApplicationFrame;
```

Once the root `PhoneApplicationFrame` loads, the first UI displayed after the splash screen is a `PhoneApplicationPage` identified as the default task in `WMAppManifest.xml`, named `MainPage.xaml` with its corresponding code-behind file named `MainPage.xaml.cs`. The code-behind partial class inherits from `PhoneApplicationPage`. `MainPage.xaml` is linked to the code-behind via the `Class` attribute on the root `PhoneApplicationPage` root element.

The root element includes several namespace declarations to bring in common namespaces, like the **phone** namespace alias that pulls in the `Microsoft.Phone.Controls` namespace. I cover options related to `PhoneApplicationPage` in the next sections.

Orientation

The root element of the page declaration includes two attributes related to page layout, SupportedOrientations and Orientation. SupportedOrientations has three options:

- Landscape

- Portrait

- PortraitOrLandscape

The Orientation attribute can be set to any of the SupportedOrientations permissible values. For the ConfigSettingsDemo project, SupportedOrientations is set to PortraitOrLandscape in order to test orientation changes. When SupportedOrientations is set to PortraitOrLandscape, the page automatically changes the display depending on how you hold the phone. We set SupportedOrientations to PortraitOrLandscape for the ConfigSettingsDemo project.

The page does not automatically change the layout of controls. So, if the page has more than 480 pixels of content when held in Portrait mode, the content will run off the screen when held in Landscape mode. An application has an opportunity to react to orientation changes by adjusting the layout content in the PhoneApplicationPage.OrientationChanged event. I cover how to handle orientation changes in detail in Chapter 6, but for this demo, I will use a simple switch statement to reposition the single UI element, the divideByZeroBtn Button object:

```
private void PhoneApplicationPage_OrientationChanged(object sender, ↵
 OrientationChangedEventArgs e)
{
  switch (e.Orientation)
  {
    case PageOrientation.Landscape:
      divideByZeroBtn.Margin = new Thickness(12, 200, 235, 0);
      break;
    case PageOrientation.LandscapeLeft:
      divideByZeroBtn.Margin = new Thickness(12, 200, 235, 0);
      break;
    case PageOrientation.LandscapeRight:
      divideByZeroBtn.Margin = new Thickness(12, 200, 235, 0);
      break;
    //default is Portrait
    default:
      divideByZeroBtn.Margin = new Thickness(12, 400, 235, 0);
      break;
  }
}
```

SystemTray

The system tray is the bar across the top of the screen in Portrait mode that displays the connection signal strength, Wi-Fi, and current time. According to the *UI Design and Interaction Guide for Windows Phone*, the system tray or status bar is 32 pixels high in Portrait mode and 72 pixels width in Landscape mode. Developers can set it to not display by editing the XAML for the page to this value:

```
shell:SystemTray.IsVisible="False"
```

It is not recommended to hide the SystemTray, as users consider it to be valuable information. Letting the SystemTray display is helpful to the user who wants to see the current time without having to exit the application. Probably the most common reason to hide the system tray is for a XNA Game Studio game.

Application Bar

The Application Bar is located at bottom of the screen to provide menu icon buttons for actions and views related to the content presented on the page. You can put up to four icon buttons at any time. If you have additional actions, you can place them into the Application Bar Menu instead. The Application Bar Menu item text will run off the screen. The recommendation is between 14 and 20 characters.

By default, XAML for the Application Bar is available in a new page but commented it out. The default XAML is un-commented for the ConfigSettingsDemo project. Two of the Application Bar IconButton images that are installed by default in the C:\Program Files (x86)\Microsoft SDKs\Windows Phone\v7.0\Icons folder are dropped into an Images folder for the project and set as the icon for two of the objects. Figure 2–14 shows the Application Bar after swiping up on the Application Bar to display the Application Bar menu items.

Figure 2–14. *Expanded Application Bar*

If you click the back button when the Application Bar is expanded, the Application Bar will close down. The application bar height is 72 pixels both in portrait and landscape mode and cannot be changed. The Application Bar can be displayed and hidden.

Developers should resist the temptation to use the Application Bar for navigation. Developers should not put a Home button into the Application Bar either, because it breaks the back stack. Users should navigate your application via the content and the hardware Back button.

In Windows Phone 7, the Application Bar was not available to developers in the Panorama, and it was also not recommended to use the Application Bar in the Panorama control. This lead to developers plopping icons all over the UI, which in the end went against the clean look end users expect in Windows Phone. With Windows Phone OS 7.1 (Mango), the Application Bar is supported and encouraged to be used in the Panorama Control.

Another issue with the Application Bar has been screen real estate, even when closed. With Windows Phone OS 7.1, the Application Bar has a "low profile" mode that renders the Application Bar to less than half its previous size when closed. Simply add this attribute to the `shell:ApplicationBar` Application Bar XAML element:

```
Mode="Minimized"
```

In Windows Phone OS 7.1, developers can also set the Opacity and Background color on the Application Bar, helping it to blend in much better with the application UI and theme. While you usually configure the Application Bar in XAML, this link to MSDN explains how to create the Application Bar in code:

```
http://msdn.microsoft.com/en-us/library/ff431786(v=VS.92).aspx
```

Page Navigation

Most Windows Phone applications will consist of more than one page. Silverlight for Windows Phone leverages the built-in navigation framework available as part of Silverlight. Pages navigation occurs within the hosting `Application PhoneApplicationFrame` object via the `Page.NavigationService` instance of the `System.Windows.Navigation.NavigationService` object.

In addition to the `NavigationService`, the page has two methods to override called `OnNavigatedTo` and `OnNavigatedFrom`. I cover these options in the next two sections.

NavigationService

The `NavigationService` has several properties and methods to aid in application navigation listed in Table 2–2.

Table 2–2. *NavigationService Key Properties and Methods*

Member	Description
CanGoBack	Indicates whether there is an entry in the back stack to navigate to backward in the stack.
CanGoForward	Indicates whether there is an entry in the forward navigation history to navigate to forward to in the navigation history.
GoBack	Navigate to the most recent page in the back stack. Throws an exception if there isn't an entry to navigate back to in the back stack.

Member	Description
GoForward	Navigate to the most recent page in the forward navigation history. Throws an exception if there isn't an entry to navigate forward to in the navigation history.
Navigate Method	Navigates to the page specified by the passed in Uri object. This Uri must be of type UriKind.Relative.
Navigated Event	Event fires when content that is being navigated to has been located and is available.
Navigating Event	Event fires when a new navigation is requested.
NavigationFailed Event	Event fires when a navigation request encounters an error.
NavigationStopped Event	Event fires when a new navigation is requested with an existing navigation in progress. It also occurs if the StopLoading method is called. Also called when StopLoading is called.
StopLoading Method	Stops asynchronous navigations that have not yet been processed.

The NavigationService provides full control over application flow but the most common member called is the Navigate method. In this chapter's solution PageNavigation project, MainPage.xaml contains a TextBlock that when clicked navigates to Page2.xaml:

```
private void NavToPage2_MouseLeftButtonDown(object sender, MouseButtonEventArgs e)
{
  this.NavigationService.Navigate(new Uri("/Page2.xaml", UriKind.Relative));
}
```

When the project is run and the TextBlock with the Text "Navigate to Page 2" is clicked, the event fires and Page2.xaml is displayed. Developers can pass parameters to the navigation target using standard Query string parameters with the question mark and paramname=paramdata notation like this:

```
this.NavigationService.Navigate(
  new Uri(String.Format("/Page2.xaml?page2data={0}",textBox1.Text), UriKind.Relative));
```

Pass multiple parameters like this: Page2.xaml?ParamName1=ParamData1&ParamName2=ParamData2 and so on with an ampersand between parameter values. Generally parameters consist of keys or object IDs such that the page can look up the full object or object collection of data for rendering.

In Table 2–3, the events like Navigating and Navigated provide opportunities to display progress to the user as navigation events fire. To test this, add the below line of code to the constructor for Page2.xaml:

```
System.Threading.Thread.Sleep(5000);
```

The effect is that when the TextBlock is clicked, the UI appears frozen for about five seconds before the navigation occurs. To provide feedback to the user, a ProgressBar is added to the UI and IsIndeterminate is set to False and Visibility to Collapsed.

■ **Note** IsIndeterminate should be set to false anytime the ProgressBar is not needed in order to conserve CPU resources. The Silverlight for Windows Phone toolkit includes a performance optimized PerformanceProgressBar control as well.

Navigation.Navigating and Navigation.Navigated are wired up to an event handler in the PhoneApplicationPage_Loaded event in MainPage.xaml.cs in the PageNavigation project. The Navigating event handler enables and makes visible the ProgressBar. The Navigated event handler hides the ProgressBar and sets IsIndeterminate to false. Here is the code from the PageNavigation project's MainPage.xaml.cs code file:

```
private void PhoneApplicationPage_Loaded(object sender, RoutedEventArgs e)
{
  NavigationService.Navigating += new navigation.NavigatingCancelEventHandler↵
(NavigationService_Navigating);
  NavigationService.Navigated += new navigation.NavigatedEventHandler↵
(NavigationService_Navigated);
}

void NavigationService_Navigating(object sender, navigation.NavigatingCancelEventArgs e)
{
  progressBar1.Visibility = Visibility.Visible;
  progressBar1.IsIndeterminate = true;
}

void NavigationService_Navigated(object sender, navigation.NavigationEventArgs e)
{
  progressBar1.Visibility = Visibility.Collapsed;
  progressBar1.IsIndeterminate = false;
}
```

The performance of the ProgressBar is choppy because, by default, it runs on the UI thread, which is put to sleep in the Page2 constructor. I cover the PerformanceProgressBar in Chapter 6 when I go over the Silverlight for Windows Phone toolkit.

■ **Tip** In Silverlight there are two threads that draw to the screen, the UI thread and the Render thread. Storyboard animations run on the Render thread. User code runs on the UI thread. Any animations that run on the UI thread can become choppy if the UI thread is very busy doing application work. Developers should strive to offload as much work as possible from the UI thread and keep an eye on the Render thread and UI thread frame rate counters to see how code changes affect render performance.

This sample so far shows how to use the `NavigationService` to navigate to a page, as well as hook into navigation related events. The next section covers the `PhoneApplicationPage` overrides available that allow additional hooks into the navigation system.

OnNavigated Overrides

There are two PhoneApplicationPage method overrides available to further plug into the navigation system:

- `OnNavigatedFrom`: Event fires when navigating from the current page.

- `OnNavigatedTo`: Event fires when navigating to the current page.

Both methods take a `NavigationEventArgs` object. This object includes two properties:

- `Uri`: Uri of the target for navigation.

- `Content`: The content of the target being navigated to.

The `OnNavigatedFrom` override is the method where you can take any final actions when the page has become inactive. The `OnNavigatedTo` override is called when the page becomes active in the navigation frame. Developers can access query parameters on `OnNavigatedTo` with code similar to the following from `MainPage.xaml.cs` in the `PageNavigation` project:

```
protected override void OnNavigatedTo(System.Windows.Navigation.NavigationEventArgs e)
{
  if (NavigationContext.QueryString.ContainsKey("page2data"))
    dataFromMainPageTextBlock.Text = NavigationContext.QueryString["page2data"];

  base.OnNavigatedTo(e);
}
```

In this code, we first check to make sure that the parameter is present and then retrieve the value. Otherwise, if you attempt to retrieve data for a non-existing key, it results in an error. We will explore navigation further in Chapters 6 and 7, but many of the examples leverage navigation so this section provides an overview. This completes the discussion on the navigating events.

Up to now, this chapter focused on overall design and then dove into project organization covering the `Application` object, `PhoneApplicationFrame`, `PhoneApplicationPage`, and an overview of the navigation framework. In the next section I step back a bit and provide an overview of the .NET Framework for Silverlight and programming XAML, to help prepare for more advanced topics such as data binding, control templates, and control customization.

.NET Framework for Silverlight

As I mentioned previously, Silverlight for Windows Phone 7 was based on Silverlight 3 with some key features pulled forward from Silverlight 4, such as the `WebBrowser` control and offline DRM for Silverlight Smooth Streaming Support, which means you can play DRM'd content when in airplane mode. I cover DRM and Smooth Streaming in more detail in Chapter 7.

Now with full Silverlight 4 compatibility, except for features that do not make sense like browser Interop, Windows Phone developers have the full power of the same framework used to build everything from rich media experiences on the Web to building mission critical Line-Of-Business applications behind the firewall in corporations.

Since this chapter is focused on building application user experience in Silverlight for Windows Phone, it provides a deeper look at the .NET Framework for Silverlight. Here is a summary of the major .NET Framework namespaces available in Silverlight for Windows Phone:

- System
- System.Collections
- System.Collections.Generic
- System.Diagnostics
- System.Globalization
- System.IO
- System.Linq
- System.Media
- System.NET
- System.Reflection

- System.Runtime
- System.Security
- System.ServiceModel
- System.Text
- System.Threading
- System.Windows
- System.Windows.Controls
- System.Windows.Input
- System.Windows.Shapes
- System.XML

If you are at all familiar with Silverlight and the .NET Framework in general, you can see that much of your existing skills will translate right over. If you are new to Silverlight, this book strives to help you get up to speed. However, consider reviewing an Introduction or Silverlight reference book for additional background information.

■ **Tip** Check out *Silverlight Recipes: A Problem-Solution Approach*, Second Edition, co-authored by Jit Ghosh and me (Apress, 2010), for more on general Silverlight development.

For Windows Phone, Microsoft adds additional assemblies and namespaces related to phone specific functionality that I cover in this chapter and throughout this book:

- Microsoft.Devices
- Microsoft.Phone
- Microsoft.Phone.Controls
- Microsoft.Phone.Shell

These assemblies and namespaces identify a rich set of APIs available to developers in order to build powerful Silverlight for Windows Phone mobile applications.

Next let's take a deeper look at Xml Application Markup Language (XAML) and how it relates to the .NET Framework for Silverlight.

XAML Overview

There are a lot of great references available on Silverlight development, but it is important to provide fundamentals on the XAML language itself in case you are a mobile developer from another platform and not familiar with Windows Presentation Foundation (WPF) or Silverlight development. As XAML is based on XML, it is hierarchical in nature, which lends itself to tooling because it is simple XML manipulation under the covers. Expression Blend 4 takes advantage of this by providing a GUI interface to XAML development that you will want to take advantage of when building animation storyboards and data binding.

Since this section is focused on XAML as a markup language, I explore the capabilities of XAML using Visual Studio 2010. We could just as easily explore XAML capabilities in Expression Blend 4. Expression Blend 4 includes syntax highlighting and IntelliSense as shown in Figure 2–15.

Figure 2–15. *Expression Blend 4 syntax highlighting and IntelliSense*

We will be looking at some C# code as well, so Visual Studio serves our purposes better in this section. But unlike with previous versions of Expression Blend, you don't have to leave Blend in order to hand-edit XAML with syntax Highlighting and IntelliSense support.

Importing a .NET Class into XAML

As you can see in Figure 2–15, the XAML markup for the XAMLBasics project includes several namespace imports using `xmlns`, including the `xmlns:phone` import that is used to declare the root element `phone:PhoneApplicationPage`. What may not be completely obvious at first glance is that `PhoneApplicationPage` is a class in the `Microsoft.Phone.Controls` namespace, contained in the `Microsoft.Phone.dll` assembly reference. Here is the `xmlns` import for the phone namespace:

```
xmlns:phone="clr-namespace:Microsoft.Phone.Controls;assembly=Microsoft.Phone"
```

In the `xmlns` import above, you see the .NET namespace, `Microsoft.Phone.Controls`, and the assembly name, `Microsoft.Phone`. This corresponds to a `using` clause in .NET code:

```
using Microsoft.Phone.Controls
```

The point is that markup written in XAML corresponds to objects in C# code. For example, you can create a button in C# using the code `Button btn = new Button()`. In XAML, you create a button with this markup: `<Button />`. You can essentially consider XAML as a human editable serialization format for .NET Framework for Silverlight.

With this background in hand, you can deduce that making custom C# classes available within XAML is as simple as creating a xmlns namespace import, which is correct. One consideration is that for a .NET classes to be brought in to a XAML markup page, it must have a parameter-less constructor so that you can simply declare it as `<foo />` in XAML without needing parameters in the constructor, which is not supported.

Programming XAML

With the appropriate namespaces in place, creating a user experience in XAML is simple XML editing with XML Elements and Attributes. Elements generally represent a class or object such as a `Button` declared as `<Button />`. To set properties on the `Button`, you can add XML `Attributes` such as `Height` and `Width`: `<Button Height="40" Width="100" />`.

Some properties are of type `System.Object` or some other complex type, which could be difficult to set via an attribute depending on the value. The `Button`'s `Content` property is of type `System.Object`, which means that it can point to pretty much anything. For a `Button`'s `Content` property, it can be set as an attribute like so:

```
<Button Height="40" Width="100" Content="Hello Reader" />
```

For a not so simple type, The Button.Content property can be set using XML property element syntax:

```
<Button>
    <Button.Content>
        <MediaElement />
    </Button.Content>
</Button>
```

Remember that the `Button.Content` property is of type `System.Object,` so you could actually play a video as the "content" of a `Button` object via a `MediaElement`. With property element syntax, more complex objects such as a `MediaElement` playing a video named **video1.wmv** can be set as the value for the Content:

```
<Button>
```

```
    <Button.Content>
        <MediaElement Source="video1.wmv" />
    </Button.Content>
</Button>
```

Other properties can be set to an enumerated type such as a `System.Windows.Media.Color` value configured on a `Brush` type such as a `SolidColorBrush` object. In the example below, how does XAML know what do to with the text value `"Blue"` in this example?

```
<Button Background="Blue" />
```

Intuitively, the developer understands what this means, however, there is a little bit of magic to support this simplified syntax. In the XAML above, the text "Blue" is converted to a `System.Windows.Media.Color` value via a built in `System.ComponentModel.TypeConverter` for the `Brush` type. Without the type converter, the full property element syntax is required:

```
<Button>
  <Button.Background>
    <SolidColorBrush Color = "Blue" />
  </Button.Background>
</Button>
```

`TypeConverter` objects are intrinsic to straightforward XAML programming. Developers can create their own custom `TypeConverter` objects to simplify data binding between two XAML objects with two different types allowing the developer to avoid cluttering event handlers in the code-behind file for a XAML page.

The last XAML concept I will cover in this overview is markup extensions. Markup extensions are similar to type converters in that they allow for more straightforward XAML development. Markup extensions allow a string value to be converted into a configured object, which can greatly reduce the amount of XAML that must either be hand-written or generated by a tool.

In order to identify and parse a markup extension, since it is configured as attribute property text, a special syntax is required that uses curly braces: `attribute="{ extension goes here}"`. The curly braces tell the XAML parser that a markup extension is inbound for parsing.

The two most common markup extensions are used for specifying a resource for an object property or attribute value and for configuring data binding for an object property or attribute value. Listing 2–5 shows the `MainPage.xaml` file for the `XAMLBasics` project where you can see Style attributes configured using the markup extension syntax:.

```
<TextBlock x:Name="ApplicationTitle" Text="MY APPLICATION"
    Style="{StaticResource PhoneTextNormalStyle}"/>
```

Listing 2–5. *XamlBasics MainPage.xaml File*

```
<phone:PhoneApplicationPage
    x:Class="XAMLBasics.MainPage"
    xmlns="http://schemas.microsoft.com/winfx/2006/xaml/presentation"
    xmlns:x="http://schemas.microsoft.com/winfx/2006/xaml"
    xmlns:phone="clr-namespace:Microsoft.Phone.Controls;assembly=Microsoft.Phone"
    xmlns:shell="clr-namespace:Microsoft.Phone.Shell;assembly=Microsoft.Phone"
    xmlns:d="http://schemas.microsoft.com/expression/blend/2008"
    xmlns:mc="http://schemas.openxmlformats.org/markup-compatibility/2006"
    mc:Ignorable="d" d:DesignWidth="480" d:DesignHeight="768"
    FontFamily="{StaticResource PhoneFontFamilyNormal}"
    FontSize="{StaticResource PhoneFontSizeNormal}"
```

```
    Foreground="{StaticResource PhoneForegroundBrush}"
    SupportedOrientations="Portrait" Orientation="Portrait"
    shell:SystemTray.IsVisible="True">
  <phone:PhoneApplicationPage.Resources>
    <Style x:Key="TestTextBlockStyle" TargetType="TextBlock">
      <Setter Property="Foreground" Value="#FFD49696"/>
      <Setter Property="FontSize" Value="16"/>
    </Style>
  </phone:PhoneApplicationPage.Resources>

  <!--LayoutRoot is the root grid where all page content is placed-->
  <Grid x:Name="LayoutRoot" Background="Transparent">
    <Grid.RowDefinitions>
      <RowDefinition Height="Auto"/>
      <RowDefinition Height="*"/>
    </Grid.RowDefinitions>

    <!--TitlePanel contains the name of the application and page title-->
    <StackPanel x:Name="TitlePanel" Grid.Row="0" Margin="12,17,0,28">
      <TextBlock x:Name="ApplicationTitle" Text="MY APPLICATION"
                      Style="{StaticResource PhoneTextNormalStyle}"/>
      <TextBlock x:Name="PageTitle" Text="page name" Margin="9,-7,0,0"
                      Style="{StaticResource PhoneTextTitle1Style}"/>
    </StackPanel>


    <!--ContentPanel - place additional content here-->
    <Grid x:Name="ContentPanel" Grid.Row="1" Margin="12,0,12,0" >
      <TextBox Height="72" HorizontalAlignment="Left" Margin="12,66,0,0"
        Name="textBoxOriginal" Text="Original" VerticalAlignment="Top"
        Width="374" />
      <TextBlock Height="30" Margin="35,185,0,0" Name="textBlock1"
        Text="{Binding Text, ElementName=textBoxOriginal}"
        VerticalAlignment="Top" Width="374"
        Style="{StaticResource TestTextBlockStyle}" />
      <TextBox Height="72" HorizontalAlignment="Left" Margin="12,280,0,0"
        Text="{Binding Text, ElementName=textBoxOriginal, Mode=TwoWay}"
        VerticalAlignment="Top" Width="374" Name="textBox2" />
    </Grid>
  </Grid>
</phone:PhoneApplicationPage>

<Button Style="{StaticResource CustomButtonStyle}" />
```

The next question is where is CustomButtonStyle defined? It can be defined either in App.xaml or the current XAML page in the Resources collection like this:

```
<phone:PhoneApplicationPage.Resources>
    <Style x:Key="CustomButtonResource" TargetType="Button" >
        <Setter Property="Margin" Value="20,20,0,0" />
    </Style>
</phone:PhoneApplicationPage.Resources>
```

Figure 2–16 shows the UI in the emulator for the XamlBasics project.

Figure 2–16. *XAML Basics UI*

The UI is pretty simple, but it helps me explain the concept of markup extensions for resources and data binding. The TextBlock has a style resource applied to it via a markup extension that makes the text very small and a reddish color. Here is the style resource wrapped in the PhoneApplicationPage.Resources element from Listing 2–1:

```
<phone:PhoneApplicationPage.Resources>
  <Style x:Key="TestTextBlockStyle" TargetType="TextBlock">
    <Setter Property="Foreground" Value="#FFD49696"/>
    <Setter Property="FontSize" Value="16"/>
  </Style>
</phone:PhoneApplicationPage.Resources>
```

The style is named TestTextBlockStyle via the x:Key attribute. The style is applied to the TextBock via the StaticResource markup extension as shown here:

```
<TextBlock Height="30" Margin="32,187,50,0" Name="textBlock1" ….
Style="{StaticResource TestTextBlockStyle}" />
```

This syntax applies to all types of resources, not just element styles. It allows for consistent UX by sharing resources across an application. Resources can be stored at the Page level or the Application level in `App.xaml`. Resources can also be stored in external files in Resource Dictionaries. I explore the `StaticResource` markup extension further when I cover Expression Blend later in this chapter, but for now this section provides solid background to help you understand how to program in XAML with resources.

Let's now move on to an overview of the data binding markup extension with Element Data binding. Element data binding allows one control's property to data bind to another control's property value. The stylized `TextBlock` and the `TextBox` below it in Figure 2–16 databind to the first `TextBox` via element data binding. Run the project and enter text in the first TextBox, notice the other two change values as you type.

▓ **Tip** If you would like to use your keyboard when typing in the emulator, click the "pause" button on your physical keyboard. This allows the emulator OS to capture the physical keyboard and can save a lot of time typing. Exit the element and click "pause" again to switch back to the soft key keyboard within the emulator.

Element Data binding is a powerful concept, but at its simplest level it saves the developer from writing simple event handlers that do nothing but copy values from one control to another. How this works is that when you type in the first `TextBox` on the screen shown in Figure 2–12, the reddish text `TextBlock` and the `TextBox` below it get the same value automatically via Element Data binding. Here is the XAML for the `TextBlock` that uses the `Binding` markup extension to element databind:

```
<TextBlock Height="30" Margin="32,187,50,0" Name="textBlock1"
  Text="{Binding Text, ElementName=textBoxOriginal}"
  VerticalAlignment="Top" Width="374"
  Style="{StaticResource TestTextBlockStyle}" />
```

The Binding markup extension first identifies the target property that the property is binding to, in this case `TextBlock.Text` is binding to `TextBox.Text`. The `ElementName` attribute value within the `Binding` markup extension specifies `textBoxOriginal.Text` as the target control/property that `textBlock1.Text` is databound to by default as one-way or read-only data binding.

The third control on the page in Figure 2–16, the TextBox, also databinds to the first TextBox as shown here:

```
<TextBox Height="72" HorizontalAlignment="Left" Margin="12,280,0,0"
  Text="{Binding Text, ElementName=textBoxOriginal, Mode=TwoWay}"
  VerticalAlignment="Top" Width="374" Name="textBox2" />
```

The Binding markup extension for the textBox2 TextBox looks very similar to the TextBlock's Binding, except that it also specifies `Mode=TwoWay` in the Binding markup extension. This means that if you type a value in the third TextBox named `textBox2`, the same value propagates back to the original TextBox named `textBoxOriginal`, which then updates the TextBlock's value via one-way Element data binding.

Data binding in XAML is an incredibly powerful construct that extends beyond Element data binding to object data binding via collections of data retrieved from a server via web service calls. I explore data binding further in a later section in this chapter on Expression Blend.

Combining `TypeConverters` with Element Data binding can provide a powerful XAML construct that avoids writing what would normally be a lot of boilerplate code. As an example, you could Element Databind a `TextBlock` to the Position property of a `MediaElement` that is playing either an audio or video segment. There is a type mismatch between the `TextBlock.Text` property's type of String and the `MediaElement.Position` property's type of `TimeSpan`. You can get around this by writing a simple event handler that manually converts from a `TimeSpan` value to a `String` value. A more elegant way to handle this is to create a simple `ValueConverter` that is applied as part of the Element Data binding markup extension. TypeConverter objects are used by the XAML parser at compile time; however, ValueConverter objects apply at runtime for converting values when data binding. I cover ValueConverters in detail in Chapter 7.

This section concludes the XAML overview. The next section dives into the class model available within Silverlight for Windows Phone and is the underlying objects behind the XAML markup.

Key Silverlight UI Base Classes

Silverlight for Windows Phone is similar to Silverlight for the desktop and traces its roots back to Windows Presentation Foundation. As such it has a similar control tree to support functionality endemic to XAML UIs such as data binding, styling, and animation to name a few.

As with all of .NET, the root base class is `Object`. Next in line from Object is `DependencyObject`, which you will find in Windows Presentation Foundation (WPF) and Silverlight. `DependencyObject` provides dependency property system services to derived classes. The `DependencyObject` includes the concept of dependency properties to enable automatic data binding, animation, and styling. Dependency Properties support three major functions over standard .NET properties: Change notification, Property value inheritance, and value providers.

The `UIElement` class inherits from the `DependencyObject` class and serves as the base class for most objects that have visual appearance and that can process basic input. Example properties and events are Visibility, Opacity, Clip, `GotFocus`, `KeyDown`, and `MouseLeftButtonDown`, etc. Check out the MSDN documentation for a full list of properties and methods:

http://msdn.microsoft.com/en-us/library/system.windows.uielement(v=VS.95).aspx

The `FrameworkElement` class is the common base class for `System.Windows.Shapes` namespace classes like Shape, Ellipse, and Rectangle and `System.Windows.Controls` namespace classes like Control, Button, and `TextBox`. `FrameworkElement` implements layout, data binding, and the visual object tree functionality. Properties and events implemented in `FrameworkElement` include Margin, Padding, Height, Width, `SizeChanged`, and `LayoutUpdated`. The next section covers graphic primitives followed by an overview on controls. Check out the MSDN documentation for a full list of properties and methods:

http://msdn.microsoft.com/en-us/library/system.windows.frameworkelement(v=VS.95).aspx

Graphics Primitives

Silverlight for Windows Phone supports 2D graphics primitives such as rectangles, ellipses, lines, and paths. Generally these objects have been used in Silverlight to build up images, separate UI areas, as well as incorporated within controls. One of the key reasons to use XAML primitives is to take advantage of the infinite scaling capabilities of vector-based graphics.

On Windows Phone, UI design is all about the content, not UI "chrome" – so you won't see a heavy use of UI control chrome in most applications. Where graphics primitives can be useful on Windows Phone is in game development when you need to draw game scenes for 2D game development.

For game development, vector graphics primitives or raster images can be used to draw the scene – so which one should you use? Vector-based graphics require a level of CPU processing to convert from a vector to raster format so that the GPU can render the scene. Therefore, wherever possible, it is recommended to use a raster format like .png files to avoid the additional format conversation, saving battery. Given the fixed screen size of a mobile device, little fidelity is lost by sing raster graphics.

I cover the graphics primitives in more detail with a sample application called `GraphicsPrimitives` in the Chapter 2 Solution. Figure 2–17 shows the UI.

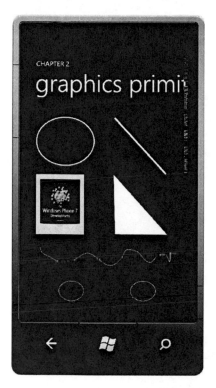

Figure 2–17. *Graphics Primitives UI*

Listing 2–6 shows the XAML markup for the `GraphicsPrimitives` project.

Listing 2–6. *GraphicsPrimitives MainPage.xaml File*

```
<phone:PhoneApplicationPage
    x:Class="GraphicsPrimitives.MainPage"
    xmlns="http://schemas.microsoft.com/winfx/2006/xaml/presentation"
    xmlns:x="http://schemas.microsoft.com/winfx/2006/xaml"
    xmlns:phone="clr-namespace:Microsoft.Phone.Controls;assembly=Microsoft.Phone"
    xmlns:shell="clr-namespace:Microsoft.Phone.Shell;assembly=Microsoft.Phone"
    xmlns:d="http://schemas.microsoft.com/expression/blend/2008"
    xmlns:mc="http://schemas.openxmlformats.org/markup-compatibility/2006"
    mc:Ignorable="d" d:DesignWidth="480" d:DesignHeight="768"
    FontFamily="{StaticResource PhoneFontFamilyNormal}"
    FontSize="{StaticResource PhoneFontSizeNormal}"
    Foreground="{StaticResource PhoneForegroundBrush}"
    SupportedOrientations="Portrait" Orientation="Portrait"
    shell:SystemTray.IsVisible="True">
```

```xml
<!--LayoutRoot is the root grid where all page content is placed-->
<Grid x:Name="LayoutRoot" Background="Transparent">
  <Grid.RowDefinitions>
    <RowDefinition Height="Auto"/>
    <RowDefinition Height="*"/>
  </Grid.RowDefinitions>

  <!--TitlePanel contains the name of the application and page title-->
  <StackPanel x:Name="TitlePanel" Grid.Row="0" Margin="12,17,0,28">
    <TextBlock x:Name="ApplicationTitle" Text="CHAPTER 2"
      Style="{StaticResource PhoneTextNormalStyle}"/>
    <TextBlock x:Name="PageTitle" Text="graphics primitives"
      Margin="9,-7,0,0" Style="{StaticResource PhoneTextTitle1Style}"/>
  </StackPanel>

  <!--ContentPanel - place additional content here-->
  <Grid x:Name="ContentPanel" Grid.Row="1" Margin="12,0,12,0">
    <Ellipse Height="146" HorizontalAlignment="Left" Margin="12,28,0,0"
        x:Name="ellipse" Stroke="White" StrokeThickness="3"
        VerticalAlignment="Top" Width="176" />
    <Rectangle x:Name="Rectangle" Fill="LightGray" HorizontalAlignment="Left"
        Margin="12,200,0,227" Stroke="White" Width="145"/>
<Image HorizontalAlignment="Left" Margin="21,213,0,0"
        x:Name="image1" VerticalAlignment="Top"
        Source="images/bookcover.png" Stretch="None" />
<Path x:Name="Line" Data="M245,28 L404,200" Fill="#FFF4F5"
        HorizontalAlignment="Right" Height="173" Margin="0,28,51,0"
        Stretch="Fill" UseLayoutRounding="False" VerticalAlignment="Top"
        Width="160" Stroke="White" StrokeThickness="5" />
    <Path Data="M406,307 L244,306 L239,187" Fill="White"
        HorizontalAlignment="Right" Margin="0,200,49.5,227" Width="161.5"
        Stretch="Fill" Stroke="White" UseLayoutRounding="False" Name="Pen" />
    <Path x:Name="pencil"   Height="55" Margin="24,0,19,93.143"
        Stretch="Fill" Stroke="White" UseLayoutRounding="False"
        VerticalAlignment="Bottom" Data="M31,396 C36.294918,415.62234 34.544609,412.77231↵
57,424
 C67.599434,429.29971 74.964737,436.59296 87,439 C91.685699,439.93713 97.165527,439 102,439
C131.96695,439 133.0285,434.60718 158,419 C181.28416,404.44739 192.78926,421.84195 221,443
C236.51602,454.63702 255.19547,455.07272 274,430 C290.42596,408.09872 279.30313,393.7677↵
 319,407
C334.2662,412.08875 343.0755,439.55231 359,441 C369.82889,441.98444 372.32379,433.58371↵
 379,425
C383.57141,419.12247 397.35007,414.1167 406,417 C419.57794,421.52597 422,469.74692 422,412
C428.6496,413.32993 435.72543,412.92343 443,413"/>
<Canvas Height="104" HorizontalAlignment="Left" Margin="6,495,0,0" Name="canvas1"
            VerticalAlignment="Top" Width="444">
        <Ellipse Canvas.Left="75" Canvas.Top="24" Height="60"
            x:Name="ellipseCanvas1" StrokeThickness="1" Width="76" Stroke="White" />
        <Ellipse Canvas.Left="290" Canvas.Top="24" Height="60"
            x:Name="ellipseCanvas2" StrokeThickness="1" Width="76" Stroke="White" />
```

```
        </Canvas>
      </Grid>
    </Grid>
</phone:PhoneApplicationPage>
```

The Ellipse and Rectangle controls are pretty straightforward except that, as a developer, you might be wondering what is setting the top and left values for the Ellipse and Rectangle objects at the top. How are they positioned?

```
<Ellipse Height="146" HorizontalAlignment="Left" Margin="12,28,0,0"
    x:Name="ellipse" Stroke="White" StrokeThickness="3"
    VerticalAlignment="Top" Width="176" />
<Rectangle x:Name="Rectangle" Fill="LightGray" HorizontalAlignment="Left"
    Margin="12,200,0,227" Stroke="White" Width="145"/>
```

Since I mentioned game development earlier, it is worth spending a little bit of time on the layout system. Silverlight includes a layout system as part of the rendering engine that places objects based on the Margin property for the Grid and StackPanel layout controls. The Margin property takes four values representing the distance from the Left, Top, Right, and Bottom sides of the containing control, in this case the ContentPanel Grid object. Notice that just the first two values are configured for the Ellipse. If the other values are not set, the Width and Height values determine sizing for the object.

For game development, it would be odd to draw game scenes using just Margin values to place game sprites or images. Silverlight includes another layout control, the Canvas object, which allows the developer to set Top and Left directly on the object. This may seem strange because graphics primitives and even controls do not include a Top or Left property. Check the Properties Tool window in Visual Studio 2010 for any object to confirm.

We added a Canvas at the bottom of the Grid and place two Ellipse objects in it. Here is the markup for the Ellipse objects.

```
<Canvas Height="104" HorizontalAlignment="Left" Margin="6,495,0,0" Name="canvas1"
        VerticalAlignment="Top" Width="444">
  <Ellipse Canvas.Left="75" Canvas.Top="24" Height="60"
      x:Name="ellipseCanvas1" StrokeThickness="1" Width="76" Stroke="White" />
  <Ellipse Canvas.Left="290" Canvas.Top="24" Height="60"
      x:Name="ellipseCanvas2" StrokeThickness="1" Width="76" Stroke="White" />
</Canvas>
```

The Ellipse objects are placed using Attached Property syntax, i.e., Canvas.Top and Canvas.Width properties. Attached properties are a special dependency property that allows the attached property to be configured on and apply to a contained object in the XAML tree. I cover attached properties in the next section, but they provide a powerful extensibility mechanism without having to create custom objects. Given that Silverlight objects tend to have many more properties then their Windows Forms counterparts already, attached properties allows controls to take advantage of additional properties without having to actually declare them in every object

The last item I'll cover here are the two <Path /> objects named Pen and Pencil. The controls have those named because that is the tool I used to draw them in Expression Blend. I cover Expression Blend later in this chapter. The Path objects include a Data property that is set to what looks like a code.

The Data property is set to a value that follows the syntax of the Path Mini-Language. The Path Mini-Language has a similar syntax as the Scalable Vector Graphics (SVG) markup Path object. Please refer to a SVG reference for more info on the syntax if interested. Otherwise, use Expression Blend to visually draw objects without worrying about the underlying Data value generated for the Path object.

The other object that is part of the GraphicsPrimitives project is the Image object. It takes an image file such as a .png as the value for its Source property. It can be configured to stretch and scale an image by setting the Stretch property to Fill or UniformtoFill. The Image object is the most common graphics primitive a developer will work with. I cover working with the Image object in detail in Chapter 7.

This wraps up the overview of the .NET Framework for Silverlight and XAML. Now let's dive into the details on controls.

Controls

Silverlight for Windows Phone includes a rich set of controls that are already templated with the Metro theme" by default. Figure 2–18 shows a quick search of controls available on my laptop.

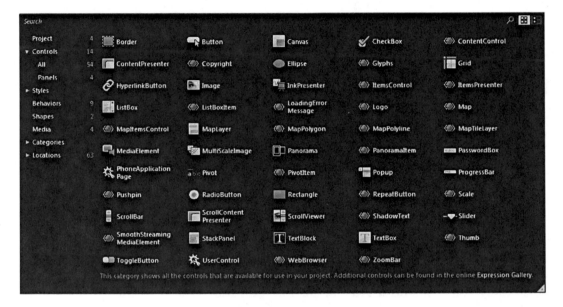

Figure 2–18. Avaialble controls on the author's laptop

Some of the controls are "sub" controls that are generally associated with a primary control. As an example, the ListBoxItem control always sits within a ListBox control. The ZoomBox control is part of the Bing Maps Map control, etc. Still, as you can see, there are a rich set of controls available for Windows Phone developers.

___

■ **Note** I cover the additional controls available in the Silverlight for Windows Phone Toolkit in Chapter 6.

___

The Chapter 2 solution in the code download has a project named BuiltInControls to demonstrate a few of the controls that ship with the Windows Phone Developer Tools. One control in Figure 2–18 that may not be on your system is the SmoothStreamingMediaElement control. This control plays media like the built-in MediaElement, but it also supports IIS Smooth Streaming adaptive streaming technology, which allows you to chunk up a media stream to different sizes depending on available bandwidth conditions.

Smooth Streaming is especially important on mobile devices where bandwidth can vary greatly by optimizing the user experience for available conditions. You can learn more about Smooth Streaming at IIS.net. I cover media playback in Chapter 7.

There's an additional control available as part of the Microsoft Advertising SDK for Windows Phone. You can download it here:

`www.microsoft.com/downloads/en/confirmation.aspx?FamilyID=b0f00afc-9709-4cc2-ba2c-57728db6cbd6`

The download installs the control and API documentation here:

`C:\Program Files (x86)\Microsoft Advertising SDK for Windows Phone`

All that's needed is to add a reference to the control and a few lines of code to generate revenue from your free applications. I cover how to integrate advertising into your application in Chapter 7. Other controls shown in Figure 2–18 are pulled in by the Silverlight for Windows Phone Toolkit, which is covered Chapter 6.

User Interface Development with Expression Blend 4

In this section we build on the introduction to Expression Blend 4 for Windows Phone provided in Chapter 1 by delving into key concepts such as the layout system, sample data, data binding, and control templates. I provide coverage of the Silverlight for Windows Phone Toolkit and then return to an overview of the Panorama and Pivot controls.

Layout System

The Silverlight for Windows Phone layout system is based on the desktop Silverlight layout system, so it behaves in a similar manner. The Silverlight layout system enables dynamic positioning of vector-based UI elements using device-independent units or pixels that default to 96 units per inch, regardless of display resolution.

For example, if you set a rectangle to be 96 units high and 96 units wide in Visual Studio 2010 or Expression Blend 4, the rectangle will be one-inch square by default, because the Windows Phone default is 96 dpi.

The Silverlight for Windows Phone layout system includes containers that manage the size and position of controls placed within the container. UI elements are placed into one of three primary containers that inherit from the Panel base class:

- **Canvas:** Defines an area within which you can explicitly position child elements by coordinates relative to the Canvas area.

- **StackPanel:** Arranges child elements into a single line that can be oriented horizontally or vertically.

- **Grid:** Defines an area containing rows and columns where elements can be placed.

I cover the container controls over the next few sections, but first let's look at the layout system in more detail. This is a critically important topic when laying out UI. The layout system is a recursive operation that first sizes, then positions, and finally draws elements onscreen.

The layout system is a two-pass system that is applied starting at the top of the visual XAML tree and then works its way through the Children collection of each control. During the Measure pass, the desired size of each child element is determined. In the Arrange pass, each child element's size and position are finalized.

Two closely related properties with respect to layout are `Margin` and `Padding`. Whereas all `FrameworkElements` have the `Margin` property, only objects that inherit from `Control` and the `Border` `FrameworkElement` have a Padding property. The difference is that `Margin` defines the extra space placed around the outside edges of the element, and `Padding` defines the extra spaced placed around the inside edges of the control.

You can use `Margin` and `Padding` to force mandatory separation between controls; it is applied by the layout system as the UI is resized, either programmatically or as the user resizes the browser.

Values for `Margin` and `Padding` can be specified using three notations: a unique value for each edge, such as "1,2,3,4"; two numbers, such as "3,5", which applies 3 for the left and right and 5 for the top and bottom; or a single value such as "4." If you set the property to a single value, that Margin or Padding will be applied to the left, top, right, and bottom edges of the control. If you set each edge explicitly to "1,2,3,4", the order applied is left, top, right, bottom.

Canvas

The `Canvas` object may feel most comfortable to developers who are not familiar with WPF or Silverlight and have built UIs in technologies similar to .NET Windows Forms. The `Canvas` container enables absolute positioning of UI elements – very similar to Windows Forms or other layout technologies.

StackPanel

The `StackPanel` arranges controls side-by-side, either vertically or horizontally, via the `Orientation` property, taking into account the configured `Margin` and `Padding` for each control nested within the `StackPanel` control.

Grid

The `Grid` control is similar to an HTML table in laying out controls. It supports multiple rows and columns in the `RowDefinitions` and `ColumnDefinitions` collections. By default, if a control is nested inside a `Grid` without any rows or columns defined, the control renders in the upper left-hand corner, which represents row zero and column zero.

When you define columns and rows on a `Grid`, you can specify the Width in the `ColumnDefinition` object for a column and the `Height` in the `RowDefinitions` object for a row in pixels. You can also leave `Width` and Height set at their default value of `Auto` or specify `Auto` explicitly for each.

Leaving `Width` and `Height` set to `Auto` causes the `Grid` to size rows and columns equally as much as possible; however, the ultimate size is determined by the layout system, which takes into account the size of the content. For example, if a `Grid` has two rows defined with the default of `Auto`, but the content in the first row has a minimum size that is twice that of the content in the second row, the layout system causes the first row to be twice the width of the second.

The `Grid` supports a much more powerful method of sizing columns and rows: star sizing. When you specify a star (*) as the `Width` or `Height` of a column or row, the column or row receives a proportional amount of space relative to the other columns or rows, respectively. This XAML has the same effect as setting `Width` and `Height` to the default of Auto:

```
<Grid.ColumnDefinitions>
  <ColumnDefinition Width="*"/>
```

```
<ColumnDefinition Width="*"/>
</Grid.ColumnDefinitions>
<Grid.RowDefinitions>
  <RowDefinition Height="*"/>
  <RowDefinition Height="*"/>
</Grid.RowDefinitions>
```

It gets interesting when you prepend an integer to * for `Width` or `Height`. For example, to give up to twice the amount of available space to the second column and second row, specify 2* for both the `Width` and `Height`, like this:

```
<Grid.ColumnDefinitions>
  <ColumnDefinition Width="*"/>
  <ColumnDefinition Width="2*"/>
</Grid.ColumnDefinitions>
<Grid.RowDefinitions>
  <RowDefinition Height="*"/>
  <RowDefinition Height="2*"/>
</Grid.RowDefinitions>
```

Note that I said "up to twice the amount." That is because the layout system takes into account the minimum size required for content. If the second column wants twice as much space as the first column, the content in the first column may prevent the second column from getting all the requested space, depending on the minimum width values configured on the content in the first column.

Layout Controls Sample and Blend Behaviors

The project LayoutControls in the Chapter 2 solution demonstrates how the `Canvas`, `StackPanel`, and `Grid` layout controls work. Since this section is focused on Expression Blend, I introduce a new concept called Behaviors to provide navigation without writing any C# code.

Behaviors Overview

WPF introduced the concept of Triggers, which allowed actions to happen such as starting an animation `StoryBoard` object by clicking a button without writing any C# code. Behaviors were introduced in Silverlight 3 and take the concept of Triggers even further while including full Expression Blend support with drag-and-drop support to apply behaviors.

Behaviors allow developers to add logic to a control visually in Blend. You can think of them as code-less events or actions meaning no C# code is needed to utilize a Behavior. To find behaviors in Expression Blend, click on the Assets tab and select Behaviors to filter to the list of items. Figure 2–19 shows a list of available behaviors.

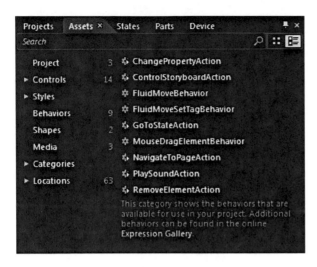

Figure 2–19. Expression Blend built-in behaviors

Additional Silverlight behaviors can be found at the Expression Blend Gallery located here:

`http://gallery.expression.microsoft.com/en-us/site/search`

For the `LayoutControls` sample project, three `TextBlock` controls are put into the UI of `MainPage.xaml` with text of `Canvas`, `StackPanel`, and `Grid`, respectively. Three pages are added to the project named `CanvasPage.xaml`, `StackPanelPage.xaml`, and `GridPage.xaml`. Switch back to `MainPage.xaml` to drag-and-drop a `NavigateToPageAction` behavior onto the `TextBlock` with the text `Canvas`. Figure 2–20 shows the Properties window for the behavior. The `EventName` property indicates the event to kick off the action, in this case touching the label will navigate to the page configured for the `TargetPage` property.

Figure 2–20. NavigateToPageAction behavior configuration

Without writing any code, when the `Canvas` `TextBlock` is touched, the `MouseLeftButtonDown` event fires and the `PhoneApplicationFrame` will navigate to the `TargetPage` of `CanvastPage.xaml`. We do the same for the other two labels so that they navigate to the `StackPanelPage.xaml` and `GridPage.xaml` pages respectively. Here is a snippet of the XAML added to the Canvas textbox as a result of dragging-and-dropping the behavior:

```
<TextBlock HorizontalAlignment="Left" TextWrapping="Wrap" Text="Canvas"
 VerticalAlignment="Top" Margin="12,43,0,0">
  <Custom:Interaction.Triggers>
    <Custom:EventTrigger EventName="MouseLeftButtonDown">
      <ic:NavigateToPageAction TargetPage="/CanvasPage.xaml"/>
    </Custom:EventTrigger>
  </Custom:Interaction.Triggers>
</TextBlock>
```

Under the hood, behaviors are just XAML markup programmed visually with Expression Blend. The navigation actions do not include animations but this quick demo touches upon just the beginning of what Silverlight Behaviors can offer in terms of simplifying code with standardized behaviors and actions. Chapter 6 covers how to add animations to page transitions.

Layout Controls

Now that the navigation has been visually programmed with Behaviors, it is time to add the layout controls starting with the `Canvas` control to `CanvasPage.xaml`. By default the `Canvas` control is not listed in the Asset Bar. As covered in Chapter 1, click and hold the chevron at the bottom of the Asset Bar on the left to pop-out the search UI, or click and hold on the `Grid` icon in the Asset Bar and the UI to switch to `Canvas` is presented.

Double-click on `Canvas` to add it to the `CanvasPage.xaml` UI. Type Shift-V to go back to Selection mode and then right-click on the `Canvas` and select **Auto-Size ➤ Fill**. The `Canvas` now occupies the content area. The interesting part is when an object is placed inside a `Canvas` such as an `Ellipse`. Click-and-Hold the `Rectangle` to switch to `Ellipse`, double-click as before to add the `Ellipse` to the `Canvas`. The `Ellipse` is added to the `Canvas` instead of the `Grid` named `ContentPanel`, because `Canvas` was the control selected (blue rectangle) in the Object and Timeline Tool Window.

Move the Ellipse to about the middle of the `ContentPanel` Grid's area. Notice that the `Margin` value did not change as what is normally the case when objects are placed within a `Grid` layout control. Because the `Ellipse` is within a `Canvas` layout control, objects are absolutely positioned using `Canvas.Left` and `Canvas.Top` attached properties instead of via `Margin`. Here is the XAML for the ellipse:

```
<Ellipse Fill="#FFF4F4F5" Height="100" Stroke="Black" Width="100" Canvas.Left="176"
 Canvas.Top="279"/>
```

The `Canvas` layout control operates differently with respect to the Silverlight Layout system. Controls are absolutely positioned within a `Canvas`, making it the ideal layout control for Silverlight-based game development. Developers can apply `Margin` to controls within a `Canvas` but the `Margin` is applied relative to the `Canvas.Top` and `Canvas.Left` properties, not to the bounds of the Canvas, which is different behavior compared to a `Grid`.

Grid Page

For `GridPage.xaml`, we don't add an additional `Grid`, because there is already a `Grid` control named `ContentPanel` by default when adding a new page to the project. Click and hold the `Rectangle` to switch to `Ellipse`, and double-click as before to add the `Ellipse` to the `Grid`. By default it is placed in `Grid.Row = 0` and `Grid.Column=0`. Initially the `ContentPanel` does not have any additional `Rows` or `Columns` so let's add a couple visually to make a tic-tac-toe type grid layout as shown in Figure 2–21.

Figure 2–21. *GridPage.xaml at desig time*

The `Ellipse` is placed in the center position in the `Grid` control resulting in this Xaml:

```
<Ellipse Fill="#FFF4F4F5" Stroke="Black" Grid.Column="1" Grid.Row="1" Width="100"↵
 Height="100"/>
```

We see two additional attached properties used to position the `Ellipse` within the `Grid` Control: `Grid.Column` and `Grid.Row`.

StackPanel Page

Double-click on `StackPanel` to add it to the `StackPanelPage.xaml` UI. Press Shift-V to go back to Selection mode, and then right-click on the `StackPanel` and select Auto-Size ➤ Fill. The `StackPanel` now occupies the content area. The interesting part is what happens when multiple objects are placed inside a `StackPanel` such as an `Ellipse`. Click and hold the `Rectangle` to switch to `Ellipse`, and double-click as before to add an `Ellipse` to the `StackPanel`. This time, double-click on the `Ellipse` icon in the Asset Bar five more times. Notice how each `Ellipse` is automatically added under the previous Ellipse or "stacked" on top of one another.

The StackPanel control does not support absolute positioning like the Canvas. Developers can use Margin and Padding to adjust the display within the StackPanel. Remove two of the six `Ellipses` so that four are stacked. Multi-select the remaining four `Ellipse` controls and then set the `Top` and `Bottom` `Margin` values to 10. This results in the `Ellipses` separating from each other a bit but still within the behavior of the `StackPanel`.

Now set a `Width` on all four `Ellipse` controls of 100 pixels to remove the stretch. By default, we now have four circles stacked and spaced. Finally, add a 100 `Left Margin` to the second `Ellipse` and 100 `Right Margin` to the third `Ellipse` resulting in Figure 2–22.

Figure 2–22. *StackPanel.xaml at design time*

Layout Tips

The layout controls provide an immense amount of flexibility within the layout system. Developers should use the controls to lay out UI as much as possible initially. As an example, use a Grid with Rows and Columns to separate UI first. For items that are lined up either horizontally or vertically, use a `StackPanel`. Adjust `HorizontalAlignment` and `VerticalAlignment` as needed.

Once the general layout is in place, Apply `Margin` and `Padding` as needed to space controls within containers. Resist the temptation to set `Width` and `Height` on every control initially. `Width` and `Height` override all other layout configurations and can result in odd layout behavior where controls appear to be cut off. Only set `Width` or `Height` when needed to ensure correct display of content.

With all that said, the Silverlight Layout System takes CPU cycles to determine positioning. In most cases following the above recommendations works fine and provides maximum flexibility with great performance. Only in cases when frame rates are dropping should a developer consider absolute positioning to reduce layout calculations and even then the gains may be marginal. In the next section, I shift gears over to another major topic in XAML development: data binding.

Data Binding

Support for data binding is engineered directly into XAML-based programming languages like WPF and Silverlight. This means most properties are of type DependencyProperty, which includes built-in support for change notifications and data binding. It would be nearly impossible to cover Silverlight user experience without also covering data binding. There are three main categories for data binding:

- Element data binding

- Object data binding

- XML data binding

Silverlight for Windows Phone OS 7.1 includes full data binding support comparable to what is related in Silverlight 4. Improvements over Windows Phone 7 include the following:

- Binding to `DependencyObject` instances

- Binding to `String` indexers

- Ability to specify `String` formatting options through the `StringFormat` property. This is very helpful and can help reduce the need for `IValueConverter` instances, which I cover in Chapter 7.

- Ability to specify default display values through the `FallbackValue` and `TargetNullValue` properties to reduce coding logic to handle blank or null data values

- Ability to group collection items through the `GroupDescriptions` property of the `CollectionViewSource` class

- Support for the `ICollectionViewFactory` interface, which enables custom data-entity collections to provide custom `ICollectionView` implementations to the `CollectionViewSource` and `DataGrid` classes

- Support for complex, multi-property validation of bound objects that implement the `INotifyDataErrorInfo` or `IDataErrorInfo` interface, which can greatly help with error handling. I cover these interfaces in Chapter 7

In order to create sample code, some demo live data is needed. The next section covers the `DemoLiveData` project available in the Chapter 2 solution.

Demo Live Data

In addition a separate project named `DemoLiveData` is available to provide an object collection and an xml data file to work with for the rest of this chapter. The project contains two simple classes, a `Customer` class and a `Customers` class to serve as the live data. Listings 2–7 and 2–8 show the `Customer` and `Customers` classes.

Listing 2–7. *Customer.cs Code File*

```
namespace SampleData.LiveData
{
  public class Customer
  {
    public string FirstName { get; set; }
    public string LastName { get; set; }
    public string PhoneNumber { get; set; }
```

```
        public string Address { get; set; }
        public string City { get; set; }
        public string State { get; set; }
        public string Zip { get; set; }
    }
}
```

Listing 2–8. *Customers.cs Code File*

```
using System.Collections.Generic;

namespace SampleData.LiveData
{
  public class Customers
  {
    private List<Customer> _customerList;

    public Customers()
    {
      _customerList = new List<Customer>()
      {
        new Customer(){FirstName="Rob",LastName="Cameron",PhoneNumber="555-555-5555",
                        Address="123 Main Street", City="Atlanta",State="GA", Zip="30042"},
        new Customer(){FirstName="Amanda",LastName="Cam",PhoneNumber="555-555-5555",
                        Address="123 Main Street", City="Philadephia",State="PA",↵
Zip="19111"},
        new Customer(){FirstName="Anna",LastName="Ron",PhoneNumber="555-555-5555",
                        Address="123 Main Street", City="New York",State="NY", Zip="10001"},
        new Customer(){FirstName="John",LastName="Smith",PhoneNumber="555-555-5555",
                        Address="123 Main Street", City="Chicago",State="IL", Zip="20011"},
        new Customer(){FirstName="Jane",LastName="Doe",PhoneNumber="555-555-5555",
                        Address="123 Main Street", City="San Francisco",State="CA",↵
Zip="30333"},
        new Customer(){FirstName="Daniel",LastName="Booth",PhoneNumber="555-555-5555",
                        Address="123 Main Street", City="Dallas",State="TX", Zip="79999"},
        new Customer(){FirstName="Arthur",LastName="Olson",PhoneNumber="555-555-5555",
                        Address="123 Main Street", City="Seattle",State="WA", Zip="50000"},
        new Customer(){FirstName="Janet",LastName="Rich",PhoneNumber="555-555-5555",
                        Address="123 Main Street", City="Portland",State="OR", Zip="43334"},
        new Customer(){FirstName="Janus",LastName="Poor",PhoneNumber="555-555-5555",
                        Address="123 Main Street", City="Sacramento",State="CA", Zip="85755"},
        new Customer(){FirstName="Alice",LastName="Mer",PhoneNumber="555-555-5555",
                        Address="123 Main Street", City="Kansas City",State="KA", Zip="48488"}
      };
    }
    public List<Customer> CustomerList { get { return _customerList; } }
  }
}
```

105

To instantiate the data, simply create the `Customers` class and data bind to the `CustomerList`. The XML file named `ApressBooks.xml` lists details on about 20 books that have been published by Apress over the years. I won't list the full XML file, but here is a summary of the schema with one of the sample book data present:

```
<ApressBook>
  <ID>4</ID>
  <ISBN>1-4302-2435-5</ISBN>
  <Author>Jit Ghosh and Rob Cameron</Author>
  <Title>Silverlight Recipes: A Problem-Solution Approach, Second Edition</Title>
    <Description>Silverlight Recipes: A Problem-Solution Approach, Second Edition is your
practical companion to developing rich, interactive web applications with Microsoft's
latest technology. This book tackles common problems and scenarios that on-the-job
developers face every day by revealing code and detailed solutions. You'll quickly be able
to integrate real-world, functioning code into your applications—and save hours of coding
time.</Description>
  <DatePublished>2010-07-15T00:00:00</DatePublished>
  <NumPages>1056</NumPages>
  <Price>$49.99</Price>
</ApressBook>
```

The next three sections cover the scenarios listed previously and demonstrated in the Chapter 2 solution. That includes a project named Data Binding, which includes a `MainPage.xaml` and a folder named **pages** that includes three pages to cover each topic that follows.

Element Data Binding

Element data binding is when a property on one control data binds to the value of a property on another control. To demonstrate this, we add a `Rectangle` and a `Slider` control to the page named `ElementDataBindingPage.xaml` with the `Rectangle` on the left and the `Slider` control oriented vertically.

The experience we want to create is that when the `Slider` is positioned, the `Opacity` on the `Rectangle` is modified. The `Slider` has a `MinimumValue` of zero and `MaximumValue` of one, with a default of one. The `LargeChange` property is changed to .1 and the `SmallChange` property is changed to .01 to keep the value consistent with what are valid values for the `Opacity property`.

What we want to do is data bind the `Rectangle`'s `Opacity` value to the `Value` property of the `Slider`. To do this, select the `Rectangle` object and click the small button to the right of the field in the Properties Window to bring up the menu shown in Figure 2–23 to select the Element Property Binding... menu item.

Figure 2–23. Expanded menu options for the Opacity property

The menu shown in Figure 2–23 is mostly the same for any Property selected for a control. When Element Property Binding… is clicked, the Artboard switches to Element Property Binding mode, allowing the developer to select a control to then choose a property. Figure 2–24 shows the UI. Notice that it indicates that the `Slider` control will be given a name of `slider`. This is because the control must be named for Element Binding to work.

Figure 2–24. Element Binding mode with mouse over the slider

Once the `Slider` control is clicked, it is named `slider` and you can select the property to bind to as shown in Figure 2–25.

Figure 2–25. *Element Binding – Create Binding dialog*

The `Slider.Value` property is the desired property so click OK to create the element binding. The XAML or the `Rectangle` is updated to include element binding for the `Opacity` value as shown here:

```
<Rectangle Fill="#FF0000E0" Height="134" Margin="30,44,0,0" Stroke="Black"↵
VerticalAlignment="Top"
HorizontalAlignment="Left" Width="188" Opacity="{Binding Value, ElementName=slider}"/>
```

The `Binding` markup extension indicates that the `Opacity` property for the `Rectangle` should get its value from the UI element named "`slider`." Markup extensions are identified by the braces within the quotes as covered above in the XAML overview. `Binding` is a class in the .NET Framework for Silverlight that connects the property, in this case `Opacity`, to the data source, in this case the `Value` property on the `Slider` control.

Object Data Binding

Data binding to collection of objects is a very typical scenario. Silverlight for Windows Phone has rich support for data binding to object collections, as is the case with Silverlight. We continue to customize the `DataBinding` project by adding a `ListBox` onto the `ObjectDataBindingPage.xaml` `ContentPanel` `Grid`. Add a reference to the `DemoLiveData` project to provide an object data source.

In Expression Blend, right-click on the `ListBox` and select the "Data bind ItemSource to Data…" menu item. Click the "+CLR Object" button in the Create Data Binding dialog shown in Figure 2–26.

Figure 2–26. *Create Data Binding dialog*

This brings up the Create Object Data Source dialog shown in Figure 2–27, where we select SampleData.LiveData.Customers and click OK.

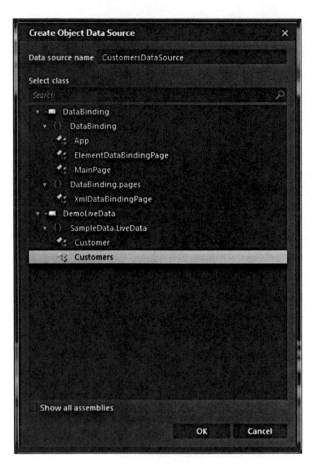

Figure 2–27. *Create Object Data Source dialog*

This returns us back to the Create Data Binding dialog with an object data source pointing to the custom object collection. Select the `CustomerList` Field to data bind it to the `ItemSource` as shown in Figure 2–28 and click OK.

Figure 2–28. *Create Data Binding with Object data source*

Figure 2–29 shows the ListBox now data bound to the object data source.

Figure 2–29. Data-bound ListBox

In Figure 2–29, the data source is configured but it just displays the `ToString()` value for the `Customer` object, which defaults to the full type name. This is because an `ItemTemplate` is not configured on the `ListBox`. The ItemTemplate is used to layout the individual `Customer` records. Listing 2–9

Listing 2–9. ObjectDataBindingPage.xaml Code File

```
<phone:PhoneApplicationPage
    xmlns="http://schemas.microsoft.com/winfx/2006/xaml/presentation"
    xmlns:x="http://schemas.microsoft.com/winfx/2006/xaml"
    xmlns:phone="clr-namespace:Microsoft.Phone.Controls;assembly=Microsoft.Phone"
    xmlns:shell="clr-namespace:Microsoft.Phone.Shell;assembly=Microsoft.Phone"
    xmlns:d="http://schemas.microsoft.com/expression/blend/2008"
    xmlns:mc="http://schemas.openxmlformats.org/markup-compatibility/2006"
    xmlns:SampleData_LiveData="clr-namespace:SampleData.LiveData;assembly=DemoLiveData"
    x:Class="DataBinding.ObjectDataBindingPage"
    SupportedOrientations="Portrait" Orientation="Portrait"
    mc:Ignorable="d" d:DesignHeight="768" d:DesignWidth="480"
    shell:SystemTray.IsVisible="True">

    <phone:PhoneApplicationPage.Resources>
        <SampleData_LiveData:Customers x:Key="CustomersDataSource" d:IsDataSource="True"/>
    </phone:PhoneApplicationPage.Resources>

    <phone:PhoneApplicationPage.FontFamily>
```

```xml
      <StaticResource ResourceKey="PhoneFontFamilyNormal"/>
    </phone:PhoneApplicationPage.FontFamily>
    <phone:PhoneApplicationPage.FontSize>
      <StaticResource ResourceKey="PhoneFontSizeNormal"/>
    </phone:PhoneApplicationPage.FontSize>
    <phone:PhoneApplicationPage.Foreground>
      <StaticResource ResourceKey="PhoneForegroundBrush"/>
    </phone:PhoneApplicationPage.Foreground>

    <!--LayoutRoot is the root grid where all page content is placed-->
    <Grid x:Name="LayoutRoot" Background="Transparent" DataContext="{Binding↵
Source={StaticResource CustomersDataSource}}">
      <Grid.RowDefinitions>
        <RowDefinition Height="Auto"/>
        <RowDefinition Height="*"/>
      </Grid.RowDefinitions>

      <!--TitlePanel contains the name of the application and page title-->
      <StackPanel x:Name="TitlePanel" Grid.Row="0" Margin="12,17,0,28">
        <TextBlock x:Name="ApplicationTitle" Text="CHAPTER 2 - DATA BINDING"↵
Style="{StaticResource PhoneTextNormalStyle}"/>
        <TextBlock x:Name="PageTitle" Text="object data binding" Margin="9,-7,0,0"↵
Style="{StaticResource PhoneTextTitle1Style}"/>
      </StackPanel>

      <!--ContentPanel - place additional content here-->
      <Grid x:Name="ContentPanel" Grid.Row="1" Margin="12,0,12,0">
        <ListBox Margin="12,0" ItemsSource="{Binding CustomerList}"/>
      </Grid>
    </Grid>
</phone:PhoneApplicationPage>
```

The Expression Blend work results in the following XAML changes:

- Added an xmlns namespace import to the SampleData.LiveData namespace at the top of the XAML page

- Added a CustomersDataSource resource to the PhoneApplicationPage.Resources section.

- Set the DataContext attribute for the LayoutRoot Grid to the CustomersDataSource resource via a Binding markup extension.

- Bind the ListBox ItemSource attribute to the CustomerList property of the Customers class.

It is important to note that by setting the DataContext on the LayoutRoot Grid, it makes the data source collection, individual records, and fields available to nested XAML controls automatically. As an example, an ItemTemplate can be added to the ListBox that Binds TextBlock control Text properties to the FirstName and LastName properties of the Customer class just by specifying the data field name in the Binding markup extension. I demonstrate how to do this visually next.

Right-click on the ListBox, select Edit Additional Templates, then Edit Generated Items, and finally click Create Empty. This puts the Artboard into template editing mode with an empty Grid. Drag two TextBlock controls next to each other with some spacing to fit the FirstName and LastName fields. Next click the more actions button next to the Text property in the Properties Window for the first TextBlock to bring up Figure 2–30.

Figure 2–30. *Create data binding*

Expression Blend understands that we are creating an ItemTemplate to display individual Customer records in the ListBox that is **data bound** to the CustomersList so the fields available for controls in the ItemTemplate are Customer class fields. We select FirstName for the left TextBlock and LastName for the second TextBlock. Adding the ItemTemplate results in the much more useful display of first name and last name for each record. Here is the resulting XAML:

```
<DataTemplate x:Key="CustomersListBoxDataTemplate">
  <Grid>
    <TextBlock Margin="0" TextWrapping="Wrap"
    Text="{Binding FirstName}"
    d:LayoutOverrides="Height" Width="75"/>
    <TextBlock Margin="0,0,-148,0" TextWrapping="Wrap"
    Text="{Binding LastName}"
    d:LayoutOverrides="Height" HorizontalAlignment="Right" Width="118"/>
  </Grid>
</DataTemplate>
```

XML Data Binding

The first step to data binding to XML is to obtain the XML file, which can be retrieved from a remote server or embedded as part of the application. For this demonstration, the XML file is retrieved from the application, because I don't cover remote server access until Chapter 4.

There are two ways to parse XML data in Silverlight: the XmlReader class and LINQ to XML, which is one of the new technologies that became available in .NET Framework 3.5 and later. The XmlReader class is a fast-forward–only, non-caching XML parser. For processing large XML files, XmlReader is better suited than LINQ to XML for performance reasons. LINQ to XML provides rich object-based XML processing using the common LINQ syntax.

The work in this section is focused on the XmlDataBindingPage.xaml page, which has two ListBox controls: a ListBox named XmlDataLinqListBox that is loaded via data binding with LINQ to XML and another ListBox named XmlDataReaderListBox that is loaded via XmlReader in Code.

The ApplicationBar control is enabled with two icon buttons, one to switch between the two ListBox controls by alternatively hiding and making visible the controls. The other icon button loads data into the XmlDataReaderListBox ListBox. We configure an icon for the icon button that loads the data via XmlReader by simply browsing the list of icons available as resources and configure the Refresh icon. The other icon was created by combining the default next and back icons into one. The second icon button switches between the two ListBox controls using the Visibility property.

Now that we have the sample project set up, the next two sections cover the code to load the XML data using both methods.

LINQ to XMLs

The Silverlight XmlReader works in a similar manner as the XmlReader in the full version of the .NET Framework. Visit this site for details on the differences between the .NET Framework and the .NET Framework for Silverlight versions of XmlReader:

http://msdn.microsoft.com/en-us/library/cc189053(VS.95).aspx

Silverlight for Windows Phone is a rich subset of the full .NET Framework 3.5 and that it includes LINQ. There are many web sites, blogs, and books that cover LINQ, so I won't dive into all the details here.

■ **Tip** A great resource on LINQ is Joseph C. Rattz Jr.'s *Pro LINQ: Language Integrated Query in C# 2008* (Apress, 2007).

Since the XML file is embedded into the application, we use an XmlResolver. In this case the XmlXapResolver, which extracts XML from the xap, and then loads the XML data into an XDocument object.

We call XDocument.Load(XmlReader) to load the contents into an XDocument so that it can be queried using LINQ. The XDocument class, located in the System.Xml.Linq namespace, is the key object in LINQ to XML functionality.

The XmlReader class can be used to read XML data from the IsolatedStorage file system as well as from streams retrieved via the network just like in the full .NET Framework. A unique Silverlight for Windows Phone ability that we take advantage of in this section is to use an XmlXapResolver to retrieve XML data embedded into the application's .xap file, which is the container for Silverlight applications. An XML resolver in .NET resolves, or evaluates, external XML resources. An XmlUrlResolver is used to resolve the Url location passed into XmlReader.Create. The XmlXapResolver looks for the name passed into XmlReader.Create within the .xap file for the application:

```
XmlReaderSettings XmlRdrSettings = new XmlReaderSettings();
XmlRdrSettings.XmlResolver = new XmlXapResolver();
```

```
XmlReader reader = XmlReader.Create("ApressBooks.xml",
XmlRdrSettings);
```

The resolver is configured for the XmlReaderSettings object that is passed into the Create method. For more information on the XmlReaderSettings class, refer to the MSDN documentation here:

http://msdn.microsoft.com/en-us/library/system.xml.xmlreadersettings(VS.95).aspx

The LINQ to XML code is encapsulated in the ApressBooks class that is part of the DemoLiveData project shown in Listing 2–10.

Listing 2–10. APressBooks.cs Code File

```
using System;
using System.Collections.Generic;
using System.Linq;
using System.Xml;
using System.Xml.Linq;
using System.Collections;

namespace DemoLiveData
{
  public class ApressBooks
  {
    private List<ApressBook> _apressBookList;
    public List<ApressBook> ApressBookList
    {
      get
      {
        if (null == _apressBookList)
          RetrieveData();
        return _apressBookList;
      }
    }

    private void RetrieveData()
    {
      XmlReaderSettings XmlRdrSettings = new XmlReaderSettings();
      XmlRdrSettings.XmlResolver = new XmlXapResolver();
      XmlReader reader = XmlReader.Create("ApressBooks.xml", XmlRdrSettings);

      XDocument xDoc = XDocument.Load(reader);

      _apressBookList =
        (from b in xDoc.Descendants("ApressBook")
         select new ApressBook()
         {
           Author = b.Element("Author").Value,
           Title = b.Element("Title").Value,
           ISBN = b.Element("ISBN").Value,
           Description = b.Element("Description").Value,
           PublishedDate = Convert.ToDateTime(b.Element("DatePublished").Value),
           NumberOfPages = b.Element("NumPages").Value,
```

```
            Price = b.Element("Price").Value,
            ID = b.Element("ID").Value
        }).ToList();
    }
  }
}
```

It is similar to the `Customers` class in the same project in that it just returns a list of objects to databind. The object type is ApressBook shown here:

```
using System;

namespace DemoLiveData
{
  public class ApressBook
  {
    public string Author { get; set; }
    public string Title { get; set; }
    public string ISBN { get; set; }
    public string Description { get; set; }
    public DateTime PublishedDate { get; set; }
    public string NumberOfPages { get; set; }
    public string Price { get; set; }
    public string ID { get; set; }
  }
}
```

The significant difference between the `Customers` class and the `ApressBooks` class is the LINQ to XML code that parses out an `ApressBook` object from the XML. Otherwise, the data binding process is the same within Expression Blend so we how all of the dialogs to data bind `ApressBooks` to the `XmlDataLinqListBox` ListBox control on the `XmlDataBindingPage.xaml` page. The next section covers reading the XML data and loading it directly into the `Items` collection of the `ListBox` control.

XmlReader

For this section, the XML records are added to the `ListBox.Items` collection for the `XmlDataReaderListBox` on the `XmlDataBindingPage.xaml` page without using an `ItemTemplate`. In Silverlight 4 `XPath` is supported so that you can create a Data Template that parses the bound XML object but for now we just bind the XML object as is without a template. Here is the code to load up the data:

```
private void XmlReaderIconButton_Click(object sender, EventArgs e)
{
  XmlReaderSettings XmlRdrSettings = new XmlReaderSettings();
  XmlRdrSettings.XmlResolver = new XmlXapResolver();
  XmlReader reader = XmlReader.Create("ApressBooks.xml", XmlRdrSettings);

  // Moves the reader to the root element.
  reader.MoveToContent();

  while (!reader.EOF)
  {
    reader.ReadToFollowing("ApressBook");
```

```
    // Note that ReadInnerXml only returns the markup of the node's children
    // so the book's attributes are not returned.
    XmlDataReaderListBox.Items.Add(reader.ReadInnerXml());
  }
  reader.Close();
  reader.Dispose();
}
```

Figure 2–31 shows both methods in action.

Figure 2–31. *Xml Data Binding UI*

In this section I covered the Silverlight for Windows Phone data binding capabilities. When live data is not available, developers can take advantage of the sample data capabilities available in Expression Blend, which I cover in the next section.

Sample Data

It is difficult to build out a user experience without the content available in a usable format. Quite often, a project will have development and test services and classes to make data available within an application. Still, this means that you must have an Internet connection available, or have VPN configured to access services. Being able to work with a local copy of the data is more convenient and probably quicker in terms of iterative development than connecting over and over to a data service.

Expression Blend 4 includes a Data Panel on the right in the Blend UI as shown in Figure 2–32 where developers and designers can add or import sample data.

Figure 2–32. *The Data Panel in Expression Blend 4*

Table 2–3 identifies key aspects of the Data Panel with a couple of fake data sources configured to help explain the various capabilities.

Table 2–3. *Expression Blend 4 Data Panel Features*

Annotation	Description
A	Selected by default, list mode for the Data panel lets you drag the Customers collection shown in Figure 2–32 onto the Artboard and generates a `ListBox` data-bound to the `Customers` design-time datasource.
B	Details mode lets you drag a collection item like `FirstName` to the Artboard to create a control data-bound to that collection item. This action also configures the `DataContext` property of the parent container to the collection, in this example Customers.
C	This is a document-level datasource collection named Customers. In addition, a datasource named ProjectSampleDataSource is defined at the Project level.
D	Click this button to edit and further customize the collection. You can specify the type of value (`String`, `Number`, `Boolean`, or `Image`) as well as the format (for `String`, how many words; for `Number`, how many digits; and for `Image`, a folder location).

Annotation	Description
E	The "Create data source" button allows you to add a live or real datasource to the application to display at runtime.
F	The "Create sample data" button allows you to create a design-time datasource to help working with UI elements that display data in Expression Blend
G	You can define datasources at the document and project levels of an application.
H	Click the plus sign to add a simple property to a datasource collection, or click the down-arrow next to the plus sign to choose whether to add a simple property, a complex property, or a collection property to the design-time datasource.
I	Click the down-arrow for an individual property to edit the attributes for the property, such as its type and format, depending on the type of the property.

The Data Panel allows developers and designers to work with the design-time data in Expression Blend while also displaying the design-time data at runtime for testing and demonstration purposes. Developers can also add a live datasource to the UI that pulls data from a live datasource for display at runtime, by clicking item E in Figure 2–32.

As long as your schema is compatible between the design-time datasource and the live datasource, a developer can use both a design-time and a runtime data source in an application. The steps to use both are pretty straightforward. Start working with a design-time datasource to build an application. Next add a live datasource to the Data panel in Expression Blend. Drag items from the live datasource, and drop them onto the control displaying the corresponding sample data. This will bind the control to design-time data at design-time and runtime data at runtime.

■ **Note** Clear the check box next to Enable When Running Application in the design-time datasource properties to allow the live datasource to display data at runtime.

As long as the data schemas match, the sample data displays on the Artboard in Expression Blend and the live data displays when the application executes. This is because the sample datasource bindings are not removed or overwritten when the run-time datasource is added. Once you create a sample data source, you can work with it just like with live data as demonstrated above in the section on Data Binding.

Control Styling

By default, Windows Phone controls are styled to fit the Metro design language intrinsic to Windows Phone. You can apply the built-in styles to your application's user interface as well as create your own styles. Silverlight styles allow you to define a set of properties related to UI that can be reused throughout an application to create a standardized look and feel.

Expression Blend 4 can apply Metro text styles as shown in Figure 2–33 by right-clicking on the control and selecting Edit Style ➤ Apply Resource ➤ and selecting a style.

Figure 2–33. Applying built-in Metro text styles

After visually applying the style, the XAML is updated with a `StaticResouce` markup extension applied to the `Style` property.

```
<TextBlock Margin="12,273,31,270" TextWrapping="Wrap" Text="Apply a Built in Style"
    Style="{StaticResource PhoneTextExtraLargeStyle}"/>
```

You can create your own styles tailored to your brand or application theme but otherwise try to use the built-in Metro styles. To create a custom Text style right-click on a TextBlock and select Edit Style as before but this time select "Create Empty…" to bring up the dialog box shown in Figure 2–34.

Figure 2–34. Create Style Resource dialog

The Name (Key) attribute is how you reference the resource when applying it as a style with this syntax Style="{StaticResource ResourceKeyNameHere}".

Resources can be defined at the application level in the `<Application.Resources>` element, at the page level in the `<phone:PhoneApplicationPage.Resources>` element, or in a separate Resource Dictionary by clicking the "New.." button. Clicking the "New..." button brings up the Resource Dictionary dialog shown in Figure 2–35.

Figure 2–35. Resource Dictionary New Item dialog

Clicking OK to the dialog in Figure 2–35 enables the Resource Dictionary option and sets the name on the dropdownlist box in the dialog shown in Figure 2–34. Clicking OK to that dictionary adds an entry to the `Application.Resources` element in `App.xaml`.

```
<Application.Resources>
  <ResourceDictionary>
    <ResourceDictionary.MergedDictionaries>
      <ResourceDictionary Source="Chapter2ControlStylesResourceDictionary.xaml"/>
    </ResourceDictionary.MergedDictionaries>
  </ResourceDictionary>
</Application.Resources>
```

Resource dictionaries are a great way to segregate XAML markup to keep markup files from becoming unwieldy and achieve better project organization. Now that you understand how styles are referenced and stored, let's move on to creating a custom text style that we can apply to the `TextBlock` named `CustomStyleTextBlock`.

We continue visually editing the `TextBlockStyle1` style now located in the `Chapter2ControlStylesResourceDictionary.xaml` resource dictionary. We set the `Foreground` color to `Gold` and the `Opacity` to 70%. Here is the resulting XAML markup:

```
<Style x:Key="TextBlockStyle1" TargetType="TextBlock">
        <Setter Property="Foreground" Value="Gold"/>
        <Setter Property="Opacity" Value="0.7"/>
</Style>
```

Tip Implicit styles are introduced in Silverlight 4, but they are not supported in Silverlight for Windows Phone, which is based on Silverlight 4. Implicit styles are defined without an x:key so that the style is applied to all controls that match the `TargetType` without an explicit `Style` value configured.

A style consists of a `TargetType` and nested series of `Setter` property elements. The `TargetType` must be a control that inherits from the `FrameworkElement` base class. Each `Setter` consists of a `Property` name and a `Value`. These identify what control properties the settings apply to as well as what the value should be. For a complex property, the `<Setter.Value>` `</Setter.Value>` syntax like this:

```
<Style x:Key="TextBlockStyle2" TargetType="TextBlock">
  <Setter Property="Foreground">
    <Setter.Value>
      <LinearGradientBrush EndPoint="0.5,1" StartPoint="0.5,0">
        <GradientStop Color="Gold" Offset="0"/>
        <GradientStop Color="White" Offset="1"/>
      </LinearGradientBrush>
    </Setter.Value>
  </Setter>
  <Setter Property="Opacity" Value="0.7"/>
</Style>
```

Another attribute available on the **Style** element is the **BasedOn** attribute, which allows a **Style** to inherit from another Style. The **TextBlockStyle2** is modified to inherit from the built-in Metro style using this attribute setting on the **Style** element:

```
BasedOn="{StaticResource PhoneTextExtraLargeStyle}"
```

The last option I will cover is inline styles, where the **Style** is nested within the XAML markup for the control. Here is an example with a single property:

```
<TextBlock Height="57" HorizontalAlignment="Left" Margin="42,427,0,0"•
 Name="InlineStyleTextBlock" Text="TextBlock" VerticalAlignment="Top" Width="162">
  <TextBlock.Style>
    <Style TargetType="TextBlock" BasedOn="{StaticResource PhoneTextLargeStyle}">
      <Setter Property="Foreground" Value="Orange" />
    </Style>
  </TextBlock.Style>
</TextBlock>
```

Any control that inherits from the **FrameworkElement** base class has a **Style** property that can be standardized across the application, though not all controls support visual editing of styles via menu items. To create a custom style for a **Button**, edit the XAML in the **Chapter2ControlStyleResourceDictionary.xaml** file to start a custom **Style** with a **TargetType** of **Button** and a name of **ButtonStyle**. Once the custom **Style** is manually created, you can visual edit styles using the **Resources** window as shown in Figure 2–36 with the **ButtonStyle** selected and ready to be edited visually.

Figure 2–36. *Resources window*

Once the custom **Button** style is completed, you can apply it to an existing **Button** control by selecting the **Button**, finding the **Style** property in the Properties window, and clicking the button to apply a Local Resource named **ButtonStyle**. See Figure 2–37.

In Figure 2–37, the Properties Window is filtered by typing Style in the filter box at the top of the Properties Window.

Figure 2–37. *Applying ButtonStyle via Properties window Style property*

The Style is already applied to the Button but the arrows highlight the small green button, which is usually black until the property is customized. Green around a property indicates that a resource is applied. Additional menu items light up such as Edit Resource… and Convert to New Resource… Here is the final XAMLfor the ButtonStyle Style:

```
<Style x:Key="ButtonStyle" TargetType="Button" >
  <Setter Property="Foreground">
    <Setter.Value>
      <LinearGradientBrush EndPoint="0.5,1" StartPoint="0.5,0">
        <GradientStop Color="Gold" Offset="0"/>
        <GradientStop Color="White" Offset="1"/>
      </LinearGradientBrush>
    </Setter.Value>
  </Setter>
  <Setter Property="Opacity" Value="0.7"/>
  <Setter Property="BorderBrush" Value="Red"/>
</Style>
```

This completes the overview on Control Styles and customization. The next section provides background on control templates.

Control Templates

In most "real" software development projects, custom controls are needed to customize data presentation, customize how a control appears, as well as how a control functions. In Silverlight, developers generally do not create custom controls. Instead, Silverlight developers modify existing controls vial control templates.

Right-click on the `ListBox` control on the `ListBoxTemplatePage.xaml` page and you will see two menu items related to Templates: Edit Template and Edit Additional Templates. I cover both menu items in the next two sections.

Edit Template Menu Item

This menu item enables direct modification of the control for maximum customization. There are two sub-menu items "Create Empty…" and "Edit a Copy…" to create a customized control. Selecting the "Create Empty…" menu item is essentially starting from scratch. The template contains a Grid to start create a new control UI.

Most customizations start with the "Edit a Copy…" menu item, which extracts the Control's internal visual tree, including visual states and animations, and makes it available for customization. This is very similar to inheriting from an existing control in other languages but much more powerful.

Edit Additional Templates

The Edit Additional Templates menu item can have one or more options depending on the control. For example, a `ListBox` control has the following options:

- Edit Generated Items (ItemTemplate)

- Edit Generated Item Container (ItemContainerStyle)

- Edit Layout of Items (ItemsPanel)

The Generated Items `ItemTemplate` is the template applied to the data bound list of items. Without customization, the `ListBox` displays the `.ToString()` value for the data bound type. This is the most common – and necessary – customization for a `ListBox` control.

The `ItemContaineStyle` is also a customization applied to the data bound list of items. This style is applied to the container element generated for each item. For a `ListBox`, the generated container control is a `ListBoxItem` control. I don't cover `ItemsContainerStyle` in this section. I will discuss customizations in Chapter 6 when I cover the Visual State Manager.

The last additional template for the `ListBox` is the `ItemsPanel` template, which just has a "Create Empty…" option. This template customizes the container that all of the `ListBoxItem` controls exist in.

As mentioned, different types of controls can have different options for additional templates to edit. As another example, the progress bar does not have any additional templates to edit but the `Button` Control has a `ContentTemplate` that customizes content rendering for the `Button` control by applying a data template to the content.

I discuss editing the control template and additional templates in the next couple of sections to demonstrate these concepts with the `ListBox`, `Button`, and `ProgressBar` controls.

ListBox Customization

The ListBox control needs to data bind with a collection of data to be interesting. We create a sample data source at the Project level named **ProductsSampleData** that has 100 items. The sample data text, a url, and an image in order to make it interesting. Next up is working with the **ItemTemplate** in the first section.

Working with ItemTemplate

The first step we take is to drag the Products collection to the ListBox, which data binds the collection and creates an **ItemTemplate** automatically that can be used as a starting point as shown in Figure 2–38.

Figure 2–38. *Generated ItemTemplate for Products sample data*

Here is the XAML markup for the ItemTemplate that we customize in Blend shortly:

```
<DataTemplate x:Key="ProductsItemTemplate">
  <StackPanel>
    <TextBlock Text="{Binding Description}"/>
    <TextBlock Text="{Binding Name}"/>
    <TextBlock Text="{Binding Price}"/>
    <Image Source="{Binding ProductImage}" HorizontalAlignment="Left" Height="64" Width="64"/>
    <TextBlock Text="{Binding Url}"/>
  </StackPanel>
</DataTemplate>
```

To edit the template, click the drop-down arrow next to (ListBox) at the top of the ArtBoard under where the filenames are displayed and select Edit Additional Templates ➤ Edit Generated Items (ItemTemplate) ➤ Edit Current to go into template editing mode.

The first modification is to add 40px bottom margin to the root StackPanel to create space between the items. Next the items are re-arranged to present a better display with the item name, price, image, and URL at the top. Do this by re-arranging the controls in the first item visually.

■ **Note** Because it is a repeated template for each item, the ItemTemplate is dynamically applied to the items below the first item as the first item is visually edited.

To improve the display and better utilize space, multi-select the Name and Price fields, right-click, select Group Into, and pick a container control. Any one of the containers can be used to arrange the Name and Price fields, but choose the StackPanel with Orientation set to Horizontal in this case to flow the content across the screen. Grab the lower right-hand corner of the Image to increase the Image size. We next apply built-in styles to further refine the UI. Finally, set the Description TextBox TextWrapping property to Wrap. Figure 2–39 shows the final modifications to the generated template shown in Figure 2–38.

Figure 2–39. Customized ItemTemplate for Products sample data

This completes our overview on working with the ItemTemplate customization for the ListBox. Let's turn to the ItemsPanel customization next.

Custom ItemsPanel

By default, the ListBox uses a VirtualizedStackPanel as the ItemsPanel. The VirtualizedStackPanel enables much faster data refresh with very long lists, because only the visible elements are drawn. For a list that is tens of items or low hundreds of items, the VirtualizedStackPanel may not provide much benefit and can potentially impact scroll performance.

If scrolling is not smooth for your application, select the ListBox control and go to the breadcrumb menu up top of the ArtBoard near the filenames and click on ListBox, select Edit Additional Templates, Edit Layout of Items (ItemsPanel), and then "Create Empty…" to get started. The Create ItemsPanelTemplate Resource dialog box pops up. Provide a name and store the template in This Document to place the template in the Resources section. By default it creates this ItemsPanelTemplate with a StackPanel.

```
<ItemsPanelTemplate x:Key="ItemsPanelTemplate1">
        <StackPanel/>
</ItemsPanelTemplate>
```

Because there is a few hundred items, you can experience the performance differences. Without the custom ItemsPanelTemplate modification, when you click Customize ListBox, the ListBoxTemplatePage.xaml page loads immediately, because the data is virtualized in the ListBox with the default VirtualizedStackPanel items container.

When you modify the ItemsPanelTemplate to be a StackPanel, the page takes noticeably longer to load –about four or five seconds. Scrolling appears smoother, but the load time may be unacceptable. This is because all of the items, a couple of hundred, must be created before rendering, i.e., the data is no longer virtualized.

As you can see, there are always trade-offs with performance recommendations to consider and test before implementation.

Button Customization

In this section I cover some additional control customizations available to developers. Next we transform a standard rectangle Button to an ellipse Button via a custom control template.

Custom Control Template

To get started, drag a Button on the ArtBoard, right-click on the Button, and select Edit Template, then "Edit a Copy…" to go into control template editing mode. The ButtonBackground Layer is a Border. You may be tempted replace the Border with an Ellipse control, but that would make the necessary changes much more complex due to animation dependencies and the fact that the Border is actually a container control whereas the Ellipse is not.

Instead, make a simple modification by adjusting the CornerRadius property for the Border by setting it to 50. The Button now has rounded corners and can take on various elliptical shapes depending on the Height and Width properties. Figure 2–40 shows the Button in action.

Figure 2–40. *Custom Button control template*

There are much more complex modifications possible that involve editing the Visual States defined in the template. I cover modifying states in Chapter 6, when I discuss the Visual State Manager. For this section I will expose you to control customizations by modifying the internal visual tree via a control template.

Animation Fundamentals

Silverlight has powerful animation capabilities that allow the designer or developer to animate any property value of type `Double`, `Color`, or `Point`. Animation lets you vary a property between two values over a specified period of time, thus providing the illusion of motion or transformation.

In Silverlight for Windows Phone, the animation engine is left to interpret how to change the value over the specified period of time between the configured values for the property that is being animated. To apply an animation to a UI element, create a `Storyboard`, which I describe in the next section and then move on to key frame animations.

Creating an Animation Storyboard

In the Chapter 2 project `BasicAnimations`, we add a navy blue `Rectangle` control named `NavyRect` to animate using a `Storyboard`. To apply an animation to a UI element, create a `Storyboard` in XAML, and set TargetName and TargetProperty to specify the element and the property of the element to animate. Nest the animation within the Storyboard element in XAML in phone:PhoneApplicationPage.Resource like this:

```
<Storyboard x:Name="NavyRectMouseClick">
  <DoubleAnimation BeginTime="00:00:00.5" From="1" To="7"
  AutoReverse="True" Duration="00:00:00.5"
  Storyboard.TargetName="Rect1"
  Storyboard.TargetProperty="(Shape.StrokeThickness)"/>
</Storyboard>
```

The TargetName and TargetProperty attributes are attached properties for the Storyboard class. Storyboard objects are usually created as resources within either the Application.Resources or UserControl.Resources element, making it easy to interact with the Storyboard by referencing it by the x:Name value.

This XAML contains a DoubleAnimation object, which can animate a value of type Double between the values configured in the From and To properties. An additional property configured here is AutoReverse, which indicates whether the animation should automatically reverse itself and animate in the opposite direction starting at the To value and ending at the From value. BeginTime indicates how long after starting the Storyboard should the animation actually begin. Duration specifies how long the animation should take to animate between the From and To values for the property of type Double. Also, a Storyboard can contain more than one animation, allowing one Storyboard to animate multiple objects and properties.

The Storyboard class provides Begin, Pause, Stop, and Resume methods you can use to control the Storyboard programmatically. The following code starts the animation when you touch the Rectangle:

```
private void NavyRect_MouseEnter(object sender, MouseEventArgs e)
{
    NavyRectMouseClick.Begin();
}
```

The Loaded event is the only RoutedEvent supported in a Trigger for Silverlight. You can read more about RoutedEvents in the Silverlight documentation:

http://msdn.microsoft.com/en-us/library/system.windows.routedevent(VS.96).aspx

Triggers provide an elegant way of firing an animation. Silverlight for Windows Phone supports Triggers like WPF, where an animation is kicked off via XAML code only; but currently, the only supported event that can be associated with a trigger is the Loaded event. Here is an example from the BasicAnimations project:

```
<Rectangle.Triggers>
  <EventTrigger RoutedEvent="Rectangle.Loaded">
    <BeginStoryboard>
      <Storyboard>
        <DoubleAnimation Storyboard.TargetName="NavyRect"
          BeginTime="00:00:00" From="0.0" To="1.0" Duration="0:0:0.5"
          Storyboard.TargetProperty="(UIElement.Opacity)" />
      </Storyboard>
    </BeginStoryboard>
  </EventTrigger>
</Rectangle.Triggers>
```

The Loaded event is very handy to have UI fade into view as the XAML loads. Run the sample to see the effect. You may wonder why the Storyboard is embedded in the Rectangle declaration and not configured as a Resource on the Page. The reason is that Silverlight does not support loading a value for Storyboard using the StaticResource markup extension within a Trigger.

In addition to the DoubleAnimation, developers can also create ColorAnimation and PointAnimation objects within a Storyboard object. To demonstrate this, add an Ellipse named GoldEllipse to the XAML:

```
<Ellipse Name="GoldEllipse" Stroke="Navy" Height="100" Fill="Gold" Width="100"
  Margin="30,162,0,0" HorizontalAlignment="Left" StrokeThickness="1"
  VerticalAlignment="Top" MouseEnter="GoldEllipse_MouseEnter"
  MouseLeave="GoldEllipse_MouseLeave" />
```

Here are several ColorAnimation examples that are started in the MouseEnter event and stopped in the MouseLeave event. Because there isn't a mouse pointer in Windows Phone, these events fire when your finger touches and then is moved off of the Ellipse.

```
<Storyboard x:Name="EllipseMouseEnter">
  <ColorAnimation BeginTime="00:00:00" Duration="00:00:00.3"
                  From="#FFC18125" To="#FF2DBD43"
                  Storyboard.TargetName="GoldEllipse"
                  Storyboard.TargetProperty=
                  "(Shape.Fill).(SolidColorBrush.Color)"/>
</Storyboard>
<Storyboard x:Name="EllipseMouseLeave">
  <ColorAnimation BeginTime="00:00:00" Duration="00:00:00.3" To="#FFFFD700"
                  Storyboard.TargetName="GoldEllipse"
                  Storyboard.TargetProperty="(Shape.Fill).(SolidColorBrush.Color)"/>
</Storyboard>
```

To demonstrate PointAnimation, add a Path object with the shape defined by a PathGeometry:

```
<Path Name="OlivePath" Fill="Olive" Margin="46,380,75,6"
  MouseLeftButtonDown="OlivePath_MouseLeftButtonDown" >
  <Path.Data>
    <PathGeometry>
      <PathFigure>
        <ArcSegment x:Name="animatedArcSegment" Point="50,50" Size="50,150"
        RotationAngle="-20" IsLargeArc="False"
              SweepDirection="Clockwise"/>
      </PathFigure>
    </PathGeometry>
  </Path.Data>
</Path>
```

Here is the related PointAnimation that is invoked by touching the Path object via the MouseLeftButtonDown event:

```
<Storyboard x:Name="PathClick">
  <PointAnimation AutoReverse="True"
    Storyboard.TargetProperty="Point"
    Storyboard.TargetName="animatedArcSegment"
    Duration="0:0:2" To="200,200"/>
</Storyboard>
```

This section covered the basics of Storyboard animation. The next section introduces key frame animation with Expression Blend.

Creating Animations in Blend

I covered the basics of animation in the previous section using Storyboard objects. In this section we will dive deeper into creating animations using keyframe objects to explore animating multiple controls and properties in the same Storyboard, configuring the interpolation type for the animation, as well as configuring easing in, easing out, i.e., acceleration for overall animation to provide fine-tuned animation control.

To create and manage animations, you work in the Objects and Timeline Tool Window as shown in Figure 2–41.

Figure 2–41. Animation management in the Objects and Timeline tool window

Clicking the "plus" sign to create a new Storyboard prompts for a name, name it RectStoryboard, and then click OK. With our new Storyboard, let's create an animation that re-positions and rotates the Rectangle vertically. Select just the Rectangle in the Storyboard editor as shown in Figure 2–42.

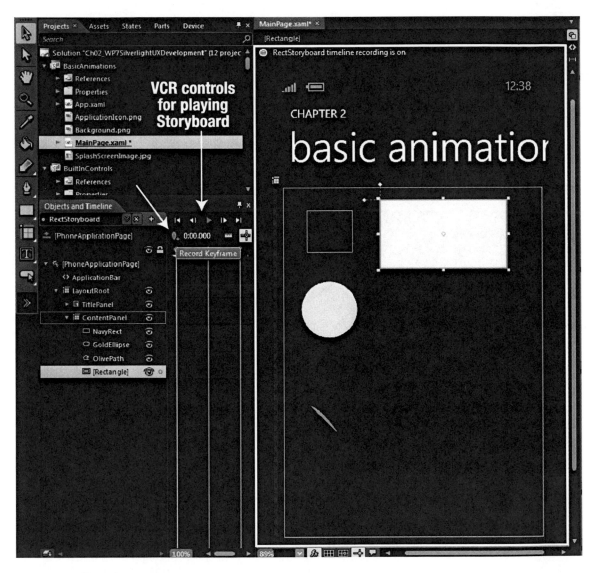

Figure 2–42. Storyboard editor

Clicking the record keyframe button (the small blue oval with the plus sign pointed to by the arrow) adds a keyframe for the selected or multiple selected objects on the Artboard. Recording a `Storyboard` is a matter of adding keyframes at different points of time, slide the yellow timeline marker to later on the timeline, reposition the object(s), and then click the add keyframe button again. Silverlight will interpret the animation behavior between keyframes. You simply have to position objects and record keyframes to create an animation.

Click the close animation button (the "x" button) to exit timeline recording mode. You don't want to accidentally record random editing as part of an animation.

■ **Tip** You can always undo accidental modifications by clicking Edit ➤ Undo or Ctrl-Z.

Open the Chapter 2 BasicAnimation project to explore the Storyboard editor and play the RectStoryboard animation. Clicking on one of the keyframe objects in the timeline brings up the visual keyframe editor as shown in Figure 2–43.

Figure 2–43. Individual Keyframe editor

Select the second keyframe at one second and change the easing from the default straight line to a `Cubic Out Easing Function` to improve the animation's behavior towards the end of the animation. Select an "In" animation to affect the beginning of the animation. The EasingFunction options provide a quick and easy way to visually identify how the changes will affect the animation.

The other options available are `KeySpline` and `Hold In`. The `Hold In` easing modification holds the animation and then adjusts position very quickly at the end. The KeySpline easing modification allows for more fine grained control by adjusting the yellow control handles to modify the values as shown in Figure 2–44.

Figure 2–44. KeySpline easing customization

Add a `TextBlock` and then drop the `ControlStoryboardAction` behavior on to the `TextBlock`. Leave the `EventName` to `MouseLeftButtonDown` and the `ControlStoryboardOption` to `Play`. All that has to be changed is the name of the Storyboard. Change it to `RectStoryboard`, which means that when the `TextBlock` is clicked or touched on a device, the white `Rectangle` will animate. Listing 2–11 has the generated XAML from the work in Expression Blend.

Listing 2–11. RectStoryboard Code Fragment

```
<Storyboard x:Name="RectStoryboard">
  <DoubleAnimationUsingKeyFrames Storyboard.TargetProperty="(UIElement.RenderTransform)↵
.(CompositeTransform.TranslateY)" Storyboard.TargetName="rectangle">
    <EasingDoubleKeyFrame KeyTime="0" Value="0"/>
    <EasingDoubleKeyFrame KeyTime="0:0:1" Value="198.876">
        <EasingDoubleKeyFrame.EasingFunction>
                <CubicEase EasingMode="EaseOut"/>
        </EasingDoubleKeyFrame.EasingFunction>
    </EasingDoubleKeyFrame>
  </DoubleAnimationUsingKeyFrames>
  <DoubleAnimationUsingKeyFrames Storyboard.TargetProperty="(UIElement.RenderTransform)↵
.(CompositeTransform.TranslateX)" Storyboard.TargetName="rectangle">
    <EasingDoubleKeyFrame KeyTime="0" Value="0"/>
    <EasingDoubleKeyFrame KeyTime="0:0:1" Value="-35.955">
        <EasingDoubleKeyFrame.EasingFunction>
                <CubicEase EasingMode="EaseOut"/>
        </EasingDoubleKeyFrame.EasingFunction>
    </EasingDoubleKeyFrame>
  </DoubleAnimationUsingKeyFrames>
  <DoubleAnimationUsingKeyFrames Storyboard.TargetProperty="(UIElement.RenderTransform)↵
.(CompositeTransform.Rotation)" Storyboard.TargetName="rectangle">
    <EasingDoubleKeyFrame KeyTime="0" Value="0"/>
    <EasingDoubleKeyFrame KeyTime="0:0:1" Value="89.949">
        <EasingDoubleKeyFrame.EasingFunction>
                <CubicEase EasingMode="EaseOut"/>
        </EasingDoubleKeyFrame.EasingFunction>
    </EasingDoubleKeyFrame>
  </DoubleAnimationUsingKeyFrames>
</Storyboard>
```

As you can see in the generated XAML, The animation class is `DoubleAnimationUsingKeyFrames`. Just like `DoubleAnimation`, `ColorAnimation,` and `PointAnimation` objects, the `keyframe` animations work on certain types, including `Color`, `Double`, `Point,` and `Object` with the corresponding `keyframe` class of `ColorAnimationUsingKeyFrames`, `DoubleAnimationUsingKeyFrames`, `PointAnimationUsingKeyFrames`, and `ObjectAnimationUsingKeyFrames`.

Each of these classes includes a `KeyFrames` collection containing `keyframe` objects that correspond to the type being animated, with an additional wrinkle of the algorithm used to interpolate between `keyframes`.

The available animation interpolation options are `linear`, `discrete`, and `splined`. `Linear` interpolation animates at a constant rate for the duration of the segment and is the default. `Discrete` or `Hold` interpolation animates at discrete intervals without interpolation over time.

`KeySpline` interpolation is more similar to linear than discrete but provides the ability to accelerate or decelerate the animation within the duration of a segment. The spline interpolation method has an additional property called `KeySpline` that defines a Bezier curve to create more realistic effects. The `KeySpline` property defines a Bezier curve with two control points that go from (0,0) to (1,1). The first control point defines the curve factor of the first half of the curve, and the second control point defines the curve factor for the second half of the curve; the curve factor defines the rate of change or acceleration for the spline keyframe as shown in Figure 2–44.

This concludes my exploration of animations in Blend. I will build on this work throughout the text as needed to demonstrate more advanced concepts such as handling orientation changes in Chapter 6. The next section covers an example of how to create animation in code.

Creating Animations in Code

On Windows Phone, such as when you click a tile or other objects in the phone UI, there is a Tilt animation to give visual feedback that the action was registered. This link provides an overview of the Tile Effect sample in the Windows Phone documentation.

`http://msdn.microsoft.com/en-us/library/ff941094(v=VS.92).aspx`

This link references a code sample that contains a file named TiltEffect.cs. This link describes how to use the TilfEffect code sample but I'll also cover the steps here:

`http://msdn.microsoft.com/en-us/library/ff941108%28v=VS.92%29.aspx`

We add `TiltEffect.cs` code file to the `BasicAnimations` project and change the namespace to `BasicAnimations`. We add the `xmlns:tilt="clr-namespace:BasicAnimations"` namespace to MainPage.xaml. We also add this line to the PhoneApplicationPage element to enable Tilt: `tilt:TiltEffect.IsTiltEnabled="True"`. We also add a `ListBox` control with a few items to test the `TiltEffect`. Run the sample to see the `TiltEffect` in action. Note that it only applies to controls that inherit from `ButtonBase` or `ListBoxItem` by default. Developers can add additional control types programmatically via code:

`TiltEffect.TiltableItems.Add(typeof("AdditionalControl"))`

Application Layout

Windows Phone 7 provides a differentiated user experience with unique interaction models. In Chapter 1 and at the beginning of Chapter 2, I discussed the Metro design language with examples provided by the "Hubs" like People, music+video, and so on. Hub experiences are based on a `Panorama` control. The built in Outlook application is based on a `Pivot` control. I cover both the `Panorama` and `Pivot` controls in the next two sections.

Panorama

The `Panorama` control allows Windows Phone developers to build "Hub-like" experiences within their own applications. Generally an application will have one `Panorama` as the first screen in the application. It is not recommended to have multiple Panorama controls within an application.

▓ **Tip** Don't forget to take advantage of the new support in the Application Bar in the Panorama control, leveraging the `Mode="Minimized"` configuration and setting Background color and Opacity.

Think of the as the magazine cover and table of contents of an application. From a design perspective, a Panorama control should not be jammed-packed with content. Rather an application's Panorama page should highlight top items, favorites, and a menu to navigate to the details of an application hosted on Pivot pages for detailed lists of items or regular pages for individual item details.

The control provides full design-time experience to switch between PanoramaItem panes and visually edit content. The built-in Panorama control matches the look and behavior of the built-in Windows Phone experience, including the gesture-and-flick support.

A Panorama control includes automatic page animations so that transitioning between panes, with different layers moving at different speeds, providing a nice parallax effect. The layers consist of a Title layer at the top left-aligned on the PanoramaItem pane furthest to the left by default. The next layer is the header for the individual PanoramaItem panes.

A Panorama control consists of multiple panes or PanoramaItem objects that span beyond the phone screen horizontally. Generally a Panorama application spans between three and five PanoramaItem objects wide, though four is the recommended maximum. The number of PanoramaItem panes that perform well depends on the content weight in each Pane. Having four PanoramaItem controls richly packed with images and content may well bog down an application with performance issues. Keep an eye on the UI performance counters when working with the Panorama control especially.

■ **Caution** Keep an eye on transitions, animations, and scrolling. If transitions and animations cut short or don't render, that's an indication of too much work on the UI thread. Poor scrolling performance is also an indicator. Reduce rendering complexity as well as offload work from the UI thread wherever possible in these situations.

In situations where performance is suffering, developers can hide individual PanoramaItems until content is visible. Dynamically loading and unloading PanoramaItems may help in some cases as well. Pay attention to the graphic performance counters covered previously to see the impact of changes as content is added.

PanoramaItem panes overlap onscreen such that 24 pixels of the pane to the right show on the current pane in view as shown in Figure 2–45. The content to the right of the line with arrows overlaid on to the screenshot is from the PanoramaItem item to the right, giving a hint to swipe right and reveal the content.

Figure 2–45. The "peek" on a PanoramaControl

Notice the straight edges and grid like nature of content on the screen. It is perfectly OK for a `PanoramaItem` object to extend into two panes such as the "History" section of the music+video Hub on a Windows Phone device. You can set the `PanoramaItem` control's `Orientation` property to `Horizontal` to flow into additional panes and achieve the same effect.

■ **Note** Across Windows Phone applications, whether Panorama or not, content should align on the left margin at 24px. In general, examine margin values and try to apply margin to the largest container possible in order to achieve alignment while reducing calculations.

A `Panorama` can have a background image. It is recommended to keep a `Panorama` background image less than 2,000 pixels wide and 800 pixels in height. If the image is not 800 pixels in height, the image will be stretched automatically without consideration to aspect ratio. The background image should span the entire width of the `Panorama` control or be a single-colored background. I demonstrate how to add a custom image as well as correct the Title layer positioning in the next section.

Correct Title Position

We start by creating a new project named PanoramaApp using the Windows Phone Panorama Application project template. This template is a fully functioning application that is based on the Panorama control leveraging sample data.

A 2272 wide x 1704 in height photo from a recent vacation is added to the project. We modify the photo to be 800 pixels in height, maintaining aspect ratio, in Paint.NET to prevent stretching the image when the project is debugged. In the emulator, the image fits nicely but the White text doesn't show very well against the image – it needs more contrast. Open the image in any editing too, such as Paint.NET and add a layer that is 30% Black over the entire of the image to provide more contrast with the White text while allowing the background image to show through when the project is run again in the emulator.

Notice though that, when you swipe over to the second pane, part of the text is clipped in the Title, as shown in Figure 2–46. The lower case 'l' and 'I' are clipped at the top.

Figure 2–46. *Clipped Title text*

To fix this, you can modify the control template in Expression Blend. Select the Panorama control, right-click, select Edit Template, Edit a Copy to create a Style resource. Click OK to the dialog box to go into Style editing mode. Select the TitleLayer in the Objects and Timeline Tool Window. Adjust the Top Margin to slide the title down a bit by changing the value from -76 to -68. When you run the application, this puts the top of the 'l' right against the top of the screen to fully display the text. Otherwise, the application behaves just as before.

Image as Title and Themes

Let's say you want to put your company name and logo as the title for a Panorama application. Once again, we can edit the Panorama control's template to create a custom Style to support this. First we add a new wrinkle to the sample code. The image for the Title in the Panorama will be an Apress logo. In the spirit of customizing the design to fit the logo, the Panorama background is changed to a solid color to a yellow similar to Apress' logo yellow.

In Expression Blend, the Device tab shown in Figure 2–47 can help you test out your application by changing the Orientation, Theme, and Accent color at design time. It also allows you to choose to preview the application in the emulator or device.

Figure 2–47. *Device tab in Expression Blend*

Switching the Theme from the default of Dark to Light changes the font from White to Black. The darker font of the Light theme looks much better; however, this is a setting that a user can change on a whim. By default Windows Phone obey the theme settings automatically because of the default control styles applied to controls.

Applications can override the default theme by setting custom values for Foreground color and the like on individual controls but that can be error prone. A better way to do this is to redefine the built-in Metro styles to force the foreground color to Color.Black regardless of theme setting, making the change in effect for the entire application with just a few lines of code.

In the App Application object constructor, remove the pre-defined resource and then add back the resource with modifications. Here is example code to redefine the pre-defined styles:

```
this.Resources.Remove("PhoneForegroundColor");
this.Resources.Add("PhoneForegroundColor", Colors.Black);

this.Resources.Remove("PhoneAccentColor");
this.Resources.Add("PhoneAccentColor",Color.FromArgb(200,200,200,200));
```

```
this.Resources.Remove("PhoneBackgroundColor");
this.Resources.Add("PhoneBackgroundColor ",  Colors.White);
```

Now that the resources are redefined to better fit the branding colors, we will now convert the title from a text title to an image. You can make this modification two different ways. The simplest method is to set Panorama.Title to an Image without editing the control template using code like this:

```
<controls:Panorama.Title>
  <Image Source="images/panorama_title.png" Height="80" Width="420" Margin="-20,80"/>
</controls:Panorama.Title>
```

The other way to modify the Title is to edit the Panorama's TitleTemplate by right-clicking on the Panorama, select Edit Additional Templates, and then Create Empty… to enter template editing mode in Expression Blend. This updates the Panorama's TitleTemplate to point to a resource:

```
<controls:Panorama  Background="#FFFFCC00"
TitleTemplate="{StaticResource PanoramaTitleDataTemplate}">
```

Here is the XAML for PanoramaTitleDataTemplate:

```
<DataTemplate x:Key="PanoramaTitleDataTemplate">
  <Grid>
    <Image HorizontalAlignment="Left" VerticalAlignment="Top"
        Source="images/panorama_title.png" Margin="-20,80,0,0"/>
  </Grid>
</DataTemplate>
```

Dynamic Background Image

A nice application customization is to make the Panorama.Background image dynamic. The Title property can be databound to a Brush type, which can be a png image or color Brush or it could simply be set when the page is Loaded or Activated via a background thread. If the Image is downloaded dynamically, you would not want to perform the download in the main UI thread. For the same reason, the background image could be configured on a Timer control as well.

Programmatically Set the Current PanoramaItem

The Panorama control lands on the most left PanoramaItem by default. Many applications implement a navigation menu on the left most pane but want the user to land on a PanoramaItem with content by default. We modify the PanoramaImageTitle project by adding a PanoramaItem to the left of the two existing PanoramaItem objects and mock up a menu.

The new PanoramaItem is named MenuPanoramaItem. The second PanoramaItem with the first set of content is named DefaultPanoramaItem, and will be displayed when the application first loads. A line of code is added to the MainPage_Loaded event to display the DefaultPanoramaItem upon load:

```
MainPanorama.DefaultItem = DefaultPanoramaItem;
```

When the user loads the application, it lands on the content page as before, but when wiping right the user will find the second set of content and then swiping again brings up the menu. The circular page scrolling in the Panorama control makes discoverability of the navigation menu via the menu very easy.

Now that I've discussed the Panorama control, let's switch over to the other major navigation control, the Pivot control.

Pivot

Upon initial examination, the Pivot control appears to be very similar to the Panorama control. It has a title and header, and swipes left and right to view additional content. However, upon closer examination, you will find significant differences. Create a new project and name it PivotApp based on the Windows Phone Pivot Application project template to get started. Figure 2–48 shows the default UI for the PivotApp project.

Figure 2–48. Visual differences for a Pivot compared with a Panorama

As you can see in Figure 2–48, there are visual differences compared to the Panorama. Also, note that while the Panorama has "peek" to indicate content to the right, the Pivotcontrol header items show the selected PivotItem in the normal font Foreground color and additional PivotItem controls to the right or left in a faded font Foreground color.

The other significant difference for the Pivot control is that PivotItem objects are dynamically created as they are scrolled to, which is unlike the Panorama control that loads all PanoramaItem objects upfront. This has implications in terms of start-up behavior, page weight, memory consumption, and so on.

Generally, a Pivot control can hold more containers of data than a Panorama control because of the dynamic memory allocation. Also, the Pivot is used more often to present a denser view of content as compared to the Panorama control. I cover additional differences below in the section titled Panorama vs. Pivot.

Pivot Background Image

Like the Panorama control, the Pivot control supports having a Background configured as a Brush (Color or Gradient), as well as an image in the same way that a Panorama can be configured. This includes data binding the background image as well as dynamically loading the image.

Pivot Title Customization

The Pivot Title property can be modified exactly like the Panorama as demonstrated in the section above covering either modifying the TitleTemplate or simply setting the value onto the Title property via element property syntax.

Programmatically Set the Current PivotItem

The Pivot control exposes a SelectedItem property that can be set in order to display a particular PivotItem other than the default leftmost PivotItem. Simply provide a name to the Pivot and PivotItem controls so that they can be identified in code. This code in MainPage_Loaded in MainPage.xaml sets the second PivotItem as the default:

```
MainPivot.SelectedItem = SecondPivotItem;
```

In the next section I conclude this chapter with a comparison of the Pivot Control vs. the Panorama control.

Pivot vs. Panorama

As mentioned, the Panorama and Pivot controls have a lot in common in terms of base functionality. Both controls mimic the built-in native control versions in terms of behavior and animations yet provide a simple programming interface with strong customization available. The controls include built-in touch navigation with support for flick and pan for a great navigation experience.

From a programming standpoint both controls function like tab controls with an Items collection for either Panorama or PivotItem controls allowing rich content presentation in compact amount of space. Both controls allow the developer to focus on building the content within the Item control panes, which is usually a matter of customizing a `ListBox` control, greatly simplifying programming tasks while providing a rich user experience.

The controls themselves can be data bound with content template properties and item container styles for the Title, Header, and Item Panel, and so on. The controls also include full Blend support such as control template modification and visual states.

In terms of usage, the vast majority of Windows Phone Silverlight applications will open to an initial page containing either a Panorama or Pivot control. For rich initial content presentation, the Panorama control is usually the better choice. For denser content presentation, or larger amounts of content, the Pivot control is ideal.

Many applications will consist of a root Panorama control with a PanoramaItem dedicated to a menu. The menu items then use the navigation framework to navigate the UI to sub-pages consisting of Pivot controls or plain old page depending on content needs. The hardware Back button provides navigation back to the root Panorama control and is in incredibly important part of the navigation framework.

Windows Phone 7.5 User Experience Enhancements

From a user experience perspective, Windows Phone 7.5 includes Silverlight 4 compatibility, improving upon Windows Phone 7's Silverlight 3 compatibility. As with Windows Phone 7, Silverlight for Windows Phone 7.5 does not include APIs related to browser integration or other browser related features (i.e., the general programming model remains the same).

New Controls

There are new user experience controls available in Silverlight including the `RichTextBox` control, though it is a read-only control on Windows Phone. Still, it allows you to display text with character or paragraph formatting, hyperlinks, and inline images.

The RichTextBox control supports a block-based content model where each block is represented by the `Paragraph` markup. Within each `Paragraph` block you can have the following inline elements:

- `Span`
- `Bold`
- `Italic`
- `Underline`
- `Hyperlink`
- `InlineUIContainer`

When you use an inline element from this list, a `Run` element is implicitly created. You can also use a Run element explicitly to contain unformatted text. A `Span` element groups other inline content elements together.

Another control also available to developers is the `Viewbox` control, which will take a single child control (that can contain additional child controls) and stretch it to fit the `Viewbox`. Not a new control, but the existing WebBrowser control has been updated to support Internet Explorer 9, which includes HTML5 support.

New Controls Demonstration

To test out the new controls, I added a project named New7.1Controls to the Chapter 2 solution. I added a couple of pages to a pages folder, one each for the RichTextBox, IE9 WebBrowser control, and the Viewbox control. I next wired up navigation from MainPage.xaml to the three new pages and dropped a RichTextBox control on RichTextBox.xaml. I set IsReadOnly to false and ran the sample. I received an UnSupportedException because on Windows Phone the RichTextBox control is a read-only control.

You may wonder what the value of this control is if it is a read-only control. There are many instances where the control can be useful, such as the following:

- Display large amounts of text within a native control instead of the WebBrowser control

- Displaying formatted text such as Books using the RTF format

I added some example inline formatted text as shown in Listing 2-12.

Listing 2–12. *RichTextFormat with inline Formatted Text*

```
<RichTextBox Name="richTextBox1" Margin="12,0,0,0" >
  <Paragraph>
    This is an RTF document created in WordPad.  RTF documents can contain images as well.
Here is an image of the first edition of this book.
  </Paragraph>
  <Paragraph>
    <InlineUIContainer>
      <Image Source="../BookImage.png" Width="123"/>
    </InlineUIContainer>
    You can wrap text around the Image using an InlineUIContainer.  RTF also supports text
formatting such as
    <Bold>Bold</Bold> ,
    <Italic>Italic</Italic>, and
    <Underline>Underline</Underline>, or
    <Bold>
      <Italic>
        <Underline>combine all three together</Underline>
      </Italic>
    </Bold>.
  </Paragraph>
  <Paragraph>
    You can also have an inline hyperlink as well such as this
    <Hyperlink TargetName="_new" NavigateUri="http://www.apress.com/mobile/windows-
phone/9781430232193">one</Hyperlink>.
  </Paragraph>
</RichTextBox>
```

It displays the text shown in Figure 2-49.

Figure 2–49. *RichTextBox in the Emulator*

One item to note is that the rendered text in the emulator does not quite match what is rendered at run-time on the phone. Figure 2-50 shows the designer with the RichTextBox content.

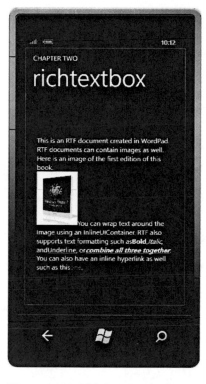

Figure 2–50. *RichTextBox in the Visual Studio Designer*

Notice that the space in the format around the commas and periods is not rendered properly, so it is important to check it at run-time on the phone.

The text in the `RichTextBox` control has a hyperlink at the end that opens up the web page in Internet Explorer 9 for the first edition of this book. For this to work you need to add the `TargetName` attribute to the `Hyperlink` element:

```
<Hyperlink TargetName="_new"
 NavigateUri="http://www.apress.com/mobile/windows-phone/9781430232193">one</Hyperlink>
```

Just like with any other XAML, you can create the object tree for the RichTextBox content in code. The `RichTextBox` control provides a nice alternative to having to go to the `WebBrowser` control when you need formatted text.

The next demo is the Internet Explorer 9 `WebBrowser` control. It is configured with the Microsoft IE9 mobile test site URL. IE9 supports HTML 5 just like the full browser application but within your Windows Phone applications. The `IE9WEbBrowserControl.xaml` page in the pages folder shows how the `WebBrowser` control works by loading the IE9 mobile test drive web site:

```
http://ie.microsoft.com/testdrive/mobile/
```

You must also configure this attribute on the WebBrowser control for it to render many of the demos because they require script:

```
IsScriptEnabled="True"
```

I cover the browser control in more detail in Chapter 4, but this demo gives a high-level overview of this greatly enhanced control in Windows Phone OS 7.1.

The last demo in the New7.1Controls project is the `Viewbox` control. The `Viewbox` control can be used to scale UI by setting its height and width. The Viewbox will force whatever UI it contains to fit within its area, scaling it.

For the demo I put a `RichTextBox` control with some text inside of the `Viewbox` control. I added a `Slider` control to the page UI. The `Height` of the `Viewbox` control is data bound to the `Slider` so that as you adjust the `Slider` control it scales the `RichTextBox` content. Listing 2-13 shows the XAML for the UI.

Listing 2–13. *RichTextFormat with inline Formatted Text*

```
<Grid x:Name="LayoutRoot" Background="Transparent">
    <Grid.RowDefinitions>
        <RowDefinition Height="Auto"/>
        <RowDefinition Height="*"/>
    </Grid.RowDefinitions>

    <!--TitlePanel contains the name of the application and page title-->
    <StackPanel x:Name="TitlePanel" Grid.Row="0" Margin="12,17,0,28">
        <TextBlock x:Name="ApplicationTitle" Text="CHAPTER TWO" Style="{StaticResource
PhoneTextNormalStyle}"/>
        <TextBlock x:Name="PageTitle" Text="viewbox" Margin="9,-7,0,0" Style="{StaticResource
PhoneTextTitle1Style}"/>
    </StackPanel>

    <!--ContentPanel - place additional content here-->
    <Grid x:Name="ContentPanel" Grid.Row="1" Margin="12,0,12,0">
  <Viewbox Name="viewbox1" VerticalAlignment="Top" Height="{Binding Value,
ElementName=slider}" >
        <RichTextBox x:Name="richTextBox1" Width="330" VerticalAlignment="Top" Height="438">
        <Paragraph><Run Text="This is an RTF document created in WordPad. RTF documents can
contain images as well. Here is an image of the first edition of this book."/></Paragraph>
            <Paragraph><InlineUIContainer>
                    <Image Source="../BookImage.png" Width="123"/>
            </InlineUIContainer><Run Text=" You can wrap text around the Image using an
InlineUIContainer. RTF also supports text formatting such as "/><Bold><Run
Text="Bold"/></Bold>
<Run Text=" , "/><Italic><Run Text="Italic"/></Italic><Run Text=" , and "/><Underline><Run
Text="Underline"/></Underline><Run Text=" , or "/><Bold><Italic><Underline>
<Run Text="combine all three together"/></Underline></Italic></Bold><Run Text="
."/></Paragraph>
            <Paragraph><Run Text="You can also have an inline hyperlink as well such as this
"/><Hyperlink TargetName="_new" NavigateUri="http://www.apress.com/mobile/windows-
phone/9781430232193"><Run Text="one"/></Hyperlink><Run Text=" ."/></Paragraph>
        </RichTextBox>
  </Viewbox>
</Grid>
    <Slider x:Name="slider" HorizontalAlignment="Right" Margin="0,8,35,0"
Orientation="Vertical" Maximum="607" Value="607" Height="153" />
</Grid>
```

Figure 2-51 shows the UI zoomed out so as you adjust the `Slider` control to a smaller value; the content also shrinks.

Figure 2–51. *ViewboxZoomed UI*

For situations where you need to have a scalable user interface, the `Viewbox` may be the tool of choice for your scenario. In the next section I cover implicit styles.

Implicit Styles

With Silverlight 4 compatibility, you can set a style implicitly similar to what is possible in Cascading Style Sheets (CSS) where you define a style and it can automatically apply to every control of that type. In Silverlight for Windows Phone, an implicit style can be defined that applies to every `UIElement` of that type.

I create a new project in the Chapter 2 part 2 solution named `ImplicitStyles`. I drop several `TextBlock` controls on to `MainPage.xaml` that we will use to demonstrate how implicit styles work.

The easiest way to quickly create an implicit style is to create a new style for the target control type as you normally would do. Once you are satisfied with the style, edit the XAML to remove the `x:Key` value for the Style. Next edit the control that you originally created the style for and reset it to no style. Here is an example implicit style:

```
<Style TargetType="TextBlock">
  <Setter Property="Foreground" Value="Yellow" />
  <Setter Property="FontStyle" Value="Italic"  />
  <Setter Property="FontSize" Value="30"  />
</Style>
```

Notice that no **x:key** value is set. Also, the four **TextBlock** controls added do not have a style set except for one to show how the implicit style is overridden. Figure 2-52 shows the UI.

Figure 2–52. *Implicit styles*

Implicit styles are an excellent addition to Windows Phone development. One use for implicit styles that can save a lot of time and code is to define them for controls where you must override the theme support. As an example, if you need to keep Font color black regardless of theme, Implicit styles can be used.

Conclusion

In this chapter I provide a sweeping overview of the Silverlight user experience controls starting with layout controls, data binding, and a demonstration of how to take advantage of sample data. I then move on to a discussion of control templates and an overview of animation in Expression Blend. In the next section I cover an overview of the Panorama and Pivot controls, which are the major navigation controls in Windows Phone. I conclude by providing coverage on what's new for Windows Phone now that it has Silverlight 4 compatibility. In the next chapter I will cover input on Windows Phone 7.

CHAPTER 3

■ ■ ■

Handling Input on Windows Phone

Handling input is a critical aspect of any application, but it is an especially unique challenge on a mobile device. The first consideration is that the user is most likely not sitting in a comfortable chair sipping coffee, casually browsing the Internet. A mobile application user is most likely on the go, looking to just get a task done or find the needed information and be on their way.

The second consideration is that user input on a mobile device is quite different than handling input on the PC or even on the XBOX 360 for XNA Framework game development. A Windows Phone mobile device may or may not have a physical keyboard, so you cannot author your application to depend on it. Even at 800px x480px screen resolution, screen real estate is still at a premium.

Mobile devices have unique hardware input capabilities for innovative user experiences, such as capacitive touch, accelerometer, and location. With Windows Phone 7 OS 7.1, available sensors are expanded to include compass, camera capture, gyroscope, and motion sensor. You may be wondering about existing devices. Many existing devices ship with compass hardware already but not a gyroscope.

The motion sensor Microsoft provides uses a combination of accelerometer, compass, and gyroscope inputs to produce a nice, clean API to determine yaw, pitch, and roll of a device. For hardware without a gyroscope but with a compass, the API simulates it using the accelerometer. It is not as good as having a gyroscope, but it still allows you to build for scenarios like augmented reality with camera capture and have them run acceptably on existing hardware if it includes a compass.

■ **Note** In Windows Phone 7.5 compass and gyroscope are optional, but if a device includes a gyroscope it also includes a compass. Applications should identify the dependency as part of the application description in marketplace.

In this chapter, I cover handling user input in both Silverlight and XNA Windows Phone applications starting first with keyboard, touch input, including single touch and multi-touch. Then we dive into the individual sensors including coverage of the new capabilities available in Windows Phone OS 7.1.

■ **Note** The gesture samples use the Silverlight for Windows Phone Toolkit, available at http://silverlght.codeplex.com. Please download the toolkit to compile the sample code.

> ■ **Note** This code in this chapter is broken up into two separate Solutions in the sample source code: Ch03_HandlingInput and Ch03_HandlingInput_Part2. Sample code starting in the location sample on forward is in the Part 2 solution.

The Keyboard

The last thing a mobile user wants to do is type on a mobile keyboard, but it is inevitable for many applications to require some form of text input. In this section I discuss keyboard capabilities and API enhancements to ease typing on the keyboard on Windows Phone devices.

Physical Keyboard

Windows Phone devices may also have a hardware slide-out keyboard, but your application will not pass certification in AppHub if it is dependent upon the hardware keyboard. Otherwise, from a software development perspective, programming for hardware keyboard input "just works." Of the six devices available at Windows Phone launch, only one had a full slide-out keyboard, and another had a vertical QWERTY keyboard. The other four devices were pure touch devices without a physical keyboard.

Soft Input Panel (SIP) Keyboard

All Windows Phone devices have a SIP keyboard used for entering text. Typing on the SIP keyboard built into Windows Phone is a pretty comfortable means of entering text; however, it is still a small keyboard, so anything that a developer can do to ease typing can really help improve the overall user experience.

Programming with the Keyboard

Typing text on a mobile phone should be minimized as much as possible, but if text input is required, a developer should take advantage of capabilities to make typing as simple as possible. In the next section I cover InputScope, which is a must-have feature to take advantage of when typing is required in your Windows Phone applications.

When testing keyboard input, you will be tempted to type on your PC keyboard; however, it does not work. You must use the mouse with the SIP keyboard in the Emulator for input.

> ■ **Tip** Click the Pause/Break button on your PC keyboard to enable typing in the emulator with your PC keyboard instead of having to use the mouse to "touch" the SIP.

InputScope

The InputScope property is available on the TextBox control, which is the primary control for text input. InputScope lets the developer customize the keyboard for the expected type of input. For example, the default behavior is that when you click into a TextBox, the SIP keyboard pops up, as shown in Figure 3–1.

Figure 3–1. *Default SIP keyboard*

The second TextBox has an InputScope of Text, which enables word selection just above the keyboard, as shown in Figure 3–2.

Figure 3–2. *InputScope of Text SIP keyboard with word suggestion*

With just one simple attribute, text input becomes much easier for the end user. Figure 3–3 shows three additional text input options, which I explain just after the figure.

| Search | Password | TelephoneNumber |

Figure 3–3. Search, Password, and TelephoneNumber InputScope customizations

Configuring an InputScope of Search turns the Enter key into a GO key with the idea that the user enters a search keyword and then clicks Enter to kick off a search. Password is not actually an InputScope. It is a custom TextBox class named PasswordBox that automatically hides data entry as the user types. An InputScope of TelephoneNumber brings up a phone keypad. As you can see, all of these could come in handy as you develop your application UI and optimize input for the end user. Table 3–1 lists the available InputScope options and their descriptions, reprinted here for your convenience from the Windows Phone documentation.

Table 3–1. Available InputScope Options

Input Scope	Description
AddressCity	The text input pattern for a city address.
AddressCountryName	The text input pattern for the name of a country/region.
AddressCountryShortName	The text input pattern for the abbreviated name of a country/region.
AddressStateOrProvince	The text input pattern for a state or province.
AddressStreet	The text input pattern for a street address.
AlphanumericFullWidth	The text input pattern for alphanumeric full-width characters (East-Asian languages only).

Input Scope	Description
AlphanumericHalfWidth	The text input pattern for alphanumeric half-width characters (East-Asian languages only).
Chat	The SIP layout for text messaging, which recognizes pre-defined abbreviations. Supported only in Silverlight for Windows Phone.
CurrencyAmount	The text input pattern for amount of currency.
CurrencyAmountAndSymbol	The text input pattern for amount and symbol of currency.
CurrencyChinese	The text input pattern for Chinese currency.
Date	The text input pattern for a calendar date.
DateDay	The text input pattern for the numeric day in a calendar date.
DateDayName	The text input pattern for the name of the day in a calendar date.
DateMonth	The text input pattern for the numeric month in a calendar date.
DateMonthName	The text input pattern for the name of the month in a calendar date.
DateYear	The text input pattern for the year in a calendar date.
Default	The default handling of input commands.
Digits	The text input pattern for digits.
EmailNameOrAddress	The SIP layout for an e-mail name or address. Supported only in Silverlight for Windows Phone.
EmailSmtpAddress	The text input pattern for a Simple Mail Transfer Protocol (SMTP) e-mail address.
EmailUserName	The text input pattern for an e-mail user name.
FileName	The text input pattern for a file name.
FullFilePath	The text input pattern for the full path of a file.
Hanja	The text input pattern for Hanja characters (Korean characters).
Hiragana	The text input pattern for the Hiragana writing system (a Japanese syllabary).

Input Scope	Description
KatakanaFullWidth	The text input pattern for full-width Katakana characters (a Japanese syllabary).
KatakanaHalfWidth	The text input pattern for half-width Katakana characters (a Japanese syllabary).
LogOnName	The text input pattern for a log on name.
Maps	The SIP layout for entering a map location. Supported only in Silverlight for Windows Phone.
NameOrPhoneNumber	The SIP layout for SMS To field. Supported only in Silverlight for Windows Phone.
Number	The text input pattern for a number.
NumberFullWidth	The text input pattern for a full-width number.
OneChar	The text input pattern for one character.
Password	The text input pattern for a password.
PersonalFullName	The text input pattern for a person's full name.
PersonalGivenName	The text input pattern for a person's given name.
PersonalMiddleName	The text input pattern for a person's middle name.
PersonalNamePrefix	The text input pattern for the prefix of a person's name.
PersonalNameSuffix	The text input pattern for the suffix of a person's name.
PersonalSurname	The text input pattern for a person's surname.
PhraseList	The text input pattern for a phrase list.
PostalAddress	The text input pattern for a postal address.
PostalCode	The text input pattern for a postal code.
RegularExpression	The text input pattern for a regular expression.
Search	The SIP layout for a search query. Supported only in Silverlight for Windows Phone.

Input Scope	Description
Srgs	The text input pattern for the Speech Recognition Grammar Specification (SRGS).
TelephoneAreaCode	The text input pattern for a telephone area code.
TelephoneCountryCode	The text input pattern for a telephone country/region code.
TelephoneLocalNumber	The text input pattern for a telephone local number.
TelephoneNumber	The text input pattern for a telephone number.
Text	The software input panel (SIP) layout for standard text input. Supported only in Silverlight for Windows Phone.
Time	The text input pattern for the time.
TimeHour	The text input pattern for the hour of the time.
TimeMinorSec	The text input pattern for the minutes or seconds of time.
Url	The text input pattern for a Uniform Resource Locator (URL).
Xml	The text input pattern for XML.

Let's now shift gears and explore the available keyboard events.

Keyboard Events

There are two keyboard events available on the TextBox, as well as pretty much any other object that inherits from UIElement: the KeyDown and KeyUp events. Both events have a KeyEventArgs class in its parameters that provides access to the Key and PlatformKeyCode values native to the platform. It also provides access to the OriginalSource property that represents the control that raised the Keyboard event, as well as a Handled member to indicate that the key has been processed.

This completes our discussion of keyboard events. In general, typing should be minimized in a mobile application for the reasons listed previously, i.e., small screen, small keyboard, and so on. Mobile devices are optimized for touch input, especially modern devices with highly responsive capacitive touch screens that do not require a stylus. Let's now focus on touch input.

Touch Input

Most modern mobile devices that have touch screens do not require a stylus, which was necessary for resistive touch-based screens. Modern mobile devices are capacitive touch and respond very well to touch with a finger.

Windows Phone supports up to four multi-touch contact points for XNA Framework development. Silverlight for Windows Phone supports two multi-touch contact points. As part of the platform, there is a touch driver and gesture engine under the covers that provides a consistent detection capability across hardware device OEMs and across applications.

As mentioned previously, Silverlight for Windows Phone is based on Silverlight 3. The Windows Phone product team took the Silverlight 3 controls and APIs and optimized the controls for performance, for look and feel via control templates and styles and for input. The next section covers single-point touch as it relates to the controls optimized for Windows Phone.

Single-Point Touch

When a user clicks a Button control, TextBox control, ListBox control and the like on Windows Phone, it is single-point touch. For consistency, single-point touch events are translated to the Mouse events that you are familiar with when programming desktop Silverlight, Windows Forms, or other application frameworks. For example, touching a button appears as a Click event. Tapping to type text in a TextBox or touch a TextBlock control fires a MouseEnter, a MouseLeftButtonDown, a MouseLeftButtonUp, and a MouseLeave event.

The Chapter 3 SinglePointTouch project TextControlsMouseEventsPage.xaml page shows these events firing when you interact with the TextBox and TextBlock controls. You will notice when testing on a device that sometimes multiple MouseEnter/MouseLeave pairs can fire. You can also see multiple MouseMove events fire as well as a result of small movements in your finger when interacting with the controls. It's something to consider when using these events with touch, as opposed to mouse clicks on the desktop, and why discrete events like listening for click or gestures is recommended except when discrete touch points are required. Figure 3–4 shows the UI with the mouse events trace.

Figure 3–4. *Text controls mouse events demo*

Listing 3–1 shows the TextControlsMouseEventPage.xaml code file with the XAML markup.

Listing 3–1. *WMAppManifest.xml Configuration File*

```
<phone:PhoneApplicationPage
  x:Class="SinglePointTouch.Pages.TextBoxMouseEventPage"
  xmlns="http://schemas.microsoft.com/winfx/2006/xaml/presentation"
  xmlns:x="http://schemas.microsoft.com/winfx/2006/xaml"
  xmlns:phone="clr-namespace:Microsoft.Phone.Controls;assembly=Microsoft.Phone"
  xmlns:shell="clr-namespace:Microsoft.Phone.Shell;assembly=Microsoft.Phone"
  xmlns:d="http://schemas.microsoft.com/expression/blend/2008"
  xmlns:mc="http://schemas.openxmlformats.org/markup-compatibility/2006"
  FontFamily="{StaticResource PhoneFontFamilyNormal}"
  FontSize="{StaticResource PhoneFontSizeNormal}"
  Foreground="{StaticResource PhoneForegroundBrush}"
  SupportedOrientations="Portrait" Orientation="Portrait"
  mc:Ignorable="d" d:DesignHeight="768" d:DesignWidth="480"
  shell:SystemTray.IsVisible="True">

  <!--LayoutRoot is the root grid where all page content is placed-->
  <Grid x:Name="LayoutRoot" Background="Transparent">
```

```xml
<Grid.RowDefinitions>
  <RowDefinition Height="Auto"/>
  <RowDefinition Height="*"/>
</Grid.RowDefinitions>

<!--TitlePanel contains the name of the application and page title-->
<StackPanel x:Name="TitlePanel" Grid.Row="0" Margin="12,17,0,28">
  <TextBlock x:Name="ApplicationTitle" Text="CHAPTER 3 - SINGLE POINT TOUCH"
             Style="{StaticResource PhoneTextNormalStyle}"/>
  <TextBlock x:Name="PageTitle" Text="textbox mouse events" Margin="9,-7,0,0"
             Style="{StaticResource PhoneTextTitle1Style}"/>
</StackPanel>
<!--ContentPanel - place additional content here-->
<Grid x:Name="ContentPanel" Grid.Row="1" Margin="12,0,12,0">
  <StackPanel Orientation="Vertical">
    <TextBox HorizontalAlignment="Left" x:Name="MouseEventsTextBox"
      Text="TextBox Mouse Events Demo" Width="460" Height="72"
      MouseEnter="MouseEventsTextBox_MouseEnter"
      MouseLeave="MouseEventsTextBox_MouseLeave"
      MouseLeftButtonDown="MouseEventsTextBox_MouseLeftButtonDown"
      MouseLeftButtonUp="MouseEventsTextBox_MouseLeftButtonUp"
      MouseMove="MouseEventsTextBox_MouseMove"
      MouseWheel="MouseEventsTextBox_MouseWheel" />
    <TextBlock Height="30" HorizontalAlignment="Left" Margin="12,0,0,0"
               x:Name="MouseEventStatusText" Text="Mouse Events Log"
               Width="438" />
    <ListBox Height="217" x:Name="MouseEventLogListBox" />
    <Rectangle Fill="#FFF4F4F5" Height="10" Stroke="Black" Margin="0,0,6,0"/>
    <TextBlock TextWrapping="Wrap" Text="TextBlock Mouse Events Demo"
      Margin="0" Name="TextBlockMouseEventsDemo"
      MouseEnter="TextBlockMouseEventsDemo_MouseEnter"
      MouseLeave="TextBlockMouseEventsDemo_MouseLeave"
      MouseLeftButtonDown="TextBlockMouseEventsDemo_MouseLeftButtonDown"
      MouseLeftButtonUp="TextBlockMouseEventsDemo_MouseLeftButtonUp"
      MouseMove="TextBlockMouseEventsDemo_MouseMove"
      MouseWheel="TextBlockMouseEventsDemo_MouseWheel" />
    <TextBlock Height="30" HorizontalAlignment="Left" Margin="12,0,0,0"
      x:Name="MouseEventStatusTextBlock" Text="Mouse Events Log"
      Width="438" />
    <ListBox Height="220" x:Name="MouseEventLogListBox2" />
  </StackPanel>
</Grid>
</Grid>
</phone:PhoneApplicationPage>
```

In Listing 3–1, you can see the event handler assignments like this one assigning an event handler to the MouseEnter event for the MouseEventsTextBox object

```
MouseEnter="MouseEventsTextBox_MouseEnter"
```

The code-behind file has the related event handlers that simply write a text message to the MouseEventLogListBox like this one:

```
private void MouseEventsTextBox_MouseEnter(object sender, MouseEventArgs e)
{
  MouseEventLogListBox.Items.Add("MouseEnter event fired.");
}
```

Now that we have covered the mouse events, we will next look at how to use the mouse events for raw touch.

Raw Touch with Mouse Events

In addition to indicating a "click" or touch even, mouse events can be used for raw touch. An example of raw touch is drawing with your finger, where you need individual touch locations. What enables raw touch with mouse events is the MouseEventArgs class passed into the mouse events. The following are the key properties of the MouseEventArgs class:

- **GetPosition(UIElement relativeTo):** Gets the position of the mouse event in relation to the passed in object. Returns a Point object.

- **OriginalSource:** Provides a reference to the object that raised the event.

- **StylusDevice:** Returns a StylusDevice object that includes the set of stylus points associated with the input.

The StylusDevice object contains a GetStylusPoints method that returns a StylusPointsCollection that we can draw an object onscreen to represent user touches. The StylusPoint class is enhanced over the Point class with the StylusPoint.PressureFactor property. Because PressureFactor is a float, we can assign it to the Opacity property of the object we draw onscreen to represent touches such that the Opacity indicates whether it is a light or heavy press on the screen. So a light pressure press will have a lower opacity when drawn on screen.

In the next couple of sections we will build a mini finger drawing application that includes multicolor selection, ListBox customizations, animations, the application bar, and basic drawing functionality.

Setting Up the Basic UI

Add a Windows Phone Portrait Page new item to the SinglePointTouch project. Uncomment the sample ApplicationBar code at the bottom of the page. We will use the ApplicationBar to implement commands to clear the drawing canvas, set the touch object size, and so on.

At the top we set the title and subtitle for the page. In the default ContentPanel Grid object, we add a Canvas object. On top of the Canvas object is a Rectangle that receives the mouse events. We take advantage of absolute positioning in the Canvas object to place the objects that represent user touches using X and Y coordinates provided by StylusPoint objects. The following is a XAML snippet of the TitlePanel and ContentPanel:

```
<!--TitlePanel contains the name of the application and page title-->
<StackPanel x:Name="TitlePanel" Grid.Row="0" Margin="12,17,0,28">
  <TextBlock x:Name="ApplicationTitle" Text="CHAPTER 3 - SinglePointTouch"
             Style="{StaticResource PhoneTextNormalStyle}"/>
  <TextBlock x:Name="PageTitle" Text="finger painting" Margin="9,-7,0,0"
             Style="{StaticResource PhoneTextTitle1Style}"/>
</StackPanel>
```

```xml
<!--ContentPanel - place additional content here-->
<Grid x:Name="ContentPanel" Grid.Row="1" Margin="24,0,0,0">
  <Canvas x:Name="DrawCanvas"  >
    <Rectangle Fill="White"  Stroke="Black"
        MouseMove="Rectangle_MouseMove" Width="456" Height="535"  />
  </Canvas>
</Grid>
```

The following is the Rectangle_MouseMove event handler on the Rectangle object and related helper method:

```csharp
private void Rectangle_MouseMove(object sender, MouseEventArgs e)
{
  foreach (StylusPoint p in e.StylusDevice.GetStylusPoints(DrawCanvas))
  {
    Ellipse ellipse = new Ellipse();
    ellipse.SetValue(Canvas.LeftProperty, p.X);
    ellipse.SetValue(Canvas.TopProperty, p.Y);
    ellipse.Opacity = p.PressureFactor;
    ellipse.Width = 20d;
    ellipse.Height = 20d;
    ellipse.IsHitTestVisible = false;
    ellipse.Stroke = new SolidColorBrush(Colors.Black);
    ellipse.Fill = new SolidColorBrush(Colors.Black);
    DrawCanvas.Children.Add(ellipse);
  }
}
```

The application uses the MouseMove event and the StylusPointsCollection to draw small Ellipse objects to the screen as you drag the mouse on the emulator or finger on a device across the screen. Figure 3–5 shows the UI in action.

Figure 3–5. *Basic finger painting UI*

Finger painting without multiple colors is boring. Let's add a ListBox and populate it with the built-in System.Windows.Media.Colors collection so that the user can select an item and change the "finger paint" color. We first create a couple of classes to encapsulate the System.Windows.Media.Colors collection since we cannot data bind directly to it. See Listing 3–2.

Listing 3–2. *The ColorClass Code File*

```
public class ColorClass
{
  public Brush ColorBrush { get; set; }
  public String ColorName { get; set; }
}
```

It contains a Brush to represent the RGB values for the color and a text name for the color. We need a collection of ColorClass objects to bind to. Listing 3–3 has the simple class that generates a collection of ColorClass objects.

Listing 3–3. *The ColorsClass Code File*

```
public class ColorsClass
{
  List<ColorClass> _colors;
```

```csharp
public ColorsClass()
{
  _colors = new List<ColorClass>();
  _colors.Add(new ColorClass() {
    ColorBrush = new SolidColorBrush(Colors.Blue), ColorName = "Blue" });
  _colors.Add(new ColorClass() {
    ColorBrush = new SolidColorBrush(Colors.Brown), ColorName = "Brown"});
  _colors.Add(new ColorClass() {
    ColorBrush = new SolidColorBrush(Colors.Cyan), ColorName = "Cyan"});
  _colors.Add(new ColorClass() {
    ColorBrush = new SolidColorBrush(Colors.DarkGray),
    ColorName = "DarkGray"});
  _colors.Add(new ColorClass() {
    ColorBrush = new SolidColorBrush(Colors.Gray), ColorName = "Gray"});
  _colors.Add(new ColorClass() {
    ColorBrush = new SolidColorBrush(Colors.Green), ColorName = "Green"});
  _colors.Add(new ColorClass() {
    ColorBrush = new SolidColorBrush(Colors.LightGray),
    ColorName = "LightGray" });
  _colors.Add(new ColorClass() {
    ColorBrush = new SolidColorBrush(Colors.Magenta),
    ColorName = "Magenta" });
  _colors.Add(new ColorClass() {
    ColorBrush = new SolidColorBrush(Colors.Orange), ColorName="Orange"});
  _colors.Add(new ColorClass() {
    ColorBrush = new SolidColorBrush(Colors.Purple), ColorName="Purple"});
  _colors.Add(new ColorClass() {
    ColorBrush = new SolidColorBrush(Colors.Red), ColorName = "Red"});
  _colors.Add(new ColorClass() {
    ColorBrush = new SolidColorBrush(Colors.White), ColorName = "White"});
  _colors.Add(new ColorClass() {
    ColorBrush = new SolidColorBrush(Colors.Yellow), ColorName = "Yellow"});
  _colors.Add(new ColorClass() {
    ColorBrush = new SolidColorBrush(Colors.Black), ColorName = "Black"});
}

public List<ColorClass> ColorsCollection
{
  get { return _colors; }
}
}
```

All of the work is done in the constructor using abbreviated syntax to create the collection. Data bind the ColorListBox.ItemsSource to the ColorsClass.ColorsCollection either manually in Visual Studio or with Expression Blend. By default the ColorListBox scrolls vertically. To have the ColorListBox scroll horizontally, right-click on the ColorListBox in Expression Blend and select Edit Additional Templates Edit Layout of Items (ItemsPanel), Edit a Copy…to edit the template. Drop a StackPanel on to the root ItemsPanelTemplate object. Configure the StackPanel to have Orientation set to Horizontal and that's it: the ColorListBox will scroll horizontally. The last bit of customization is to create an ItemTemplate for ColorListBox. ColorListBox.ItemsSource data binds to the collection. The ItemTemplate has that as its context, so the ItemTemplate data binds to individual records. The following is the ItemTemplate:

```
<DataTemplate x:Key="FingerPaintingColorTemplate">
  <StackPanel Orientation="Vertical">
    <Rectangle Fill="{Binding ColorBrush}" HorizontalAlignment="Left"
      Height="95" Stroke="Black" VerticalAlignment="Top" Width="95" Margin="4,4,4,0"/>
    <TextBlock HorizontalAlignment="Center" TextWrapping="Wrap"
      Text="{Binding ColorName}" VerticalAlignment="Center" Margin="0"/>
  </StackPanel>
</DataTemplate>
```

The ColorListBox DataTemplate consists of a Rectangle that displays the color based on the ColorClass.ColorBrush property and a TextBlock that displays the name of the color based on the ColorClass.ColorName property. Figure 3–6 shows the resulting work.

Figure 3–6. *Finger painting UI with ColorListBox*

In PhoneApplicationPage_Loaded, set the SelectedIndex on ColorListBox so that a color is always selected.. The drawing code is updated to obtain the ColorListBox.SelectedItem object in order to set the brush color for the Ellipse.

```
private void Rectangle_MouseMove(object sender, MouseEventArgs e)
{
  foreach (StylusPoint p in e.StylusDevice.GetStylusPoints(DrawCanvas))
  {
```

```
    Ellipse ellipse = new Ellipse();
    ellipse.SetValue(Canvas.LeftProperty, p.X);
    ellipse.SetValue(Canvas.TopProperty, p.Y);
    ellipse.Opacity = p.PressureFactor;
    ellipse.Width = 20d;
    ellipse.Height = 20d;
    ellipse.IsHitTestVisible = false;
    ellipse.Stroke = ((ColorClass)ColorListBox.SelectedItem).ColorBrush;
    ellipse.Fill = ((ColorClass)ColorListBox.SelectedItem).ColorBrush;
    DrawCanvas.Children.Add(ellipse);
  }
}
```

The application will now allow finger painting using the selected color in the ColorListBox. In the next section we will expand the painting functionality in the application.

Expand Painting Functionality

Let's now add additional painting functionality to make the application more usable, such as to clear the drawing surface, increase the touch pencil size, decrease the touch pencil size, show/hide the color palate to change drawing color, and to set the background for the image. Here is how the UI is set up:

- **Clear:** Erase the drawing surface (trashcan icon).

- **Touch color:** Shows the color palate to set the drawing color (edit pencil icon).

- **Pencil size:** Increases pencil size (plus sign icon).

- **Pencil size:** Decreases pencil size (minus sign icon).

- **Set background color menu item:** Shows the color palate to set the background color.

In Expression Blend, edit the Application Bar to provide four application bar icons and one menu item. Expression Blend provides access to the built-in icons, as shown in Figure 3–7.

Figure 3–7. *Finger painting UI with ColorListBox*

Once the application bar icons and menu item are configured visually in Blend, set the ColorListBox control's Visibility to Visibility.Collapsed so that it is only visible when needed. We switch over to Visual Studio to add the event handlers in XAML for the Application Bar button icons and menu item. Listings 3–4 and 3–5 have the full source code of the mini-application.

Listing 3–4. *The FingerPaintingPageMouseEvents.xaml Code File*

```
<phone:PhoneApplicationPage
  xmlns="http://schemas.microsoft.com/winfx/2006/xaml/presentation"
  xmlns:x="http://schemas.microsoft.com/winfx/2006/xaml"
  xmlns:phone="clr-namespace:Microsoft.Phone.Controls;assembly=Microsoft.Phone"
```

```xml
xmlns:shell="clr-namespace:Microsoft.Phone.Shell;assembly=Microsoft.Phone"
xmlns:d="http://schemas.microsoft.com/expression/blend/2008"
xmlns:mc="http://schemas.openxmlformats.org/markup-compatibility/2006"
xmlns:SinglePointTouch="clr-namespace:SinglePointTouch"
x:Class="SinglePointTouch.Pages.FingerPaintingPageMouseEvents"
SupportedOrientations="Portrait" Orientation="Portrait"
mc:Ignorable="d" d:DesignHeight="696" d:DesignWidth="480"
shell:SystemTray.IsVisible="True" Loaded="PhoneApplicationPage_Loaded">
<phone:PhoneApplicationPage.Resources>
  <SinglePointTouch:ColorsClass x:Key="ColorsClassDataSource"
   d:IsDataSource="True"/>
  <DataTemplate x:Key="FingerPaintingColorTemplate">
    <StackPanel Orientation="Vertical">
      <Rectangle Fill="{Binding ColorBrush}" HorizontalAlignment="Left"
        Height="95" Stroke="Black" VerticalAlignment="Top" Width="95"
        Margin="4,4,4,0"/>
      <TextBlock HorizontalAlignment="Center" TextWrapping="Wrap"
        Text="{Binding ColorName}" VerticalAlignment="Center" Margin="0"/>
    </StackPanel>
  </DataTemplate>
  <ItemsPanelTemplate x:Key="FingerPaintingColorsListBoxItemsPanel">
    <StackPanel Orientation="Horizontal"/>
  </ItemsPanelTemplate>
</phone:PhoneApplicationPage.Resources>

<phone:PhoneApplicationPage.ApplicationBar>
  <shell:ApplicationBar IsVisible="True" IsMenuEnabled="True">
    <shell:ApplicationBarIconButton x:Name="AppBarClearButton"
     IconUri="/icons/appbar.delete.rest.png" Text="clear"
     Click="AppBarClearButton_Click" />
    <shell:ApplicationBarIconButton x:Name="AppBarChangeTouchColorButton"
     IconUri="/icons/appbar.edit.rest.png" Text="touch color"
     Click="AppBarChangeTouchColor_Click"/>
    <shell:ApplicationBarIconButton x:Name="AppBarIncreaseButton"
     IconUri="/icons/appbar.add.rest.png" Text="pencil size"
     Click="AppBarIncreaseButton_Click"/>
    <shell:ApplicationBarIconButton x:Name="AppBarDecreaseButton"
     IconUri="/icons/appbar.minus.rest.png" Text="pencil size"
     Click="AppBarDecreaseButton_Click"/>
    <shell:ApplicationBar.MenuItems>
      <shell:ApplicationBarMenuItem  Text="Set Background Color"
        x:Name="SetBackgroundColorMenuItem"
        Click="SetBackgroundColorMenuItem_Click" />
    </shell:ApplicationBar.MenuItems>
  </shell:ApplicationBar>
  </phone:PhoneApplicationPage.ApplicationBar>

<phone:PhoneApplicationPage.FontFamily>
  <StaticResource ResourceKey="PhoneFontFamilyNormal"/>
</phone:PhoneApplicationPage.FontFamily>
<phone:PhoneApplicationPage.FontSize>
  <StaticResource ResourceKey="PhoneFontSizeNormal"/>
```

```xml
  </phone:PhoneApplicationPage.FontSize>
  <phone:PhoneApplicationPage.Foreground>
    <StaticResource ResourceKey="PhoneForegroundBrush"/>
  </phone:PhoneApplicationPage.Foreground>
  <Grid x:Name="LayoutRoot" Background="Transparent" DataContext=
        "{Binding Source={StaticResource ColorsClassDataSource}}" >
    <Grid.RowDefinitions>
      <RowDefinition Height="Auto"/>
      <RowDefinition Height="*"/>
    </Grid.RowDefinitions>

    <!--TitlePanel contains the name of the application and page title-->
    <StackPanel x:Name="TitlePanel" Grid.Row="0" Margin="12,17,0,28">
      <TextBlock x:Name="ApplicationTitle" Text="CHAPTER 3 - SinglePointTouch"
                 Style="{StaticResource PhoneTextNormalStyle}"/>
      <TextBlock x:Name="PageTitle" Text="finger painting" Margin="9,-7,0,0"
                 Style="{StaticResource PhoneTextTitle1Style}"/>
    </StackPanel>

    <!--ContentPanel - place additional content here-->
    <Grid x:Name="ContentPanel" Grid.Row="1" Margin="24,0,0,0">
      <Canvas x:Name="DrawCanvas"  >
                <Rectangle Fill="White"  Stroke="Black" Name="BlankRectangle"
                       MouseMove="Rectangle_MouseMove" Width="456" Height="535"  />
      </Canvas>
      <ListBox x:Name="ColorListBox" Margin="0"
        ScrollViewer.HorizontalScrollBarVisibility="Auto"
        ScrollViewer.VerticalScrollBarVisibility="Disabled"
        ItemsPanel="{StaticResource FingerPaintingColorsListBoxItemsPanel}"
        VerticalAlignment="Top" ItemsSource="{Binding ColorsCollection}"
        ItemTemplate="{StaticResource FingerPaintingColorTemplate}"
        Background="Black" SelectedIndex="-1" HorizontalAlignment="Right"
        Width="456" RenderTransformOrigin="0.5,0.5"
        SelectionChanged="ColorListBox_SelectionChanged" Visibility="Collapsed">
      </ListBox>
    </Grid>
  </Grid>
</phone:PhoneApplicationPage>
```

Listing 3–5. *The FingerPaintingPageMouseEvents.xaml.cs Code File*

```csharp
using System;
using System.Windows;
using System.Windows.Controls;
using System.Windows.Input;
using System.Windows.Media;
using System.Windows.Shapes;
using System.Windows.Threading;
using Microsoft.Phone.Controls;

namespace SinglePointTouch.Pages
{
```

```csharp
public partial class FingerPaintingPageMouseEvents : PhoneApplicationPage
{
  private Rectangle _backgroundRectangle;
  private double _touchRadius = 20d;
  private bool ColorBackgroundMode = false;
  private int TouchPaintingSelectedColorIndex;

  public FingerPaintingPageMouseEvents()
  {
    InitializeComponent();

    _backgroundRectangle = BlankRectangle;
  }

  private void Rectangle_MouseMove(object sender, MouseEventArgs e)
  {
    foreach (StylusPoint p in e.StylusDevice.GetStylusPoints(DrawCanvas))
    {
      Ellipse ellipse = new Ellipse();
      ellipse.SetValue(Canvas.LeftProperty, p.X);
      ellipse.SetValue(Canvas.TopProperty, p.Y);
      ellipse.Opacity = p.PressureFactor;
      ellipse.Width = _touchRadius;
      ellipse.Height = _touchRadius;
      ellipse.IsHitTestVisible = false;
      ellipse.Stroke = ((ColorClass)ColorListBox.SelectedItem).ColorBrush;
      ellipse.Fill = ((ColorClass)ColorListBox.SelectedItem).ColorBrush;
      DrawCanvas.Children.Add(ellipse);
    }
  }

  private void PhoneApplicationPage_Loaded(object sender, RoutedEventArgs e)
  {
    ColorListBox.SelectedIndex = 0;

    //Setup memory tracking timer
    DispatcherTimer DebugMemoryTimer = new DispatcherTimer();
    DebugMemoryTimer.Interval = new TimeSpan(0, 0, 0, 0, 5000);
    DebugMemoryTimer.Tick += DebugMemoryInfo_Tick;
    DebugMemoryTimer.Start();
  }

  // Track memory Info
  void DebugMemoryInfo_Tick(object sender, EventArgs e)
  {
    //GC.GetTotalMemory(true);
    long deviceTotalMemory =
     (long)Microsoft.Phone.Info.DeviceExtendedProperties.GetValue(
     "DeviceTotalMemory");
    long applicationCurrentMemoryUsage =
     (long)Microsoft.Phone.Info.DeviceExtendedProperties.GetValue(
     "ApplicationCurrentMemoryUsage");
```

```
    long applicationPeakMemoryUsage =
      (long)Microsoft.Phone.Info.DeviceExtendedProperties.GetValue(
      "ApplicationPeakMemoryUsage");

    System.Diagnostics.Debug.WriteLine("--> " +
      DateTime.Now.ToLongTimeString());
    System.Diagnostics.Debug.WriteLine("--> Device Total : " +
      deviceTotalMemory.ToString());
    System.Diagnostics.Debug.WriteLine("--> App Current : " +
      applicationCurrentMemoryUsage.ToString());
    System.Diagnostics.Debug.WriteLine("--> App Peak : " +
      applicationPeakMemoryUsage.ToString());
  }

  private void AppBarClearButton_Click(object sender, EventArgs e)
  {
    DrawCanvas.Children.Clear();
    DrawCanvas.Children.Add(BlankRectangle);
    BlankRectangle.Fill = new SolidColorBrush(Colors.White);
  }

  private void AppBarIncreaseButton_Click(object sender, EventArgs e)
  {
    if (_touchRadius <= 30d)
    {
      _touchRadius += 5;
    }
  }

  private void AppBarDecreaseButton_Click(object sender, EventArgs e)
  {
    if (_touchRadius > 20d)
    {
      _touchRadius -= 5;
    }
  }

  private void SetBackgroundColorMenuItem_Click(object sender, EventArgs e)
  {
    ColorListBox.Visibility = Visibility.Visible;
    ColorBackgroundMode = true;
    TouchPaintingSelectedColorIndex = ColorListBox.SelectedIndex;
  }

  private void ColorListBox_SelectionChanged(object sender,
    SelectionChangedEventArgs e)
  {
    ColorListBox.Visibility = Visibility.Collapsed;
    if (ColorBackgroundMode == true)
    {
      _backgroundRectangle.Fill =
        ((ColorClass)ColorListBox.SelectedItem).ColorBrush;
```

```
          ColorBackgroundMode = false;
          ColorListBox.SelectedIndex = TouchPaintingSelectedColorIndex;
        }
    }

    private void AppBarChangeTouchColor_Click(object sender, EventArgs e)
    {
      ColorListBox.Visibility = Visibility.Visible;
    }
  }
}
```

In Listing 3–5 there is memory-tracking code to help analyze memory consumption that I cover in the next section.

Analyzing Memory

In Listing 3–5 there is an event handler named DebugMemoryInfo_Tick, as well as code in the PhoneApplicationPage_Loaded method to fire the Tick event for a DispatcherTimer object named TrackMemoryTimer. The DebugMemoryInfo_Tick event handler generates this text to the Output window in Visual Studio when the finger painting page is launched in the SinglePointTouch project.

```
--> 7:14:50 PM
--> Device Total : 497618944
--> App Current : 11014144
--> App Peak : 12492800
```

Next, draw a sample image, such as that shown in Figure 3–8.

Figure 3–8. Finger painting sample image

What follows is the resulting memory consumption:

```
--> 7:14:36 AM
--> Device Total : 390012928
--> App Current : 24748032
--> App Peak : 24748032
```

The emulator has essentially unlimited memory so consuming almost 250MB of RAM runs fine. You could finger paint a similar image on a physical device with 512MB, and it would be fine as well. However, for certification in AppHub, applications need to stay under 90MB to pass. This is because on a device with 256MB of RAM, consuming more than that could impact performance.

Tracking memory using this script or something similar is a very important aspect of performance tuning Windows Phone applications, especially when testing on the emulator that essentially has unlimited resources.

■ **Tip** Applications can momentarily go over 90MB and not crash, so don't panic if your application peaks over 90MB, but settles in below 90MB.

The reason the finger painting application consumes memory is that it is a purely vector-based drawing consisting of Ellipse objects. The Ellipse objects can yield an impressionistic effect with careful drawing but it does result in high memory consumption. As a user moves the mouse, new Ellipse objects are drawn to screen. When drawing over an area that is already colored, the old color is still present underneath in Ellipse objects. Options to investigate are to use Silverlight geometry primitives instead of Ellipse objects. Another option to reduce memory consumption is to use the WritableBitmap class to "burn" the objects into the background as a way to collapse the vector objects into simple raster bitmaps.

The Mouse and Touch events are familiar to developers and easy to work with; however, they should only be used when absolutely necessary, such as when you need individual touch points. The MSDN documentation has a section titled "Performance Considerations in Applications for Windows Phone" available here

http://msdn.microsoft.com/en-us/library/ff967560(v=VS.92).aspx

This white paper has a section titled "User Input" that recommends using Manipulation Events instead of mouse and touch events or performance and compatibility reasons for all scenarios other than when you need individual points. This chapter covers gestures and manipulation events next as part of multi-point touch.

Multi-Point Touch

As mentioned previously, Silverlight applications are generally based on the control framework and single touch when interacting with controls. There are parts of applications that may require multi-touch. Windows Phone supports up to four touch points, which are available to both Silverlight- and XNA Framework-based applications. Examples of multi-touch in Silverlight would be image manipulation, zooming in or out on a news article to adjust the font, and so on.

In the XNA Framework, multi-touch is essential, since game-based user experiences are generally highly customized. One example of multi-touch in the XNA Framework are having one thumb manipulating a virtual accelerator and the other thumb manipulating a virtual brake in a driving game. Another example is one thumb manipulating a virtual joystick and the other thumb touching buttons to jump or shoot.

Controls

A couple of controls that are part of the Windows Phone development platform include support for multi-touch. The WebBrowser control supports pinch/zoom and pan gestures. Another control that has built-in support for multi-touch is the Bing Maps control, which also supports pinch/zoom and pan gestures.

The other control that is more generic than the WebBrowser and Bing Maps controls is the ScrollViewer panel control, which supports flick and pan gestures for contained content. The ScrollViewer project in the Chapter 3 solution demonstrates the ScrollViewer Control. Once the solution is created, drag a ScrollViewer control onto the ContentPanel Grid control in Expression Blend. Reset the Height and Width on the Image control to Auto. Also reset layout on the ScrollViewer so that it fills the ContentPanel.

Drag an Image control onto the ScrollViewer control. Set the Source property of the Image control to point to the France.jpg image in the images folder of the ScrollViewer solution. Set the Stretch property on the Image control to None so that it expands beyond the screen bounds to full size. On the containing ScrollViewer control, set the HorizontalScrollBarVisibility property to Auto from Disabled. We want to be able to pan and flick the image in all directions.

Once layout is configured property for the controls as detailed in the previous paragraphs, we are ready to test. When you run the application, you can see that you get pan and flick gestures "for free," provided by the ScrollViewer control. In the next couple of sections I cover multi-touch programming, gestures, and manipulation events.

Raw Touch with Touch.FrameReported

The mouse events covered in the previous section may work fine for many cases, but may feel a bit clunky. In this section we will implement the finger-painting application using Touch.FrameReported for more fine-grained raw touch development.

We start with a copy of the previous finger painting application but change the Page class from FingerPaintingPageMouseEvents to FingerPaintingPageTouchEvents to prevent compilation errors with duplicate names. We keep both pages in the SinglePointTouch project, though System.Windows.Input.Touch supports multi-touch, which is an advantage over the mouse events. The next step is to remove the MouseMove event handler from the Rectangle and comment out the Rectangle_MouseMove event handler in the code behind.

In the PhoneApplicationPage_Loaded event, wire-up the FrameReported event like this

```
System.Windows.Input.Touch.FrameReported += new TouchFrameEventHandler(Touch_FrameReported);
```

To prevent exceptions when navigating back and forth to the page, the event is disconnected in the unload event here

```
private void PhoneApplicationPage_Unloaded(object sender, RoutedEventArgs e)
{
  System.Windows.Input.Touch.FrameReported -= Touch_FrameReported;
}
```

The Touch_FrameReported event is where the touch action happens and directly replaces the Rectangle_MouseMove event from the previous example. The FrameReported event TouchFrameEventArgs class provides a rich set of properties to provide fine-grained control over touch development. Table 3–2 provides a summary of its properties and events.

***Table 3–2.** Available InputScope Options*

Member	Description
GetPrimaryTouchPoint	Returns the primary or first finger touch point for the reported frame as a TouchPoint class value.
GetTouchPoints	Returns a collection of all of the TouchPoint class objects from the reported frame.
SuspendMousePromotionUntilTouchUp	Disables promoting the low-level touch events from becoming mouse events. Useful if you want to override mouse event behavior in an application.
Timestamp	Determines how much time has passed between touch events.

Unlike with the mouse events StylusPoint class, the TouchPoint class does not support PressureFactor values, so Opacity is not varied by pressure. The TouchPoint class does support a Size value for the touch action but the size resolves to a very small value regardless of whether drawing with a small finger or larger finger, making the Size value less useful. The following is the final Touch_FrameReported event handler:

```
void Touch_FrameReported(object sender, TouchFrameEventArgs e)
{
  foreach (TouchPoint p in e.GetTouchPoints(DrawCanvas))
  {
    if ((InDrawingMode) && (p.Action == TouchAction.Move))
    {
      Ellipse ellipse = new Ellipse();
      ellipse.SetValue(Canvas.LeftProperty, p.Position.X);
      ellipse.SetValue(Canvas.TopProperty, p.Position.Y);
      ellipse.Width = _touchRadius;
      ellipse.Height = _touchRadius;
      ellipse.IsHitTestVisible = false;
      ellipse.Stroke = ((ColorClass)ColorListBox.SelectedItem).ColorBrush;
      ellipse.Fill = ((ColorClass)ColorListBox.SelectedItem).ColorBrush;
      DrawCanvas.Children.Add(ellipse);
    }
  }
}
```

Notice that this code has an additional check on the Boolean variable InDrawingMode. The value of InDrawingMode is set to false when showing the color selector ColorListBox. This is because the Touch.FrameReported event fires no matter what control has focus. So without additional checks, selecting or scrolling colors would generate additional touch events on the DrawCanvas Canvas object. Raw touch with Touch.FrameReported is truly raw touch processing.

The mouse events have a nice benefit over Touch.FrameReported. The mouse events generate StylusPoint objects, which include a PressureFactor value instead of the TouchPoint objects for Touch.FrameReported. This allows varying the Opacity, for a better drawing experience. However, for other touch-related programming where Gestures or Manipulations cannot provide needed functionality, raw touch with Touch.FrameReported is recommended over mouse events

Multi-Touch with Raw Touch

One capability that Touch.FrameReported provides over mouse events is multi-touch capabilities via the TouchPoint class. The TouchPoint class has the following two members that allow tracking of state and history:

- **Action:** Identifies whether the touch action is Down, Move, or Up.

- **TouchDevice:** Contains an ID that represents the "finger" as it moves about the screen.

With these two properties it is possible to track the state of the touch as well as associated history as the user moves their finger around the screen. The MultiTouchwithRawTouch project is a simple program that tracks up to four touch actions by a user. Essentially you can place four fingers on the screen and watch the Rectangle objects follow your fingers on the screen. The XAML for the project is a generic page that has Rectangle objects dynamically added to a Canvas panel added to the default ContentPanel Grid. Listing 3–6 contains the source code for the code-behind file.

Listing 3–6. *MultiTouchwithRawTouch MainPage.xaml.cs Code File*

```
using System.Collections.Generic;
using System.Linq;
using System.Windows;
using System.Windows.Controls;
using System.Windows.Input;
using System.Windows.Media;
using System.Windows.Shapes;
using Microsoft.Phone.Controls;

namespace MultiTouchwithRawTouch
{
  public partial class MainPage : PhoneApplicationPage
  {
    List<TrackedTouchPoint> trackedTouchPoints = new List<TrackedTouchPoint>();

    // Constructor
    public MainPage()
    {
      InitializeComponent();

      Touch.FrameReported += new TouchFrameEventHandler(Touch_FrameReported);
    }

    void Touch_FrameReported(object sender, TouchFrameEventArgs e)
    {
      foreach (TouchPoint tp in e.GetTouchPoints(DrawCanvas))
      {
        tp.TouchDevice.
        TrackedTouchPoint ttp = null;
        var query = from point in trackedTouchPoints
                    where point.ID == tp.TouchDevice.Id
                    select point;
        if (query.Count() != 0)
          ttp = query.First();

        switch (tp.Action)
        {
          case TouchAction.Down: ttp = new TrackedTouchPoint();
            ttp.ID = tp.TouchDevice.Id;
            if (trackedTouchPoints.Count == 0)
            {
              ttp.IsPrimary = true;
              DrawCanvas.Children.Clear();
            }
            trackedTouchPoints.Add(ttp);
            ttp.Position = tp.Position;
            ttp.Draw(DrawCanvas);
```

```
                  break;

             case TouchAction.Up: ttp.UnDraw(DrawCanvas);
                trackedTouchPoints.Remove(ttp);
                break;
             default:
                ttp.Position = tp.Position;
                ttp.Draw(DrawCanvas);
                break;
         }
      }
      CleanUp(e.GetTouchPoints(DrawCanvas));
   }

   private void CleanUp(TouchPointCollection tpc)
   {
      List<int> ToDelete = new List<int>();
      foreach (TrackedTouchPoint ttp in trackedTouchPoints)
      {
         var query = from point in tpc
                     where point.TouchDevice.Id == ttp.ID
                     select point;
         if (query.Count() == 0)
            ToDelete.Add(ttp.ID);
      }

      foreach (int i in ToDelete)
      {
         var query = from point in trackedTouchPoints
                     where point.ID == i
                     select point;
         if (query.Count() != 0)
            trackedTouchPoints.Remove(query.First());
      }
      if (trackedTouchPoints.Count == 0)
      {
         DrawCanvas.Children.Clear();
      }
   }
}

class TrackedTouchPoint
{
   public TrackedTouchPoint()
   {
      Rect = new Rectangle() { Height = 50, Width = 50 };
      Position = new Point(0, 0);
      IsPrimary = false;
      BrushColor = new SolidColorBrush(Colors.Yellow);
   }

   private Rectangle Rect { get; set; }
```

```
    public int ID { get; set; }

    public Brush BrushColor
    {
      set
      {
        Rect.Fill = value;
      }
    }
    public Point Position { get; set; }

    public bool IsPrimary { get; set; }

    public void Draw(Canvas canvas)
    {
      if (IsPrimary)
        BrushColor = new SolidColorBrush(Colors.Blue);

      Rect.SetValue(Canvas.LeftProperty, Position.X);
      Rect.SetValue(Canvas.TopProperty, Position.Y);
      if (Rect.Parent == null)
        canvas.Children.Add(Rect);
    }

    public void UnDraw(Canvas canvas)
    {
      canvas.Children.Remove(Rect);
    }
  }
}
```

Raw touch with Touch.FrameReported gives full access to every touch event; however, it is cumbersome to work with when you just need to detect gestures or a set of gestures. For multi-touch programming Touch.FrameReported is not recommended. The next couple of sections cover gesture detection in the XNA Framework and Silverlight as well as manipulations, which are recommended for multi-touch.

Programming with Gestures

A gesture is a one or two finger action that is a pre-defined touch interaction. Gestures on Windows Phone are similar to gestures that are defined on Windows 7, iPhone, Android, or pretty much any other touch device. What makes gestures useful is their consistency, which means that they should not be altered or "enhanced" in a way that will confuse users.

I cover single-touch and raw touch in the previous section titled "Single-Point Touch," but I did not speak to it in terms of gestures. Single-touch gestures consist of the following interactions:

- **Tap:** Select an object in a ListBox, touch to click a button, or text to navigate to another screen.

- **Double Tap:** Successive taps in a row that happen with a time duration such as one second and are therefore recognized as a double-tap, not two single-tap gestures.

- **Pan:** Use a single feature to move an object across the screen.

- **Flick:** Similar to a pan gesture except that the finger moves quickly across the screen, acceleration is detected, and the object moves with inertia relative to the amount of acceleration applied.

- **Touch and Hold:** Touch on an area of screen for a period of time, say a second, and a touch and hold gesture is detected. Used to open context menus.

The two-finger gestures are Pinch and Stretch. The pinch gesture consists of placing two fingers on the screen and moving them closer. `Pinch` is used to zoom out as well as to make an object smaller. The `Stretch` gesture consists of placing two fingers on the screen and moving them further away. `Stretch` is used to zoom in as well as to make an object larger. In the next two subsections I cover how to support gestures in Windows Phone Applications.

Multi-Touch with XNA Framework Libraries

The XNA Framework on Windows Phone includes the `Microsoft.Xna.Framework.Input.Touch` namespace. This is a non-graphical, non-rendering namespace, so it can be leveraged in both Silverlight and XNA Game Studio. The primary class for the namespace is the `TouchPanel` static class, which receives touch input that is automatically interpreted into a gesture for developers.

To process gestures, developers call `TouchPanel.IsGestureAvailable` to determine if a Gesture is pending. If one is, developers then call `TouchPanel.ReadGesture`. The `Microsoft.Xna.Framework.Input.Touch` namespace includes an enumeration named GestureType that identifies the supported gestures, DoubleTap, Flick, FreeDrag, HorizontalDrag, VerticalDrag, Hold, Pinch, and Tap.

The Chapter 3 project `GesturesTouchPanelXNA` demonstrates how simple it is to use the `TouchPanel` class to determine gestures. In the `Initialize()` method of Game1.cs, the code enables all possible gestures.

```
TouchPanel.EnabledGestures = GestureType.DoubleTap | GestureType.Flick |
  GestureType.FreeDrag | GestureType.Hold | GestureType.HorizontalDrag |
  GestureType.None | GestureType.Pinch | GestureType.PinchComplete |
  GestureType.Tap | GestureType.VerticalDrag | GestureType.DragComplete;
```

We want to draw text to the screen in the XNA Framework project so we right-click on the `GesturesTouchPanelXNAContent` Content project and select Add New Item…and then select Sprite Font. You can edit the `FontName` tag to be a different font name as long as you have rights to redistribute the font. It is changed to `Pescadero` because that is one of the fonts available for redistribution via XNA Game Studio. For more details on font redistribution, visit http://msdn.microsoft.com/en-us/library/bb447673.aspx. The project declares a `SpriteFont` object named `spriteFontSegoeUIMono` to represent the font.

In the `LoadContent()` method of Game1.cs, this code loads the font and defines a position in the middle of the screen to draw the font.

```
spriteFontSegoeUIMono = Content.Load<SpriteFont>("Segoe UI Mono");
spriteFontDrawLocation = new Vector2(graphics.GraphicsDevice.Viewport.Width / 2,
  graphics.GraphicsDevice.Viewport.Height / 2);
```

In the Update() method, here is the code to check for a gesture:

```
if (TouchPanel.IsGestureAvailable)
{
  gestureSample = TouchPanel.ReadGesture();
  gestureInfo = gestureSample.GestureType.ToString();
}
```

The gestureInfo variable is printed to the screen using the imported font with these lines of code in the Draw() method.

```
spriteBatch.Begin();
// Draw gesture info
string output = "Last Gesture: " + gestureInfo;

// Find the center of the string to center the text when outputted
Vector2 FontOrigin = spriteFontSegoeUIMono.MeasureString(output) / 2;
// Draw the string
spriteBatch.DrawString(spriteFontSegoeUIMono, output, spriteFontDrawLocation,
  Color.LightGreen,0, FontOrigin, 1.0f, SpriteEffects.None, 0.5f);
spriteBatch.End();
```

Run the application on a device and gesture on the screen to see the gesture recognized and the name of the gesture action drawn onscreen. Now that we have an easy way to detect a gesture, let's use it to do something useful.

The GestureSample class provides six properties to provide useful information regarding the gesture, GestureType, Timestamp, Position, Position2, Delta, and Delta2. You know what GestureType does from the discussion in the preceding paragraphs. Timestamp indicates the time of the gesture sample reading. The Timestamp values are continuous for readings to they can be subtracted to determine how much time passed between readings. The other four values are Vector2 values related to the position of the finger on the screen. Position represents the first finger. Position2 represents the second finger if a two-finger gesture. The Delta and Delta2 values are like Timestamp, in that they indicate the changes in finger position relative to the last finger position, not between fingers if a multi-touch gesture. Table 3–3 relates gestures to the applicable fields with relevant notes.

Table 3–3. *Gestures and Applicable GestureSample Members*

Gesture	Applicable Members	Notes
Tap	Position	
DoubleTap	Position	
Hold	Position	
FreeDrag	Position, Delta	
VerticalDrag Position, Delta	Delta values are constrained to the direction of movement, either vertical (X=0) or horizontal (Y=0).	
HorizontalDrag	Position, Delta	
DragComplete	N/A	All vector2 values set to zero.
Flick	Delta	The Delta member represents flick speed (and direction) as pixels per second.
Pinch	Position, Position2, Delta, Delta2	Position/Delta represent the first finger. Position2/Delta2 represents the second finger. Negative values indicate the Pinch gesture is moving fingers closer together.
PinchCompete	N/A	All vector2 values set to zero.

Debug info is added to write out the data from the GestureSample instance named gestureSample to help with development. The following is an example from the beginning of a Pinch gesture:

```
gesture Type:      Pinch
gesture Timestamp: 03:27:37.3210000
gesture Position:  {X:425.2747 Y:287.3394}
gesture Position2: {X:523.077 Y:366.6055}
gesture Delta:     {X:0 Y:0}
gesture Delta2:    {X:0 Y:0}
```

A short expanding Pinch gesture results in about 30 gesture samples over just less than half a second, providing a rich set of data to apply to objects as a result of user touches. Run the sample and perform gestures on blank portions of the screen to see how position and delta values change.

To make the sample more interesting stickman figure manipulation is added to the GesturesTouchPanelXNA project. The stickman figure responds to Hold, Flick, Drag, and Pinch gestures.

Figure 3–9 shows the simple UI but you will want to run this on a device to try out the supported gestures.

Figure 3–9. *Multi-Touch with the XNA Framework UI*

If you tap and hold (Hold GestureType) on the stickman, the figure rotates 90 degrees. If the stickman is flicked (Flick GestureType), the stickman will bounce around the screen and will eventually slow down. Tap on the stickman to stop movement. Finally, drag (FreeDrag GestureType) to slide the stickman around the screen.

There is a little bit of XNA Framework development in the sample to create a basic GameObject class to represent the stickman sprite. This keeps the game code clean without using a bunch of member variables to track state in the Game1.cs file. Listing 3–7 shows the GameObject class.

Listing 3–7. *GameObject.cs Code File*

```
using Microsoft.Xna.Framework;
using Microsoft.Xna.Framework.Graphics;

namespace GesturesTouchPanelXNA
{
  class GameObject
  {
    private const float _minScale = .4f;
    private const float _maxScale = 6f;
    private const float _friction = .7f;
    private const float _bounceVelocity = .9f;


    private float _scale = 1f;
    private Vector2 _velocity;
    private Vector2 _position;

    public GameObject(Texture2D gameObjectTexture)
    {
      Rotation = 0f;
      Position = Vector2.Zero;
      SpriteTexture = gameObjectTexture;
      Center = new Vector2(SpriteTexture.Width / 2, SpriteTexture.Height / 2);
```

```
    Velocity = Vector2.Zero;
    TintColor = Color.White;
    Selected = false;
}

public Texture2D SpriteTexture { get; set; }
public Vector2 Center { get; set; }
public float Rotation { get; set; }
public Rectangle TouchArea { get; set; }
public Color TintColor { get; set; }
public bool Selected { get; set; }
public float Scale
{
  get { return _scale; }
  set
  {
    _scale = MathHelper.Clamp(value, _minScale, _maxScale);
  }
}
public Vector2 Position
{ get { return _position; }
  set { _position = value ; } //Move position to Center.
}
public Vector2 Velocity
{
  get {return _velocity;}
  set { _velocity = value; }
}

public Rectangle BoundingBox
{
  get
  {
    Rectangle rect =
      new Rectangle((int)(Position.X - SpriteTexture.Width / 2 * Scale),
      (int)(Position.Y - SpriteTexture.Height / 2 * Scale),
      (int)(SpriteTexture.Width * Scale),
      (int)(SpriteTexture.Height * Scale));
      //Increase the touch target a bit
      rect.Inflate(10, 10);
    return rect;
  }
}

public void Update(GameTime gameTime, Rectangle displayBounds)
{
  //apply scale for pinch / zoom gesture
  float halfWidth = (SpriteTexture.Width * Scale) / 2f;
  float halfHeight = (SpriteTexture.Height * Scale) / 2f;

  // apply friction to slow down movement for simple physics when flicked
  Velocity *= 1f - (_friction * (float)gameTime.ElapsedGameTime.TotalSeconds);
```

```
        // Calculate position
        //position = velocity * time
        //TotalSeconds is the amount of time since last update in seconds
        Position += Velocity * (float)gameTime.ElapsedGameTime.TotalSeconds;

        // Apply "bounce" if sprite approaches screen bounds
        if (Position.Y < displayBounds.Top + halfHeight)
        {
          _position.Y = displayBounds.Top + halfHeight;
          _velocity.Y *= -_bounceVelocity;
        }
        if (Position.Y > displayBounds.Bottom - halfHeight)
        {
          _position.Y = displayBounds.Bottom - halfHeight;
          _velocity.Y *= -_bounceVelocity;
        } if (Position.X < displayBounds.Left + halfWidth)
        {
          _position.X = displayBounds.Left + halfWidth;
          _velocity.X *= -_bounceVelocity;
        }

        if (Position.X > displayBounds.Right - halfWidth)
        {
          _position.X = displayBounds.Right - halfWidth;
          _velocity.X *= -_bounceVelocity;
        }
      }
    }

    public void Draw(SpriteBatch spriteBatch)
    {
      spriteBatch.Draw(SpriteTexture, Position, null, TintColor, Rotation,
        Center,Scale,
        SpriteEffects.None,0);
    }
  }
}
```

The vast majority of the `GameObject` class is basic math calculations for checking screen boundaries, velocity, position, and so on. The one item to point out is the handy `MathHelper` static class that includes numerous helpful methods. The `Clamp` method is used to limit the zooming via the `Pinch GestureType` to be between a min and max scale value.

The other interesting code is the `ProcessTouchInput()` method in Game1.cs that is called in the `Update()` method. The method checks for touches first in order to determine if the stickman was touched on screen. To perform the check, each touch is converted to a `Point` object mapped into the screen coordinates. Next, we create a `Rectangle` object that encapsulates the stickman. The `Rectangle.Contains` method is passed in the Point object that represents the touch to determine if the touch was within the bounding box of the stickman. If the `Point` object is within the bounds of the `Rectangle` object, `Selected` is set to `true` on the `StickMan` sprite and gestures are applied. Otherwise, if a gesture is performed outside of the stickman, the gesture info is displayed to the screen as before but the `StickMan` sprite is not affected. The following is the code to determine selection:

```
TouchCollection touches = TouchPanel.GetState();
```

```
if ((touches.Count > 0) && (touches[0].State == TouchLocationState.Pressed))
{
  // map touch to a Point object to hit test
  Point touchPoint = new Point((int)touches[0].Position.X,
                               (int)touches[0].Position.Y);

  if (StickManGameObject.BoundingBox.Contains(touchPoint))
  {
    StickManGameObject.Selected = true;
    StickManGameObject.Velocity = Vector2.Zero;
  }
}
```

A switch statement is added to the while (TouchPanel.IsGestureAvailable) loop. As a GestureType is identified, it is applied to the StrawMan sprite. The switch statement is shown in Listing 3–8.

Listing 3–8. *ProcessInput Method GestureType Switch Statement*

```
if (StickManGameObject.Selected)
{
  switch (gestureSample.GestureType)
  {
    case GestureType.Hold:
      StickManGameObject.Rotation += MathHelper.Pi;
      break;
    case GestureType.FreeDrag:
      StickManGameObject.Position += gestureSample.Delta;
      break;
    case GestureType.Flick:
      StickManGameObject.Velocity = gestureSample.Delta;
      break;
    case GestureType.Pinch:
      Vector2 FirstFingerCurrentPosition = gestureSample.Position;
      Vector2 SecondFingerCurrentPosition = gestureSample.Position2;
      Vector2 FirstFingerPreviousPosition = FirstFingerCurrentPosition -
              gestureSample.Delta;
      Vector2 SecondFingerPreviousPosition = SecondFingerCurrentPosition -
              gestureSample.Delta2;
      //Calculate distance between fingers for the current and
      //previous finger positions.  Use it as a ration to
      //scale object.  Can have positive and negative scale.
      float CurentPositionFingerDistance = Vector2.Distance(
        FirstFingerCurrentPosition, SecondFingerCurrentPosition);
      float PreviousPositionFingerDistance = Vector2.Distance(
        FirstFingerPreviousPosition, SecondFingerPreviousPosition);

      float zoomDelta = (CurentPositionFingerDistance -
                        PreviousPositionFingerDistance) * .03f;
      StickManGameObject.Scale += zoomDelta;
      break;
  }
}
```

For the `GestureType.Hold` gesture, the `StickMan`'s `Rotation` property on the sprite is altered by `MathHelper.PiOver2` radians, which is equal to 90 degrees. For the `GestureType.FreeDrag` gesture, the `StickMan`'s `Position` property is updated by the `Delta` value, which is a `Vector2` in the direction and magnitude of movement since the last time a gesture sample was provided. For `GestureType.Flick`, the `StickMan`'s `Velocity` is updated by the `Delta` as well, which in this case represents a flick speed that is added.

The `GestureType.Pinch` gesture requires a bit more calculation, but it is fairly straightforward. Essentially, the distance between fingers in screen coordinates is calculated for the current finger position and previous finger position. The differences are used to calculate scale factor. Increasing finger distance is a positive scale factor. Decreasing finger distance is a negative scale factor. If the distance greatly increases (either to be bigger or smaller), that determines the size of the scale factor.

Touch input and Gestures are a key component to game development for Windows Phone. This section covered a lot of ground from gesture recognition to applying gestures to a game object, taking advantage of the gesture capabilities available in the XNA Framework libraries. We will now cover how to work with gestures in Silverlight.

Multi-Touch with Silverlight

We can take the information above regarding XNA Framework multi-touch and apply it to Silverlight. Because Silverlight and XNA Framework share the same application model, you can share non-drawing libraries across programming models. This is demonstrated in the `GesturesTouchPanelSilverlight` project. To get started, add a reference to the `Microsoft.Xna.Framework` and `Microsoft.Xna.Framework.Input.Touch` namespaces.

In the `MainPage()` constructor in `MainPage.xaml.cs`, add the following code to enable Gestures, just as before:

```
TouchPanel.EnabledGestures = GestureType.DoubleTap | GestureType.Flick |
        GestureType.FreeDrag | GestureType.Hold | GestureType.HorizontalDrag |
        GestureType.None | GestureType.Pinch | GestureType.PinchComplete |
        GestureType.Tap | GestureType.VerticalDrag | GestureType.DragComplete;
```

In XNA Game Studio, the game loop `Update` method is called 30 times a second so it is a single convenient place to capture touch input. In Silverlight there isn't a game loop. A polling loop could be simulated with a `DispatcherTimer` that fires every 1000/30 milliseconds. This is the cleanest approach, because it exactly simulates how the XNA Framework works.

Another method is to hook into the mouse or manipulation events. I cover the manipulation events in the next section so we use the mouse events instead. This will work fine most of the time, but some gesture events fire in `MouseLeftButtonDown` and `MouseButtonUp` as well as `MouseMove` so you have to be careful if it causes you a bug if you are just tracking events in `MouseMove`, and so on. The following is the code to capture gesture events in Silverlight mouse events:

```
private void PhoneApplicationPage_MouseLeftButtonDown(object sender, MouseButtonEventArgs e)
{
  while (TouchPanel.IsGestureAvailable)
  {
    GestureActionsListBox.Items.Add("LeftBtnDown
"+TouchPanel.ReadGesture().GestureType.ToString());

  }
}
```

```
private void PhoneApplicationPage_MouseLeftButtonUp(object sender, MouseButtonEventArgs e)
{
  while (TouchPanel.IsGestureAvailable)
  {
    GestureActionsListBox.Items.Add("LeftBtnUp " +
TouchPanel.ReadGesture().GestureType.ToString());
  }
}

private void PhoneApplicationPage_MouseMove(object sender, MouseEventArgs e)
{
  while (TouchPanel.IsGestureAvailable)
  {
    GestureActionsListBox.Items.Add("MouseMove " +
TouchPanel.ReadGesture().GestureType.ToString());
  }
}
```

Once the gestures are detected in the mouse events, you can perform similar programming using a Canvas panel as with the XNA Framework ample to react to gestures. One additional item to consider when comparing the XNA Framework and Silverlight is the coordinate system. In the XNA Framework, all objects are absolutely positioned relative to the upper left hand corner so the math to calculate position is straightforward. In Silverlight, objects can be placed within containers. For example, a Rectangle can have margin top and left margin of 10,10, but be contained within a Grid that has margin of 100,100 relative to the screen so coordinate mapping is necessary to translate the touch location to an actual control position.

Another method to detect gestures in Silverlight is available within the Silverlight for Windows Phone Toolkit at Silverlight.codeplex.com. The toolkit includes the GestureService/GestureListener components to detect gestures, so you will want to download the toolkit to test out the sample

Once the Silverlight for Windows Phone Toolkit is installed, browse to the toolkit library and add a reference. On my system it is located here: C:\Program Files (x86)\Microsoft SDKs\Windows Phone\v7.0\Toolkit\Nov10\Bin. The GesturesSilverlightToolkit project demonstrates how to use the GestureListener control. The toolkit library is added as a reference and made available in MainPage.xaml via an xml namespace import:

```
xmlns:toolkit="clr-namespace:Microsoft.Phone.Controls;assembly=↵
Microsoft.Phone.Controls.Toolkit"
```

A Rectangle object containing a GestureListener control is added to the ContentPanel Grid:

```
<toolkit:GestureService.GestureListener>
  <toolkit:GestureListener />
</toolkit:GestureService.GestureListener>
```

Figure 3–10 shows the events available on the GestureListener.

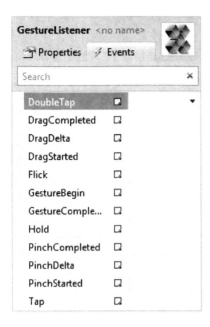

Figure 3–10. *GestureListener events*

An event handler is added for all the possible supported gestures, Tap, DoubleTap, Drag, Flick, TapAndHold, and Pinch to the GesturesSilverlightToolkit project to allow you to explore the events. Figure 3–11 shows the test UI.

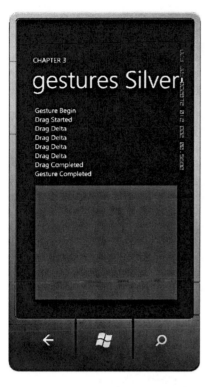

Figure 3–11. *Multi-Touch with the XNA Framework UI*

An important item to note, each event has unique EventArgs to provide the information developers need to apply the gesture to objects. As an example, the FlickGestureEventArgs class includes Angle, Direction, GetPosition, Handled, HorizontalVelocity, and VerticalVelocity members. The properties are more tailored toward Silverlight development, which may simplify gesture processing over using the XNA Framework libraries.

This concludes the discussion of gesture processing. The next section covers manipulation events.

Programming with Manipulation Events

Manipulations permit more complex interactions. They have two primary characteristics: Manipulations consists of multiple gestures that appear to happen simultaneously. The other characteristic is that manipulations consist of a set of transforms resulting from the user touch actions. The Manipulation events are very helpful because they interpret the user touch interaction into a set of transforms like translate and scale that you as the developer can apply to objects onscreen.

Windows Presentation Foundation 4.0 introduced Manipulation events to provide a high-level touch programming model that simplifies touch programming when compared to using low-level raw touch input. A subset of the manipulation events is available in Silverlight for Windows Phone with some differences. WPF manipulation events support translation, scaling, and rotation. Silverlight for Windows Phone does not include rotation.

Manipulation events do not distinguish between fingers. The events interpret finger movement into translation and scaling as well as an indication of velocity to implement physics.

Windows Phone includes three manipulation events: ManipulationStarted, ManipulationDelta, and ManipulationCompleted defined on the UIElement base class. Each manipulation event includes a custom EventArgs class with the following members in common:

- **e.OriginalSource:** The original object that raised the event.

- **e.ManipulationContainer:** The container object or panel that defines the coordinate system for the manipulation. This property will stay consistent through all three events.

- **e.ManipulationOrigin:** The point from which the manipulation originated. Indicates the location of the finger relative to the ManipulationContainer object. For two-finger manipulations, the ManipulationOrigin represents roughly the center point between the two fingers.

The events include unique EventArgs members as well, listed in the following:

- **ManipulationStarted:** The ManipulationStartedEventArgs class includes a Complete method that completes the manipulation without inertia, and a Handled property to indicate that the routed event is handled so that other controls don't attempt to handle the event again.

- **ManipulationDelta:** The ManipulationDeltaEventArgs class includes a Complete method. The IsInertial method indicates whether the Delta events has occurring during inertia. Other properties are DeltaManipulation and CumulativeManipulation, which represent the discrete (delta) and cumulative changes since ManipulationStarted resulting from the manipulation. The other EventArgs property is Velocities, which indicates the most recent rate of change for the manipulation.

- **ManipulationCompleted:** The ManipulationCompletedEventArgs include a FinalVelocities and TotalManipulation properties. It also includes a Handled and IsInertial properties.

As we saw before with gesture development there is one "started" event followed by zero or more ManipulationDelta events, and then a ManipulationCompleted "completed" event. To test manipulations, we created the ManipulationEvents project using the StickMan sprite from the GesturesTouchPanelXNA project. Figure 3–12 shows the UI.

Figure 3–12. *Manipulations test app UI*

The project implements drag and scale via the ManipulationsDelta event. Here is the code for the ManipulationsDelta event.

```
private void StickManImage_ManipulationDelta(object sender,
  ManipulationDeltaEventArgs e)
{
  ReportEvent("Manipulation Delta Event: ");
  Image image = sender as Image;
  CompositeTransform compositeTransform =
    image.RenderTransform as CompositeTransform;

  if ((e.DeltaManipulation.Scale.X > 0) || (e.DeltaManipulation.Scale.Y > 0))
  {
    double ScaleValue = Math.Max(e.DeltaManipulation.Scale.X,
      e.DeltaManipulation.Scale.Y);
    System.Diagnostics.Debug.WriteLine("Scale Value: " +
      ScaleValue.ToString());

    //Limit how large
    if ((compositeTransform.ScaleX <= 4d) || (ScaleValue < 1d))
    {
      compositeTransform.ScaleX *= ScaleValue;
```

```
        compositeTransform.ScaleY *= ScaleValue;
    }
}
System.Diagnostics.Debug.WriteLine("compositeTransform.ScaleX: " +
    compositeTransform.ScaleX);
System.Diagnostics.Debug.WriteLine("compositeTransform.ScaleY: " +
    compositeTransform.ScaleY);

compositeTransform.TranslateX += e.DeltaManipulation.Translation.X;
compositeTransform.TranslateY += e.DeltaManipulation.Translation.Y;
e.Handled = true;
}
```

The code modifies a CompositeTransform based on the DeltaManipulation values, Scale for Pinch gestures and Translation for movement. The CompositeTransform is declared in the XAML for the StickMan Image tag, as shown in the following:

```
<Image x:Name="StickManImage" Source="/images/StickMan.png"
    ManipulationCompleted="StickManImage_ManipulationCompleted"
    ManipulationDelta="StickManImage_ManipulationDelta"
    ManipulationStarted="StickManImage_ManipulationStarted">
 <Image.RenderTransform>
    <CompositeTransform />
 </Image.RenderTransform>
</Image>
```

The Silverlight for Windows Phone Toolkit GestureListener control is the preferred method for detecting gestures in Silverlight for Windows Phone. Manipulation events should be a second or third choice if for some reason the GestureListener or XNA Framework libraries do not suit your needs. For non-gesture detection multi-touch development, the manipulation events are recommended. Let's now shift gears to discuss other forms of application input on Windows Phone 7.

Accelerometer

As far as fun goes, the accelerometer can be an entertaining and engaging method of input, especially for game development with XNA Game Studio or Silverlight. We all have seen the car racing games on mobile phone or mobile gaming devices where the user is tilting the device like a steering wheel. The next section covers how to work with the Accelerometer sensor.

Understanding How It Works

The Accelerometer sensor detects acceleration in all three axes, X, Y, Z, to form a 3D vector. You may wonder in what direction and magnitude does the vector point? Collect a few Accelerometer readings using this line of code:

```
        System.Diagnostics.Debug.WriteLine(AccelerometerHelper↵
.Current2DAcceleration.ToString());
```

The following are a few samples from the Output window when debugging:

```
{X:0.351 Y:-0.002 Z:0.949} (Magnatude is approximately 1.02)
{X:0.401 Y:0.044 Z:0.984} (Magnatude is approximately 1.06)
{X:0.378 Y:0.04 Z:1.023} (Magnatude is approximately 1.09)
{X:0.386 Y:0.022 Z:0.992} (Magnatude is approximately 1.06)
{X:0.409 Y:0.03 Z:0.992} (Magnatude is approximately 1.07)
```

You can calculate the magnitude of the vector using the Pythagorean Theorem, which is the $Sqrt(X^2+Y^2+Z^2)$ = magnitude of the vector. The value should be about one but as you can see from the above samples, it can vary by location or could possibly be an error deviation. Either way, this is why applications like a level suggest that you calibrate the level against a known flat surface before using the virtual level.

If you run the application in the emulator, this reading is returned every time: {X:0 Y:0 Z:-1}, unless you use the accelerometer simulation tool available in the Winodows Phone OS 7.1 SDK to simulate acceleration.

Holding the phone flat in my unsteady hand yields similar values with Z near one and X, and Y near zero.

```
{X:0.039 Y:0.072 Z:-1.019}
{X:0.069 Y:0.099 Z:-1.047}
{X:0.012 Y:0.056 Z:-1.008}
{X:0.016 Y:0.068 Z:-1.019}
```

This suggests that the vector is oriented to point towards the center of the earth, which for the above readings is the bottom of the phone or a negative Z when the phone is lying flat on its back. Flipping the phone in my hand yields the following values:

```
{X:-0.043 Y:0.08 Z:1.019}
{X:-0.069 Y:0.111 Z:1.093}
{X:-0.069 Y:0.099 Z:1.093}
{X:-0.039 Y:0.107 Z:1.031}
```

This time the vector is pointing out from the glass toward the ground, because the phone is lying face down. This information is useful if you need to determine how the phone is oriented in the users hand when say taking a photograph.

Figure 3–13 shows the accelerometer coordinate system. This is important because developers must translate readings into the coordinate system for the application.

Figure 3–13. *Accelerometer fixed coordinate system*

As an example, in the XNA Framework, the default 2D coordinate system has positive Y going down, not up, so you cannot just take the Y component of acceleration and apply it to the Y value for a game object in 2D XNA.

■ **Note** The default coordinate system for 3D in the XNA Framework has positive Y going up. Chapter 8 covers 3D XNA Game Studio development.

With this background in hand, the next section covers development with the accelerometer sensor.

Programming with the Accelerometer

Accessing the Accelerometer sensor is pretty straightforward. We start with an XNA project, adding a reference to the Microsoft.Devices.Sensors assembly, and declaring instance of the Accelerometer class. In the Game1.Initialize() method, create an instance of the Accelerometer and call the Start() method to generate readings.

■ **Note** Turn off the Accelerometer if not needed to save battery power.

Create an event handler for ReadingChanged as well. The following is the code to create the event handler:

```
accelerometer = new Accelerometer();
accelerometer.Start();
accelerometer.ReadingChanged +=
  new EventHandler<AccelerometerReadingEventArgs>(accelerometer_ReadingChanged);
```

The accelerometer_ReadingChanged event handler event arguments AccelerometerReadingEventArgs class exposes acceleration in three dimensions via the X, Y, and Z member variables of type double. There is also a TimeStamp variable to allow measurement of acceleration changes over time.

A private member Vector3 variable named AccelerometerTemp is added to the Game1 class to collect the reading so that the code in the event handler does not have to new up a Vector3 each time a reading is collected. We create a helper static class named AccelerometerHelper that takes the accelerometer reading and assigns it to a Vector3 property named Current3DAcceleration. The following is the ReadingChanged event handler:

```
private Vector3 AccelerometerTemp = new Vector3();
void accelerometer_ReadingChanged(object sender, AccelerometerReadingEventArgs e)
{
  //
  AccelerometerTemp.X = (float)e.X;
  AccelerometerTemp.Y = (float)e.Y;
  AccelerometerTemp.Z = (float)e.Z;

  AccelerometerHelper.Current3DAcceleration = AccelerometerTemp;
  AccelerometerHelper.CurrentTimeStamp = e.Timestamp;
}
```

The AccelerometerHelper class takes the Vector3 and parses the values up in the "setter" function for the Current3DAcceleration property into the class members listed in Figure 3–14.

- Current2DAcceration
- Current3DAcceration
- CurrentTimeStamp
- Orientation
- Previous2DAcceration
- Previous3DAcceration
- PreviousTimeStamp
- XDelta
- YDelta
- ZDelta

Figure 3–14. AccelerometerHelper class members

Most of the code in the AccelerometerHelper class is properties and private member variables to hold values. Private backing variables are optional with the {get ; set ;} construct in C# but we use them here in order for all other member variables to be derived from just setting the Current3DAcceleration property. Listing 3–9 has the code for the AccelerometerHelper class.

Listing 3–9. *AccelerometerHelper Class Code File*

```csharp
using System;
using System.Collections.Generic;
using System.Linq;
using System.Text;
using Microsoft.Xna.Framework;

namespace AccelerometerInputXNA
{
  static public class  AccelerometerHelper
  {
    static private Vector3 _current3DAcceleration;
    static public Vector3 Current3DAcceleration
    {
      get
      {
        return _current3DAcceleration;
      }
      set
      {
        //Set previous to "old" current 3D acceleration
        _previous3DAcceleration = _current3DAcceleration;

        //Update current 3D acceleration
        //Take into account screen orientation
        //when assigning values
        switch (Orientation)
        {
          case DisplayOrientation.LandscapeLeft:
            _current3DAcceleration.X = -value.Y;
            _current3DAcceleration.Y = -value.X;
            _current3DAcceleration.Z = -value.Z;
            break;
          case DisplayOrientation.LandscapeRight:
            _current3DAcceleration.X = value.Y;
            _current3DAcceleration.Y = value.X;
            _current3DAcceleration.Z = value.Z;
            break;
          case DisplayOrientation.Portrait:
            _current3DAcceleration.X = value.X;
            _current3DAcceleration.Y = value.Y;
            _current3DAcceleration.Z = value.Z;
            break;
        }
```

```csharp
      //Update current 2D acceleration
      _current2DAcceleration.X = _current3DAcceleration.X;
      _current2DAcceleration.Y = _current3DAcceleration.Y;
      //Update previous 2D acceleration
      _previous2DAcceleration.X = _previous3DAcceleration.X;
      _previous2DAcceleration.Y = _previous3DAcceleration.Y;
      //Update deltas
      _xDelta = _current3DAcceleration.X - _previous3DAcceleration.X;
      _yDelta = _current3DAcceleration.Y - _previous3DAcceleration.Y;
      _zDelta = _current3DAcceleration.Z - _previous3DAcceleration.Z;
    }
}

static private Vector2 _current2DAcceleration;
static public Vector2 Current2DAcceleration
{
  get
  {
    return _current2DAcceleration;
  }
}

static private DateTimeOffset _currentTimeStamp;
static public DateTimeOffset CurrentTimeStamp
    {
  get
  {
    return _currentTimeStamp;
  }
  set
  {
    _previousTimeStamp = _currentTimeStamp;
    _currentTimeStamp = value;
  }
}

static private Vector3 _previous3DAcceleration;
static public Vector3 Previous3DAcceleration
{ get { return _previous3DAcceleration; } }

static private Vector2 _previous2DAcceleration;
static public Vector2 Previous2DAcceleration
{ get { return _previous2DAcceleration; } }

static private DateTimeOffset _previousTimeStamp;
static public DateTimeOffset PreviousTimeStamp
{ get { return _previousTimeStamp; } }

static private double _xDelta ;
static public double XDelta { get { return _xDelta;} }

static private double _yDelta;
```

```
        static public double YDelta { get { return _yDelta; } }

        static private double _zDelta;
        static public double ZDelta { get { return _zDelta; } }

        public static DisplayOrientation Orientation { get; set; }
    }
}
```

Notice in the setter function for the Current3DAcceleration property, there is a switch statement that flips the sign as needed based on device orientation, whether landscape left or landscape right, because the accelerometer coordinate system is fixed. This ensures that behavior is consistent when the XNA Framework flips the screen based on how the user is holding the device

To test the helper class, we copy over the GameObject class and assets, StickMan and the font, from the GesturesTouchPanelXNA project as well as the code to load up the assets and draw on the screen. The gesture code is not copied over since the input for this project is the Accelerometer. As before, the Game1.Update() method in the game loop is the place to handle input and apply it to objects. This line of code is added to the Update method to apply acceleration to the StickMan GameObject instance:

```
StickManGameObject.Velocity += AccelerometerHelper.Current2DAcceleration;
```

Run the application and the application behaves as expected: tilt the phone left, and the StickMan slides left, and vice versa when holding the phone in landscape orientation. If you tilt the phone up far enough, the screen flips to either DisplayOrientation.LandscapeLeft or DisplayOrientation.LandscapeRight and the behavior remains consistent.

The main issue with this calculation of just adding the Current2DAcceleration to the StickMan's velocity results in a very slow acceleration. This can be easily remedied by scaling the value like this

```
StickManGameObject.Velocity +=30* AccelerometerHelper.Current2DAcceleration;
```

The UI "feels" much better with this value and is more fun to interact with. Depending on the game object's desired behavior, you could create a ratchet effect by having fixed positions when the accelerometer values are between discrete values instead of the smooth application of accelerometer values to position in this code sample.

The Accelerometer sensor works equally well in Silverlight. The difference is mapping Accelerometer sensor changes to X/Y position values directly (instead of applying Vectors) using a CompositeTransform object just like what was done in the Silverlight sample with Manipulations in the previous section on multi-touch. Next up is the Location sensor.

Accelerometer Simulation

In the Windows Phone OS 7.1 development tools, the Windows Phone Emulator now exposes the ability to simulate the accelerometer when running your code in the emulator, a productivity boon for developers.

To test this out, I run the AccelerometerInputXNA sample in the Windows Phone Emulator. Figure 3-15 shows the tool.

Figure 3–15. *Windows Phone accelerometer simulator*

As you can see in the UI, a virtual phone is presented in a window next to the emulator. As you move the mouse while dragging the virtual phone, it updates the readings sent to the simulated accelerometer sensor.

Notice that the bottom part of the simulator allows you to set the orientation of the device to match how the application is expected to work. In this case, it is set to Landscape Flat, which matches the orientation of the emulator. Make sure the emulator orientation and the simulator orientation match for best results.

You can also send a "Shake" to the emulator via the other option at the bottom of the simulation control UI. The accelerometer simulation tool provides a very easy-to-use interface to help you get the most out of your accelerometer-based applications.

In the next section, I cover the location sensor as well as the simulation tool to help you build great location-based application with the emulator without having to walk-around with your PC while debugging.

Location

The location sensor is a very useful capability, given that mobile devices are generally on the go with their owner. Location provides context for applications that can make life easier on the user by automatically adjusting for the user's current location. A great example is the Search button on the phone. Enter or speak a keyword and click search. The local tab finds relevant items nearby. So a search for "Starbucks" gives the user exactly what they want on the local tab—which café is closest.

Understanding How It Works

The location sensor is a service that can use cell tower locations, wireless access point locations, and GPS to determine a user's location with varying degree of accuracy and power consumption.

Determining location with GPS is highly accurate, but it takes a while to spin up the GPS, and it consumes relatively more battery. Determining location using cell tower location is very fast, doesn't consume additional battery, but may not be accurate depending on how many cell towers are in range and their relative distance from each other in relation to the phone. Determining location with wireless access points can be accurate depending on how many wireless access points are in range and their relative position. If only one wireless access point is available location data will have a large error ring. Turning on Wi-Fi can consume additional battery power as well.

Programming with Location

You may try to guess that the Location namespace is in the Microsoft.Devices.Sensors namespace, but that would not be correct. It is located in the System.Device.Location namespace. The primary class for location is the GeoCoordinateWatcher class with the following class members:

- **DesiredAccuracy:** Can have a value of GeoPositionAccuracy.Default or GeoPositionAccuracy.High. The latter value forces the use of GPS, which can delay readings and consume battery. Use with care.

- **MovementThreshold:** This has a type of double. It indicates how far you have to move in order to generate a location reading in meters.

- **Permission:** Level of access to the location service.

- **Position:** Latest position obtained from location service.

- **PositionChanged:** Event that fires when a new position is available.

- **Start:** Starts location data acquisition from the location service.

- **Status:** Current status of the location service.

- **StatusChanged:** Event that fires when the status of the location changes.

- **Stop:** Stops location data acquisition from the location service.

- **TryStart:** Attempts to start location data acquisition with a timeout parameter passed in. The method returns false if the timeout expires before data is acquired. This call is synchronous and will block the thread it is called on – call on a background thread.

For this section topic on forward for the rest of the chapter, we start a new solution named Ch03_HandlingInput_Part2. The sample in that solution for this section is titled LocationSensorSilverlight. In the MainPage() constructor for the LocationSensorSilverlight project, the LocationService is instantiated and events for PositionChanged and StatusChanged are wired up. Here is the code:

```
LocationService = new GeoCoordinateWatcher();
LocationService.PositionChanged +=
  new EventHandler<GeoPositionChangedEventArgs<GeoCoordinate>>
    (LocationSensor_PositionChanged);

LocationService.StatusChanged +=
  new EventHandler<GeoPositionStatusChangedEventArgs>
    (LocationSensor_StatusChanged);
```

The rest of the application is just UI to display the LocationService information. The code uses the Bing Maps Map object to center the map on the user's current location. Here is the event handler to plot and zoom in on the map a bit:

```
private void PlotLocation_Click(object sender, EventArgs e)
{
  BingMap.Center = LocationService.Position.Location;
  BingMap.ZoomLevel = 15;
}
```

For more information we cover the Bing Maps control in detail in Chapter 5, but the most important property for the Map control is to set the CredentialsProvider key in XAML.

■ **Note** Obtain a free CredentialsProvider developer key from the Bing Maps account management web site located at www.bingmapsportal.com.

The UI implements the Application Bar to start and stop the Location Service as well as plot current location. The Application Bar also has a menu item to change the location accuracy. It is not possible to change accuracy after instantiating the GeoCoordinateWatcher variable. You have to instantiate a new GeoCoordinateWatcher variable and wire-up the event handlers again. Here is the code that handles this:

```
private void SetAccuracy_Click(object sender, EventArgs e)
{
  if (LocationService.DesiredAccuracy == GeoPositionAccuracy.Default)
    if (MessageBox.Show(
      "Current Accuracy is Default.  Change accuracy to High?"
      +"This may take some time and will consume additional battery power.",
      "Change Location Accuracy", MessageBoxButton.OKCancel)
      == MessageBoxResult.OK)
    {
      LocationService.Dispose();
      LocationService = new GeoCoordinateWatcher(GeoPositionAccuracy.High);
      LocationService.PositionChanged +=
    new EventHandler<GeoPositionChangedEventArgs<GeoCoordinate>>
      (LocationSensor_PositionChanged);

  LocationService.StatusChanged +=
    new EventHandler<GeoPositionStatusChangedEventArgs>
      (LocationSensor_StatusChanged);
    }
  else
    if (MessageBox.Show(
      "Current Accuracy is High.  Change accuracy to Default?"+
      "This wll be faster but will reduce accuracy.",
      "Change Location Accuracy", MessageBoxButton.OKCancel)
      == MessageBoxResult.OK)
    {
      LocationService.Dispose();
      LocationService =
        new GeoCoordinateWatcher(GeoPositionAccuracy.Default);
      LocationService.PositionChanged +=
    new EventHandler<GeoPositionChangedEventArgs<GeoCoordinate>>
      (LocationSensor_PositionChanged);
```

```
    LocationService.StatusChanged +=
      new EventHandler<GeoPositionStatusChangedEventArgs>
        (LocationSensor_StatusChanged);
      }
}
```

The XAML for the MainPage class implements a simple status panel that displays Location Service data. The code also uses the Silverlight Toolkit GestureListener to allow the user to drag the status panel over the map. Here is the markup:

```
<Border x:Name="LocationStatusPanel" HorizontalAlignment="Left"  VerticalAlignment="Top"
  Background="#96000000" Padding="2" >
  <toolkit:GestureService.GestureListener>
    <toolkit:GestureListener  DragDelta="GestureListener_DragDelta"/>
  </toolkit:GestureService.GestureListener>
  <Border.RenderTransform>
    <CompositeTransform/>
  </Border.RenderTransform>
    <StackPanel Orientation="Horizontal" Width="200" >
...Xaml for TextBoxes here.
    </StackPanel>
</Border>
```

Here is the GestureListener_DragDelta event handler code that repositions based on the user dragging the status panel.

```
private void GestureListener_DragDelta(object sender, DragDeltaGestureEventArgs e)
{
  Border border = sender as Border;
  CompositeTransform compositeTransform = border.RenderTransform as CompositeTransform;
  compositeTransform.TranslateX += e.HorizontalChange;
  compositeTransform.TranslateY += e.VerticalChange;
  e.Handled = true;
}
```

Windows Phone Emulator Location Simulation

Also in the Windows Phone 7.1 OS development tools, the Windows Phone Emulator includes another simulation tool, this time for location. This simulator is a very powerful and useful debugging and testing tool with the ability to set location as well as create a set of points for playback to ensure more consistent testing. Figure 3-16 shows the location UI with the emulator located where the plot point was added to the map on the simulator UI.

Figure 3–16. *Windows Phone location simulator*

Notice in the top left you can search for a location; in this case, it's Atlanta, GA. The location simulator has three points plotted roughly along Interstate 85 in Atlanta, GA. You place points by clicking on the map, which you can save for playback later. The mouse cursor is hovering over the play button.

You can set how often play back fires for a new location, allowing you to control the speed changing positions as well as the locations themselves. As you can see, this is incredibly helpful and probably the best way to develop, debug, and test a location-based application.

This concludes the overview of the Location Service available for Windows Phone. The next section covers how to capture Microphone input and play it back.

Microphone Input

The XNA Framework libraries make the `Microphone` available programmatically to applications. Add a reference to `Microsoft.Xna.Framework` assembly and a using clause for the `Microsoft.Xna.Framework.Audio`. The class of interest is the `Microphone` class that provides access to available microphones on the device.

The audio produced by the `Microphone` sensor is 16-bit raw PCM. The audio can be played using the `SoundEffect` object without issue. To play recorded audio in a `MediaElement` control, the raw audio needs to be put into a .wmv file format.

For the sample project named `MicrophoneWithSilverlight` in the `Ch03_HandlingInput_Part2` solution file the code uses the `SoundEffect` object to playback the audio.

In order to work with the microphone, some boilerplate XNA Framework code is required. Visit here for more info:

http://forums.create.msdn.com/forums/p/56995/347982.aspx

App.xaml.cs is modified to include the XNAAsyncDispatcher class and add an instance to this.ApplicationLifetimeObjects. With the boiler code in place, the application builds out a simple UI to record, stop, and play microphone audio. A slider is configured as a pitch selector so that you make your voice sound like Darth Vader or a Chipmunk. Figure 3–17 shows the UI.

Figure 3–17. *Microphone with Silverlight*

Listing 3–10 shows the source code.

Listing 3–10. *MainPage.xaml.cs Code File*

```
using System;
using System.IO;
using System.Windows;
using Microsoft.Phone.Controls;
using Microsoft.Xna.Framework.Audio;

namespace MicrophoneWithSilverlight
{
  public partial class MainPage : PhoneApplicationPage
  {
```

```
Microphone microphone = Microphone.Default;
MemoryStream audioStream;

// Constructor
public MainPage()
{
  InitializeComponent();

  microphone.BufferReady +=
    new EventHandler<EventArgs>(microphone_BufferReady);
  SoundEffect.MasterVolume = 1.0f;

  MicrophoneStatus.Text = microphone.State.ToString();
}

void microphone_BufferReady(object sender, EventArgs e)
{
  byte[] audioBuffer = new byte[1024];
  int bytesRead = 0;

  while ((bytesRead = microphone.GetData(audioBuffer, 0, audioBuffer.Length)) > 0)
    audioStream.Write(audioBuffer, 0, bytesRead);

  MicrophoneStatus.Text = microphone.State.ToString();
}

private void recordButton_Click(object sender, RoutedEventArgs e)
{
  if (microphone != null)
    microphone.Stop();

  audioStream = new MemoryStream();

  microphone.Start();
  MicrophoneStatus.Text = microphone.State.ToString();
}

private void stopRecordingButton_Click(object sender, RoutedEventArgs e)
{
  if (microphone.State != MicrophoneState.Stopped)
    microphone.Stop();

  audioStream.Position = 0;
  MicrophoneStatus.Text = microphone.State.ToString();
}

private void playButton_Click(object sender, RoutedEventArgs e)
{
  SoundEffect recordedAudio =
    new SoundEffect(audioStream.ToArray(), microphone.SampleRate,
      AudioChannels.Mono);
```

```
        recordedAudio.Play(1f, (float)pitchSlider.Value, 0f);
    }
  }
}
```

With the `Microphone` class, developers can create fun applications that allow a user to record and playback recorded audio with pitch modifications.

Compass Sensor

The compass sensor has been a part of many Windows Phone devices since RTM in the original devices. However, no API was available to developers. The Windows Phone OS 7.1 and Tools (Mango) now provides an API to access compass data if a compass is available. You will need a physical device to test the compass. There isn't built-in compass simulation in the emulator. The next section provides more details on the compass sensor.

Compass Background

The compass sensor is actually a magnetometer sensor. It can be used to determine the angle by which the device is rotated relative to the Earth's magnetic North Pole. You can also use raw magnetometer readings to detect magnetic forces around the device. This is something to consider when testing and programming the compass sensor—it can be affected by magnetic objects such as magnets, speakers, and monitors, as well as large metal objects.

▓ **Note** The compass sensor is not required for all Windows Phone devices. It is important that you consider this when designing and implementing your application. Your application should always check to see whether the sensor is available and either provide an alternative input mechanism or fail gracefully if it is not.

You need to understand how the compass works in order to build applications for it. Figure 3-18 describes the compass functionality.

Figure 3–18. *Compass functionalty*

As you can see in Figure 3-18, the device is meant to be held flat in your hand with the top of the phone pointing in the direction of the current magnetic heading. As you rotate the phone about the "Z" axis with the phone flat in your hand, you change the current heading relative to magnetic north.

■ **Note** Magnetic north can be different than true north found via GPS by several degrees.

The compass sensor can become inaccurate over time, especially if exposed to magnetic fields. There is a simple user action to recalibrate the compass that you can show the user how to do. I demonstrate how to work with the compass as well as the calibration process in the next section.

Coding with the Compass

In this sample we create a basic compass UI to demonstrate how to work with the compass. We create the UI in XAML and use Layout, Margin, and Padding to build out a simple compass UI that leverages the phone Accent color. You can just as easily create a nice image of compass rose and use that instead for the rotation.

I create a new project named CompassSensor and add it to the Chapter 3 part 2 solution in the Chapter 3 folder. The first thing I do is create a compass rose in XAML with the cardinal directions identified. I start with an Ellipse object named BoundingEllipse set to 200 Height and Width. I mark each cardinal direction using TextBlock control with alignment and Padding to position each TextBlock.

I group all of the controls into a Grid and name the Grid XamlCompass. I apply a RotationTransform to the Grid like this:

```
<Grid x:Name="XamlCompass" Margin="128,204,128,203" RenderTransformOrigin="0.5,0.5">
  <Grid.RenderTransform>
    <CompositeTransform x:Name="Angle" Rotation="0"/>
  </Grid.RenderTransform>
</Grid.RenderTransform>
```

The idea is that you use the Rotation to always point the north cardinal direction toward magnetic north based on the orientation of the device and compass sensor or true north if using the TrueHeading reading. The last item I add is an orange line using a Rectangle to show the device heading, which is always the top direction of the phone if held in Portrait mode flat in your hand. Figure 3-19 shows testing the XamlMagCompass in Blend with the mouse by manipulating the Rotation value for the transform.

Figure 3–19. *Testing rotation in Expression Blend*

To use the compass sensor, add a reference to Microsoft.Devices.Sensors assembly. Next I declare a private compass property of type Compass as well as add a using Microsoft.Devices.Sensors statement at the top of MainPage.xaml.cs. I next create a new instance of the Compass object in the Initialize method and assign an event handler to the CurrentValueChanged event. In the compass_CurrentValueChanged event handler you get access to these items:

- HeadingAccuracy
- MagneticHeading
- MagnetometerReading
- Timestamp
- TrueHeading

You may be wondering what TrueHeading represents. TrueHeading represents the angle in degrees from Earth's geographic north whereas MagneticHeading represents the angle in degrees from Earth's magnetic north. The two North Poles generally do not align due to the irregular shape of Earth's magnetic core and can vary by your geographic location due to local magnetic interferences.

■ **Tip** You will find TrueHeading to be much more accurate than MagneticHeading.

I make a copy of the compass and name it TrueHeadingCompass and re-arrange the UI to show the other available values as shown in Figure 3-20.

Figure 3–20. *Compass sensor test UI in action*

In testing the compass application, the TrueHeading value does align pretty well with actual bearings, using my street as a reference and testing by pointing the phone parallel to the direction of my street. I obtained a rough bearing of my street heading using Bing Maps.

For most purposes, the TrueHeading value is what you and your users will want. MagneticHeading will generally vary wildly from geocoordinate references due to the Earth's magnetic north not aligning with true north. There are special situations for highly localized maps that actually use magnetic headings instead so it is always good to give your users an option of which value to use. Listing 3-11 shows the code that captures the compass reading and sets the values to the UI.

Listing 3–11. *compass_CurrentValueChanged from MainPage.xaml.cs*

```
void compass_CurrentValueChanged(object sender, SensorReadingEventArgs<CompassReading> e)
{
  if (compass.IsDataValid)
    ContentPanel.Dispatcher.BeginInvoke(() =>
      {
        XamlMagCompassAngle.Rotation = e.SensorReading.MagneticHeading* -1;
        XamlTrueCompassAngle.Rotation = e.SensorReading.TrueHeading*-1;
        MagHeadingValue.Text = String.Format("{0} degrees", e.SensorReading.MagneticHeading);
        TrueHeadingValue.Text = String.Format("{0} degrees", e.SensorReading.TrueHeading);
```

```
        HeadingAccuracy.Text = "Heading Accuracy: " + e.SensorReading.HeadingAccuracy +"
degrees";
        MagnetometerReading.Text =
            String.Format("Magnetometer: {0:0.00} microteslas",
            e.SensorReading.MagnetometerReading.Length());
        calibrationTextBlock.Text = e.SensorReading.HeadingAccuracy.ToString();
        if (e.SensorReading.HeadingAccuracy > 10d)
            calibrationTextBlock.Foreground = new SolidColorBrush(Colors.Red);
        else
            calibrationTextBlock.Foreground = new SolidColorBrush(Colors.Green);
    });

}
```

The `compass_CurrentValueChanged` event handler fires on a background thread, so we need to call the `Dispatcher.BeginInvoke(()=>{})` method to fire an anonymous delegate on the UI thread in order to safely access the UI controls and not encounter an exception.

In order to position the north axis with either true or magnetic north depending on which value is being used, you need to subtract the value returned from `TrueHeading` / `MagneticHeading` to determine which direction is north. In our case I use a `CompositeTransform` with a `Rotation` value, so I first multiply the returned value for `TrueHeading` / `MagneticHeading` by negative one and then set that to the `Rotation` value to push north "back" to the direction it points to, since heading is always fixed to the top of the phone in Portrait position.

The rest of the code is pretty straightforward, using String.Format to build out the values. Note that in this method it also updates the calibration UI as well even though it is not visible by default. The `compass_Calibrate` event is fired when the phone determines that the compass needs to be calibrated. You can force this by placing the phone near a large magnet—do this at your own risk! placed my phone near a pair of speakers and the `compass_Calibrate` event fires:

```
void compass_Calibrate(object sender, CalibrationEventArgs e)
{
  Dispatcher.BeginInvoke(() =>
    { calibrationStackPanel.Visibility = Visibility.Visible; });
}
```

This results in showing the UI listed in Figure 3-21.

Figure 3–21. Compass calibration UI

If you move the phone in the figure eight pattern a few times you will see the heading accuracy value drop down to below 10 degrees and the heading accuracy number will turn green. Click the Back button to close the calibration dialog.

When you try the compass, it is somewhat jittery. The Compass class has a property named TimeBetweenUpdates. It defaults at 20ms, which is a fairly high sampling rate. One way to smooth it out is to sample less frequently. Experimenting with the value, I set it to 100 ms, which resulted in less jitter. Here is the initialization code:

```
public MainPage()
{
  InitializeComponent();
  if (Compass.IsSupported)
  {
    compass = new Compass();
    compass.TimeBetweenUpdates = TimeSpan.FromMilliseconds(100);
    compass.CurrentValueChanged += compass_CurrentValueChanged;
    compass.Calibrate += compass_Calibrate;
  }
}
```

Dead Reckoning Navigation

Dead Reckoning, or DR, navigation is the process of calculating your current position using a previously determined position, or "fix," advancing position based on upon actual or estimated speed for a period of time and in a compass direction. DR navigation is one of the oldest forms of navigation but still a very useful form of navigation, especially when in locations where the location sensor and GPS are not available.

A compass can be used to perform basic DR navigation using your own walking speed, the compass for direction, and the clock. As you move in a direction, record the compass heading and amount of time on that course. When you make a turn, record the new bearing and restart the timer.

This type of navigation can be used to create mobile applications such as "find my car" in a large covered parking lot at the airport or navigation inside a large building or any other enclosed location where GPS is not available. In this section I create a basic DR navigation sample that we will enhance by adding support for the gyroscope and then rewrite it to take advantage of the motion sensor.

DRNavigation Sample

In this sample I demonstrate basic DR navigation using a compass and time. The assumption is that the user's walking speed is constant and the device is held flat in your hand when walking like you would hold a compass.

The application has minimal UI, just displaying the recorded "steps" in a databound ListBox to demonstrate data capture and turn detection. Since this must be tested on a device and not in the emulator, deploy this sample to your Windows Phone OS 7.1 device and give it a try following the instructions.

If you walk in a well-defined shape by say making 90 degree turns to form a square, you may still see quite a few steps when you might expect to see just four steps. However, if you look closely at the steps, you can group them together into four distinct sets representing the four 90 degree turns. The additional steps are a result of jitter as you are walking and holding a device, as well as compass accuracy.

You could employ a smoothing algorithm to further refine the steps down to just four steps by evaluating the compass and perhaps the accelerometer sensors, but that may not be completely necessary as we continue on with the chapter and cover the additional sensors available in Windows Phone 7.5.

DRNavigation with Compass Code

There is quite a bit of code in the DRNavigation sample so we cover the overall structure and then the key points that we will modify in subsequent sections as we add more sensors to the code. The UI consists of a ListBox control and the Application Bar. The ListBox is databound to an instance of the DeadReckoner class, which is where all the logic exists for navigation.

The DeadReckoner class consists of two DispatcherTimer instances, one that collects the sensor data and the other that processes the sensor data. The DispatcherTimer is a special timer class where the Tick event fires on the UI thread. The _fixTimer collects sensor data every 100 milliseconds, and the _processTimer processes SensorsFix records collected by the _fixTimer. Here is the SensorFix class declaration:

```
public class SensorsFix
{
  public int NavStepID;
  public AccelerometerReading AccelerometerReading;
```

```
    public CompassReading CompassReading;
    public GyroscopeReading GyroScopeReading;
    public MotionReading MotionReading;
    public DateTime FixTime;
    public TimeSpan TimeSinceLastFix;
    public bool Processed;
}
```

The class is a bit lazy in that it saves the "reading" value for each sensor. It could be made leaner to just collect the values of interest in a full application, but for now I picked simplicity.

The _processTimer evaluates the unprocessed SensorsFix objects to determine current motion (i.e., detecting whether the user is going straight or making a left or right turn). Time is tracked between readings and then added together to determine how long a particular navigation step lasts. Remember that direction (course) and time were the basic key components of dead reckoning navigation.

The unprocessed SensorsFix objects are combined into a single DRNavigationStep record with this class declaration:

```
public class DRNavigationStep
{
  //Link each reading to a Nav Step
  //This could allow additional post-processing
  //to make sure that the ultimate direction of turns
  //is correct by doing a full run through all steps
  //at the end of the captures
  static private int _nextStepID;
  static public int NextStepID
  {
    get
    {
      _nextStepID++;
      return _nextStepID;
    }
    set { _nextStepID = value; }
  }

  public int NavStepID { get; set; }
  public TimeSpan Time { get; set; }
  //if Direction is straight, maintain bearing
  //in a turn this is the new bearing to turn to
  public double Bearing { get; set; }
  public double Speed { get; set; }
  public DRDirection Direction { get; set; }
  public DRMovementState MovementState { get; set; }
}
```

The class has properties to track bearing or course, speed, and direction of type DRDirection. This is an enumeration type with values of TurningLeft, TurningRight, GoingStraight, and Unknown. DRMovementState indicates whether the user is Stopped, Moving, or Unknown.

The bulk of the logic, albeit not complex, is located in the _processTimer.Tick event handler named processTimer_Tick. Listing 3-12 has the code for this event handler.

Listing 3–12. The processTimer_Tick Event Handler in DeadReckoner.cs

```
void processTimer_Tick(object sender, EventArgs e)
{
  Debug.WriteLine("Eval Fixes Ticks" + DateTime.Now.Ticks.ToString());
  //Detect new DR fixes
  var unprocessedFixes = from reading in _fixReadings
                         where reading.Processed == false
                         select reading;

  if (unprocessedFixes.Count<SensorsFix>() == 0)
  {
    //No longer collecting data
    _processTimer.Stop();
  }
  else
  { //Process fixes
    //detect when going straight
    //detect when makng a turn
    //detect when coming out of a turn
    double currentBearing;
    double newBearing;
    double bearingDelta;

    DRNavigationStep currentNavStep;
    DRNavigationStep newStep;
    foreach (SensorsFix reading in unprocessedFixes)
    {
      //Always get latest in case a new step was added while processing
      currentNavStep = NavigationInstructions.Last();
      //bearing is changing
      newBearing = reading.CompassReading.TrueHeading;
      currentBearing = currentNavStep.Bearing;
      bearingDelta = currentBearing - newBearing;
      if (!(Math.Abs(bearingDelta) < BEARING_ACCURACY_LIMIT))
        //Adjust  direction based on current state
        switch (currentNavStep.Direction)
        {
          case DRDirection.TurningLeft:
            if (bearingDelta > 0)//still moving left
              currentNavStep.Bearing = reading.CompassReading.TrueHeading;
            else //stopped turning left
            {
              //done turning, add a new step to go straight
              newStep = new DRNavigationStep();
              newStep.NavStepID = DRNavigationStep.NextStepID;
              newStep.Bearing = reading.CompassReading.TrueHeading;
              newStep.Direction = DRDirection.GoingStraight;
              NavigationInstructions.Add(newStep);
            }
            currentNavStep.Time += reading.TimeSinceLastFix;
            break;
          case DRDirection.TurningRight:
            if (bearingDelta < 0)//still moving right
```

219

```
            currentNavStep.Bearing = reading.CompassReading.TrueHeading;
          else //stopped turning right
          {
            //done turning, add a new step to go straight
            newStep = new DRNavigationStep();
            newStep.NavStepID = DRNavigationStep.NextStepID;
            newStep.Bearing = reading.CompassReading.TrueHeading;
            newStep.Direction = DRDirection.GoingStraight;
            NavigationInstructions.Add(newStep);
          }
          currentNavStep.Time += reading.TimeSinceLastFix;
          break;
        case DRDirection.GoingStraight:
          if (OnCurrentCourse(currentNavStep, reading))
          {
            currentNavStep.Time += reading.TimeSinceLastFix;
          }
          else
          {
            newStep = new DRNavigationStep();
            newStep.NavStepID = DRNavigationStep.NextStepID;
            newStep.Bearing = reading.CompassReading.TrueHeading;
            //update direction based on changes
            if (bearingDelta > 0)
              newStep.Direction = DRDirection.TurningLeft;
            else
              newStep.Direction = DRDirection.TurningRight;
            NavigationInstructions.Add(newStep);
          }
          currentNavStep.Time += reading.TimeSinceLastFix;
          break;
        case DRDirection.Unknown:
          break;
        default:
          break;
      }
      reading.Processed = true;
    }
  }
}
```

The first part of the event handler gathers up the unprocessed readings. If there are not any unprocessed readings, the code stops the timer. Otherwise the code enters a foreach loop to process the readings via a switch statement. The bearingDelta property represents the difference between the current reading and the current navigation step. To calculate it we have a constant named BEARING_ACCURACY_LIMIT.

If the delta between the current course and the new course obtained from the SensorsFix is greater than the BEARING_ACCURACY_LIMIT, it is detected as a turn. Otherwise, the time is added to the current navigation step as it is detected as continuing on course:

```
if (Math.Abs(bearingDelta) < BEARING_ACCURACY_LIMIT)
```

```
{
  currentNavStep.Time += reading.TimeSinceLastFix;
}
else
  //Adjust  direction based on current state
  switch (currentNavStep.Direction)
...
```

Check out the code to understand how it works. Notice that it implements two interfaces, IDisposable and INotifyPropertyChanged. The IDisposable interface is necessary because the sensors all implement IDisposable because they work with unmanaged resources (i.e., the sensors themselves). MainPage.xaml.cs calls Dispose on the DeadReckoner class when navigating away from the MainPage.

The INotifyPropertyChanged interface is necessary to support data binding, which is covered in Chapter 6. This completes the coverage of the compass sensor. Let's now move next to a discussion of the gyroscope sensor as well as what scenarios it enables.

Gyroscope Sensor

The gyroscope sensor is a new hardware sensor available on Windows Phone 7.5, though not mandatory. Windows Phone 7 devices do not have a gyroscope. This may cause concern with fragmentation of the Windows Phone ecosystem. Microsoft went to extra lengths to mitigate this issue by also providing the motion sensor, which abstracts out the gyroscope to provide sensor data with just accelerometer and compass, though in a slightly degraded mode. I cover the motion sensor in the next section. I'll first provide background on how a gyroscope works.

Gyroscope Background

The gyroscope sensor measures the rotational velocity of the device along its three primary axes. When the device is still, the readings from the gyroscope are zero for all axes. If you rotate the device around its center point as it faces you, like an airplane propeller, the rotational velocity on the Z axis will elevate above zero, growing larger as you rotate the device faster. Figure 3-22 shows the axis orientation for the gyroscope in relation to the phone.

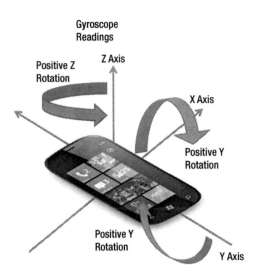

Figure 3–22. Gyrscope readings on 3-dimentional axis

The rotational velocity is measured in units of radians per second, where 2 * Pi radians are a full rotation. In Figure 3-22, if you hold the phone pointing away from you flat in your hand and then roll the phone from left to right, you will see positive Y rotation. If you flip the phone head to toe in your hand, you will see positive X rotation. Finally, if you rotate the phone flat in your hand counterclockwise, you will see positive Z rotation. If you are interested in determining the device's absolute orientation in space (yaw, pitch, and roll), you should use the combined Motion API, accessed using the Motion class, which I cover later in this chapter.

The gyroscope sensor is not required for all Windows Phone devices. Your application should always check to see whether the sensor is available and either provide an alternative input mechanism or fail gracefully if it is not. Also, be sure to mention that your application requires a gyroscope in the Marketplace description if that is the case.

Gyroscope Sample

The MSDN documentation has a useful walkthrough to help you understand how moving the phone in space affects the gyroscope readings. The walkthrough is available here:

http://msdn.microsoft.com/en-us/library/hh202943(v=VS.92).aspx

A modified version of the gyroscope code from MSDN is available in the GyroscopeSensor project as part of the Chapter 3 part 2 solution so that you can get a good feel for how the gyroscope values are affected by moving the device. Figure 3-23 shows the UI in the emulator.

Figure 3–23. *Gyroscope sensor project UI*

The gyroscope is not supported in the emulator currently, so the three Line objects at the top all have a length of zero since there isn't a reading. Likewise, the three Lines on the bottom are on top of each other and not moving since there isn't a reading available. Still, Figure 3-23 gives you an idea of how it works.

The Line objects at the top indicate current readings in radians per second with positive length to the right and negative length to the left. The Line objects at the bottom rotate as the device rotates, depending on orientation, showing cumulative rotation. Try moving the device fast and slow around each access to get a feel for how the gyroscope is affected by moving the phone.

Gyroscope Readings

The gyroscope has a CurrentValueChanged event just like the other sensors on Windows Phone. In the event handler gyroscope_CurrentValueChanged, the e.SensorReading value includes the Timestamp value as for all sensor readings. The unique value to the Gyroscope SensorReadingEventArgs instance is the RotationRate property of type Vector3. A Vector3 consists of X, Y, and Z values of type float. The real-world units for the sensor readings are radians/second. 2*pi radians is equal to 360 degrees.

The gyroscope_CurrentValueChanged event handler also updates another Vector3 named cumulativeRotation. This is calculated by multiplying the current rotation rate Vector3, with units of radians per second, by the number of seconds since the last reading. This sets the cumulativeRotation Vector3 to have units of just radians:

```
cumulativeRotation += currentRotationRate * (float)(timeSinceLastUpdate.TotalSeconds);
```

The next subsection covers how the readings are used in the timer_Tick event for the Timer object to update the position of the Line objects that represent the current rotation values as well as the cumulative rotation values around the X, Y, and Z axes.

Visualizing the Gyroscope

The math behind it is pretty simple. For the upper portion of the UI of the sample that represents the current rotation, the X2 value for each Line object is changed depending on the current reading with a scaling factor of 100. The centerX value is calculated by taking the width of the Grid layout container and halving it. The centerX value applies the rotation value at the proper offset:

```
currentXLine.X2 = centerX + currentRotationRate.X * 100;
currentYLine.X2 = centerX + currentRotationRate.Y * 100;
currentZLine.X2 = centerX + currentRotationRate.Z * 100;
```

For the bottom portion of the UI, the Line objects need to change direction, which means that both the X2 and Y2 values must vary. Leaving, X1 and Y1 for each Line object in the same location while changing the X2 and Y2 values rotates the line around the center point, giving the visualization of the line changing as the phone rotates.

Taking this into account, the cumulative rotation values on the bottom half of the UI come from slightly more complicated calculations to determine the X2 and Y2 values for each Line object:

```
cumulativeXLine.X2 = centerX - centerY * Math.Sin(cumulativeRotation.X);
cumulativeXLine.Y2 = centerY - centerY * Math.Cos(cumulativeRotation.X);
cumulativeYLine.X2 = centerX - centerY * Math.Sin(cumulativeRotation.Y);
cumulativeYLine.Y2 = centerY - centerY * Math.Cos(cumulativeRotation.Y);
cumulativeZLine.X2 = centerX - centerY * Math.Sin(cumulativeRotation.Z);
cumulativeZLine.Y2 = centerY - centerY * Math.Cos(cumulativeRotation.Z);
```

With the use of the Sin and Cos functions in the Math namespace, the code calculates the X and Y end point for the line so that it presents the cumulative angle of turn relative to the start position.

Now that you understand how the gyroscope works, you can see that it enables a number of new types of applications. You can precisely detect the angle of turn using the gyroscope, even for small turns. This is in fact one of the ways that the Motion API leverages the gyroscope.

Another use for the raw gyroscope readings are to detect walking steps for a pedometer type of application. To see how it can be used, walk around while running the gyroscope sensor and you will see a pattern on how each step affects the gyroscope. These are just a few of the ways that a gyroscope can be used within an application. Now that you understand the gyroscope, let's jump straight to the motion sensor, because as you will see it has advantages over working with the raw sensors.

Motion "Sensor"

The motion sensor is not a physical sensor. It is an API that abstracts the compass, accelerometer, and gyroscope sensors with quite a bit of math by Microsoft Research to present a single integrated motion reading. The Motion API can account for the lack of a gyroscope in older devices and instead simulates the gyroscope using the accelerometer, compass, and complex mathematics. This allows developers to target both original and new Windows Phone codename 'Mango' devices with a single application.

Motion API Background

The Motion API is useful for creating Windows Phone applications that use the device's orientation and movement in space as an input mechanism. The Motion API reads the raw accelerometer, compass, and gyroscope input and performs the complex math necessary to combine the data from these sensors to produce easy-to-use values for the device's altitude and motion.

In general, Microsoft recommends using the Motion API instead of direct sensor readings to provide maximum compatibility between devices. However, you always have the option to get access to the direct sensor data if needed. Cases where you may want direct access to hardware sensor readings are for custom motion algorithms where you need to interpret the data directly. Another example is if you need to detect something like a phone shake being used as a gesture for an application.

Motion API Benefits

The major benefit of the Motion API is that it attempts to leverage the strengths of each physical sensor while minimizing the weaknesses. The accelerometer can tell you the orientation of the phone by measuring gravitational forces to generate a 3D vector. The gyroscope cannot measure orientation, but it can tell you how much the orientation changes.

You saw this in the previous gyroscope sample. When you clicked start and turned 90 degrees, the Z component of the sensor reading also changed 90 degrees. The Motion API combines these two values to generate a single view of the device's orientation. It starts with the accelerometer as a baseline and then uses the gyroscope sensor to adjust these values. A weakness with the gyroscope is that it tends to drift over time. The accelerometer sensor can be used to "calibrate" the gyroscope readings.

Likewise, the gyroscope can be combined with the compass sensor to provide a more accurate sensor reading. A major benefit of the gyroscope is that it is unaffected by magnetic fields, which contributes to its having a smoother reading than the compass sensor.

The Motion API uses the compass to obtain true north and then uses the gyroscope's smoother movement to adjust the bearing. However, as mentioned previously, the gyroscope can drift, so the compass can be used to re-calibrate the reading. Taking advantage of multiple sensors allows the Motion API to provide smooth, accurate bearing change with the gyroscope while waiting for the slower compass sensor to catch up and settle on the current actual bearing. This is then used to re-calibrate the reading in case the gyroscope drifts over time.

You may conclude that technically the gyroscope is not required to obtain device orientation, which is correct. The accelerometer and compass are enough, which is why the Motion API can function on older devices without a gyroscope. However, the gyroscope is very fast and smooth, providing less jittery and more accurate readings, even for small changes.

Coding with the Motion API once again, the MSDN documentation provides a handy walkthrough to demonstrate how the motion sensor functions at this link:

http://msdn.microsoft.com/en-us/library/hh202984(v=VS.92).aspx

Grab the code at this link to see the code in action, but in reality you should have a pretty solid understanding at this point. The Motion API SensorReadingEventArgs returns the following values:

- Attitude: Consists of Yaw, Pitch, and Roll values

- DeviceAcceleration: Returns the same Vector3 as the acceleration sensor covered previously

- DeviceRotationRate: Returns the same Vector3 as the gyroscope sensor covered previously

- Gravity: Returns the direction of Gravity as a Vector3, essentially pointing to the center of the Earth (i.e., pointing to the ground, just like with the accelerometer sensor)

- Timestamp: Same as with previous sensors, it is the timestamp when the reading was calculated

The one value that the Motion API does not provide is current bearing, either magnetic or true. This is easily obtained by the compass, whereas the Motion API is focused on providing information on the device's altitude and movement in space.

You may be asking how yaw, pitch, and roll relate to the device's coordinate system. Figure 3-24 shows yaw, pitch, and roll with respect to the device's coordinate system.

Motion API Attitude Readings

Figure 3–24. Motion API attitude values

With this background in hand, you could go and enhance the DRNavigation sample to have more precise readings regardless of the phones aspect. For example, the Yaw reading is the same whether the phone is in a horizontal/flat position or sitting vertical in your pocket. This simplifies creating a "Find My Car" application for Windows Phone in addition to the smoother turn detection available with the combined sensor Motion API.

I don't have a sample here with the motion sensor, as it is more interesting when used in combination with other sensors such as the new camera sensor to provide augmented reality scenarios as well as with the XNA Framework. I next discuss the camera sensor and how to take advantage of its capabilities. Later in Chapter 9 I cover how to use the motion sensor to create augmented reality scenarios that include 3D objects rendered by the XNA Framework. In Chapter 10 I cover how to build an augmented reality application that leverages both the Motion API and the camera sensor.

Camera Sensor

There is at least one camera on every Windows Phone device with a minimum of five megapixels in resolution. The camera on Windows Phone is accessible to developers. Developers could programmatically capture a photo but not video in Windows Phone 7. With Windows Phone 7.5 and the Windows Phone OS 7.1 developer tools, you can capture video, build your own custom camera UI, and build augmented reality scenarios using the camera sensor.

Camera Sensor Background

You can use the camera sensor to capture a photo. The simplest way to do that is with the CameraCaptureTask in the Microsoft.Phone.Tasks tasks and choosers API, which provides a simple method to capture a photo. I cover the camera task in Chapter 5. This is the basic functionality currently available in Windows Phone 7.

The base Camera class provides methods to determine CameraType, Orientation, PreviewResolution, and Resolution of the camera. The CameraType property determines the location of the camera on the device.

The PhotoCamera class allows you to develop applications that take high-resolution photographs, use the hardware shutter button, and access the flash mode or focus functionality. You can create a custom picture-taking application that provides additional features over the built-in camera functionality. The next section explores the PhotoCamera object in detail.

PhotoCamera

With Windows Phone 7.5 and the Windows Phone OS 7.1 developer tools, developers have an additional option available to capture a photo and programmatically modify the settings using the PhotoCamera class. The PhotoCamera class provides programmatic access to the camera settings like focus, resolution, and flash mode as well as events for camera focus, image capture, and image availability.

You use the CameraButtons class to detect when the hardware shutter button is half-pressed, pressed, and released. The GetPreviewBuffer method provides frames from the camera preview buffer in two formats, ARGB and YCbCr. ARGB is the format used to describe color in Silverlight UI. YCbCr enables efficient image processing but cannot be used by Silverlight. In order to manipulate a YCbCr frame you must convert it to ARGB.

Coding with the PhotoCamera

In this section I cover coding with the PhotoCamera object to demonstrate the flexibility available to you as a developer. I add a new project to the Chapter 3 part 2 solution named CameraSensor. I next add a folder named pages to put each test page starting with a landscape-oriented page named CustomCamera.xaml.

On the CustomCamera.xaml page, I create a custom camera UI that captures photos and adds them to the media library on the phone. To get access to the camera, add a using Microsoft.Devices statement to CustomCamera.xaml.cs. This brings in the PhotoCamera object, which is declared as photoCamera in CustomCamera.xaml.cs.

A variable of type MediaLibrary is declared as mediaLibrary in CustomCamera.xaml.cs to gain access to the MediaLibrary.SavePictureToCameraRoll API call. This allows your custom camera application to save photos to the camera roll and sync with the Zune client just like the built-in camera. The MediaLibrary is actually part of the Microsoft.Xna.Framework.Media namespace, so you also need to add a reference to Microsoft.Xna.Framework in CustomCamera.xaml.cs.

To display the camera preview in the UI, you use a VideoBrush object. In CustomCamera.xaml, I modify the LayoutRoot Grid object like this:

```xml
<Grid x:Name="LayoutRoot">
<Grid.Background>
  <VideoBrush x:Name="cameraViewFinder" />
</Grid.Background>
</Grid>
```

Windows Phone supports two types of cameras, `CameraType.Primary` and `CameraType.FrontFacing`. If a Windows Phone 7.5 device supports both types of camera, you can let the user choose which one he wants to use.

In the `CustomCamera.xaml.cs` code behind, I call `VideoBrush.SetSource` and pass in the `PhotoCamera` object to create the viewfinder:

```csharp
void CustomCamera_Loaded(object sender, RoutedEventArgs e)
{
    _photoCamera = new PhotoCamera(CameraType.Primary);
    cameraViewFinder.SetSource(_photoCamera);
}
```

Figure 3-25 shows the viewfinder in the emulator.

Figure 3–25. *Camera viewfinder*

In Windows Phone OS 7.1 developer tools, the emulator supports camera emulation by moving a black square over a white background. This allows you to test photo apps in the emulator. Now let's build the UI to wrap the Camera API.

I add a Grid with a Rectangle object to the bottom of the UI. I then add a Flash button to the Grid with the idea that if you tap on the screen the Grid containing the UI to change the camera configuration animates into view.

The `CustomCamera_Loaded` event is expanded to wire up the camera events as well as the physical camera button on the phone to events that fire within the application:

```csharp
void CustomCamera_Loaded(object sender, RoutedEventArgs e)
{
    //Can set to CameraType.FrontFacing if available
    _photoCamera = new PhotoCamera(CameraType.Primary);
    //wire up event handlers
    _photoCamera.AutoFocusCompleted += _photoCamera_AutoFocusCompleted;
    _photoCamera.CaptureCompleted += _photoCamera_CaptureCompleted;
```

```
_photoCamera.CaptureImageAvailable += _photoCamera_CaptureImageAvailable;
_photoCamera.CaptureStarted += _photoCamera_CaptureStarted;
_photoCamera.CaptureThumbnailAvailable += _photoCamera_CaptureThumbnailAvailable;
_photoCamera.Initialized += _photoCamera_Initialized;

//Wire up camera button
CameraButtons.ShutterKeyHalfPressed += CameraButtons_ShutterKeyHalfPressed;
CameraButtons.ShutterKeyPressed += CameraButtons_ShutterKeyPressed;
CameraButtons.ShutterKeyReleased += CameraButtons_ShutterKeyReleased;

//Set up view finder
cameraViewFinder.SetSource(_photoCamera);

LayoutRoot.Tap += LayoutRoot_Tap;

//Create MediaLibrary object
_mediaLibray = new MediaLibrary();

ThumbImages = new ObservableCollection<BitmapImage>();
ThumbImageLB.ItemsSource = ThumbImages;
}
```

The code sample for this section builds out a camera UI to demonstrate the features available to developers. Each picture you take with the sample will be added to the pictures hub as part of the camera roll section, just like with the built-in camera. The custom camera application will also show thumbnails of captured images in a ListBox on the right side of the UI just to demonstrate how to work with that section of the API. Figure 3-26 shows the full camera UI in the Windows Phone Emulator.

Figure 3–26. *Full camera UI in the emulator*

The black square floats around the screen to simulate a viewfinder. In Figure 3-26 the black square is behind photos taken using the Take Pic Button. The ListBox to the left of the Take Pic Button allows you to select the image capture resolutions. The other two buttons allow you to switch between the flash options like Off, On, and Auto. The second button allows you to focus the camera lens, if supported.

There is quite a bit of code in MainPage.xaml.cs, but most of the code simply wraps the PhotoCamera API. For example, this line of code captures an image:

```
_photoCamera.CaptureImage();
```

To change to a different flash type, always call the IsFlashModeSupported method before modifying the FlashMode property. The code to save an image to the pictures hub is pretty simple:

```
void _photoCamera_CaptureImageAvailable(object sender, ContentReadyEventArgs e)
{
  _mediaLibray.SavePictureToCameraRoll("TestPhoto" +
            DateTime.Today.Date.ToString(), e.ImageStream);
  this.Dispatcher.BeginInvoke(() =>
  {
    cameraStatus.Text = "Image saved to camera roll...";
  });
}
```

The last few lines of code are sprinkled throughout the code. Dispatch.BeginInvoke marshals the anonymous delegate (()=>{...}) call back to the UI thread. Otherwise you will get a cross-thread access not authorized exception if you just tried to update the CameraStatus.Text outside of the anonymous delegate passed into the BeginInvoke method.

The other interesting code captures the thumbnail and data binds it in a ListBox control on the right side of the viewfinder UI. Here is the CaptureThumbnailAvailable event:

```
void _photoCamera_CaptureThumbnailAvailable(object sender, ContentReadyEventArgs e)
{
  this.Dispatcher.BeginInvoke(() =>
    {
      BitmapImage bitmap = new BitmapImage();
      bitmap.CreateOptions = BitmapCreateOptions.None;
      bitmap.SetSource(e.ImageStream);
      ThumbImages.Add(bitmap);
    });
}
```

ThumbImages is a simple ObservableCollection containing BitmapImage objects declared at the top of CustomCamera.xaml.cs:

```
ObservableCollection<BitmapImage> ThumbImages;
```

The data binding for this collection requires a simple "trick" to have the DataTemplate simply render the image. Here is the ListBox declaration from CustomCamera.xaml:

```
<ListBox x:Name="ThumbImageLB" Margin="0,6,8,2"
ItemTemplate="{StaticResource ThumbsDataTemplate}" HorizontalAlignment="Right" Width="133" />
```
Here is the data template:

```
<DataTemplate x:Key="ThumbsDataTemplate">
    <Grid Margin="0,0,0,30">
            <Image Height="100" Source="{Binding}"  Stretch="UniformToFill"/>
    </Grid>
</DataTemplate>
```

Notice in the DataTemplate that the Image.Source property simply has the value {Binding} without a property or field name. Usually in a ListBox, it data binds to an object with properties that are then configured in the DataTemplate. In this case, the object in the collection is what we want to render so the empty Binding call data binds the item directly in the DataTemplate.

Camera Examples

The MSDN documentation has two interesting camera samples that I recommend you check out if you are building a camera application. One covers how to convert the native camera YCbCr image format, which is highly efficient for the camera's use but not usable directly by image viewing programs. The sample covers converting the YCbCr format to ARGB so you can then display directly in the Silverlight UI:

http://msdn.microsoft.com/en-us/library/hh394035(v=VS.92).aspx

The other camera sample in the MSDN docs covers how to take an image and turn it into a black and white image:

http://msdn.microsoft.com/en-us/library/hh202982(v=VS.92).aspx

This concludes coverage of the camera sensor in this chapter. I cover how to build an augmented reality application using the camera sensor and Motion API in Chapter 10. The next couple of sections cover how to capture video using the camera and the new WebCam APIs available in Windows Phone OS 7.1 (Mango).

Video Capture

Another exciting capability in the Windows Phone OS 7.1 SDK is the ability to capture video within a custom application. There are two methods available to capture video in Windows Phone. One uses the camera CaptureSource object to get access to the camera video stream. The other method is via the Silverlight WebCam APIs ported from the desktop.

Camera CaptureSource Video Recording

The MSDN documentation covers how to use the CaptureSource object to capture video and pass it to a FileSink that records video output to Isolated Storage via the IsolatedStorageFIleStream object.

You can also capture an image using the CaptureSource.CaptureImageAsync method call. The image is returned in the CaptureImageCompleted event as a WritableBitmap. This capability is interesting because it provides a means to create bar code reader-type applications. Here is the link to the code sample:

http://go.microsoft.com/fwlink/?LinkId=226290

WebCam APIs Video Recording

If you are more interested in capturing video in a format that can be played back by a user on his PC, the WebCam APIs are the way to go. The APIs allow you to capture both video and audio using the Silverlight 4 WebCam APIs but with enhancements for use on Windows Phone.

This link provides an overview of the Silverlight 4 class support available for video and audio capture:

http://msdn.microsoft.com/en-us/library/ff602282(VS.95).aspx

The WebCam APIs will generate an .MP4 file. This link provides a walkthrough of the process:

http://msdn.microsoft.com/en-us/library/hh394041(v=VS.92).aspx

PhotoCamera vs. WebCam APIs

It may seem odd to have two separate APIs interacting with the same piece of hardware. This section provides background on when you might want to use the PhotoCamera object vs. when you might want to use the WebCam APIs ported from Silverlight 4 with enhancements.

Use the PhotoCamera API when you need to obtain high quality photos, want support for the camera hardware button, and need to customize flash mode and camera focus.

The PhotoCamera class provides support for a "point and shoot" programming model as I described earlier and provides lower-level control over your polling rate. However, use the Silverlight 4 APIs now available on Windows Phone to encode the video.

■ **Note** The Silverlight 4 APIs do not enable rate limiting, so you may be consuming more battery than necessary if you don't require 100% of frames. You can efficiently poll for frames by using PhotoCamera GetPreviewBuffer methods.

For best performance when using the VideoSink class in the Silverlight 4 APIs, specify the ReuseBuffer allocation mode. With ReuseBuffer, a new buffer is created for each sample capture. This can improve performance by reducing the amount of garbage collection that is required.

Conclusion

In the last chapter I covered Silverlight output. In this chapter I covered input for both Silverlight and XNA Game Studio, covering text input and the value of InputScope. I next moved on to touch and multi-touch, covering the range of APIs available to developers, and I covered accelerometer input for both Silverlight and the XNA Framework. The next sections focused on location and fun with the microphone.

With the introduction of new sensor APIs available in the Windows Phone OS 7.1 developer tools, I also covered the new Compass, Gyroscope, and Motion APIs, which greatly enhance the types of applications you can build for Windows Phone.

The new Camera Sensor API provides the ability to build rich photo and video capture applications. The Camera API also enables the ability to create bar code scanner-type applications for Windows Phone.

With the overview in Chapter 1, rendering in Chapter 2, and input in Chapter 3 out of the way, I next dive deep into the application programming model in Chapter 4.

CHAPTER 4

■ ■ ■

Windows Phone Data Persistence and Networking Programming Model

In the previous chapter, we covered handing input in a Windows Phone application, and in Chapter 2, we covered rendering UI. With the fundamentals covered for input and output, let's now take a closer look at the Windows Phone programming model with a focus on data persistence and network programming.

In this chapter, we start first with covering local file persistence within isolated storage, which is great for working with file-based data such as XML and HTML files. Windows Phone OS 7.1 (Mango) introduces support for local database functionality to store structured data using LINQ to SQL. We then cover asynchronous programming to prepare for programming with remote services in Windows Phone. We will cover Windows Communications Foundation, web services and REST as well as OData. A related topic is data serialization, which we cover as well.

This chapter also covers the web-browser control, which can be used to load local and remote HTML data hosted in a Windows Phone application. Another control that can rely heavily on data and remote services is the Bing Maps control.

When it comes to data, application lifecycle management is critical since the user can switch applications at any time. Windows Phone optimizes for battery so you as a developer must have a solid understanding of application lifecycle management, otherwise known as tombstoning. This is a critical concept that will be a constant consideration. We will demonstrate how and when it plays a role with application development.

Application Data Persistence

Saving data to the file system is a necessity for most real applications. On Windows Phone, each application can access an isolated file system to read and write data that is only accessible to that application. This means that applications cannot share data with each other via the file system. It also means that one application cannot access or overwrite data from another application in the file system.

■ **Note** Windows Phone OS 7.1 (Mango) introduces background agents, which can access the same isolated store as the related Windows Phone application.

There are several namespaces related to data persistence that are available on Windows Phone. These namespaces include the following:

- **System.Data.Linq**: Contains classes that provide local database support in Windows Phone OS 7.1 (Mango) applications.

- **System.IO**: Provides access to base **Stream**, **StreamWriter**, and **StreamReader** classes.

- **System.IO.IsolatedStorage**: Provides access to Isolated Storage.

- **System.Runtime.Serialization**: Must add a reference to System.Runtime.Serialization assembly.

- **System.Xml**: Provides access to **XMLReader** stream class, as well as other core XML related classes.

- **System.Xml.Linq**: Must add a reference to System.Xml.Linq assembly. Provides access to **XDocument** class for XML manipulation as well as LINQ language constructs.

- **System.Xml.Serialization**: Provides access to XML serialization attributes that you can apply to .NET classes.

If you are a .NET developer, most of these look familiar, as they are the standard .NET classes related to serializing .NET objects, as well as reading and writing data to the file system. In Windows Phone OS 7.1 (Mango), developers now have access to the **System.Data.Linq** namespace, providing LINQ to SQL support with a local database in Windows Phone.

The one exception that may not be familiar to developers is possibly **System.IO.IsolatedStorage**, which is available via Silverlight on the desktop and also on Windows Phone. Isolated Storage represents the physical file system made available via the **IsolatedStorage** classes.

Unlike with Silverlight for the Web, there isn't an Isolated Storage quota on Windows Phone; however, it is recommended to not exceed two Gigabytes of data for an application if you are to be a good citizen and not abuse available space. Also, applications should make users aware of estimated file space requirements and try to give an option to delete data if needed. Keeping the user informed and in control is paramount.

The **System.IO.IsolatedStorage** namespace provides two possible methods to access the file system. The first is a key-value pair of type string-object where the key is a string and the value is of type object available in the static class **IsolatedStorageSettings** via its single property named **ApplicationSettings**. The **Dictionary** class stores object values, so essentially any class that can be serialized can be stored in the **IsolatedStorageSettings.ApplicationSettings** object. It is not limited to just simple values.

The other method to access the file system is via file and folder management using the **IsolatedStorageFile static** class. The method that provides access to the application's file system area is the **GetUserStoreForApplication()** method With a reference to the user store in hand, you can create files to serialize objects to the file system.

In addition to the general file storage area, isolated storage contains several special folders for specific scenarios listed in Table 4-1.

Table 4–1. *Frame Rate Counters*

Name	Purpose	Notes
Shared	Used to host the Media, ShellContent, and Transfers folders.	This folder is created when your application is installed, but it can be deleted.
Shared/Media	Album Art: Applications can use this folder to display album art in the Universal Volume Control (UVC) while playing background audio.	This folder is created when your application is installed, but it can be deleted.
Shared/ShellContent	Tiles can display background images on the front and back of each Tile. Background images can be stored in isolated storage but must be located in this folder or a subfolder of it.	This folder is created when your application is installed, but it can be deleted. I cover live Tiles in Chapter 10.
Shared/Transfers	Background file transfer: Applications can save files to isolated storage in the background, even when the application is no longer running in the foreground.	This folder is created when your application is installed, but it can be deleted. I cover background processing in Chapter 10.

The next two sections provide code samples for isolated storage. The first example covers fundamental isolated storage operations, and the second example covers object persistence and serialization.

IsoStore File IO

In the Chapter 4 solution DataPersistence project is a MainPage page that has a menu to three additional pages, the first named IsoStoreFileIO.xaml. Figure 4–1 has the UI.

Figure 4–1. DataPersistence IsoStoreFileIO UI

The UI has several controls that store fake settings and data values. The sample uses both the `ApplicationSettings` object and an `IsolatedStorageFileStream` object to store and retrieve the values.

■ **Note** All of the data could persist within the `ApplicationSettings` object, but the sample shows how to work with the `IsolatedStorageFileStream` to prepare for more complex scenarios.

The code is straightforward `Dictionary` object access and file IO. See Listing 4–1.

Listing 4–1. IsoStoreFileIO.xaml.cs Code File

```
using System;
using System.IO;
using System.IO.IsolatedStorage;
using Microsoft.Phone.Controls;

namespace DataPersistence.pages
{
  public partial class IsoStoreFileIO : PhoneApplicationPage
  {
```

```csharp
private const string fileName = "notes.dat";

public IsoStoreFileIO()
{
  InitializeComponent();
}

private void saveAppBarIcon_Click(object sender, EventArgs e)
{
  SaveData();
}

private void loadAppBarIcon_Click(object sender, EventArgs e)
{
  LoadData();
}

private void LoadData()
{
  //Load "settings"
  if (IsolatedStorageSettings.ApplicationSettings.Contains("EnablePush"))
    enableNotifications.IsChecked =
      (bool)IsolatedStorageSettings.ApplicationSettings["EnablePush"];
  if (IsolatedStorageSettings.ApplicationSettings.Contains("FavColor"))
    colorListBox.SelectedIndex =
      (int)IsolatedStorageSettings.ApplicationSettings["FavColor"];
  if (IsolatedStorageSettings.ApplicationSettings.Contains("NickName"))
    nicknameTextBox.Text =
      (string)IsolatedStorageSettings.ApplicationSettings["NickName"];

  //Load "notes" text to file
  using (IsolatedStorageFile isf = IsolatedStorageFile.GetUserStoreForApplication())
  {
    if (isf.FileExists(fileName))
    {
      using (IsolatedStorageFileStream fs =
        isf.OpenFile(fileName, System.IO.FileMode.Open))
      {
        using (StreamReader reader = new StreamReader(fs))
        {
          notesTextBox.Text = reader.ReadToEnd();
          reader.Close();
        }
      }
    }
  }
}

private void SaveData()
{
  //Save "settings"
```

```
IsolatedStorageSettings.ApplicationSettings["EnablePush"] =
    enableNotifications.IsChecked;
IsolatedStorageSettings.ApplicationSettings["FavColor"] =
    colorListBox.SelectedIndex;
IsolatedStorageSettings.ApplicationSettings["NickName"] =
    nicknameTextBox.Text;

//Save "notes" text to file
using (IsolatedStorageFile isf = IsolatedStorageFile.GetUserStoreForApplication())
{
  using (IsolatedStorageFileStream fs =
    isf.OpenFile(fileName, System.IO.FileMode.Create))
  {
    using (StreamWriter writer = new StreamWriter(fs))
    {
      writer.Write(notesTextBox.Text);
      writer.Flush();
      writer.Close();
    }
  }
}
}
}
}
}
```

There are two application bar icons to load and save data. Loading data is a matter of checking that a key exists using ApplicationSettings.Contains, and then accessing the value via the key. The ApplicationSettings class is of type Dictionary that takes a key value of type String and stores the passed-in class as a type of Object. This permits you to pass any class into a Dictionary object, since all classes inherit from type Object. You must, however, type convert the retrieved object to the original type. Otherwise a runtime error will occur.

Loading the "Notes" TextBox data checks that the file exists and just reads the data using a StreamReader object. You may be tempted to put the filename into the StreamReader constructor directly. This will result in a code security access violation if you do. The only valid constructor parameter for an instance of StreamReaderor StreamWriter is an object of type IsolatedStorageFile.

Saving the data is very similar code to loading the data. Note the use of the using construct for all objects that have a Dispose method. The following is the pseudo code:

```
using (TextReader textReader = new StreamReader(streamResourceInfo.Stream)  // create.
 instance
{
//...code that leverages the instance....
}//Disposed called automatically when the block is exited
```

■ **Note** Only .NET objects that have handles to non-managed objects like a physical file handle have Dispose methods in .NET.

The `using` clause ensures that `Dispose` is called and that unmanaged resources are released. Otherwise, memory will not be freed immediately, and the runtime memory load will slowly increase until either Garbage Collection occurs or until the memory threshold limit is exceeded, and the app fails or until the application exits. Now that we've covered how to access isolated storage, we move on next to object persistence.

Object Persistence

In the previous section, we demonstrated how to store and retrieve individual values. In this section, we add some realism by serializing objects instead of individual values. The `ObjectSerialization.xaml` sample starts with almost the same UI and values as the `IsoStoreFileIO` sample, but this time the controls data bind to a sample class named `AppClass`, as shown in Listing 4–2.

Listing 4–2. `AppClass.cs` Code File

```
using System.Xml.Serialization;

namespace DataPersistence
{
  [XmlRootAttribute("AppClass")]
  public class AppClass
  {
    public AppClass()
    {
      FavoriteColor = -1;
    }

    //Settings
    [XmlElement]
    public bool EnablePushNotifications { get; set; }

    [XmlElement]
    public int FavoriteColor { get; set; }

    [XmlElement]
    public string NickName { get; set; }

    //Data
    [XmlElement]
    public string Notes { get; set; }
  }
}
```

The sample `AppClass` class that we serialize in this example includes attributes from the `System.Xml.Serialization` namespace to provide support for serializing the object to the file system. The MSDN documentation covers all of the possible XML serialization attribute values:

http://msdn.microsoft.com/en-us/library/83y7df3e(v=VS.100).aspx

Configuring the data binding with Blend using sample data based on the AppClass is straightforward, as demonstrated in Chapter 2. A sample data source is added to the project that is based on the .NET AppClass class. This facilitates design-time data binding without causing issues at run-time.

In order to save and load the data, the code-behind for ObjectSerialization.xaml has modified Save and Load methods that serialize and deserialize an instance of the AppClass object, and configures it as the DataContext for the LayoutRoot Grid object. For the SaveData method, I take an extra step to programmatically update the data binding in the event that the user clicks the Save Application Bar button, which does not take away the focus. Without the code to update the bindings, there is a chance that an edit is not persisted. The following are the LoadData and SaveData methods:

```
private void LoadData()
{
  using (IsolatedStorageFile isf = IsolatedStorageFile.GetUserStoreForApplication())
  {
    if (isf.FileExists(fileName))
    {
      using (IsolatedStorageFileStream fs =
        isf.OpenFile(fileName, System.IO.FileMode.Open))
      {
        XmlSerializer serializer = new XmlSerializer(typeof(AppClass));
        LayoutRoot.DataContext = (AppClass)serializer.Deserialize(fs);
      }
    }
  }
}

private void SaveData()
{
  //The app bar button does not take focus
  //Force update of data bindings in case either TextBox has focus
  var binding = notesTextBox.GetBindingExpression(TextBox.TextProperty);
  binding.UpdateSource();
  binding = nicknameTextBox.GetBindingExpression(TextBox.TextProperty);
  binding.UpdateSource();
  //Save object to isolated storage
  using (IsolatedStorageFile isf = IsolatedStorageFile.GetUserStoreForApplication())
  {
    using (IsolatedStorageFileStream fs =
      isf.OpenFile(fileName, System.IO.FileMode.Create))
    {
      XmlSerializer xs = new XmlSerializer(typeof(AppClass));
      xs.Serialize(fs, ((AppClass)LayoutRoot.DataContext));
    }
  }
}
```

The serialization attributes attached to the AppClass object tell the XmlSerializer object how to read and write the class in XML format. From there, the rest of the code in SaveData and LoadData methods is boilerplate, isolated storage file I/O, as in the previous sample.

The samples in this section exposed data management issues when you run the sample application to test the samples. If you navigate away from the sample, such as going to the Start screen, and then navigate back, the UI resets to what it is at startup. The data that was displayed is not preserved.

Serializing out UI objects and settings is a critically important requirement for Windows Phone applications. The concepts covered in this section lay the groundwork for the section titled Application Life Cycle Management.

In that section, application and data architecture is discussed, such that the data can be made to appear to be preserved, and to the user it will appear that the application was waiting in the background for the user to return to it. We next cover the new Isolated Storage Explorer feature available in the Windows Phone OS 7.1 (Mango) Tools SDK.

Isolated Storage Explorer

The Isolated Explorer tool allows you to list, copy, and replace files and directories in isolated storage. This functionality allows developers to validate that files are being saved to the correct location with the correct data. This tool is installed with the Windows Phone Developer Tools 7.1 and will work with both the emulator and physical devices as long as the device is developer unlocked with an App Hub account.

Tool Functionality

In this section I cover the tool's command-line and available options. The tool is installed to one of these directories depending on whether you are on an x86 or x64 operating system:

```
Program Files\Microsoft SDKs\Windows Phone\v7.1\Tools\IsolatedStorageExplorerTool
Program Files (x86)\Microsoft SDKs\Windows Phone\v7.1\Tools\IsolatedStorageExplorerTool
```

Table 4-2 explains the parameters, but here is the command-line syntax:

```
ISETool.exe <ts|rs|dir[:device-folder]> <xd|de> <Product GUID> [<desktop-path>]
```

Table 4-2. Isolated Storage Command-Line Tool Options

Option	Description
ts	(Take snapshot) Copies the files and directories in isolated storage from the device or emulator to your computer
rs	(Restore snapshot) Replaces the files and directories in isolated storage on the device or emulator with files and directories from your computer
dir	Lists the files and directories in the specified directory of isolated storage. If a directory is not specified, the files and directories in the root are listed.
device-folder	Specifies the directory in isolated storage on the device or emulator that you want to target
xd	Indicates to target the emulator
de	Indicates to target a tethered device

Option	Description
Product GUID	Specifies the ProductID from the WPAppManifest.xml file for the application you want to test
desktop-path	Specifies the directory on your computer where isolated storage files are written to or copied from. A subdirectory named IsolatedStore is created in desktop-path when files are copied using the ts command. If the specified directory already exists a ts command will overwrite the contents of the directory with no warning.

Using the Tool

Let's use the tool to explore the emulator file system after running the DataPersistence sample we just created. Run the Chapter 4 solution to deploy the DataPersistence project to the emulator and be sure to click Save in the application bar to persist data to isolated storage.

Launch a command-line window and navigate to the folder containing the isolated storage tool and run this command-line: ISETool.exe ts xd {02ae1c3c-0f6e-45e9-9f40-747c38da4648} c:\test\]

This creates a folder named IsolatedStore in the c:\test\ folder containing three files. Now you can inspect the data files by changing the extension to .txt and opening the files in Notepad. For more complex, file-intensive applications, this tool is invaluable for debugging and troubleshooting data persistence bugs, allowing you to validate exactly what is happening.

Local Database

Windows Phone OS 7.1 (Mango) introduces local database support via LINQ to SQL. This was a sorely missed feature by developers in Windows Phone 7. Let's cover how it works now that it is available in the latest version. You can store relational data in a local database that resides in your application's isolated storage container. The database is accessed exclusively via LINQ to SQL from database definition, schema modifications, to basic create, update, and delete (CRUD) operations.

Architecture

Database access is greatly simplified in Windows Phone via LINQ to SQL. You create a System.Data.Linq.DataContext object to bridge between your application's object set and the underlying relational data stored in the local database. The DataContext object contains a set of Table objects representing a table in the database. Each Table object consists of Entity objects that correspond to database rows.

When your application executes LINQ to SQL statements, the run-time converts the API calls to Transact-SQL statements and then updates the local database. The API is purely object-based, without any support for executing Transact-SQL statements directly. LINQ to SQL consists of a very capable query language with plenty of power for database operations. A couple of additional items to note: The database does not run in a separate process, and the database is only available when the application runs. Because of this restriction, it is not possible to share a database among applications.

Local Database Sample

Developers have two options to work with a local database. An application can create a database on the fly and add data either locally or via remote service call. Another option is to deploy a pre-loaded local database with the application upon installation. This section will demonstrate both options.

The first sample will create a database on the fly. We then will take this database and add it to another sample application as a pre-loaded database deployed at installation. This is actually the recommended process to create a pre-populated database. You use the Isolated Storage Tool to copy the database from local storage to your development computer and then add it to the production application that requires the pre-populated database. Let's dive in to the code.

Create Database Sample

In this sample I show how to create a database on-the-fly and then retrieve it from the emulator using the Isolated Storage Tool. A new project is added to the Chapter 4 part 1 solution named DBCreateSample:

```
string DBConnectionString = "Data Source=isostore:/RecipesDb.sdf";
```

I start by adding a reference to System.Data.Linq and then add several using clauses at the top of MainPage.xaml.cs:

```
using System.Data.Linq;
using System.Data.Linq.Mapping;
using System.ComponentModel;
using System.Collections.ObjectModel;
```

The System.Data.Linq namespace brings in LINQ to SQL and the DataContext class. The System.Data.Linq.Mapping namespace brings in the attributes used to decorate object classes so that LINQ to SQL understands to map objects to data rows in a table, and vice versa. This namespace includes attributes to define a Table, Column, Index, and Association between Table objects as well as other mappings defined at this link:

```
http://msdn.microsoft.com/en-us/library/system.data.linq.mapping(VS.96).aspx
```

The System.ComponentModel namespace brings in the INotifyPropertyChanged and INotifyPropertyChanging Interfaces. These are key interfaces for data binding to work. They let the data binding plumbing know when a property is changing or has changed. I cover these interfaces in more detail in Chapter 6, but LINQ to SQL and local database functionality need these to be implemented to work.

Note that for .NET developers familiar with the INotifyPropertyChanged interface, the INotifyPropertyChanging Interface may be new. Implementing this second interface reduces memory consumption required for change tracking, which is critical on a mobile device.

I add another class named Recipe to the project. Add the previous using statements and have the Recipe class implement the INotifyPropertyChanged and INotifyPropertyChanging interfaces. Add the boiler-plate code from the documentation to implement those interfaces, or just copy from this file going forward.

The Recipe class contains properties for a recipe's Name, CookingTime, and MealType. The MealType property is an enumeration containing Breakfast, Lunch, Dinner, and Dessert values. There are two string values to store Ingredients and recipe Steps as well. As mentioned before, I need to decorate this class with mapping attributes so that LINQ to SQL knows how to handle the recipe objects and its properties when storing into a local database.

For example, the Recipe class itself is decorated with the [TableAttribute] to identify that it is stored as its own separate table. In .NET, you can omit the "Attribute" portion of the class name and just use [Table]. For each property, add the [Column] attribute to identify the Properties that should be stored in the database. You could have properties that are part of an object but that do not need to be stored. An example is a calculated read-only property. In those cases simply do not add the [Column] attribute to the property. Listing 4-3 contains the Recipe class after right-clicking on the code-file and selecting Organize Usings ➤ Remove and Sort operation. The Recipe class declares an index on the Name property to speed sorting on a common field.

Listing 4–3. *Recipe Class from Recipe.cs Code File*

```
using System;
using System.ComponentModel;
using System.Data.Linq;
using System.Data.Linq.Mapping;
namespace DbCreateSample
{
  //Create an index on the Name property
  [Table,Index(Columns = "Name ASC", Name="IDX_Name")]
  public class Recipe : INotifyPropertyChanged, INotifyPropertyChanging
  {
    public Recipe()
    {
    }

    // Define ID: private field, public property, and database column.
    private int _recipeId;
    [Column(DbType = "INT NOT NULL IDENTITY", IsDbGenerated = true,
     IsPrimaryKey = true, CanBeNull = false, AutoSync = AutoSync.OnInsert)]
    public int RecipeId
    {
      get { return _recipeId; }
      set
      {
        NotifyPropertyChanging("RecipeId");
        _recipeId = value;
        NotifyPropertyChanged("RecipeId");
      }
    }

    private string _name;
    [Column]
    public string Name
    {
      get { return _name; }
      set
      {
        if (_name != value)
        {
          NotifyPropertyChanging("Name");
          _name = value;
```

```
      NotifyPropertyChanged("Name");
    }
  }
}

private TimeSpan _cookingTime;
[Column]
public TimeSpan CookingTime
{
  get { return _cookingTime; }
  set
  {
    if (_cookingTime != value)
    {
      NotifyPropertyChanging("CookingTime");
      _cookingTime = value;
      NotifyPropertyChanged("CookingTime");
    }
  }
}

private MealType _mealType;
[Column]
public MealType MealType
{
  get { return _mealType; }
  set
  {
    if (_mealType != value)
    {
      NotifyPropertyChanging("MealType");
      _mealType = value;
      NotifyPropertyChanged("MealType");
    }
  }
}

private string _ingredients;
[Column]
public string Ingedients
{
  get { return _ingredients; }
  set
  {
    if (_ingredients != value)
    {
      NotifyPropertyChanging("Ingedients");
      _ingredients = value;
      NotifyPropertyChanged("Ingedients");
    }
  }
}
```

245

```csharp
    private string _steps;
    [Column]
    public string Steps
    {
      get { return _steps; }
      set
      {
        if (_steps != value)
        {
          NotifyPropertyChanging("Steps");
          _steps = value;
          NotifyPropertyChanged("Steps");
        }
      }
    }

    [Column(IsVersion=true)]
    private Binary _version;

    #region INotifyPropertyChanged Members

    public event PropertyChangedEventHandler PropertyChanged;

    // Used to notify the page that a data context property changed
    private void NotifyPropertyChanged(string propertyName)
    {
      if (PropertyChanged != null)
      {
        PropertyChanged(this, new PropertyChangedEventArgs(propertyName));
      }
    }

    #endregion

    #region INotifyPropertyChanging Members

    public event PropertyChangingEventHandler PropertyChanging;

    // Used to notify the data context that a data context property is about to change
    private void NotifyPropertyChanging(string propertyName)
    {
      if (PropertyChanging != null)
      {
        PropertyChanging(this, new PropertyChangingEventArgs(propertyName));
      }
    }

    #endregion
}

public enum MealType
```

```
{
    Breakfast, Lunch, Dinner, Dessert
  }
}
```

Notice in Listing 4-3 that there is an additional property defined named `RecipeID`. It has an expanded `Column` attribute with named property assignments:

```
[Column(DbType = "INT NOT NULL IDENTITY", IsDbGenerated = true,
IsPrimaryKey = true, CanBeNull = false, AutoSync = AutoSync.OnInsert)]
```

The `RecipeID` property represents the Primary Key for the `Recipe` Table definition, so you may want to take advantage of the database capabilities to auto-generate the key and add some constraints to the field. You can add constraints to other properties as well, such as setting `CanBeNull` to `false`, in order to have your database better model reality. Another `private` property present in the class is the `Version` property. This property enables fast updates when performing updates and is specific to LINQ to SQL on Windows Phone.

To connect to a local database, you must create a `DataContext` object, which lives in the `System.Data.Linq` namespace. This class takes a connection string and provides the run time between the object collections and underlying database store. Listing 4-4 shows the `RecipeDataContext` implementation.

Listing 4–4. RecipeDataContext Class from Recipe.cs Code File

```
public class RecipeDataContext : DataContext
{
  //Using static makes the connection string available anywhere in the code
  //but let's us keep it close to where it is used within the code
  public static string DBConnectionString = "Data Source=isostore:/Recipes.sdf";

  public RecipeDataContext(string connectionString)
    : base(connectionString)
  { }

  public Table<Recipe> Recipes;

}
```

In the `RecipeDataContext` class I define one table to contain the `Recipe` objects named `Recipes`. Since we want the database to be available prior to working with it, create it in `App.xaml.cs` within the constructor `App()` using this code:

```
// Create the Recipe database if it does not exist.
using (RecipeDataContext RecipeDB = new
RecipeDataContext(RecipeDataContext.DBConnectionString))
{
  try
  {
    if (RecipeDB.DatabaseExists() == false)
    {
      RecipeDB.CreateDatabase();

      CreateInitialRecords(RecipeDB);
```

```
      }
    }
    catch
    {
      RecipeDB.DeleteDatabase();
    }
  }

  private void CreateInitialRecords(RecipeDataContext recipeDB)
  {
    Recipe recipe = new Recipe()
    {
      Name = "Hot Dog",
      MealType = MealType.Lunch,
      CookingTime = new TimeSpan(0, 10, 0),
      Ingedients = "Hotdog, Hotdog Roll, Mustard, Relish",
      Steps = "1. Put water in a pot and bring to a boil.\n" +
              "2. Add hotdogs to pot and cook for 5 minutes.\n" +
              "3. Heat hotdog roll in pre-heated oven for 4 minutes at 350 degrees.\n" +
              "4. Remove roll from oven and place hotdog in roll.\n" +
              "5. Add mustard and relish to taste.\n"
    };
    recipeDB.Recipes.InsertOnSubmit(recipe);

    recipeDB.SubmitChanges();
  }
```

This code will run just once to create the database and populate it with some data. Note the try/catch block within the using clause. If for some reason an error occurs in creating the tables and data, I want to simply delete the database to prevent invalid operations.

Now let's shift gears and focus on working within the database in MainPage.xaml. Modify MainPage.xaml.cs to support database operations. In a real-world application you would use Model-View-ViewModel (MVVM) architecture to separate concerns and not clutter the UI with this code. I cover MVVM in Chapter 6, but at this point in the book I want to show you how to work with the local database as well as provide background on how to implement data management in code. This will make learning MVVM easier.

We have the MainPage class implement the INotifyPropertyChanged interface to allow it to support data management operations. It contains one property named RecipeItems declared like this:

```
private ObservableCollection<Recipe> _recipeItems;
public ObservableCollection<Recipe> RecipeItems
{
  get
  {
    return _recipeItems;
  }
  set
  {
```

```
    if (_recipeItems != value)
    {
      _recipeItems = value;
      NotifyPropertyChanged("RecipeItems");
    }
  }
}
```

Instantiate the `RecipeDB` in the `MainPage` constructor using this line of code:

```
RecipeDB = new RecipeDataContext(RecipeDataContext.DBConnectionString);
```

In `OnNavigatedTo` I grab the `Recipe` records from the database and assign to the `RecipeItems` property on the `MainPage` class:

```
protected override void OnNavigatedTo(
  System.Windows.Navigation.NavigationEventArgs e)
{
  if (RecipeDB.DatabaseExists())
  {
    //Grab all of the recipes from the Recipe database
    var recipesFromDb = from Recipe recipe in RecipeDB.Recipes
                        select recipe;
    //Instantiate the RecipeItems collection with the database items
    //This is the collection that we actually work with in code or via
    //databinding visually with Blend
    RecipeItems = new ObservableCollection<Recipe>(recipesFromDb);
  }
  base.OnNavigatedTo(e);
}
```

In `OnNavigatedFrom` call `SubmitChanges` to commit any pending changes prior to navigating away from the page.

```
protected override void OnNavigatedFrom(System.Windows.Navigation.NavigationEventArgs e)
{
  if (RecipeDB.DatabaseExists())
  {
    //Commit changes if moving from page
    RecipeDB.SubmitChanges();
  }
  base.OnNavigatedFrom(e);
}
```

I add a little bit more code to the `CreateInitialRecords` method to have a bit more data to work with. Running the application as it is coded will generate a new recipe database and add one record to it. While the code runs fine and no errors or exceptions are generated, that does not always mean that no errors exist. To proactively validate the data you can use the Isolated Storage Tool to copy over the isolated storage contents and attach the database in Visual Studio. I create a short batch file to copy it over. Here is the batch file content:

```
"c:\Program Files (x86)\Microsoft SDKs\Windows
      Phone\v7.1\Tools\IsolatedStorageExplorerTool\isetool.exe" ts xd
      {8539e37d-5f0e-47ef-8263-e9d09c82e107} c:\test\
pause
```

This puts the folder contents into `c:\test\IsolatedStore`, including the file Recipes.sdf. In Visual Studio, go to View ➤ Server Explorer if not already displayed. Add a new Data Connection by right-clicking on Data Connections and select Add Connection. When the "Add Connection" dialog shows, click Change.. to select 'Microsoft SQL Server Compact 3.5' and click OK.

■ **Note** You must select 'Microsoft SQL Server Compact 3.5' or else you will upgrade the database to 'Microsoft SQL Server Compact 4.0,' which is not compatible with Windows Phone.

Next click Browse.., navigate to `c:\test\IsolatedStore` in my case, and select `Recipes.sdf`. Click OK to finish creating the data source. When prompted for a password, just click OK as the password is currently blank. To create a secure database, review the section covering how to encrypt a local database.

Next expand the folder tree to view the column details for the `Recipe` table. Right-click on Recipes.sdf and select Show Table Data. You can also manually enter data as well. Figure 4-2 shows the UI in Visual Studio.

Figure 4–2. Exploring `Recipes.sdf` *in Visual Studio*

In MainPage.xaml.cs the application simply updates a `TextBlock` to show how many records are present in the database. Now that we have created a simple Recipes database and we can pull the database from the emulator, let's use this database to demonstrate how to ship and utilize a pre-populated database.

Pre-Populated Database Sample

In this sample I demonstrate how to ship and use a pre-created local database as part of a Windows Phone application. I will use the Recipes.sdf from the previous sample as the pre-created sample local database. I add a reference to `System.Data.Linq` as before to bring in the correct namespace and classes.

The first step is to add the pre-populated database to the project. Copy Recipes.sdf to the project folder and then add it to the DBPrePropSample project. Right-click on the project in Solution Explorer and select Add ➤ Existing Item.. and select Recipes.sdf. Make sure it is configured as `Content` and set to "Copy Always."

When Recipe.sdf is deployed with the application, it is stored in the installation folder after deployment, which is read-only. The application has two options, connect to it in read-only mode from that location or copy it to Isolated Storage for read-write operations. The next two sections cover both options.

Read-Only Access

To read from the database when it is deployed in the installation folder as content, you use a special connections string to access it. Here is an example:

```
RecipesDataContext RecipesDB =
new RecipesDataContext ("Data Source = 'appdata:/Recipes.sdf'; File Mode = read only;");
```

You reference the database from the `appdata:` location and the `File Mode` must be set to `read only`. Otherwise an error will occur. In the next section we copy to isolated storage and access the database normally.

Copy to Isolated Storage

Many applications will start with a pre-populated database to save bandwidth and provide the user with some start up data, updating the database from the cloud. The first step is to copy the database to isolated storage from the installation folder.

We start with a new project named `DBPrePropSample` that will ship with the Recipes.sdf database file, copy it to isolated storage, and then present a master – a details view of the Recipes database. The first step is to add two using clauses needed to copy over the database:

```
using System.IO.IsolatedStorage;
using System.IO;
```

The next step is to modify App.xaml.cs to first check to see if Recipes.sdf exists. If it does not already exist, copy over the pre-populated database to isolated storage. This method is called at the end of the App class constructor in `App.xaml.cs`:

```
private void CheckAndCopyDBToIsoStore()
{
  // Obtain a reference to the application's isolated storage
  IsolatedStorageFile iso = IsolatedStorageFile.GetUserStoreForApplication();

  //Only copy db file over if it does not already exist
  if (!iso.FileExists("Recipes.sdf"))
    using (Stream input = Application.GetResourceStream(new Uri("Recipes.sdf",
UriKind.Relative)).Stream)
    {
      using (IsolatedStorageFileStream output = iso.CreateFile("Recipes.sdf"))
      {
        byte[] readBuffer = new byte[4096];
        int bytesRead = -1;
        // Copy the file from the install folder to isolated storage.
        while ((bytesRead = input.Read(readBuffer, 0, readBuffer.Length)) > 0)
        {
          output.Write(readBuffer, 0, bytesRead);
        }
      }
    }
}
```

We copy over the code from the `DbCreateSample` Main.xaml.cs to `DBPrePropSample`'s Main.xaml.cs so that we have the `RecipeItems` collection loaded up from the local database in the `OnNavigatedTo` event.

The `DataContext` for the page is configured to point to itself to get access to the `RecipeItems` collection in this line of code from the `MainPage` constructor:

```
this.DataContext = this;
```

The next step is to data bind a `ListBox` to the `RecipeItems` collection in the `MainPage` class. I add a `ListBox` control to `MainPage.xaml` and configure the `ItemsSource` property to point to `RecipeItems`. I add an inline `DataTemplate` to the `ListBox` as well. Here is the final XAML:

```
<ListBox BorderThickness="12,0,0,0" ItemsSource="{Binding RecipeItems}"
  SelectionChanged="ListBox_SelectionChanged">
  <ListBox.ItemTemplate>
    <DataTemplate>
      <StackPanel Margin="0,0,0,40">
        <TextBlock Text="{Binding Name}" Style="{StaticResource PhoneTextLargeStyle}" />
        <TextBlock Text="{Binding MealType}" Style="{StaticResource PhoneTextNormalStyle}" />
        <TextBlock Text="{Binding CookingTime}" Style="{StaticResource PhoneTextAccentStyle}"
/>
      </StackPanel>
    </DataTemplate>
  </ListBox.ItemTemplate>
</ListBox>
```

When you run the `DBPrePropSample` in the emulator, the resulting UI shown in Figure 4-3.

Figure 4–3. DBPrePropSample MainPage.Xaml

Let's now add a details page to view the full recipe details when one of the recipes is selected. I add a new item named `Details.xaml` to the `DBPrePropSample` project. In MainPage.xaml I add this code to the `ListBox_SelectionChanged` event:

```
private void ListBox_SelectionChanged(object sender,
    System.Windows.Controls.SelectionChangedEventArgs e)
{
  if ((sender as ListBox).SelectedItem != null)
  {
    //Cast Sender to ListBox and the SelectedItem to a Recipe object
    NavigationService.Navigate(new Uri("/Details.xaml?id=" +
      ((Recipe)(sender as ListBox).SelectedItem).RecipeId, UriKind.Relative));
  }
}
```

This will pass the `RecipeID` for the selected item to the `Details` page as part of the query string. Since I am not using MVVM architecture for this sample I need to create a database connection in `Details.xaml.cs`. I create a `RecipeDataContext` named `RecipeDB` as before, but I do not need the `RecipeItems` collection. I also need to modify `OnNavigatedTo` to retrieve the `RecipeID` from the query string and set the `DataContext` to the selected `Recipe` object. Here is the code for `Details.xaml.cs` `OnNavigatedTo` and then we will go through it:

```
protected override void OnNavigatedTo(
  System.Windows.Navigation.NavigationEventArgs e)
{
  int id = Convert.ToInt16(NavigationContext.QueryString["id"]);
  if (RecipeDB.DatabaseExists())
  {
    //Grab all of the recipes from the Recipe database
    var selectedRecipe = from Recipe recipe in RecipeDB.Recipes
                         where recipe.RecipeId == id
                         select recipe;

    this.DataContext = selectedRecipe.First<Recipe>();
  }
  base.OnNavigatedTo(e);
}
```

The `RecipeID` is obtained from the `NavigationContext.QueryString` value and then a LINQ query is executed to retrieve the selected recipe data from the database. The value returned is an `IEnumerable` of one record so I use the `First` method to obtain a reference to the correct `Recipe` object and set the `DetailsPage`'s `DataContext`.

The XAML is pretty straightforward. Each `TextBlock` data binds to a field in the `Recipe` object configured on the `DataContext` property. Here is the XAML.

```
<Grid x:Name="ContentPanel" Grid.Row="1" Margin="12,0,12,0">
  <TextBlock Name="Name" Text="{Binding Name}" HorizontalAlignment="Left"
    VerticalAlignment="Top" Width="436" Margin="12,23,0,0"
    Style="{StaticResource PhoneTextLargeStyle}"/>
  <TextBlock Name="CookingTime" Text="{Binding CookingTime}" HorizontalAlignment="Left"
    VerticalAlignment="Top" Width="150" Margin="12,66,0,0"
    d:LayoutOverrides="HorizontalAlignment" Style="{StaticResource PhoneTextAccentStyle}"/>
  <TextBlock Name="MealType" Text="{Binding MealType}" HorizontalAlignment="Left"
```

```
              VerticalAlignment="Top" Width="150" Margin="12,109,0,0"
              d:LayoutOverrides="HorizontalAlignment" Style="{StaticResource PhoneTextLargeStyle}"/>
        <TextBlock HorizontalAlignment="Left" TextWrapping="Wrap" Text="Ingredients:"
              VerticalAlignment="Top" Margin="12,160,0,0" Style="{StaticResource
    PhoneTextSubtleStyle}"/>
        <TextBlock Name="Ingredients" Text="{Binding Ingedients}" HorizontalAlignment="Left"
              VerticalAlignment="Top" Width="444" Margin="12,187,0,0" Height="51"/>
        <TextBlock HorizontalAlignment="Left" TextWrapping="Wrap" Text="Steps:"
              VerticalAlignment="Top" Margin="12,242,0,0" Style="{StaticResource
    PhoneTextSubtleStyle}"/>
        <TextBlock Name="Steps" Text="{Binding Steps}" HorizontalAlignment="Left"
              Width="425" Margin="12,269,0,123"/>
    </Grid>
```

Figure 4-4 shows the data bound UI in action.

Figure 4–4. *Data bound Details.Page UI*

This concludes the local database sample. In the next couple of sections I cover additional considerations when working with a local database as part of a Windows Phone application.

Application Updates and Local Database

Local database capabilities in Windows Phone OS 7.1 can be very helpful for managing large data sets on Windows Phone. As your application evolves, it is likely that your local database will need to evolve as well. This section provides a short overview and pointers on what to consider when it comes to database management.

Adding associations, indexes, tables, and columns to a local database is pretty simple to do using the `DatabaseSchemaUpdater` class. It can also assist with more complex migrations where data needs to be copied into a new database and database versioning is used via the `DatabaseSchemaVersion` property. This link has more info with a code sample walkthrough performing a local database migration:

`http://msdn.microsoft.com/en-us/library/hh394022(v=VS.92).aspx`

Local Database Security and Connection String Options

Local database functionality in Windows Phone OS 7.1 provides password protection and encryption to add another level of security to your application. To create a secure database, simply add the Password option to the connection string like in this example:

```
RecipesDataContext RecipesDB = new RecipesDataContext ("Data
Source='isostore:/Recipes.sdf';Password='password'");
```

As far as where to store the password, the recommendation is to not store the password in the application code or file system. For maximum security, prompt for the password every time the application is launched. This isn't the most convenient requirement for users so you have to decide what is best for your application. The Windows Phone SDK 7.1 provides access to a set of security APIs including an Encrypted Credential Store. We cover this functionality later in this chapter.

For other connection string options, you can also specify max buffer size, max database size, file mode, culture info, and case sensitivity options via the connections string as well. For more information check out this link:

`http://msdn.microsoft.com/en-us/library/hh202861(v=VS.92).aspx`

Web Browser Control

The `WebBrowser` control allows you to display remote and local HTML within a Windows Phone XAML+.NET application. In Windows Phone OS 7.1, the `WebBrowser` control supports `HTML5` including the `HTML5 Canvas` object. The `WebBrowser` control is based on Internet Explorer 9 mobile, which is compatible with Internet Explorer 9 on the desktop. To see the capabilities of Internet Explorer 9 mobile, open the following page in the emulator or on a device:

`http:// ie.microsoft.com/testdrive/mobile`

The `WebBrowser` control is much more programmable than the `WebBrowserTask` covered in the next chapter. The `WebBrowser` control can be embedded within the XAML of an application, so the content appears more integrated with the application itself. It is still a full browser, so you can navigate away from content if following hyperlinks, but you can configure how it behaves. The following is a list of the `WebBrowser` control class members to help guide capabilities:

- **Base:** Sets the base directory in isolated storage that is used to resolve relative URLs.

- **CacheMode:** Determines whether content should be cached when possible.

- **InvokeScript:** Executes a function in the script for the currently loaded content.

- **IsScriptEnabled:** Set to true to enable scripting. Applies to the next document navigated to, not the current document.

- **LoadCompleted:** Event fires when the content is fully loaded. Permits having a loading animation.

- **Navigate:** Navigates the browser control to the provided URI. Two overloads with the second taking post data and additional headers.

- **Navigated:** Fires after successful navigation.

- **Navigating:** Fires when browser is navigating

- **NavigateToString:** Allows loading the provided HTML string into the browser.

- **ScriptNotify:** Fires when JavaScript calls `window.external.Notify(<data>)`.

The `WebBrowserControl` project sample in the Chapter 4 solution exercises the `WebBrowser` control with two pages. The first sample page demonstrates basic use. The second sample page demonstrates scripting interoperability between Silverlight and the hosted HTML code.

WebBrowser Control Sample

In the `WebBrowserControlPage.xaml`, there is a `WebBrowser` control, a `TextBox` to enter a URL, and a load button in the application bar. There is also a semi-transparent `Rectangle` to demonstrate transparency support in the `WebBrowser` control.

The project includes a simple animation named `AnimateGreenRect` that spins and animates the size of the green `Rectangle` while loading content into the `WebBrowser` control. The `Storyboard` object is built using Expression Blend. First a keyframe is added at 0 seconds with the configured position. The yellow timeline indicator is slid over to 500ms and another keyframe is added by clicking the small circle with a plus sign in the Object and Timeline window as shown in Figure 4–5.

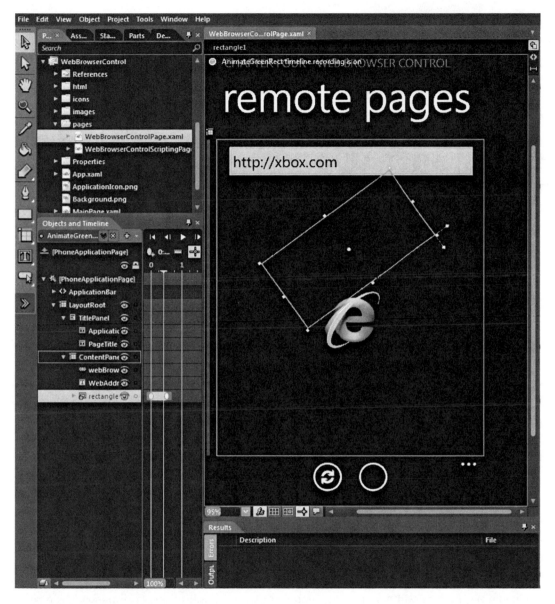

Figure 4–5. *Creating the animation*

With the yellow timeline indicator over the half second keyframe, move over to the Properties window and expand the Transform section. Select the `Rotate` tab and set the `Angle` property to about 144 degrees. Next, select the `Scale` tab and set `X` and `Y` to .5. Click on the name of the `Storyboard` at the top of the Object and Timeline window to select the newly created `Storyboard` and move over to the Properties window. Check the `AutoReverse` checkbox and set the `RepeatBehavior` to `Forever`.

It takes just a little bit of code to wire-up playing the animation while loading the web page. Listing 4–5 has the code.

Listing 4–5. *WebBrowserControlPage.xaml.cs Code File*

```
public partial class WebBrowserControlPage : PhoneApplicationPage
  {
    public WebBrowserControlPage()
    {
      InitializeComponent();
      webBrowserControl.LoadCompleted += new
        System.Windows.Navigation.LoadCompletedEventHandler(webBrowserControl_LoadCompleted);
      webBrowserControl.Navigating += new
        EventHandler<NavigatingEventArgs>(webBrowserControl_Navigating);
    }

    void webBrowserControl_Navigating(object sender, NavigatingEventArgs e)
    {
      System.Diagnostics.Debug.WriteLine(e.Uri);
    }

    private void loadUrlAppBarButton_Click(object sender, EventArgs e)
    {
      AnimateGreenRect.Begin();
      webBrowserControl.Navigate(new Uri(WebAddressTextBox.Text));
    }

    void webBrowserControl_LoadCompleted(object sender, System.Windows.Navigation.
.NavigationEventArgs e)
    {
      AnimateGreenRect.Stop();
    }
  }
```

You can hook into the various events available listed above in XAML as we have done previously. Using the += syntax, Visual Studio will automatically generate the correct event handler just by hitting the tab key to generate it:

```
webBrowserControl.Navigating += new
  EventHandler<NavigatingEventArgs>(webBrowserControl_Navigating);
```

An important capability of the WebBrowser control is to load HTML fragments using the WebBrowser.NavigateToString() method. Another important capability is the WebBrowser.Base property allows relative URLs for items such as images to be loaded locally. Caching items to the file system can save download time and bandwidth for the user, improving overall application performance. The next section covers interacting with the HTML content via scripting.

WebBrowser Control Scripting Sample

The WebBrowser control supports HTML5, CSS, and JavaScript. To support JavaScript, set the IsScriptEnabled property to true in XAML or in the code-behind. The

`WebBrowserControlScriptingPage.xaml` sample contains a `WebBrowser` control that is loaded with an HTML page stored in the xap as content. The HTML page contains two `JavaScript` script functions; one that sets the content on a DIV, the other script sets the source to an IMG tag in the HTML. Listing 4–8 has the HTML file that is stored in the xap as content.

Listing 4–6. *The* `content.html` *Code File*

```html
<html>
<head>
  <title>Test Script</title>
  <script type="text/javascript">

    function PassData(data) {
      content1.innerHTML = data;
    }

    function SetImageSource(source) {
      image1.src = source;
    }
    <style type="text/css">
    body {
      font-family: "Segoe WP";
      font-size: medium;
      color: #FFFFFF;
      background-color: #000000;
    }
  </script>
</head>
<body>
  <h3>
    Page Loaded</h3>
  <img alt="image goes here" src="" id="image1" />
  <h4>
    Text appears below:</h4>
  <div id="content1">
  </div>
</body>
</html>
```

You can see the two JavaScript functions in Listing 4–6 as well as the div and image that are updated by the functions. The HTML file has a little bit of formatting to help the HTML file blend in with the UI. The style was creating using the Visual Studio Manage Styles dialog box by clicking the new style button. You can see the styling in the CSS style applied to the HTML BODY tag. The style does the following:

- Sets the font to match the Windows Phone font (`Segoe WP`)

- Font Size to medium and a foreground color of `White`

- Set the background color to `Black`

When using the `WebBrowser` control, try to have the content blend into the UI with styling. Windows Phone supports two themes, light and dark, so you should dynamically apply styles based on the theming, which you will see is not difficult to do via the scripting bridge.

259

The WebBrowser Control supports invoking script. Listing 4–7 has the code-behind file where the Silverlight code calls the two scripts.

Listing 4–7. *The* WebBrowserControlScriptingPage.xaml.cs *Code File*

```
using System;
using System.IO;
using System.IO.IsolatedStorage;
using System.Windows;
using Microsoft.Phone.Controls;

namespace WebBrowserControl.pages
{
  public partial class WebBrowserControlScriptingPage : PhoneApplicationPage
  {
    public WebBrowserControlScriptingPage()
    {
      InitializeComponent();
      Loaded += new RoutedEventHandler(WebBrowserControlScriptingPage_Loaded);
    }

    void WebBrowserControlScriptingPage_Loaded(object sender, RoutedEventArgs e)
    {
      SetUpWebBrowserControlContent();
      webBrowserControl.Base = "home";
      webBrowserControl.Navigate(new Uri("content.html", UriKind.Relative));
    }

    private void SetUpWebBrowserControlContent()
    {
      //Copy content out of xap and into isolated storage
      using (IsolatedStorageFile isf =
             IsolatedStorageFile.GetUserStoreForApplication())
      {
        //if (!isf.DirectoryExists("home"))
        //{
        isf.CreateDirectory("home");
        //create base html file
        using (IsolatedStorageFileStream fs =
          isf.OpenFile("home/content.html", System.IO.FileMode.Create))
        {
          byte[] buffer = new byte[256];
          int count = 0;
          Stream resourceStream =
            Application.GetResourceStream(
                    new Uri("html/content.html", UriKind.Relative)).Stream;
          count = resourceStream.Read(buffer, 0, 256);
          while (count > 0)
          {
            fs.Write(buffer, 0, count);
            count = resourceStream.Read(buffer, 0, 256);
```

```
      }
    }
    //Create Image directory
    isf.CreateDirectory("home/images");
    //Create image file
    using (IsolatedStorageFileStream fs =
      isf.OpenFile("home/images/image.jpg", System.IO.FileMode.Create))
    {
      byte[] buffer = new byte[256];
      int count = 0;
      Stream resourceStream = Application.GetResourceStream(
        new Uri("images/image.jpg", UriKind.Relative)).Stream;
      count = resourceStream.Read(buffer, 0, 256);
      while (count > 0)
      {
        fs.Write(buffer, 0, count);
        count = resourceStream.Read(buffer, 0, 256);
      }
    }
  }
}

private void loadUrlAppBarButton_Click(object sender, EventArgs e)
{
  //Invoke script
  webBrowserControl.InvokeScript(
      "PassData", "This is the data.  Hello from Silverlight.");
  webBrowserControl.InvokeScript(
      "SetImageSource", "images/image.jpg");
}
  }
}
```

The InvokeScript method on the WebBrowser control takes the name of the JavaScript method and a string array for parameters. When the refresh button is clicked, the loadUrlAppBarButton_Click shown in Listing 4–8 event fires resulting in the UI shown in Figure 4–6.

Figure 4–6. WebBrowser control scripting page

When you use Internet Explorer 9 mobile, either browsing or with the WebBrowser control, you can see a huge speed improvement over the previous version.

HTML5 Support

Mentioned earlier, Internet Explorer 9 mobile supports HTML5 just like its big brother on the desktop. This book doesn't go into detail on HTML5. There are plenty of books out there covering the topic including *Pro HTML5 Programming*, 2nd Edition, from Apress.

If you need to include support for HTML5 in your applications, PhoneGap announced support to bring its framework to Windows Phone. As of this writing, PhoneGap has created APIs for this functionality so far:

- Accelerometer

- Camera

- Compass

- Contacts

- Events

- Geolocation

- MediaCapture

- Connection

- Notification

This link announced PhoneGap support for Windows Phone OS 7.1 and provides details on how to get started:

`http://blogs.nitobi.com/jesse/2011/09/08/pg-wp7mango/`

This concludes our coverage of the `WebBrowser` control. Next up is asynchronous programming and then on to accessing remote services.

Asynchronous Programming

This section covers asynchronous programming, which is the preferred method do to work in Silverlight. Asynchronous programming is preferred, because it takes work off of the UI thread, which should be a priority in order to maximize UI performance for animation and transitions.

Rendering performance can be improved two ways: pushing work from the UI thread to the `Render` thread and pushing work such as processing remote data to a separate background thread. We cover various ways to push work off of the UI thread in this section.

Background Threads

You can use the standard .NET multithreading class `Thread.Start` and `ThreadPool.QueueUserWorkItem` to perform background work that writes data to isolated storage, and it will work fine. If you try to access the XAML from the standard classes without taking extra steps, it will throw an exception. Silverlight includes classes that make it easier to perform background work that interacts with the user interface.

Fire and Forget Background Processing

The `Dispatcher` class offers a safe way to call a method that updates the UI asynchronously from a background thread by providing services for managing the queue of work items for a thread. Both the `Dispatcher` and the `BackgroundWorker` classes can perform work on a separate thread. The `BackgroundWorker` class supports progress reporting and cancellation, which we cover in detail in the next section. The `Dispatcher` class is useful when you need a simple way to queue up background work without progress reporting or cancellation.

You can create a delegate and then user `Dispatcher.BeginInvoke` to fire the delegate, which then updates the UI. As an example, if you have a `TextBlock` named `TextBlock1` that you need to update from a background thread, obtain the `Dispatcher` from that control and perform the update. Here is an example of using C# lambda syntax (=>).

```
TextBlock1.Dispatcher.BeginInvoke(() =>
  {
    TextBlock1.Text = "Data Updated";
  };
```

You can call `Dispatcher.CheckAccess` to determine if the calling thread is on the same thread as the control or the UI thread. Use `BeginInvoke` it if returns false. It is recommended to obtain the `Dispatcher` instance from the control closest to the controls being updated. So if multiple controls need to be updated and they are contained in a `Grid` panel, obtain the Dispatcher from the `Grid`.

Our sample for this section will retrieve an xml file from the services project named `WcfRemoteServices` that is part of the Chapter 4 solution. Remote services are covered in detail in the section titled "Connecting Windows Phone to Services and Feeds" later in this chapter. A file named `ApressBooks.xml` is added to the `AsynchronousProgramming` project. This XML file contains a simple xml schema with a few book titles in it. Here is one record from the XML file:

```
<ApressBook>
  <ID>4</ID>
  <ISBN>1-4302-2435-5</ISBN>
  <Author>Jit Ghosh and Rob Cameron</Author>
  <Title>Silverlight Recipes: A Problem-Solution Approach, Second Edition</Title>
  <Description>Silverlight Recipes: A Problem-Solution Approach, Second Edition is your
practical
    companion to developing rich, interactive web applications with Microsoft's latest
  technology.
</Description>
  <DatePublished>2010-07-15T00:00:00</DatePublished>
  <NumPages>1056</NumPages>
  <Price>$49.99</Price>
</ApressBook>
```

The UI for the `DispatcherPage.xaml` contains a `ListBox` with an `ItemTemplate` to display the above data and an application bar with one button to load the data. When the button is clicked, the `LoadDataAppBarButton_Click` event handler spins up a `WebRequest` object that points to the local developer web server from the `WcfRemoteServices` Project to retrieve the XML file. Here is the code snippet for the application bar button event handler:

```
private void LoadDataAppBarButton_Click(object sender, EventArgs e)
{
  Uri location =
      new Uri("http://localhost:9090/xml/ApressBooks.xml", UriKind.Absolute);
  WebRequest request = HttpWebRequest.Create(location);
  request.BeginGetResponse(
      new AsyncCallback(this.RetrieveXmlCompleted), request);
}
```

All remote service calls MUST be executed asynchronously, so the callback function named `RetrieveXmlCompleted` is where the results are actually returned to the application. Here is the `RetrieveXmlCompleted` method:

```
void RetrieveXmlCompleted(IAsyncResult ar)
{
  List<ApressBook> _apressBookList;
  HttpWebRequest request = ar.AsyncState as HttpWebRequest;
  WebResponse response = request.EndGetResponse(ar);
  Stream responseStream = response.GetResponseStream();
  using (StreamReader streamreader = new StreamReader(responseStream))
  {
    XDocument xDoc = XDocument.Load(streamreader);
```

```
  _apressBookList =
  (from b in xDoc.Descendants("ApressBook")
    select new ApressBook()
    {
      Author = b.Element("Author").Value,
      Title = b.Element("Title").Value,
      ISBN = b.Element("ISBN").Value,
      Description = b.Element("Description").Value,
      PublishedDate = Convert.ToDateTime(b.Element("DatePublished").Value),
      NumberOfPages = b.Element("NumPages").Value,
      Price = b.Element("Price").Value,
      ID = b.Element("ID").Value
    }).ToList();
}
//Could use Anonymous delegate (does same as below line of code)
// BooksListBox.Dispatcher.BeginInvoke(
// delegate()
// {
//    DataBindListBox(_apressBookList);
// }
// );
//Use C# 3.0 Lambda
BooksListBox.Dispatcher.BeginInvoke(() => DataBindListBox(_apressBookList));
}
```

The xml file is received and then loaded into an XDocument object for some basic LINQ to XML manipulation to turn it into a collection of APressBook .NET objects. Once that little bit of work is completed, the collection needs to be pushed back to the UI thread. This is where the BooksListBox.Dispatcher is finally used to fire the DataBindListBox method to perform the data binding.

The previous code snippet includes an alternative method of passing the _apressBookList to the UI thread and databind. It could be reduced further to the following:

```
BooksListBox.Dispatcher.BeginInvoke(() =>
{
  BooksListBox.ItemsSource = _apressBookList;
});
```

To test the Dispatcher using WebRequest, both the WCFRemoteServices project and the AsynchronousProgramming project must be running. Right-click on the Ch04_WPProgrammingModel Solution and configure it to have multiple startup projects, as shown in Figure 4–7.

Figure 4–7. *WebBrowser control scripting page*

If you still want to use standard .NET Framework threading, You can call `SynchronizationContext.Current` to get the current `DispatcherSynchronizationContext`, assign it to a member variable on the `Page`, and call `Post(method, data)` to fire the event back on the UI thread. Calling `Send(method, data` instead of `Post` will make a synchronous call, which you should avoid doing if possible as it could affect UI performance.

Supporting Progress Reporting and Cancellation

For long running processes, having the ability to cancel work as well as show work progress is necessary for a good user experience. A convenient class that provides a level of abstraction as well as progress updates is the `System.ComponentModel.BackgroundWorker` class. The `BackgroundWorker` class lets you indicate operation progress, completion, and cancellation in the Silverlight UI. For example, you can check whether the background operation is completed or canceled and display a message to the user.

The Chapter 4 sample `AsynchronousProgramming` project test page named BackgroundWorkerPage.xaml explores the `BackgroundWorker` class. To use a background worker thread, declare an instance of the `BackgroundWorker` class at the class level, not within an event handler:

```
BackgroundWorker bw = new BackgroundWorker();
```

You can specify whether you want to allow cancellation and progress reporting by setting one or both of the `WorkerSupportsCancellation` and `WorkerReportsProgress` properties on the `BackgroundWorker` object to `true`. The next step is to create an event handler for the `BackgroundWorker.DoWork` event. This is where you put the code for the time-consuming operation. Within the `DoWork` event, check the `CancellationPending` property to see if the user clicked the `Cancel` button. You must set `e.Cancel = true` in `DoWork` so that `WorkCompleted` can check the value and finish correctly if the work was completed.

266

If the operation is not cancelled, call the ReportProgress method to pass a percentage complete value that is between 0 and 100. Doing this raises the ProgressChanged event on the BackgroundWorker object. The UI thread code can subscribe to the event and update the UI based on the progress. If you call the ReportProgress method when WorkerReportsProgress is set to false, an exception will occur. You can also pass in a value for the UserState parameter, which in this case is a string that is used to update the UI.

Once the work is completed successfully, pass the data back to the calling process by setting the e.Result property of the DoWorkerEventArgs object to the object or collection containing the data resulting from the work. The DoWorkerEventArgs.Result is of type object and can therefore be assigned any object or collection of objects. The value of the Result property can be read when the RunWorkerCompleted event is raised upon completion of the operation and the value can be safely assigned to UI object properties. Listing 4–8 shows the XAML modifications in the ContentPanel Grid.

Listing 4–8. The BackgroundWorkerPage.xaml ContentPanel XAML

```
<Grid x:Name="ContentPanel" Grid.Row="1" Margin="12,0,12,0">
  <StackPanel Orientation="Vertical" d:LayoutOverrides="Height">
    <StackPanel x:Name="StatusStackPanel" Orientation="Vertical">
      <StackPanel Orientation="Horizontal" d:LayoutOverrides="Width">
        <TextBlock x:Name="processingStateTextBlock" TextWrapping="Wrap"
            VerticalAlignment="Top" Width="190" Margin="12,34,0,0"/>
        <Button x:Name="cancelButton" Content="Cancel Operation"
            VerticalAlignment="Top" Click="cancelButton_Click" Width="254" />
      </StackPanel>
      <ProgressBar x:Name="BookListDownloadProgress" Width="456"
                      HorizontalAlignment="Left" />
    </StackPanel>
    <ListBox x:Name="BooksListBox" ItemsSource="{Binding ApressBookList}"
      Height="523" ItemTemplate="{StaticResource BookListBoxDataTemplate}" />
  </StackPanel>
</Grid>
```

The StatusStackPanel container that has the status info is made visible when the work is started, and is then hidden since the work is completed. Figure 4–8 has the UI.

Figure 4–8. WebBrowser control scripting page

One additional wrinkle is that the code overrides `OnNavigateFrom`. If the `BackgroundWorker` thread is busy, the code cancels the operation, since the user navigated away. Listing 4–9 has the full source code.

Listing 4–9. The `BackgroundWorkerPage.xaml.cs` Code File

```
using System.ComponentModel;
using System.Windows;
using Microsoft.Phone.Controls;

namespace AsynchronousProgramming.pages
{
  public partial class BackgroundWorkerPage : PhoneApplicationPage
  {
    private BackgroundWorker _worker = new BackgroundWorker();

    public BackgroundWorkerPage()
    {
      InitializeComponent();
      //Configure BackgroundWorker thread
      _worker.WorkerReportsProgress = true;
      _worker.WorkerSupportsCancellation = true;
```

```csharp
  _worker.DoWork +=
    new DoWorkEventHandler(worker_DoWork);
  _worker.ProgressChanged +=
    new ProgressChangedEventHandler(worker_ProgressChanged);
  _worker.RunWorkerCompleted +=
    new RunWorkerCompletedEventHandler(worker_RunWorkerCompleted);

  //Kick off long running process
  //Make status visible
  _worker.RunWorkerAsync();
  StatusStackPanel.Visibility = Visibility.Visible;
}

protected override void OnNavigatedFrom(
              System.Windows.Navigation.NavigationEventArgs e)
{
  //Cancel work if user navigates away
  if (_worker.IsBusy)
    _worker.CancelAsync();

  base.OnNavigatedFrom(e);
}

void worker_DoWork(object sender, DoWorkEventArgs e)
{
  ApressBooks books = new ApressBooks();
  books.LoadBooks();
  int progress;
  string state = "initializing...";
  //Do fake work to retrieve and process books
  for (int i = 1; i <= books.ApressBookList.Count;i++ )
  {
    if (_worker.CancellationPending == true)
    {
      e.Cancel = true;
      break;
    }
    else
    {
      progress = (int)System.Math.Round((double)i /
                  books.ApressBookList.Count * 100d);

      if ((progress > 15) && (progress < 90))
        state = "processing..." ;
      if (progress > 85)
        state = "finishing..." ;
      if (progress == 95)
        state = "Loading complete.";

      _worker.ReportProgress(progress, state);
      System.Threading.Thread.Sleep(250);
    }
```

```
      }
      e.Result = books;
    }

    void worker_ProgressChanged(object sender, ProgressChangedEventArgs e)
    {
      BookListDownloadProgress.Value = e.ProgressPercentage;
      processingStateTextBlock.Text = e.UserState as string;
    }


    void worker_RunWorkerCompleted(object sender, RunWorkerCompletedEventArgs e)
    {
      if (e.Cancelled == true)
        MessageBox.Show("Operation cancelled.","Cancelled",MessageBoxButton.OK);
      else
        LayoutRoot.DataContext = e.Result as ApressBooks;

      //Clean up status UI
      BookListDownloadProgress.Value = 0;
      processingStateTextBlock.Text = "";
      StatusStackPanel.Visibility = Visibility.Collapsed;
    }

    private void cancelButton_Click(object sender, RoutedEventArgs e)
    {
      _worker.CancelAsync();
    }
  }
}
```

Silverlight includes the standard .NET locking primitives, such as Monitor or lock, as well as the ManualResetEvent class where deadlocks can occur. A deadlock occurs when two threads each hold on to a resource while requesting the resource that the other thread is holding. A deadlock will cause the application to hang. It is easy to create a deadlock with two threads accessing the same resources in an application.

The BackgroundWorker class tries to prevent deadlocks or cross-thread invocations that could be unsafe.

Any exceptions that can occur must be caught within the background thread, because they will not be caught by the unhandled exception handler at the application level. If an exception occurs on the background thread, one option is to catch the exception and set Result to null as a signal that there was an error. Another option is to set a particular value to Result as a signal that a occurred.

Connecting Windows Phone to Services and Feeds

In this section, we cover the supported networking and service protocols available to Windows Phone applications. These include Windows Communication Foundation (WCF), HttpWebRequest, and WebClient. Windows Communication Foundation is Microsoft's service development framework for SOAP, REST, Data Services (OData), and Feed-based services. HttpWebRequest and WebClient are straightforward HTTP request and response classes.

A command-line tool available to work with remote services is the Silverlight Service Model Proxy Generation Tool (SLsvcUtil.exe), used to generate proxy classes based on a web service WSDL file. New with Windows Phone OS 7.1 is the ability to use the Visual Studio Add Service Reference Feature to generates proxy classes based on either a web service WSDL file or a data service CSDL file. Another command-line tool to list is the WCF Data Service Client Utility (DataSvcUtil.exe) to generate proxy classes based on a data service CSDL file.

HttpWebRequest and WebClient

We demonstrated how to use `HttpWebRequest` earlier, when we discussed the `Dispatcher` and how it helps to marshal data back over to the UI thread. `WebClient` has similar functionality as `HttpWebRequest` and is fine for doing small amounts of work if preferred.

In Silverlight for Windows Phone, you can set the User-agent string and Headers for requests like using this syntax:

```
request.Headers.Add(HttpRequestHeader.UserAgent, "appname");
```

In Windows Phone OS 7.1, the `WebClient` class returns on the calling thread so there is no need to marshal data back to the UI thread.

Windows Communication Foundation Support

Windows Phone WCF includes client-side libraries to call services and a server-side programming model to create services. You can use the WCF libraries to connect to services implemented in other programming models and languages, as long as it is a supported network and wire protocol.

There is a fair amount of networking capability available in Windows Phone for Silverlight developers, including SOAP, REST, and Basic Authentication. Now with Silverlight 4 compatibility, the networking capabilities available in Windows Phone are much improved, adding support for `Sockets` and UDP Multicast clients as well as an improved `WebClient` class that returns on the calling thread for better performance.

Web Services

To have some data and services to work with, a new project solution named `WcfRemoteServices` is added to the Chapter 4 project. It is a `WCF Service Application` project type. When run, it launches the development web server to host the service. The project also includes an ADO.NET Entity Framework model to represent the `AdventureWorks` sample database available from Microsoft. The EF model is located in the model folder.

The database server used in the sample is SQL Server 2008 Express R2, which is available for free here:

www.microsoft.com/express/Database/

The sample database is available from CodePlex here:

http://msftdbprodsamples.codeplex.com/

The default `Service1` WCF class is removed, and one service class is added to the project in the `services` folder named, `AdventureWorks`. To create the service, edit the corresponding `IAdventureWorks`

Interface, and then implement the Interfaces in the **AdventureWorks.svc** class by editing the **AdventureWorks.svc.cs** file.

The service methods implement the Interfaces using LINQ queries against the **AdventureWorksModel** EF model. Listings 4–10 and 4–11 have the code for the Interface and concrete implementation of the **AdventureWorks** service.

Listing 4–10. *The IAdventureWorks Interface for the SOAP WCF Service*

```
using System;
using System.Collections.Generic;
using System.ServiceModel;
using WcfRemoteServices.model;
using System.Runtime.Serialization;

namespace WcfRemoteServices.services
{
    // NOTE: You can use the "Rename" command on the "Refactor" menu to change the
    //interface name "IProducts" in both code and config file together.
    [ServiceContract]
    public interface IAdventureWorks
    {
        [OperationContract]
        List<Product> FullProductList();

        [OperationContract]
        List<ProductCategory> ProductCategoryList();

        [OperationContract]
        List<ProductSubcategory> ProductSubcategoryList();

        [OperationContract]
        List<Product> GetProductsByCategory(Int32 CategoryID);

        [OperationContract]
        List<Product> GetProductsBySubcategory(Int32 SubCategoryID);

        [OperationContract]
        int CheckInventory(Int32 ProductID);
        [OperationContract]
        List<Vendor> FullVendorList();

        VendorGeoLocation GetVendorAddress(Int32 VendorID);
    }

    [DataContract]
    public class VendorGeoLocation
    {
        [DataMember]
        public double Latitude { get; set; }

        [DataMember]
        public double Longitude { get; set; }
```

```
    }
}
```

Listing 4–11. The `AdventureWorks.svc.cs` *Class Implementation for the WCF Service*

```
using System;
using System.Collections.Generic;
using System.ServiceModel;
using WcfRemoteServices.model;
using System.Runtime.Serialization;

namespace WcfRemoteServices.services
{
    // NOTE: You can use the "Rename" command on the "Refactor" menu to change the
    //interface name "IProducts" in both code and config file together.
    [ServiceContract]
    public interface IAdventureWorks
    {
        [OperationContract]
        List<Product> FullProductList();

        [OperationContract]
        List<ProductCategory> ProductCategoryList();

        [OperationContract]
        List<ProductSubcategory> ProductSubcategoryList();

        [OperationContract]
        List<Product> GetProductsByCategory(Int32 CategoryID);

        [OperationContract]
        List<Product> GetProductsBySubcategory(Int32 SubCategoryID);

        [OperationContract]
        int CheckInventory(Int32 ProductID);
        [OperationContract]
        List<Vendor> FullVendorList();

        VendorGeoLocation GetVendorAddress(Int32 VendorID);
    }

    [DataContract]
    public class VendorGeoLocation
    {
        [DataMember]
        public double Latitude { get; set; }

        [DataMember]
        public double Longitude { get; set; }
    }
}
```

In the `AdventureWorks` service, the interface has a method named `GetVendorAddress` that uses the Bing Maps Geocode service to obtain a latitude and longitude. The developer environment is located here:

`http://dev.virtualearth.net/webservices/v1/geocodeservice/geocodeservice.svc/mex`

The staging environment is here:

`http://staging.dev.virtualearth.net/webservices/v1/geocodeservice/geocodeservice.svc`

The production environment is here:

`http://dev.virtualearth.net/webservices/v1/geocodeservice/geocodeservice.svc`

Once the WCF services are created, use the WCF Service Configuration Editor tool in the Visual Studio Tools menu to create the configuration for the services, which is located in the `WcfRemoteServices Web.Config` file. The most important item to keep in mind is that Silverlight for Windows Phone only supports `basicHttpBinding` and `webHttpBinding`. For security, Windows Phone supports `Basic Authentication` for credentials (SSL is always recommended if using Basic Authentication).

To access a remote service in Visual Studio 2010, you can generate a proxy class for the remote service using the Add Service Reference in the Windows Phone application as shown in Figure 4–9.

Figure 4–9. Add service reference menu

Silverlight includes a command-line tool for complete control when generating proxy classes. For Silverlight for Windows Phone, use the Silverlight 3 version of the tool called slsvcutil.exe, located at c:\Program Files (x86)\Microsoft SDKs\Silverlight\v3.0\Tools. The following is an example command-line for the two services we just created:

```
slsvcutil.exe http: //localhost:9090/services/AdventureWorks.svc
/out:c:\test\AdventureWorksProxy.cs
```

One advantage of using the command-line tool is that you can customize the proxy generation. For this sample, the slsvcutil.exe is used to generate the proxy class.

With the server-side service SOAP service created and the client proxy in hand, I add another project to the Chapter 4 Part 1 solution named CallingRemoteServices. MainPage.xaml is customized to display a menu that navigates to individual sample pages that demonstrate how to call SOAP, OData, and JSON remote services.

We start with the SOAP example, adding a page named WebServicePage.xaml to the pages folder. The WebServicePage.xaml page is customized to call the SOAP service. A ListBox control with an inline DataTemplate is added to the XAML of the WebServicePage.xaml page (see the following):

```
<ListBox x:Name="ProductsListBox" HorizontalAlignment="Left" VerticalAlignment="Top" >
  <ListBox.ItemTemplate>
    <DataTemplate>
      <StackPanel Margin="0,0,0,20">
        <TextBlock Text="{Binding Name}" Style="{StaticResource PhoneTextLargeStyle}" />
        <TextBlock Text="{Binding ProductNumber}" Style=.
"{StaticResource PhoneTextSmallStyle}" />
        <TextBlock Text="{Binding ListPrice}" Style="{StaticResource PhoneTextAccentStyle}" />
      </StackPanel>
    </DataTemplate>
  </ListBox.ItemTemplate>
</ListBox>
```

Listing 4–12 has the code-behind file that calls the service asynchronously and then data binds the list box with the product info.

Listing 4–12. The WebServicePage.xaml.cs Code File

```
using Microsoft.Phone.Controls;

namespace CallingRemoteServices.pages
{
  public partial class WebServicePage : PhoneApplicationPage
  {
    public WebServicePage()
    {
      InitializeComponent();
    }

    private void PhoneApplicationPage_Loaded(object sender, RoutedEventArgs e)
    {
      AdventureWorksClient adventureWorksClient = new AdventureWorksClient();
      adventureWorksClient.FullProductListCompleted +=
        new EventHandler<FullProductListCompletedEventArgs>(
          adventureWorksClient_FullProductListCompleted);
      adventureWorksClient.FullProductListAsync();
    }

    void adventureWorksClient_FullProductListCompleted(
      object sender, FullProductListCompletedEventArgs e)
    {
      ProductsListBox.ItemsSource = e.Result;
    }
  }
}
```

When you run the sample, it takes a good 10 seconds to download and data bind the data, as it is a long list, but it demonstrates how to call a SOAP service in Windows Phone. Figure 4–10 has the UI.

Figure 4–10. *WebServicePage.xaml in action*

This concludes the demonstration on how to call SOAP web services. In the next section, we cover ADO.NET Data Services, and demonstrate accessing REST services with the OData client for Windows Phone.

REST+OData

We now switch to demonstrating how Windows Phone can access REST services using an OData client. A new WCF Data Service item named AdventureWorksRestOData.svc is added to the WcfRemoteServices project and the class is edited to look like the following:

```
namespace WcfRemoteServices.services
{
  public class AdventureWorksREST : DataService<AdventureWorksEntities>
  {
    public static void InitializeService(DataServiceConfiguration config)
    {
            config.SetEntitySetAccessRule("*", EntitySetRights.All);
      config.DataServiceBehavior.MaxProtocolVersion = DataServiceProtocolVersion.V2;
      config.SetEntitySetPageSize("*", 20);
    }
  }
}
```

Notice that the `DataService` class also uses the `AdventureWorksEntities` Entity Framework model as the basis for which objects it makes available via REST. A similar URL is used to access the service:

`http://localhost:9090/services/AdventureWorksRestOData.svc`

To retrieve the `Vendors` list, append the text `Vendors` to the end of this URL. Other REST operations are supported as well, but that's all it takes to create the REST Service.

In the Windows Phone client project named `CallingRemoteServices`, a new page is added, named `RestDataServicesODataPage.xaml`, where the `AdventureWorksREST` service is called. We need to generate a client proxy class for the REST service. We can use the new support for OData via the Visual Studio ➤ Add Service Reference functionality. Figure 4-11 shows the UI.

Figure 4–11. *Visual Studio Add Service Reference for OData Client*

After creating the reference, add the following using statement to `RestDataServicesODataPage.xaml.cs`:

`using CallingRemoteServices.AdventureWorksRestOData;`

Now that we have everything set up, we add a `ListBox` named `VendorsListBox` control to the `ContentPanel` Grid control in `RestDataServicesODataPage` XAML. We create a simple `DataTemplate` as well. Here is the XAML:

```xml
<ListBox.ItemTemplate>
  <DataTemplate>
    <StackPanel Margin="0,0,0,30">
      <TextBlock Text="{Binding Name}" />
      <TextBlock Text="{Binding AccountNumber}" />
      <StackPanel Orientation="Horizontal">
        <TextBlock Text="Credit Rating:" Margin="0,0,4,0"/>
        <TextBlock Text="{Binding CreditRating}" />
      </StackPanel>
    </StackPanel>
  </DataTemplate>
</ListBox.ItemTemplate>
</ListBox>
```

Listing 4–13 shows the code-behind for `RestDataServicesOdataPage.xaml`.

Listing 4–13. *The* `RestDataServicesOdataPage.xaml.cs` *Code File*

```csharp
using System;
using System.Data.Services.Client;
using System.Windows;
using Microsoft.Phone.Controls;
using CallingRemoteServices.AdventureWorksRestOData;

namespace CallingRemoteServices.pages
{
  public partial class RestDataServicesODataPage : PhoneApplicationPage
  {
    public RestDataServicesODataPage()
    {
      InitializeComponent();
    }

    private void PhoneApplicationPage_Loaded(object sender, RoutedEventArgs e)
    {
      AdventureWorksEntities context =
        new AdventureWorksEntities(
          new Uri("http://localhost:9090/services/AdventureWorksRestOData.svc"));

      DataServiceCollection<Vendor> vendors =
        new DataServiceCollection<Vendor>(context);
      //Add REST URL for collection
      VendorsListBox.ItemsSource = vendors;
      vendors.LoadAsync(new Uri("/Vendors", UriKind.Relative));
    }
  }
}
```

As you can see, it is pretty straightforward to connect to REST services with the OData client. You can support viewing collections of data, as well as inserting and deleting records. The sample named ODataClient_WinPhone7SampleApp.zip located at this link demonstrates viewing collections as well as inserting and deleting records:

`http://odata.codeplex.com/releases/view/54698#DownloadId=161862`

In the next section we cover accessing REST+JSON services directly.

Plain Old REST+JSON

There will be scenarios where you will build an application that connects to services created on non-Microsoft platforms that deliver JSON data over REST services. Another scenario is that you have a data-tier to retrieve data already created, and you just need to plug in that data-tier into a service that publishes the data via REST+JSON. This section provides an example of connecting to JSON data in those situations.

To have a completely fresh look at service creation for this scenario, another WCF Service Application project is added to the Chapter 4 solution named WcfRemoteServicesSimpleRestJSON. Use the refactoring capabilities in Visual Studio 2010 to change IService1 to IAdventureWorksRestJSON and to change the implementation from Service1 to AdventureWorksRestJSON. The IAdventureWorksRestJSON Interface is further modified to return rest data and it is provided a UriTemplate for the underlying GetVendors method. Listing 4–14 is the Interface IAdventureWorksRestJSON.

Listing 4–14. *The* IAdventureWorksRestJSON *Interface Code File*

```
using System.Collections.ObjectModel;
using System.ServiceModel;
using System.ServiceModel.Web;
using WcfRemoteServicesSimpleRestJSON.Models;

namespace WcfRemoteServicesSimpleRestJSON
{
  [ServiceContract]
  public interface IAdventureWorksRestJSON
  {
    [OperationContract]
    [WebGet(UriTemplate = "/Vendors",
      BodyStyle = WebMessageBodyStyle.Bare,
      ResponseFormat = WebMessageFormat.Json)]
    ObservableCollection<Vendor> GetVendors();

  }
}
```

Listing 4–15 provides the concrete implementation of the Interface.

Listing 4–15. *The* `IAdventureWorksRestJSON` *Interface Code File*

```
using WcfRemoteServicesSimpleRestJSON.Models;
using System.Collections.ObjectModel;

//TEST THE SERVICE: http://localhost:9191/AdventureWorksRestJSON.svc/Vendors

namespace WcfRemoteServicesSimpleRestJSON
{
  public class AdventureWorksRestJSON : IAdventureWorksRestJSON
  {

    public ObservableCollection<Vendor> GetVendors()
    {
      //Replace with real data layer here
      ObservableCollection<Vendor> vendors = new ObservableCollection<Vendor>()
      {
        new Vendor(){AccountNumber="111111", CreditRating=65,
          Name="Frabrikam Bikes" },
        new Vendor(){AccountNumber="222222", CreditRating=40,
          Name="Contoso Sports" },
        new Vendor(){AccountNumber="333333", CreditRating=30,
          Name="Duwamish Surfing Gear" },
      };

      return vendors;
    }

  }
}
```

The implementation simply creates an `ObservableCollection` of `Vendor` objects inline and returns the collection. Plug in your data layer here and using the refactoring capabilities to rename namespaces and classes in order to customize to your needs.

Using the refactoring capabilities in Visual Studio will automatically update the `web.config` that is in the project to match the new class names. Listing 4–16 shows the complete `web.config` file.

Listing 4–16. *Web.config file for AdventureWorksRestJSON Service*

```
</system.web>
<system.serviceModel>
  <behaviors>
    <serviceBehaviors>
      <behavior name="RestDataServiceBehavior">
        <serviceMetadata httpGetEnabled="true"  policyVersion="Policy15"/>
        <serviceDebug includeExceptionDetailInFaults="true" />
      </behavior>
    </serviceBehaviors>

    <endpointBehaviors>
      <behavior name="REST">
```

```
            <webHttp helpEnabled="true"/>
          </behavior>
        </endpointBehaviors>
      </behaviors>
      <services>
        <service behaviorConfiguration="RestDataServiceBehavior"
                name="WcfRemoteServicesSimpleRestJSON.AdventureWorksRestJSON">
        <endpoint address="" behaviorConfiguration="REST" binding="webHttpBinding"
          contract="WcfRemoteServicesSimpleRestJSON.IAdventureWorksRestJSON" />
        <endpoint address="mex" binding="mexHttpBinding" name="RestDataMetaData"
          contract="IMetadataExchange" />
        </service>
      </services>
      <serviceHostingEnvironment multipleSiteBindingsEnabled="true" />

    </system.serviceModel>
    <system.webServer>
      <modules runAllManagedModulesForAllRequests="true" />
      <directoryBrowse enabled="true" />
    </system.webServer>
</configuration>
```

Notice the address attribute for the <endpoint> element under the <services> element. There are two endpoints configured for the service: one to return data with an attribute of **address=""** and the other to return metadata with an **address="mex."** These addresses are relative to where the service is hosted. In this case, the project is hosted in the file **AdventureWorksRestJSON.svc**, which is part of the URL where the service is hosted:

http://localhost:9191/AdventureWorksRestJSON.svc

The WcfRemoteServicesSimpleRestJSON project's Web tab defines where the project is hosted, such as the port number. Now that we have a functioning service, we add a label to MainPage.xaml in the CallingRemoteServices project that navigates to a new page named AdventureWorksRestJSONPage.xaml. Save the project and switch to Expression Blend to edit the page. Uncomment the application bar, and four application bar buttons are added. A ListBox named VendorsListBox is added to the ContentPanel Grid. Two buttons titled "Add" and "Delete" are added beneath the VendorsListBox. The sample demonstrates the following things:

- Application bar button to show the returned JSON

- Application bar button that retrieves the JSON, parses it into a collection, and then data binds with the VendorsListBox

- Application bar button to save the current object list to isolated storage

- Application bar button to load from isolated storage the saved object list

- The Add button adds a record to the collection displayed in the VendorsListBox

- The Delete button deletes the currently selected record in the VendorsListBox

To test calling the REST+JSON service the leftmost application bar button calls the service and displays the returned JSON in a MessageBox:

```
#region Get Raw JSON data
HttpWebRequest request;
private void GetRawJSONDataAppBarBtn_Click(object sender, EventArgs e)
{
  request = WebRequest.CreateHttp("http://localhost:9191/AdventureWorksRestJSON.svc/Vendors");
  request.BeginGetResponse(new AsyncCallback(ReceiveRawJSONData), null);
}

string returnedResult;
void ReceiveRawJSONData(IAsyncResult result)
{
  WebResponse response = request.EndGetResponse(result);
  using (StreamReader reader = new StreamReader(response.GetResponseStream()))
  {
    returnedResult = reader.ReadToEnd();
  }
  LayoutRoot.Dispatcher.BeginInvoke(() =>
  {
    MessageBox.Show(returnedResult);
  });
}
#endregion
```

Figure 4–12 displays the returned JSON when the leftmost application bar is clicked.

Figure 4-12. *Raw JSON from the REST service*

The application bar button second to the left makes the same web call, but this time it serializes the JSON into a collection of Vendor objects. Here is the code:

```
#region Retrieve Vendors Data
private void GetVendorsAppbarBtn_Click(object sender, EventArgs e)
{
  request = WebRequest.CreateHttp("http://localhost:9191/AdventureWorksRestJSON.svc/Vendors");
  request.BeginGetResponse(new AsyncCallback(GetVendors), null);
}

//add a reference to System.Servicemodel.web to get DataContractJsonSerializer
void GetVendors(IAsyncResult result)
{
  DataContractJsonSerializer ser = null;
  WebResponse response = request.EndGetResponse(result);
  ser = new DataContractJsonSerializer(typeof(ObservableCollection<Vendor>));
  DataStore.Instance.Vendors = ser.ReadObject(response.GetResponseStream()) as
ObservableCollection<Vendor>;
  VendorsListBox.Dispatcher.BeginInvoke(() =>
  {
    VendorsListBox.ItemsSource = DataStore.Instance.Vendors;
  });
}
#endregion
```

This code uses the `DataContractJsonSerializer` class to deserialize the JSON data into `Vendor` objects. A Lambda expression (the =>) is used to fire an anonymous delegate back on the UI thread to data bind the Vendors collection to the `VendorsListBox`. The anonymous delegate is represented by the block created by the braces.

JSON.NET is very popular in the development community as an alternative JSON serializer to the `DataContractJsonSerializer` class. Many blog posts also claim that JSON.NET is faster at performing serialization over DataContractJsonSerialize. It also provides additional features, such as LINQ to JSON. Here is a link: `http://json.codeplex.com/`

In the previous code, you may have noticed the DataStore.Instance.Vendors object, which we will now explain. Windows Phone OS 7.1 SDK includes support for local database, which we covered earlier in the chapter. There are several third-party and open source solutions available to provide object persistence support, as well as an abstraction layer to hide boilerplate code. In this sample, we have a simple object database implementation as a lightweight alternative for situations where full database support isn't needed. See Listing 4–17 for the code.

Listing 4–17. The DataStore and Vendor Class Code File

```
using System;
using System.Collections.ObjectModel;
using System.ComponentModel;
using System.IO.IsolatedStorage;
using System.Runtime.Serialization;
using System.Runtime.Serialization.Json;

namespace RestJSON.DataModel
{
  sealed public class DataStore
  {
    //Declare suported collection types here
    public ObservableCollection<Vendor> Vendors { get; set; }

    //Provide a static read-only instance
    private static readonly DataStore instance = new DataStore();

    //Private Constructor for Singleton
    public DataStore() { }

    //The entry point into this Database
    public static DataStore Instance
    {
      get
      {
        return instance;
      }
    }

    //Deserialize ObservableCollection from JSON
    public T LoadCollection<T>(T collectionToLoad, string collectionName)
    {
      using (IsolatedStorageFile store =
              IsolatedStorageFile.GetUserStoreForApplication())
```

```csharp
      {
        if (store.FileExists(collectionName + ".txt"))
        {
          using (IsolatedStorageFileStream stream = store.OpenFile(
            collectionName + ".txt", System.IO.FileMode.Open))
          {
            DataContractJsonSerializer serializer =
              new DataContractJsonSerializer(typeof(T));
            return (T)serializer.ReadObject(stream);
          }
        }
        else
        {
          throw new Exception("Table not found");
        }
      }
    }

    //Serialize ObservableCollection to JSON
    public void SaveCollection<T>(T collectionToSave, string collectionName)
    {
      if (collectionToSave != null)
      {
        using (IsolatedStorageFile store =
              IsolatedStorageFile.GetUserStoreForApplication())
        {
          using (IsolatedStorageFileStream stream =
            store.CreateFile(collectionName + ".txt"))
          {
            DataContractJsonSerializer serializer =
              new DataContractJsonSerializer(typeof(T));
            serializer.WriteObject(stream, collectionToSave);
          }
        }
      }
    }

    //Delete ObservableCollection from Iso Storage
    public void DeleteCollection(string tableName)
    {
      using (IsolatedStorageFile store =
            IsolatedStorageFile.GetUserStoreForApplication())
      {
        if (store.FileExists(tableName + ".txt"))
        {
          store.DeleteFile(tableName + ".txt");
        }
      }
    }
  }
}

[DataContract()]
```

```
public class Vendor : INotifyPropertyChanged
{
  private string AccountNumberField;
  private byte CreditRatingField;
  private string NameField;

  [DataMemberAttribute()]
  public string AccountNumber
  {
    get
    {
      return this.AccountNumberField;
    }
    set
    {
      this.AccountNumberField = value;
      NotifyPropertyChanged("AccountNumber");
    }
  }

  [DataMemberAttribute()]
  public byte CreditRating
  {
    get
    {
      return this.CreditRatingField;
    }
    set
    {
      this.CreditRatingField = value;
      NotifyPropertyChanged("CreditRating");
    }
  }

  [DataMemberAttribute()]
  public string Name
  {
    get
    {
      return this.NameField;
    }
    set
    {
      this.NameField = value;
      NotifyPropertyChanged("Name");
    }
  }

  public event PropertyChangedEventHandler PropertyChanged;
  private void NotifyPropertyChanged(String propertyName)
  {
    if (null != PropertyChanged)
```

```
      {
          PropertyChanged(this, new PropertyChangedEventArgs(propertyName));
      }
    }
  }
}
```

The DataStore class shown in Listing 4–17 is not a lot of code, and it includes the Vendor class as well; but it provides a simple layer of abstraction that makes the code in the event handler much cleaner. Figure 4–13 shows the UI after the button second from the left is clicked.

Figure 4–13. *Vendor" data databound to ListBox*

The last two buttons use the DataStore class to save to isolated storage and retrieve the data from isolated storage. Here are the event handlers:

```
private void SaveVendorsAppbarBtn_Click(object sender, EventArgs e)
{
  DataStore.Instance.SaveTable<ObservableCollection<Vendor>>(
    DataStore.Instance.Vendors, "Vendors");
}

private void LoadVendorsAppbarBtn_Click(object sender, EventArgs e)
{
```

```
    DataStore.Instance.Vendors =
      DataStore.Instance.LoadTable<ObservableCollection<Vendor>>(
      DataStore.Instance.Vendors, "Vendors");
    VendorsListBox.ItemsSource = DataStore.Instance.Vendors;
}
```

The Vendors save and load functionality turns into simple code with the help of the `DataStore` class. When the data is loaded into the `VendorsListBox`, save the data, click the Start hardware button, and then click the back button. The Resuming… screen is displayed, and the data is not loaded. You can click the Load button to load the data from isolated storage and data bind it with the `VendorsListBox`. We cover how to manage application life cycle, also known as tombstoning, next.

The last two buttons in the UI are `Add` and `Delete`. Note that while the `Vendors` object collection that is part of the `DataStore` object is `read-only`, you can still add and remove objects from the collection. The read only modifier applies to the `Vendors` instance, not its underlying collection. The following is the code for the `Add` and `Delete` button:

```
private void addVendorButton_Click(object sender, RoutedEventArgs e)
{
  if (DataStore.Instance.Vendors != null)
  {
    DataStore.Instance.Vendors.Add(
    new Vendor()
    {
      AccountNumber = "555555",
      CreditRating = 45,
      Name = "Frabrikam Sports"
    });
  }
}

private void deleteButton_Click(object sender, RoutedEventArgs e)
{
  if (DataStore.Instance.Vendors != null)
  {
    DataStore.Instance.Vendors.Remove((Vendor)VendorsListBox.SelectedItem);
  }
}
```

The `Add` button is hard-coded to demonstrate how simple the operation is, but you could just as easily create a page with a set of controls that data bind to a new `Vendor` instance's properties and, upon clicking save, add the `Vendor` instance to the collection. The delete button removes the `Vendor` item selected in the `VendorsListBox` control from the underlying collection.

This concludes our discussion on connecting to remote services. Next up is the Bing Maps Control for Windows Phone, where we demonstrate adding pins to the map programmatically and via data binding tocollection.

Sockets

Windows Phone adds support for socket programming via the `System.Net.Sockets` namespace with support for UDP multicast clients. Multicast enables network clients to take advantage of multicast applications that more efficiently use network resources, which is critical with today's mobile data speeds.

I do not go into detail on socket development in this book. So many topics, so little time. Here are several links to help you get started:

Working with Multicast

```
http://msdn.microsoft.com/en-us/library/ee707325(v=VS.96).aspx
```

Working with Sockets

```
http://msdn.microsoft.com/en-us/library/cc296248(v=VS.96).aspx
```

For code samples check out these two links to code samples starting with a Tic-Tac-Toe Over Sockets Sample:

```
http://go.microsoft.com/fwlink/?LinkId=219075
```

The other sample is a Multicast sockets code sample available at this link:

```
http://go.microsoft.com/fwlink/?LinkId=221143
```

Bing Maps Control

The \Bing Maps control provides full mapping capabilities on Windows Phone. The control is optimized for mobile performance, including map tiles optimized for mobile bandwidth speeds.

The Bing Maps control fully supports Silverlight data binding for pushpin data with templates for plotting information. Users can pinch zoom the map, so it is not recommended to implement buttons for zooming in and out.

A new project named `BingMapsControl` is added to the Chapter 4 part 1 solution. A Bing Maps control is dropped into the `ContentPanel Grid` control, and two application bar buttons are enabled. The next three sections cover licensing, how to add a pin programmatically, and how to data bind to a collection of locations and plot on the Bing Maps control.

Licensing

As of this writing, the Bing Maps control is free to use for consumer-facing applications. This means if you are building a store locator, points of interest application, and so on that consumers would use, there is no licensing cost. To get started go to this URL to obtain an application key:

`www.bingmapsportal.com`

Set the `Application Type` to mobile for your mobile application. Next, set the key value in XAML, either directly or via data binding, for the `CredentialProvider` attribute:

```
<bing:Map Name=" TestBingMapsControl"
    CredentialsProvider="AppKeyGoesHere" />
```

It is really that simple to gain access to what is a very powerful Silverlight-based mapping control. The next two sections cover plotting data on the Bing Maps control.

Programmatically Add a Pin

There are many mobile scenarios where your application just needs to plot a single point, or a small number of points, and center the map on a point. In the `BingMapsControl` project's `MainPage.xaml` code file, the application bar is enabled. The left button plots a single point on the map by setting the location on a Pushpin object configured in the XAML. The following is the XAML for the Bing Maps Control:

```
<bing:Map Name="TestBingMapsControl"
  CredentialsProvider="…" >
  <bing:Pushpin x:Name="SinglePushpin" Visibility="Collapsed">
    <bing:Pushpin.Content>
      <Ellipse Width="25" Height="25" Fill="#FF00FF4A"/>
    </bing:Pushpin.Content>
  </bing:Pushpin>
</bing:Map>
```

Notice the `<bing:Pushpin>` object named `SinglePushpin` nested within the `Map` object The `Content` property for the Pushpin is set to an `Ellipse` object. Notice that `Visibility` is set to `Collapsed` initially. All that's missing is a location.

The event handler for the left application bar button titled "add a pin" sets the position on the `Pushpin` object by name and then configures `Visibility` to `Visible`. Here is the code:

```
private void AddaPinAppBarBtn_Click(object sender, EventArgs e)
{
  //SinglePushpin is defined in XAML
  GeoCoordinate location = new GeoCoordinate(34d, -84d);
  SinglePushpin.Location = location;
  SinglePushpin.Visibility = Visibility.Visible;

  //Center and Zoom in on point
  TestBingMapsControl.Center = location;
  TestBingMapsControl.ZoomLevel = 11;
  //Turn on zoom bar for emulator testing
  TestBingMapsControl.ZoomBarVisibility = Visibility.Visible;
}
```

The `Location` property for the `Pushpin` object is set and `Pushpin` made visible. The `Map` control is also centered on the configured `Location` and zoomed in a bit. Figure 4–14 shows the results of clicking the application bar button.

Figure 4–14. *Plot a single Pushpin object*

You could add another `Pushpin` object, and have one represent current location and the other represent desired location. Using `Pushpin` objects is a quick and easy way to get data on the `Map` control. For a large number of positions to plot, a `MapItems` control is recommended. We cover that in the next section.

Note that the zoom-in (+) and zoom-out (-) buttons are just there to ease development within the Emulator. You should have zoom-in and zoom-out buttons in a real application. The user should use pinch-zoom instead.

Data Bind to a Collection

In this section, we use the same `MainPage.xaml` and `TestBingMapsControl` Bing Maps control to plot a collection of points. A `<bing:MapItemsControl` is nested within the `TestBingMapsControl`. The `MapItemsControl` represents a collection of points to plot on the Bing Maps control.

Two classes are added to the project: `PushpinCollection` and `PlotPoint`. The class `PushpinCollection` publishes a list of `PlotPoint objects,` and provides a method to initialize the collection. The `PlotPoint` class represents a point that is plotted, containing `Quantity` and `Location` properties. `Quantity` is what is displayed and `Location` represents where to plot the point. Listing 4–18 contains the source for the classes.

Listing 4–18. The PushpinCatalog and PlotPoints Classes

```
using System.Collections.Generic;
using System.Device.Location;

namespace BingMapsControl
{
  public class PushpinCollection
  {
    private List<PlotPoint> points;
    public List<PlotPoint> Points { get { return points; } }

    public void InitializePointsCollection()
    {
      //Generate sample data to plot
      points = new List<PlotPoint>()
      {
        new PlotPoint()
        { Quantity = 50,
          Location= new GeoCoordinate(35d, -86d)
        },
        new PlotPoint()
        { Quantity = 40,
          Location= new GeoCoordinate(33d, -85d)
        },
         new PlotPoint()
        { Quantity = 60,
          Location= new GeoCoordinate(34d, -83d)
        },
        new PlotPoint()
        { Quantity = 20,
          Location= new GeoCoordinate(40d, -120d)
        },
      };
    }
  }

  public class PlotPoint
  {
    public int Quantity { get; set; }
    public GeoCoordinate Location { get; set; }
  }
}
```

Expression Blend is used to data bind the MapItemsControl to the Points collection of the PushpinCatalog class. A DataTemplate is created to render the PlotPoint items into a customized Pushpin template. Listing 4–19 the XAML for the BingMapsControl project's MainPage.xaml page.

Listing 4–19. The BingMapsControl's MainPage.xaml

```xml
<phone:PhoneApplicationPage
    xmlns="http://schemas.microsoft.com/winfx/2006/xaml/presentation"
    xmlns:x="http://schemas.microsoft.com/winfx/2006/xaml"
    xmlns:phone="clr-namespace:Microsoft.Phone.Controls;assembly=Microsoft.Phone"
    xmlns:shell="clr-namespace:Microsoft.Phone.Shell;assembly=Microsoft.Phone"
    xmlns:d="http://schemas.microsoft.com/expression/blend/2008"
    xmlns:mc="http://schemas.openxmlformats.org/markup-compatibility/2006"
    xmlns:bing="clr-namespace:Microsoft.Phone.Controls.Maps;assembly=Microsoft.
.Phone.Controls.Maps"
    xmlns:local="clr-namespace:BingMapsControl"
    x:Class="BingMapsControl.MainPage"
    mc:Ignorable="d" d:DesignWidth="480" d:DesignHeight="696"
    SupportedOrientations="Portrait" Orientation="Portrait"
    shell:SystemTray.IsVisible="True"
    >

  <phone:PhoneApplicationPage.Resources>
    <local:PushpinCollection x:Key="PushpinCollectionDataSource" d:IsDataSource="True"/>
    <DataTemplate x:Key="PlotPointDataTemplate">
      <Grid>
        <bing:Pushpin Location="{Binding Location}"
         ToolTipService.ToolTip="{Binding Quantity}" />
      </Grid>
    </DataTemplate>
  </phone:PhoneApplicationPage.Resources>
  <phone:PhoneApplicationPage.FontFamily>
    <StaticResource ResourceKey="PhoneFontFamilyNormal"/>
  </phone:PhoneApplicationPage.FontFamily>
  <phone:PhoneApplicationPage.FontSize>
    <StaticResource ResourceKey="PhoneFontSizeNormal"/>
  </phone:PhoneApplicationPage.FontSize>
  <phone:PhoneApplicationPage.Foreground>
    <StaticResource ResourceKey="PhoneForegroundBrush"/>
  </phone:PhoneApplicationPage.Foreground>
  <phone:PhoneApplicationPage.ApplicationBar>
    <shell:ApplicationBar IsVisible="True" IsMenuEnabled="True">
      <shell:ApplicationBarIconButton x:Name="AddaPinAppBarBtn"
                IconUri="/icons/appbar.favs.addto.rest.png"
                Text="add a pin" Click="AddaPinAppBarBtn_Click"/>
      <shell:ApplicationBarIconButton x:Name="DatabindAppBarBtn"
                IconUri="/icons/appbar.refresh.rest.png"
                Text="data bind" Click="DatabindAppBarBtn_Click"/>
    </shell:ApplicationBar>
  </phone:PhoneApplicationPage.ApplicationBar>

  <!--LayoutRoot is the root grid where all page content is placed-->
  <Grid x:Name="LayoutRoot" Background="Transparent"
    DataContext="{Binding Source={StaticResource PushpinCollectionDataSource}}">
    <Grid.RowDefinitions>
      <RowDefinition Height="Auto"/>
```

```xml
      <RowDefinition Height="*"/>
    </Grid.RowDefinitions>

    <!--TitlePanel contains the name of the application and page title-->
    <StackPanel x:Name="TitlePanel" Grid.Row="0" Margin="12,17,0,28">
      <TextBlock x:Name="ApplicationTitle" Text="CHAPTER 4"
              Style="{StaticResource PhoneTextNormalStyle}"/>
      <TextBlock x:Name="PageTitle" Text="bing maps control" Margin="9,-7,0,0"
                Style="{StaticResource PhoneTextTitle1Style}"/>
    </StackPanel>

    <!--ContentPanel - place additional content here-->
    <Grid x:Name="ContentPanel" Grid.Row="1" Margin="12,0,12,0">
      <bing:Map x:Name="TestBingMapsControl"
        CredentialsProvider="your bing maps AppID goes here" >
        <bing:MapItemsControl Name="mapLayer"
          ItemTemplate="{StaticResource PlotPointDataTemplate}"
          ItemsSource="{Binding Points}"/>
        <bing:Pushpin x:Name="SinglePushpin" Visibility="Collapsed">
          <Ellipse Width="25" Height="25" Fill="#FF00FF4A"/>
        </bing:Pushpin>
      </bing:Map>
    </Grid>
  </Grid>
</phone:PhoneApplicationPage>
```

The following is the application bar button event handler that loads the Points collection:

```csharp
private void DatabindAppBarBtn_Click(object sender, EventArgs e)
{
  PushpinCollection collection = LayoutRoot.DataContext as PushpinCollection;
  if (collection != null)
    collection.InitializePointsCollection();
}
```

This code needs to grab the instance of the PushpinCollection that is configured as the DataContext of the LayoutRoot Grid object. See Figure 4–15.

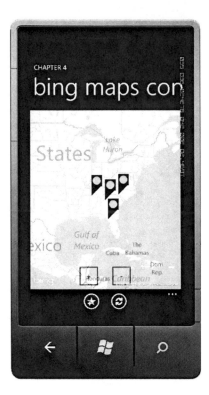

Figure 4-15. Plot a collection of points

Application Execution Model

We cover Application Execution Model, aka tombstoning, in this chapter since it relates to restoring the application UI, which will generally include data retrieved via network APIs. While Windows Phone adds support for background processing via agents, applications executing in the foreground still need to handle situations when moving from the active to an inactive application.

Windows Phone OS 7.1 adds support for Fast App Switching (FAS), which keeps applications in memory until memory pressure requires that an application tombstone. In many situations where users are switching back and forth between applications, tombstoning is averted with FAS. Still, it is not guaranteed so developers must understand how to implement FAS with tombstoning together for the best application experience.

We start with an overview of the user experience without Fast Application Switching, and then detail what happens under the hood. Finally the section explains how to manage application state within the available framework, as well as how to implement Fast Application Switching, which is available in Windows Phone OS 7.1 for the best experience.

User Experience

If you have a Windows Phone device, you are familiar with the navigation model. You know that the `Start` and the `Back` hardware button play an important role in the navigation model. The navigation model is similar to web browser navigation, which suggests that the phone maintains a `back-stack` of pages previously visited. Given that third-party applications do not multitask with other third-party applications in the current release, this brings up an intriguing question: what happens when you navigate back to a previous third-party application?

You probably noticed in previous examples that if you dynamically loaded data either via code or a remote service call, if you hit the Start button and then the Back button, the blank Resuming… screen is displayed and the application UI is rendered, but is missing the dynamic data. This happens because, while the operating system keeps a record in the back-stack of which apps have run previously, it does not maintain application state. Applications have the responsibility with the operating system to restore the application to its previous state.

Event Lifecycle

If you are a Windows Forms or WPF developer, you are familiar with these four events related to application life cycle:

- `Launching`: Application initially loads

- `Closing`: Application is excited by the user

- `Activated`: Application comes to the foreground

- `Deactivated`: Application loses focus

On Windows Phone, these events retain their general meaning, but with a twist. `Launching` and `Closing` work as expected. The `Launching` event fires upon initially launching the application. `Closing` fires upon exit.

The `Deactivated` event fires when the application loses focus when a hardware button is tapped, a phone call comes in, and so on. But the twist is that instead of continuing to run, the application is shut down, and an entry in the back-stack is made.

If the user navigates back to the application via the placeholder in the back-stack, the `Activated` event fires and the application resumes. Even though the application is no longer running when the `Deactivated` event fires, the `Closing` event does not fire. Same when the application launches upon resume in the `Activated` event; the Launching event does not fire.

For this section, the code for calling REST+JSON services in the `CallingRemoteServices` project is copied into this project to give us some interesting data to work with. We add additional code to log what is happening via the Visual Studio Output window using `Debug.WriteLine,` so as to not interfere with basic application functionality, but to let us know what is happening.

■ **Note** Configure both the `WcfRemoteServicesSimpleRestJSON` and `AppExecutionModel` projects as startup projects for the solution to ensure the service is running.

The application lifecycle events are not attached to the individual pages, like `MainPage.xaml`. Instead, the events are attached to the Application object directly via the `Microsoft.Phone.Shell.PhoneApplicationService` class as part of the `Application.ApplicationLifetimObjects` collection. The lifecycle events are already created for you when you start a new project. In this project a few more events are added to the code:

- Application_Startup

- Application_Exit

- MainPage - PhoneApplicationPage_Loaded

- MainPage - PhoneApplicationPage_Unloaded

- MainPage - PhoneApplicationPage_BackKeyPress

The application uses `Debug.WriteLine("")` to log when in an event handler. Let's now run the application, close the application, and then review the logged events in the Output Window.

```
In App constructor
In Application_Startup
In Application_Launching
In MainPage Constructor
In PhoneApplicationPage_Loaded
In PhoneApplicationPage_BackKeyPress
In Application_Closing
In Application_Exit
```

Let's next load the application, click the Start button, navigate back, and then hit the back button again to exit the application.

```
In App constructor
In Application_Startup
In Application_Launching
In MainPage Constructor
In PhoneApplicationPage_Loaded
In Application_Deactivated
'taskhost.exe' (Managed): Loaded 'System.Runtime.Serialization.dll'
In Application_Exit
…navigate to Start screen,application tombstones, and then navigate back to application
In App constructor
In Application_Startup
In Application_Activated
In MainPage Constructor
In PhoneApplicationPage_Loaded
In PhoneApplicationPage_BackKeyPress
In Application_Closing
In Application_Exit
```

You can see that the `Page` and `Application` constructors and `Page_Loaded` fire every time, whether as part of initial launch or when resuming from tombstoning. Same for `Application_Exit`. It fires whether tombstoning or actually exiting the application. You will really want to understand this event cycle to ensure that you place code in the appropriate event handler, depending on what's desired. The next section discusses how to maintain state.

Managing State

Let's now add state management to the code copied from the `AdventureWorksRestJSONPage` page in the `CallingRemoteServices` project. First, let's generate random state in the App() constructor and store in a variable named `randomState` as a string. The state will be the current `DateTime.Now` value when the application is launched. It will be saved in `Application_Deactivated`, and restored in `Application_Activated`. The application will use `Debug.WriteLine` to log the state in `App.xaml.cs`. Here is the code to initialize state:

```
if (PhoneApplicationService.Current.StartupMode ==
    StartupMode.Launch)
{
  Debug.WriteLine("In App constructor");
  randomState = DateTime.Now.ToString();
  Debug.WriteLine("Random State: = " + randomState);
}
```

Notice that the code in App() to initialize state checks to ensure the application is Launching and not Activating. This is because the constructor is called in both cases as shown in the previous section.

The recommended location to store application state is in `PhoneApplicationService.Current.State`, which is of type `IDictionary<string, object>`. The "key" is a `string`, and the state is of type `object`, which means it can store any serializable object, including complex objects that contain objects. Here is the code to save in `Application_Deactivated` and restore in `Application_Activated`:

```
// Code to execute when the application is activated (brought to foreground)
// This code will not execute when the application is first launched
private void Application_Activated(object sender, ActivatedEventArgs e)
{
  Debug.WriteLine("Activating - load state");
  IDictionary<string, object> state =
    PhoneApplicationService.Current.State;
  if (state.ContainsKey("Random State"))
  {
    randomState = state["Random State"] as String;
  }
  Debug.WriteLine("Random State Restore - " + randomState);
  Debug.WriteLine("In Application_Activated");
}


// Code to execute when the application is deactivated (sent to background)
// This code will not execute when the application is closing
private void Application_Deactivated(object sender, DeactivatedEventArgs e)
{
  Debug.WriteLine("Deactivating - save state");
  IDictionary<string, object> state =
    PhoneApplicationService.Current.State;
  state["Random State"] = randomState;
  Debug.WriteLine("In Application_Deactivated");
}
```

The `Application_Deactivated` event adds the data to the State object. The `Application_Activated` event restores state, but first uses `State.ContainsKey` to make sure the state information is present before trying to retrieve the state using the key value.

▓ **Caution** Applications have 10 seconds in both Application_Deactivated and Application_Activated to complete work. If saving or loading data goes beyond 10 seconds, the operating system will end the event handler.

The following is the data from the Output window after launching the app, clicking the Start button, and then the Back button:

```
In App constructor
Random State: = 1/24/2011 11:59:26 PM
In Application_Startup
In Application_Launching
In MainPage Constructor
In PhoneApplicationPage_Loaded
Deactivating - save state
In Application_Deactivated
In Application_Exit
In Application_Startup
Activating - load state
Random State Restore - 1/24/2011 11:59:26 PM
In Application_Activated
In MainPage Constructor
In PhoneApplicationPage_Loaded
In PhoneApplicationPage_BackKeyPress
In Application_Closing
In Application_Exit
```

As an alternative, you can handle state management at the page level. In many ways, this method makes more sense, because it is easier to restore the data as close to where it is needed, as opposed to restoring in App.xaml.cs and then passing it along. The code in MainPage.xaml.cs overrides the OnNavigatedFrom and OnNavigatedTo methods as shown here:

```
protected override void OnNavigatedFrom(
  System.Windows.Navigation.NavigationEventArgs e)
{
  base.OnNavigatedFrom(e);
  IDictionary<string, object> state = PhoneApplicationService.Current.State;
  state["Selected Item"] = VendorsListBox.SelectedIndex;
  DataStore.Instance.SaveCollection<ObservableCollection<Vendor>>(
    DataStore.Instance.Vendors, "Vendors");
}

protected override void OnNavigatedTo(
  System.Windows.Navigation.NavigationEventArgs e)
{
  base.OnNavigatedTo(e);
  if (PhoneApplicationService.Current.StartupMode ==
    StartupMode.Activate)
  {
    //Load data from isolated storage
    DataStore.Instance.Vendors =
```

```
DataStore.Instance.LoadCollection<ObservableCollection<Vendor>>(
DataStore.Instance.Vendors, "Vendors");
VendorsListBox.ItemsSource = DataStore.Instance.Vendors;
// The state bag for  temporary state
IDictionary<string, object> state =
  PhoneApplicationService.Current.State;
// See if the bag contains the selected item
if (state.ContainsKey("Selected Item"))
{
  //Set selected item on page
  VendorsListBox.SelectedIndex = (int)state["Selected Item"];
  //Scroll to selected item
  VendorsListBox.ScrollIntoView(
    VendorsListBox.Items[VendorsListBox.SelectedIndex]);
  }
 }
}
```

Notice that the code does not save the Vendors collection to the
PhoneApplicationService.Current.State object. The application could do that, but it seems to make
sense to persist the major data collections where they would normally be saved, as opposed to being
temporary state. On the other hand, saving the selected item makes sense, because when the user
returns to the application after resume, the user will expect to see the application state just as they left it.

When you run the application, retrieve it from the service and then tombstone it by clicking a
hardware button; then click the Back button to resume. Notice that the data is restored, and the current
item is selected in the VendorsListBox control. To the user, it is as if the application continued to run
when it really hadn't.

Understanding and supporting good life-cycle management is critical to providing a robust user
interface. With good state management, a user will not even notice that the application stopped
running. While we demonstrated tombstoning and persisting data in the MainPage class, in Chapter 6 we
pick up the programming model discussion again starting with how to architect Silverlight for Windows
Phone applications correctly to manage these scenarios.

Running Under Lock Screen

You can configure an application to run under the lock screen. This means that when the phone lock
careen activates, the application continues to run in the foreground and is not tombstoned. This also
means that the application continues to consume CPU and more importantly battery when running
under the lock screen. Here is a link to the documentation:

http://msdn.microsoft.com/en-us/library/ff941090%28v=VS.92%29.aspx

In Windows Phone 7, there are some application scenarios in which running under the lock screen
greatly enhances the user experience. An application that records GPS values while running under lock
for a run tracker program is an excellent example. Many of these situations are addressed in Windows
Phone OS 7.1 via background processing such as background audio agents, file transfer agents, etc. With
these improvements it is recommended to not implement idle detection/run under lock screen in
Windows Phone 7.5

If you still need to run under lock screen, it is pretty straightforward to implement. Essentially
configure ApplicationIdleDetectionMode to disabled in App.xaml.cs:

PhoneApplicationService.Current.ApplicationIdleDetectionMode = IdleDetectionMode.Disabled;

Handle the Application's `RootFrame Obscured` and UnObscured events. When the application is Obscured, execute code to reduce CPU cycles as much as possible to conserve battery. In the UnObscured event, restart application functionality to restore the application or game.

Fast Application Switching

In Windows Phone 7, applications are automatically terminated when the user navigates away, as covered previously. In Windows Phone OS 7.1 (Mango), applications are put into a dormant state when the user navigates away instead of being tombstoned. When dormant, the application state is preserved in memory so that if the user returns to the application, it can resume almost instantly. This is a huge improvement for applications with large memory states, like XNA Framework games.

Applications do not need to implement any code to enable Fast Application Switching (FAS); it is enabled automatically. However, it is still possible that an application will be terminated while it is dormant so you still need to implement the tombstoning code covered previously. Also, you need to detect if restoring from a dormant state (FAS), or if resuming from a tombstoned state. You do not want to do all the work to resume from tombstone if it is not needed because of FAS.

To demonstrate FAS, I copy over the AppExecutionModel project from the Chapter 4 part 1 solution and add it to the Chapter 4 part 2 solution and rename the project to FASAppExecutionModel. The first code change I made is in App.xaml.cs in the Application_Activated event. I add code to check if the application instance is preserved (was dormant) and return if that is the case:

```
if (e.IsApplicationInstancePreserved)
{
  Debug.WriteLine("Not Tombstoned - Resume from dormant state");
  return;
}
```

This code gets us partially there. We still have the restore from tombstone code in the `MainPage.xaml.cs` OnNavigatedTo method. This method will execute every time the page is navigated to so we add additional code to detect whether we have a new page instance (i.e., initial app launch/restoring from tombstone) or if we are returning from the dormant state.

I add a Boolean variable to `MainPage.xaml.cs` that I use to track whether a new page is created or whether restoring from dormant state and the page already exists:

```
bool _returnfromTombstone = false;
```

In the `MainPage` constructor, set the variable to true to indicate that this is a new instance of the page so it may be returning from tombstone or that it is the initial launch of the application:

```
public MainPage()
{
  InitializeComponent();
  Debug.WriteLine("In MainPage Constructor");

  //Add temporal state to the page
  //that a new page instance was created
  _returnfromTombstone = true;
}
```

The last bit of code is a check in the `MainPage.OnNavigatedTo` event where I check to see if the application is returning from tombstoning or initial launch. If it is returning from tombstoning or is the initial launch of the application, load up data. At the end of `OnNavigatedTo` set `_returnfromTombstone` to false. This way when the application returns from the dormant state (no tombstone), the page instance is preserved and _returnfromTombstone will remain false and the tombstoning code will not run in OnNavigatedTo because it is not needed.

Run the application with breakpoints in the constructor and OnNavigatedTo to see how it works. As you can see, Fast Application Switching is pretty easy to implement, and your end-users will appreciate it.

Conclusion

In this chapter we started by covering how to identify users, the device, network status, and application trial mode status for Windows Phone, and then investigated application data persistence with Isolated Storage. We also dove into the new Local Database functionality available in Windows Phone OS 7.1

We next covered how to access remote services with Windows Phone, including SOAP, REST, OData, and REST+JSON based services. An overview of the new socket support available in Windows Phone is provided as well.

This chapter also covered how to load HTML into the WebBrowser control, as well as how to call HTML script from Silverlight and how to call Silverlight methods from HTML script. The chapter moved on to cover the Bing Maps control and the Application Execution Model in detail including Fast Application Switching. In the next chapter, we cover how to integrate deeply with Windows Phone.

CHAPTER 5

■ ■ ■

Integrating with the Windows Phone Platform

In the previous chapter, we covered the Windows Phone programming model. We covered handing input in a Windows Phone application in Chapter 3, and rendering a UI in Chapter 2. With the fundamentals covered for input and output, let's now take a closer look at how you can integrate more closely with the Windows Phone platform.

In this chapter, we start first with the APIs available on Windows Phone to obtain information about either the device or the user. We also cover how to interact with the Clipboard, and work with ringtones and alarms.

We next cover the tasks and choosers, APIs that enable a Windows Phone application to interact with other software components on the phone, such as the web browser from within the application.

We next explore how to work with Windows Phone contacts and calendar.

Device Information

Developers need to understand the state of a device in order to provide the best experience for end users, such as letting the user know when a large download is about to begin and asking if the user would like to switch to a wireless or Ethernet connection via USB.

In this section, we cover the different pieces of device status and information that are available via the Windows Phone APIs, including user identifiers, device identifiers, network status, and device capabilities. The Chapter 5 project DeviceInfo demonstrates these APIs in action.

Most of the code for device information is simply a matter of displaying string-based properties, so the only code listed in this section is for network availability info. Otherwise, please refer to the DeviceInfo project in the source code for additional detail. The next subsection starts with user and device identification first.

Identifying Unique Users

There is a properties class for user information available in this release of Windows Phone, which is contained in Microsoft.Phone.Info.dll. It supports exactly one value, Anonymous Identifier (ANID), which can be used to identify the user. Here are the full namespace, class, and method calls to obtain a user identifier:

```
Microsoft.Phone.Info.UserExtendedProperties.GetValue("ANID")
Microsoft.Phone.Info.UserExtendedProperties.TryGetValue("ANID")
```

How unique is this ID? It identifies the user with the same value, even if the user owns multiple phones. This value is maintained across reboots. Even if you factory-reset the phone, but configure it with the same Live ID, you will get the same value for the ANID property.

■ **Note** The ANID property returns an empty string in the emulator.

Using this property requires the user identity capability and the ID_CAP_IDENTITY_DEVICE entry in the Capabilities section of WMAppManifest.xml for the application. If an application uses this class, the user will be alerted that the application requires this capability in the Windows Phone Marketplace. You should only use this capability if your application absolutely needs it, and if it provides a direct benefit to the user in some fashion; for example, if it makes it possible to store and retrieve from the cloud settings and data tied to the ID. Developers should mention the benefit in the application description; otherwise, users may be less inclined to download your application.

Device Information

There is a separate properties class for device information in Microsoft.Phone.Info.dll called DeviceExtendedProperties. It provides the ability to uniquely identify a device. Unlike the UserExtendedProperties class, the DeviceExtendedProperties class supports more than one value. The method call is the same as for the user property:

```
Microsoft.Phone.Info.DeviceExtendedProperties.GetValue()
Microsoft.Phone.Info.DeviceExtendedProperties.TryGetValue()
```

In Window Phone OS 7.1, only one value has not been deprecated, DeviceUniqueID."""" The DeviceUniqueID value will uniquely identify a device across all installed applications, even if the phone is updated with a new operating system version. This ID should not be used to identify users, because it is tied to the device, not the user.

■ **Note** Accessing DeviceUniqueID in the emulator returns false for TryGetValue.

If your application can use the DeviceUniqueID in a way that benefits the user, you should use it; be sure, however, to mention why you use it in the application description, so that the user understands the benefit. Otherwise, cautious users may shy away from downloading your application.

■ **Caution** Most of the properties in the DeviceExtendedProperties class are depreciated in Windows Phone OS 7.1. Use the DeviceStatus class instead.

In Windows Phone OS 7.1 (Mango), additional device information is available via the Microsoft.Phone.Info namespace in the DeviceStatus class. Some of the information replaces what you can obtain using the DeviceExtendedProperties, as listed here:

ApplicationCurrentMemoryUsage (replacement)

ApplicationMemoryUsageLimit (new)

ApplicationPeakMemoryUsage (replacement)

DeviceFirmwareVersion (replacement)

DeviceHardwareVersion (replacement)

DeviceManufacturer (replacement)

DeviceName (duplicate)

DeviceTotalMemory (replacement)

IsKeyboardDeployed (new)

IsKeyboardPresent (new)

PowerSource (new)

KeyboardDeployedChanged event (new)

PowerSourceChanged event (new)

The last memory reporting properties are very important to track. In Chapter 3 we mentioned using a DispatcherTimer and an event handler to track the values in the Visual Studio Output Tool window using the DeviceExtendedProperties implementation. In the Chapter 5 DeviceInfo project, an updated DebugMemoryInfo timer event is wired up as shown in Listing 5-1.

Listing 5-1. *Sample DispatcherTimer Tick Event to Record Debug Info*

```
void DebugMemoryInfo_Tick(object sender, EventArgs e)
{
  System.Diagnostics.Debug.WriteLine("<------------------->");
  //GC.GetTotalMemory(true);
  string deviceTotalMemory =
    (DeviceStatus.DeviceTotalMemory / (1024 * 1024)).ToString() + "MB";
  string applicationCurrentMemoryUsage =
    (DeviceStatus.ApplicationCurrentMemoryUsage / (1024 * 1024)).ToString() + "MB";
  string applicationPeakMemoryUsage =
  (DeviceStatus.ApplicationPeakMemoryUsage / (1024 * 1024)).ToString() + "MB";
  System.Diagnostics.Debug.WriteLine("--> " +
    DateTime.Now.ToLongTimeString());
  System.Diagnostics.Debug.WriteLine("--> Device Total : " +
    deviceTotalMemory);
  System.Diagnostics.Debug.WriteLine("--> App Current : " +
    applicationCurrentMemoryUsage);
  System.Diagnostics.Debug.WriteLine("--> App Peak : " +
    applicationPeakMemoryUsage);
  System.Diagnostics.Debug.WriteLine("");
}
```

Certification requirements dictate that memory usage remain under 90MB, because some devices can have just 256MB, and 90MB is what Microsoft has determined is optimal. Applications can temporarily go over 90MB and not fail certification in some cases, such as if the application is transitioning pages and one page is going out of memory and another is loading data structures for display. In general, with memory-constrained devices, it is important to allocate memory efficiently to maximize performance. This is true for any mobile device application, regardless of the operating system, and it is something that makes mobile development a fun challenge: squeezing out every little bit of performance possible!

System Environment Information

The System.Environment class provides the following information on the current environment via its properties:

CurrentDirectory

HasShutdownStarted

OSVersion (includes Platform and Version properties; Version has additional properties of Build, Major, Minor, and Revision)

TickCount (since last reboot)

Version (CLR version)

The next section starts with a very important topic when you are building mobile applications that depend on data in the cloud: current network status.

Network Status

Mobile applications must be thoughtful in using phone resources, such as data connectivity, and offer the user information when using the data connection. The Windows Phone namespace Microsoft.Phone.Net.NetworkInformation provides the NetworkInterface object with the following two useful static members:

NetworkInterface.GetIsNetworkAvailable method

NetworkInterface.NetworkInterfaceType property

The GetIsNetworkAvailable method returns true or false. The NetworkInterface property stores a value from the Microsoft.Phone.Net.NetworkInformation.NetworkInterfaceType enumeration. Table 5--1 lists the common values in which most developers will be interested. You can find the full list at

http://msdn.microsoft.com/en-us/library/microsoft.phone.net.networkinformation
.networkinterfacetype(VS.92).aspx

Table 5-1. *NetworkInterfaceType Enumeration Common Values*

Enumeration Value	Description
None	No interface exists to provide access to the Internet.
Ethernet	The network interface is of type Ethernet. When connected via Zune and the PC, this is the value that is returned.
MobileBroadbandGSM	This is the value returned when connected over a wireless GSM network (AT&T or T-Mobile in the U.S. and most of the world).
MobileBroadbandCdma	This is the value returned when connected over a wireless CDMA network (Verizon and Sprint in the U.S. and other regions of the world).
Wireless80211	The network interface is a wireless LAN connection.

One item to note is that when connected to the PC without Zune running, the network connection will return either MobileBroadband or Wireless80211 if a connection is available over those protocols. Zune must be running when connected to the PC in order to have an Ethernet connection.

You may be tempted to poll network status on a background thread, but that would not be battery-efficient. Instead, the code can subscribe to the System.Net.NetworkInformation.NetworkChange.NetworkAddressChanged static event. The System.Net.NetworkInformation namespace also includes a NetworkInterface class, so you will need to disambiguate namespaces.

In the DeviceInfo project, we add two TextBlock controls and two TextBox controls to store network availability and connection type, storing network availability status in the NetworkAvailableTextbox control, and network connection type in the NetworkConnectionTextbox control. Listing 5-2 has the code from the DeviceInfo project that performs network detection.

Listing 5-2. *Network Detection Method*

```
#region Network Status Check
private void SetupNetworkStatusCheck()
{
  NetworkChange.NetworkAddressChanged +=
    new NetworkAddressChangedEventHandler
        (NetworkChange_NetworkAddressChanged);
  //Initialize values
  NetworkAvailableTextBlock.Text =
    PhoneNetworkApi.NetworkInterface.GetIsNetworkAvailable().ToString();
  NetworkConnectionTextBlock.Text =
    PhoneNetworkApi.NetworkInterface.NetworkInterfaceType.ToString();
}

void NetworkChange_NetworkAddressChanged(object sender, EventArgs e)
{
  NetworkAvailableTextBlock.Text =
    PhoneNetworkApi.NetworkInterface.GetIsNetworkAvailable().ToString();
```

```
    NetworkConnectionTextBlock.Text =
        PhoneNetworkApi.NetworkInterface.NetworkInterfaceType.ToString();
}
#endregion
```

Determining the Mobile Operator

Sometimes a developer may need to determine who the mobile operator is for the device, perhaps offering additional features on a preloaded application as an example. This information is easy enough to obtain on Windows Phone with this call:

```
Microsoft.Phone.Net.NetworkInformation.DeviceNetworkInformation.CellularMobileOperator
```

I've added this call to the Network Info section of the `DeviceInfo` project in the Chapter 5 solution.

Determining Available Network Services

Quite often, a developer may need to determine the available network before performing a network operation. For example, an application may not want to kick off a large download if the user is currently roaming. Or if an application determines that Wi-Fi is not enabled, it may want to prompt the user to enable Wi-Fi prior to kicking off a large download. In Windows Phone 7.5 (Mango), you can now determine these capabilities with the following three properties:

```
DeviceNetworkInformation.IsCellularDataEnabled
DeviceNetworkInformation.IsCellularDataRoamingEnabled
DeviceNetworkInformation.IsWiFiEnabled
```

We'll use these calls in the Network Info section of the `DeviceInfo` project in the Chapter 5 solution.

Socket Network Information

The `Microsoft.Phone.Net.NetworkInformation` namespace provides extension methods to the Socket class. You can use the `GetCurrentNetworkInterface(Socket)` extension method to help determine whether the network interface is using a GSM or CDMA network, or the network is using a Wi-Fi connection.

You must establish a connection for the `GetCurrentNetworkInterface(Socket)` call to work. The sample code provides an implementation that makes a socket connection and then calls the method. This means that you need to have a server to talk to that also exposes a socket.

You can turn your PC into a socket server by enabling Simple TCP/IP services, which provide the services shown in Table 5-2.

Table 5-2. Simple TCP/IP Services

Service Name	Description	Port
Echo	Echoes back data from any messages it receives on the server port.	7
Quote of the Day	Returns a quotation of one or more lines of text taken at random from the following file: %SYSTEMROOT%\System32\Drivers\Etc\Quotes	17
Daytime	Returns day of the week, month, day, year, current time, and timezone info.	13
Character Generator	Sends data made up of the set of 95 ASCHII printable characters.	19
Discard	Discards all messages received on this port without response or acknowledgement.	9

You can add Simple TCP/IP Services to your computer by going to Start ➤ Control Panel ➤ Select Programs and Features and clicking Turn Windows Features ON or Off. In the Windows Features dialog, scroll down and select Simple TCP/IP Services and then click OK.

You will need to start the Simple TCP/IP Services. Go to the Start menu, type **View Local Services** to launch View Local Services, scroll down in the list to Simple TCP/IP Services, right-click, and select Start. With your socket server set up, the code is pretty straightforward.

In the Chapter 5 DeviceInfo project, this method establishes a socket connection and lets us check the network configuration:

```
private void EstablishSocketConnectionAndCheckNetwork()
{
  Socket socket =
    new Socket(AddressFamily.InterNetwork, SocketType.Stream,
      ProtocolType.Tcp);
  string serverName = "192.168.0.119";
  int portNumber = 7;
  //create DNS end point
  DnsEndPoint hostEntry = new DnsEndPoint(serverName, portNumber);
  //Create Event args and w.ire up completed event
  SocketAsyncEventArgs socketEventArg = new SocketAsyncEventArgs();
  socketEventArg.RemoteEndPoint = hostEntry;
  socketEventArg.UserToken = socket;
  socketEventArg.Completed += new
EventHandler<SocketAsyncEventArgs>(socketEventArg_Completed);
  //Connect to the socket
  socket.ConnectAsync(socketEventArg);
}
```

The connection is attempted and the results are fired in the socketEventArg_Completed event handler:

```
void socketEventArg_Completed(object sender, SocketAsyncEventArgs e)
{
  // When ConnectAsync is called, the socket object is passed in as part
  // of the socketEventArg UserToken value.
  Socket socket = e.UserToken as Socket;
  if (e.SocketError == SocketError.Success)
  {
    PhoneNetworkApi.NetworkInterfaceInfo netInterfaceInfo =
      socket.GetCurrentNetworkInterface();
    Dispatcher.BeginInvoke(() =>
    {
      SocketInterfaceNameTextBlock.Text = netInterfaceInfo.InterfaceName;
      SocketInterfaceNameTextBlock.Text = netInterfaceInfo.InterfaceName;
      SocketNetworkStateTextBlock.Text = netInterfaceInfo.InterfaceState.ToString();
      SocketNetworkTypeTextBlock.Text = netInterfaceInfo.InterfaceType.ToString();
      SocketNetworkSubTypeTextBlock.Text = netInterfaceInfo.InterfaceSubtype.ToString();
    });
  }
}
```

When you run the application connected via USB, it successfully connects to port 8 on my PC and returns the connected network interface info.

DeviceInfo Code

The project named DeviceInfo in the Chapter 5 code demonstrates all of the settings just discussed. This code requires the following using statements for these namespaces:

```
using System.Net.NetworkInformation;
using PhoneNetworkApi = Microsoft.Phone.Net.NetworkInformation;
using Microsoft.Phone.Info;
using System.Net;
using System.Net.Sockets;
using System.Windows.Threading;
```

The code uses a namespace alias to disambiguate between the two namespaces for the NetworkInterface class that is present in both namespaces, though the Phone version includes the NetworkInterfaceType property. Figure 5-1 shows the UI displaying device and network info that we have covered in the previous sections.

Figure 5-1. *Windows Phone device information and network status*

Most of the sample code consists of simple API calls to retrieve device or system info. The `DeviceStatus.PowerSourceChanged` and `DeviceStatus.KeyboardDeployedChanged` events are simple event handlers that fire as state changes.

A `DispatcherTimer` is used to fire two events, one that updates memory info in the `DeviceInfo` sample project UI and another that writes memory info out to the debug console so that it shows up in the Output window of Visual Studio.

The other interesting code related to networking and sockets is covered in the preceding sections.

System Tray

The system tray appears at the top of the screen in portrait mode. Figure 5-2 is a clip from the Windows Phone Design Template file named `StatusBar_PSD.psd,` which shows possible status information.

Figure 5-2. *Windows Phone system tray indicators*

The Windows Phone development guidelines recommend leaving the system tray visible within applications, because it shows useful information without having to force the user to exit the application. The system tray does take up a little bit of screen real estate, so for games and media players, it makes sense to disable the system tray.

The system tray can be disabled on a page-by-page basis by editing the `phone:PhoneApplicationPage` element and setting `shell:SystemTray.IsVisible` to `False`.

This concludes our discussion of device information. Next up is application data persistence using isolated storage on Windows Phone 7.

Marketplace Status and Trial Mode

Windows Phone 7 supports building a single application that includes both trial and full functionality. The `Microsoft.Phone.Marketplace.LicenseInformation` class provides one method named `IsTrial()` that the application can use to determine if the application has been fully purchased or is in trial mode.

As a developer, you get to determine what is the right trial experience for your application. For a game, it might be a certain number of tries or just the first level. For an application, it might be filtering to a subset of information, display advertising, or lack of personalization.

Application developers in Silverlight can use the `MarketplaceDetailTask` class to display the purchase experience. The `MarketplaceDetailTask` is discussed in the following section, "Tasks," covering launchers and choosers.

For XNA Game Studio developers, the `Microsoft.Xna.Framework.GamerServices.Guide` class has a method named `IsTrialMode` to get current license information. Developers call `Guide.ShowMarketplace` to display the purchase experience. The `Guide.SimulateTrialMode` property allows developer to test their game under trial mode conditions. Chapters 7 and 8 cover XNA Framework development in more detail.

■ **Tip** Trial mode is a great way to encourage end users to try out your application, enjoy it, and purchase the full version. If you plan to sell your application, implement and test trial mode.

Silverlight developers may be wondering how they can simulate trial mode. The good news is that Silverlight developers can also use the `Microsoft.Xna.Framework.GamerServices.Guide` class and the `SimulateTrialMode` property. Set it to true to permit testing trial mode functionality.

When testing trial mode by setting `SimulateTrialMode` to true, a call to `Guide.IsTrialMode` returns the current value of `SimulateTrialMode`. Calling `Guide.ShowMarketplace` simulates making a purchase.

■ **Caution** You must set `SimulateTrialMode` to `false` in release code. Place the code that sets it to true in `#if DEBUG` to ensure it is not available in a released application submitted to Marketplace.

In this section, we covered how to identify users, the device, network status, and application trial mode status for Windows Phone. In the next section, we move to the next major topic, settings and data storage in isolated storage.

Tasks

Windows Phone third-party applications run in a sandbox that is isolated from other third-party applications, as well as from the underlying operating system and hardware, except where APIs are surfaced.

One of the primary namespaces where a developer can integrate with the hardware and software platform is the `Microsoft.Phone.Tasks` namespace. The namespace consists of launchers and choosers. Launchers do not return any data back to your application; they are "fire and forget." Choosers can return data and status to your application.

The following are the launchers:

`BingMapsDirectionsTask`

`BingMapsTask`

`ConnectionSettingsTask`

`EmailComposeTask`

`MarketplaceDetailTask`

`MarketplaceHubTask`

`MarketplaceReviewTask`

`MarketplaceSearchTask`

`MediaPlayerLauncher`

`PhoneCallTask`

`SearchTask`

`ShareLinkTask` (Social Network Sharing)

`ShareStatusTask` (Social Network Sharing)

`SMSComposeTask`

WebBrowserTask

Here are the choosers:

AddressChooserTask

CameraCaptureTask

EmailAddressChooserTask

GameInviteTask (Xbox LIVE titles only)

PhoneNumberChooserTask

PhotoChooserTask

SaveContactTask

SaveEmailAddressTask

SavePhoneNumberTask

SaveRingtoneTask

Many of the launchers and choosers must be tested on a device, because the emulator does not include the full Windows Phone user experience with e-mail accounts, marketplace, and the like.

Application Execution Model (Tombstoning)

It is important to note that showing a launcher or chooser deactivates your application. Usually this puts your application in a dormant state, such that when the user returns to your application, the UI is as it was prior to launching the task. Figure 5-3 shows two launchers, BingMapsTask, and ConnectionSettingsTask, as well as the Chapter 5 sample application in the Fast Application Switching UI.

Figure 5-3. *Launcher and chooser tasks in fast application switching*

As you can see from Figure 5-3, launchers and choosers are almost like separate applications. Therefore, it is possible that your application will become tombstoned and terminated. In this case the user will return to a new instance of the application, and you as the developer must restore the application state. I covered the Windows Phone Application Execution Model at the end of Chapter 4.

Debugging Launchers and Choosers

When debugging many of the launchers and choosers, the connection to Zune may prevent the application from running. To debug your application, you must use the WPConnect tool that was made available in the Windows Phone Developer Tools October and January updates. Here is a link:

http://create.msdn.com/en-us/home/getting_started

Once installed, the WPConnect tool is located here on my machine:

C:\Program Files (x86)\Microsoft SDKs\Windows Phone\v7.0\Tools\WPConnect

To use the tool, run Visual Studio 2010 and connect a device to your PC via the Zune client. Once connected, close Zune and run WPConnect via a command prompt. It will display a message that the device is connected. If you disconnect the device from the cable, you will have to repeat the process. Figure 5-4 shows a few runs just to show how easy it is to enable debugging when testing media such as the pictures hub or the MediaPlayerLauncher task.

Figure 5-4. *The WPConnect tool in action*

Most of the tasks in the Chapter 5 solution LaunchersAndChoosers sample project are launched directly by clicking on the name. Some open another page for additional configuration options, or to show how the task can be fully utilized. The following subsections describe the development of each launcher and chooser.

Launchers

Launchers display a UI to send the user to another part of the phone's functionality. When the user presses the Back hardware button, he or she is returned to your application. Launchers are "fire and forget" in that they do not return information back to the application.

BingMapsDirectionsTask

New in Windows Phone OS 7.1, the Bing Maps directions task launches the built-in Windows Phone Bing Maps application, displaying driving directions between two points. As the developer, you can specify both the start and end points, or specify only one. If you specify just one point, the user's current location is used for the other location.

The start and end points contain a string label and geographic coordinates specifying the latitude and longitude of the location. If you omit the geographic coordinates, the label string is used by the Bing Maps application as a search term to find the location.

To use the BingMapsDirectionsTask, first add a reference to the System.Device assembly. The BingMapsDirectionsTask allows you to specify Start and End points of type LabeledMapLocation. The LabeledMapLocation object has a Label property of type string and a Location property of type GeoCoordinateLocation.

You must set the Label property, but you can leave the Location property null. Bing Maps will perform a search using the Label string to find the geo-coordinate and then plot the point with the Label value on the map. Also, you only have to specify one location. The BingMapsDirectionsTask will use the Windows Phone user's location as the other location value. Here is the code for this task:

```
private void BingMapsDirectionsTask_MouseLeftButtonDown(object sender, MouseButtonEventArgs e)
{
 BingMapsDirectionsTask task = new BingMapsDirectionsTask();
 //Use the Windows Phone user's current location as Start by not
 //specifying a Start location on the BingMapsDirectionsTask instance
 //Use a search term of "Gwinnett Arena" as the End location.
 //Leave GeoCoordinate location value as null to have Bing first find the location
 LabeledMapLocation DirectionsEndPoint = new LabeledMapLocation();
 DirectionsEndPoint.Label = "Gwinnett Arena";
 //or pass in a geolocation...
 // LabeledMapLocation DirectionsEndPoint = new LabeledMapLocation("Gwinnett Arena",
 // new GeoCoordinate(33, 98764, -84.09148));
 task.End = DirectionsEndPoint;
 task.Show();
}
```

You might think that you must test this task on a device, but it is actually pretty easy to test using the Location simulation tool in the Emulator. Before launching the task, I opened the Additional Tools in the emulator, searched for my current location, and set a pin point there to simulate using my current location. Figure 5-5 shows the results. By starting with my location set via the Location simulation tool, I got the results that I expected.

Figure 5-5. *The BingMapsDirectionsTask in action*

BingMapsTask

New in Windows Phone OS 7.1, the BingMapsTask class lets you specify a Center property (or leave it blank to use the current user's location) and a Search Term. In this example, I specify the latitude and longitude for the Gwinnett Arena near where I live and search for restaurants in case I am hungry after attending a concert or event. Here is the code:

```
private void BingMapsTask_MouseLeftButtonDown(object sender, MouseButtonEventArgs e)
{
  BingMapsTask task = new BingMapsTask();
  //Search for restaurants near the Gwinnett Arena
  //Leave the Center property blank to use the user's current location
  //Use location simulation in the Emulator to help you test
  task.Center = new GeoCoordinate(33.98764, -84.09148);
  task.SearchTerm = "restaurants";
  task.Show();
}
```

Figure 5-6 shows the Bing Maps search results with one of my favorite restaurants highlighted.

Figure 5-6. *BingMapsTask in action*

ConnectionSettingsTask

New in Windows Phone OS 7.1, the ConnectionsSettingsTask class allows you to show settings related to AirplaneMode, Bluetooth, Cellular, and Wi-Fi connections from within your application. You may want to do this to allow the user to quickly enable Wi-Fi so that the application can begin a long download operation. You set the ConnectionsettingsType property from an enumeration of the same name prior to calling the Show() method:

```
private void ConnectionSettingsTask_MouseLeftButtonDown(object sender, MouseButtonEventArgs e)
{
  ConnectionSettingsTask task = new ConnectionSettingsTask();
  //Other options besides WiFi are AirplaneMode, Bluetooth, and Cellular
  task.ConnectionSettingsType = ConnectionSettingsType.WiFi;
  task.Show();
}
```

EmailComposeTask

The EmailComposeTask class allows the user to send e-mail from an application. You can configure the To, Cc, Subject, and Body of the e-mail message via properties. It is not possible to attach a file to the e-mail. Also, the Body property takes a string of text, so formatting such as HTML formatting the e-mail message is not supported. Listing 5-3 has the code for the EmailComposeTask sample.

Listing 5-3. *EmailComposeTask Code*

```
private void textBlock1_MouseLeftButtonUp(object sender, MouseButtonEventArgs e)
{
  //cause an exception and then send an error report.
  try
  {
    int num1 = 3;
    int num2 = 3;
    int num3 = num1 / (num1 - num2);
  }
  catch (Exception err)
  {
    EmailComposeTask task = new EmailComposeTask();
    task.To = "support@WP7isv.com";
    task.Subject = "Customer Error Report";
    //Size StringBuilder appropriately
    StringBuilder builder;
    if (null == err.InnerException)
      builder = new StringBuilder(600);
    else //need space for InnerException
      builder = new StringBuilder(1200);
    builder.AppendLine("Please tell us what you were doing when the problem occurred.\n\n\n");
    builder.AppendLine("EXCEPTION DETAILS:");
    builder.Append("message:");
    builder.AppendLine(err.Message);
    builder.AppendLine("");
    builder.Append("stack trace:");
```

```
      builder.AppendLine(err.StackTrace);
      if (null != err.InnerException)
      {
        builder.AppendLine("");
        builder.AppendLine("");
        builder.AppendLine("inner exception:");
        builder.Append("inner exception message:");
        builder.AppendLine(err.InnerException.Message);
        builder.AppendLine("");
        builder.Append("inner exception stack trace:");
        builder.AppendLine(err.InnerException.StackTrace);
      }
      task.Body = builder.ToString();
      task.Show();
    }
```

MarketplaceHubTask

The MarketplaceHubTask class launches into the Marketplace Hub. The only parameter is ContentType, which determines whether the application view or music view of the Marketplace is displayed. The following is the code to show the music view:

```
private void MarketplaceHubTask2_MouseLeftButtonDown(object sender, MouseButtonEventArgs e)
{
  marketplaceHubTask = new MarketplaceHubTask();
  marketplaceHubTask.ContentType = MarketplaceContentType.Music;
  marketplaceHubTask.Show();
}
```

There are no return properties or events. This task simply shows the Marketplace Hub, and allows the user to interact with the hub and then return back to the application by pressing the Back hardware button.

MarketplaceSearchTask

The MarketplaceSearchTask also has a ContentType property to filter by either Applications or Music. It also has a SearchTerms property to pass in search terms to kick off the search. The following is the code to kick off search:

```
private void MarketplaceSearchTask_MouseLeftButtonDown(object sender, MouseButtonEventArgs e)
{
  MarketplaceSearchTask marketplaceSearchTask = new MarketplaceSearchTask();
  marketplaceSearchTask.ContentType = MarketplaceContentType.Music;
  marketplaceSearchTask.SearchTerms = "driving music";
  marketplaceSearchTask.Show();
}
```

Figure 5-7 shows the task displayed after calling the Show() method.

Figure 5-7. *MarketplaceSearchTask in action*

MarketplaceDetailTask

The MarketplaceDetailTask class displays the Marketplace details page for an application, which allows you to purchase the currently running application if it is in trial mode. You can also show the Marketplace details for your other applications so you can promote them. The ContentIdentifier property determines which application to show details for. This property is the product ID for the application found in the Marketplace when an application is certified.

▓ **Tip** Leave the property null if you wish to display the Marketplace details for the currently running application.

The product ID is generated when an application is submitted to Marketplace, so if you have a family of applications that you wish to cross-promote, you can simply plug in the product ID for each application to display the Marketplace details page. Here is the code:

```
private void MarketplaceDetailTask_MouseLeftButtonDown(object sender, MouseButtonEventArgs e)
{
  MarketplaceDetailTask marketplaceDetailTask = new MarketplaceDetailTask();
  marketplaceDetailTask.ContentType = MarketplaceContentType.Applications;
  //AppID for the youtube application
  marketplaceDetailTask.ContentIdentifier = "dcbb1ac6-a89a-df11-a490-00237de2db9e";
  marketplaceDetailTask.Show();
}
```

MarketplaceReviewTask

The Marketplace ReviewTask class allows you to display the Marketplace Review page for your application from within the application itself. This is a convenient way to encourage users to provide a review of your application. This task does not include a ContentIdentifier property, meaning that you can only display the review page for the currently running application. Here is the code:

```
private void MarketplaceReviewTask_MouseLeftButtonDown(object sender, MouseButtonEventArgs e)
{
  MarketplaceReviewTask marketplaceReviewTask = new MarketplaceReviewTask();
  marketplaceReviewTask.Show();
}
```

MediaPlayerLauncher

The MediaPlayerLauncher class has three properties of interest. The Controls property identifies which media player buttons to display. You can pick MediaPlaybackControls.All for full media controls, or you can use the bitwise "or" operator to combine a custom set of playback controls. The MediaPlayerLauncher has a property named Location that lets the player know how to resolve the URL if the media is located in isolated storage, or as part of the application's .xap file. The most important property is Media, where you set the URL for the media location. Here is code to play a Channel 9 video:

```
private void MediaPlayerLauncher_MouseLeftButtonDown(object sender, MouseButtonEventArgs e)
{
  MediaPlayerLauncher mediaPlayerLauncher = new MediaPlayerLauncher();
  mediaPlayerLauncher.Controls = MediaPlaybackControls.FastForward |
    MediaPlaybackControls.Pause | MediaPlaybackControls.Rewind |
    MediaPlaybackControls.Skip | MediaPlaybackControls.Stop;
  mediaPlayerLauncher.Location = MediaLocationType.Data;
  mediaPlayerLauncher.Media = new Uri("http://files.ch9.ms/ch9/f2c3/b59b6efb-3c70-4bc2-b3ff-
9e650007f2c3/wp7ces_high_ch9.mp4");
  mediaPlayerLauncher.Show();
}
```

PhoneCallTask

The PhoneCallTask class has two properties: DisplayName and PhoneNunber. When the PhoneCallTask.Show() method is called, a dialog box is displayed that says, "Dial DisplayName at PhoneNumber." Here is the code to dial a phone number with the user's consent:

```
private void PhoneCallTask_MouseLeftButtonDown(object sender, MouseButtonEventArgs e)
{
  PhoneCallTask phoneCallTask = new PhoneCallTask();
  phoneCallTask.DisplayName = "Rob Cameron";
  phoneCallTask.PhoneNumber = "555-555-1111";
  phoneCallTask.Show();
}
```

SearchTask

The SearchTask class performs the same search as pushing the hardware Search button. It has a SearchQuery property to pass a search string for the search. Here is the code for the SearchTask:

```
private void SearchTask_MouseLeftButtonDown(object sender, MouseButtonEventArgs e)
{
  SearchTask searchTask = new SearchTask();
  searchTask.SearchQuery = "driving music";
  searchTask.Show();
}
```

ShareLinkTask

New in Windows Phone OS 7.1, the ShareLinkTask allows you to share a link with status to social networks via the IinkUri, Message, and Title properties. This is a fantastic addition to Windows Phone, as it helps developers avoid having to write the social network sharing integration code themselves. Here is an example:

```
private void ShareLinkTask_MouseLeftButtonDown(object sender, MouseButtonEventArgs e)
{
  ShareLinkTask task = new ShareLinkTask();
  task.LinkUri = new Uri("http://www.windowsphone.com");
  task.Title = "Check out Windows Phone.";
  task.Message = "Now in the Mango edition:-)";
  task.Show();
}
```

This task only works on an actual device. The ShareLinkTask displays with the prepopulated fields via the properties. If you tap on the last option displayed in the task UI, it brings up a list of which social networks to share, leaving the user in control.

ShareStatusTask

New in Windows Phone OS 7.1, the SharedStatusTask takes a Status property of type string to post to the user's chosen social networks. Here is the code:

```
private void ShareStatusTask_MouseLeftButtonDown(object sender, MouseButtonEventArgs e)
```

```
{
  ShareStatusTask task = new ShareStatusTask();
  task.Status = "Check out Windows Phone";
  task.Show();
}
```

SMSComposeTask

The SmsComposeTask class sends an SMS based on the configured properties: the To property and the Body property. Calling the Show() method brings up the SMS application on the phone with the SMS ready to go. Note that the user can decide not to send. As with other launchers, there is no way to determine whether a user cancels or goes through with the action. Here is the code:

```
private void SMSComposeTask_MouseLeftButtonDown(object sender, MouseButtonEventArgs e)
{
  Microsoft.Phone.Tasks.SmsComposeTask smsComposeTask = new SmsComposeTask();
  smsComposeTask.To = "555-555-5555";
  smsComposeTask.Body = "Meet me for pizza.";
  smsComposeTask.Show();
}
```

WebBrowserTask

The WebBrowserTask class opens the full browser experience based on the configured property, URL, which takes a string. Here is the code:

```
private void WebBrowserTask_MouseLeftButtonDown(object sender, MouseButtonEventArgs e)
{
  WebBrowserTask webBrowserTask = new WebBrowserTask();
  webBrowserTask.Uri = "http://create.msdn.com";
  webBrowserTask.Show();
}
```

There is a known issue that if you try running this code under the debugger, it quite often displays the web browser with a blank URI. Sometimes if you click in the address bar and then click outside the address bar, it starts working. Running the code normally without the debugger seems to work much better.

■ **Note** Microsoft announced at Mobile World Conference in February 2011 that Internet Explorer 9 with support for HTML5 will be added to Windows Phone later in 2011.

Choosers

While the launchers are fire-and-forget, choosers return information back to the application, such as an image from the camera, a phone number, or e-mail address. As with the launchers, users can cancel the action; however, the application will know if the action was canceled. If the action is not canceled, the information will be returned to the application with the user's consent.

Choosers have a Show() method, like the launchers, but choosers also have a Completed event where data is returned. Developers wire up the Completed event in order to process the returned values.

AddressChooserTask

New in Windows Phone OS 7.1, the AddressChooserTask allows the user to choose a contact, and the task returns the associated address. The Address property is returned as a simple string, which could be passed into the BingMapsTask as an example. The DisplayName returned by the AddressChooserTask could also be passed in to the BingMapsTask to serve as the pushpin label.

This task does work in the Emulator for testing purposes with a few prepopulated contacts. Here is the code:

```
private void AddressChooserTask_MouseLeftButtonDown(object sender, MouseButtonEventArgs e)
{
  AddressChooserTask task = new AddressChooserTask();
  task.Completed += new EventHandler<AddressResult>(task_Completed);
  task.Show();
}

void task_Completed(object sender, AddressResult e)
{
  if (e.TaskResult == TaskResult.OK)
  {
    MessageBox.Show("Display Name: " + e.DisplayName +
      "\n Address: " + e.Address);
  }
  else
    MessageBox.Show("No address was selected: "+e.Error);
}
```

Figure 5-8 shows the "choose a contact" Ui displayed after launching the task, and then a message box from the AddressChooserTask.Completed event that displays the captured address information.

Figure 5-8. *AdressChooserTask in action*

CameraCaptureTask

This task allows the user to take a picture. The task returns a stream to the taken photo. One potential "gotcha" with this task is that you cannot invoke the camera on a device while syncing with Zune, because a photo is media, and media interaction is not allowed while synching with Zune. This is another example of where the WPConnect tool comes in handy. Because the sample is a little more involved, it has its own page for a UI. Listing 5-4 shows the code.

Listing 5-4. *CameraTaskPage.xaml.cs Code File*

```
using System;
using System.IO;
using System.IO.IsolatedStorage;
using System.Windows;
using System.Windows.Media.Imaging;
using Microsoft.Phone.Controls;
using Microsoft.Phone.Tasks;

namespace LaunchersAndChoosers.TaskPages
{
  public partial class CameraTaskPage : PhoneApplicationPage
  {
    private CameraCaptureTask cameraTask;
    private BitmapImage capturedImage;
```

```csharp
    string fileName = "capturedimage.jpg";

    public CameraTaskPage()
    {
      InitializeComponent();
      cameraTask = new CameraCaptureTask();
      capturedImage = new BitmapImage();

      cameraTask.Completed += new EventHandler<PhotoResult>(cameraTask_Completed);
      PreviewImage.Source = capturedImage;
    }

    void cameraTask_Completed(object sender, PhotoResult e)
    {
      if ((null == e.Error) && (null != e.ChosenPhoto))
        capturedImage.SetSource(e.ChosenPhoto);
      else
      {
        MessageBox.Show(e.Error.Message);
      }
    }

    private void TakePictureButton_Click(object sender, EventArgs e)
    {
      cameraTask.Show();
    }

    private void SavePictureButton_Click(object sender, EventArgs e)
    {
      WriteableBitmap bmp = new WriteableBitmap(capturedImage);

      using (IsolatedStorageFile iso = IsolatedStorageFile.GetUserStoreForApplication())
      {
        using (IsolatedStorageFileStream fs =
          iso.OpenFile(fileName, System.IO.FileMode.Create))
        {
          bmp.SaveJpeg(fs, bmp.PixelWidth, bmp.PixelHeight, 0, 100);
          savedImage.Source = bmp;
        }
      }
    }
  }
}
```

The sample application shows the CameraCaptureTask chooser to take a picture. Once the user accepts the picture, the image is displayed in the bottom Image object. When the user clicks the Save Application bar button, the sample saves the image to isolated storage and displays the image in the UI in the top Image object.

EmailAddressChooserTask

The EmailAddressChooserTask class allows the user to pick an e-mail for an application action, such as sharing a link or other information in the application. The task shows the phone UI with a list of contacts to choose once the Show() method is called.

The e-mail address is made available in the Completed event. It could be used as part of launching the EmailComposeTask. Here is the code:

```
private void EmailAddressChooserTask_MouseLeftButtonDown(object sender,↩
 MouseButtonEventArgs e)
{
  EmailAddressChooserTask emailAddressChooserTask = new EmailAddressChooserTask();
  emailAddressChooserTask.Completed += new EventHandler<EmailResult>↩
(emailAddressChooserTask_Completed);
  emailAddressChooserTask.Show();
}

void emailAddressChooserTask_Completed(object sender, EmailResult e)
{
  if ((null == e.Error) && (TaskResult.OK == e.TaskResult))
  {
    MessageBox.Show("Email Address Returned is: " + e.Email);
  }
}
```

PhoneNumberChooserTask

The PhoneNumberChooserTask class allows the user to pick a phone number for an application action, such as to open the PhoneCallTask launcher. The task shows the phone UI with a list of contacts to choose once the Show() method is called. The phone number is made available in the Completed event. Here is the code:

```
private void PhoneNumberChooserTask_MouseLeftButtonDown(object sender, MouseButtonEventArgs e)
{
  PhoneNumberChooserTask phoneNumberChooserTask = new PhoneNumberChooserTask();
  phoneNumberChooserTask.Completed += new EventHandler<PhoneNumberResult>↩
(phoneNumberChooserTask_Completed);
  phoneNumberChooserTask.Show();
}

void phoneNumberChooserTask_Completed(object sender, PhoneNumberResult e)
{
  if ((null == e.Error) && (TaskResult.OK == e.TaskResult))
  {
    MessageBox.Show("Phone number returned is: " + e.PhoneNumber);
  }
}
```

GameInviteTask

New in Windows Phone OS 7.1, the GameInviteTask class allows Xbox LIVE game developers to pass in a game session ID so that the user can invite friends to a game. This task is only useful and available to game developers working with an Xbox LIVE publisher, such as Microsoft Game Studios or one of the other major game publishers.

PhotoChooserTask

The PhotoChooserTask class is very similar to the CameraCaptureTask, in that it returns a photo image. The PhotoChooserTask has a property named ShowCamera to give the user an option of choosing an existing photo or capturing a new photo. After calling the Show() method to launch the UI, the Completed event fires when the user is done, and the picture is loaded into an Image control in the UI. Here is the code:

```
private void PhotoChooserTask_MouseLeftButtonDown(object sender, MouseButtonEventArgs e)
{
  PhotoChooserTask photoChoserTask = new PhotoChooserTask();
  photoChoserTask.ShowCamera = true;
  photoChoserTask.Completed += new EventHandler<PhotoResult>(photoChoserTask_Completed);
  photoChoserTask.Show();
}

private BitmapImage capturedImage;
void photoChoserTask_Completed(object sender, PhotoResult e)
{
  if ((null == e.Error) && (TaskResult.OK == e.TaskResult))
  {
    capturedImage = new BitmapImage();
    capturedImage.SetSource(e.ChosenPhoto);
    ChosenPhotoImage.Source = capturedImage;
  }
}
```

SaveContactTask

New in Windows Phone OS 7.1, the SaveContactTask class allows you to save a contact to the user's contacts in the People hub, with the user's consent. The task takes all the typical properties you would expect to set on a new contact record. Here is the code:

```
private void SaveContactTask_MouseLeftButtonDown(object sender, MouseButtonEventArgs e)
{
  SaveContactTask task = new SaveContactTask();
  task.Completed += new EventHandler<SaveContactResult>(task_Completed);
  //A few properties available are populated below
  //Full contact data fields are available
  task.Company = "Test Company";
  task.FirstName = "Robert";
  task.LastName = "Cameron";
  task.HomePhone = "555-555-1111";
  task.WorkPhone = "555-555-2222";
```

```
    task.Website = "http://blogs.msdn.com/robcamer";
    task.JobTitle = "Author";
    task.Nickname = "Rob";
    task.PersonalEmail = "test@personalemail.com";
    task.WorkEmail = "test@test.com";
    task.MobilePhone = "555-555-3333";
    task.Show();
}

void task_Completed(object sender, SaveContactResult e)
{
  if (e.TaskResult == TaskResult.OK)
    MessageBox.Show("Contact saved.");
  else
    MessageBox.Show("Error savign contact: " + e.Error);
}
```

SaveEmailAddressTask

The SaveEmailAddressTask class shows the built-in contacts application. It allows the code to save the provided e-mail address to a new or existing contact via the Email property. Use the Completed event to determine whether an error occurred and that the task completed successfully. Here is the code:

```
private void SaveEmailAdressTask_MouseLeftButtonDown(object sender, MouseButtonEventArgs e)
{
  SaveEmailAddressTask saveEmailAddressTask = new SaveEmailAddressTask();
  saveEmailAddressTask.Completed += new EventHandler<TaskEventArgs>↵
(saveEmailAddressTask_Completed);
  saveEmailAddressTask.Email = "email@domain.com";
  MessageBox.Show("Saving this email: " + saveEmailAddressTask.Email);
  saveEmailAddressTask.Show();
}

void saveEmailAddressTask_Completed(object sender, TaskEventArgs e)
{
  if ((null == e.Error) && (TaskResult.OK == e.TaskResult))
  {
    MessageBox.Show("Email address saved");
  }
}
```

SavePhoneNumberTask

The SavePhoneNumberTask class works very similarly to SaveEmailAddressTask, except that it passes in a phone number instead of an e-mail address. Here is the code:

```
private void SavePhoneNumberTask_MouseLeftButtonDown(object sender, MouseButtonEventArgs e)
{
  SavePhoneNumberTask savePhoneNumberTask = new SavePhoneNumberTask();
  savePhoneNumberTask.Completed += new EventHandler<TaskEventArgs>↵
(savePhoneNumberTask_Completed);
```

```
    savePhoneNumberTask.PhoneNumber = "555-555-5555";
    MessageBox.Show("Saving this phone number: " + savePhoneNumberTask.PhoneNumber);
    savePhoneNumberTask.Show();
}
void savePhoneNumberTask_Completed(object sender, TaskEventArgs e)
{
    if ((null == e.Error) && (TaskResult.OK == e.TaskResult))
    {
        MessageBox.Show("Phone number saved");
    }
}
```

SaveRingToneTask

New in Windows Phone OS 7.1, the SaveRingToneTask class allows the user to select an available music track or clip downloaded as part of the application as a ringtone. Users cannot select music from their Zune music library. (It's a digital rights issue and is consistent with other mobile platforms.) Instead, an application can do one of two things:

License music clips and tracks from musicians or music companies and provide a store as part of the application.

Provide an upload service that allows a user to upload a track or clip that they own to a server-side application that is part of your offering. When the user logs into the Windows Phone application, they could then download the clips and tracks that they originally uploaded (but not anyone else's clips or tracks).

There are also technical requirements regarding the ringtone file itself. Ringtone audio files must meet the following requirements:

Files must be of type MP3 or WMA.

Files must be less than 1 MB in size.

Files must be less than 40 seconds in length.

Files must not have digital rights management (DRM) protection.

You can create a ringtone yourself, but you'll need to ensure that it meets all the criteria; or you can use one of the sample ringtone files available here on Windows:
C:\ProgramData\Microsoft\Windows\Ringtones. I grabbed a sample ringtone named Ringtone 01.wma from that directory and added it to the Chapter 5 Launchers and Choosers project. It is added to the project as content and will be deployed within the XAP file.

Ringtones deployed this way are considered part of application data. The sample ringtone I added to the project can be added via the SaveRingtoneTask.Source property using this line of code:

```
    task.Source = new Uri("appdata:/Ringtone01.wma");
```

Ringtones downloaded from the web would be stored as files in isolated storage, where they can be accessed via URIs. Here is the full code:

```
private void SaveRintoneTask_MouseLeftButtonDown(object sender, MouseButtonEventArgs e)
{
    SaveRingtoneTask task = new SaveRingtoneTask();
```

333

```
    task.Completed += new EventHandler<TaskEventArgs>(task_Completed);
    task.DisplayName = "My Fav Ringtone";
    task.IsShareable = true; //shareable with other applications
    task.Source = new Uri("appdata:/Ringtone01.wma");
    task.Show();
}

void task_Completed(object sender, TaskEventArgs e)
{
    if (e.TaskResult == TaskResult.OK)
      MessageBox.Show("Ringtone saved.");
    else
      MessageBox.Show("Error savign Rington: " + e.Error);
}
```

The task UI has a checkbox to allow users to make the saved ringtone the user's current ringtone. If the user goes into settings to configure their ringtone, the newly added ringtone would be displayed in the standard Windows Phone settings as well. This concludes our coverage of the launchers and choosers. We next cover Clipboard access, alarms, and contacts and calendar access available in Windows Phone 7.5.

Clipboard

Windows Phone 7.5 provides support to integrate with the system Clipboard object, allowing you to copy text within your application. As background, Windows Phone 7 with the NoDo update offered in the spring of 2011 enabled Clipboard copy and paste at the system level without any programmatic support.

In Windows Phone OS 7.1 you now have programmatic access to the system Clipboard. The Clipboard object offers three static methods:

Clipboard.ContainsText returns true if text is present on the Clipboard.

Clipboard.GetText returns a string containing the current text on the Clipboard.

Clipboard.SetText accepts a string of text to add to the Clipboard.

On Windows Phone one item to note is that invoking the Clipboard.GetText method results in a SecurityException. On Windows Phone you can call the SetText and ContainsText methods only. To demonstrate this, create a simple test application with a TextBlock and two TextBox controls. The TextBlock has a ContextMenu from the Silverlight for Windows Phone Toolkit associated with it to enable tap-and-hold Copy operations from the TextBlock control. Normally this behavior is not enabled on the TextBlock and RichTextBox controls, but it is something that a developer may need on occasion. Here is the XAML for the ContextMenu control:

```
<TextBlock Height="30" HorizontalAlignment="Left" Margin="12,53,0,0" Name="TextBlock1"
    Text="This is some text. Tap and Hold to Copy or Paste." VerticalAlignment="Top">
  <toolkit:ContextMenuService.ContextMenu>
  <toolkit:ContextMenu HorizontalAlignment="Left" Margin="52,62"
  Name="ClipboardContextMenu" VerticalAlignment="Top" Width="200">
  <toolkit:MenuItem Name="CopyMenuItem"  Header="Copy" Tag="COPY"
    Click="CopyMenuItem_Click"/>
```

```
</toolkit:ContextMenu>
  </toolkit:ContextMenuService.ContextMenu>
</TextBlock>
```

As a developer, you do not have to worry about showing or hiding the ContextMenu control. The ContextMenuService handles that for you by wiring things up with the tap-and-hold gesture on the control. When the Copy ContextMenuItem is selected, the TextBlock's Text property is copied to the Clipboard and made available to paste into the TextBox controls in the UI. Here is the copy code:

```
private void CopyMenuItem_Click(object sender, RoutedEventArgs e)
{
    Clipboard.SetText(TextBlock1.Text);
}
```

The Clipboard UI in action is shown in Figure 5-9.

Figure 5-9. *The Clipboard Test application in action*

In the next section, you'll see another of the new scheduled notification integration points in Windows Phone 7.5, with custom alarms and reminders.

Alarms and Reminders

New in Windows Phone OS 7.1, the ADK provides the programmatic ability to create and manage scheduled notifications, a small but important value-add feature for many application scenarios. Examples are reminders to work out, to take a pie out of an oven in a cooking application, or to start driving before a meeting to get there on time.

This feature is a great addition to the platform because Windows Phone applications cannot run continuously in the background, and not all scenarios can be served via push notification toast functionality. Scheduled notifications allow your application to provide the user information when not running at all.

In Chapter 10 we cover the new background processing available in Windows Phone OS 7.1, but it is scenario-based as well, with a scheduled process that can run about every 30 minutes, which cannot replace the functionality provided by scheduled notifications.

A scheduled notification is a dialog box that pops up on the screen at a specified time even when the application is not running, similar to the notifications displayed by the phone's built-in applications. The dialog box displays some customizable text information to the user and allows the user to dismiss the notification or postpone it until later.

If the user taps a notification you created within your application, your application will be launched. Notifications can be configured to launch once or multiple times on a recurring schedule.

▓ **Note** The schedules for notifications are only accurate to within a range of one minute, that is, a notification can launch up to one minute after its scheduled time.

There are two types of scheduled notifications, Alarm and Reminder objects. An application can have up to 50 Alarm and Reminder objects active at a time. We cover both in the next two subsections.

THE ALARM CLASS

An Alarm object lets you specify a sound file to play when the notification is launched with the user interface shown in Figure 5-10.

Figure 5-10. The Alarm object system UI

An Alarm system notification always displays the text "Alarm" in the title as well as the name of the application that created it and the content provided by the application to indicate the reason for the Alarm.

If the user taps the Alarm system UI anywhere but the Snooze or Dismiss button, the application is launched and the initial page is shown; there are no deep link capabilities available with Alarm objects.

The Reminder Class

A Reminder object accepts a deep link within your application, including query string parameters for context. Figure 5-11 shows the Reminder system UI.

Figure 5-11. *The Reminder Object system UI*

The Reminder object system UI displays the name of the application that created the Reminder object as well as a reminder title provided by the application. The application can provide additional detail about the Reminder object in the reminder content section as well.

Reminder objects use the default system sound for notifications configured by the user. If the user taps the Reminder system UI anywhere but the Snooze or Dismiss button, the application is launched with a deep link that includes the navigation URI and query string provided when the Reminder was created.

In the next subsection I show how to work with Alarm and Reminder scheduled notifications.

Alarms and Reminder Sample Project

The Alarm class inherits from the ScheduledNotification class, and the Reminder class inherits from the ScheduledActionService class. The primary difference is that the Reminder class accepts a deep link into the application.

To demonstrate these elements, we add a new project named AlarmsAndReminders to the Chapter 5 solution. The first page of the application will display a list of all of the Alarm and Reminder objects created within the application. Another page, named ReminderDeepLinkPage.xaml, is added to the AlarmsAndReminders project, which will be the landing page for the deep link capability available with the Reminder class.

In MainPage.xaml.cs, add a using clause for the Microsoft.Phone.Scheduler namespace. This makes the Alarm and Reminder objects available in the project. We also declare a collection to hold all of the created Reminder and Alarm objects at the top of the MainPage class in MainPage.xaml.cs:

```
IEnumerable<ScheduledNotification> _notifications;
```

The Alarm class can take a custom audio file to play, so we add the C:\ProgramData\Microsoft\Windows\Ringtones\Ringtone 07.wma sample ringtone to the

AlarmsAndReminders project as content. We wire up the Loaded event to call a method we are about to create, named RefreshScheduledNotificationsList, that will retrieve the created Alarm and Reminder objects and populate the _notifications collection.

The RefreshScheduledNotificationsList makes a call to this method to obtain scheduled notifications created by the application:

ScheduledActionService.GetActions<ScheduledNotification>()

The notifications are displayed in a ListBox control with the following DataTemplate in Listing 5-5.

Listing 5-5. *NotificationListBox.DataTemplate from MainPage.Xaml.cs*

```
<DataTemplate>
  <Grid Background="Transparent" Margin="0,0,0,35">
    <Grid.ColumnDefinitions>
      <ColumnDefinition Width="380"/>
      <ColumnDefinition Width="50"/>
    </Grid.ColumnDefinitions>
    <Grid Grid.Column="0">
      <StackPanel Orientation="Vertical" Margin="12,0,0,0">
        <TextBlock Text="{Binding Title}" TextWrapping="NoWrap" FontWeight="Bold"
            Style="{StaticResource PhoneTextLargeStyle}" Margin="0,0,12,0"/>
        <TextBlock Text="{Binding Content}" TextWrapping="Wrap"
            Style="{StaticResource PhoneTextSubtleStyle}" Margin="0,0,12,0"/>
        <StackPanel Orientation="Horizontal" Margin="0,6,0,0">
          <TextBlock Text="begin "/>
          <TextBlock Text="{Binding BeginTime}" HorizontalAlignment="Right"/>
        </StackPanel>
        <StackPanel Orientation="Horizontal">
          <TextBlock Text="expiration "/>
          <TextBlock Text="{Binding ExpirationTime}" HorizontalAlignment="Right"/>
        </StackPanel>
        <StackPanel Orientation="Horizontal">
          <TextBlock Text="recurrence "/>
          <TextBlock Text="{Binding RecurrenceType}" HorizontalAlignment="Right"/>
        </StackPanel>
        <StackPanel Orientation="Horizontal">
          <TextBlock Text="is scheduled? "/>
          <TextBlock Text="{Binding IsScheduled}" HorizontalAlignment="Right"/>
        </StackPanel>
      </StackPanel>
    </Grid>
    <Grid Grid.Column="1">
      <Button Tag="{Binding Name}" Click="deleteNotificationButton_Click"
            VerticalAlignment="Top" BorderThickness="0" Padding="0,0,0,0"
            HorizontalAlignment="Center">
        <Image Source="icons/RemoveNotification.png" Stretch="UniformToFill"/>
      </Button>
    </Grid>
  </Grid>
</DataTemplate>
```

The most interesting aspect of the DataTemplate is the Delete button in the upper-right corner of each reminder, as shown in Figure 5-12.

Figure 5-12. *The List of Reminders UI*

In the ListBox's DataTemplate, the Button.Tag property is bound to the Name property for the reminder. The Delete button in the DataTemplate is bound to the same event handler in MainPage.Xaml.cs. The Tag property on the Button cast from the Sender parameter for the event handler is used to find the right notification to delete. Here is the shared deleteNotificationButton_Click:

```
private void deleteNotificationButton_Click(object sender, RoutedEventArgs e)
{
  // The scheduled action name is stored in the Tag property
  // of the delete button for each notification
  string name = (string)((Button)sender).Tag;
  // Call Remove to unregister the scheduled notification with the service.
  ScheduledActionService.Remove(name);
  // Reset the NotificationListBox items
  RefreshScheduledNotificationsList();
}
```

Notice how the code above casts the Button.Tag property back to a string, which is then used to delete the notification. This is a handy technique to use when possible to avoid having to write a custom user control to enable Buttons in a DataTemplate.

The other interesting part of the code is the CreateTextButton_MouseLeftButtonDown method. Notice in Figure 5-12 that there is an Add button in the Application Bar. This method shows a collapsed Grid object containing the UI to create a Reminder or Alarm item. Figure 5-13 shows the Add UI with the Create button visible at the bottom of the ScrollViewer.

Figure 5-13. The add scheduled notification UI

The CreateTextButton_MouseLeftButtonDown event handler creates either a Reminder or an Alarm using the entered values. Notice at the bottom of Figure 5-13 that you can set query parameters; these are attached to the deep link that can be processed by the deep link page. Listing 5-6 has the code for the CreateTextButton_MouseLeftButtonDown event handler.

Listing 5-6. CreateTextButton_MouseLeftButtonDown Event Handler from MainPage.Xaml.cs

```
private void CreateTextButton_MouseLeftButtonDown(object sender, MouseButtonEventArgs e)
{
  String name = System.Guid.NewGuid().ToString();
  DateTime date = (DateTime)beginDatePicker.Value;
  DateTime time = (DateTime)beginTimePicker.Value;
  DateTime beginTime = date + time.TimeOfDay;
  // Make sure that the begin time has not already passed.
  if (beginTime < DateTime.Now)
  {
```

```
  MessageBox.Show("The begin date must be in the future.");
  return;
}

// Get the expiration time for the notification.
date = (DateTime)expirationDatePicker.Value;
time = (DateTime)expirationTimePicker.Value;
DateTime expirationTime = date + time.TimeOfDay;
// Make sure that the expiration time is after the begin time.
if (expirationTime < beginTime)
{
  MessageBox.Show("Expiration time must be after the begin time.");
  return;
}
// Determine which recurrence radio button is checked.
RecurrenceInterval recurrence = RecurrenceInterval.None;
if (dailyRadioButton.IsChecked == true)
{
  recurrence = RecurrenceInterval.Daily;
}
else if (weeklyRadioButton.IsChecked == true)
{
  recurrence = RecurrenceInterval.Weekly;
}
else if (monthlyRadioButton.IsChecked == true)
{
  recurrence = RecurrenceInterval.Monthly;
}
else if (endOfMonthRadioButton.IsChecked == true)
{
  recurrence = RecurrenceInterval.EndOfMonth;
}
else if (yearlyRadioButton.IsChecked == true)
{
  recurrence = RecurrenceInterval.Yearly;
}

string param1Value = param1TextBox.Text;
string param2Value = param2TextBox.Text;
string queryString = "";
if (param1Value != "" && param2Value != "")
{
  queryString = "?param1=" + param1Value + "&param2=" + param2Value;
}
else if (param1Value != "" || param2Value != "")
{
  queryString = (param1Value != null) ? "?param1=" + param1Value : "?param2=" + param2Value;
}
Uri navigationUri = new Uri("/ReminderDeepLinkPage.xaml" + queryString, UriKind.Relative);
if ((bool)reminderRadioButton.IsChecked)
{
  Reminder reminder = new Reminder(name);
```

341

```
      reminder.Title = titleTextBox.Text;
      reminder.Content = contentTextBox.Text;
      reminder.BeginTime = beginTime;
      reminder.ExpirationTime = expirationTime;
      reminder.RecurrenceType = recurrence;
      reminder.NavigationUri = navigationUri;

      // Register the reminder with the system.
      ScheduledActionService.Add(reminder);
    }
    else
    {
      Alarm alarm = new Alarm(name);
      alarm.Content = contentTextBox.Text;
      alarm.Sound = new Uri("/Ringtone 07.wma", UriKind.Relative);
      alarm.BeginTime = beginTime;
      alarm.ExpirationTime = expirationTime;
      alarm.RecurrenceType = recurrence;

      ScheduledActionService.Add(alarm);
    }
    //Since save clicked, close dialog and refresh list
    AddNotificationGrid.Visibility = Visibility.Collapsed;
    ApplicationBar.IsVisible = true;
    RefreshScheduledNotificationsList();
}
```

When the Add button is clicked in the Application Bar, AddNotificationGrid.Visibility is set to Visibility.Visible. When the CreateTextButton_MouseLeftButtonDown method finishes, it sets Visibility back to false to hide the AddNotificationGrid and sets IsVisible to true on the Application Bar to return the UI to normal.

The correct way to close a dialog in Windows Phone is to select the hardware Back key. In this case, that cancels the add operation. You must catch the Back click to check if the AddNotificationGrid is visible and set e.Cancel to true to prevent the page from navigating back or exiting the application. Here is the code for the override:

```
protected override void OnBackKeyPress(System.ComponentModel.CancelEventArgs e)
{
    if (AddNotificationGrid.Visibility == Visibility.Visible)
    {
        AddNotificationGrid.Visibility = Visibility.Collapsed;
        ApplicationBar.IsVisible = true;
        e.Cancel = true;
    }
    base.OnBackKeyPress(e);
}
```

The rest of the application is boilerplate UI, data binding, and navigation logic, but as you can see, the ability to create alarms and reminders is pretty straightforward, enabling functionality that adds high value for many scenarios with minimal effort.

Contacts and Calendar

New in Windows Phone OS 7.1, the SDK provides read-only access to the user's contacts and calendar data. You can query the user's data to build highly customized applications with the ability for users to choose from a list of contacts, send email, and find birthdays or appointment times, as well as many other scenarios.

The People hub in Windows Phone integrates a user's contacts across Windows Live, Outlook, Facebook, Twitter, LinkedIn, Yahoo! Mail, and Google Gmail. When you query contacts in a user's contact database, the information can originate from the Phone, Windows Live, Outlook, or Facebook. Not all data from all service providers is exposed publicly through the contacts and calendar API. The StorageKind enumeration can indicate how a contact was pulled in. Table 5-3 lists the properties available from each provider.

Table 5-3. *Simple TCP/IP Services*

Data Provider	Contact Name	Contact Picture	Contact Data	Calendar Appointments	Storage Kind
Windows Phone Device	Yes	Yes	Yes	Yes	Phone
Windows LiveSocial	Yes	Yes	Yes	Yes	WindowsLive
WindowsLive Rolodex	Yes	Yes	Yes	Yes	WindowsLive
Exchange Accounts (local address book only)	Yes	Yes	Yes	Yes	Outlook
Mobile Operator Address Book	Yes	Yes	Yes	No	Other
Facebook	Yes	Yes	No	No	Facebook
WindowsLive Aggregated Networks (Twitter, LinkedIn, etc.)	No	No	No	No	None

Contacts and Calendar Background

There are a few things you must do to be able to publish an application to the Marketplace. Applications must obtain the user's permission as well as provide a privacy policy on how the data will be used per section 2.11 in Windows Phone Application Policies:

```
http://msdn.microsoft.com/en-us/library/hh184841(v=VS.92).aspx
```

There are WmAppManfiest.xml capabilities that are required in order to access contact and calendar data. To access contacts, you must add the ID_CAP_CONTACTS capability to WmAppManifest.xml. To access calendar data, you must add the ID_CAP_APPOINTMENTS capability to WmAppManifest.xml.

Contacts data is provided as a read-only snapshot. You must manually re-query the data to access any recent changes. Also, a user's contact data can vary greatly in size and number of records. Always expect a large contact list and display a loading message just in case.

Finally, when you query contacts and calendar, use the preconfigured search filters, which are pre-indexed. Using LINQ may result in less than optimal performance.

Coding with Contacts and Calendar

To demonstrate how to query and work with contacts and calendar, we next add a project named ContactsAndCalendar to the Chapter 5 solution. By default, the WMAppManifest.xml file located in the Properties folder for the project includes the necessary ID_CAP_CONTACTS and ID_CAP_APPOINTMENTS capabilities.

We add a folder named pages and then add two pages, ContactsPage.xaml and AppointmentsPage.xaml. We add two TextBlock controls to MainPage.xaml and apply the NavigateToPageAction Behavior in Expression Blend. In both ContactsPage.xaml and AppointmentsPage.xaml, we add a using clause for the Microsoft.Phone.UserData namespace to pull in the classes related to Contact and Appointment objects.

We next add a ProgressBar control to both the calendar and contacts page, configuring each ProgressBar with its Indeterminate property set to true and the Visibility property set to Collapsed. We also add a ListBox to each page, named contactsListBox and calendarListbox respectively. In case there is a large amount of data, we set the ProgressBar.Visibility property to Visible before loading the data by calling SearchAsync and then set the Visibility property back to Visibility.Collapsed in the SearchCompleted event handler. Here is the search code:

```
void ContactsPage_Loaded(object sender, RoutedEventArgs e)
{
  _contacts = new Contacts();
  _contacts.SearchCompleted += new
EventHandler<ContactsSearchEventArgs>(_contacts_SearchCompleted);
  //Apply initial filter on contacts
  _contactsFilter = String.Empty;
  //Refresh contact list
  RefreshAppBarBtn_Click(sender, e);
}

void _contacts_SearchCompleted(object sender, ContactsSearchEventArgs e)
{
  _contactsList = e.Results.ToList<Contact>();
  contactsListBox.ItemsSource = _contactsList;
  contactsLoadProgressBar.Visibility = Visibility.Collapsed;
}
```

The contact's variable of type Contacts is instantiated. The default filter is set to no filter with a value of String.Empty. The SearchCompleted event is wired up to the Contacts object. The Loaded event handler reuses the RefreshAppBarBtn_Click(sender, e); method to call Contacts.SearchAsync as shown here:

```
private void RefreshAppBarBtn_Click(object sender, EventArgs e)
{
  contactsLoadProgressBar.Visibility = Visibility.Visible;
  //Retrieve contacts based on filter
  _contacts.SearchAsync(_contactsFilter, FilterKind.DisplayName, null);
}
```

You can set the filter string, in this case the contactsFilter variable, and the FilterKind. Other options besides DisplayName are EmailAddress, None, PhoneNumber, and PinnedToStart. Figure 5-14 shows the contacts UI.

Figure 5-14. *List of contacts sorted by displayName*

The left Application Bar button calls the Refresh event handler. Remember that you present a snapshot to the user, so you may need to periodically refresh the list of Contact objects. The right Application Bar button gives the ability to search on DisplayName by typing in a letter or two to filter the list. Figure 5-15 shows the filter UI.

Figure 5-15. *Add Scheduled Notification UI*

Typing a few characters and tapping the Back button brings you back to the contact list filter to contacts starting with R for the DisplayName property. Tapping one of the built-in contacts, such as Roan Kan, navigates to the ContactsDetails.xaml page as shown in Figure 5-16.

Figure 5-16. *Contact details UI*

The contactsListBox.SelectionChanged method handles the navigation to the ContactDetails.xaml page that supplies the query parameters for lookup. Here is the SelectionChanged event handler:

```
private void contactsListBox_SelectionChanged(object sender, SelectionChangedEventArgs e)
{
  if (e.AddedItems.Count > 0)
  {
    Contact contact = (Contact)e.AddedItems[0];
    NavigationService.Navigate(new Uri("/pages/ContactDetails.xaml?DisplayName=" +
contact.DisplayName, UriKind.Relative));
  }
}
```

The ContactDetails.xaml.cs OnNavigatedTo override processes the query parameters on the URL, finds the contact, and data-binds it to the page in this code:

```
protected override void OnNavigatedTo(System.Windows.Navigation.NavigationEventArgs e)
{
  base.OnNavigatedTo(e);
  string contactDisplayName = (string)NavigationContext.QueryString["DisplayName"];
  Contacts _contacts;
  _contacts = new Contacts();
```

```
  _contacts.SearchCompleted += new
EventHandler<ContactsSearchEventArgs>(_contacts_SearchCompleted);
  _contacts.SearchAsync(contactDisplayName, FilterKind.DisplayName, null);
}
```

Check out the ContactsAndCalendar sample project to see the code, but the calendar and appointments code works exactly the same way as the Contacts code, so I don't dive into it here. As you can see, this functionality provides a great new capability to pull in a user's Contacts and Appointments into your custom application experience to provide more tailored functionality for the user.

Conclusion

This chapter introduces you to the many ways that your application can integrate with the overall Windows Phone experience. We started out by exploring the information available regarding the mobile device and the Windows Phone environment.

Next up was extensive coverage of the Windows Phone launchers and choosers. There are many new choosers including the very useful BingMapsDirectionsTask, BingMapsTask, and AddressChooserTask introduce with Windows Phone OS 7.1. I switched gears to quickly cover the Clipboard functionality now available.

The chapter wraps up with coverage of the system notifications functionality, including alarms and reminders, concluding with extensive coverage of the contacts and calendar functionality. If you are an existing Windows Phone developer, there is a lot of new functionality that you can leverage to provide a more personalized application user experience.

CHAPTER 6

■ ■ ■

Windows Phone Advanced UI Development

Building a great user interface for a professional application is challenging, given all of the competing priorities, such as presenting data, interaction models, network connectivity, security, managing background tasks, and localization. It's important to build a rich application on a solid architecture that helps the different pieces work together.

This chapter delves more deeply into user interface development with Silverlight, covering a wide range of topics. It builds on previous chapters, but especially on Chapter 2, which covered Silverlight user interface development. This chapter extends the topic of user interface development to include how to architect an application with separation of concerns without sacrificing support for tooling or ease of development.

This chapter starts with an introduction of the most prevalent application architecture model in Silverlight development, Model-View-ViewModel (MVVM), which provides excellent support for well-designed user interfaces with separation of concerns. With Windows Phone OS 7.1 (Mango), Windows Phone adds compatibility with the Silverlight 4 programming model including much improved commanding support.

After MVVM, the Silverlight for Windows Phone Toolkit is next, covering the additional controls and capabilities including the new controls available in the update for Windows Phone OS 7.1 (Mango). The section following is on creating transitions and interactivity in Expression Blend. The final section is on the Microsoft Advertising SDK, which provides an excellent vehicle to monetize applications.

The Model-View-ViewModel Architecture

The Model-View-ViewModel (MVVM) architecture originated when the Microsoft Windows Presentation Foundation (WPF) team were building the first version of Expression Blend. WPF is Microsoft's desktop XAML development model, and Expression Blend is written in WPF. MVVM is similar to other separation-of-concerns architectures, like the tried-and-true Model-View-Controller (MVC) model; however, MVVM is optimized to take advantage of XAML's rich data binding, data templates, commands, and event routing capabilities. The next section covers the architecture in more detail.

MVVM Overview

In this section, the MVVM pattern is defined to help you grasp how it works with XAML. If you are familiar with MVC, MVVM will look somewhat familiar to you—but it is much more than just MVC. MVVM relies heavily on XAML data-binding capabilities to allow the UI to bind to both data and commands. Figure 6-1 depicts the MVVM architecture.

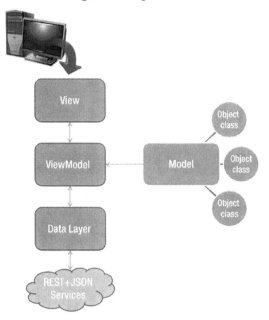

Figure 6-1. *The MVVM architecture*

In Chapter 4, there is a simple example that displays a list of fake `Vendor` data made available via JSON. The REST+JSON service project, named `WcfRemoteServicesSimpleRestJSON,` is added to the Chapter 6 solution. The `BasicMVVM` sample re-architects the `AdventureWorksRestJSONPage.xaml` page from the Chapter 4 `CallingRemoteServices` project to use MVVM in the Chapter 6 project named `BasicMVVM`.

The `BasicMVVM` and the `WcfRemoteServicesSimpleRestJSON` projects are configured as the startup project. Three folders are added to the project, named `Model`, `View`, and `ViewModel`. The sections that follow cover the major components of MVVM in the `BasicMVVM` example.

BasicMVVM - Model

The Model contains the building blocks of the application. It consists of the underlying data objects that are populated via a data access layer. Examples of Model classes are `Customer`, `Store`, `Product`, and so on. When you create a class to represent an object in an application, it most likely belongs as part of the Model. The Model sits behind the ViewModel. The View will data bind to lists or individual objects based on classes in the Model.

To get started, copy over the `Vendor` class from the `WcfRemoteServicesSimpleRestJSON` services project to the `BasicMVVM` Models folder. The class implements the `INotifyPropertyChanged` interface to support data binding at the class level. The INotifyPropertyChanged interface ensures that changes to the underlying object are propagated to the UI and vice versa. See Listing 6-1 for the code.

Listing 6-1. Vendor Model Class Code File

```
using System;
using System.ComponentModel;
using System.Runtime.Serialization;

namespace BasicMVVM.Model
{
  //Copied from services project
  [DataContract()]
  public class Vendor : INotifyPropertyChanged
  {
    private string AccountNumberField;
    private byte CreditRatingField;
    private string NameField;

    [DataMemberAttribute()]
    public string AccountNumber
    {
      get
      {
        return this.AccountNumberField;
      }
      set
      {
        this.AccountNumberField = value;
        NotifyPropertyChanged("AccountNumber");
      }
    }

    [DataMemberAttribute()]
    public byte CreditRating
    {
      get
      {
        return this.CreditRatingField;
      }
      set
      {
        this.CreditRatingField = value;
        NotifyPropertyChanged("CreditRating");
      }
    }

    [DataMemberAttribute()]
    public string Name
    {
      get
```

```
    {
      return this.NameField;
    }
    set
    {
      this.NameField = value;
      NotifyPropertyChanged("Name");
    }
  }

  public event PropertyChangedEventHandler PropertyChanged;
  private void NotifyPropertyChanged(String propertyName)
  {
    if (null != PropertyChanged)
    {
      PropertyChanged(this, new PropertyChangedEventArgs(propertyName));
    }
  }
}
}
```

BasicMVVM - ViewModel

The fact that the View or UI data binds to the ViewModel suggests that a ViewModel consists of the data containers for the application, which is correct. Lists of objects defined in the Model are created and managed by the ViewModel. In addition, the ViewModel consists of the majority of application logic as well.

Next create the VendorViewModel class. The VendorViewModel class in the BasicMVVM project supports the following four major features:

- Vendor-specific business logic

- UI Data binding via INotifyPropertyChanged

- Design-time support

- REST+JSON data loading

The Vendor-specific business logic is pretty straightforward. It consists of a read-only collection of Vendor objects from the Model and a couple of update operations that we cover in just a bit.

▓ **Note** While the VendorViewModel.Vendors collection is read-only— it has just a get property accessor— you can still add and remove Vendor objects in the collection. You just cannot assign a new collection to the property.

It is critical to implement INotifyPropertyChanged for data binding to work. Otherwise, changes are not propagated back to the UI, and vice versa. It is simple enough to do. Add an instance of the

PropertyChangedEventHandler class named PropertyChanged and a method that takes a property name as a string and then fires the PropertyChanged event instance.

To detect design time, the System.ComponentModel.DesignerProperties class has a static bool property named IsInDesignTool that indicates whether the code is running in a design-time tool. The VendorViewModel constructor checks if an instance of the class is running at design-time. If it is at design-time, the constructor calls the LoadSampleData method. Otherwise, at run-time, it calls LoadData, which invokes a remote REST+JSON service.

The VendorViewModel class implements two data operations on the Vendors collection, one to insert a vendor and another to delete a vendor. The data operations are implemented via two ICommand implementations, one to add a Vendor object and another to remove a Vendor object from the VendorViewModel.Vendors collection. The ICommand interface is newly available in Windows Phone OS 7.1, brought over from Silverlight 4. This interface enables rich control over business logic execution via data binding. Commanding is an advanced feature of Silverlight that enables stronger separation of concerns between the View and the ViewModel.

In the previous edition of the book, event handlers had to be wired up in the View's code-behind class file, and code like this executed in the handler:

```
private void insertVendorAppBarBtn_Click(object sender, EventArgs e)
{
  VendorViewModel vm = LayoutRoot.DataContext as VendorViewModel;
  vm.AddVendor();
}
```

Instead, you can now data bind in XAML to the ICommand directly without having to write any code. I'll discuss how that works when I cover the VendorsView view object. The last major functionality for the VendorsViewModel class is making the remote service call, which is covered in detail in Chapter 4. The interesting change for this scenario is that the service call and asynchronous callback live in the VendorsViewModel class, so the code does not have direct access to the View and the View UI elements as in Chapter 4. The callback cannot have code like the following:

```
vendorsListbox.Dispatcher.BeginInvoke(…);
```

The solution is to make the call using this line of code instead:

```
Deployment.Current.Dispatcher.BeginInvoke(..);
```

This code ensures that the correct Dispatcher instance is used to notify the UI that data changes occurred. The next challenge is that the callback function needs to update the Vendors collection property. Remember that Vendors is a read-only collection, because we do not want external classes to be able to assign a new collection to it. We want the data to only come from the remote services. The code instead assigns the collection to the underlying _vendors collection private member variable.

The final issue is that the code still needs to notify the UI that data changes occurred—that is, that the Vendors collection is loaded. Since the _vendors collection is updated directly, NotifyPropertyChanged("Vendors") is called in the anonymous delegate by BeginInvoke. Again, the code could make Vendors read/write and have a set accessor function like this, but maintaining data integrity is preferred, so the set function is commented out, as in the following:

```
set
{
  _vendors = value;
  NotifyPropertyChanged("Vendors");
}
```

Listing 6-2 has the full source code for VendorViewModel as well as the two ICommand implementations in the AddVendorCommand and RemoveVendorCommand classes.

Listing 6-2. *VendorViewModel Class Code File*

```
using System;
using System.Collections.ObjectModel;
using System.ComponentModel;
using System.Linq;
using System.Net;
using System.Runtime.Serialization.Json;
using System.Windows;
using BasicMVVM.Models;
using System.Windows.Input;

namespace BasicMVVM.ViewModels
{
  public class VendorViewModel : INotifyPropertyChanged
  {
    public VendorViewModel()
    {
      if (InDesignTime)
      {
        LoadSampleData();
      }
      else
      {
        LoadData();
      }
    }

    #region Design-time support
    private bool InDesignTime
    {
      get
      {
        return DesignerProperties.IsInDesignTool;
      }
    }

    private void LoadSampleData()
    {
      _vendors = new ObservableCollection<Vendor>()
      {
        new Vendor(){AccountNumber="111111", CreditRating=65,
          Name="DesignTime - Fabrikam Bikes" },
        new Vendor(){AccountNumber="222222", CreditRating=40,
          Name="Contoso Sports" },
        new Vendor(){AccountNumber="333333", CreditRating=30,
          Name="Duwamish Surfing Gear" },
        new Vendor(){AccountNumber="444444", CreditRating=65,
```

```
        Name="Contoso Bikes" },
      new Vendor(){AccountNumber="555555", CreditRating=40,
        Name="Fabrikam Sports" },
      new Vendor(){AccountNumber="666666", CreditRating=30,
        Name="Duwamish Golf" },
      new Vendor(){AccountNumber="777777", CreditRating=65,
        Name="Fabrikam Sun Sports" },
      new Vendor(){AccountNumber="888888", CreditRating=40,
        Name="Contoso Lacross" },
      new Vendor(){AccountNumber="999999", CreditRating=30,
        Name="Duwamish Team Sports" },
    };
}
#endregion

#region Vendors Data Load
HttpWebRequest httpWebRequest;
private void LoadData()
{
    httpWebRequest =
      HttpWebRequest.CreateHttp(
      "http://localhost:9191/AdventureWorksRestJSON.svc/Vendors");
    httpWebRequest.BeginGetResponse(new AsyncCallback(GetVendors), null);
}

//add a reference to System.Servicemodel.web to get DataContractJsonSerializer
void GetVendors(IAsyncResult result)
{
    HttpWebResponse response =
      httpWebRequest.EndGetResponse(result) as HttpWebResponse;
    DataContractJsonSerializer ser =
      new DataContractJsonSerializer(typeof(ObservableCollection<Vendor>));
    _vendors =
      ser.ReadObject(response.GetResponseStream()) as ObservableCollection<Vendor>;
    //Vendors is read-only so cannot set directly
    //Must call NotifyPropertyChanged notifications on UI thread
    //to update the UI and have data binding work properly
    Deployment.Current.Dispatcher.BeginInvoke(() =>
    {
      NotifyPropertyChanged("Vendors");
    });
}
#endregion

#region Vendors Business Logic
private ObservableCollection<Vendor> _vendors;
public ObservableCollection<Vendor> Vendors
{
    get
    {
      return _vendors;
    }
```

```
    //set
    //{
    //   _vendors = value;
    //   NotifyPropertyChanged("Vendors");
    //}
  }

  public Vendor GetVendorByAccountNumber(string accountNumber)
  {
    var vendor = from v in _vendors
                 where v.AccountNumber == accountNumber
                 select v;

    return vendor.First<Vendor>();
  }

  public ICommand AddVendor
  {
    get { return new AddVendorCommand(this); }
  }

  public ICommand RemoveVendor
  {

    get { return new RemoveVendorCommand(this); }
  }
  #endregion

  #region INotifyPropertyChanged interface members
  public event PropertyChangedEventHandler PropertyChanged;

  public void NotifyPropertyChanged(String property)
  {
    if (PropertyChanged != null)
    {
      PropertyChanged(this, new PropertyChangedEventArgs(property));
    }
  }
  #endregion
}

public class AddVendorCommand : ICommand
{
  VendorViewModel _vendorViewModel;
  public AddVendorCommand(VendorViewModel vendorViewModel)
  {
    _vendorViewModel = vendorViewModel;
  }

  public bool CanExecute(object parameter)
  {
    if (_vendorViewModel != null)
```

```
      return true;
    else
      return false;
  }

  public event EventHandler CanExecuteChanged;

  public void Execute(object parameter)
  {
    _vendorViewModel.Vendors.Add(new Vendor()
    {
      AccountNumber = "111111",
      CreditRating = 65,
      Name = "Fabrikam Bikes - Added"
    });
  }
}

public class RemoveVendorCommand : ICommand
{
  VendorViewModel _vendorViewModel;
  public RemoveVendorCommand(VendorViewModel vendorViewModel)
  {
    _vendorViewModel = vendorViewModel;
  }

  public bool CanExecute(object parameter)
  {
    if (_vendorViewModel != null)
      return true;
    else
      return false;
  }

  public event EventHandler CanExecuteChanged;

  public void Execute(object parameter)
  {
    Vendor vendor = parameter as Vendor;
    if (null != vendor)
      _vendorViewModel.Vendors.Remove((Vendor)vendor);
  }
}
}
```

Commanding is implemented by first declaring an ICommand object as part of the ViewModel class, in this case VendorViewModel.AddVendor and VendorViewModel.RemoveVendor. Both return an instantiation of the appropriate ICommand implementation, passing in the current instance of the VendorViewModel. The next section covers how to make the Model and ViewModel objects available to the UI as well as how to wire in the ICommand support

BasicMVVM - View

The View is the actual XAML of an application. It is the `MainPage.xaml` file in a typical Windows Phone project, and is what the user interacts with directly, presenting the underlying data and application logic. The View data binds to the ViewModel, which is covered in the previous section.

The goal when building the View is not to have any code in the code-behind for the `.xaml` file, if possible, to maximize separation of concerns. This means that all logic is in the ViewModel, which is nonvisual, making it much more unit-testable. The other advantage of the separation of concerns here is that the design team can focus on building out the View without interfering with business logic in event handlers. A View always has a reference to the ViewModel, because it data binds to it.

Remove the `MainPage.xaml` from the `BasicMVVM` project and add a new View (.xaml page) to the `Views` folder named `VendorsView.xaml`. Next, edit the WMAppManifest.xml file by changing the `NavigationPage` attribute to point to the new default task, as in the following:

```
<DefaultTask  Name ="_default" NavigationPage="Views/CustomersView.xaml"/>.
```

■ **Note** In general, the `WMAppManifest.xml` file should not be manually edited, but in this case it is required.

In Expression Blend, add a `ListBox` to `VendorsView.xaml` and configure the `ItemsSource` to data bind to the `VendorViewModel.Vendors` collection by clicking the Advanced Options button next to the `ItemsSource` property in the Expression Blend Properties window and selecting Data Binding to bring up the Create Data Binding dialog. Click the +CLR Object button, select `VendorViewModel,` and then click OK.

■ **Tip** If the `VendorViewModel` class— or any .NET CLR class that you want to data bind—does not show up in the dialog box, make sure to compile the application. Static collections will not appear either.

This generates a new Data Source named `VendorViewModelDataSource` in the left pane. Select `Vendors` in the right pane and then click OK. This configuration updates the XAML in three places. It adds a new resource to the `VendorsView` page, as in the following:

```
<phone:PhoneApplicationPage.Resources>
  <BasicMVVM_ViewModels:VendorViewModel
  x:Key="VendorViewModelDataSource" d:IsDataSource="True"/>
</phone:PhoneApplicationPage.Resources>
```

It configures `LayoutRoot Grid`'s `DataContext` property to point to the `VendorViewModel` class:

```
DataContext="{Binding Source={StaticResource VendorViewModelDataSource}}"
```

Next, Configure the `vendorsListBox ItemsSource` property to data bind to the `VendorViewModel.Vendors` collection like so: ItemsSource="{Binding Vendors}" in Expression Blend. Generally in Windows Phone, developers should use the Application Bar as much as possible as the standard UI to implement in-page functionality. In this case we use two standard buttons to demonstrate the concept of commanding. The `ListBox` configured above is added to a `StackPanel` container, and another `StackPanel` with Orientation set to Horizontal is added below the `ListBox` with two Buttons objects. Figure 6-2 shows the UI.

Figure 6-2. *BasicMVVM running in the emulator*

One of the goals of MVVM and separating concerns is to make the View as "thin" as possible. Windows Phone OS 7.1 (Mango) now supports UI element Buttons to data bind to methods on the `ViewModel` via Commanding and the `ICommand` interface. This means that instead of having event handlers in the code-behind for the view, everything is instead configured via data binding in XAML.

As mentioned above, Windows Phone OS 7.1 with Silverlight 4 compatibility includes support for Commanding. `ButtonBase` and `Hyperlink` support `Command` and `CommandParameter` properties. The `Command` property can reference an `ICommand` implementation that comes from a view-model data source, through a `{Binding}` usage. The command is then interpreted at run-time. `CommandParameter` can pass data into the `Command`, such as which record to delete.

In Expression Blend, select each button and bring up the data binding UI, and both of the `VendorViewModel ICommand` objects are displayed. For the "Remove Vendor" button, also data bind the `CommandParameter` property to the `ListBox.SelectedItem` property. Save the changes and run the project to test out Commanding support, and you'll see that it works like a charm.

While using Commanding with `Button` objects is great, unfortunately support for Commanding is not available with the Application Bar Buttons. Luckily, there are third-party, open-source frameworks that provide extensions to Silverlight that enable better support for MVVM, which we cover in the next section.

Pick an MVVM Helper SDK

Because Silverlight for Windows Phone is based on Silverlight 3, it falls short of the MVVM capabilities available in Silverlight 4 and WPF, such as full Commanding support. Luckily, there are quite a few third-party MVVM frameworks available to choose from that provide Commanding support and more. The following lists a few in no particular order:

- Caliburn

- nRoute

- Composite Application Block/PRISM

- SilverlightFX

- GalaSoft's MVVM Light Toolkit

The major benefit that these frameworks have in varying degrees is increasing separation of concerns, unit testing support, support for Messaging, and additional Commanding support. You can find arguments for and against the available frameworks, so please investigate the available options. For this example, let's take MVVM Light Toolkit for a spin, as it is this author's opinion that MVVM Light provides a nice balance of power and simplicity that is a great fit for phone application development. Many others would suggest Caliburn instead for similar reasons. The most important thing is to pick a helper SDK, learn it, and use it.

GalaSoft MVVM Light Toolkit

For Windows Phone development, my preference is GalaSoft's MVVM Light Toolkit. In my opinion it has the right combination of power and as the name says, lightness, for mobile application development.

The MVVM Light Toolkit is up to version 4 Beta, which has quite a few enhancements over the previous version. All of the code has been updated to work with this latest version as of the time of this writing.

The MVVM Light Toolkit was originally developed to address the Commanding shortfalls in Silverlight 2 and Silverlight 3. The MVVM Light Toolkit also includes customized Visual Studio 2010 templates to help you get started right away. First, download the MVVM Light Toolkit and follow the instructions at this page:

`http://galasoft.ch/mvvm/getstarted/`

If you like the MVVM Light toolkit, I encourage you to click the Donate button at the bottom of the above page, which goes towards the cost of running the site and the rest goes to charity. The source code is available in CodePlex here:

`http://mvvmlight.codeplex.com/`

Once you have the toolkit downloaded and installed, you can run the MVVMLightSample available in Chapter 6 to see it in action. The entire range of features of the MVVM Light Toolkit are not described end-to-end in this book, but the next couple of sections cover the features of MVVM Light used to migrate the BasicMVVM to MVVM Light.

MVVM Light Sample

In Visual Studio 2010, you can select File New Project, and click on Silverlight for Windows Phone to filter to the Windows Phone project templates. Select MvvmLight (WP71) as the project template to get started with the Mango version of MVVM Light. If you don't see that option, check to ensure that you installed the toolkit correctly before proceeding.

Once the project is created, run it and the screen in Figure 6-3 should appear, which indicates that all is configured correctly.

Figure 6-3. *Testing your MVVM Light installation*

The page title, subtitle, and text are all data bound to the `MainViewModel` class. Let's go through the architecture of MVVM Light so that you have a basic understanding as we migrate the `BasicMVVM` app to MVVM Light. After a new project is created, the project includes the default `App.xaml` and `MainPage.xaml` as well as the other items expected in a Silverlight for Windows Phone application but with a couple of additions. There is a Model folder with three code files present that we discuss shortly. There is also a `ViewModel` folder that contains two `ViewModel` classes named `MainViewModel` and `ViewModelLocator`. I cover these in the next section.

ViewModelLocator

The `ViewModelLocator` class contains a reference to every `ViewModel` class in the project. This provides a centralized way to manage creation and allow XAML configuration via a single application resource. By default, in `App.xaml` a resource is added for the `ViewModelLocator` class. A namespace is added to the `<Application>` object that hosts the `PhoneApplicationFrame` that contains the XAML pages or View classes as they are navigated:

```
xmlns:vm="clr-namespace:MvvmLightSample.ViewModel"
```

The `ViewModelLocator` class is configured as an application level resource like this:

```
<Application.Resources>
    <vm:ViewModelLocator x:Key="Locator"
                         d:IsDataSource="True" />
</Application.Resources>
```

This resource is available throughout the entire application, just like any other application-level resource, making the referenced `ViewModel` objects available now. Now we move on to explain how `MainPage.xaml` data binds to MainViewModel within this architecture. In the XAML, the `<PhoneApplicationPage>` element's `DataContext` property data binds to the Locator resource discussed above via this XAML code:

```
DataContext="{Binding Main, Source={StaticResource Locator}}"
```

The `Path` property for the `Binding` object is configured with the value of `Main` using the default syntax (it can also be written as `Path=Main`). This configuration makes an instance of the `MainViewModel` available within `MainPage.xaml` and allows the page title, sub-title, and text to data bind to properties available on the `MainViewModel`. Here's an example of one of the Application Title Bindings:

```
<TextBlock x:Name="ApplicationTitle"
    Text="{Binding ApplicationTitle}"
    Style="{StaticResource PhoneTextNormalStyle}" />
```

Listing 6-3 shows the default ViewModelLocator class.

Listing 6-3. *Default ViewModelLocator Class Code File*

```
namespace MvvmLightSample.ViewModel
{
  /// <summary>
  /// This class contains static references to all the view models in the
  /// application and provides an entry point for the bindings.
  /// <para>
  /// Use the <strong>mvvmlocatorproperty</strong> snippet to add ViewModels
  /// to this locator.
  /// </para>
  /// <para>
  /// See http://www.galasoft.ch/mvvm/getstarted
  /// </para>
  /// </summary>
  public class ViewModelLocator
  {
    static ViewModelLocator()
    {
      ServiceLocator.SetLocatorProvider(() => SimpleIoc.Default);

      if (ViewModelBase.IsInDesignModeStatic)
```

```
    {
      SimpleIoc.Default.Register<IDataService, Design.DesignDataService>();
    }
    else
    {
      SimpleIoc.Default.Register<IDataService, DataService>();
    }

    SimpleIoc.Default.Register<MainViewModel>();
  }

  /// <summary>
  /// Gets the Main property.
  /// </summary>
  [System.Diagnostics.CodeAnalysis.SuppressMessage("Microsoft.Performance",
    "CA1822:MarkMembersAsStatic",
    Justification = "This non-static member is needed for data binding purposes.")]
  public MainViewModel Main
  {
    get
    {
      return ServiceLocator.Current.GetInstance<MainViewModel>();
    }
  }

  /// <summary>
  /// Cleans up all the resources.
  /// </summary>
  public static void Cleanup()
  {
  }
 }
}
```

Notice in Listing 6-3 how the MainViewModel is made available. It uses the SimpleIoc class to register the class MainViewModel within the application. For the Main property, the ServiceLocator class gets the instance of MainViewModel that is available.

The class name SimpleIoc is short for Simple Inversion of Control, which is a technique to simplify the creation and the resolution of services by allowing a consumer to request an interface and have SimpleIoc provide a matching concrete class, in this case the ViewModels; it allows for a cleaner syntax in the ViewModelLocator than in previous versions of MVVM Light.

To add additional ViewModel objects, manually edit the ViewModelLocator class and follow the pattern for the MainViewModel as an example. There is a code snippet available to automate this process. Type mvvmlocatorproperty and tap the Tab key twice to quickly add the property using Visual Studio 2010's code snippet template UI. Essentially, type new values for the default and click the Tab key to move through the template to quickly add the property combination in the correct format.

The MainViewModel takes a type of IDataService in its constructor. Generally ViewModels need not take parameters for XAML support. With SimpleIoc, as long as the service is registered, in this case IDataService, and the ViewModel is registered, SimpleIoc will handle this for you and pass the registered instance into the constructor and create the MainViewModel.

Notice also in the ViewModelLocator class it registers a service for the IDataService interface in the constructor using an if statement to provide design-time or run-time data depending on the current environment. What's nice about this method is that the application can simply retrieve an instance of `IDataService` and it will be properly populated with data as needed; you won't have to worry about design-time vs. run-time. You could use the same technique to register an `IDataService` that provides different sets of data to authenticated or unauthenticated users, as well as design-time data.

MvvmLightSample – Model

A reference is added to `System.Runtime.Serialization` assembly and to `System.ServiceModel.Web` to set up the work needed to create the Model and the related data service.

A question that comes up when building MVVM is where to put the code to load up your data collections. MVVM Light provides an answer to this question with the concept of an `IDataService` and the inversion-of-control functionality provided by `SimpleIoc`. The idea is that you register your data service and ViewModels in the view model locator page, and it connects the ViewModel with the corresponding service. In MVVM Light, the service is placed with the related `Model` in the `Model` folder.

We first modify the `IDataService` provided by the default project template to return the `ApplicationTitle` and `PageName` so that the `MainPage.xaml` View has something to bind to for the Title and Page Name. Note that the data binding code is already there in the default `MainPage.xaml` View, but it is not present in the `MainViewModel` or the `IDataService`. Here is the updated interface:

```
public interface IDataService
{
  void GetApplicationTitle(Action<DataItem, Exception> callback);
  void GetPageName(Action<DataItem, Exception> callback);
}
```

The implementation class, `DataService`, is not much more complex. It simply returns the values for the properties:

```
public class DataService : IDataService
{
  public void GetApplicationTitle(Action<DataItem, Exception> callback)
  {
    var item = new DataItem("CHAPTER SIX");
    callback(item, null);
  }

  public void GetPageName(Action<DataItem, Exception> callback)
  {
    var item = new DataItem("mvvm light sample");
    callback(item, null);
  }
}
```

While a pretty simple modification, it demonstrates that the `DataService` provides a callback of the desired data. Let's now create the `IVendorService`, which will return a listing of all of the `Vendor` objects:

```
public interface IVendorsService
{
  void GetVendors(Action<IList<Vendor>, Exception> callback);
}
```

In this case, instead of returning a DataItem class object, GetVendors returns an IList containing Vendor objects. Where this gets interesting is in the concrete implementation in the VendorService class shown here:

```
using System;
using System.Collections.Generic;
using System.Collections.ObjectModel;
using System.Net;
using Newtonsoft.Json;

namespace MvvmLightSample.Model
{
  public class VendorsService : IVendorsService
  {
    private const string ServiceUri =
"http://localhost:9191/AdventureWorksRestJSON.svc/Vendors";
    public void GetVendors(Action<IList<Vendor>, Exception> callback)
    {
      var client = new WebClient();
      client.DownloadStringCompleted += ClientDownloadStringCompleted;
      client.DownloadStringAsync(new Uri(ServiceUri), callback);
    }

    private static void ClientDownloadStringCompleted(object sender,
DownloadStringCompletedEventArgs e)
    {
      var callback = e.UserState as Action<IList<Vendor>, Exception>;

      if (callback == null)
      {
        return;
      }

      if (e.Error != null)
      {
        callback(null, e.Error);
        return;
      }

      ObservableCollection<Vendor> vendors;
      vendors = JsonConvert.DeserializeObject<ObservableCollection<Vendor>>(e.Result);
      callback(vendors, null);
    }
  }
}
```

There are a few things going on in this implementation to note, but the first is that the code uses JSON.NET to deserialize the data. JSON.NET has been tested informally to have better performance than the built-in DataContractSerializer class. JSON.NET is very flexible with quite a few options that I won't go into here. I do take advantage of the very simple code it takes to deserialize a string into a collection of objects:

```
ObservableCollection<Vendor> vendors;
vendors = JsonConvert.DeserializeObject<ObservableCollection<Vendor>>(e.Result);
```

Otherwise, the code uses the new and improved `WebClient` class in Windows Phone OS 7.1 (Mango) to call the REST service and return the data in a string as shown earlier in the code. The last item I cover is the modifications to the `Vendor` class. It inherits from `ObservableObject`, a new base class available in MVVM Light version 4. Here is the updated `Vendor` class:

```
using System.Runtime.Serialization;
using GalaSoft.MvvmLight;

namespace MvvmLightSample.Model
{
  [DataContract()]
  public class Vendor : ObservableObject
  {
    private string AccountNumberField;
    private byte CreditRatingField;
    private string NameField;

    [DataMemberAttribute()]
    public string AccountNumber
    {
      get
      { return this.AccountNumberField; }
      set
      { this.AccountNumberField = value;
        RaisePropertyChanged("AccountNumber");}
    }

    [DataMemberAttribute()]
    public byte CreditRating
    {
      get
      { return this.CreditRatingField; }
      set
      {this.CreditRatingField = value;
        RaisePropertyChanged("CreditRating");}
    }

    [DataMemberAttribute()]
    public string Name
    {
      get
      {return this.NameField;}
      set
      {this.NameField = value;
        RaisePropertyChanged("Name");}
    }
  }
}
```

The other item is design-time data. The `ViewModelLocator` class checks for design time with a call to `ViewModelBase.IsInDesignModeStatic`. Depending on whether it is design time or not, the `Design` data service is registered with SimpleIoc or the production data service is registered in the ViewModelLocator constructor:

```
if (ViewModelBase.IsInDesignModeStatic)
{
  SimpleIoc.Default.Register<IVendorsService, Design.DesignVendorService>();
  SimpleIoc.Default.Register<IDataService, Design.DesignDataService>();
}
else
{
  SimpleIoc.Default.Register<IVendorsService, VendorsService>();
  SimpleIoc.Default.Register<IDataService, DataService>();
}
```

The default project template for MVVM Light has a Design folder with a default design-time data source class named DesignDataService. I modified it to return the ApplicationTitle and PageName values at design time. The design-time data class for Vendors is DesignVendorDataService.cs in the Design folder. It creates five records to have some data at design-time. As you can see, having Interface-based services allow for simplified code to instantiate the correct data source as needed. This completes coverage of the Model and data service. Next up on our MVVM journey is the ViewModel.

MvvmLightSample – VendorsViewModel

With the changes in MVVM Light version 4, I rewrote the ViewModel class from BasicMVVM to take advantage of the new features.

■ **Note** The first edition of this book leveraged MVVM Light version 3, which does not compile in the new version. Be sure to update to the latest sample code available as a download for this edition.

The VendorViewModel class inherits from ViewModelBase to take advantage of the built-in INotifyPropertyChange implementation. I've also added a reference to System.ServiceModel.Web to make the DataContractJsonSerializer class available within the VendorsViewModel.

The new VendorsViewModel class includes a Vendors property of type ObservableCollection as before. The constructor for VendorsViewModel takes an instance of IVendorsService passed in by SimpleIoc. In the constructor the data is loaded up as shown here:

```
public VendorsViewModel(IVendorsService dataService)
{
  _vendorsService = dataService;

  Vendors = new ObservableCollection<Vendor>();
  _vendorsService.GetVendors(
      (vendors, error) =>
      {
        if (error != null)
        {
          // Report error here
```

```
            return;
        }
        Vendors = (ObservableCollection<Vendor>)vendors;
    });
}
```

Whether at design time or runtime, the appropriate concrete implementation of IVendorService is provided and the appropriate data service provides data to the UI. Next up is the VendorsView object where the data is displayed.

MvvmLightSample – VendorsView

A new folder named View is added to the MVVMLightSample project, and the VendorsView.xaml page is copied from the BasicMVVM project to the MVVMLightSample view folder. Do a Find / Replace with BasicMVVM to replace it with MvvmLightSample with the "Look in" set to Current Project. That fixes up namespace references to compile the project successfully.

Next, MainViewModel is modified to return a more appropriate page title and subtitle as well as string text for the Welcome message property for the MainPage.xaml page to display the application title and page name. A TextBlock is added to MainPage.xaml to provide a link to navigate to the Vendors View page via the NavigateToPageAction behavior. Clicking on that text will navigate you to the VendorsView.xaml page. Fix up the margins so that everything aligns at 24px on the left.

If you run the project, it works as before, but let's configure the VendorsView to take advantage of the MVVM Light toolkit capabilities. First, add a property combination to the ViewModelLocator via the mvvmlocatorproperty code snippet. The code snippet quickly generates this code for you in the ViewModelLocator class:

```
static ViewModelLocator()
{
  ServiceLocator.SetLocatorProvider(() => SimpleIoc.Default);

  if (ViewModelBase.IsInDesignModeStatic)
  {
    SimpleIoc.Default.Register<IVendorsService, Design.DesignVendorService>();
    SimpleIoc.Default.Register<IDataService, Design.DesignDataService>();
  }
  else
  {
    SimpleIoc.Default.Register<IVendorsService, VendorsService>();
    SimpleIoc.Default.Register<IDataService, DataService>();
  }
  SimpleIoc.Default.Register<MainViewModel>();
  SimpleIoc.Default.Register<VendorsViewModel>();
}

public VendorsViewModel Vendors
{
  get
  {
    return ServiceLocator.Current.GetInstance<VendorsViewModel>();
  }
}
```

As you can see, if you are not familiar with Visual Studio 2010 the code snippet is quite handy! It adds an implementation of the constructor that registers the ViewModel. We delete that version and edit the existing constructor as shown above. It also adds a property that uses the `ServiceLocator` to return the `VendorsViewModel` instance.

Now that we have the `VendorsView` added to the `ViewModelLocator`, we can configure the `VendorsView` to data bind the MVVM Light Toolkit way using Expression Blend. First compile the project to make sure everything is up to date, and then remove the `DataContext` binding on the `LayoutRoot Grid`. Also remove the `VendorViewModelDataSource` from the `PhoneApplicationPage.Resources` section in the `VendorsView.xaml` file.

In Expression Blend, select the `PhoneApplicationPage` root item in the Objects and Timeline tool window. Find the `DataContext` property, click the Advanced Options button, and select Data Binding to bring up the Create Data Binding dialog. Select the `Locator` data source and then select Vendors, as shown in Figure 6-4.

Figure 6-4. *Data bind DataContext to the VendorsViewModel*

Run the application and navigate to the `VendorsView`, and it displays the data as before. We still have the event handlers in the code-behind. In the next subsection the event handlers are removed and instead the application takes advantage Commanding support provided by the MVVM Light toolkit.

Commanding and RelayCommand

The MVVM Light Toolkit supports Commanding, or data binding events to ViewModel methods, via the RelayCommand and RelayCommand<T> classes. With Windows Phone OS 7.1, the programming model is improved with full support for ICommand and Commanding within the XAML programming model. I demonstrated the command support in the BasicMVVM project. This section covers how to leverage MVVM Light's Commanding support.

In the VendorViewModel class, two RelayCommand instances are added in a region named Commanding, one that is parameter-less and one that takes a parameter. Here is the declaration:

```
#region Commanding
public RelayCommand AddAVendorCommand
{
  get;
  private set;
}

public RelayCommand<Vendor> RemoveAVendorCommand
{
  get;
  private set;
}
#endregion
```

The commands are instantiated in the VendorViewModel() constructor in this code:

```
//Instantiate Commands
AddAVendorCommand = new RelayCommand(
  () => AddVendor());

RemoveAVendorCommand = new RelayCommand<Vendor>(
  param => RemoveVendor(param));
```

The RelayCommand objects bridge between the ViewModel methods and the UI events. RelayCommand has support for one parameter only so if you need to pass more info, consider encapsulating into an object. Now it's time to data bind the commands in the UI. Currently the application uses the application bar to execute Add and Remove. Unfortunately, the ApplicationBarIconButton class does not inherit from FrameworkElement so the ButtonBaseExtension cannot be attached to a DependencyObject. You can still call the relay in code-behind as before. Here is an example from the sample:

```
private void insertVendorAppBarBtn_Click(object sender, EventArgs e)
{
  var vm = DataContext as VendorViewModel;
  if (vm != null)
  {
    vm.AddAVendorCommand.Execute(null);
  }
}
```

For this sample, the two Buttons are added so that we can demonstrate the EventToCommand Expression Blend behavior, as well as via the code-behind for the application bar buttons. In Expression Blend, switch to the Assets tab and select Behaviors to filter the list. Drag the EventToCommand behavior on to the Button objects and configure the correct command on each button. For the Remove Button, data bind the EventToCommand Command property to the RemoveAVendorCommand RelayCommand. Also data bind the CommandParameter for the Remove EventToCommand object to the vendorsListBox.SelectedItem method, which returns a Vendor object. Here is the resulting markup for Remove:

```
<Button x:Name="RemoveButton" Content="Remove" HorizontalAlignment="Right"
VerticalAlignment="Bottom" Margin="0,0,8,7">
  <Custom:Interaction.Triggers>
    <Custom:EventTrigger EventName="Click">
      <GalaSoft_MvvmLight_Command:EventToCommand Command="{Binding RemoveAVendorCommand,
Mode=OneWay}" CommandParameter="{Binding SelectedItem, ElementName=VendorsListBox}"/>
    </Custom:EventTrigger>
  </Custom:Interaction.Triggers>
</Button>
```

The RelayCommand class also supports CanExecute and CanExecuteChanged members as well to determine whether to enable or disable the element, in this case a Button object. The CanExecute method can be passed in to the constructor as a second parameter. Here's an example:

```
AddAVendorCommand = new RelayCommand(
  () => AddVendor(), () => CheckEnabled);
```

We have now completely migrated the sample over to MVVM. Listing 6-4 shows the source code for the updated VendorViewModel class.

Listing 6-4. *Updated* VendorViewModel *Code File*

```
using System.Collections.ObjectModel;
using System.Linq;
using GalaSoft.MvvmLight;
using GalaSoft.MvvmLight.Command;
using MvvmLightSample.Model;

namespace MvvmLightSample.ViewModel
{
  public class VendorsViewModel : ViewModelBase
  {
    private readonly IVendorsService _vendorsService;

    public const string VendorsPropertyName = "Vendors";
    private ObservableCollection<Vendor> _vendors = null;
    public ObservableCollection<Vendor> Vendors
    {
      get
      {
        return _vendors;
      }

      set
      {
        if (_vendors == value)
        {
          return;
```

```
    }

    _vendors = value;
    RaisePropertyChanged(VendorsPropertyName);
  }
}

/// <summary>
/// Initializes a new instance of the VendorsViewModel class.
/// </summary>
public VendorsViewModel(IVendorsService dataService)
{
  _vendorsService = dataService;

  Vendors = new ObservableCollection<Vendor>();
  _vendorsService.GetVendors(
      (vendors, error) =>
      {
        if (error != null)
        {
          // Report error here
          return;
        }
        Vendors = (ObservableCollection<Vendor>)vendors;
      });

  //Instantiate Commands
  AddAVendorCommand = new RelayCommand(
    () => AddVendor());

  RemoveAVendorCommand = new RelayCommand<Vendor>(
    param => RemoveVendor(param));

}

#region Business Logic
public Vendor GetVendorByAccountNumber(string accountNumber)
{
  var vendor = from v in Vendors
               where v.AccountNumber == accountNumber
               select v;

  return vendor.First<Vendor>();
}

public void AddVendor()
{
  Vendors.Add(new Vendor()
  {
    AccountNumber = "111111",
    CreditRating = 65,
    Name = "Fabrikam Bikes - Added"
```

```
      });
    }

    public void RemoveVendor(object vendor)
    {
      if (null != vendor)
        Vendors.Remove((Vendor)vendor);
    }
    #endregion

    #region Commanding
    public RelayCommand AddAVendorCommand
    {
      get;
      private set;
    }

    public RelayCommand<Vendor> RemoveAVendorCommand
    {
      get;
      private set;
    }
    #endregion

    ////public override void Cleanup()
    ////{
    ////    // Clean up if needed

    ////    base.Cleanup();
    ////}
}
```
}In the next couple of sections, I cover additional features of the MVVM Light Toolkit.

The MVVM Light Messenger Class

The Messenger class provides a means to communicate within an application in a decoupled way. Classes can register to receive messages of different types. The message can be anything from simple values to complex objects. Likewise, messages can specify a target type that should receive the message for fine-tuned control.

MVVM Light includes multiple message classes. The following is a list of possible messages from the docs:

- **MessageBase:** A simple message class, carrying optional information about the message's sender.

- **GenericMessage<T>:** A simple message with a Content property of type T.

- **NotificationMessage:** Used to send a notification (as a string) to a recipient. For example, define notifications as constants in a Notifications class, and then send **Notifications.Save** to recipients.

- `NotificationMessage<T>:` Same as the previous, but with a generic Content property. It can be used to pass a parameter to the recipient together with the notification.

- `NotificationMessageAction:` Sends a notification to a recipient and allows the recipient to call the sender back.

- `NotificationMessageAction<T>:` Sends a notification to a recipient and allows the recipient to call the sender back with a generic parameter.

- `DialogMessage:` Used to request that a recipient (typically a View) displays a dialog, and passes the result back to the caller (using a callback). The recipient can choose how to display the dialog, either with a standard MessageBox, with a custom popup, or something similar.

- `PropertyChangedMessage<T>:` Used to broadcast that a property changed in the message sender. Fulfills the same purpose as the `PropertyChanged` event, but in a decoupled manner.

The `Messenger` class provides a powerful means to pass data and notifications between application layers and within `ViewModels` in a decoupled way.

Silverlight for Windows Phone Toolkit

The Silverlight Toolkit has been in existence for several years. The idea behind it is to be able to more frequently release control and other updates with full source code to developers out-of-band from the normal product release cycle. The toolkit has been updated for Windows Phone OS 7.1 (Mango) in August 2011. It is available at the following URL:

`http://silverlight.codeplex.com/`

The updated version adds quite a few additional controls highlighted in Table 6.1 in the next section. It also includes improved transitions and ContextMenu performance as well as various bug fixes. The toolkit also includes localized resources to provide support for multiple languages.

Installation and Overview

Installation is simply a matter of running the MSI and making the controls available in the Toolbox within Visual Studio 2010. Right-click on the Toolbox, select Choose Items, and then put a check box next to controls you want to show up in the Toolbox. You can sort the controls alphabetically as well. The Silverlight for Windows Phone Toolkit includes several phone-specific controls that most developers will want to take advantage of to some degree; they are listed in Table 6-1.

Table 6-1. Silverlight for Windows Phone Toolkit Available Controls

Control Name	Description
AutoCompleteBox	A Metro-style auto-complete `TextBox` control.
ContextMenu	Enables a Tap-and-Hold action to bring up a Metro-style context menu.
DatePicker	A Metro-style `DatePicker` control.
DateTimeConverters	New in Mango. Converts a DateTime object into a string that represents the elapsed time relative to the present.
DateTimePickers	New in Mango. These controls provide a UI similar to the built-in UI to select a date or a time value.
ExpanderView	New in Mango. This control provides an indented view of content in a threaded view.
GestureService/GestureListener	Enables rich gesture support for Silverlight applications.
HubTile	New in Mango. Provides a nice image view similar to the Start screen including tile flip and pop-up animations.
ListPicker	A Metro-style `DropDownList` control.
LockablePivot	New in Mango. The LockablePivot lets you "lock" the Pivot control so that you can use other controls that use gestures, drawing, and so on.
LongListSelector	A turbo-charged `ListBox` control optimized for Windows Phone 7.5 that also includes "Jump List" functionality.
MultiselectList	New in Mango. This control enables multiple selection, similar to the select mode available in Outlook on Windows Phone.
Page Transitions	Set of transitions and animations. Covered in the next section.
PerformanceProgressBar	A custom progress bar control enhanced with better performance over the built-in progress bar.
PhoneTextBox	New in Mango and listed at the CodePlex site but not present in the download. It is an enhanced TextBox with the ability to display hints and a length indicator.
TIltEffect	Provides visual feedback that an item was engaged via touch.

Control Name	Description
TimePicker	A Metro-style `TimePicker` control.
ToggleSwitch	A Metro-style Toggle-button control.
WrapPanel	A phone-specific version of the Silverlight tried-and-true `WrapPanel` control.

The controls in Table 6-1 were frequently requested by developers during the beta-test phase of the Windows Phone Developer Tools. The product team created the toolkit to supplement the SDK to help match the built-in native UI controls' look and feel.

■ **Note** GestureService and GestureListener are covered in Chapter 3.

The best way to proceed is to dive right in and show you how to put the controls to work within a sample project. Luckily, the Silverlight for Windows Phone Toolkit includes a very robust sample that is included with the source code download titled "Silverlight for Windows Phone Toolkit Source & Sample - Aug 2011.zip" available here:

http://silverlight.codeplex.com/releases/view/71550

There isn't any documentation beyond the sample application, so this section provides an overview of the available additional controls available in the toolkit. There is one additional sample project in the Chapter 6 solution that demonstrates how to data bind the WrapPanel control.

When you first run the sample app that ships with the source code available for download at the link I just gave you, it launches into a menu shown in Figure 6-5.

Figure 6-5. Silverlight for Windows Phone Toolkit sample main menu

Each control is covered in the sections that follow.

The AutoCompleteBox Control

The AutoCompleteBox control allows a user to type letters, which brings up matches from the data source resource configured on the ItemSource attribute. Here is an example:

```
<toolkit:AutoCompleteBox VerticalAlignment="Top" ItemsSource="{StaticResource words}"↵
 Margin="0,12"/>
```

Figure 6-6 shows the AutoCompleteBox in action. The top AutoCompleteBox is configured with the above XAML.

Figure 6-6. *AutoCompleteBox in action*

The bottom `AutoCompleteBox` is configured with an `ItemTemplate` to display two lines of text:

```
<toolkit:AutoCompleteBox
    InputScope="Url"
    ItemsSource="{StaticResource websites}"
    Margin="0,12"
    ValueMemberPath="Item1">
    <toolkit:AutoCompleteBox.ItemTemplate>
        <DataTemplate>
            <StackPanel Margin="0,7">
                <TextBlock
                    Margin="8,0"
                    Text="{Binding Item1}"/>
                <TextBlock
                    FontSize="{StaticResource PhoneFontSizeNormal}"
                    Foreground="#ff666666"
                    Margin="8,-6,8,2"
                    Text="{Binding Item2}"/>
            </StackPanel>
        </DataTemplate>
    </toolkit:AutoCompleteBox.ItemTemplate>
</toolkit:AutoCompleteBox>
```

The words come from these resources, configured in the `PhoneApplicationPage.Resources` section:

```
<phone:PhoneApplicationPage.Resources>
    <data:LoremIpsum x:Key="words"/>
    <data:LoremIpsumWebsites x:Key="websites"/>
</phone:PhoneApplicationPage.Resources>
```

In the Data folder of the toolkit sample solution PhoneToolkitSample project, there are two classes, LoremIpsum.cs and LoremIpsumWebsites.cs, which generate a random collection of words in an IEnumerable collection. You can data bind to any collection of strings and display the values as the user types.

The AutoCompleteBox provides a great way to improve UI by populating text fields with most likely values, saving users from having to type.

The ContextMenu Control

The ContextMenu control provides a user interaction unique to Windows Phone with the tap-and-hold gesture. Figure 6-7 shows the test page with in-text hints on functionality, as well as results after tap-and-hold actions.

Figure 6-7. *ContextMenu control test page*

The ContextMenu control is bindable to ICommand objects, so it can work quite nicely with GalaSoft's MVVM support for Commanding, allowing context menu items to invoke methods on the data bound ViewModel class.

The DatePicker and TimePicker Controls

The DatePicker and TimePicker controls make it easy for users to pick date and time within a Windows Phone application. Figure 6-8 shows the controls in action.

Figure 6-8. *DatePicker and TimePicker controls in action*

You can attach an event hander to the `Click` event and assign commands to the `Command` property. Here is example XAML for `ICommand` support:

```
<toolkit:ContextMenuService.ContextMenu>
    <toolkit:ContextMenu>
        <toolkit:MenuItem
        Header="Always-on item"
        Command="{Binding AlwaysCommand}"/>
        <toolkit:MenuItem
        Header="Intermittent item"
        Command="{Binding IntermittentCommand}"/>
        <toolkit:MenuItem
        Header="Always-on item with param"
        Command="{Binding AlwaysCommand}"
        CommandParameter="param1"/>
        <toolkit:MenuItem
        Header="Intermittent item with param"
        Command="{Binding IntermittentCommand}"
        CommandParameter="param2"/>
    </toolkit:ContextMenu>
</toolkit:ContextMenuService.ContextMenu>
```

The controls are dependent on having the correct application bar icons in a folder named `Toolkit.Content`. The icons are `ApplicationBar.Cancel.png` and `ApplicationBar.Check.png` and their build action must be set to `Content`.

The ListPicker Control

The `ListPicker` control provides a full-page, touch-friendly drop-down scrollable list to select an item. Figure 6-9 shows the example.

Figure 6-9. *ListPicker control in action*

The `ListPicker` control can display a set of inline strings like this:

```
<toolkit:ListPicker Header="background">
    <sys:String>dark</sys:String>
    <sys:String>light</sys:String>
    <sys:String>dazzle</sys:String>
</toolkit:ListPicker>
```

The `ListPicker` control also has `ItemSource` and `ItemTemplate` attributes to support data binding and full customization of how items are displayed. Here is example XAML:

```
<toolkit:ListPicker ItemsSource="{Binding}" Header="accent color"
                FullModeHeader="ACCENTS" CacheMode="BitmapCache">
    <toolkit:ListPicker.ItemTemplate>
        <DataTemplate>
            <StackPanel Orientation="Horizontal">
                <Rectangle Fill="{Binding}" Width="24" Height="24"/>
                <TextBlock Text="{Binding}" Margin="12 0 0 0"/>
```

```
                </StackPanel>
            </DataTemplate>
        </toolkit:ListPicker.ItemTemplate>
        <toolkit:ListPicker.FullModeItemTemplate>
            <DataTemplate>
                <StackPanel Orientation="Horizontal" Margin="16 21 0 20">
                    <Rectangle Fill="{Binding}" Width="43" Height="43"/>
                    <TextBlock Text="{Binding}" Margin="16 0 0 0" FontSize="43"
                               FontFamily="{StaticResource PhoneFontFamilyLight}"/>
                </StackPanel>
            </DataTemplate>
        </toolkit:ListPicker.FullModeItemTemplate>
    </toolkit:ListPicker>
```

The ToggleSwitch Control

The ToggleSwitch control configures a boolean value as On or Off. It can take a simple Header attribute for a text value to display across the top above the switch and current status as shown in the first two ToggleSwitch controls in Figure 6-10.

Figure 6-10. *The ToggleSwitch control*

The last `ToggleSwitch` control is much more customized than the first two. It includes a `ToggleSwitch.HeaderTemplate` to adjust the `Font` for the header. The `ToggleSwitch.ContentTemplate` customizes the `ToggleSwitch` status info on the left with additional detail. Simply embed a `<ContentControl Content="{Binding}"/>` control inside the `ToggleSwitch.ContentTemplate` to have the On/Off status display correctly, as in the following:

```
<toolkit:ToggleSwitch Header="5:45 AM">
    <toolkit:ToggleSwitch.HeaderTemplate>
        <DataTemplate>
            <ContentControl FontSize="{StaticResource PhoneFontSizeLarge}"
                    Foreground="{StaticResource PhoneForegroundBrush}" Content="{Binding}"/>
        </DataTemplate>
    </toolkit:ToggleSwitch.HeaderTemplate>
    <toolkit:ToggleSwitch.ContentTemplate>
        <DataTemplate>
            <StackPanel>
                <StackPanel Orientation="Horizontal">
                    <TextBlock Text="Alarm: " FontSize="{StaticResource PhoneFontSizeSmall}"/>
                    <ContentControl HorizontalAlignment="Left"
                            FontSize="{StaticResource PhoneFontSizeSmall}"
Content="{Binding}"/>
                </StackPanel>
                <TextBlock Text="every schoolday"
                            FontSize="{StaticResource PhoneFontSizeSmall}"
                            Foreground="{StaticResource PhoneSubtleBrush}"/>
            </StackPanel>
        </DataTemplate>
    </toolkit:ToggleSwitch.ContentTemplate>
</toolkit:ToggleSwitch>
```

The WrapPanel Control

The `WrapPanel` control works very similarly to the same named control available in the desktop Silverlight toolkit. It arranges child items left to right, row by row or top to bottom, column by column. Figure 6-11 shows the UI.

Figure 6-11. The WrapPanel control

The `WrapPanel` control has a `Children` collection that allows you to add child items to the control via code, which is how the toolkit sample adds items. There may be situations in which you prefer to data bind to an `ItemSource` property and an `ItemTemplate`, as you can in the `ListBox` control. The `WrapPanelDataBinding` project sample in the Chapter 6 solution demonstrates how to do this.

You can use an `ItemsControl` to provide this functionality by changing the `ItemsControl.ItemsPanel` to a `WrapPanel`. Otherwise, data binding works just like with a `ListBox`. Here is the XAML markup:

```
<ItemsControl ItemsSource="{Binding Strings}">
  <ItemsControl.ItemsPanel>
    <ItemsPanelTemplate>
      <toolkit:WrapPanel ItemWidth="69"/>
    </ItemsPanelTemplate>
  </ItemsControl.ItemsPanel>
  <ItemsControl.ItemTemplate>
    <DataTemplate>
      <Grid Width="60" Height="60" Margin="4">
        <Rectangle Fill="#FF2A2AC8" Stroke="Black"/>
        <TextBlock
          Text="{Binding Text}" TextWrapping="Wrap"/>
      </Grid>
    </DataTemplate>
  </ItemsControl.ItemTemplate>
</ItemsControl>
```

The `WrapPanelDataBinding` project has a sample data source generated in Expression Blend to display random text over rectangles. The `ItemsControl.ItemsSource` points to the `Strings` collection in the sample data source. Figure 6-12 shows the output.

Figure 6-12. *Data binding the WrapPanel control*

The HubTile Control

In Table 6-1, I've listed the new controls available in the August toolkit for Windows Phone 7.5, but I do not highlight every control in this chapter. However, one control that provides an amazing UI for very little effort is `HubTile`. Figure 6-13 shows its UI.

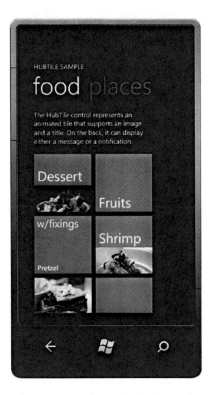

Figure 6-13. *The HubTile Control In Action*

The configuration for the control is very straightforward and can be done via data binding. Here is the XAML for the `HubTileSample.xaml` file, which is part of the Phone Toolkit sample project available for download from CodePlex:

```
<toolkit:HubTile Grid.Row="1" Grid.Column="0"
                                Margin="12,12,0,0"
                                Source="/Images/Dessert.jpg"
                                Title="Dessert"
                                Notification="2 New&#x0d;&#x0a;Receipes"
                                DisplayNotification="True"
                                GroupTag="Food"/>
                <toolkit:HubTile Grid.Row="1" Grid.Column="1"
                                Margin="12,12,0,0"
                                Source="/Images/Fruits.jpg"
                                Title="Fruits"
                                GroupTag="Food"/>
                <toolkit:HubTile Grid.Row="2" Grid.Column="0"
                                Margin="12,12,0,0"
                                Source="/Images/Pretzel.jpg"
                                Title="Pretzel"
                                Notification="w/fixings"
                                DisplayNotification="True"
```

```
                                    GroupTag="Food"/>
                <toolkit:HubTile Grid.Row="2" Grid.Column="1"
                                 Margin="12,12,0,0"
                                 Source="/Images/Shrimp.jpg"
                                 Title="Shrimp"
                                 Message="&quot;Just an amazing work by the
chef&quot;"
                                 GroupTag="Food"/>
                <toolkit:HubTile Grid.Row="3" Grid.Column="0"
                                 Margin="12,12,0,0"
                                 Source="/Images/SteakSandwich.jpg"
                                 Title="Steak&#x0d;&#x0a;Sandwich"
                                 Message="@ a great cafe"
                                 GroupTag="Food"/>
                <toolkit:HubTile Grid.Row="3" Grid.Column="1"
                                 Margin="12,12,0,0"
                                 Source="/Images/Beignets.jpg"
                                 Title="Beignets"
                                 Notification="New&#x0d;&#x0a;Orleans"
                                 DisplayNotification="True"
                                 GroupTag="Food"/>
```

As you can see, configuration of the HubTile control is very simple but can yield an amazing user interface addition to your application.

A control that we won't dive into here is PerformanceProgressBar, which was added to the toolkit in February 2011 and is now a part of the Windows Phone OS 7.1 SDK. Using the control is pretty straightforward, as it models the functionality of the built-in Progressbar control. I mention it because you will want to use the toolkit PerformanceProgressBar to improve rendering performance in your Silverlight or Windows Phone applications.

The LongListSelector Control

The LongListSelector control is the uber-ListBox control available for Windows Phone. It supports flat lists (like in a ListBox), but it can also support complex grouping and list navigation, which is very useful on the small screen. Try it for your scenario, especially in Windows Phone 7.5. The control has been completely rewritten to take advantage of performance enhancements around scrolling and off-thread touch support available in the Windows Phone OS 7.1 SDK. The LongListSelector control also supports grouped list, inline "more like these" buttons, and jump list UI.

Given the complexity and power of this control, the next couple of sections describe its visual capabilities, key properties and methods, and coding approaches.

LongListSelector - IsFlatList

The quickest way to take advantage of the LongListSelector control's potential performance and list virtualization advantages is to replace existing ListBox controls with LongListSelector controls and set the attribute IsFlatList to True. When in IsFlatList=true mode, the UI looks just like a ListBox control, though you can provide a header and footer to the list via the ListHeaderTemplate and ListFooterTemplate properties, as shown in Figure 6-14.

Figure 6-14. *LongListSelector with header and footer*

Listing 6-5 shows the XAML for the control and the three templates that are configured.

Listing 6-5. *LongListSelector XAML Markup File*

```
<phone:PhoneApplicationPage
    x:Class="LongListSelectorSample.pages.LongListSelectorPage2"
...<!--removed standard namespaces for clarity →
    SupportedOrientations="Portrait" Orientation="Portrait"
    mc:Ignorable="d" d:DesignHeight="768" d:DesignWidth="480"
    shell:SystemTray.IsVisible="True" Loaded="PhoneApplicationPage_Loaded"
    xmlns:toolkit="clr-namespace:Microsoft.Phone.Controls;assembly=↵
Microsoft.Phone.Controls.Toolkit">
  <phone:PhoneApplicationPage.Resources>
    <DataTemplate x:Key="ItemTemplate">
      <StackPanel Margin="0,0,0,20">
        <TextBlock Text="{Binding Name}"
                   Style="{StaticResource PhoneTextExtraLargeStyle}"/>
        <TextBlock Text="{Binding Description}"
                   Style="{StaticResource PhoneTextSmallStyle}"/>
        <TextBlock Text="{Binding Quantity}"
                   Style="{StaticResource PhoneTextAccentStyle}"/>
```

```xml
        </StackPanel>
      </DataTemplate>
      <DataTemplate x:Key="HeaderDataTemplate">
        <Border Background="#FF0027FF">
          <TextBlock TextWrapping="Wrap" Text="Chapter Six"
            HorizontalAlignment="Center" VerticalAlignment="Center"
            Style="{StaticResource PhoneTextLargeStyle}"/>
        </Border>
      </DataTemplate>
      <DataTemplate x:Key="FooterDataTemplate">
        <Border Background="#FF0027FF">
          <TextBlock TextWrapping="Wrap" Text="Advanced Silverlight UI"
            HorizontalAlignment="Center" VerticalAlignment="Center"
            Style="{StaticResource PhoneTextLargeStyle}"/>
        </Border>
      </DataTemplate>
    </phone:PhoneApplicationPage.Resources>
    <!--LayoutRoot is the root grid where all page content is placed-->
    <Grid x:Name="LayoutRoot" Background="Transparent"
      DataContext="{Binding Source={StaticResource longlistDataSource}}">
      <Grid.RowDefinitions>  <RowDefinition Height="Auto"/>
        <RowDefinition Height="*"/>  </Grid.RowDefinitions>
      <!--TitlePanel contains the name of the application and page title-->
      <StackPanel x:Name="TitlePanel" Grid.Row="0" Margin="12,17,0,28">
        <TextBlock x:Name="ApplicationTitle" Text="CHAPTER 6-LONGLISTSELECTORSAMPLE"
                   Style="{StaticResource PhoneTextNormalStyle}"/>
        <TextBlock x:Name="PageTitle" Text="longlistselector" Margin="9,-7,0,0"
                   Style="{StaticResource PhoneTextTitle1Style}"/>
      </StackPanel>
      <!--ContentPanel - place additional content here-->
      <Grid x:Name="ContentPanel" Grid.Row="1" Margin="12,0,12,0">
        <toolkit:LongListSelector IsFlatList="True"
          ItemTemplate="{StaticResource ItemTemplate}"
          ItemsSource="{Binding Collection}"
          ListHeaderTemplate="{StaticResource HeaderDataTemplate}"
          ListFooterTemplate="{StaticResource FooterDataTemplate}"/>
      </Grid>
    </Grid>
</phone:PhoneApplicationPage>
```

If you forget to set IsFlatList equal to True, it will generate an error when data bound to a flat list. This is because by default the LongListSelector control expects a data structure with a grouped set of items that permits the control to display the long list of content segmented by available groups.

LongListSelector via LINQ

The PhoneToolkit Sample Solution downloaded from CodePlex when you install the toolkit includes a page named LongListSelectorSample.xaml. This page demonstrates several ways a developer can implement grouping with the LongListSelector control. The UI for the LongListSelectorSample.xaml is a Pivot control with three PivotItem pages, titled linq, code, and buddies. The LongListSelector implementation for the PivotItem titled linq has the following XAML:

```
<toolkit:LongListSelector x:Name="linqMovies" Background="Transparent"
    ListHeaderTemplate="{StaticResource movieListHeader}"
    GroupHeaderTemplate="{StaticResource movieGroupHeader}"
    GroupItemTemplate="{StaticResource groupItemHeader}"
    ItemTemplate="{StaticResource movieItemTemplate}">
</toolkit:LongListSelector>
```

Note that it does not implement a GroupFooterTemplate. The PivotItem page titled linq displays movie data via Category using LINQ to demonstrate how to group items in the correct format using LINQ. The item that is displayed in the LongListSelector for both the linq and code PivotItem pages is a Movie class that has fields like Title, Description, Year, and so on. The movies are grouped by Category, which is of type string. In the code-behind file, the LoadLinqMovies method creates a flat collection of movies with random data and then builds a LINQ to Object query to group the movies by category.

The LINQ query is dazzlingly simple, taking advantage of the built-in group by support in LINQ that is based on the IGrouping Interface. Here is the LoadLinqMovies method

```
private void LoadLinqMovies()
{
    List<Movie> movies = new List<Movie>();

    for (int i = 0; i < 50; ++i)
    {
        movies.Add(Movie.CreateRandom());
    }

    var moviesByCategory = from movie in movies
                           group movie by movie.Category into c
                           orderby c.Key
                           select new PublicGrouping<string, Movie>(c);

    linqMovies.ItemsSource = moviesByCategory;
}
```

The class PublicGrouping implements the IGrouping Interface, which has this definition from metadata:

```
namespace System.Linq
{
  // Summary:
  //     Represents a collection of objects that have a common key.
  //
  // Type parameters:
  //   TKey:
  //     The type of the key of the System.Linq.IGrouping<TKey,TElement>.
  //
  //   TElement:
  //     The type of the values in the System.Linq.IGrouping<TKey,TElement>.
  public interface IGrouping<TKey, TElement> : IEnumerable<TElement>, IEnumerable
  {
    // Summary:
    //     Gets the key of the System.Linq.IGrouping<TKey,TElement>.
    //
    // Returns:
```

```
//      The key of the System.Linq.IGrouping<TKey,TElement>.
TKey Key { get; }
  }
}
```

An IEnumerable collection of PublicGrouping items is the output from the previous LINQ query:

```
var moviesByCategory = from movie in movies
                       group movie by movie.Category into c
                       orderby c.Key
                       select new PublicGrouping<string, Movie>(c);
```

The PublicGrouping class is generic: Here is the class declaration and constructor:

```
public class PublicGrouping<TKey, TElement> : IGrouping<TKey, TElement>
...
public PublicGrouping(IGrouping<TKey, TElement> internalGrouping)
{
    _internalGrouping = internalGrouping;
}
```

The LINQ query obtains the Enumerator from the LINQ Query, in this case the 'c' variable, which is defined as Category. Use the PublicGrouping class as a basis for your usage of the LongListSelector control.

Given the correctly formatted data structure, the LongListSelector class renders the UI in a grouped format. If you click a group item, it displays a menu of available groups. Figure 6-15 shows the linq PivotItem in action, with the screenshot on the right showing the results of clicking the group item. Select a new group item like Comedy to jump to the portion of the list containing the Comedy movies.

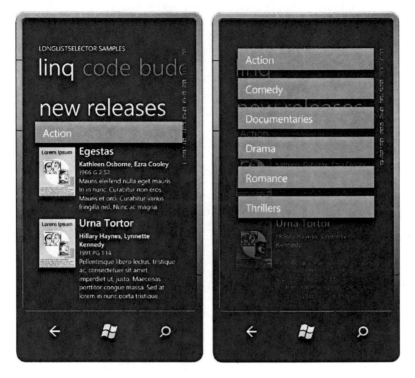

Figure 6-15. LongListSelector using LINQ

LongListSelector via Code

The "code PivotItem" in the PhoneToolkit project LongListSelectorSample.xaml page implements an additional feature with the LongListSelector control. The GroupFooterTemplate is modified to include a Button to display "more" of a particular category. Here is the XAML for the code PivotItem LongListSelector control:

```
<toolkit:LongListSelector x:Name="codeMovies" Background="Transparent"
            ItemsSource="{StaticResource movies}"
            ListHeaderTemplate="{StaticResource movieListHeader}"
            GroupHeaderTemplate="{StaticResource movieGroupHeader}"
            GroupItemTemplate="{StaticResource groupItemHeader}"
            ItemTemplate="{StaticResource movieItemTemplate}">
  <toolkit:LongListSelector.GroupFooterTemplate>
    <DataTemplate>
      <local:CommandButton DataContext="{Binding}" Content="{Binding GetMore}"
        Command="{StaticResource moreCommand}" CommandParameter="{Binding}"/>
    </DataTemplate>
  </toolkit:LongListSelector.GroupFooterTemplate>
</toolkit:LongListSelector>
```

Notice that the `GroupFooterTemplate` includes a `DataTemplate` with a `CommandButton` class instance, which is included in the sample code. The `LongListSelector` implementation on the code `PivotItem` does not use LINQ to generate the grouped item list. It binds to a `StaticResource` defined on the page named `moreCommand`, which is a class located in the `MoviesByCategory.cs` class file in the `Data` folder. More on that in a bit.

Also notice that `ItemsSource` data binds to a `StaticResource` named `movies`, which points to a class named `MoviesByCategory` located in the `Data` folder. The `MoviesByCategory` class is fairly simple. It obtains the Categories, and then randomly generates a set of fake objects for each `Category` using the `MoviesInCategory` class. It demonstrates how to create properly formatted groups in code and can provide a useful starter example.

The `MoreCommand` class implements the `ICommand` interface. The `ICommand.Execute` method adds additional random objects to the currently selected group that is passed in via a parameter. For a real implementation, some tracking is necessary to identify which records are already displayed so that the correct next set of records is retrieved, if present. Figure 6-16 shows the UI with the `More Command` button.

Figure 6-16. *LongListSelector with Command button displayed.*

The last `PivotItem,` named `buddies,` also generates a collection in code. It randomly generates a list of people names via the `AllPeople` class, sorts, them, and then generates groups by the alphabet and related group of names starting with each letter in the `PeopleByFirstName` class. The `GroupItemTemplate` in this case is the alphabet as shown in Figure 6-17.

Figure 6-17. LongListSelector with alphabetized list

In this section, we performed an in-depth review of the LongListSelector control, because it provides rich and very much needed functionality for Windows Phone applications that display lists of data. This section concludes the review of the Silverlight for Windows Phone toolkit except for the transition animations, which we cover as part of the next section.

Creating Transitions and Interactivity

In previous sections, we used the NavigateToPageAction behavior to navigate from one page to another. In this section, I focus on showing how to create more interactivity with Expression Blend for page transitions, status changes, and orientation changes. We start by investigating how to add interactivity using the Silverlight for Windows Phone Toolkit. We next focus on the Visual State Manager to create animations and transitions using a state-based management system.

Toolkit Page Transitions

The Silverlight for Windows Phone toolkit enables transitions that match the built-in native transitions available in Windows Phone, allowing your application to have the same look and feel without a lot of work. It is very simple to make the transitions available within an application, which is demonstrated in the Chapter 6 project named ToolkitTransitions.

Sample Project

The ToolkitTransitions project has three XAML pages. MainPage.xaml navigates to TestTransitionsPage.xaml, which data binds to a collection of sample data. The sample data is present to make the transitions more obvious than with just a mostly blank screen. When an item is selected in the TestTransitionsPage.xaml's sampleDataListBox, the code in the sampleDataListBox_SelectionChanged event appends the index of the selected item to a query string and then navigates to TestTransitionsPage2.xaml. The TestTransitionsPage2.xaml page displays the full details of the selected item.

An extra page is added to the project beyond MainPage.xaml because transitions from the Silverlight for Windows Phone toolkit do not override the standard application loading and exiting page transitions, so we need another page to fully demonstrate the transitions. The page in the middle, TestTransitionsPage.xaml, will have the transitions configured on it to demonstrate the full navigating to and from page transition capabilities because it is not the default item or main page for the application.

To get started, first add a project reference to the Microsoft.Phone.Controls.Toolkit assembly. Next open the App.xaml.cs file and change this line of code in the InitializePhoneApplication() method.

```
RootFrame = new PhoneApplicationFrame();
```

to this line of code:

```
RootFrame = new Microsoft.Phone.Controls.TransitionFrame();
```

Next, add a second page named toolkittransitionpage.xaml to a pages folder. A TextBlock is added to MainPage.xaml and the NavigateToPageAction behavior is applied to the TextBlock, so that when it is touched, the toolkittransitionpage.xaml is displayed. Run the project and check to make sure the navigation from MainPage to the toolkittranstiionpage.xaml is working. It is working, but it still does not have a nice transition to the second page. Now you can add any transition within the application.

Configuring Transitions

There isn't any Expression Blend support for visually applying transitions via behaviors. You edit the XAML to apply transitions. For each page, you can define four types of transitions:

- **NavigationInTransition:** Applies when navigating to the current page, either via a forward navigation to the page or via clicking the Back button to navigate back to the page.

- **NavigationOutTransition:** Applies when the current page is navigating out to another page, either via forward navigation to another page or when clicking the Back button on the current page.

- **DatePickerPage:** Applies when the current page is navigating to a DatePicker control page.

- **TimePickerPage:** Applies when the current page is navigating to a TimePicker control page.

To add a transition in XAML, add a namespace reference to the toolkit:

```
xmlns:toolkit="clr-namespace:Microsoft.Phone.Controls;assembly=↵
Microsoft.Phone.Controls.Toolkit"
```

Next, type `<toolkit:TransitionService` to bring up IntelliSense to show the five available transition types. Select `NavigationInTransition` and then close the tag to generate the ending element `</toolkit:TransitionService.NavigationInTransition>`. A warning appears: "Property 'NavigationInTransition' does not have a value," and blue squiggly lines appear as shown in Figure 6-18.

```
<toolkit:TransitionService.NavigationInTransition>
  <toolkit:
              NavigationInTransition
</toolkit:TransitionService.NavigationInTransition>
```

Figure 6-18. *XAML Intellisense for* `NavigationInTransition`

The only option that displays is `toolkit:Navigation:InTransition`. Within that element you can add the following two additional elements:

- `NavigationInTransition.Backward`

- `NavigationInTransition.Forward`

Within the `.Backward` and `.Forward` transitions, you can configure one of five options, as shown in Figure 6-19.

```
<toolkit:TransitionService.NavigationInTransition>
  <toolkit:NavigationInTransition>
    <toolkit:NavigationInTransition.Backward>
      <toolkit:
              RollTransition
              RotateTransition
              SlideTransition
              SwivelTransition
              TurnstileTransition

    </toolkit:NavigationInTransition.Backward>
  </toolkit:NavigationInTransition>
</toolkit:TransitionService.NavigationInTransition>
```

Figure 6-19. *XAML Intellisense for actual transition types*

We discuss the five possible transitions in detail in the next subsection. `NavigationOutTransition` also has a `.Backward` and `.Forward` option. Figure 6-20 describes the relationship for all four configurations.

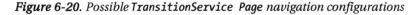

Figure 6-20. *Possible* `TransitionService` *Page navigation configurations*

In Figure 6-20, all five transitions are configured on the middle page and have independent behavior depending on the relative navigation to the middle page. This is the same configuration as in the `ToolkitTransitions` sample project's `TestTransitionsPage.xaml` page, where all five options are configured. Here is the XAML for the `ToolkitTransitions` sample transitions:

```
<toolkit:TransitionService.NavigationInTransition>
  <toolkit:NavigationInTransition>
    <toolkit:NavigationInTransition.Backward>
      <toolkit:RollTransition />
    </toolkit:NavigationInTransition.Backward>
    <toolkit:NavigationInTransition.Forward>
      <toolkit:RotateTransition  />
    </toolkit:NavigationInTransition.Forward>
  </toolkit:NavigationInTransition>
</toolkit:TransitionService.NavigationInTransition>
<toolkit:TransitionService.NavigationOutTransition>
  <toolkit:NavigationOutTransition>
    <toolkit:NavigationOutTransition.Backward>
      <toolkit:TurnstileTransition Mode="BackwardOut" />
    </toolkit:NavigationOutTransition.Backward>
    <toolkit:NavigationOutTransition.Forward>
      <toolkit:TurnstileTransition Mode="ForwardOut" />
    </toolkit:NavigationOutTransition.Forward>
  </toolkit:NavigationOutTransition>
</toolkit:TransitionService.NavigationOutTransition>
```

To help further explain, let's configure transitions on the page right. Since it is a "leaf" page without any additional forward navigation actions, only two transitions need to be configured. One is for when the page is being navigated to and the other when on the page and the back button is touched and the page is navigated from. The two transitions are the forward "in" transition,

NavigationInTransition.Forward, and the backward "out" transition, NavigationOutTransition.Backward. Here is the XAML:

```
<toolkit:TransitionService.NavigationInTransition>
  <toolkit:NavigationInTransition>
    <toolkit:NavigationInTransition.Forward>
      <toolkit:RotateTransition />
    </toolkit:NavigationInTransition.Forward>
  </toolkit:NavigationInTransition>
</toolkit:TransitionService.NavigationInTransition>
<toolkit:TransitionService.NavigationOutTransition>
  <toolkit:NavigationOutTransition>
    <toolkit:NavigationOutTransition.Backward>
      <toolkit:TurnstileTransition Mode="BackwardOut" />
    </toolkit:NavigationOutTransition.Backward>
  </toolkit:NavigationOutTransition>
</toolkit:TransitionService.NavigationOutTransition>
```

Run the project in the emulator or, better yet, on a device where the transitions are more apparent. You will see that the transitions are "chained," meaning that the NavigationOutTranstion.Forward for page TestTransitionsPage.xaml does not override the NavigationIn.Forward for page TestTransitionsPage2.xaml. Instead, the transitions are chained. Again, this is more visible on a real device than in the emulator.

Transitions in Depth

We briefly mentioned above the five possible types of transitions that can be applied in any configuration, either "in," or "out," Forward or Backward:

- RollTransition

- RotateTransition

- SlideTransition

- SwivelTransition

- TurnstileTransition

All of the transitions except the RollTransition take a Mode property that can have these values:

- BackwardIn

- BackwardOut

- ForwardIn

- ForwardOut

The Mode attribute allows you to tell the transition how it should appear based on whether it is a Forward "in" transition, and so on, so that it matches the native transitions correctly.

In addition to the `Backward` and `Forward` properties, the `NavigationInTransition` and `NavigationOutTransition` objects also have two events:

- `BeginTransition`

- `EndTransition`

These events allow you to hook into the transition at the Begin and End portion to perform actions such as data loading, unloading, and the like. Because these are events, you can use the MVVM Light Toolkit `EventToCommand` Behavior to bind the transition events to Commands declared in the ViewModel for your application.

Transitions and UI Elements

Transitions can be applied to any UI Element object. In the `ToolkitTransitions` project, click `apply transition to rectangle TextBlock` in `MainPage.Xaml` to load the corresponding page, and click the single Application Bar button. The `Rectangle` object will slide down and fade in. The Rectangle is named `targetRectangle` and its `Opacity` is set to 0 in XAML:

```
private void ApplyTransitionAppBarBtn_Click(object sender, EventArgs e)
{
  RotateTransition rotateTransition =
    new RotateTransition { Mode = RotateTransitionMode.In180Clockwise};

  ITransition transition = rotateTransition.GetTransition(targetRectangle);

  transition.Completed +=
    (s, eventarg) => { transition.Stop(); targetRectangle.Opacity = 1; };

  transition.Begin();
}
```

You can of course simply create a `Storyboard` using Expression Blend and apply it to the `Rectangle` as well, but this section demonstrates how to leverage the existing animations available in the Silverlight for Windows Phone toolkit. The next section describes how to create a transition based on a custom `Storyboard` object.

Custom Transitions

In this section I describe how to create a new transition class that leverages a custom `Storyboard` object. The steps are to implement the `ITransition` Interface with a custom class and implement another class that inherits from the `TransitionElement` base class. In the Chapter 6 Solution `ToolkitTransitions` project's `MainPage.xaml`, there is a `TextBlock` titled "custom transition" that navigates to the `CustomTransitionPage.xaml` page. This page demonstrates a custom Transition.

The first step is to create a custom Storyboard animation that applies to the entire page named `CustomPageTransitionStoryboard` in Expression Blend. The `CustomPageTransitionStoryboard` uses translation to move the Page content from off-screen lower left sliding diagonally into place. The `Storyboard` is moved into the `App.Resources` section of `App.xaml` to make it globally available throughout the application.

Next create a class named `TheTransition` that implements `ITransition,` as shown in Listing 6-6.

Listing 6-6. The Transition Class

```csharp
public class TheTransition : ITransition
{
  private Storyboard _storyboard;

  public TheTransition(Storyboard storyBoard)
  {
    _storyboard = storyBoard;
  }

  public void Begin()
  {
    _storyboard.Begin();
  }

  public event EventHandler Completed;

  public ClockState GetCurrentState()
  {
    return _storyboard.GetCurrentState();
  }

  public TimeSpan GetCurrentTime()
  {
    return _storyboard.GetCurrentTime();
  }

  public void Pause()
  {
    _storyboard.Pause();
  }

  public void Resume()
  {
    _storyboard.Resume();
  }

  public void Seek(TimeSpan offset)
  {
    _storyboard.Seek(offset);
  }

  public void SeekAlignedToLastTick(TimeSpan offset)
  {
    _storyboard.SeekAlignedToLastTick(offset);
  }

  public void SkipToFill()
  {
    _storyboard.SkipToFill();
  }
```

```
  public void Stop()
  {
    _storyboard.Stop();
  }
}
```

It is a pretty simple class that essentially wraps the `Storyboard` object. The class that is actually added in XAML is named `MyTransition,` and is shown in Listing 6-7.

Listing 6-7. MyTransition Class

```
public class MyTransition : TransitionElement
{
  public override ITransition GetTransition(UIElement element)
  {
    Storyboard myStoryboard = App.Current.Resources["CustomPageTransitionStoryboard"] as
Storyboard;

    Storyboard.SetTarget(myStoryboard, element);

    return new TheTransition(myStoryboard);
  }
```

Notice how the `MyTransition` class obtains the `Storyboard` via the `App.Current.Resources` collection. In the `CustomTransitionPage.xaml`, a namespace named `thisPage` is added, as is the custom transition:

```
xmlns:thisPage="clr-namespace:ToolkitTransitions.pages"
...
<toolkit:TransitionService.NavigationInTransition>
  <toolkit:NavigationInTransition>
    <toolkit:NavigationInTransition.Forward>
      <thisPage:MyTransition/>
    </toolkit:NavigationInTransition.Forward>
  </toolkit:NavigationInTransition>
</toolkit:TransitionService.NavigationInTransition>
```

Run the `toolkitTransitions` project to see the custom transition in action. It would make sense to add a `Mode` parameter to the `MyTransitions` class and then apply a custom `Storyboard,` depending on whether it is `Backward`, `Forward`, "in," or "out," but this sample demonstrates how to get started if you wish to create a custom transition.

This concludes coverage of the Silverlight for Windows Phone Toolkit and how to create interactivity for page transitions. The next section demonstrates how to use the Visual State Manager to provide interactivity within a page.

Visual State Manager

The Visual State Manager (VSM) is a tool available within Expression Blend. It allows the developer / designer to visually define Visual State Groups that represent UI state for controls in that state, represented as a `Storyboard`. The best way to learn how to work with the VSM is by demonstration, most of which will be in Expression Blend.

Orientation Aware

This section demonstrates how to create an `Orientation`-aware application using the VSM. A new project named **VSMVideoPlayer** is added to the Chapter 6 solution based on the MVVMLight (WP71 Application project template. The project is customized to be a basic video player that can play a list of videos from a recent vacation— videos without ownership rights issues that I can use for this example.

A Grid containing a `MediaElement` control named `mediaPlayer` is added to the `ContentPanel Grid`. Below the `Grid` containing the `MediaElement`, a `ListBox` named `videosListBox` is added and the Application Bar is enabled. The Application Bar is wired up to provide video controls for the `mediaPlayer` `MediaElement`.

A Model named `Video` is added to the `Model` folder and a collection of `Video` objects is added to the `MainViewModel` class. Finally, three videos are added to a folder named `Content` and added to the project. Figure 6-21 shows the **VSMVideoPlayer** project in Expression Blend with the States tab opened.

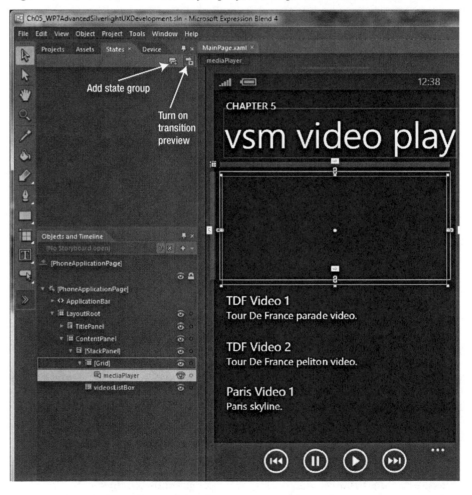

Figure 6-21. *VSMVideoPlayer and States tab*

The videosListBox is data bound to the Videos collection on the MainViewModel. The Grid containing the MediaElement is data bound to the SelectedItem of the videosListBox. The Source property for the mediaPlayer MediaElement is data bound to the Url property of the SelectedItem Video object. Run the project, and when you select a video in the videosListBox it plays in the MediaElement. Listing 6-8 shows the XAML for the Content Grid and Application Bar from MainPage.xaml.

Listing 6-8. Content Grid and Application Bar Code

```
<Grid x:Name="ContentPanel" Grid.Row="1" Margin="12,0,12,0">
  <StackPanel d:LayoutOverrides="Width">
    <Grid Height="213" DataContext="{Binding SelectedItem, ElementName=videosListBox}">
      <MediaElement Source="{Binding Url}" Margin="5,9,7,-9" Name="mediaPlayer"
MediaFailed="mediaPlayer_MediaFailed" Stretch="UniformToFill" />
    </Grid>
    <ListBox x:Name="videosListBox" ItemsSource="{Binding Main.Videos}"
     Margin="12,24,0,0" ItemTemplate="{StaticResource VideoDataTemplate}" />
  </StackPanel>
</Grid>
</Grid>
<phone:PhoneApplicationPage.ApplicationBar>
  <shell:ApplicationBar IsVisible="True" IsMenuEnabled="True">
    <shell:ApplicationBarIconButton x:Name="rewindAppBarBtn"
     IconUri="/icons/appbar.transport.rew.rest.png" Text="rewind"
     Click="rewindAppBarBtn_Click"/>
    <shell:ApplicationBarIconButton x:Name="stopAppBarBtn"
     IconUri="/icons/appbar.transport.pause.rest.png" Text="pause"
     Click="stopAppBarBtn_Click"/>
    <shell:ApplicationBarIconButton x:Name="playAppBarBtn"
     IconUri="/icons/appbar.transport.play.rest.png" Text="play"
     Click="playAppBarBtn_Click"/>
    <shell:ApplicationBarIconButton x:Name="ffAppBarBtn"
     IconUri="/icons/appbar.transport.ff.rest.png" Text="fastforward"
      Click="ffAppBarBtn_Click"/>
  </shell:ApplicationBar>
</phone:PhoneApplicationPage.ApplicationBar>
```

Listing 6-9 shows the MainPage.xaml.cs code-behind file where the event handlers control the mediaPlayer MediaElement.

Listing 6-9. MainPage.xaml.cs Code File

```
using Microsoft.Phone.Controls;
using System;
using System.Windows;

namespace VSMVideoPlayer
{
  public partial class MainPage : PhoneApplicationPage
  {
    // Constructor
    public MainPage()
```

```csharp
        {
            InitializeComponent();
        }

        private void rewindAppBarBtn_Click(object sender, System.EventArgs e)
        {
            if (mediaPlayer.CanSeek)
            {
                mediaPlayer.Position = mediaPlayer.Position - new TimeSpan(0, 0, 5);
                mediaPlayer.Play();
            }
        }

        private void stopAppBarBtn_Click(object sender, System.EventArgs e)
        {
            mediaPlayer.Pause();
        }

        private void playAppBarBtn_Click(object sender, System.EventArgs e)
        {

            mediaPlayer.Play();
        }

        private void ffAppBarBtn_Click(object sender, System.EventArgs e)
        {

            if (mediaPlayer.CanSeek)
            {
                mediaPlayer.Position = mediaPlayer.Position + new TimeSpan(0, 0, 5);
                mediaPlayer.Play();
            }
        }

        private void mediaPlayer_MediaFailed(object sender,
            System.Windows.ExceptionRoutedEventArgs e)
        {
            MessageBox.Show("Media Failed: " + e.ErrorException.Message);
        }
    }
}
```

The last item to highlight is that the SupportedOrientations attribute on the PhoneApplicationPage element in XAML is changed from Portrait to PortraitOrLandscape. This allows the page to respond to orientation changes via the PhoneApplicationPage.OrientationChanged event.

Now that everything is configured properly, let's configure the project to support a full-screen mode for video playback in Expression Blend. With the States tab opened in Expression Blend, the Add state group button creates a Visual State Group that can contain one or more Visual States. The Turn on transition preview button dynamically shows the changes when different states are selected at design time.

Click the Add State Group button and name the Visual State Group "Orientations." Next, create an "Add state" button to create a Visual State for PortraitUp. Create another state named LandscapeRight. The VSM should look like Figure 6-22.

Figure 6-22. *VSM with one State Group and two Visual States*

Figure 6-22 also defines the UI available in the VSM to create states as well as customize the transitions. EasingFunctions provide for a more realistic animation flow. EasingFunctions are literally functions like quadratic, cubic, bounce, elastic, and so on. In general, EasingFunctions are available in Storyboards. Developers can create custom EasingFunctions as well. Think of an EasingFunction as altering the animation speed from a straight line to a curve, where sharp bends represent an increase in speed so that animations appear to better model real-world movement with acceleration and bounce. Figure 6-23 shows the EasingFunction selector.

Figure 6-23. *EasingFunction selector for Storyboards*

The other buttons shown in Figure 6-23 are transition duration, which represents how long the animation should take in real time, regardless of `EasingFunction`, and a button to turn on `FluidLayout`. `FluidLayout` provides an engine that takes a look at the start state, the end state, and then creates a smooth animation between the states based on the selected `EasingFunction`. `FluidLayout` can help make animations created by non-designers look great. Now that we have the Blend functionality covered, let's create our states based on current orientation for the sample project.

Look at Figure 6-22, and you see a state at the top called "`Base`." When working in Blend previously, you may not have been aware, but this is the visual state that you were working in. "`Base`" represents the default or initial state. All other state modifications are referenced to the `Base` state.

■ **Tip** Be sure to select the `Base` state if you want to make modifications that apply across all states.

In Expression Blend, switch to Landscape in the Device tab and then switch back to the States tab. With the `LandscapeRight` Visual State selected, select the `TitlePanel Grid` and set `Visibility` to `Collapsed`, and set `Visibility` to `Collapsed` for the `videosListBox` as well. For the `Grid` that contains the `mediaPlayer MediaElement`, set the `Height` property on the `Grid` to 480px. The Objects and Timeline window indicates the changes visually in the timeline keyframe editor as shown in Figure 6-24.

Figure 6-24. Object and Timeline window

When you run the application, it works as expected when flipped to LandscapeRight, as shown in Figure 6-25.

Figure 6-25. Project running in LandScapeRight orientation

If you switch the Emulator to LandscapeLeft, the UI remains as the Portrait layout, as shown in Figure 6-26.

Figure 6-26. *Project running in LandScapeLeft orientation*

You could build another state manually, but an easier option is to right-click on the LandscapeRight state, select Copy State To, and then select New State. Rename it LandscapeLeft, and that is all that's required to have both Landscape Orientation values display correctly.

The Visual State Manager provides a powerful tool to customize transitions and animations via a state-based mechanism. The next section covers the Microsoft Advertising SDK, which supports advertising revenue for both Silverlight and XNA Framework applications.

The RichTextBox Control

Now available in Windows Phone OS 7.1 SDK is the RichTextBox control. This is a read-only control that you can use to render Rich Text Format (RTF) content. The control does not accept user input or edits, but you can update the content programmatically or via data binding.

The RichTextBox control supports formatted text, inline images, and hyperlinks. To put this into context, Windows ships with WordPad, which is a feature-rich text editor, built on the RTF format.

The RichTextBox control supports the FlowDirect property available in Silverlight 4 for localization. This means that text can flow RightToLeft or LeftToRight as needed to support the desired language. The RichTextBox control supports sub-elements for content formatting including the following:

- Paragraph: Starts a new text paragraph in the content.

- Run: Represents a discrete section of formatted or unformatted text.

- HyperLink: Web link.

- InlineUIContainer: Can be used to render an Image element.

- LineBreak: Causes a new line within the content.

- Span: Groups other Inline descendent content elements.

- Bold, Italic, Underline: Specify additional text formatting within the content.

The RichTextBox control supports a block-based content model where a block is a collection of Paragraph elements. A Paragraph element can contain elements that derive from inline such as Run, Span, text formatting like Bold, Hyperlink and InLineUIContainer. Here is an example that displays some text with an inline image:

```
<RichTextBox>
    <Paragraph>
        Displaying text with inline image
        <InlineUIContainer>
            <Image Source="./Sports.jpg" Height="75" Width="75" />
        </InlineUIContainer>
    </Paragraph>
</RichTextBox>
```

The RichTextBox control is great when you have RTF content to render, such as help documentation. In general, Microsoft recommends using the RichTextBox control instead of the WebBrowser control if possible since it presents native rendering.

The Microsoft Advertising SDK

The Microsoft Advertising SDK now ships directly in the Windows Phone OS 7.1 SDK. It provides mobile advertising support for Windows Phone. You are not required to use Microsoft's advertising SDK and associated advertising network. If you have an existing advertising network or an in-house creative and sales force, you can continue to use those resources for advertising revenue.

If you are new to mobile applications or simply want a fast and easy mobile advertising solution, the Microsoft Advertising SDK can get you up and running in about 20 minutes and about 50 lines of code. This is explained next.

Getting Started

While Windows Phone is a new platform, Microsoft's advertising solution is not. With the world's first real-time bidding Mobile Ad Exchange with targeted advertising, multiple purchase models and leading resellers including Microsoft's sales force, you can tap into the existing adCenter marketplace by simply adding the control to your application.

Register on pubCenter at the https://pubcenter.microsoft.com link to set up your advertising account. You create a software property where ads are displayed, create a mobile ad unit, and set up a targeting category. After registering in pubCenter, you will have an application ID and an Ad unit ID that you can use to request ads from the Microsoft Advertising Servers.

You can also try out the mobile advertising control and receive test ads without signing up, but you will soon want to take advantage of Microsoft's contextual advertising platform with over 20,000 advertisers and resellers to get paid.

Adding the Advertising Control

You can drag the control onto your Silverlight UI from the Toolbox window to add advertising to a Silverlight page. You can receive test ads using the test Application ID and test Ad Unit ID to get a feel for how the advertising works. There are three types of ads you can receive in your application, summarized in Table 6-2.

Table 6-2. *Advertising Types and Test Values*

Ad Type	AdControl Size (width x height)	Test ApplicationId	TestAdUnitId
Text Ad	480 × 80	test_client	TextAd
XXL Image Banner 6-1	480 × 80	test_client	Image480_80
X-Large Image Banner 6-1	300 × 50	test_client	Image300_50

Even though there is support for a 300 × 50 ad size, it is recommended to always set the size of the `AdControl` instance to 480px wide by 80px height. For the X-Large Image Banner, the control will automatically size to display the full 300 × 50, centered at the center of the `AdControl` instance.

The `AdControl` also has a `Location` property to receive targeted ads by supplying a `Latitude` and `Longitude` value as a `Location` type. You can use a `GeoCoordinateWatcher` instance to collect location data as shown in Chapter 3 on input. The AdControl class supports the following events:

- `AdControlError:` Fires when there is a problem receiving or displaying an advertisement.

- `AdEngaged:` Fires when the user clicks the ad and the action dialog appears.

- `AdDisengaged:` Fires when the user clicks any button in the action dialog to dismiss the dialog.

- `NewAd:` Fires when a new advertisement is displayed. Can use to animate the `AdControl` to catch the user's attention.

AdControl in Silverlight

In this section, the AdControl is leveraged in a sample project named AdvertisingSLSample. For the Silverlight sample project, start with the `Windows Phone Data bound Application project` template so that you have some data to display. Next, simply drag and drop the control at the bottom of the `MainPage.xaml` page, adjusting its settings so it just fits across the bottom of the screen.

It is recommended to place the `AdControl` at the top or bottom of a page. For the `Panorama` or `Pivot` controls, you can place the `AdControl` instance inside or over top of the `Panorama` or `Pivot` control. If placed inside either control, the ad will only display in a single pane. You can choose to have a unique ad on each pane if desired. To have the `AdControl` always visible, even when scrolling, place the instance outside of the `Panorama` control on top.

■ **Tip** It is not recommended to change the parent control of an `AdControl` instance at run time.

As you can see, the control is simple to configure. Here is the XAML for the configured ad control in the Silverlight AdvertisingSample project:

```
<my:AdControl  Height="80" HorizontalAlignment="Left" Margin="-16,527,0,0" Name="adControl1"
  VerticalAlignment="Top" Width="480"  ApplicationId="test_client" AdUnitId="Image480_80"
  RenderTransformOrigin="0.5,0.5"  IsAutoCollapseEnabled="True" >
<my:AdControl.RenderTransform>
  <CompositeTransform/>
</my:AdControl.RenderTransform>

</my:AdControl>
```

Figure 6-27 shows the control in action, using the test configuration in the previous XAML.

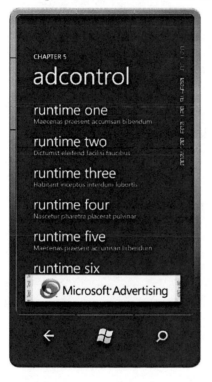

Figure 6-27. *Advertising in a Silverlight application*

We want to grab the user's attention when a new ad is available. One possible way to do that is to create an animation that indicates something happened, such as to make the control increase in size slightly and then return to its original size via a Storyboard animation.

In Expression Blend, create the `AnimateAdControl` `Storyboard` resource by clicking the New button in the Objects and Timeline window. Add a keyframe at zero time and then slide the yellow timeline over to 100 milliseconds. Click on the `Transform` section in the Properties window for the `AdControl` and switch to the `Scale` transform tab. Change `X` and `Y` to 1.1 from 1. Slide the yellow timeline bar to 200 milliseconds, right-click the first keyframe at zero seconds and then right-click and select Paste.

Switch back to Visual Studio and create an event handler for the NewAd event on the adControl1 instance and then add this code:

```
AnimateAdControl.Begin();
```

For a multi-page application, it is recommended to unload the control when a page is unloaded to minimize resource consumption. This can be done in the PhoneApplicationPage.Unloaded event handler. Simply set the AdControl instance to null.

Although this chapter is focused on Silverlight UX, the next subsection covers how to add advertising support to a Windows Phone XNA Framework-based game.

AdControl in the XNA Framework

Adding support for the AdControl in a Windows Phone XNA Framework application is just as easy. Start by adding a reference to the Microsoft.Advertising.Mobile.Xna.dll using the Add Reference functionality.

Next add a using Microsoft.Advertising.Mobile.Xna; statement to game1.cs. Next add a DrawableAd object as a private member of the Game1 class:

```
DrawableAd bannerAd;
```

In the constructor for the Game1 class, add this line of code to initialize and add the static Current AdGameContent to the Components list for the game:

```
AdGameComponent.Initialize(this, "test_client");
Components.Add(AdGameComponent.Current);
```

Notice that the same application Id, test_client, is used as before for the testing functionality. Finally, we want to load an ad, which is done in the LoadContent() method where all game assets are generally loaded for most games:

```
bannerAd = AdGameComponent.Current.CreateAd(
"Image300_50",
  new Rectangle(
    10, 390, GraphicsDevice.Viewport.Bounds.Width, 120), true);
```

That is all that is required to add advertising to a Windows Phone XNA Framework game. Figure 6-28 shows the results.

Figure 6-28. Test advertising in an XNA application

As you can see from this section, adding support for Advertising revenue to your applications is very straight-forward. For a free or trial application, advertising revenue is a great way to get paid for your hard work.

Conclusion

This chapter began with an overview of the Model-View-ViewModel pattern, which is the architecture to use in XAML-based applications. We next moved on to covering one of the third-party MVVM frameworks that improve upon the built in support for MVVM when building property architected applications.

This was followed by a discussion of the Silverlight for Windows Phone toolkit, including coverage on all of the major controls including detailed coverage on the `LongListSelector` control as well as on page transitions. We then explored how to use the Visual State Manager in your applications to greatly simplify UI development.

The coverage of advertising concludes Chapter 6 on advanced user interface development. The next chapter covers advanced programming model topics that allow you to more deeply integrate with Windows Phone, leverage media, as well as other topics.

■ ■ ■

CHAPTER 7

Advanced MVVM, Services and App Connect

In this chapter, we cover additional topics related to the programming model starting with more advanced coverage of the MVVM Architecture and data binding. The sample covers how to access RSS feeds, show a ProgressBar control from the ViewModel, how to lazy load images for better performance, and then concludes on how to data bind anything to anything using the IValueConverter Interface.

. The following section covers advanced services starting with encryption services, an important topic and critical for most professionally developed applications. This is followed by a discussion covering advanced media services.

The rest of the chapter covers App Connect. App Connect refers to the various ways that applications can integrate with Windows Phone including integration with the pictures hub, the music+video hub, as well as integration with Bing Search. Next up we start with a discussion of Advanced MVVM programming topics.

Advanced MVVM

In this section, I cover how to access Syndicated Services like RSS feeds from Windows Phone, as well as advanced Model-View-ViewModel (MVVM) techniques to incorporate page navigation, showing progress, and lazy loading images. The last subsection covers the IValueConverter interface, which allows you to data bind any data type to just about any other data.

A sample project based on the MVVM Light project template named AdvancedMVVM is added to the Chapter 7 solution. MVVM is leveraged for this example (and in many samples throughout this chapter) to demonstrate how to handle slightly additional complexity of separating concerns between the View and the ViewModel when dealing with real-world scenarios.

By default, the MainPage.xaml binds to the MainViewModel in the ViewModel folder. MainPage.xaml presents a menu of four items that navigate to individual pages corresponding to the sections that follow:

- Syndicated Services (/View/SyndicatedServices.xaml)

- Showing Progress (/View/ShowProgress.xaml)

- Lazy Load Images (/View/LazyLoadImages.xaml)

- Data Bind to Anything (/View/DatabindToAnything.xaml)

MainPage.xaml consists of a ListBox data bound to a collection of items that represent the above pages. Here is the XAML:

```
<ListBox x:Name="listBox1" Margin="24,0,0,0"
  ItemsSource="{Binding Pages}"
  ItemTemplate="{StaticResource PageItemTemplate}" />
```

In MainViewModel.cs, the ApplicationTitle and PageName properties are added to the code. A PageItems property is added to MainViewModel class that is of type List<PageItem>:

```
public const string PageItemsPropertyName = "PageItems";
private List<PageItemViewModel> _pages = null;
public List<PageItemViewModel> PageItems
{
  get
  {
    return _pages;
  }

  protected set
  {
    if (_pages == value)
    {
      return;
    }

    var oldValue = _pages;
    _pages = value;

    // Update bindings, no broadcast
    RaisePropertyChanged(PageItemsPropertyName);
  }
}
```

The MainViewModel class's constructor takes an IPageItemsDataService Interface. MVVM Light then finds a concrete class registered via the inversion of control class SimpleIoc that implements that interface and provides the needed data service and data. I cover this in Chapter 7 in the MVVMLight sample. I recommend going through that section for more details on how MVVM Light works as well as the new Inversion of Control pattern.

Here is the constructor for MainViewModel:

```
public MainViewModel(IPageItemsDataService dataService)
{
  _pageItemsService = dataService;
  PageItems = new List<PageItem>();

  _pageItemsService.GetPageItems(
      (pageItems, error) =>
      {
        if (error != null)
        {
          // Report error here
```

```
        return;
      }
      PageItems = (List<PageItem>)pageItems;
    });
}
```

ShowProgress.xaml

Normally, the PageItem class would be a simple Model class; however, it has a bit more functionality than previous model classes covered in Chapter 7 with MVVM Light since it needs to implement commanding as shown in Listing 7-1 below   The ListBox displaying the Pages data. When an item is selected in the ListBox shown in Figure 7–1, the application navigates to the associated page. We don't want to write code to do this in the MainPage.xaml.cs code-behind file. Instead we take advantage of messaging and commanding support provided by the MVVM Light toolkit.

Figure 7–1. *AdvancedMVVM MainPage.xaml UI*

The selected item in the ListBox on MainPage.xaml should perform navigation to the associated page pointed to by the selected item. This means that the Commanding support is required at the PageItem / ItemTemplate level, not at the ListBox level. To support this functionality, the PageItem model class supports GalaSoft Light Messaging and Commanding (see Chapter 6 for details on GalaSoft MVVM). Listing 7–1 shows the PageItem ,model class.

Listing 7–1. *PageItem Model Class File*

```
using System;
using GalaSoft.MvvmLight;
using GalaSoft.MvvmLight.Command;
using GalaSoft.MvvmLight.Messaging;

namespace AdvancedMVVM.Model
{
  public class PageItem : ViewModelBase
  {
    public PageItem()
    {
      NavigateToPageCommand = new RelayCommand<Uri>(
        param => SendNavigationRequestMessage(param));
    }

    #region PageItem properties
    public const string PageTitlePropertyName = "PageTitle";
    private string _pageTitle = null;
    public string PageTitle
    {
      get
      {
        return _pageTitle;
      }
      set
      {
        if (_pageTitle == value)
        {
          return;
        }

        var oldValue = _pageTitle;
        _pageTitle = value;
        RaisePropertyChanged(PageTitlePropertyName);
      }
    }


    public const string PageUriPropertyName = "PageUri";
    private Uri _pageUri = null;
    public Uri PageUri
    {
      get
      {
        return _pageUri;
      }
      set
      {
        if (_pageUri == value)
        {
```

```
      return;
    }

    var oldValue = _pageUri;
    _pageUri = value;

    // Update bindings, no broadcast
    RaisePropertyChanged(PageUriPropertyName);
  }
}
#endregion

#region Commanding and Messaging
public RelayCommand<Uri> NavigateToPageCommand
{
  get;
  private set;
}

protected void SendNavigationRequestMessage(Uri uri)
{
  Messenger.Default.Send<Uri>(uri, "PageNavRequest");
}
#endregion
  }
}
```

The PageItem Model class is broken up into two sections, one for the properties and the other for the Commanding and Messaging support available in MVVM Lite. The PageItemViewModel class has two properties, PageTitle and PageUri. The PageUri points to the appropriate XAML file to navigate to for the PageTitle property value.

The Commanding and Messaging support is pretty simple code. The NavigateToPageCommand is what the MainPage.xaml View DataBinds to when the ListBoxItem is clicked via the MVVM Light EventToCommand Behavior. The NavigateToPageCommand RelayCommand<T> is connected to the MVVM Light Messaging infrastructure via this code in the PageItemViewModel constructor:

```
NavigateToPageCommand = new RelayCommand<Uri>(
  param => SendNavigationRequestMessage(param));
```

The NavigateToPageCommand takes an Uri and passes it to the SendNavigationRequestMessage. This is a bit of indirection, as the Uri property comes from the ListBox's template and then is sent back to the View via the MVVM Light Messaging infrastructure but it does promote decoupling of the UI from the ViewModel.

The MainPage.xaml View receives the message via this line of code added to the PhoneApplicationPage constructor and uses an inline Lambda statement to call the NavigationService:

```
Messenger.Default.Register<Uri>(
        this, "PageNavRequest",
        (uri) => NavigationService.Navigate(uri));
```

I mentioned earlier that the DataTemplate data binds to the NavigateToPageCommand. Here is the ItemTemplate="{StaticResource PageItemTemplate}" for the MainPage.ListBox control:

```
<DataTemplate x:Key="PageItemTemplate">
```

```
<Grid Margin="0,15">
  <TextBlock Margin="0,0,1,0" TextWrapping="Wrap" Text="{Binding PageTitle}"
    d:LayoutOverrides="Width, Height" Style="{StaticResource PhoneTextLargeStyle}">
    <Custom:Interaction.Triggers>
      <Custom:EventTrigger EventName="MouseLeftButtonDown">
        <GalaSoft_MvvmLight_Command:EventToCommand Command="{Binding NavigateToPageCommand,
Mode=OneWay}" CommandParameter="{Binding PageUri}"/>
      </Custom:EventTrigger>
    </Custom:Interaction.Triggers>
  </TextBlock>
</Grid>
</DataTemplate>
```

The EventToCommand behavior is dragged from the Assets | Behaviors section and is dropped on the TextBlock. Figure 7–2 shows the Properties window for the EventToCommand behavior.

Figure 7–2. EventToCommand properties in Expression Blend

In Figure 7–2, the Command value is data bound to the NavigateToPageCommand property on the PageItemViewModel class. The CommandParameter is data bound to PageUri property of the selected item from the MainViewModel Pages collection of type PageItemViewModel.

This was a detailed walkthrough of relatively simple functionality, but it demonstrates the powerful capabilities of MVVM Light's Commanding and Messaging infrastructure to support decoupling UI from the ViewModel via Silverlight's data binding framework. In addition, I recommend exploring the

INotifyDataErrorInfo and IDataErrorInfo interfaces now included as part of the Windows Phone OS SDK for error tracking and reporting.

The next section covers how to access syndicated services like RSS feeds from Windows Phone.Syndicated Services

Silverlight 3 and later on the desktop includes excellent support for easily consuming syndicated feeds like RSS, ATOM, and formatted data feeds. Unfortunately, the System.ServiceModel.Syndication.dll is not available in the Silverlight for Windows Phone SDK. You can simply add a reference to the Silverlight 4 version of the assembly for Windows Phone OS 7.1 (Mango), but it is just as easy to use LINQ to XML to parse syndication feeds.

For the AdvancedMVVM project, a page named SyndicatedServices.xaml is added to the View folder and a ViewModel named SyndicatedServicesViewModel is added to the ViewModel folder. The SyndicatedServicesViewModel is added to the ViewModelLocator class in the ViewModel folder.

Clicking the syndicated services label shown in Figure 7–3 navigates to the page. The page is configured with a ListBox named feedListBox and added to the ContentPanel in SyndicatedServices.xaml. The page automatically loads the data in the SyndicatedServicesViewModel when it is created.

As before, when the SyndicatedServicesView.xaml data binds to the SyndicatedServicesViewModel class, the SyndicatedServicesViewModel ViewModel retrieves the data via the FeedItemsDataService class.

The ClientDownloadStringCompleted event has code to parse the response, load the data into an XDocument, and parse the feed into a collection of FeedItem objects that is data bound to the feedListBox.ItemsSource property. Listing 7–2 has the FeedItemDataService class.

Listing 7–2. *FeedItem Class File*

```
using System;
using System.Collections.Generic;
using System.Linq;
using System.Net;
using System.Xml.Linq;

namespace AdvancedMVVM.Model
{
  public class FeedItemsDataService : IFeedItemsDataService
  {
    private const string ServiceUri =
"http://public.create.msdn.com/Feeds/CcoFeeds.svc/CmsFeed?group=Education Catalog List";
    public void GetFeedItems(Action<IList<FeedItem>, Exception> callback)
    {
      var client = new WebClient();
      client.DownloadStringCompleted += ClientDownloadStringCompleted;
      client.DownloadStringAsync(new Uri(ServiceUri), callback);
    }
    private static void ClientDownloadStringCompleted(object sender,
DownloadStringCompletedEventArgs e)
    {
      var callback = e.UserState as Action<IList<FeedItem>, Exception>;
```

```
        XDocument doc = XDocument.Parse(e.Result);
        List<FeedItem> feedItems = (from results in doc.Descendants("item")
                                    select new FeedItem
                                    {
                                      Title = results.Element("title").Value.ToString(),
                                      Link = new Uri(results.Element("link").Value.ToString(),
UriKind.Absolute),
                                      Description =
results.Element("description").Value.ToString()
                                    }).ToList<FeedItem>();

        if (callback == null)
        {
          return;
        }

        if (e.Error != null)
        {
          callback(null, e.Error);
          return;
        }
        callback(feedItems, null);
      }
    }
}
```

Since the FeedItemDataService marshals the data via an Asynchronous call back to the
SyndicatedServicesViewModel class in the constructor, the Dispatcher.BeginInvoke method is not
necessary in order to marshal the data back to the UI thread.

Once the data is returned to the SyndicatedServicesViewModel class it populates the FeedItems
property of type List<FeedItem> FeedItems, In the SyndicatedServicesVew.xaml class, a simple
DataTemplate is configured on feedListBox.ItemTemplate that binds to FeedItem object properties:

```
<ListBox.ItemTemplate>
  <DataTemplate>
    <StackPanel Margin="0,0,0,30">
      <TextBlock Text="{Binding Title}"  Margin="0,0,12,0" FontSize="24" FontFamily="Segoe WP
Semibold" />
      <TextBlock Text="{Binding Description}" />
      <HyperlinkButton  NavigateUri="{Binding Link}" FontFamily="Segoe WP SemiLight"
        TargetName="_blank"          FontSize="18.667" FontStyle="Italic"
        Content="More..." HorizontalAlignment="Left"/>
    </StackPanel>
  </DataTemplate>
</ListBox.ItemTemplate>
```

Figure 7–3 shows the UI when the SyndicatedServicesVew.xaml loads

Figure 7–3. *AppHub RSS feed parsed and loaded*

If you click `More...` it loads the URL for the content into the Web Browser. Clicking the Back hardware button takes you back to the page. Notice in Figure 7–3 that the Description is formatted as HTML. I can change the `DataTemplate` to have a `WebBrowser` control instead of a `TextBlock` but when I do this, the HTML does not render.

The `WebBrowser` control supports navigating to an HTML fragment using the `NavigateToString` Method, but it does not have a simple HTML property that we can data bind, too. We would rather not write a lot of code to data bind to the HTML fragment. When working in Silverlight, whenever a control is missing a property, you can always add it using XAML Attached properties. The goal is to have a simple HTML property of type text for the HTML fragment from the feed that gets loaded via the `NavigateToString` method. Listing 7–3 shows the attached property class.

Listing 7–3. *WebBrowserHTMLProp Code File*

```
public static class WebBrowserHTMLProp
{
  public static readonly DependencyProperty HtmlProperty =
    DependencyProperty.RegisterAttached(
      "Html", typeof(string), typeof(WebBrowserHTMLProp),
      new PropertyMetadata(OnHtmlPropChanged));

  public static string GetHtml(DependencyObject dependencyObject)
```

```
  {
    return (string)dependencyObject.GetValue(HtmlProperty);
  }

  public static void SetHtml(DependencyObject dependencyObject, string value)
  {
    dependencyObject.SetValue(HtmlProperty, value);
  }

  private static void OnHtmlPropChanged(DependencyObject dependencyObject,
    DependencyPropertyChangedEventArgs e)
  {
    var webBrowser = dependencyObject as WebBrowser;

    if (webBrowser == null)
      return;

    var html = e.NewValue.ToString();
    webBrowser.NavigateToString(html);
  }
}
```

It is mostly boilerplate code with the important code in the OnHtmlPropChanged method where the HTML is loaded into the WebBrowser via NavigateToString. Unfortunately, because this code is part of the DataTemplate, an error is thrown stating that "You cannot call WebBrowser methods until it is in the visual tree." Because the DataTemplate is composited and then added to the Visual Tree, the Attached Property does not help us here but it can assist in situations where the WebBrowser control is embedded into the static XAML. Instead a TextBlock is placed within the DataTemplate. Figure 7–3 shows the output. Clicking "More…" loads the link into IE Mobile.

An alternative approach for this feed would be to just display the Title in the ListBox and then navigate to another page that displays the Description details in a WebBrowser control that is part of the static XAML visual tree of the page.

In this section I covered how to load an RSS feed using LINQ to XML. We will explore adding additional functionality for displaying feed data, showing progress, and lazy loading images in the following sections.

Showing Progress

In this section, I demonstrate how to have your ViewModel drive UI, such as when to show progress bars or not, via data binding. It is a quick example based on the previous example that downloads the AppHub feed but the concept is very important to help you understand how to put more code into your ViewModels and less code in your View.

The SyndicatedServicesViewModel.cs code file is copied and renamed ShowProgressViewModel as well as the constructor. The new ShowProgressViewModel property is added to the ViewModelLocator just as before, and a new View named ShowProgress.xaml is created and data bound to the ShowProgressViewModel. Run the project and it should work just as the previous sample, returning the feed items.

A new Boolean property named ShowProgressBar is added to the ShowProgressViewModel class. The ShowProgressBar property is set to true just before invoking the IFeedItemsDataService.GetFeedItems method in the ShowProgressViewModel .DownloadAppHubFeed method.

```csharp
public void DownloadAppHubFeed()
{
  ShowProgressBar = true;
  System.Threading.Thread.Sleep(3000);

  _feedItemsService.GetFeedItems(
      (feedItems, error) =>
      {
        if (error != null)
        {
          // Report error here
          return;
        }
        FeedItems = (List<FeedItem>)feedItems;
        ShowProgressBar = false;
      });
}
...
```

When the asynchronous call returns and the value assigned to the FeedItems property, ShowProgressBar is set to false. This completes the changes in the ViewModel. The progress bar should be enabled right before making the web call and then disabled once the new data is data bound to the UI. Again the property must be modified on the UI thread as shown above in the DownloadAppHubFeed code snippet. The FeedItemsDataService class performs the download and uses LINQ to XML to create the feedItems collection. Here is the FeedItemsDataService with the GetFeedItems implementation:

```csharp
public class FeedItemsDataService : IFeedItemsDataService
{
  private const string ServiceUri =
    "http://public.create.msdn.com/Feeds/CcoFeeds.svc/CmsFeed?group=Education Catalog List";
  public void GetFeedItems(Action<IList<FeedItem>, Exception> callback)
  {
    var client = new WebClient();
    client.DownloadStringCompleted += ClientDownloadStringCompleted;
    client.DownloadStringAsync(new Uri(ServiceUri), callback);
  }
  private static void ClientDownloadStringCompleted(object sender,
    DownloadStringCompletedEventArgs e)
  {
    var callback = e.UserState as Action<IList<FeedItem>, Exception>;

    XDocument doc = XDocument.Parse(e.Result);
    List<FeedItem> feedItems = (from results in doc.Descendants("item")
                                select new FeedItem
                                {
                                  Title = results.Element("title").Value.ToString(),
                                  Link = new Uri(results.Element("link").Value.ToString(),
                                    UriKind.Absolute),
                                  Description =
                                      results.Element("description").Value.ToString()
                                }).ToList<FeedItem>();
```

```
    if (callback == null)
    {
      return;
    }

    if (e.Error != null)
    {
      callback(null, e.Error);
      return;
    }
    callback(feedItems, null);
}
```

}In the ShowProgress.xaml page, add a ProgressBar control that applies to the width of the screen in the middle of the page. The ProgressBar should look like the native WP7 ProgressBar, otherwise known as "the flying dots." Luckily the Silverlight for Windows Phone Toolkit has been updated to include two new controls, TiltEffect and PerformanceProgressBar. Previously you had to create a customized version of the built-in progress bar in order to have good UI thread performance.

Once the latest Silverlight toolkit for WP7 is installed, add PerformanceProgressBar to the Toolbox window in Visual Studio and drag the control on to the ShowProgress.xaml View. Switch over to Expression Blend and set the HorizontalAlignment and VerticalAlignment to Stretch and reset Margin to zero. Next set the IsIndeterminate Property to True and you can see the flying dots at design-time in Expression Blend. We only want to see the flying dots when loading data so let's data bind the LoadingDataPerfProgressBar's Indeterminate property to the ShowProgressViewModel.ShowProgressBar property. Here is the XAML for the PerformanceProgressBar from ShowProgress.xaml:

```
<toolkit:PerformanceProgressBar Name="performanceProgressBar1" Grid.Row="1" Margin="0"
  VerticalAlignment="Stretch" Padding="0" HorizontalAlignment="Stretch"
  IsIndeterminate="{Binding ShowProgressBar}" />
```

By default, the data is obtained by ShowProgressViewModel via the constructor when the application loads and the ShowProgressViewModel is created. We modify the constructor to not automatically call the DownloadAppHubFeed() method. The ShowProgress.xaml View is modified to have an Application Bar button that manually downloads the feed. Clicking the Application Bar button to start the download will enable the progress bar, download the feed, and then disable the progress bar. Figure 7–4 shows the flying dots in the emulator.

Figure 7–4. *PerformanceProgressBar in action*

This example demonstrates the power of XAML and its data binding infrastructure to allow the ViewModel non-visual class to drive the UI based on the applications current state. This technique is critical to effective MVVM development and can be extended to other data-driven UI to indicate state and display additional UI when needed.

Lazy Load Images

When developing for a mobile device with constrained networking and hardware capabilities relative to a desktop computer, you sometimes have to take additional steps beyond the "default" programming model. As an example, loading a ListBox with data and images from a remote server can peg the UI thread resulting in a poor user experience for scrolling and animations. Anytime work can be taken off of the UI thread is a win for performance.

A Silverlight for Windows Phone team member David Anson blogged here about a way to offload image loading to a background thread that results in much better UI performance:

```
http://blogs.msdn.com/b/delay/archive/2010/09/02/keep-a-low-profile-lowprofileimageloader-
helps-the-windows-phone-7-ui-thread-stay-responsive-by-loading-images-in-the-background.aspx
```

In the blog post, Dave introduces the LowProfileImageLoader class to address the very specific issue of loading lots of images from the web simultaneously. The LowProfileImageLoader slows the loading of images but the UI remains responsive as images are loaded because the UI thread is not slammed waiting for images to load and then data bind.

To test out the LowProfileImageLoader, let's work with the Netflix API. I picked this API because it has an interesting set of images (movie art) in a well-documented API. The API is available at developer.netflix.com.

▓ **Note** You must register an account to use the Netflix APIs at

http://developer.netflix.com/member/register.

We will use the OData Client Library for Windows Phone that we covered in Chapter 4 to access the Netflix API. As before we add a reference to System.Data.Services.Client.dll. With built-in support for Odata in Windows Phone OS 7.1.(Mango) developer tools, I simply right-click on References in the AdvancedMVVM Project and select "Add Service Reference." I enter this URL in the dialog:

http://odata.netflix.com/Catalog/

I next click GO, provide a namespace name of NetflixAPI, and click OK. This adds an OData service reference to the AdvancedMVVM project. Add using AdavncedDataBinding.NetflixAPI to bring the Odata service into the LazyLoadViewModel and NetflixCatalogODataService classes.

The OData access is wired into the LazyLoadViewModel.cs class, which is a copy of the ShowProgressViewModel. It follows the GalaSoft MVMM Light 4.0 pattern in the LazyLoadViewModel that we implemented previously:

```
public void DownloadNetflixCatalog()
{
  ShowProgressBar = true;
  _netflixCatalogfeedItemsService.GetNetflixCatalogFeedItems(
     (topMovieTitles, error) =>
     {
       if (error != null)
       {
         // Report error here
         return;
       }
       TopMovieTitles = (DataServiceCollection<Title>)topMovieTitles;
       ShowProgressBar = false;
     });
}
```

Since the code needs to return a DataServiceCollection<Title> collection, the INetflixCatalogOdataService interface is modified accordingly:

```
using System;
using System.Data.Services.Client;
using AdvancedMVVM.NetflixAPI;

namespace AdvancedMVVM.Model
{
  public interface INetflixCatalogODataService
```

```
    {
      void GetNetflixCatalogFeedItems(Action<DataServiceCollection<Title>, Exception> callback);
    }
}
```

The `NetflixCatalogODataService` implementation class is where things get a little more interesting. This class must handle the asynchronous call back a little differently because of API differences with OData.

```
private NetflixCatalog ODataContext;
private Action<DataServiceCollection<Title>, Exception> _callback;
private DataServiceCollection<Title> _topMovieTitles;
```

I need to save a copy of the callback parameter passed into `GetNetflixCatalogFeedItems` at the class level so that I can use it when processing the `LoadCompleted` event handler;

```
private const string ServiceUri = "http://odata.netflix.com/Catalog/";
public void GetNetflixCatalogFeedItems(Action<DataServiceCollection<Title>, Exception>
callback)
{
  ODataContext = new NetflixCatalog(
    new Uri(ServiceUri,
        UriKind.Absolute));
  //Save a reference to the callback in this case
  //Cannot pass it via the LoadAsync method for OData
  _callback = callback;
  _topMovieTitles = new DataServiceCollection<Title>(ODataContext);
  _topMovieTitles.LoadCompleted +=
    new EventHandler<LoadCompletedEventArgs>(topMovieTitles_LoadCompleted);
  _topMovieTitles.LoadAsync(new Uri("/Titles()", UriKind.Relative));
}
private void topMovieTitles_LoadCompleted(object sender, LoadCompletedEventArgs e)
{
  if (_topMovieTitles == null)
  {
    return;
  }

  if (e.Error != null)
  {
    _callback(_topMovieTitles, e.Error);
    return;
  }
  _callback(_topMovieTitles, null);
}
```

Once you understand the Data Service pattern, it is fairly easy to customize it to your requirements so don't be tempted to avoid creating a Data Service for your View Model.

The `LazyLoad.xaml` View page is modified to include a `ListBox` with a simple `DataTemplate` that shows the movie title and image. Figure 7–5 shows the UI.

Figure 7–5. *Netflix API top titles via OData*

Not every movie title has box art, but many do. Let's now modify this application to use the LowProfileImageLoader class to asynchronously display the images. Download the source code at the blog post link above and grab the PhonePerformance.dll. Add a reference to it in the AdvancedMVVM project and then add a namespace reference to LazyLoadImage.xaml:

```
xmlns:delay="clr-namespace:Delay;assembly=PhonePerformance"
```

Next update the NetflixTopTitleDataTemplate so that the image is not loaded from the built-in Source property but instead is loaded using this XAML:

```
<Image delay:LowProfileImageLoader.UriSource="{Binding BoxArt.SmallUrl}"
HorizontalAlignment="Left" Stretch="UniformToFill" Width="150"/>
```

The performance difference is much more obvious on a physical device over 3G, but as you can see it is pretty trivial to add support for the LowProfileImageLoader to see if it can help with any performance issues related to image loading in your applications.

Data Bind to Anything

There are situations where you need to data bind to a value and the value type or format does not quite line up with what you need. The IValueConverter interface allows your application to data bind to just about anything including data that does not match the type expected for a particular control.

As an example, let's say you have a field that takes values of either Yes or No. You could use a ListPicker but a CheckBox makes more sense since it is just two values. You can implement IValueConverter to convert true to a Yes value and No value to false (and vice versa) while still using standard data binding mechanisms.

In this section, a new view is added named DatabindToAnything.xaml that data binds to the existing ShowProgressViewModel. Since the work is at the View level for this demo, there is no need to create a new ViewModel and Data Service.

I create a custom IValueConverter named HtmlToImageUriConverter. This very simple converter parses the AppHub Feed html, previously displayed as raw html text, into a URL that points to an image related to the content.

The URL is extracted from the HTML. Listing 7–4 shows the code for the converter.

Listing 7–4. *WebBrowserHTMLProp Code File*

```
using System;
using System.Windows.Data;

namespace AdvancedMVVM.Converters
{
  public class HtmlToImageUriConverter : IValueConverter
  {
    public object Convert(object value, Type targetType,
      object parameter, System.Globalization.CultureInfo culture)
    {
      string html = (string)value;
      string imageUrl = "";
      if (null != html)
      {
        string[] strings = html.Split('"');
        if (strings.Length > 3)
          imageUrl = strings[3].Trim();
      }
      return imageUrl;
    }

    public object ConvertBack(object value, Type targetType,
      object parameter, System.Globalization.CultureInfo culture)
    {
      throw new NotImplementedException();
    }
  }
}
```

The converter is somewhat brittle in that it depends on the URL value to be the fourth string when split, but one wouldn't expect the feed format to change very often, and it makes for an interesting sample. The converter is made available to the DatabindToAnything.xaml View via an xml namespace import:

```
xmlns:converters="clr-namespace:AdvancedMVVM.Converters"
```

The converter is added as a resource in this XAML:

```
<phone:PhoneApplicationPage.Resources>
  <converters:HtmlToImageUriConverter x:Key="HtmlToImageConverter"/>
</phone:PhoneApplicationPage.Resources>
```

Applying the converter is a simple modification in XAML or visually in Expression Blend. Here is the updated ListBox DataTemplate:

```
<DataTemplate>
  <StackPanel Margin="0,0,0,30">
    <TextBlock Text="{Binding Title}" Margin="0,0,12,0" Style="{StaticResource
PhoneTextLargeStyle}" />
    <Image delay:LowProfileImageLoader.UriSource=
        "{Binding Description, Converter={StaticResource HtmlToImageConverter}}"
        Margin="0,6,0,4" Width="100" HorizontalAlignment="Left" />
    <HyperlinkButton NavigateUri="{Binding Link}" FontFamily="Segoe WP SemiLight"
TargetName="_blank"
        FontSize="18.667" FontStyle="Italic" Content="More..." HorizontalAlignment="Left"
Margin="-12,0,0,0"/>
  </StackPanel>
</DataTemplate>
```

The Binding.Converter parameter is configured to the added StaticResource to apply the converter for the Image object. Note that this sample also implements the LowProfileImageLoader for better performance as well as the PerformanceProgressBar to give better visual status to the user. Figure 7–6 shows the resulting output with a nice image instead of the raw HTML that was displayed previously.

Figure 7–6. *AppHub feed with articles and corresponding images*

In this section, data binding concepts are extended to more real world scenarios while also incorporating MVVM concepts. The next section provides a quick tour of available encryption services in Windows Phone.

Encryption Services

A mobile device no matter what operating system or platform is inherently insecure. A mobile device is not locked safely in a server room within a secure data center like a web server. A mobile device is easily misplaced or stolen. For pretty much any computing platform, loss of physical control is loss of security. Therefore, it is important to minimize storing sensitive data on a mobile device.

However, there are scenarios in which it is convenient to store sensitive data on a device. As an example, a user would never use a video player application that requires the user to memorize and enter a long key to unlock DRM'd content. It is a risk management challenge that weighs the benefits and inconvenience provided by any given security solution. This section in the MSDN documentation provides a detailed overview of balancing security with convenience:

http://msdn.microsoft.com/en-us/library/ff402533(v=VS.92).aspx

In the next few sections, I provide an overview of the capabilities available in the Windows Phone platform.

Secure Sockets Layer

Many mobile applications transfer data to and from the server-side of a mobile application solution. In cases where sensitive data must be transported always use Secure Sockets Layer (SSL) to protect data in transit. This link lists SSL root certificates that ship on Windows Phone:

http://msdn.microsoft.com/en-us/library/gg521150(v=VS.92).aspx

Once sensitive data is on the device, use available encryption services on the platform to secure the data. Windows Phone supports the following cryptographic algorithms:

- AES
- HMACSHA1
- HMACSHA256
- Rfc2898DeriveBytes
- SHA1
- SHA256

The next covers how to use these algorithms to securely store data on Windows Phone.

Securely Encrypting Data

We add a project named EncryptingData to the Chapter 7 solution based on the GalaSoft MVVM project template. The UI takes some data to encrypt, a password and salt to perform the encryption, and then a couple of TextBlock controls to show the encrypted data as well as results from decrypting.

The Application Bar is enabled with four buttons:

■ Encrypt Data

■ Decrypt Data

■ Save to Isolated Storage

■ Load from Isolated Storage

All the UI data fields and event methods have corresponding properties on the MainViewModel class. The encryption operations are actually performed on MainViewModel properties with data binding bringing the results to the UI. Figure 7–7 shows the UI layout.

Figure 7–7. *EncryptData project UI*

The following using statements are added to the MainViewModel class to provide the necessary access for stream-based processing and encryption:

```
using System.IO;
using System.IO.IsolatedStorage;
using System.Security.Cryptography;
using System.Text;
```

In addition to the ViewModel data fields backing the UI MainPage.xaml View, four additional methods are added to MainViewModel:

■ EncryptData

■ DecryptData

■ SaveEncryptedDataToIsolatedStorage

■ LoadEncryptedDataFromIsolatedStorage

Each method performs the task described by the method name. These four methods are accessed via the Application Bar buttons in the View as shown in Listing 7–5.

Listing 7–5. *MainPage.Xaml.cs Code File*

```
using System.Windows;
using System.Windows.Controls;
using EncryptingData.ViewModel;
using Microsoft.Phone.Controls;

namespace EncryptingData
{
  public partial class MainPage : PhoneApplicationPage
  {
    MainViewModel vm;
    // Constructor
    public MainPage()
    {
      InitializeComponent();
      vm = this.DataContext as MainViewModel;
    }

    private void EncryptAppBarBtn_Click(object sender, System.EventArgs e)
    {
      vm.EncryptData();
    }

    private void DecryptAppBarBtn_Click(object sender, System.EventArgs e)
    {
      vm.DecryptData();
    }

    private void SaveIsoAppBarBtn_Click(object sender, System.EventArgs e)
    {
      vm.SaveEncryptedDataToIsolatedStorage();
    }

    private void LoadIsoAppBarBtn_Click(object sender, System.EventArgs e)
    {
      vm.LoadEncryptedDataFromIsolatedStorage();
    }

    private void PasswordBox_LostFocus(object sender,
      System.Windows.RoutedEventArgs e)
    {
```

```
        if (((PasswordBox)sender).Password.Length < 8)
          MessageBox.Show("Salt Value must be at least eight characters.",
            "Minimum Length Error",MessageBoxButton.OK);
      }
    }
}
```

The four encryption related methods in MainViewModel code are shown in Listing 7–6.

Listing 7–6. *Methods from MainViewModel.cs Code File*

```csharp
public void EncryptData()
{
  using (AesManaged aes = new AesManaged())
  {
    Rfc2898DeriveBytes rfc2898 = new Rfc2898DeriveBytes(Password,
      Encoding.UTF8.GetBytes(SaltValue), 10000);
    aes.Key = rfc2898.GetBytes(32);
    aes.IV = rfc2898.GetBytes(16);
    using (MemoryStream memoryStream = new MemoryStream())
    {
      using (CryptoStream cryptoStream = new CryptoStream(memoryStream,
        aes.CreateEncryptor(), CryptoStreamMode.Write))
      {
        //Encrypt Data with created CryptoStream
        byte[] secret = Encoding.UTF8.GetBytes(DataToEncrypt);
        cryptoStream.Write(secret, 0, secret.Length);
        cryptoStream.FlushFinalBlock();
        aes.Clear();
        //Set values on UI thread
        Deployment.Current.Dispatcher.BeginInvoke(() =>
        {
          EncryptedData = Convert.ToBase64String(memoryStream.ToArray());
        });
      }
    }
  }
}

public void DecryptData()
{
  MemoryStream memoryStream = null;

  using (AesManaged aes = new AesManaged())
  {
    //Generate Key and IV values for decryption
    Rfc2898DeriveBytes rfc2898 = new Rfc2898DeriveBytes(Password,
Encoding.UTF8.GetBytes(SaltValue), 10000);
    aes.Key = rfc2898.GetBytes(32);
    aes.IV = rfc2898.GetBytes(16);

    using (memoryStream = new MemoryStream())
```

```csharp
    {
      using (CryptoStream cryptoStream =
        new CryptoStream(memoryStream, aes.CreateDecryptor(),
                          CryptoStreamMode.Write))
      {
        //Decrypt Data
        byte[] secret = Convert.FromBase64String(EncryptedData);
        cryptoStream.Write(secret, 0, secret.Length);
        cryptoStream.FlushFinalBlock();
        byte[] decryptBytes = memoryStream.ToArray();
        aes.Clear();
        //Update values on UI thread
        Deployment.Current.Dispatcher.BeginInvoke(() =>
        {
          DecryptedData = Encoding.UTF8.GetString(decryptBytes, 0, decryptBytes.Length);
          DataToEncrypt = Encoding.UTF8.GetString(decryptBytes, 0, decryptBytes.Length);
        });
      }
    }
  }
}

public void SaveEncryptedDataToIsolatedStorage()
{
  //Save secret to Application Settings
  if (EncryptedData != "")
  {
    if (IsolatedStorageSettings.ApplicationSettings.Contains(StorageKeyName))
    {
      IsolatedStorageSettings.ApplicationSettings[StorageKeyName] =
        EncryptedData;
    }
    else
    {
      IsolatedStorageSettings.ApplicationSettings.Add(
        StorageKeyName, EncryptedData);
    }
  }
}

public void LoadEncryptedDataFromIsolatedStorage()
{
  //Retrieve secret from Application Settings
  if (IsolatedStorageSettings.ApplicationSettings.Contains(StorageKeyName))
  {
    Deployment.Current.Dispatcher.BeginInvoke(() =>
    {
      EncryptedData =
        IsolatedStorageSettings.ApplicationSettings[StorageKeyName].ToString();
    });
  }
  else
```

```
  {
    Deployment.Current.Dispatcher.BeginInvoke(() =>
    {
      EncryptedData = "";
    });
  }
}
```

The code generates a Key for AES based on the Password and Salt values provided by the user. The Rfc2898DeriveBytes class is used to generate the HMACSHA1 random number (iteration count of 1,000) for the AES Key and IV values. What's handy with implementing encryption via the ViewModel is that it is easily reusable. The MainViewModel class has zero dependencies on UI.

Saving confidential data in a phone's isolated storage is not secure. Encrypting the data will not increase the security if the decryption key resides on the phone, no matter how well the key is hidden.

In Windows Phone 7.5, an encryption method is made available to developers via the unmanaged DPAPI. DPAPI solves the problem of explicitly generating and storing a cryptographic key by using the user and phone credentials to encrypt and decrypt data. I add DPAPI support to the project via the System.Securty.Cryptography.ProtectedData static class.

■ **Tip** If upgrading a project to Windows Phone 7.5, you must add a reference to the mscorlib.Extensions assembly for the ProtectedData class to be available.

A new bool property named SavePasswordAndSalt is added to the MainViewModel class. A CheckBox control with the Content set to "Check to save the Password and Salt" is added to the MainPage.xaml UI. This allows you to maintain the code that determines whether to save or unsave the credentials on the device to the MainViewModel class in Listing 7-7.

Listing 7–7. Encryption Services MainViewModel.cs Methods

```
public const string SavePasswordAndSaltPropertyName = "SavePasswordAndSalt";
private bool _savePasswordAndSalt = false;
public bool SavePasswordAndSalt
{
  get
  {
    return _savePasswordAndSalt;
  }

  set
  {
    if (_savePasswordAndSalt == value)
    {
      return;
    }
    //Do not check the box unless
    //Password and Salt values are configured
```

```
    if ((Password == String.Empty) ||
        (Salt == String.Empty))
    {
      _savePasswordAndSalt = false;
      RaisePropertyChanged(SavePasswordAndSaltPropertyName);
      return;
    }
    _savePasswordAndSalt = value;
    RaisePropertyChanged(SavePasswordAndSaltPropertyName);
    ProcessSaltAndPasswordValues();
  }
}
```

If both the Password and Salt TextBox controls have data and the user checks the savePasswordandSaltCheckBox CheckBox control, the ProcessSaltAndPasswordValues method is called via data binding in the Setter for the SavePasswordAndSalt property. This method checks whether the user wants to save settings or not based on whether SavePasswordAndSalt is true or false. The password and salt are encrypted and then added to the Application's IsolatedStorageSettings collection. If the user does not want to persist the Password and Salt values, the code checks if the Password and Salt values are saved and then removes them from IsolatedStorageSetings:

```
private void ProcessSaltAndPasswordValues()
{
  if (SavePasswordAndSalt)
  {
    if (settings.Contains("Password"))
      settings.Remove("Password");
    if (settings.Contains("Salt"))
      settings.Remove("Salt");
    //Set Entropy to null in the Protect method for this demo.
    //You could instead collect a user PIN and use that value
    //for entropy to provide stronger security.
    settings.Add("Password", ProtectedData.Protect(Encoding.UTF8.GetBytes(Password), null));
    settings.Add("Salt", ProtectedData.Protect(Encoding.UTF8.GetBytes(Salt), null));
  }
  else
  {
    if (settings.Contains("Password"))
      settings.Remove("Password");
    if (settings.Contains("Salt"))
      settings.Remove("Salt");
  }
}
```

The last item is initializing the UI with the Password and Salt values when first launching the UI. The MainViewModel Constructor checks to see if the Password and Salt are persisted in settings. The code first has to convert the value to a byte[] array and then decrypt using the ProtectedData.Unprotect method, returning a byte[] array of characters, which is then turned into a string. Here is the code:

```
public MainViewModel()
{
  if (!ViewModelBase.IsInDesignModeStatic)
  {
```

```
    if (settings.Contains("Password"))
    {
      byte[] encryptedPasswordBytes = (byte[])settings["Password"];
      byte[] decryptedPasswordBytes = ProtectedData.Unprotect(encryptedPasswordBytes, null);
      Password = Encoding.UTF8.GetString(decryptedPasswordBytes, 0,
decryptedPasswordBytes.Length);

    }
    if (settings.Contains("Salt"))
    {
      byte[] encryptedSaltBytes = (byte[])settings["Salt"];
      byte[] decryptedSaltBytes = ProtectedData.Unprotect(encryptedSaltBytes, null);
      Salt = Encoding.UTF8.GetString(decryptedSaltBytes, 0, decryptedSaltBytes.Length);
    }
    if (Password != String.Empty)
      SavePasswordAndSalt = true;
  }
}
```

Testing this out, you will find that the Password and Salt values are persisted correctly. When testing the UI overall, be sure to follow the pattern of filling in the fields, clicking Encrypt, and then save to isolated storage. Likewise, be sure to click load and then decrypt if launching the app after previously encrypting data.

Data encryption needs to be easily accessible and of course secure. The new ProtectedData class available in Windows Phone OS 7.1 fits the bill for your encryption needs. In the next section we switch gears, covering phone integration with the picture hub and images.

Working with Images on Windows Phone

Windows Phone supports BMP, TIF, GIF, JPEG, and PNG formats in general. However, from a development perspective JPG and PNG are supported for viewing in the Silverlight Image control. The JPG and PNG formats are recommended for displaying images within an application. JPG is preferred when the image will remain opaque. The PNG format supports transparency and is preferred for this scenario.

Images Classes

The Image control is the Silverlight class for displaying images in applications. A related Silverlight object that us very useful is the ImageBrush object. As an example, setting the background on a Panorama object is via an ImageBrush like this:

```
<controls:Panorama.Background>
  <ImageBrush  ImageSource="PanoramaBackground.png" Opacity="0.785" />
</controls:Panorama.Background>
```

Note that for the Opacity value to have an effect with an ImageBrush object, the image pointed to via the ImageSource property must be a .PNG file.

The BitmapImage is the utility class that provides the class for the Image.Source property. The BitmapImage supports the JPEG and PNG format. The BitmapImage has two constructors, one that takes a

URI and the other that takes a Stream. You can set Image.Source via a BitmapImage without having to save the file to disk, which is better for performance.

The WriteableBitmap class is a versatile class that provides a BitmapSource that can be written to and updated. The WriteableBitmap class has properties to retrieve DPI, Format, Metadata, Palette, and Pixel size. The WriteableBitmap class provides methods to CopyPixels and to WritePixels into the WriteableBitmap. It is possible to generate an image within your application using the WriteableBitmap's constructor that takes a UIElement:

```
WriteableBitmap bmp =
new WriteableBitmap(element, transform)
```

The WriteableBitmap class allows you to generate images on the client when needed. One example would be if you need to add branding to an image or somehow modify it before rendering, such as when creating a music+video hub application, covered later in this chapter.

This is a short section highlighting key classes, properties, and capabilities when working with images. These classes are leveraged in the next couple of sections including the next section that demonstrates how to work with the media library on Windows Phone.

The Windows Phone Media Library

The MediaLibrary class provides access to the media available on the device as part of the music+video hub and corresponding Zune service. So if a user rips their CD collection, purchases some music from Zune, and so on, and the content is available in the music+video hub on the device, the MediaLibrary class provides the ability to enumerate and index the content but you cannot add media content to the Media Library except for images, which can be added to the Pictures collection. If you download audio or video content in your application you can only save it to your application's isolated storage area.

The MediaLibrary class does not provide access to media content stored in individual third-party application's isolated storage area. Here is a list of the available media collections on Windows Phone:

- **Albums:** AlbumCollection class

- **Artists:** ArtistCollection class

- **Genres:** GenreCollection class

- **Pictures:** PictureCollection class

- **Playlists:** PlaylistCollection class

- **Songs:** SongCollection class

To gain access to the MediaLibrary class add a reference to the Microsoft.Xna.Framework assembly. The MediaLibrary class was originally available as part of the XNA Game Studio development environment for the Zune music player, and that is how it is made available on Windows Phone. Add a using clause for the Microsoft.Xna.Framework.Media namespace to get started.

■ **Note** To run this sample while debugging, shutdown Zune and run the WPConnect.exe tool from a command-line to enable debugging when accessing media content on a physical device.

The Chapter 7 sample code has a project named WorkingWithMediaLibrary to demonstrate how to access media content. The project is once again based on the MVVM Light SDK and data bound to the UI. This time we use a Panorama control as the main page with a background based on a photo from a recent vacation. There are four PanoramaItem panels:

■ Albums

■ Artists

■ Playlists

■ Songs

Each PanoramaItem includes a ListBox that data binds to a collection of these items. You might be tempted to do something like this for making the media available to the UI:

```
public AlbumCollection Albums
{
  get { return _mediaLibrary.Albums; }
}
```

Data binding to this property does not return any data. This is because there could be many artists, albums, and songs in a collection. Instead you must access each item via indexed access into the collection. To make the media items available, declare properties of type List<Album>, and so on, for each property just like with other samples.

The interesting aspect to this code sample is the constructor that loads the data like we have seen before when using GalaSoft MVVM Light as shown in Listing 7–8.

Listing 7–8. *MainViwModel Constructor that Populates the Media Collections*

```
public MainViewModel(IMediaLibraryAlbumsService mediaLibraryAlbumsService,
  IMediaLibraryArtistsService mediaLibraryArtistsService,
  IMediaLibraryPlayListsService mediaLibraryPlaylistsService,
  IMediaLibrarySongsService mediaLibrarySongsService)
{
  _mediaLibraryAlbumsService = mediaLibraryAlbumsService;
  _mediaLibraryArtistsService = mediaLibraryArtistsService;
  _mediaLibraryPlaylistsService = mediaLibraryPlaylistsService;
  _mediaLibrarySongsService = mediaLibrarySongsService;
  //Albums
  _mediaLibraryAlbumsService.GetData(
      (albums, error) =>
      {
        if (error != null)
        {
          // Report error here
          return;
        }
        Albums = (List<Album>)albums;
      });
  //Artists
  _mediaLibraryArtistsService.GetData(
(artists, error) =>
{
```

```
    if (error != null)
    {
      // Report error here
      return;
    }
    Artists = (List<Artist>)artists;
  });
    //Playlists
    _mediaLibraryPlaylistsService.GetData(
    (playlists, error) =>
    {
      if (error != null)
      {
        // Report error here
        return;
      }
      Playlists = (List<Playlist>)playlists;
    });
    //Songs
    _mediaLibrarySongsService.GetData(
    (songs, error) =>
    {
      if (error != null)
      {
        // Report error here
        return;
      }
      Songs = (List<Song>)songs;
    });
}
```

I had a choice to make for this sample. Should I implement one MainViewModel and load all of the data there, or should each category (Song, Artist, Album, etc.) get its own ViewModel class. I opted for one single MainViewModel class that calls all of the data services but you could easily do it the other way and have individual View Model classes.

The primary change to use multiple View Model classes, one for each category, would be to not set the DataContext for the ViewModelLocator at the Page level for MainPage.xaml. Instead, set the DataContext for each PanoramaItem (or containing Grid control) separately. Here is an example for loading Artist data via its Data Service:

```
using System;
using System.Collections.Generic;
using Microsoft.Xna.Framework.Media;

namespace WorkingWithMediaLibrary.Model
{
  public class MediaLibraryArtistsService : IMediaLibraryArtistsService
  {
    private MediaLibrary _mediaLibrary;
    public void GetData(Action<List<Artist>, Exception> callback)
    {
      _mediaLibrary = new MediaLibrary();
```

```
      List<Artist> artists = new List<Artist>();
      Artist artist = null;
      for (int i = 0; i < _mediaLibrary.Artists.Count; i++)
      {
        artist = _mediaLibrary.Artists[i];
        artists.Add(artist);
      }

      callback(artists, null);
      _mediaLibrary.Dispose();
    }
  }
}
```

You must access the media item by index into a local variable and then add it to the List<Artist> collections, as shown in Listing 7–8, for each media type in order to have an actual object reference. Note that adding the entire collection as in the sample can be risky from a memory consumption standpoint if the user has a large media collection.

The MediaLibrary.Albums collection has a reference to album art available but it is not directly published as a property on the Album object. The Album object does have a HaveArt property with a GetAlbumArt method. Remember from the previous sample that IValueConverter data converters allow you to data bind to anything. For this sample a simple data converter that creates a BitmapImage object to hold the image returned by the Album.GetAlbumArt() method call. The BitmapImage is then returned as the value for the Image.Source property to display the album art. Listing 7–9 shows the data converter.

Listing 7–9. AlbumArtConverter Code File

```
using System;
using System.Windows.Data;
using System.Windows.Media.Imaging;
using Microsoft.Xna.Framework.Media;

namespace WorkingWithMediaLibrary.Converters
{
  public class AlbumArtConverter : IValueConverter
  {
    public object Convert(object value, Type targetType, object parameter,
      System.Globalization.CultureInfo culture)
    {
      try
      {
        BitmapImage artImage = new BitmapImage();
        Album album = value as Album;
        if (album.HasArt)
        {
          artImage.SetSource(album.GetAlbumArt());
        }
        return artImage;
      }
      catch (Exception err)
      {
        return "";
```

```
    }
  }

  public object ConvertBack(object value, Type targetType, object parameter,
    System.Globalization.CultureInfo culture)
  {
    throw new NotImplementedException();
  }
 }
}
```

The last item to cover is that you can play Song or SongCollection objects via the MediaPlayer.Play() method, which is covered in more detail below. Figure 7–8 shows the UI in the emulator, which has just test data for a single album and a few songs so you will want to run on a real device with a populated library.

Figure 7–8. *WorkingWithMediaLibrary UI in the Emulator*

This concludes our coverage of the Windows Phone media library programmable API. Next up is how to create a Photo Extras application.

Working with Video and Audio Media

So far, we have discussed working with the Media Library and the Picture hub with Photo Extras applications. In this section, we discuss video and audio media. As mentioned previously, Windows Phone third-party applications cannot add media to the Media Library but third-party applications can add content to Isolated Storage in addition to playing video and audio content in memory.

In this section we cover supported codecs, playing video, audio, and DRM considerations within the context of the programming model.

Supported Codecs and Containers

Windows Phone has extensive codec and container support as detailed at this link:

http://msdn.microsoft.com/en-us/library/ff462087%28VS.92%29.aspx

Container support for a variety of media includes WAV, MP3, WMA, 3GP, MP4, 3G2, M4A, WMV, M4V, 3G2, JPG, and PNG. Of note, GIF, BMP, and TIF are not supported in the Image control in Silverlight.

Decoder support is a long list at the above link, but of note support is available for MP3, WMA Standard v9, AAC-LC, HE-AAC v1, HE-AAC v2, AMR-NB, WMV (VC-1, WMV9) simple, main, and advanced. Also supported are MPEG-4 Part 2, Simple, Advanced Simple, MPEG-4 Part 10 Level 3.0 Baseline, Main, High, and H.263. There are specific requirements in terms of bitrate, constant bitrate vs. variable bitrate, as well as methods of playback, so check the above link when troubleshooting playback issues on a device to see if a capability or playback method is not correct.

Video and Audio in the Emulator

The emulator does not support all of the codecs supported on a device. Specifically, AAC-LC, HE-AAC v1, HE-AAC v2, AMR-NB, MPEG-4 Part 2 simple, MPEG-4 Part 2 advanced, MPEG-4 Part 10 level 3 baseline, main or high, and H.263 are all not supported.

The following codecs are supported but with caveats:

- ▓ WMV (VC-1, WMV9) – Simple Profile – Unsupported above 320 x 176 pixels.

- ▓ WMV (VC-1, WMV9) - Main Profile – Unsupported above 800 x 488 pixels.

- ▓ WMV (VC-1, WMV9) - Advanced Profile – Unsupported above 720 x 480 pixels.

When investigating video support for your content, it is recommended to test on a real device first to ensure that an accurate assessment is made.

Progressive Download Video

Progressive download is generally used for short form video, clips, music videos, and the like. The file is completely downloaded over HTP while playback begins immediately.

We create a project named WorkingWtihVideo in the Chapter 7 solution. The MainPage.xaml page is a menu page to launch additional pages to test out functionality starting with testing progressive play back in the MediaPlayerLauncher, which was covered in Chapter 4 in the LaunchersAndChoosers sample.

Progressive Video with MediaPlayerLauncher

Silverlight supports both progressive and streaming video via the MediaElement control, but a simple way to play progressive non-DRM video is via the Microsoft.Phone.Tasks.MediaPlayerLauncher task. A page named MediaPlayeTask.xaml is added to the WorkingWithVideo project that has a single button titled play video.private void textBlock1_MouseLeftButtonDown(object sender, MouseButtonEventArgs e)

```
{
  MediaPlayerLauncher mediaPlayerLauncher = new MediaPlayerLauncher();
  mediaPlayerLauncher.Controls = MediaPlaybackControls.FastForward |
    MediaPlaybackControls.Pause | MediaPlaybackControls.Rewind |
    MediaPlaybackControls.Skip | MediaPlaybackControls.Stop;
  mediaPlayerLauncher.Location = MediaLocationType.Data;
  mediaPlayerLauncher.Media = new
Uri("http://ecn.channel9.msdn.com/o9/ch9/8/9/6/6/3/5/WP7Xbox_ch9.mp4");
  mediaPlayerLauncher.Show();
}
```

As you can see, it is possible to configure what trickplay controls are visible during playback. In the next section, we cover playing video with the MediaElement, which is pretty simple as well – but you will need to build up your own media player for best user experience. This is because the MediaElement is a blank canvas with a highly programmable API. By default, it does not have any media controls and the like. Unless you need specific functionality or want complete control over the playback UI the MediaPlayerLauncher task is easiest.

One situation where the MediaPlayerLauncher is not a good choice is with DRM'd content. I cover DRM'd video later in the chapter. The next section covers playing progressive video with the MediaElement control.

Progressive Video with MediaElement

The MediaElement is a very powerful control with a rich API to provide fined-grained control during playback with a rich event model. We create a simple example that hooks into the interesting events as well as displays values for video related properties.

A new page named MediaElement.xaml is added to the WorkingWithVideo project. A MediaElement control is added to the page. The application bar is available to host a play and pause button that will programmatically control the MediaElement control. Several TextBlock controls are laid out to display values from various MediaElement properties as shown in Figure 7–9.

Figure 7–9. *MediaElement.xaml UI*

There are several interesting events available with the MediaElement control. Listing 7–10 shows the available media-related events.

Listing 7–10. *PictureEditorView .xaml.cs Code File*

```
using System;
using System.Windows;
using System.Windows.Threading;
using Microsoft.Phone.Controls;

namespace WorkingWithVideo.pages
{
  public partial class MediaElement : PhoneApplicationPage
  {
    public MediaElement()
    {
      InitializeComponent();
      DispatcherTimer timer = new DispatcherTimer();
      timer.Tick += new EventHandler(timer_Tick);
      timer.Interval = new TimeSpan(0, 0, 1);
      timer.Start();
```

```csharp
}

void timer_Tick(object sender, EventArgs e)
{
  CanSeekTextBlock.Text = mediaPlayer.CanSeek.ToString();
  CanPauseTextBlock.Text = mediaPlayer.CanPause.ToString();
  DroppedFramesTextBlock.Text =
    mediaPlayer.DroppedFramesPerSecond.ToString();
}

private void mediaPlayer_MediaOpened(object sender, RoutedEventArgs e)
{
  mediaPlayer.Play();
}

private void mediaPlayer_MediaFailed(object sender,
  ExceptionRoutedEventArgs e)
{
  MessageBox.Show("Media Failed: " + e.ErrorException.Message);
}

private void mediaPlayer_MediaEnded(object sender, RoutedEventArgs e)
{

}

private void PlayAppBarBtn_Click(object sender, EventArgs e)
{
  mediaPlayer.Source =
    new Uri("http://ecn.channel9.msdn.com/o9/ch9/8/9/6/6/3/5/WP7Xbox_ch9.wmv",
      UriKind.Absolute);
}

private void PauseAppBarBtn_Click(object sender, EventArgs e)
{
  mediaPlayer.Pause();
}

private void mediaPlayer_CurrentStateChanged(object sender,
  RoutedEventArgs e)
{
  CurrentStateTextBlock.Text = mediaPlayer.CurrentState.ToString();
}

private void mediaPlayer_BufferingProgressChanged(object sender,
  RoutedEventArgs e)
{
  BufferingProgressTextBlock.Text = mediaPlayer.BufferingProgress.ToString();
}

private void mediaPlayer_DownloadProgressChanged(object sender,
  RoutedEventArgs e)
```

```
        {
            DownloadProgressChangedTextBlock.Text = mediaPlayer.DownloadProgress.ToString();
        }
    }
}
```

Notice that clicking play doesn't start playback. Instead, it sets the Source property on the MediaElement control. If the video configured on the Source property is successfully opened, the MediaOpened event fires, which is where Play is actually called.

MediaStreamSource

For custom video delivery, you can use the MediaElement.SetSource() method in your code to specify the media to be played. One overload of SetSource() accepts a System.IO.Stream, which is suited for the scenario where you decide to acquire the media through some other mechanism rather than have the MediaElement handle the download. When you acquire the media file, you can create a Stream around it (using a more concrete type like System.IO.IsolatedStorage.IsolatedStorageFileStream) and pass it to SetSource().

The second overload of SetSource() accepts an instance of the System.Windows.Media.MediaStreamSource type. The MediaStreamSource type is actually a way to plug a video container file format into Silverlight, for which the MediaElement does not come with a built-in parser. Video container file formats and related specifications are complex topics, and consequently a treatment of MediaStreamSource implementations is beyond the scope of this book.

When the Source is set by either mechanism, for progressive download scenarios the MediaElement immediately starts to download the media. The MediaElement.DownloadProgressChanged event is raised repeatedly as the download progresses. The MediaElement.DownloadProgress property reports the download progress as a percentage value (actually a double between 0 and 1 that you can convert to percentage) that you can use to track and report the download progress in the DownloadProgressChanged event handler.

■ **Note** For more information on Silverlight and MediaStreamSource check out *Silverlight Recipes: A Problem-Solution Approach*, Second Edition: http://apress.com/book/view/1430230339.

Streaming Video

In addition to progressive download video, streaming video is another technique used to deliver media to a player. Streaming does not require downloading the media file locally, and it is well suited for scenarios involving either live or on-demand broadcasts to a large population of viewers.

Microsoft provides Smooth Streaming, an IIS Media Services extension that enables adaptive streaming of media to Silverlight and other clients over HTTP. Smooth Streaming provides a high-quality viewing experience that scales massively on content distribution networks, making true HD 1080p media experiences a reality.

Smooth Streaming is the productized version of technology first used by Microsoft to deliver on-demand video for the 2008 Summer Olympics at NBCOlympics.com. By dynamically monitoring both local bandwidth and video rendering performance, Smooth Streaming optimizes playback of content by switching video quality in real-time to match current network conditions resulting in a better viewing experience.

Smooth Streaming uses the simple but powerful concept of delivering small content fragments (typically two seconds worth of video) and verifying that each has arrived within the appropriate time and played back at the expected quality level. If one fragment does not meet these requirements, the next fragment delivered will be at a somewhat lower quality level. Conversely, when conditions allow it, the quality of subsequent fragments will be at a higher level if network conditions improve.

▓ **Note** For more information on IIS Smooth Streaming go to `http://learn.iis.net/page.aspx/558/getting-started-with-iis-smooth-streaming/`.

SmoothStreamingMediaElement

The `Microsoft.Web.Media.SmoothStreaming.SmoothStreamingMediaElement` is a customized version of the `MediaElement` that works directly with IIS Smooth Streaming technology. The `SmoothStreamingMediaElement` available in Windows Phone is compatible with the IIS Smooth Streaming Client 1.1. Windows Phone is a subset of the full client support. The phone icon in the API reference identifies members of classes in the `Microsoft.Web.Media.SmoothStreaming` namespace that are available for Windows Phone development. Review the documentation at the following link:

`http://msdn.microsoft.com/en-us/library/microsoft.web.media.smoothstreaming(v=VS.90).aspx`

IIS Smooth Streaming combined with the `SmoothStreamingMediaElement` provide an incredibly powerful and flexible streaming capability with support for multiple video and audio tracks, multiple languages, subtitles, Timeline Markers, Fast Forward and Rewind, and metadata in tracks for "pop-up" information during playback for a rich media experience. Please refer to this link for details on capabilities:

`http://msdn.microsoft.com/en-us/library/ee958035(v=VS.90).aspx`

Microsoft Media Framework Player Framework

The Silverlight Media Framework (SMF), renamed the Microsoft Media Platform Play Framework (MMP PF), is an open source CodePlex project that provides a robust, scalable customizable media player for IIS Smooth Streaming media delivery. The MMP PF builds on the core functionality of the Smooth Streaming Client (formerly known as the Smooth Streaming Player Development Kit) and adds a large number of additional features, including an extensibility API that allows developers to create plug-ins for the framework. The MMP PF also now includes full support for Windows Phone so developers can incorporate high-end video playback experiences in their Windows Phone applications. Please check out the MMP PF at this link:

`http://smf.codeplex.com/`

DRM

Most long form video, whether it be TV show episodes, movies, or live TV, has some form of Digital Rights Management (DRM). As the goal of DRM is to prevent illegal copying of digital content, securely storing licenses to content is of paramount concern.

Silverlight for Windows Phone supports DRM via Microsoft PlayReady. Microsoft PlayReady is a platform independent DRM content access technology that is optimized for broad use across a range of devices. Microsoft PlayReady supports subscription, purchase, rental, and pay-per-view business models that can be applied to many digital content types and to a wide range of audio and video formats.

On Windows Phone, there is support for Microsoft PlayReady built into the platform including a secure key store for online and offline DRM key storage. After DRM media is accessed the first time, the license is stored offline enabling offline playback of DRM'd content.

A full discussion of DRM is beyond this book but here is a link for more information on Microsoft PlayReady technology:

`www.microsoft.com/PlayReady/Default.mspx`

When it comes to DRM protected content available via the Zune Service, either purchased or subscription, you can play that content within Silverlight applications using the `MediaElement` as well as the `MediaPlayer` object available in the XNA Framework. License acquisition occurs behind the scenes with no additional work necessary by the developer. For content that is not owned by the end-user, you can use the `MarketplaceDetailsTask` to show UI that allows the user to purchase the content.

Audio Support

Because audio is critical to video playback, audio support is covered in pretty good detail in concert with what has been discussed above regarding video playback. However, in addition to the `MediaElement` and `SmoothStreamingMediaElement`, developers can play audio using the `Microsoft.Xna.Framework.Media.MediaPlayer` object. We demonstrated this in the Chapter 7 `WorkingWithMediaLibrary` project in this event handler from `MainPanoramaPage.xaml.cs`:

```
private void ListBox_SelectionChanged(object sender, SelectionChangedEventArgs e)
{
  object obj = (sender as ListBox).SelectedItem;
  MediaLibrary library = new MediaLibrary();
  try
  {
    switch (obj.GetType().ToString())
    {
      case "Microsoft.Xna.Framework.Media.Album": MediaPlayer.Play(((Album)(obj)).Songs);
break;
      case "Microsoft.Xna.Framework.Media.Song": MediaPlayer.Play((Song)(obj)); break;
      case "Microsoft.Xna.Framework.Media.Playlist":
MediaPlayer.Play(((Playlist)(obj)).Songs); break;
      case "Microsoft.Xna.Framework.Media.Artist": MediaPlayer.Play(((Artist)(obj)).Songs);
break;
    }
  }
  catch (Exception ex)
  {
```

```
    MessageBox.Show("Error: " + ex.Message);
  };
}
```

The MediaPlayer object can play by Album, Song, Playlist, and Artist objects, but only one of these items at a time. So, for example, for a custom play list you must provide one song at a time. The MediaPlayer object has two events that you can hook, MediaStateChanged and ActiveSongChanged. MediaStateChanged fires when state changes from Paused, Playing, or Stopped to another MediaState value. Here is a code example, not from a specific project but provided as reference:

```
public MainPage()
{
  InitializeComponent();
  MediaPlayer.MediaStateChanged += new EventHandler<EventArgs>(MediaPlayer_MediaStateChanged);
  MediaPlayer.ActiveSongChanged += new EventHandler<EventArgs>(MediaPlayer_ActiveSongChanged);
}

void MediaPlayer_ActiveSongChanged(object sender, EventArgs e)
{
  if (MediaPlayer.Queue.Count == 0)
  {
    //add a song to Play
    MediaPlayer.Play(nextSong);
  }
}

void MediaPlayer_MediaStateChanged(object sender, EventArgs e)
{
  switch (MediaPlayer.State)
  {
    case MediaState.Paused:
      break;
    case MediaState.Playing:
      break;
    case MediaState.Stopped:
      break;
  }
}
```

On a related note, you can prompt the user to purchase additional music using MarketplaceSearchTask and passing in a search string containing the artist, album, and song title. You can also use the WebBrowserTask and Zune Http links for content if you have the ID for the content. Here is an example:

```
WebBrowserTask task = new WebBrowserTask();
task.URL = HttpUtility.UrlEncode("http://social.zune.net/External/LaunchZuneProtocol.aspx?
                  pathuri=navigate%3FalbumID%3Dd1935e06-0100-11db-89ca-0019b92a3933");
task.Show();
```

You can then use the MediaLibrary object covered above and demonstrated in the WorkingWithMediaLibrary project to find acquired content and show album art as well as purchase the media.

You might guess that the `MarketplaceDetailsTask` could also show the purchase UI but it is not supported in this release.

For more information on music playback, check out Chapter 10 where I cover background audio playback now available in Windows Phone OS 7.1

App Connect -Extending the picture Hub

Developers always ask about ways to integrate with the underlying platform. This is especially true for a mobile device where mobile devices users want to perform actions with as little effort as possible. In Windows Phone 7.5, Microsoft introduced App Connect to encompass application extensions that integrate with the Windows Phone, including integrating with the pictures Hub, music+video Hub, and Bing Search. In this section I focus on picture Hub integration.

■ **Note** In Windows Phone 7, extending the pictures Hub was called a "Photos Extra" application.

One popular use case is manipulating pictures taken with the built-in camera. Many applications allow photo manipulation directly on the device so integrating these applications as much as possible with the pictures Hub benefits the end-user.

An application that extends the pictures Hub is accessible from within the pictures Hub's Single Photo Viewer (SPV) UI. When in the SPV, swipe up the Application Bar to expose the apps… menu item. Select the apps… menu to see the available third-party applications.

Note that images are the only media type that can be added to the Media Library, so once a picture Hub extension performs its magic on an image; it can be saved back to the media library to be shared with others. Figure 7–10 shows the Photos Extra UI.

Figure 7–10. *Photos Extensibility via the Share… Menu*

The next section covers how an application can extend the pictures Hub.

Extending the pictures Hub

This section covers how easy it is to integrate with the pictures Hub. Extending the pictures Hub includes the following two major steps:

- Modifying the WMAppManifest.xml file
- Retrieving the selected photo

A new project named AppConnectPhoto is added to the Chapter 7 solution. We will turn this project into a picture Hub extension and use MVVM Light as part of the sample. We will take advantage of messaging to communicate between the image editing View named ImageEditorView.xaml and the backing ViewModel class named PictureEditingViewModel.cs. We also will use a few IValueConverter classes as well. First we need to edit the project so that it shows up in the SPV "Apps..." menu. The next section covers the steps.

Apps... Menu

For an application that extends the pictures Hub to appear in the Apps... menu, you must add this XML element to the WMAppManifest.xml file:

```
<Extensions>
    <Extension ExtensionName="Photos_Extra_Hub"
        ConsumerID="{5B04B775-356B-4AA0-AAF8-6491FFEA5632}" TaskID="_default" />
    <Extension ExtensionName="Photos_Extra_Viewer"
        ConsumerID="{5B04B775-356B-4AA0-AAF8-6491FFEA5632}" TaskID="_default" />
</Extensions>
```

Add the above Xml just past the <Tokens> element within the <App> element in the WmAppManifest.xml file. The first <Extension> element adds the application to the picture Hub Apps menu. The second <Extension> adds support for the Share... menu in the SVP.

The TaskID in the <Extension> element matches the DefaultTask's Name property, "_default", defined in the WMAppManifest.xml file. This means the extension will launch the DefaultTask, usually MainPage.xaml.

Retrieving the Selected Photo

Retrieving the selected photo is performed in the OnNavigatedTo method override of the application. A set of parameters are passed in when the application is launched from the Single Photo Viewer in the Pictures hub. This allows the application to know when it is launched as a picture Hub extension or when the application is simply launched from the application list or Start screen tile if pinned to the Start screen because no query parameters are present.

To retrieve the query parameters, you use the NavigationContext.QueryString property. The QueryString object is a Dictionary<string, string> object. Look for the pre-defined QueryString["token"] to know that the application was launched from the SVP. Use the query value to also obtain a handle to the image.

To get started, we override OnNavigatedTo in Main.xaml.cs in order to capture the query string value to set the correct picture on PictureEditingViewModel.PictureToEdit property. Listing 7–11 has the code for the AppConnectPhoto MainPage.xaml.cs code file.

Listing 7–11. AppConnectPhoto MainPage.xaml.cs Code File

```csharp
using System;
using System.Collections.Generic;
using System.Windows.Controls;
using GalaSoft.MvvmLight.Messaging;
using Microsoft.Phone.Controls;
using Microsoft.Xna.Framework.Media;
namespace AppConnectPhoto
{
  public partial class MainPage : PhoneApplicationPage
  {
    // Constructor
    public MainPage()
    {
      InitializeComponent();
    }
    protected override void OnNavigatedTo(System.Windows.Navigation.NavigationEventArgs e)
    {
      base.OnNavigatedTo(e);

      //Process query string
      IDictionary<string, string> queryStrings = this.NavigationContext.QueryString;
      if (NavigationContext.QueryString.Count > 0 &&
        NavigationContext.QueryString.ContainsKey("token"))
      {
        MediaLibrary library = new MediaLibrary();
        Picture picture = library.GetPictureFromToken(queryStrings["token"]);
        //Remove this query string item so that when the user clicks
        //"back" from the ImageEditorView page the app doesn't loop back
        //over to the ImageEditorView in an endless loop of navigation because
        //the query string value is still present and picked up by
        //MainPage.OnNavigateTo each time...
        NavigationContext.QueryString.Remove("token");

        //Send Message with Picture object
        SetPictureAndNavigate(picture);
      }
    }

    private void ListBox_SelectionChanged(object sender,
System.Windows.Controls.SelectionChangedEventArgs e)
    {
      ListBox lb = sender as ListBox;SetPictureAndNavigate(lb.SelectedItem as Picture);
    }

    void SetPictureAndNavigate(Picture picture)
    {
      Messenger.Default.Send<Picture>(picture, "PictureToEdit");
      NavigationService.Navigate(new Uri("/ImageEditorView.xaml", UriKind.Relative));
    }
  }
}
```

The query string value for the token parameter is obtained and the
MediaLibrary.GetPictureFromToken method is called to obtain the correct image from the Picture hub.
The picture is passed to the SetPictureAndNavigate method shown in Listing 7–11. This same method is
called when an image is selected from the ListBox in MainPage.xaml via the ListBox_SelectionChanged
method also in Listing 7–11.

Notice in the SetPictureAndNavigate method, it uses the MVVM Light Messenger.Default.Send to
pass the picture as a message. The message is registered for and received in the
PictureEditingViewModel class constructor in this line of code:

```
Messenger.Default.Register<Picture>(
  this, "PictureToEdit",
  (picture) => { PictureToEdit = picture; });
```

The PictureEditorView.xamlView data binds to the MainViewModel's PictureEditingVM property,
which is an instance of PictureEditingViewModel that is created when MainViewModel is constructed.
This ensures that an instance of the PictureEditingViewModel is available when the message is sent.
Otherwise, if PictureEditorView.xaml data binded to an instance when constructed, the message would
have already been sent resulting in a bug that the first time you navigate to a photo the message is lost.

When the message is received by the PictureEditingViewModel, it updates the
PictureEditingViewModel.PictureToEdit property so that the Image control on that page can data bind
to the PictureToEdit property. This allows the UI to data bind to a ViewModel without directly accessing
the ViewModel by using MVVM Light Toolkit Messaging.

Let's finish discussing the MainPage.xaml functionality before diving further into the picture edit
page. The ListBox in MainPage.xaml data binds to the List<Picture> Pictures property in the
MainViewModel class. The interesting part of the MainViewModel class is loading the images:

```
private void CreateDataCollections()
{
  Pictures = new List<Picture>();
  Picture picture = null;
  for (int i = 0; i < _mediaLibrary.Pictures.Count; i++)
  {
    picture = _mediaLibrary.Pictures[i];
    Pictures.Add(picture);
    if (i > 30)
      break;
  }
}
```

The CreateDataCollections method is hard coded to just load the first 30 pictures found into the
MainViewModel.Pictures property. Figure 7–11 shows the MainPage.xaml UI with sample images from the
Emulator rendered in a basic data template that shows the name, the image, and the album it is from.

Figure 7–11. *PhotosExtra main page UI*

The ListBox data binds to the `List<Picture>` `Pictures` collection. The data template includes an Image control. It leverages a value converter named `ImageSourceConverter` that calls `Picture.GetImage()` and sets it on the Source property for the Image control in the `DataTemplate`. The `Picture.GetThumbnail` property would be a better choice for the `ListBox` template, because it is a small image but we use the same converter when displaying the image on the edit screen and `GetImage` returns the full image and so looks better when full screen.

MainPage.xaml only displays when launched from the App List. When an image is tapped, it opens to the picture editing View named `PictureEditorView.xaml`, which data binds to an instance of `PictureEditingViewModel` that is a property named `PictureEditingVM` on the `MainViewModel`.

When launched from the Photos Extra menu with the QueryStrings value present, the application goes straight to the picture editing view as shown in Figure 7–12.

Figure 7–12. *PhotosExtra picture editing UI*

Notice that in both Figure 7–11 and Figure 7–12 that the name does not include the extension. The TextBlock data binds to the Picture.Name property that includes the extension but it is parsed out. This is accomplished by a simple value converter named ImageNameConverter that has a simple line of code to obtain just the name portion:

```
return ((string)value).Split('.')[0];
```

Notice also that in Figure 7–11, when the UI is in Landscape mode the text title disappears to maximize space for image viewing and editing. This is also achieved via a value converter. The TextBlock's Visibility property Element data binds to the Orientation of the Page. The value converter sets Visibility to Collapsed if the phone is in Landscape mode. Otherwise the TextBlock control's Visibility is configured to Visible. The PictureEditorView data binds to the PictureEditingViewModel class shown in Listing 7–12.

Listing 7–12. *PictureEditingViewModel.cs Code File*

```
using System.IO;
using System.Windows.Media.Imaging;
using GalaSoft.MvvmLight;
using GalaSoft.MvvmLight.Command;
using GalaSoft.MvvmLight.Messaging;
using Microsoft.Xna.Framework.Media;

namespace AppConnectPhoto.ViewModel
{
    public class PictureEditingViewModel : ViewModelBase
    {
```

```csharp
private MediaLibrary mediaLibrary;

public PictureEditingViewModel()
{
  mediaLibrary = new MediaLibrary();

  //Register to receive message with picture object from Picture Hub
  //This message is sent from MainPage.xaml.cs in OnNavigateTo
  Messenger.Default.Register<Picture>(
   this, "PictureToEdit",
   (picture) => { PictureToEdit = picture; });

  //Instantiate Commands
  SaveImageCommand = new RelayCommand(
    () => SaveImage());

  SaveImageAsCommand = new RelayCommand<string>(
    param => SaveImageAs(param));

  RevertToSavedImageCommand = new RelayCommand(
    () => EditImage());
  EditImageCommand = new RelayCommand(
    () => RevertToSavedImage());
}

#region Image State
public const string PictureToEditPropertyName = "PictureToEdit";
private Picture _pictureToEdit = null;
public Picture PictureToEdit
{
  get
  {
    return _pictureToEdit;
  }

  set
  {
    if (_pictureToEdit == value)
    {
      return;
    }
    var oldValue = _pictureToEdit;
    _pictureToEdit = value;
    RaisePropertyChanged(PictureToEditPropertyName);
  }
}


public const string ModifiedPicturePropertyName = "ModifiedPicture";
private WriteableBitmap _modifiedPicture = null;
public WriteableBitmap ModifiedPicture
{
```

```csharp
    get { return _modifiedPicture; }
    set
    {
      if (_modifiedPicture == value)
      { return; }
      var oldValue = _modifiedPicture;
      _modifiedPicture = value;
      RaisePropertyChanged(ModifiedPicturePropertyName);
    }
  }

  //Property to data bind to for SaveAs input UI
  //Used for SaveAs command
  public const string ImageSaveAsNamePropertyName = "ImageSaveAsName";
  private string _imageSaveAsName = null;
  public string ImageSaveAsName
  {
    get { return _imageSaveAsName;}
    set
    {
      if (_imageSaveAsName == value)
      { return; }
      var oldValue = _imageSaveAsName;
      _imageSaveAsName = value;
      RaisePropertyChanged(ImageSaveAsNamePropertyName);
    }
  }

  public const string ImageIsDirtyPropertyName = "ImageIsDirty";
  private bool _imageIsDirety = false;
  public bool ImageIsDirty
  {
    get { return _imageIsDirety; }
    set
    {
      if (_imageIsDirety == value)
      { return; }

      var oldValue = _imageIsDirety;
      _imageIsDirety = value;
      RaisePropertyChanged(ImageIsDirtyPropertyName);
    }
  }
#endregion

#region Image Actions for RelayCommand Objects
private void EditImage()
{
  //Editing, unsaved changes pending
  ImageIsDirty = true;
}
```

```
//View must set the writable bitmap area
//prior to executing this command
//This Save action takes a new name
private void SaveImageAs(string saveAsName)
{
  using (MemoryStream jpegStream = new MemoryStream())
  {
    //Tell the UI to update the WriteableBitmap property
    Messenger.Default.Send<bool>(true, "UpdateWriteableBitmap");
    ModifiedPicture.SaveJpeg(jpegStream, ModifiedPicture.PixelWidth,
      ModifiedPicture.PixelHeight, 0, 100);
    //Update current Picture to reflect new modified image
    PictureToEdit = mediaLibrary.SavePicture(saveAsName, jpegStream);
    //Saved, not editing
    ImageIsDirty = false;
  };
}


//PictureEditingView registers to receive this message
//It would clear out any edits at the UI level.
private void RevertToSavedImage()
{
  Messenger.Default.Send<bool>(true, "UndoImageChanges");
}
#endregion

#region Image Editing Commmands
public RelayCommand SaveImageCommand { get; private set; }
public RelayCommand<string> SaveImageAsCommand { get; private set; }
public RelayCommand EditImageCommand { get; private set; }
public RelayCommand RevertToSavedImageCommand { get; private set; }
#endregion
  }
}
```

The PictureEditingViewModel class has two primary data properties: PictureToEdit of type Picture and the ModifiedPicture of type WriteableBitmap. The idea is to display the selected picture to be modified in an Image control.

■ **Note** The sample doesn't actually modify the control, but you could enable drawing, etc., just like what was demonstrated in Chapter 2.

The user can then edit the image in the UI. The modifications under the covers would result in additional Silverlight controls added to the XAML with the Grid WritableBitMapSourceArea as the top-level parent. When the user clicks save, the Grid is passed into the WriteableBitmap to turn it into a bitmap image.

You can pass any UIElement into the WriteableBitmap.Render method and it will turn the element and its children into an image. In the SaveImageCommand (SaveImage()) and SaveImageAsCommand (SaveImageAs()) commands, a message is sent to the UI to update the ModifiedPicture property on the VM prior to saving. We could do this in a way without tying the View to the ViewModel via additional messages, but for our example this is sufficient.

The PictureEditingViewModel class also sends a message to the UI to ask the View to undo modifications to the image. Listing 7–13 has the PictureEditorView code-behind file.

Listing 7–13. *PictureEditorView .xaml.cs Code File*

```
using System.Windows.Controls;
using GalaSoft.MvvmLight.Messaging;
using Microsoft.Phone.Controls;
using AppConnectPhoto.ViewModel;

namespace AppConnectPhoto
{
  /// <summary>
  /// Description for ImageEditorView.
  /// </summary>
  public partial class PictureEditorView : PhoneApplicationPage
  {
    PictureEditingViewModel vm;
    /// <summary>
    /// Initializes a new instance of the ImageEditorView class.
    /// </summary>
    public PictureEditorView()
    {
      InitializeComponent();

      vm = DataContext as PictureEditingViewModel;

      //Register for message to undo changes
      Messenger.Default.Register<bool>(
        this, "UndoImageChanges",
        (param) => UndoImageChanges());

      Messenger.Default.Register<bool>(
        this, "UpdateWriteableBitmap",
        (param) => UpdateWriteableBitmap());
    }

    private void UpdateWriteableBitmap()
    {
      //Update WriteableBitmap so it is ready to save
      vm.ModifiedPicture.Render(WriteableBitmapSourceArea, null);
    }

    private void UndoImageChanges()
```

```
  {
    //Undo Image changes
    //Reset WriteableBitmapSourceArea Grid to just hold
    //the original image content only
    Image img = ImageToEdit;
    WriteableBitmapSourceArea.Children.Clear();
    WriteableBitmapSourceArea.Children.Add(img);
  }

  private void EditAppBarBtn_Click(object sender, System.EventArgs e)
  {
    vm.EditImageCommand.Execute(null);
  }

  private void saveAppBarBtn_Click(object sender, System.EventArgs e)
  {
    vm.SaveImageCommand.Execute(null);
  }

  private void SaveAsAppMenItem_Click(object sender, System.EventArgs e)
  {
    vm.SaveImageAsCommand.Execute(vm.ImageSaveAsName);
  }

  private void RevertToLastSaveMenuItem_Click(object sender, System.EventArgs e)
  {
    vm.RevertToSavedImageCommand.Execute(null);
  }
 }
}
```

This code walkthrough demonstrates how to set up all the infrastructure for a picture modifying Photos Extra application. It does not actually perform edits, that we leave to the enterprising reader to build the next great Photos Extra application.

App Connect - music+videos Hub Integration

Applications that play music or video can integrate more deeply into the Windows Phone user experience. This helps to provide consistent quick access to content for the end user, while also allowing your application to surface content and the application itself within the music+videos hub in addition to the App List. Figure 7–13 shows the music+videos hub panorama for reference.

Figure 7–13. Microsoft Windows Phone music+videos hub

The music+videos hub has an apps, history, and new section that a music or video application can integrate into for a richer user experience.

An application that calls the Microsoft.Devices.MediaHistory or Microsoft.Devices.MediaHistoryItem classes is considered as a Music + Videos hub application and will appear in the apps list in the hub when installed on the phone. When an application is submitted to the Windows Phone Marketplace, the marketplace detects that the application uses these classes and will automatically update the hub type to Music + Videos in the application's Windows Phone application manifest.

The Windows Phone Certification Requirements Document covers music+videos hub application certification requirements in section 6.5. In this section, we build a sample music+videos hub application that you can use to guide you when building your own applications.

Additional Assets

As you can see in Figure 7–13 that shows the music+videos hub, applications and content are represented by tiles. Here are the rules for tiles:

- Tile images must be a .jpg image.

- The application title or logo must be present on each tile.

- The now playing tile must be 358 pixels x 358 pixels in size.

- Other tiles shown on the hub must be 173 pixels x 173 pixels in size.

- The Title property of the MediaHistoryItem class must be set to text that represents the content, such as a station name or video title.

We create two tiles to represent the videos, named ParisVideoTile.jpg and tdfVideoTile.jpg, to correspond to the videos of the Paris skyline video and Tour De France video. We also create two now playing tiles appropriately named NowPlayingParisTile.jpg and NowPlayingtdfTile.jpg.

All of the image tiles are passed into the MediaHistoryItemAPI as a System.IO.Stream object.

■ **Tip** In an application retrieving images from server-apis, use the WriteableBitmap class to create images that are branded to your application.

Testing music+videos Hub Applications

When an application is ingested into marketplace, marketplace detects if the application makes calls to the MediaHistory and MediaHistoryItem classes and updates the application manifest so that the application is ready for publishing. We cover how to work with these APIs in the next section.

You can test music+videos hub applications with Visual Studio and an actual device, but you must edit the manifest file manually. Set the HubType attribute on the <App> element to a value of 1 and be sure to disconnect from Zune when testing if not using the WPConnect tool to allow media interaction, and debugging, while connected via Zune. The APIs will throw an exception if syncing with Zune.

Because the emulator does not ship with the full Windows Phone experience (i.e., the music+videos hub is not available), it is not possible to test music+videos hub applications in the emulator in this release.

Debugging music+videos Hub Applications

There's a tool that allows Visual Studio 2010 to connect to a device without the Zune Client software running. This functionality is especially necessary for applications that play media because it is not possible to play media when connected to the Zune Client. It is also not possible to update music+videos hub items like the "History," "Now playing," and "New" sections while connected to Zune.

To enable debugging without the Zune client running, download the WPConnect tool available with the Zune Client in this directory: The steps are as follows:

a. Connect the device.

b. Close the Zune software.

c. Run either the 32-bit or 64-bit version of the WPConnect tool from the command-line based on your operating system

Disconnecting the device reverts back to normal Zune functionality with the device.

music+videos Hub Sample Application

We start with a Windows Phone Application project named AppConnectMusicPlusVideo in the Chapter Six solution. We create a simple UI with two videos from a recent vacation to play as shown in Figure 7–14.

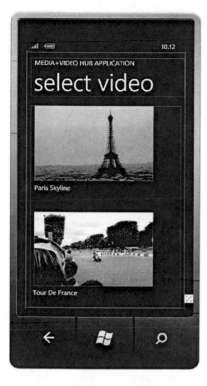

Figure 7–14. *AppConnectMusicPlusVideo sample application*

We add another page to the application called VideoPlayerPage.xaml that contains a MediaElement where the content is actually played. When one of the thumbnails shown in Figure 7–14 is clicked, the associated video is passed as part of the query string and the application navigates to the VideoPlayerPage.xaml page to actually play the video. Here is the method handler for the top thumbnail image when touched or clicked:

```
private void PlayParisImage_MouseLeftButtonUp(object sender, MouseButtonEventArgs e)
{
  NavigationService.Navigate(new Uri(
    "/VideoPlayerPage.xaml?video=Paris",UriKind.Relative));
}
```

■ **Note** The videos are royalty-free because the author recorded them, but the videos were shot with an old camera at 320 x 240, resulting in terrible quality on a high-resolution device like Windows Phone. But they are still useful to demonstrate the concepts.

The VideoPlayerPage.xaml page does not manifest any video playing UI as we are laser focused on just the code to create a music+videos hub application. Listing 7–13 has the code for VideoPlayerPage.xaml.cs.

Listing 7–13. Initial VideoPlayerPage.xaml.cs Code File

```
using System;
using System.Windows;
using Microsoft.Phone.Controls;

namespace AppConnectMusicPlusVideo
{
  public partial class VideoPlayerPage : PhoneApplicationPage
  {
    public VideoPlayerPage()
    {
      InitializeComponent();
    }

    protected override void OnNavigatedTo(System.Windows.Navigation.NavigationEventArgs e)
    {
      VideoPlayer.Source = new
          Uri(@"/video/"+NavigationContext.QueryString["video"]+".wmv",UriKind.Relative);

      base.OnNavigatedTo(e);
    }

      private void VideoPlayer_MediaOpened(object sender, RoutedEventArgs e)
      {
        VideoPlayer.Play();
      }

      private void VideoPlayer_MediaFailed(object sender, ExceptionRoutedEventArgs e)
      {
        MessageBox.Show(e.ErrorException.Message);
      }
  }
}
```

In Listing 7–13, we process the query string with the video name in the OnNavigatedTo event handler. If the media is successfully opened we play it. If it fails to open the application displays a MessageBox with the error message.

We now focus on modifying the code to become a music+videos hub application. From the Windows Phone application certification requirements, the application needs to do these items:

■ The application must update the "New" section of the music+videos hub when media is added to the device.

■ The application must update the "Now playing" section of the music+videos hub when the application plays media.

■ The application must update the "History" section of the music+videos hub when the application plays media.

■ The application must launch the playback experience when the user taps on a hub tile in the "History" or "Now playing" area of the music+videos hub.

■ **Note** The "Now playing" tile must update for each media item played, i.e., you cannot have one "Now playing" tile for the entire application or for a video series or an album.

Before proceeding, let's add a using clause for the Microsoft.Devices and System.IO namespaces to MainPage.xaml.cs and VideoPlayerPage.xaml.cs code files. The Microsoft.Devices namespace provides access to the MediaHistory and MediaHistoryItem classes, which we use to update the "Now playing," "New," and "History" sections of the music+videos hub. We pass in the image tiles as a System.IO.Stream object.

Update the music+videos "New" Section

When the application acquires new content such as user-selected favorite radio stations or videos, it must update the "New" section in the music+videos hub for each content item individually. For our sample application, we add code to the MainPage.xaml.cs code file for the two media items available, a video of the Paris skyline and a short clip taken by the author at the 2010 Tour De France.

Add a call to the UpdateMusicPlusVideosHub_NewSection() method in the MainPage constructor. In this method we have the following code shown in Listing 7–14.

Listing 7–14. UpdateMusicPlusVideosHub_NewSection Method Code

```
StreamResourceInfo ParisTileStreamResource =
    Application.GetResourceStream(new Uri("images/hubTiles/ParisTile.jpg",
        UriKind.Relative));
//Create the MediaHistoryItem that has been newly aquired
MediaHistoryItem ParisVideoMediaHistoryItem = new MediaHistoryItem();
ParisVideoMediaHistoryItem.ImageStream = ParisTileStreamResource.Stream;
ParisVideoMediaHistoryItem.Source = "xap";
ParisVideoMediaHistoryItem.Title = "Paris Skyline Video";
//Set State for situation when navigating via click in Music+Videos Hub
ParisVideoMediaHistoryItem.PlayerContext.Add("videoHub", "Paris");
//This method call writes the history item to the 'New' section
MediaHistory.Instance.WriteAcquiredItem(ParisVideoMediaHistoryItem);

//NEW Tour De France Video
StreamResourceInfo tdfTileStreamResource =
Application.GetResourceStream(new Uri("images/hubTiles/TDFTile.jpg",
  UriKind.Relative));
//Create the MediaHistoryItem that has been newly aquired
MediaHistoryItem tdfVideoMediaHistoryItem = new MediaHistoryItem();
tdfVideoMediaHistoryItem.ImageStream = tdfTileStreamResource.Stream;
tdfVideoMediaHistoryItem.Source = "xap";
tdfVideoMediaHistoryItem.Title = "Tour De France Video";
//Set State for situation when navigating via click in Music+Videos Hub
```

```
tdfVideoMediaHistoryItem.PlayerContext.Add("videoHub", "TDF");
//This method call writes the history item to the 'New' section
MediaHistory.Instance.WriteAcquiredItem(tdfVideoMediaHistoryItem);
```

In the UpdateMusicPlusVideosHub_NewSection method code shown in Listing 7–14, we retrieve a stream that contains the desired image using Application.GetResourceStream. Since the images are stored as content in the XAP file, we simply pass in an Uri to the content based on the project folder structure. Images retrieved from server-side APIs work just as well and can be customized with a brand using the WriteableBitmap class as shown previously.

Once we have a stream to the image, we can create a MediaHistoryItem object. We assign the stream pointing to the tile image that we obtained via Application.GetResourceStream to the MediaHistoryItem.ImageStream property. According to IntelliSense, the MediaHistoryItem .Source property is not used but we set it to "xap." We set MediaHistoryItem.Title to the desired name of the object, "Paris Skyline Video" and "Tour De France Video" for our two videos.

The MediaHistoryItem class contains a dictionary of key/value pairs stored in the PlayerContext property. The values stored in the PlayerContext property are made available to the application when the item is touched in the music+videos hub in the OnNavigatedTo method of the XAML page configured as the DefaultTask for the application in WMAppManifest.xml. I cover how to leverage this information in the section titled "Implement Playback from music+videos hub" later in this chapter.

We add a key/value pair to the MediaHistoryItem.PlayerContext Dictionary object. For our simple application, we just need one value to be stored with the MediaHistoryItem. For a more complex implementation, multiple values may be stored in order to facilitate accessing the media content when the item is selected in the music+videos hub.

The last bit of code is to add the new media item to the "New" section of the music+videos hub by calling the MediaHistory.Instance.WriteAcquiredItem method and passing in our newly created MediaHistoryItem. The next two subsections covers the code added to the VideoPlayerPage.xaml file in order to update the "Now playing" and "History" sections.

Update the music+videos "Now playing" Section

In VideoPlayerPage.xaml.cs we follow the same process as we did in the previous section and create a MediaHistoryItem each time content is played in the UpdateMusicPlusVideoAppNowPlaying() method. This method is called when the media is successfully opened in the VideoPlayer_MediaOpened event where playback begins with a call to VideoPlayer.Play.

We create a MediaHistoryItem but with a few modifications. The tile image is different for "Now playing" in terms of size, which is 358 x 358 pixels square. The other change is that we add a different key/value pair to MediaHistoryItem.PlayerContext using a key name of "videoHub". This helps us distinguish between values passed within app versus a value made available as a result of clicking on an item in the music+videos hub.

As covered in the previous section, the MediaHistoryItem object makes the PlayerContext values available to the music+videos hub and passes those values back to the application upon activation. The last bit of code in the UpdateMusicPlusVideoAppNowPlaying() method is that we assign the newly created MediaHistoryItem to the MediaHistory.Instance.NowPlaying property.

Update the music+videos "History" Section

In VideoPlayerPage.xaml.cs we follow the same process as we did in the previous section and create a MediaHistoryItem each time content is played in the UpdateMusicPlusVideoAppHistory() method. This method is called when the media is successfully opened in the VideoPlayer_MediaOpened event where playback begins with a call to VideoPlayer.Play.

As before the code acquires an image, this time the same 173 x 173 pixel tile that we display in the "New" section of the music+videos hub. This image includes the book logo in the upper left corner so that the content is associated with the application. This method also adds the "videoHub" key to the PlayerContext as before:

```
VideoMediaHistoryItem.PlayerContext.Add("videoHub", video);
```

The other code that is different when adding an item to the music+videos "History" section is a call to MediaHistory.Instance.WriteRecentPlay() method where the code passes in the newly created MediaHistoryItem.

Implement Playback from music+videos Hub

According to the AppHub certification requirements, the play back experience should display when media associated with the application is selected in the music+videos hub. This helps to provide the seamless experience of selecting media and having it immediately start playing without having to find the media by navigating the application.

The application implements a simple scheme to provide this experience by passing in to the application an ID that identifies the correct video. In the sample application, either "Paris" or "TDF" are passed in to identify the correct video. This value is captured in the OnNavigatedTo event of the DefaultTask XAML page, which in this application is MainPage.xaml. Here is the code from MainPage.xaml.cs:

```
protected override void OnNavigatedTo(
  System.Windows.Navigation.NavigationEventArgs e)
{
  base.OnNavigatedTo(e);

  if (NavigationContext.QueryString.Count > 0 &&
    NavigationContext.QueryString.ContainsKey("videoHub"))
  {
    NavigationService.Navigate(new Uri("/VideoPlayerPage.xaml?video=" +
        NavigationContext.QueryString["videoHub"], UriKind.Relative));
    NavigationContext.QueryString.Remove("videoHub");
  }
}
```

In general, there are two reasons why the MainPage.OnNavigatedTo event will fire for a XAML page. It will fire as a result of normal application startup with the passed-in query values if launched from the music+video hub, or because the Mainpage.xaml was activated as a result of a "Back" navigation from the VideoPlayerPage as part of normal application back stack function. If it is activated as a result of selecting media in the music+videos hub, the QueryString Dictionary object will contain the videoHub key/value pair that was associated with the item when it was initially added to the hub.

In the OnNavigatedTo method, the code checks to see if there are any values available in the NavigationContext.QueryString dictionary. If there is, it indicates that the page was activated from the music+videos hub as part of application start up. If this is the case, the application navigates to the VideoPlayerPage.xaml file, passing in the video name. It also removes the videoHub key so that we don't enter an endless loop of navigating back and forth between MainPage.xaml and VideoPlayerPage.xaml.

This completes our implementation of a music+videos hub application. In the next section, we shift gears and cover remote media consumption.

App Connect – Bing Search Integration

This is the last section on App Connect, focused on how applications can integrate with the Bing Search functionality on Windows Phone 7.5. This is an exciting new capability that allows your application to be offered in search results on the device, even if the application is not currently installed.

The way it works from an end-user perspective is that when a user performs a web search using the hardware Search button on the phone, it can launch a relevant page in your application based on the Bing search results. Figure 7-15 shows the end-user experience:

Figure 7–15. App Connect Bing Search End-User Experience

In Figure 7-15, the end user performs a search for baby doll strollers. The Product Quick Card is returned in the results. The user can view search information and then swipe over to the apps pivot item. Selecting the application will install it if not installed and then the parameters are passed into the application and relevant information is displayed.

From a developer perspective, you register your applications for search extensions that make sense for your application. Extensions are associated by Bing to "quick cards." Here is a list of available extensions:

- Product Card – Items listed under the "product" heading in the web pivot page of search results.

- Place Card – Locations listed in the "local" pivot page of search results.

- Movie Card – Movies currently playing in theaters listed under the "Movies near…" heading the web pivot page of search results.

There are several extensions associated with each card type. For example, some Product Card extensions are Bing_Products_Arts_and_Crafts, Bing_Products_Baby_and_Nursery, Bing_Products_Beauty_and_Fragrance, etc.

■ **Note** Applications that over-register for non-applicable search extensions risk being pulled from marketplace. Applications must use the App Connect URI parameters in a meaningful way.

Each card type receives launch parameters relevant to the card type. For example, the Product Card returns two parameters:

- ProductName – The name of the product.

- Category – A coma-delimited list of extensions related to the product

Here is an example deep link URI with the parameters returned to an application from an end-user product search for "Xbox 360":

```
app://046B642D-C70D-4D8D-95E2-D92236763294/_default#/SearchExtras?
ProductName=XBox 360&Category=Bing_Products_Electronics,Bing_Products_Office_Products
```

Applications parse the query string parameters to process the values and display information relevant to the end-user. This link provides details on the available Quick Card extensions and parameters that are returned:

http://msdn.microsoft.com/en-us/library/hh202958.aspx

Building App Connect Search Applications Overview

Just like with the pictures Hub integration, you modify WMAppManifest.xml for your application. You also add an Extras.xml file where you identify the Quick Card extensions. The application must have at least one page that can process the deep link URI.

Your application needs to surface relevant information for display in the apps pivot page for a quick card. Here is a summary of the modifications that are required.

- WMAppManifest.xml – Edit the Extensions element to list each Quick Card extension your application can handle.

- Extras.Xml – Create an Extras.xml to hold the AppTitle element, which is the title displayed in the Quick Card. You can also display caption text below the AppTitle in Bing Search results. You can specify unique caption strings in the CaptionString element for particular Quick Card extensions.

App Connect Search Application Code Sample

In this section I go through the process of adding App Connect for Bing Search to an application. I add a project named AppConnectSearch to the Chapter 7 solution to start. The first step is to review your application requirements and capabilities to identify which Quick Card extensions your application should register for in WMAppManifest.xml. This will ensure the best experience for end users.

With the Quick Card extensions identified, the next step is to update the WMAppManifest.xml file with the supported extensions as shown here:

```xml
<Extensions>
    <!-- Production extensions, for products: video games -->
    <Extension
      ExtensionName="Bing_Products_Video_Games"
      ConsumerID="{5B04B775-356B-4AA0-AAF8-6491FFEA5661}"
      TaskID="_default"
      ExtraFile="Extensions\\Extras.xml" />

    <!-- Production extensions, for movies. -->
    <Extension
      ExtensionName="Bing_Movies"
      ConsumerID="{5B04B775-356B-4AA0-AAF8-6491FFEA5661}"
      TaskID="_default"
      ExtraFile="Extensions\\Extras.xml" />

    <!-- Production extensions, for places: travel, food, and dining. -->
    <Extension
      ExtensionName="Bing_Places_Food_and_Dining"
      ConsumerID="{5B04B775-356B-4AA0-AAF8-6491FFEA5661}"
      TaskID="_default"
      ExtraFile="Extensions\\Extras.xml" />
  </Extensions>
```

Next create an Extras.xml in a new folder named Extensions. This allows us to specify the captions that will appear in the apps pivot page for the Quick Card. You can also specify the AppTitle element in multiple languages for the user as well. Listing 7-15 has the Extras.xml file.

Listing 7–15. *Example Extras.xml File*

```xml
<?xml version="1.0" encoding="utf-8" ?>
<ExtrasInfo>
  <!-- Application title -->
  <AppTitle>
    <default>Display App Connect URI Parameters</default>
  </AppTitle>

  <!-- Search-related captions -->
  <Consumer ConsumerID="{5B04B775-356B-4AA0-AAF8-6491FFEA5661}">
    <!-- Products caption for video games -->
    <ExtensionInfo>
      <Extensions>
        <ExtensionName>Bing_Products_Video_Games</ExtensionName>
      </Extensions>
      <CaptionString>
        <default>Product URI Details</default>
      </CaptionString>
    </ExtensionInfo>

    <!-- Movies caption -->
```

```
<ExtensionInfo>
  <Extensions>
    <ExtensionName>Bing_Movies</ExtensionName>
  </Extensions>
  <CaptionString>
    <default>Movie URI Details</default>
  </CaptionString>
</ExtensionInfo>

<!-- Places caption for food and dining -->
<ExtensionInfo>
  <Extensions>
    <ExtensionName>Bing_Places_Food_and_Dining</ExtensionName>
  </Extensions>
  <CaptionString>
    <default>Place URI Details</default>
  </CaptionString>
</ExtensionInfo>
  </Consumer>
</ExtrasInfo>
```

The next step is to configure URI mapping for deep link support so that when the user is on the Quick Card in Bing Search and clicks the app, the user is taken to the deep link target page within the application. Add an xmlns namespace to bring in System.Windows.Navigation to App.xaml:

```
xmlns:nav="clr-namespace:System.Windows.Navigation;assembly=Microsoft.Phone"
```

This markup below is needed to configure URI mapping by adding this XAML to the Application.Resources element:

```
<nav:UriMapper x:Key="UriMapper">
  <nav:UriMapper.UriMappings>
    <nav:UriMapping Uri="/SearchExtras" MappedUri="/View/AppConnectSearchTargetPage.xaml"/>
  </nav:UriMapper.UriMappings>
</nav:UriMapper>
```

In App.xaml.cs in the App class constructor, add this code to declare a UriMapper instance. The UriMapper class converts a URI deep link into a new URI based on rules declared within the UriMapper class. The class is instantiated based on the XAML resource declared just above.

```
RootFrame.UriMapper = Resources["UriMapper"] as UriMapper;
```

Now it is time to create a basic MVVM architecture to handle the URI parameters, following guidance on MSDN. Listing 7-16 has the AppConnectSearchUriParams model that can store URI parameters.

Listing 7–16. The AppConnectSearchUriParams Model Class Code File

```
using System.ComponentModel;

namespace AppConnectBingSearch.Model
{
```

```
public class AppConnectSearchUriParams
{
  public AppConnectSearchUriParams(string Name, string Value)
  {
    _paramName = Name.Trim();

    if (_paramName == "Category")
    {
      _paramValue = Value.Replace(",", ",\n");
    }
    else
    {
      _paramValue = Value;
    }
  }

  private string _paramName;
  public string ParamName
  {
    get { return _paramName; }
    set
    {
      if (_paramName != value)
      {
        _paramName = value;
        NotifyPropertyChanged("ParamName");
      }
    }
  }

  private string _paramValue;
  public string ParamValue
  {
    get { return _paramValue; }
    set
    {
      if (_paramValue != value)
      {
        _paramValue = value;
        NotifyPropertyChanged("ParamValue");
      }
    }
  }

  #region INotifyPropertyChanged Members
  public event PropertyChangedEventHandler PropertyChanged;

  private void NotifyPropertyChanged(string propertyName)
  {
    if (PropertyChanged != null)
    {
      PropertyChanged(this,
```

```
                  new PropertyChangedEventArgs(propertyName));
          }
      }
      #endregion
  }
}
```

With the Model class declared, next I create a View Model class to back the page that will be displayed after processing the deep link. The AppConnectSearchViewModel class uses an instance of the AppConnectUriParameters to receive the values from the deep link and display them on the page.

Listing 7–17. The *QuickCardTargetPageViewModel ViewModel Class Code File*

```
using System.Collections.Generic;
using System.Collections.ObjectModel;
using System.ComponentModel;
using AppConnectBingSearch.Model;

namespace AppConnectBingSearch.ViewModel
{
  public class QuickCardTargetPageViewModel : INotifyPropertyChanged
  {
    public QuickCardTargetPageViewModel()
    {
      AppConnectUriParameters =
        new ObservableCollection<AppConnectSearchUriParams>();
    }

    private ObservableCollection<AppConnectSearchUriParams>
      _AppConnectUriParameters;
    public ObservableCollection<AppConnectSearchUriParams>
      AppConnectUriParameters
    {
      get { return _AppConnectUriParameters; }
      set
      {
        if (_AppConnectUriParameters != value)
        {
          _AppConnectUriParameters = value;
          NotifyPropertyChanged("AppConnectUriParameters");
        }
      }
    }

    public void LoadUriParameters(IDictionary<string, string> QueryString)
    {
      AppConnectUriParameters.Clear();

       foreach (string KeyName in QueryString.Keys)
       {
         // Default value for parameter
         string KeyValue = "<no value present in deep link>";
```

477

```
        QueryString.TryGetValue(KeyName, out KeyValue);

        AppConnectUriParameters.Add(
          new AppConnectSearchUriParams(KeyName, KeyValue));
    }
}

    #region INotifyPropertyChanged Members
    public event PropertyChangedEventHandler PropertyChanged;

    private void NotifyPropertyChanged(string propertyName)
    {
      if (PropertyChanged != null)
      {
        PropertyChanged(this, new PropertyChangedEventArgs(propertyName));
      }
    }
    #endregion
  }
}
```

The next step is to add a folder named View and a new page named
AppConnectSearchTargetPage.xaml to present the UI and data bind it to the
QuickCardTargetPageViewModel class, which I do in Expression Blend. The
AppConnectSearchTargetPage.Loaded event handler loads the deep link parameters into the ViewModel:

```
void AppConnectSearchTargetPage_Loaded(object sender, RoutedEventArgs e)
{
  ((AppConnectSearchViewModel)DataContext).LoadUriParams(this.NavigationContext.QueryString);
}
```

Testing an App Connect Search Application

In this section I cover how to test an App Connect Bing Maps search application, which requires an
Internet connection to work. The first step is to start debugging to deploy the application to the
Emulator or a tethered device for debugging. Once the application is running on the emulator, click the
Bing Search hardware button and enter "gears of war 3" or some other search related to video game
products. Figure 7-16 shows the first search page with the products heading in the results. The middle
screenshot shows the products page on the apps pivot. The right screenshot shows the results after
clicking the Display App Connect URI Parameters item in the apps pivot page.

Figure 7–16 Testing Bing Search App Connect

Integrating with App Connect Bing Search is pretty straightforward to do. The more difficult aspect is to process the query parameters to provide the best experience for the user that is relevant with what they are trying to accomplish.

Conclusion

This chapter covers a lot of ground on advanced integration with Windows Phone. First it starts off with a discussion of necessary MVVM Techniques to help you build real world applications, covering how to drive the user interface from the ViewModel as well as how to data bind any type to any other type via the IValueConverter Interface.

The chapter next moves on to a discussion of advanced services such as Encryption Services and Audio and Media services. We cover the new DataProtected class available in Windows Phone OS 7.5 to encrypt secrets.

The chapter concludes with a discussion of the various App Connect scenarios such as picture Hub integration, music+video hub integration, and Bing Search integration.

In the next chapter this book shifts gears focusing on 2D game development with the XNA Framework.

■ ■ ■

CHAPTER 8

XNA Framework for Games and Applications

In this and the next chapter, we cover programming with the XNA Framework. With Windows Phone 7.5, XNA Framework development was limited to game development for the most part. You can share the nonvisual APIs between the XNA Framework and Silverlight, but you could not share rendering. In Windows Phone 7.5.5, this changes with the XNA Framework shared graphics manager, which supports blended rendering of XNA Framework and Silverlight content. We cover blended rendering at the end of this chapter.

If you jumped straight to this chapter in the book, first please review the extensive introduction to XNA Game Studio development in Chapter 1. Chapter 3 focuses on user input. It also contains several examples based on XNA Game Studio development related to touch and accelerometer input. In Chapter 7, we discussed how to work with the XNA Media Library APIs, playing music, displaying image art, and the like. I recommend reviewing those chapters prior to diving in here.

In general, it is impossible to cover the full range of game development in just two chapters, so we take an optimized approach that builds on existing samples available at Microsoft's AppHub website, which is located at http://create.msdn.com with the primary goal of helping Silverlight developers learn enough XNA to bring it into their Silverlight applications as well as get started with game development if desired. There are quite a few samples based on the XNA Framework that we leverage in this chapter to jumpstart game development. Why reinvent a game screen or menu framework when there are tried and true samples that we can leverage while covering key concepts of game development?

■ **Note** The AppHub samples are available under the Microsoft Permissive License (Ms-PL) license, which you can download and review at http://create.msdn.com/downloads/?id=15.

I'm not a lawyer, so I won't provide an opinion on the license—but please do download and read it.

Xbox LIVE Gamer Services

A hot topic of interest to indie game developers is access to Xbox LIVE gamer services. Xbox LIVE gamer services provide support for matchmaking, Achievements, Leaderboards, and the like to Xbox games. You can find more information here:

http://msdn.microsoft.com/en-us/library/microsoft.xna.framework.gamerservices.aspx

On Windows Phone, a subset of Xbox LIVE gamer services is available to Xbox LIVE publishers. Example Xbox LIVE game publishers are Microsoft Game Studios, Electronic Arts, and Gameloft. Generally, a game developer works with an existing Xbox LIVE game publisher to ship a game that includes Xbox LIVE gamer services. It is difficult for a new game developer to immediately become an Xbox LIVE game publisher. It is a high bar; just look at the names of existing publishers.

So for an indie game developer, create an awesome game or possibly a fully fleshed-out concept as the first step to gain access to Xbox LIVE gamer services. The next step is to get your game in front of an existing Xbox LIVE game publisher. Microsoft Game Studios currently has an e-mail alias to which you can send proposals: wpgame@microsoft.com. The other way to get noticed is to submit your finished game to AppHub and climb the popularity charts. An existing proven success as an indie publisher will help you get noticed.

Don't lose hope if you have your heart set on Xbox LIVE gamer services. Initially, the services were not available to Xbox Indie game publishers as part of create.msdn.com, but the services were eventually made available to indie game publishers on big Xbox. One can hope that in the future more Xbox LIVE gamer services become available to indie developers on Windows Phone 7.5 as well.

In the next section we will begin a journey of taking the HelloXNA project from Chapter 1 and turn it into a full-fledged game with a menu system, score keeping, options, tombstone support, and the like—all of the things you need to consider when building a game for Windows Phone 7.5.

Alien Shooter

Back in Chapter 1, we covered XNA Game Studio development fundamentals in the HelloXNA sample. The sample covered game loop basics with a very simple UI that had a hero ship that shot a missile at the alien attacker ship. As you recall, XNA is not event driven. Rather, it checks status on objects and input (polls) in a type loop that tries to ensure that the screen is drawn at 30 frames/second. Frame rate can drop if a game spends too much time "thinking" when updating objects. Here is a summary of how this works:

```
while (Game.IsRunning)
{
  Update();  //Perform calculations, update objects, handle input
  Draw();  //Draw background, objects, effects
}
```

The HelloXNA sample from Chapter 1 isn't really much of a "game," because there wasn't any interactivity. It essentially loaded up content and initialized state in the Game.LoadContent method. The Update method did some screen bounds checking and reset objects when they flew off the screen, and then the objects were rendered in the Draw method. In the HelloXNA sample, you cannot move the hero ship, and the one attacker appears on the screen at the same place. In this section we will turn it into a "real" game with a menu, score, movable hero ship, and more worthy opponents in the alien attackers.

In the next section, we turn the HelloXNA game into a real game in the Chapter 8 AlienShooter sample project. The AlienShooter game will include a main menu, options menu, and actual game play.

We introduce a Game Management sample that provides a ScreenManager class, a Menu class, and GameScreen objects to manage game functions. The game is modularized into individual screen classes, so you can have a screen that shows the main menu, a screen that shows the options for the game, and so on, as well as a screen that actually handles game play. By following these best practices you give your game a professional look and feel, and make it more maintainable. In subsequent sections we cover how to add basic animations and effects to provide more interesting game play.

From Demo to Game

This section covers how to add the game management and screens to the AlienShooter sample project. We start by creating the Chapter 8 code solution with a project named AlienShooter based on the XNA Game Studio 4.0 Windows Phone 7.5 Game (4.0) project template. The best way to start creating a "real" game is to base it on the Game State Management sample, which includes a main menu, an options screen, some gameplay, and a pause menu. It displays a loading screen between menus and gameplay with a popup message box to confirm that a user intends to quit. You can download the sample here:

http://create.msdn.com/en-US/education/catalog/sample/game_state_management

---

▨ **Tip** Right-click on the .zip and select "unblock" to ensure that security checks don't prevent you from being able to compile and run the application.

When you deploy the GameStateManagementSample (Phone) sample, notice that the game does not show up in the Games Hub, but is instead in the application list. The Genre attribute on the App element in the WMManifest.xml file determines where an application appears. The default is Genre="Apps.Normal" so that the application appears in the Application List. Change the genre attribute to Genre="Apps.Games" to have the game show up in the Games Hub.

Run the GameStateManagementSample (Phone) sample project to see the nice animations and transitions available with this sample. Let's get started by transitioning the AlienShooter sample to this format and then we will add in the code from Chapter 1's sample named HelloXNA. From there we will refactor to make the game more interactive.

▨ **Tip** Close the Toolbox tool window to give yourself more space when working with XNA Game Studio games, since there aren't components relevant in the Toolbox tool window.

With both the AlienShooter and GameStateManagementSample (Phone) sample projects open, we first create two new folders in AlienShooter named Screens and GameManagement. Copy the contents of the ScreenManager folder in the GameStateManagementSample (Phone) sample project to the GameManagement folder in the AlienShooter project. Copy the Screens folder content to the Screens folder content in the AlienShooter project.

Once everything is copied over, select the option to Show All Files at the top of the Solutions Tool Window in Visual Studio. The next step is to right-click the files in Visual Studio and select Include In

Project to add them to the AlienShooter project. Be sure to fix up the namespaces by changing them from GameStateManagement to AlienShooter.GameManagement for the GameManagement folder content and to AlienShooter.Screens for the Screens folder content. You will also need to add a using AlienShooter.GameManagement; statement to all of the code files in the Screens folder as well. After everything is fixed up, the application should compile without any errors or warnings.

Next open the GameStateManagementSample (Phone) Content project folder and, using Windows Explorer, copy over all of the content files to the AlienShooterContent project folder except for the Content.contentproj file. As before, select the option to Show All Files in Visual Studio 2010, and then include the files into the AlienShooterContent project folder. We decide to split the content between GameManagement content and actual game content. Create a new folder in the AlienShooterContent project named GameManagement and copy menufont.spritefont and blank.png into the AlienShooterContent project GameManagement folder. The rest of the content is related to game play, which we will eventually replace anyway.

Next we go through the GameStateManagementSample (Phone) project's Game1.cs and modify the AlienShooter Game1.cs file to match the game state sample's Game.cs file. First, rename the Game1 class to AlienShooterGame and rename the code file Game1.cs to AlienShooterGame.cs. You will notice right away that the default spriteBatch private variable is not present in the game state sample, which suggests that the Game1.Draw and Game1.Update methods must not perform any game logic in this code file. Instead, there is a private field variable named screenManager of type ScreenManager that is added. Add a using AlienShooter.GameManagement; statement to the top of AlienshooterGame.cs as well.

We next move to the Constructor AlienShooterGame() and modify it to match the game state sample's GameStateManagementGame constructor as shown in Listing 8-1.

Listing 8-1. *AlienShooterGame Constructor*

```
public AlienShooterGame()
{
  graphics = new GraphicsDeviceManager(this);
  Content.RootDirectory = "Content";
  TargetElapsedTime = TimeSpan.FromTicks(333333);

  // You can choose whether you want a landscape or portrait
  // game by using one of the two helper functions defined below
  InitializePortraitGraphics();
  // InitializeLandscapeGraphics();

  // Create the screen manager component.
  screenManager = new ScreenManager(this);

  Components.Add(screenManager);

  // Attempt to deserialize the screen manager from disk. If that
  // fails, we add our default screens.
  if (!screenManager.DeserializeState())
  {
    // Activate the first screens.
    screenManager.AddScreen(new BackgroundScreen(), null);
    screenManager.AddScreen(new MainMenuScreen(), null);
  }
}
```

The code file defines two helper functions that set whether the game is a portrait or landscape game. Listing 8-2 has the code for the two helper functions.

Listing 8-2. *Helper Functions to Configure Portrait or Landscape Game*

```
private void InitializePortraitGraphics()
{
  graphics.PreferredBackBufferWidth = 480;
  graphics.PreferredBackBufferHeight = 800;
}

private void InitializeLandscapeGraphics()
{
  graphics.PreferredBackBufferWidth = 800;
  graphics.PreferredBackBufferHeight = 480;
}
```

The next bit of code in Listing 8-1 for the AlienShooterGame constructor creates the ScreenManager and then adds it to the Components collection for the Microsoft.Xna.Framework.Game base class. Component classes inherit from the Microsoft.Xna.Framework.DrawableGameComponent class, which attempts to modularize game development by providing the ability to have objects Update and Draw themselves without forcing all of that logic into the default Game.Draw and Game.Update methods. The ScreenManager class inherits from DrawableGameComponent and handles all of the actual Draw and Update logic for the game. I cover the ScreenManager class in detail in just a bit, so let's continue updating our AlienShooterGame (formerly Game1.cs) code file to get our game up and running. The last section of the AlienShooterGame constructor attempts to load the ScreenManager instance from disk. If it cannot, it loads the default screens to start the game.

The code overrides Game.OnExiting to serialize game state to disk in this event handler to set up state for the next time the game launches.

```
protected override void OnExiting(object sender, System.EventArgs args)
{
  // serialize the screen manager whenever the game exits
  screenManager.SerializeState();

  base.OnExiting(sender, args);
}
```

Unlike in Chapter 1, where all of our code was packed into Game1.cs, AlienShooterGame.cs does not perform any code in Update or in Draw. For our new version of the application, we use the ScreenManager to do the work for us, so we remove the LoadContent, UnloadContent, and Update methods from AlienShooterGame.cs. We modify Game.Draw to set the background color to Color.Black from Color.CornflowerBlue but otherwise this completes our edits for this file.

In order to test our work, we need to modify where GameManagement content is loaded from; remember that we placed that content inside a GameManagement folder in the AlienShooterContent project. Open up the ScreenManager class and find the LoadContent override. Modify the load locations like this:

```
font = content.Load<SpriteFont>("GameManagement/menufont");
blankTexture = content.Load<Texture2D>("GameManagement/blank");
```

Once these edits are completed, test and run and the AlienShooter project. It should work just like the GameStateManagementSample (Phone) sample project with a bit of code and content reorganization under the covers. You can choose to follow these steps by hand in your project or simply grab the AlienShooter project and rename the namespaces, game class, and screen classes to match your application. In the next section we go through the Game Management–related classes located in the GameManagement folder to help you understand what's going on under the covers so that you can further customize the game to meet your needs.

Game Management

The GameManagement folder contains three class files, GameScreen.cs, InputState.cs, and ScreenManager.cs. The ScreenManager class orchestrates loading GameScreen objects and transitions between GameScreen objects for you. The GameScreen abstract base class contains all of the underlying plumbing code to plug into the Game Management framework and is the base class for objects declared in the Screens folder. The InputState class collects Keyboard, Gamepad, and TouchPanel inputs. For Windows Phone 7.5, TouchPanel input is primary, though some devices support a keyboard as well. Figure 8-1 shows the class diagram for the Game Management classes.

Figure 8-1. *Game Management framework*

The ScreenManager class is a DrawableGameComponent, while the GameScreen base class is not. The ScreenManager manages one or more screen classes that inherit from GameScreen. ScreenManager maintains a stack of screens, calls their Update and Draw methods at the appropriate times, and automatically routes input to the top most active screen.

You will notice that DrawableGameComponent looks very similar to the Game class. There are method overrides available for LoadContent, UnloadContent, Update, and Draw, much like the Game class. Under the covers the XNA Framework keeps the main Game class and available DrawableGameComponents in sync with respect to the Update and Draw methods, so that the developer can just focus on each individual component and screen.

In the ScreenManager.Draw and ScreenManager.Update methods, each screen is given an opportunity to process input, and either Update or Draw itself if it is the active screen. The ScreenManager's framework provides nice transition support for fade-in and fade-out of screens as the user navigates the game. If you like the way things work as is, you can just focus on your menu, options, game play screen, and so on, and the framework takes care of the rest.

Screens and Menus

Now that we have covered the game management plumbing provided by the ScreenManager class, we will switch focus to the UX aspects of screens and menu. There are several screens in the project that were copied over from the Game Management sample that provide the starter UI. We go through these screens in this section.

The BackgroundScreen class sits behind all of the other menu screens. It draws a background image that remains fixed in place regardless of whatever transitions that other screens may implement. The content that is loaded is the background.png. Swap the background.png file with your default background image.

The MainMenuScreen class is the first screen that is loaded by the game. It displays the main menu items of Play and Options. The OptionsMenuScreen class is displayed over the main menu screen. It provides the user a chance to configure the game. Figure 8-2 shows the default Main Menu and Options Menu screens.

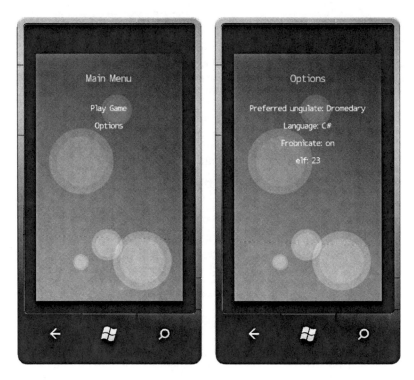

Figure 8-2. *Main Menu and Options Menu*

The menu items have a nice Metro transition when flying in and out. Individual menu items are still graphic items with additional logic to detect a touch and fire an event. The MenuEntry class provides menu item functionality. Here is the constructor for the OptionsMenuScreen class:

```
public OptionsMenuScreen()
    : base("Options")
{
    // Create our menu entries.
    ungulateMenuEntry = new MenuEntry(string.Empty);
    languageMenuEntry = new MenuEntry(string.Empty);
    frobnicateMenuEntry = new MenuEntry(string.Empty);
    elfMenuEntry = new MenuEntry(string.Empty);

    SetMenuEntryText();

    // Hook up menu event handlers.
    ungulateMenuEntry.Selected += UngulateMenuEntrySelected;
    languageMenuEntry.Selected += LanguageMenuEntrySelected;
    frobnicateMenuEntry.Selected += FrobnicateMenuEntrySelected;
    elfMenuEntry.Selected += ElfMenuEntrySelected;

    // Add entries to the menu.
    MenuEntries.Add(ungulateMenuEntry);
```

```
        MenuEntries.Add(languageMenuEntry);
        MenuEntries.Add(frobnicateMenuEntry);
        MenuEntries.Add(elfMenuEntry);
}
```

The MenuEntries collection in the OptionsMenuScreen constructor is a protected member of the MenuScreen base class for the MainMenuScreen and OptionsMenuScreen classes. The MenuScreen.Draw and MenuScreen.Update methods measure and position menu entries for drawing to the screen. The MenuScreen class includes the sliding transitions logic for menu items in case you want to modify it.

Click on a menu item to view the transition to a new screen. The loading screen inherits from the GameScreen class coordinates transitions between the menu system and the game itself. Normally one screen will transition off at the same time as the next screen is transitioning on, but for larger transitions that can take a longer time to load their data; we want the menu system to be entirely gone before we start loading the game. This is done as follows:

- Tell all the existing screens to transition off.

- Activate a loading screen, which will transition on at the same time.

- The loading screen watches the state of the previous screens.

- When the loading screen sees they have finished transitioning off, it activates the real next screen, which may take a long time to load its data. The loading screen will be the only thing displayed while this load is taking place.

This concludes the overview of the Game Management ScreenManager, GameScreen, MenuScreen, and MenuEntry classes. In the next section we dive in and start to customize the template game for the AlienShooter game.

AlienShooter Game Structure

In this section, we begin customizing the game management starter project with content and game logic. We start by adding the content from the original game in Chapter 1 to AlienShooter. We copy over the Sprites and Textures folder and remove background.png, which is the generic XNA Framework sample image.

The Content Project

When you create a new XNA project, it always creates two projects, one project for your game and the other for your content. The Content project provides compile-time processing for game assets, including detecting missing assets, asset conversion, compression, and preprocessing. The key component to the Content project is the Content Pipeline.

The Content Pipeline

The content pipeline does the work of preparing assets for use within an XNA Framework game. Assets are processed in two steps. The first step is importing the content. For the majority of formats, XNA has Content Importer classes to convert content into a common intermediate format. The second step converts the imported content into a final compiled, compressed, format via a Content Processor.

Importing the Content

Importing content is as simple as adding new items to the Content project. In most cases, the content pipeline automatically detects the asset type and assigns the correct Content Importer and Content Processor. It is also possible to create custom Content Importer and Content Processor classes for assets not supported by the built-in classes.

In the Chapter 1 HelloXNA sample we demonstrate how to load content a single texture at a time using this code from the LoadContent method:

```
HeroShip = this.Content.Load<Texture2D>("Sprites/heroship");
SpaceShip = this.Content.Load<Texture2D>("Sprites/spaceship");
Missile = this.Content.Load<Texture2D>("Sprites/missile");
```

Each content item is loaded into a single texture. When drawn, each item requires its texture to be loaded by the GPU and rendered. The items just defined are drawn to the screen with these three lines of code in the Draw method:

```
spriteBatch.Draw(SpaceShip, SpaceShipPosition, Color.White);
spriteBatch.Draw(Missile, MissilePosition, Color.White);
spriteBatch.Draw(HeroShip, HeroShipPosition, Color.White);
```

Loading each texture is a performance hit for the GPU. A better way is to load a single texture that contains all of the images, and then just tell Draw which area of the texture to draw for that item. This type of texture is called a *sprite sheet* and is very common to use in game development, especially when creating sprite animation, which we will cover later in the chapter. There are two challenges with using sprite sheets: you have to take all of your individual images and mash them into a larger image, and you have to remember which part of the single large texture contains the particular image you want to draw to the screen.

Luckily AppHub comes to the rescue again with a ready-to-go custom Content Importer and Content Processor that can take a collection of images and automatically turn them into a single sprite sheet, solving the first challenge. For the complete background on the sample, download it here:

```
http://create.msdn.com/en-US/education/catalog/sample/sprite_sheet
```

The sample also includes a runtime class to include in your game named SpriteSheet, which allows either named or indexed access to images so that you do not have to remember the exact pixel location, solving the second challenge listed previously.

We implement the SpriteSheet sample in AlienShooter by copying over the SpriteSheetPipeline and SpriteSheetRuntime (Phone) projects from the AppHub SpriteSheetSample and adding them to the Chapter 8 Solution. Right-click the References folder in the AlienShooterContent project, select Add Reference, choose the Projects tab, and select the SpriteSheetPipeline project. Next, right-click on the References folder in the AlienShooter project and select Add Reference, choose the Projects tab, and select the SpriteSheetRuntime (Phone) project.

In the AlienShooterContent project, navigate to the Sprites folder and exclude from the project these assets: heroship.tga, missile.tga, and spaceship.tga. We don't want to add the textures twice, so they should not be included as individual assets any more. Next, right-click on the Sprites folder and select Add ➤ New Item and choose XML File with a name of AlienShooterSpriteSheet.xml. Listing 8-3 shows the edited XML file.

Listing 8-3. *AlienShooterSpriteSheet.xml Sprite Sheet XML File*

```
<?xml version="1.0" encoding="utf-8" ?>
<XnaContent>
  <Asset Type="System.String[]">
    <Item>Sprites/heroship.tga</Item>
    <Item>Sprites/missile.tga</Item>
    <Item>Sprites/spaceship.tga</Item>
  </Asset>
</XnaContent>
```

If you don't edit the file correctly, you will get a compile error if the SpriteSheetPipeline Content Processor cannot find an asset listed in the XML file. Notice in this example that the folder location is included relative to the AlienShooterContent project to correctly identify the asset location. Figure 8-3 shows the Solution tool window with the AlienShooterContent project expanded and the Properties dialog for the AlienShooterSpriteSheet.xml.

Notice in Figure 8-3 that the individual sprite images are hidden and not part of the project in the Sprites folder, though they need to be accessible in the file system to the SpriteSheetProcessor Content Processor so that it can turn them into a single sprite sheet. The only content that is part of the Sprites folder is the AlienShooterSpriteSheet.xml XML file. Also in Figure 8-3, notice that the custom SpriteSheetProcessor Content Processor is configured for the XML file. Let's now draw-update the GamePlay screen to start to render our new AlienShooter assets. A using SpriteSheetRuntime statement is added to the top of the GamePlay.cs code file. Three new private fields are added at the top of the GamePlayScreen class:

```
SpriteSheet alienShooterSpriteSheet;
Texture2D backgroundTexture;
Rectangle screenRect;
```

The alienShooterSpriteSheet variable will let us render the entire sprite sheet to the screen for debug purposes. The backgroundTexture variable represents our game background as with the HelloXNA sample and the screenRect variable holds a variable that points to the Rectangle object that is the size of the draw area.

Figure 8-3. *Solution and Content project after SpriteSheet modifications*

The LoadContent method is updated to load the alienShooterSpriteSheet SpriteSheet and backgroundTexture Texture2D variables:

```
alienShooterSpriteSheet = content.Load<SpriteSheet>("Sprites/AlienShooterSpriteSheet");
backgroundTexture = content.Load<Texture2D>("Textures/background");
```

Most of the code in the Update and HandleInput methods is commented out since we no longer want the placeholder code. The placeholder draw code is modified in the Draw method, and the following two additional items are added to draw the backgroundTexture and the alienShooterSpriteSheet to the screen:

```
spriteBatch.Begin();
//Draw background
spriteBatch.Draw(backgroundTexture, screenRect, Color.White);
//Draw Sprite Sheet
spriteBatch.Draw(alienShooterSpriteSheet.Texture,
  new Rectangle(screenRect.Width / 2, screenRect.Height / 2,
            alienShooterSpriteSheet.Texture.Width / 2,
```

```
                    alienShooterSpriteSheet.Texture.Height / 2),
        Color.White);
spriteBatch.End();
```

Everything should compile, and the game now shows AlienShooter assets on the GamePlayScreen, as shown in Figure 8-4.

Figure 8-4. *AlienShooter SpriteSheet and background textures*

Notice how tightly the Hero Spaceship, Missile, and Alien Ship are automatically packed in Figure 8-4 by the custom Content Processor. Just to close the loop, the code to draw an individual image from the AlienShooterSpriteSheet is very simple. Here is the code to just draw the Hero Spaceship at a point in the middle of the screen:

```
spriteBatch.Draw(alienShooterSpriteSheet.Texture,
    new Vector2((screenRect.Width / 2)-
                alienShooterSpriteSheet.SourceRectangle("heroship").Width / 2,
                    (screenRect.Height / 2)-
                alienShooterSpriteSheet.SourceRectangle("heroship").Height / 2),
    alienShooterSpriteSheet.SourceRectangle("heroship"),
```

There is a verbose computation to create a Vector2 for the screen center minus the center of the Hero Ship, but otherwise it is the standard Draw(texture, Vector, SourceRectangle, Color) method. Notice how easy it is to identify the Rectangle on the alienShooterSpriteSheet where the Hero Ship resides. Just pass in the asset name and the SpriteSheet class will locate it. More on drawing later in the chapter, but I wanted to close out how to completely work with the SpriteSheet class.

When you download the SpriteSheet Sample from AppHub, it includes an example extension on how to add a compression option to the Content Processor. Unfortunately the extension does not work for the XNA Game Studio 4.0 Reach profile. It just works for the HiDef profile.

■ **Tip** The Reach profile limits XNA Game Studio to a subset of functions supported on Windows Phone, Xbox, and Windows for maximum compatibility. The HiDef profile supports only Xbox and Windows. It includes support for custom HLSL shaders as well as additional features.

We dive into creating a more robust game below, but first let's cover some of the other constructs for a real game such as displaying game status text and menus, which is covered in the next section.

Text and Menus

Displayed text, such as game status and menus, is an important component of game development. Users want a nice clean menu system to navigate. Game status is critical to game play; it makes the game interesting such as how much life is left, high score, rounds of ammunition available, and the like.

There are two methods to display text in the XNA Framework. The first is via the SpriteFont class. The SpriteFont class leverages the built-in Font classes on your PC to create the font texture to display letter character images when rendered. The SpriteFont class is covered in the next section.

The other method to display text in the XNA Framework is with customized bitmap fonts. This method is more advanced, which means it is highly customizable but also requires additional work. To demonstrate working with fonts a new project named FontsSample is added to the Chapter 8 solution.

SpriteFont

The SpriteFont class takes a built-in font and rasterizes it based on configuration parameters. To add a text Font for rendering in XNA Game Studio, right-click on the FontsSampleContent project and select Add ➤ Item ➤ Sprite Font, and enter a name. Usually, you name the Sprite Font item the same as the Font Name. If you include multiple sizes append the size to the end, which will make more sense in a bit.

While we take fonts for granted when working in Microsoft Word or in Outlook, fonts are licensed content. You must have redistribution rights to include a font in your game. Search the Web for "purchase fonts online" and quite a few sites show up. Some include free fonts with others for purchase.

Luckily XNA Game Studio 4.0 includes a set of OpenTypefonts you can use in your games. Figure 8-5 shows the fonts that are licensed by Microsoft for your use. The image is taken from the AppHub education catalog.

Andy Bold - ABC abc 123
JING JING - ABC ABC 123
Kootenay - ABC abc 123
Lindsey - ABC abc 123
Miramonte, Miramonte Bold - ABC abc 123
Moire Bold, Moire ExtraBold, Moire Light, Moire Regular - ABC abc 123
MOTORWERK - ABC ABC 123
News Gothic, **NewsGothic Bold** - ABC abc 123
OCRA Extended - ABC abc 123
PERICLES, PERICLES LIGHT - ABC ABC 123
Pescadero, **Pescadero Bold** - ABC abc 123
QUARTZ MS - ABC ABC 123
⌑s⌑e⌑g⌑o⌑e⌑⌑k⌑e⌑y⌑c⌑a⌑p⌑s⌑. *Segoe Print,* **Segoe Print Bold** - ABC abc 12
Segoe UI Mono Bold, Segoe UI Mono - ABC abc 123
Wasco Sans Bold, *Wasco Sans Bold Italic*, *Wasco Sans Italic,* Wasco Sans - ABC abc

Figure 8-5. *Fonts provided by XNA Game Studio for use in XNA framework games*

For our sample, name the new Sprite Font item SegoeKeycaps24 and click Add. A new item named SegoeKeycaps16.spritefont is added to the FontSampleContent project. What may surprise you is that the SegoeKeycaps16.spritefont file is an XML file. Listing 8-4 shows the contents of the newly added file.

Listing 8-4. *SpriteFont XML File Format*

```xml
<?xml version="1.0" encoding="utf-8"?>
<XnaContent xmlns:Graphics="Microsoft.Xna.Framework.Content.Pipeline.Graphics">
  <Asset Type="Graphics:FontDescription">
    <FontName>Segoe UI Mono</FontName>
    <Size>14</Size>
    <Spacing>0</Spacing>
    <UseKerning>true</UseKerning>
    <Style>Regular</Style>
    <!-- <DefaultCharacter>*</DefaultCharacter> -->
    <CharacterRegions>
      <CharacterRegion>
        <Start>&#32;</Start>
        <End>&#126;</End>
      </CharacterRegion>
    </CharacterRegions>
  </Asset>
</XnaContent>
```

The XML file describes the parameters for what should be rendered when text is drawn using this SpriteFont. For our example, change the FontName element to Segoe Keycaps. Change the Size to 16 and leave everything else at the default values.

You can edit the Spacing element to increase the space between characters, as well as modify the UseKerning item to modify how the font is laid out. Kerning adjusts the spacing between characters to be more pleasing to the eye. An example of kerning is when a capital "W" overhangs a neighboring "e" slightly when typing the word "Well." Without kerning, letters do not overhang or underhang as the case may be. The Style element indicates whether it should be Regular, Bold, or Italic.

The last element to discuss is the CharacterRegions element, which controls what letters are available in the font. The default range is 32 (ASCII space) to 126 (ASCHII '~'). This reduces the number of characters rasterized as part of the content import process.

To draw the SegoeKeycaps16 Sprite Font, add a new private member named segoeKeycaps16 of type SpriteFont to the Game1 class in the FontSample project. Next add this line of code to the Game1.LoadContent method:

```
segoeKeycaps16 = Content.Load<SpriteFont>("SegoeKeycaps16");
```

We used the SpriteBatch.Draw method to draw textures to the screen. The SpriteBatch.DrawString method has six overloads to provide flexibility in drawing text to the screen. Here are a couple of examples:

```
spriteBatch.DrawString(segoeKeycaps24, text, new Vector2(24, 130), Color.Yellow);
```

```
spriteBatch.DrawString(segoeKeycaps24, text, new Vector2(24, 450), Color.Orange,
    -.25f * (float)Math.PI, Vector2.Zero, 3, SpriteEffects.None, 0);
```

You can tinge the font color by adjusting the fourth parameter with a color value such as Color.Yellow. The second DrawString call above applies a negative 45 degree rotation in the fifth parameter and a 300 percent scale in the sixth parameter, with an orange tinge applied to the Sprite Font. Another font is added to the project named Miramonte with Italics style, and a few more DrawString calls are in the code, but Figure 8-6 shows the results.

Figure 8-6. *DrawString examples with the SpriteFont class*

The scaled font renders pretty well but you can see some stretching in the letter "e" in Figure 8-6 that could be more obvious with other fonts. In the next section we cover how to create a bitmap font.

Bitmap Fonts

Bitmap fonts are not dependent on a built-in font. Instead, the fonts are loaded from a texture similar to what is shown in Figure 8-7.

Figure 8-7. *Bitmap font texture example*

The example in Figure 8-7 was copied from MSDN by zooming in the browser by 200% and taking a screenshot, but you can create a custom bitmap font texture using any drawing program by following the conventions specified in the documentation.

The character order matters, with a space as the upper-left character. You can use a solid white or black background color for monochrome characters. In the previous example, black is used as the background color. Multicolored characters are supported with an alpha channel.

The space between characters must be filled with Magenta color (Red:255 Green:0 Blue:255 Alpha:255). The FontTextureProcessor class is applied to the texture instead of the default processor. The FontTextureProcessor will pack the characters in as close as possible so you don't have to worry about exact spacing between characters.

A new project named BitmapFontSample is added to the Chapter 8 solution. The bitmap font texture in Figure 8-7 is added to the BitmapFontSampleContent project with a name of BitmapFont.bmp. The Content Processor is configured to Sprite Font Texture - XNA Framework from the default of Texture - XNA Framework.

The SpriteFont class is still used as the member type for the bitmapFont object and the bitmap font is loaded in LoadContent just like for a regular SpriteFont content:

```
SpriteFont bitmapFont;
…//Load Content
bitmapFont = Content.Load<SpriteFont>("BitmapFont");
```

Drawing is the same as well with the DrawString method:

```
spriteBatch.Begin();
spriteBatch.DrawString(bitmapFont, text, new Vector2(24, 70), Color.White);
spriteBatch.End();
```

In summary, the primary differences when using a custom bitmap font is that you must draw out the characters correctly in the proper order and you configure the Content Processor to Sprite Font Texture - XNA Framework for the bitmap font texture.

MenuScreen Class

The MenuScreen class is part of the GameStateManagementSample (Phone) sample project. It is the base class for the MainMenu.cs and OptionsMenu.cs screen objects that are part of the AlienShooter game project.

The MenuScreen class takes advantage of a helper class named MenuEntry, which draws the text and publishes a Selected event. The MenuEntry class does not detect the touch. Instead, the MenuScreen does most of the work to draw, detect a touch, and associate the touch with the correct `MenuEntry` item. A good way to understand how this works is to look at the constructor for the `MainMenuScreen` class:

```
public MainMenuScreen()
    : base("Main Menu")
{
    // Create our menu entries.
    MenuEntry playGameMenuEntry = new MenuEntry("Play Game");
    MenuEntry optionsMenuEntry = new MenuEntry("Options");

    // Hook up menu event handlers.
    playGameMenuEntry.Selected += PlayGameMenuEntrySelected;
    optionsMenuEntry.Selected += OptionsMenuEntrySelected;

    // Add entries to the menu.
    MenuEntries.Add(playGameMenuEntry);
    MenuEntries.Add(optionsMenuEntry);
}
```

The `MainMenuScreen` class creates the menu entries and associates event handlers with the menu entries. The base class `MenuScreen` handles the animation and positioning. A developer can customize the animation and layout by modifying the base `MenuScreen` class.

One way to customize the menu screens is to change the Font in the `AlienShooterContent` project. Open the `/GameManagement/menufont.spritefont` file and change the `FontName` element to Quartz MS listed in Figure 8-5 and change the `Size` to 24. The font has a science fiction look to it, which suites a game named AlienShooter pretty well.

We also modify the `GamePlayScreen` class to have Score and Lives text across the top with a `SlateBlue` color background. This is achieved via the `SpriteBatch.DrawString` method as well as adjusting the background color to `SlateBlue` and drawing the `backgroundTexture` 34 pixels lower via the added `backgroundPosition` Vector2 object. Figure 8-8 shows both the updated menu screen and game play screen.

Figure 8-8. *Updated Menu and Game screens for AlienShooter*

When you run the project on a device, the animations and transitions look pretty nice. These can certainly be customized as well once you understand how to create animations and transitions in XNA Game Studio. We cover both topics in detail to create the actual game play.

AlienShooter Game Play

In this section we focus on building out the game. Remember in Chapter 1 that we drew all of the objects directly in the Game1.cs class. In this chapter we will build up an object hierarchy to add better organization to the game structure. We start with an explanation of how sprite animation works so that we can then encapsulate the work in a GameObject class.

Sprite Animation

In this section we cover spite animation, which is the technique that brings a 2D game to life. Sprite animation is a matter of showing frames or individual sprites at set intervals to give the illusion of motion, no different than flipping a drawing book that has pictures of a stick man running. Each picture is static, but when drawn in the correct order with the right position, the stick man appears animated when you flip through the images.

A new project named SpriteAnimation is added to the Chapter 8 solution. Project references to the SpriteSheetRuntime and SpriteSheetPipeline are added to the SpriteAnimation and

SpriteAnimationContent projects respectively in order to take advantage of the automatic sprite sheet creation and easy sprite access via file name within the sprite sheet without having to remember coordinates or the math to track frames.

The sprite sheet is created from the AlienShooter textures. For the hero ship, we want to add rocket engine exhaust animations as well as for the missile. For the alien spaceship, a bit of glow is added underneath that shimmers and some tilt to the left and right is added to the ship. To create these effects I fired up Paint.NET and created 10 sprites for each object, varying the patterns enough to make cartoonish flame for the hero ship and missile as well as the glow and tilt for the spaceship. Figure 8-9 shows the individually edited sprite files in the file system.

Figure 8-9. Individual sprite files

The files are added to the Sprite Sheet XML file as shown in Listing 8-5.

Listing 8-5. SpriteAnimationSpriteSheet.xml Content File

```xml
<?xml version="1.0" encoding="utf-8" ?>
<XnaContent>
  <Asset Type="System.String[]">
    <Item>Sprites/heroship0.tga</Item>
    <Item>Sprites/heroship1.tga</Item>
    <Item>Sprites/heroship2.tga</Item>
    <Item>Sprites/heroship3.tga</Item>
    <Item>Sprites/heroship4.tga</Item>
```

```
    <Item>Sprites/heroship5.tga</Item>
    <Item>Sprites/heroship6.tga</Item>
    <Item>Sprites/heroship7.tga</Item>
    <Item>Sprites/heroship8.tga</Item>
    <Item>Sprites/heroship9.tga</Item>
    <Item>Sprites/spaceship0.tga</Item>
    <Item>Sprites/spaceship1.tga</Item>
    <Item>Sprites/spaceship2.tga</Item>
    <Item>Sprites/spaceship3.tga</Item>
    <Item>Sprites/spaceship4.tga</Item>
    <Item>Sprites/spaceship5.tga</Item>
    <Item>Sprites/spaceship6.tga</Item>
    <Item>Sprites/spaceship7.tga</Item>
    <Item>Sprites/spaceship8.tga</Item>
    <Item>Sprites/spaceship9.tga</Item>
    <Item>Sprites/missile0.tga</Item>
    <Item>Sprites/missile1.tga</Item>
    <Item>Sprites/missile2.tga</Item>
    <Item>Sprites/missile3.tga</Item>
    <Item>Sprites/missile4.tga</Item>
    <Item>Sprites/missile5.tga</Item>
    <Item>Sprites/missile6.tga</Item>
    <Item>Sprites/missile7.tga</Item>
    <Item>Sprites/missile8.tga</Item>
    <Item>Sprites/missile9.tga</Item>
  </Asset>
</XnaContent>
```

The Content Processor is configured to SpriteSheetProcessor, which instructs the Content Pipeline to collect the individual files and mash them together into a single texture, as shown in Figure 8-10.

Figure 8-10. Generated textures

Personally, I would find it tedious to hand-create a sprite texture as shown in Figure 8-10, and prefer drawing individual images and letting the SpriteSheet sample code do the hard work for me. Once you see how easy it is to animate sprites using this method, I think you will agree.

Drawing the frames so that it animates between the images is pretty straightforward. In the Game1 class for the SpriteAnimation sample, the following private fields are declared:

```
SpriteSheet SpriteAnimationSpriteSheet;
int spriteIndex = 0;
Rectangle screenRect;
TimeSpan timeToNextFrame = new TimeSpan();
TimeSpan frameTime = TimeSpan.FromMilliseconds(50d);
```

The spriteIndex variable is used to append a number from 0 to 9 to the sprite names of heroship, missile, and spaceship. Note in Figure 8-9 and Listing 8-5 how the sprite images are named. Incrementing spriteIndex steps over to the next sprite by name shown visually in Figure 8-10.

The timeToNextFrame field is used to sum elapsed time for the game. The frameTime field stores how often the spriteIndex should change over to the next frame. Here is the code from Game1.Update that performs this calculation:

```
protected override void Update(GameTime gameTime)
{
  // Allows the game to exit
  if (GamePad.GetState(PlayerIndex.One).Buttons.Back == ButtonState.Pressed)
    this.Exit();

  // TODO: Add your update logic here
  // Add elapsed game time between calls to Update
  // Once enough time has passed, i.e. timeToNextFrame > frameTime
  //increment sprite index.
  timeToNextFrame += gameTime.ElapsedGameTime;
  if (timeToNextFrame > frameTime)
  {
    if (spriteIndex < 9)
      spriteIndex++;
    else spriteIndex = 0;
      frameElapsedTime = TimeSpan.FromMilliseconds(0d);  }
  base.Update(gameTime);
}
```

Essentially, the frameTime variable is how long any given frame is displayed. If you want the frames to animate more slowly, increase the value of the frameTime variable, currently set to 50.

Drawing a frame is pretty straightforward as well. Here is the code to draw the center of the hero ship at the center of the screen:

```
spriteBatch.Draw(SpriteAnimationSpriteSheet.Texture,
  new Vector2((screenRect.Width / 3) -
        SpriteAnimationSpriteSheet.SourceRectangle("spaceship" +
spriteIndex.ToString()).Width / 2,
      (screenRect.Height / 3) -
        SpriteAnimationSpriteSheet.SourceRectangle("spaceship" +
spriteIndex.ToString()).Height / 2),
  SpriteAnimationSpriteSheet.SourceRectangle("spaceship" + spriteIndex.ToString()),
  Color.White);
```

The previous code takes the entire sprite sheet and uses this parameter for the source rectangle to select which sprite to draw:

```
SpriteAnimationSpriteSheet.SourceRectangle("spaceship" + spriteIndex.ToString())
```

You can only see the actual animation by running the code, but Figure 8-11 provides a snapshot.

Figure 8-11. *Animated sprites*

We copy over all of the `heroship`, `alienship`, and `missile` images and `SpriteSheet` XML file to the `AlienShooterContent` content project's `Sprites` folder so that we can leverage the assets we created in our primary game.

Now that you understand how to animate sprites, we can move forward and create a `GameObject` class that handles the animation logic, as well as other object state allowing the code to focus more on game play and let the `GameObject` class handle rendering and state management.

Remember from our `ScreenManager` coverage that the actual game functionality exists in the `GameplayScreen` class. The rest of this chapter focuses on the code in the `GameplayScreen` class that manages the game objects as well as the game object code itself. The goal is that you come away with a solid understanding of how to go about creating your own games.

Game Object Class

We create a class named `GameObject` to be our base class for game assets, which includes the hero ship, the missiles, and the alien ships. The `GameObject` class handles the animation, Update, and Drawing for each object. We copied over the assets and sprite sheet logic from the `SpriteAnimation` sample project. Here is the `GameObject` constructor:

```
public GameObject(SpriteSheet loadedTexture, string spriteName, Rectangle screenRect)
{
  SpriteAnimationSpriteSheet = loadedTexture;
  SpriteCenter = new Vector2(
    SpriteAnimationSpriteSheet.SourceRectangle(spriteName + 0).Width / 2,
    SpriteAnimationSpriteSheet.SourceRectangle(spriteName + 0).Height / 2);
  //Used to access sprite in SpriteSheet
  //Assume starts at 0 so SpriteName+0 is first Sprite frame for animation
  //NumberOfAnimationFrames is how many sprite frames are available
```

503

```
        SpriteName = spriteName;
        _screenRect = screenRect;

        //Default initialization
        FrameTime = TimeSpan.FromMilliseconds(100d);
        NumberOfAnimationFrames = 10;
        Position = Vector2.Zero;
        ElapsedFrameTime = TimeSpan.FromMilliseconds(0d);
        Velocity = Vector2.Zero;
        Rotation = 0f;
        Alive = false;
    }
```

The constructor for GameObject takes the following parameters:

- `SpriteSheet loadedTexture`

- `string spriteName`

- `Rectangle screenRect`

Just as with the `SpriteAnimation` sample, all of the individual object frames are combined into a single texture shared by all of the objects, which is more efficient than loading individual textures and switching textures when rendering. The `loadedTexture` parameter represents the single texture and is passed in to the constructor. The `spriteName` parameter is used by the animation code so that the correct object frames can be found in the `loadedTexture`. This code assumes a naming convention starting at `spriteName+0` through `spriteName+NumberOfAnimationFrames`, which is hard-coded to 10 frames for all objects. The `screenRect` parameter is used to check when objects collide with screen bounds.

Properties

The `GameObject` class has quite a few public properties declared that are used to animate the sprite and to hold information on Sprite such as the center point, position, velocity and rotation. Here are the declarations:

```
public SpriteSheet SpriteAnimationSpriteSheet { get; set; }
public string SpriteName { get; private set; }
public int NumberOfAnimationFrames { get; set; }
public TimeSpan FrameTime { get; set; }
public TimeSpan ElapsedFrameTime { get; set; }
public Vector2 SpriteCenter { get; set; }
public bool Alive { get; set; }
public Vector2 Position { get; set; }
public Vector2 Velocity { get; set; }
public float Rotation { get; set; }
```

There is an additional property related to collision detection that we will cover next.

Collision Detection

The `BoundingRect` property of type `Rectangle` is used to return the `Rectangle` area that contains the sprite on screen. This property is used for collision detection. If you have ever played a video game where the objects seemed to touch but nothing happen, it is a result of imperfect collision detection, as shown in Figure 8-12 where a regular shaped object, like a rectangle, is used to define the area of an irregularly shaped object.

Figure 8-12. *Bounding box collision detection*

There are more than a few algorithms for sprite collision detection that can be found in books focused on the topic that range in accuracy from bounding rectangles to resource-intensive point by point comparison. Probably the best answer lies somewhere between those extremes, such as using more than one bounding box or only performing point-by-point comparison on sides that could collide, and so on. For our purposes, we check for intersection using the BoundingRect property defined in GameObject:

```
public virtual Rectangle BoundingRect
{
  get
  {
    return new Rectangle((int)Position.X, (int)Position.Y,
      SpriteAnimationSpriteSheet.SourceRectangle(SpriteName + 0).Width,
      SpriteAnimationSpriteSheet.SourceRectangle(SpriteName + 0).Height);
  }
}
```

One trick to that you can use to adjust collision detection is to call the Inflate(horizontalAmount,verticalAmount) method to individually increase or decrease (with a negative value) the sides of the Rectangle to better match the object shape.

GameObject Methods

The rest of the GameObject class contain its individual methods to reset its position if the object flies off the screen, update the object state, and draw the object to screen. Methods are marked with the virtual keyword so that they can be overridden in inherited classes as needed:

```
public virtual void ResetGameObject()
{
  Position = Vector2.Zero;
  Velocity = Vector2.Zero;
  Alive = false;
}
```

```
public virtual void Update(GameTime GameTime)
{
  if (Alive)
  {
    Position += Velocity;
    //Check screen bounds
    if ((Position.X < 0) ||
        (Position.X > _screenRect.Width) ||
        (Position.Y < 0) ||
        (Position.Y > _screenRect.Height))
      ResetGameObject();
    //Update animation
    UpdateAnimation(GameTime);
  }
}

private void UpdateAnimation(GameTime gameTime)
{
  ElapsedFrameTime += gameTime.ElapsedGameTime;
  if (ElapsedFrameTime > FrameTime)
  {
    if (_spriteIndex < NumberOfAnimationFrames - 1)
      _spriteIndex++;
    else _spriteIndex = 0;
    ElapsedFrameTime = TimeSpan.FromMilliseconds(0d);
  }
}

public virtual void Draw(GameTime gameTime, SpriteBatch spriteBatch)
{
  if (Alive)
  {
    spriteBatch.Draw(SpriteAnimationSpriteSheet.Texture, Position - SpriteCenter,
      SpriteAnimationSpriteSheet.SourceRectangle(SpriteName + _spriteIndex.ToString()),
      Color.White);
  }
}
```

The ResetGameObject is called when an object is "destroyed" or flies off the screen. The method is pretty simple in just setting Position and Velocity to a zero vector and Alive to false.

The Update method checks to see if the object is Alive before updating Position by adding Velocity to it and then checking screen bounds. The Update method also calls the UpdateAnimation method, which leverages the code we developed in the SpriteAnimation sample. Finally, the Draw method simply applies the same logic we used in the SpriteAnimation sample to draw the correct frame to screen as part of the animation sequence.

Now that we have our base class out of the way, we move on to cover the enemy alien class and then move on to the user-controlled hero ship and missile classes.

Enemy Class

The AlienGameObject class that represents the frenzied aliens is remarkably simple. The class inherits from the GameObject class and uses the inherited constructor with some modifications:

```
public AlienGameObject(SpriteSheet loadedTexture,
          string spriteName, Rectangle screenRect)
  : base(loadedTexture, spriteName, screenRect)
{
  Alive = true;
  ResetGameObject();
}
```

The Alive property is set to true because we want enemies to keep dropping. There is a customized ResetGameObject method that overrides the base class version as well:

```
public override void ResetGameObject()
{
  //Randomize animation
  _spriteIndex = (int)(randomNumber.NextDouble() * NumberOfAnimationFrames);
  //Randomize initial position
  Position = new Vector2(randomNumber.Next(_screenRect.Width), 35);

  //Apply default alien speed
  Velocity = new Vector2(randomNumber.Next(alienVelocityArc), alienSpeed);
  Alive = true;
}
```

The alien spaceship has a unique shape. For better collision detection we override the BoundingRect property and call Rectangle.Inflate(0,2); to inflate the Rectangle on the Y axis resulting in much better collision detection for this game:

```
public override Rectangle BoundingRect
{
  get
  {
    Rectangle rect = new Rectangle((int)Position.X, (int)Position.Y,
      SpriteAnimationSpriteSheet.SourceRectangle(SpriteName + 0).Width,
      SpriteAnimationSpriteSheet.SourceRectangle(SpriteName + 0).Height);
    rect.Inflate(0,20);
    return rect ;
  }
}
```

That's it for this class. All of the lively action is a result of the animation code handled by the base class and the ResetGameObject method. This method does a couple of things:

- It starts the animation at a random index, so that the objects don't appear to be animating in sync, which would be boring.

- It randomly picks an 'X' value for the initial Position Vector2 to start the drop.

- Finally, it applies a random but very small 'X' value to the Velocity so that the alien space ships don't appear to just fall straight down.

Figure 8-13 shows an army of aliens invading.

Figure 8-13. *Alien invasion*

You will want to play on a real device to get a full sense of the game, but as you can see in Figure 8-13, the aliens strike different drop lines and fall fairly randomly for such little code. The animation code helps to keep things lively as well. In the next section, we cover the hero ship class, which takes accelerometer and touch input to move and fire missiles at the invasion.

The Hero Ship Class

We create another class named UserGameObject that inherits from the GameObject class. This class represents the player, which is the Hero Ship in AlienShooter, which makes it unique compared to the other classes since it takes user input in the form of accelerometer and touch. The accelerometer input will move the ship left or right by tilting the phone. It has a window so that if the phone is relatively flat the ship does not move. Touching the screen will fire missiles.

User Input

By default, the Game Management sample does not include support for accelerometer input. The GamePlayScreen class has a HandleInput method that takes a parameter of type InputState, which is a class that captures keyboard, controller, and touch input. It does not capture accelerometer input by default. In the source code for the book, you will find a modified InputState class, as well as a new class named AccelerometerState, which is shown in Listing 8-6.

Listing 8-6. AccelerometerState Class File

```
public class AccelerometerState
{
  public double X;
  public double Y;
  public double Z;
  public DateTimeOffset Timestamp;
}
```

The modifications to the InputState class are pretty straightforward:

```
//robcamer - Add a private instance of AccelerometerState
public AccelerometerState CurrentAccelerometerState { get; private set; }
//robcamer - Add private field for the accelerometer
private Accelerometer accelerometer;
```

The constructor for the InputState class is modified to instantiate the previous two private variables, as well as add an event handler to the Accelerometer:

```
CurrentAccelerometerState = new AccelerometerState();
//Robcamer - initialize accelerometer
accelerometer = new Accelerometer();
accelerometer.ReadingChanged +=
  new System.EventHandler<AccelerometerReadingEventArgs>(accelerometer_ReadingChanged);
accelerometer.Start();
```

The values of CurrentAccelerometerState are updated in the accelerometer_ReadingChanged event handler:

```
void accelerometer_ReadingChanged(object sender, AccelerometerReadingEventArgs e)
{
  CurrentAccelerometerState.X = e.X;
  CurrentAccelerometerState.Y = e.Y;
  CurrentAccelerometerState.Y = e.Z;
  CurrentAccelerometerState.Timestamp = e.Timestamp;
}
```

Processing Input

Now that we have the modifications in place for the InputState class, two private fields related to user input are added to the UserGameObject class.

```
private AccelerometerState _accelerometerState;
private Vector2 _leftRightVector = new Vector2(5, 0);
```

The _accelerometerState and _leftRightVector fields are modified in the UserGameObject.HandleInput method.

```
public void HandleInput(InputState input)
{
  //Must check for TouchLocationState as wel as Count
  //Otherwise, FireMissile will be called twice
  //Once for 'Pressed' and once for 'Released'
  if ((input.TouchState.Count > 0) &&
    input.TouchState[0].State == TouchLocationState.Pressed)
  {
    FireMissile();
  }

  _accelerometerState = input.CurrentAccelerometerState;
  if (_accelerometerState.X > .1)
  {
    Velocity = _leftRightVector;
  }
  if (_accelerometerState.X < -.1)
  {
    Velocity = -_leftRightVector;
  }
  //near Zero tilt left or right so
  //set velocity to zero
  if ((_accelerometerState.X < .1) &&
    (_accelerometerState.X > -.1))
    Velocity = Vector2.Zero;
}
```

If the _accelerometerState X component is greater than .1, a positive or negative velocity is applied to the Velocity vector via the leftRightVector variable in the proper tilt direction. Likewise, if the user holds the phone close to neutral, Velocity is set to zero. If you don't like how it responds, play with the .1 value to see what feels good to you.

The other part of the HandleInput session is to detect if the screen is touched. Each touch fires to TouchState values, one for TouchLocationState.Pressed and one for TouchLocationState.Released. If the screen is touched the FireMissile method is fired.

The UserGameObject class manages a collection of Missile objects since they are closely associated with the hero ship:

```
public List<MissileGameObject> Missiles;
public int MaxNumberofMissiles;
```

The Missile related properties are public properties because the GameplayScreen will need to check collisions between missiles and enemy alien ships. Also, the number of available missiles could be adjusted dynamically as part of game play for a "blitz" mode, where the hero ship can fire more than three at a time as an example. The Missiles collection is instantiated in the UserGameObject constructor:

```
MaxNumberofMissiles = 3;
Missiles = new List<MissileGameObject>();
for (int i=0;i < MaxNumberofMissiles; i++)
  Missiles.Add(new MissileGameObject(loadedTexture,"missile",screenRect));
```

When the screen is touched, the FireMissile method code searches for an available missile; only three are available by default. It then sets the missile property to Alive and the Missile Position property to the same Position value for the hero ship / UserGameObject class. Note that once the Missile is set to Alive, it automatically starts moving based on the default logic implemented in the GameObject class.

UserGameObject Class Core Methods

The UserGameObject class overrides the Update method with custom code to position the spaceship correctly with user input. It also manages the Missiles collection by calling Update for missiles where Alive is true; that is, they are in flight. Here is the UserGameObject.Update method:

```
public override void Update(GameTime gameTime)
{
  base.Update(gameTime);

  if (Position.X < SpriteCenter.X)
    Position = new Vector2(SpriteCenter.X,Position.Y);
  if (Position.X > (_screenRect.Width - SpriteCenter.X))
    Position = new Vector2(_screenRect.Width-SpriteCenter.X,Position.Y);


  for (int i = 0; i < MaxNumberofMissiles; i++)
  {
    if (Missiles[i].Alive == true)
      Missiles[i].Update(gameTime);
  }
}
```

The Draw method is overridden as well:

```
public override void Draw(GameTime gameTime, Microsoft.Xna.Framework.Graphics.SpriteBatch
spriteBatch)
{
  for (int i = 0; i < MaxNumberofMissiles; i++)
  {
    if (Missiles[i].Alive == true)
      Missiles[i].Draw(gameTime, spriteBatch);
  }
  base.Draw(gameTime, spriteBatch);
}
```

The Draw method checks to see if each Missile is Alive and then calls Draw for the Missile object. The last item in the UserGameObject class to cover is the LoadContent method. In this method, the ContentManager instance is passed in so that the UserGameObject can make a sound effect when a missile is fired from the hero ship. Here is the method:

```
public void LoadContent(ContentManager content)
{
  _missileLaunchSoundEffect =
              content.Load<SoundEffect>("SoundEffects/MissileLaunch");
}
```

Sound Effects

XNA Game Studio has very rich audio mixing capabilities to support Dolby-quality sound. For our game the SoundEffect class provides a quick and easy way to play audio during a game with the Play method. We add three sound effects to the AlienShooterContent project in the SoundEffects folder:

- Explosion.wma

- HeroShipDamage.wma

- MissileLaunch.wma

One item to note is that I recorded the sounds using the Windows 7 Recorder tool, which generates a .wma file. When added to the Content project, the XNA Framework automatically chose the Song - XNA Framework Content Processor. This format cannot be played by the SoundEffect class. Simply change the Content Processor to Sound Effect - XNA Framework and the audio plays fine.

Let's now move on to a discussion of the Missile class.

The Missile Class

The Missile class is pretty straightforward, shown in Listing 8-7.

Listing 8-7. Missile GameObject Class File

```
using System;
using System.Collections.Generic;
using System.Linq;
using System.Text;
using SpriteSheetRuntime;
using Microsoft.Xna.Framework;

namespace AlienShooter.GameObjects
{
  class MissileGameObject : GameObject
  {
    public MissileGameObject(SpriteSheet loadedTexture,
            string spriteName, Rectangle screenRect)
      : base(loadedTexture, spriteName, screenRect)
    {
      ResetGameObject();
    }

    public override void ResetGameObject()
    {
      Position = new Vector2(-SpriteCenter.X, _screenRect.Height + SpriteCenter.Y);
      Velocity = new Vector2(0,-5);
      Alive = false;
    }
  }
}
```

The next class we cover is the GameStatusBoard class.

The Game Status Board Class

The GameStatusBoard class keeps track of and displays the score and lives available during the game. This class also plays sound effects when an enemy ship is destroyed and when the hero ship takes a hit from an enemy ship. The GameStatusBoard class also vibrates the phone when an alien ship hits the hero ship using the VibrateController class. Figure 8-14 shows the status board in action.

Figure 8-14. Alien invasion status board

In the following two sections, we cover keeping score and tracking lives functionality in the GameStatusBoard class.

Keeping Score

Each time a hero ship missile intercepts an alien space ship, 5 points are added to the GameStatusBoard.Score property. The Score property is modified in the GamePlay screen, which we cover later.

Within the GameStatusBoard class, updating the score results in a SoundEffect.Play call for the Explosion.wma file:

```
public int Score
{
```

```
    get { return _score; }
    set
    {
      _score = value;
      _alienExplosionSoundEffect.Play();
    }
}
```

The GameStatusBoard.Update method has a switch statement to display a message based on current score:

```
switch (Score)
{
  case 50: _displayMessage = true;
    _message = "Nice Start!";
    break;
  case 60: _displayMessage = false;
    break;
  case 100: _displayMessage = true;
    _message = "Keep It Up!";
    break;
  case 120: _displayMessage = false;
    break;
  default: break;
}
```

When the _displayMessage field is true based on score, GameStatusBoard.Draw displays the message in the Status Board with this call:

```
if (_displayMessage)
  spriteBatch.DrawString(_gameFont, _message, new Vector2(175, 0),
    _livesTextColor);
```

That's it for score keeping. We next cover tracking hero ship lives and game over functionality.

Tracking Lives

Be default, when playing the Alien Shooter game, you get three lives to start. Each time an alien ship intersects the hero ship, a life is deducted. At two lives a message of "Warning!" is displayed. At one life, a message of "Danger!" is displayed. Finally, when zero lives are the state, a "Game Over!" message is displayed at top and in the middle of the screen. Also, each time a life is deducted, the phone is briefly vibrated. Here is the declaration and instantiation of the VibrateController class:

```
private VibrateController _vibrateController = VibrateController.Default;
private TimeSpan _vibrateTimeSpan = TimeSpan.FromMilliseconds(400);
```

Here is the Lives property where the sound is played and phone vibrated when the Lives property is modified:

```
public int Lives
{
  get { return _lives; }
  set
```

```
  {
    _lives = value;
    _heroShipDamageSoundEffect.Play();
    _vibrateController.Start(_vibrateTimeSpan);
  }
}
```

Here is the code from the GameStatusBoard.Update method that determines what message to display, and in what color:

```
switch (_lives)
{
  case 3: _livesTextColor = Color.LightGreen;
          break;
  case 2: _livesTextColor = Color.Yellow;
          _displayMessage = true;
          _message = "Warning!";
          break;
  case 1: _livesTextColor = Color.Red;
          _displayMessage = true;
          _message = "Danger!";
          break;
  case 0: _livesTextColor = Color.Red;
          _displayMessage = true;
          _message = "Game Over!";
          GameOver = true;
          break;
}
```

Here is the corresponding code from the GameStatusBoard.Draw method that determines when to display a message about the hero ship help on the screen:

```
if (_displayMessage)
  spriteBatch.DrawString(_gameFont, _message, new Vector2(175, 0),
    _livesTextColor);
if (GameOver)
  spriteBatch.DrawString(_gameFont, _message, new Vector2(175, 370),
    _livesTextColor);
```

Having an informative game status board is an important component of any game development effort. This section covered how simple it is to provide the basics. In the next section, we cover the overall logic in the GamePlayScreen class that pulls together all of the game objects we just covered.

Updated GameplayScreen Class

When you click New Game in the main menu, the GameplayScreen is the screen that loads and the GameplayScreen class is where all of the game action occurs. The following sections cover how the GameplayScreen class manages the game objects, collision detection, and scoring.

GamePlay Screen Initialization

Now we are ready to modify the GameplayScreen class to manage the game objects. We declare the object instances needed:

```
//Game objects
GameStatusBoard statusBoard;
List<AlienGameObject> enemies;
int maxEnemies = 5;
UserGameObject heroShip;
int maxMissiles = 3;
//Indicates to draw game over frame;
bool drawGameOverFrame = false ;
```

The maxMissiles and maxEnemies variables are not constants, because we may want to change them dynamically during the game as part of the game play. Otherwise, one UserGameObject named heroShip and a List of AlienGameObjects are the other key components of the game. Another potential modification would be to increase the number of AlienGameObjects in the game as the score gets higher to make it more interesting. Otherwise, a player will get bored if nothing changes.

Next we load and initialize assets in LoadContent():

```
public override void LoadContent()
{
  if (content == null)
    content = new ContentManager(ScreenManager.Game.Services, "Content");

  gameFont = content.Load<SpriteFont>("gamefont");
  alienShooterSpriteSheet = content.Load<SpriteSheet>("Sprites/AlienShooterSpriteSheet");
  backgroundTexture = content.Load<Texture2D>("Textures/background");
  backgroundPosition = new Vector2(0, 34);
  //Get a pointer to the entire screen Rectangle
  screenRect = ScreenManager.GraphicsDevice.Viewport.Bounds;

  //Initialize Enemies collection
  enemies = new List<AlienGameObject>();
  for (int i = 0; i < maxEnemies; i++)
  {
    enemies.Add(new AlienGameObject(alienShooterSpriteSheet, "spaceship", screenRect));
  }

  //Initialize Player Object
  heroShip = new UserGameObject(alienShooterSpriteSheet, "heroship", screenRect, maxMissiles);
  heroShip.Position = new Vector2(screenRect.Width / 2, 720);
  heroShip.LoadContent(content);

  //Initialize Status Board
  statusBoard = new GameStatusBoard(gameFont);
  statusBoard.LoadContent(content);

  // A real game would probably have more content than this sample, so
  // it would take longer to load. We simulate that by delaying for a
  // while, giving you a chance to admire the beautiful loading screen.
  Thread.Sleep(1000);
```

```
  // Once the load has finished, we use ResetElapsedTime to tell the game's
  // timing mechanism that we have just finished a very long frame, and that
  // it should not try to catch up.
  ScreenManager.Game.ResetElapsedTime();
}
```

Breaking out our game assets into objects greatly unclutters the code in the GameplayScreen class. As an example, initializing the enemies object is a matter of passing in the texture information for the animations:

```
//Initialize Enemies collection
enemies = new List<AlienGameObject>();
for (int i = 0; i < maxEnemies; i++)
{
  enemies.Add(new AlienGameObject(alienShooterSpriteSheet, "spaceship", screenRect));
}
```

GameplayScreen Update and Draw Methods

Adding support for the heroShip and the AlienGameObject to the GameplayScreen.Update method is pretty straightforward now that we have nice objects that manage work for us:

```
public override void Update(GameTime gameTime, bool otherScreenHasFocus,
                                               bool coveredByOtherScreen)
{
  if (IsActive)
  {
    if (!statusBoard.GameOver)
    {
      CheckForCollisions();

      heroShip.Update(gameTime);
      statusBoard.Update(gameTime);

      for (int i = 0; i < maxEnemies; i++)
      {
        enemies[i].Update(gameTime);
      }
    }
  }
  base.Update(gameTime, otherScreenHasFocus, coveredByOtherScreen);
}
```

If StatusBoard.GameOver is not true, and the hero ship has lives available, the game action continues. Otherwise, the code is straightforward, calling Update for each object. Notice the call to the CheckForCollisions method. We cover collision detection in the next subsection.

Adding support for user input is just as easy by adding a call to heroShip.HandleIpnut(input) just after the else in the GameplayScreen.HandleInput method. For the GameplayScreen.Draw method, the Draw method is called for each object. If StatusBoard.GameOver is true, the Draw method is not called for the enemies any further, and the game is over.

```
public override void Draw(GameTime gameTime)
{
  ScreenManager.GraphicsDevice.Clear(ClearOptions.Target,
                                     Color.SlateBlue, 0, 0);

  // Our player and enemy are both actually just text strings.
  SpriteBatch spriteBatch = ScreenManager.SpriteBatch;

  spriteBatch.Begin();
  //Draw Background
  spriteBatch.Draw(backgroundTexture, backgroundPosition, Color.White);
  //Draw Status Board
  statusBoard.Draw(gameTime, spriteBatch);
  //Draw Hero Ship
  heroShip.Draw(gameTime, spriteBatch);
  //Draw enemies
  if (!statusBoard.GameOver)
  {
    for (int i = 0; i < maxEnemies; i++)
    {
      enemies[i].Draw(gameTime, spriteBatch);
    }
  }
  spriteBatch.End();

  // If the game is transitioning on or off, fade it out to black.
  if (TransitionPosition > 0)
    ScreenManager.FadeBackBufferToBlack(1f - TransitionAlpha);
}
```

Collision Detection and Memory Management

In the GameplayScreen.Update method, there is a call to the CheckForCollisions method. This method detects collisions between inflight missiles and enemy alien ships (a score) as well as collisions between enemy alien ships and the hero ship (lose a life). Here is the code for the CheckForCollisions method:

```
private void CheckForCollisions()
{
  //Checking for two major collisions
  //1 - Has an in flight missile intersected an alien spaceship - score 5 pts
  for (int i = 0; i < heroShip.MaxNumberofMissiles; i++)
    if (heroShip.Missiles[i].Alive)
      for (int j = 0; j < maxEnemies; j++)
        if ((enemies[j].Alive) &&
            (enemies[j].BoundingRect.Intersects(heroShip.Missiles[i].BoundingRect)))
        {
          statusBoard.Score += 5;
          enemies[j].ResetGameObject();
          heroShip.Missiles[i].ResetGameObject();
        }
  //2 - Has an alien spaceship intersected the hero ship? - deduct a life
```

```
for (int j = 0; j < maxEnemies; j++)
  if ((enemies[j].Alive) && (enemies[j].Position.Y > 600) &&
      (enemies[j].BoundingRect.Intersects(heroShip.BoundingRect)))
  {
    statusBoard.Lives -= 1;
    for (int i = 0; i < maxEnemies; i++)
      enemies[i].ResetGameObject();
    for (int i = 0; i < heroShip.MaxNumberofMissiles; i++)
      heroShip.Missiles[i].ResetGameObject();
  }
}
```

For detecting a hit by a missile from an alien ship, each missile's bounding box must be compared with each enemy alien ship's bounding box. The same goes for detecting a collision between an enemy ship and the hero ship to lose a life. Each one must be compared every frame for the most part. This means that every time two objects are compared, which could be every frame, two new bounding boxes must be constructed. Remember that the bounding box includes a position for the bounding box as well as height and width. Here is the code to return a bounding box in the GameObject base class as a refresher:

```
public virtual Rectangle BoundingRect
{
  get
  {
    return new Rectangle((int)Position.X, (int)Position.Y,
      SpriteAnimationSpriteSheet.SourceRectangle(SpriteName + 0).Width,
      SpriteAnimationSpriteSheet.SourceRectangle(SpriteName + 0).Height);
  }
}
```

In a mobile application you want to try to minimize memory allocations to reduce garbage collection activity. In a mobile game, it is especially important to watch memory allocations. As an example, when an enemy is destroyed by a hit, the AlienGameObject for that enemy has its Alive property set to false. We could instead set the object to null and then instantiate a new object but that just wastes CPU cycles on garbage collection.

Another way to minimize CPU cycles is to do work only if needed. Notice in the CheckforCollisions method that the if statements are structured to only perform work and get a BoundingRect when needed. As an example, an enemy alien ship can only intersect the hero ship after it has fallen about two-thirds of the way down the screen, so a check is made to perform the collision calculations only if the alien ship is below 600 pixels on the screen:

```
if ((enemies[j].Alive) && (enemies[j].Position.Y > 600) &&
    (enemies[j].BoundingRect.Intersects(heroShip.BoundingRect)))
```

Part of game development is always looking for ways to do things smartly. For me, it is one of the most enjoyable parts of the effort. Now that we have covered XNA Framework development, we move on to the new shared rendering capability available in Windows Phone 7.5 that allows XNA Framework and Silverlight composited rendering.

XNA and Silverlight Composite Rendering

With Windows Phone 7 RTM, developers had to choose a rendering method, either Silverlight or the XNA Framework. Starting with Windows Phone OS 7.1, you can combine Silverlight and XNA Framework rendering into a single application.

When taking advantage of XNA Framework shared graphics, you create a Silverlight application, with an `App.xaml`, `page.xaml`, navigation, and so on. The full Silverlight application programming model is available to you with the additional capability of rendering XNA Framework content such as a 3D model. This enables developers to have Silverlight-rendered content in an XNA Framework game, as well as bring XNA Framework content, such as a 3D model, into a Silverlight application. This is an incredibly exciting capability now available to developers, enabling unique user interfaces such as actually seeing a 3D model of a product for a mobile marketplace, 3D augmented reality, and much more.

How Does Shared Graphics Work?

As background, Silverlight runs in "retained mode" on the GPU, where it has a nice object model that is processed to determine the look and layout, and is then rendered by the GPU. XNA Framework runs in *immediate mode* on the GPU, directly accessing the GPU buffers to render. When thinking about rendering both XNA Framework and Silverlight content, performance invariably comes to mind—how are GPU resources managed with both runtimes trying to render?

In "shared graphics" mode, the XNA Framework handles all rendering. You can declare Silverlight controls within the XAML markup for a page with shared graphics enabled, but the markup does not render automatically—the XNA Framework is in control to maximize memory. To render Silverlight content, you load it into a `UIElementRenderer` class, which takes the `UIElement` content and generates a texture based on current look and layout processing. This ensures that only the needed Silverlight content is actually rendered within the XNA Framework.

The actual rendering is performed within the XNA Framework game loop, provided by the `GameTimer` class so that the Silverlight UI loaded into the `UIElementRender` is sampled 30 times per second. This means that as the Silverlight UI layout and look changes, via animation or otherwise, the modifications are picked up each time the `UIElementRender` texture is generated and drawn in the game loop.

Performance is maximized by evicting all Silverlight resources from memory when using XNA Framework rendering. Silverlight content renders only when specified by the `UIElementRenderer`. A related performance topic is XNA Framework content loading, which can take some time. XNA Framework content is not dumped from memory when, say, navigating to a Silverlight-based high score page and then navigating back to the game page. Users would not want to sit through reloading content if that was the case.

As you can see, while the performance hit to use shared graphics is not zero, it is very small. The product team has also taken steps to maximize memory usage efficiency and not to exact a usability penalty on users for reloading content.

With the background out of the way, we next cover the project templates and then dive into the various classes mentioned in this section in detail so that you can start using shared graphics in your own applications.

Shared Graphics Project Templates

With the updated Windows Phone Developer Tools for Mango, two project templates are available: the Windows Phone Rich Graphics Application in the Silverlight for Windows Phone section, and the

Windows Phone Silverlight and XNA Application project template. Both are essentially the same project template to get you started, but let's first provide background on how shared rendering works by first covering the SharedGraphicsDeviceManager class.

The SharedGraphicsDeviceManager Class and Rendering

In the previous part of this chapter and in Chapter 1, we covered XNA Framework development, including the GraphicsDeviceManager class, which managed the device adapter, orientation, screen size, as well as the low-level graphics management under the covers. The SharedGraphicsDeviceManager class does the same for a composite rendering application, bringing XNA Framework rendering to Silverlight.

This line of code in OnNavigatedTo on a Silverlight XAML page will enable shared rendering:

```
SharedGraphicsDeviceManager.Current.GraphicsDevice.SetSharingMode(true);
```

This line of code in OnNavigatedFrom on a Silverlight XAML page will disable shared rendering:

```
SharedGraphicsDeviceManager.Current.GraphicsDevice.SetSharingMode(false);
```

You might ask at this point, "What about the game loop?" We cover that in the next section.

Silverlight and the Game Loop

Silverlight is an event-driven programming model, while the XNA Framework runs in an infinite loop, calling the Update and Draw methods until the user quits the game. To bridge the gap between the two programming models, a new class named GameTimer has been added to the XNA Framework to enable the game loop within Silverlight.

The GameTimer class has Start and Stop methods, just like the standard Timer class, but it also includes the game loop heartbeat methods in Update and Draw events. These events will fire based on the value configured on GameTimer.UpdateInterval. Generally games try to run at 60 frames per second. Many Windows Phone devices do not support rendering at that high a frame rate, so usually a value of 30 frames per second is configured in code like this:

```
timer.UpdateInterval = TimeSpan.FromTicks(333333);
```

Once the GameTimer Update and Draw events are wired up like this, you can start to code the XNA Framework rendering portion, just like in a regular XNA Framework application:

```
gameTimer.Update += OnUpdate;
gameTimer.Draw += OnDraw;'
```

In the next section I cover loading content and general initialization for XNA Framework development within the Silverlight application model.

Loading Content and Initialization

There isn't a LoadContent method in the XNA Framework Shared Graphics project templates, because these are Silverlight applications. Instead, developers can load content in the OnNavigateTo event for the page. Declare a ContentManager object in the XAML page and then obtain a reference to the App.Content ContentManager object for the application in the page constructor:

```
contentManager = (Application.Current as App).Content;
```

By having the ContentManager declared at the App.xaml class level, we keep all loaded XNA content in memory when navigating between the game page and a high score or setting page. This is what prevents having to reload the XNA Framework content when navigating the application. Having a reference to the App.Content property in the page is simply a convenience for loading the content within the XAML page.

The other item in App.xaml is the SharedGraphicsDeviceManager declaration as part of the ApplicationLifetimeObjects collection in XAML:

```
<xna:SharedGraphicsDeviceManager />
```

This makes the SharedGraphicsDeviceManager object available to the entire project. By implementing the IApplicationService interface, it allows the class to work well with the lifetime of the application and appropriately clean up resources as needed.

With the background out of the way, let's get started with a simple demonstration of how this works in the next section with a basic shared graphics demonstration project.

Basic Shared Graphics Demo

In this sample you can start with either shared graphics project template, the Windows Phone Silverlight or the XNA Application template under the XNA Game Studio 4.0 folder in Visual Studio 2010, and name the project SharedGraphicsBasic in the Chapter 8 solution.

On the MainPage.xaml page, we replace the ugly Button object with a TextBlock and copy over the navigation code to get to the gameplay in GamePage.xaml. The "game" will be based on the Chapter 3 sample named GesturesTouchPanelXNA. For now let's get it working within this new framework. With the modifications to MainPage.xaml in place, the rest of the modifications are on GamePage.xaml.

We first copy over the StickMan.png and Pescadero.spritefont files to the SharedGraphicsBasicLibContent project, which is the XNA Framework content project for the SharedGraphicsBasic project. We next copy these field variables from GesturesTouchPanelXNA.Game1.cs over to GamePage.xaml.cs in the Chapter 8 SharedGraphicsBasic project:

```
GestureSample gestureSample;
string gestureInfo;
SpriteFont spriteFontSegoeUIMono;
Vector2 spriteFontDrawLocation;
Texture2D StickManTexture;
GameObject StickManGameObject;
```

We next copy over the GameObject.cs code file to the SharedGraphicsBasic project and then copy over the code from GesturesTouchPanelXNA Game1.cs to SharedGraphicsBasic GamePage.xaml, starting with the code in the Game1.Initialize method to enable gestures over to GamePage's constructor:

```
TouchPanel.EnabledGestures = GestureType.DoubleTap | GestureType.Flick |
    GestureType.FreeDrag | GestureType.Hold | GestureType.HorizontalDrag |
    GestureType.None | GestureType.Pinch | GestureType.PinchComplete |
    GestureType.Tap | GestureType.VerticalDrag | GestureType.DragComplete;.
```

Next is the code to load content and initialize variables in Game1.LoadContent. GamePage.xaml does not have a load content page, so instead we copy the code over to the SharedGraphicsBasic.OnNavigateTo method:

```
spriteFontSegoeUIMono = Content.Load<SpriteFont>("Pescadero");
spriteFontDrawLocation = new Vector2(40, 40);
//Load StickMan texture
```

```
StickManTexture = Content.Load<Texture2D>("StickMan");
//Create StickMan sprite object
StickManGameObject = new GameObject(StickManTexture);
//Position in the middle of the screen
StickManGameObject.Position = new Vector2(graphics.GraphicsDevice.Viewport.Width / 2,
graphics.GraphicsDevice.Viewport.Height / 2);
```

Next up are the Update and Draw events. In a regular XNA Framework project, Update is a method override with this signature:

```
protected override void Update(GameTime gameTime)
{
  // Allows the game to exit
  if (GamePad.GetState(PlayerIndex.One).Buttons.Back == ButtonState.Pressed)
    this.Exit();
  // TODO: Add your update logic here
  base.Update(gameTime);
}
```

In a SharedGraphics project with the GameTimer events, the Update event has this signature:

```
private void OnUpdate(object sender, GameTimerEventArgs e)
{
    // TODO: Add your update logic here
}
```

As you can see, they have different parameter types, so modifications are required to the GameObject class for the Update method to take the GameTimerEventArgs event handler parameter instead of the GameTime parameter, and we must also modify ElapsedGameTime to just ElapsedTime in the GameObject.Update method.

Some additional modifications are required, such as changing the graphics variable in the XNA Framework project to the SharedGraphicsDeviceManager.Current variable in the Shared Graphics project. Other modifications are related to adding and resolving namespaces. Listing 8-8 shows the OnUpdate and OnDraw methods.

Listing 8-8. *GamePage.xaml.cs OnUpdate and OnDraw Event Handlers*

```
private void OnUpdate(object sender, GameTimerEventArgs e)
{
    // TODO: Add your update logic here
  ProcessTouchInput();
  StickManGameObject.Update(e,
    SharedGraphicsDeviceManager.Current.GraphicsDevice.Viewport.Bounds);
}

private void OnDraw(object sender, GameTimerEventArgs e)
{
    SharedGraphicsDeviceManager.Current.GraphicsDevice.Clear(Color.CornflowerBlue);

    // TODO: Add your drawing code here
    spriteBatch.Begin();
    // Draw gesture info
    string output = "Last Gesture: " + gestureInfo;
```

```
    // Draw the string
    spriteBatch.DrawString(spriteFontSegoeUIMono, output, spriteFontDrawLocation,
      Color.LightGreen, 0, Vector2.Zero, 1.0f, SpriteEffects.None, 0.5f);
    //Draw the stickman
    StickManGameObject.Draw(spriteBatch);
    spriteBatch.End();
}
```

Once the modifications are complete and everything compiles, run the SharedGraphicsBasic project and click the Load Game text. This brings up the same UI as shown in the GesturesTouchPanelXNA project in Chapter 3, and everything works as expected. In the next section we replace the SpriteFont display with Silverlight controls by using the UIElementRender object.

Shared Graphics with UIElementRenderer

In this section I cover how to use the UIElementRender class, starting by first moving all of the modifications in the SharedGraphicsBasic project over the new sample project for this section named UIElementRendererDemo so that it has the exact same behavior. The functionality is working just like in the SharedGraphcisBasic sample project, so now it is ready for additional modification to draw the gesture text with Silverlight instead of using the SpriteFont class.

In the UIElementRendererDemo project, open up GamePage.xaml and remove the "No XAML content" comment. Add this XAML to the page just inside the <phone:PhoneApplicationPage> tag:

```
<Grid>
<TextBlock Name="GestureStatus" Text="Gesture Type Here" />
</Grid>
```

Figure 8-15 shows the not very fancy XAML Expression Blend.

Figure 8-15. *UIElementRenderer Xaml*

Switch back to Visual Studio and declare a UIElmentRenderer object at the top of GamePage.xaml.cs and comment out the gestureInfo string declaration:

```
//Declare a UIElementRenderer
 UIElementRenderer xamlRenderer;
```

Remember that we copied over all of the code to load the XNA Framework content into the OnNavigatedTo method. We first comment out the code to load the SpriteFont and then add the code to create the UIElementRender just before the timer.Start() code. Here is the full OnNavigatedTo method:

```
protected override void OnNavigatedTo(NavigationEventArgs e)
{
  // Set the sharing mode of the graphics device to turn on XNA rendering.
  SharedGraphicsDeviceManager.Current.GraphicsDevice.SetSharingMode(true);

  // Create a new SpriteBatch, which can be used to draw textures.
  spriteBatch = new SpriteBatch(SharedGraphicsDeviceManager.Current.GraphicsDevice);

  // TODO: use this.content to load your game content here
  //spriteFontSegoeUIMono = contentManager.Load<SpriteFont>("Pescadero");
  spriteFontDrawLocation = new Vector2(40, 40);
  //Load StickMan texture
  StickManTexture = contentManager.Load<Texture2D>("StickMan");
  //Create StickMan sprite object
```

```
    StickManGameObject = new GameObject(StickManTexture);
    //Position in the middle of the screen
    StickManGameObject.Position = new
Vector2(SharedGraphicsDeviceManager.Current.GraphicsDevice.Viewport.Width / 2,
    SharedGraphicsDeviceManager.Current.GraphicsDevice.Viewport.Height / 2);

    //Create UIElementRenderer
    xamlRenderer = new UIElementRenderer(
      GestureStatus,
      (int)GestureStatus.ActualWidth, (int)GestureStatus.ActualHeight);

    // Start the timer
    timer.Start();

    base.OnNavigatedTo(e);
}
```

The UIElementRenderer constructor takes the Xaml element, in this case the GestureStatus
TextBlock, and a height and width value that is used to generate the texture for rendering. You may be
tempted to pass in GestureStatus.Width and GestureStatus.Height.

As described in Chapter 2, the layout system computes ActualHeight and ActualWidth for a control
based on Margin, Padding, Height and Width settings, as well as the settings on the parent layout control.
Therefore, it is important to pass in the ActualWidth and ActualHeight properties instead of Width and
Height.

We could have configured GestureStatus.Text in the Xaml to an empty string, which would then
cause ActualHeight and ActualWidth to be zero as well. This results in a runtime error because you must
have a positive integer for the UIElement's constructor's Height and Width parameters. Note that it is not
possible to change the UIElement's Height and Width properties at runtime. You must create a new
UIElementRenderer object or hard code the UIElementRenderer's Height and Width values to a value large
enough to draw the desired content. This can result in overdraw if drawing a lot of empty space over and
over, which has a performance cost. It is a trade-off to evaluate creating new UIElementRender objects as
needed or have one that is sized large enough that is drawn over and over.

Now on to configuring the current gesture type and drawing the string to the screen. The code in the
ProcessTouchInput method is updated to set the current GestureType name to GestureStatus.Text:

```
GestureStatus.Text = "Last Gesture: " + gestureSample.GestureType.ToString();
```

That's it for the update code. Here is the code to draw the UIElementRenderer in OnDraw:

```
if (xamlRenderer != null  && GestureStatus.Text != "")
{
  xamlRenderer.Render();
  spriteBatch.Draw(xamlRenderer.Texture, spriteFontDrawLocation, Color.White);
}
```

The code first checks to make sure that the UIElement is created and that there is text to draw.
UIElementRenderer.Render() creates the texture to be drawn. This texture is based on the current status
of the Sivlerlight UI, which could include Storyboard animations and other dynamic changes.

Calling UIElementRenderer.Render takes a snapshot of the Silverlight UX at that moment, 30 times a
second in the OnDraw method so dynamic changes render smoothly as if just rendering within a plain
Silverlight application. Next the code calls SpriteBatch.Draw to render the texture. Figure 8-16 shows the
UX.

Figure 8-16. *UIElementRenderer in action*

Nothing fancy yet, so let's make it more interesting. Let's say you want to jazz up the text. This gets a bit more tricky in the XNA Framework. As shown in the earlier section titled "Bitmap Fonts," you have to hand-draw each letter you need in order to create a more customized version of the text.

With shared graphics we can instead use Expression Blend to make things more interesting. In Expression Blend I changed the font to Algerian and increased the size to 36pt. In about a minute I created a simple animation that changes the color of the Font for the text every 100ms and runs forever or until stopped.

Once you are satisfied with the Storyboard, switch over to Visual Studio to create a MouseLeftButtonDown event like this:

```
private void GestureStatus_MouseLeftButtonDown(object sender, MouseButtonEventArgs e)
{
  if (AnimateTextBlcokFontColor.GetCurrentState() ==
System.Windows.Media.Animation.ClockState.Stopped)
    AnimateTextBlcokFontColor.Begin();
  else
    AnimateTextBlcokFontColor.Stop();
}
```

When you run the application and click anywhere on the screen, you get a nice effect, which would have taken a lot more code if authored purely in the XNA Framework. Note that you can click anywhere to generate the tap event. Remember that for the current configuration on the TextBlock, height and

527

width are not configured, resulting in the TextBlock essentially filling the entire Xaml page, as well as the entire screen at runtime (most of the control is transparent, except the text). So when you run the project, anytime you touch the screen, you fire TouchPanel events in the XNA Framework *and* the MouseLeftButtonDown event for the TextBlock.

To fix this, configure a height and width on the TextBlock so that it looks like this in Xaml:

```
<TextBlock Name="GestureStatus" Text="Gesture Type Here"
    FontSize="48" FontFamily="Algerian" Width="468" Height="64"
    MouseLeftButtonDown="GestureStatus_MouseLeftButtonDown" />
```

Running the application results in some interesting behavior. Now when you tap the screen, it no longer fires the MouseLeftButtonDown event; however, the touch area where you must tap to start/stop the Storyboard is not the same location where the TextBlock is drawn. Figure 8-17 illustrates the situation.

Design-Time Position   **Run-Time Behavior**

Figure 8-17. Disconnect between touch input and draw location.

If you change the UIElementRender to load the Grid and reposition the GestureStatus TextBlock to the top, it works fine but then you create overdraw for the entire page, which could impact performance. It may not matter depending on the application but is something to consider for a more demanding application.

Give the Grid control a name of XamlGrid and update the code to create the UIElementRenderer control:

```
xamlRenderer = new UIElementRenderer(
  XamlGrid,
  (int)XamlGrid.ActualWidth, (int)XamlGrid.ActualHeight);
```

Next change the draw location in OnDraw Vector2.Zero:

```
if (xamlRenderer != null  && GestureStatus.Text != "")
{
  xamlRenderer.Render();
  spriteBatch.Draw(xamlRenderer.Texture, Vector2.Zero, Color.White);
}
```

Another option to work around this issue of input at one part of the screen but rendering at another part of the screen at runtime is to revert to drawing only the GestureStatus TextBlock to remove the overdraw and position the control at design-time in Silverlight at the same location as where it will be drawn at run-time.

One option is to choose to just use XNA Framework touch input because we need to let the user manipulate the stickman via the TouchPanel input. Remove the MouseLeftButtonDown event so that the GestureStatus TextBlock Xaml looks like this:

```
<TextBlock Name="GestureStatus" Text="Gesture Type Here"
  FontSize="48" FontFamily="Algerian" />
```

To test for TouchPanel touches, first create a bounding box for the xamlRenderer in OnNavigateTo:

```
xamlRendererRect =
  new Microsoft.Xna.Framework.Rectangle(
    (int)spriteFontDrawLocation.X, (int)spriteFontDrawLocation.Y,
    (int)GestureStatus.ActualWidth,
    (int)GestureStatus.ActualHeight);
```

Next we need to modify the ProcessTouchInput method to check to see if the user touched the area where the UIElementRender xamlRenderer will be drawn. We add this code just before the code checks to see if the stickman is touched:

```
if (xamlRendererRect.Contains(touchPoint))
{
  if (AnimateTextBlcokFontColor.GetCurrentState() ==
    System.Windows.Media.Animation.ClockState.Stopped)
    AnimateTextBlcokFontColor.Begin();
  else
    AnimateTextBlcokFontColor.Stop();
}
```

When you run the application, it works as expected. Tap on the text to enable / disable the Storyboard animation. Using the TouchPanel is fine in this instance because the Xaml rendered by the UIElementRenderer control is fine; it contains a single control that runs the animation. If there were multiple controls that needed individual input, you should stick to using Silverlight input for the Silverlight controls and position them correctly on the screen so that it matches the position at runtime.

As you can see, combining Silverlight and XNA Framework enables you to use the best of both worlds when rendering your user experience. This section took you through some of the considerations for taking advantage of the UIElementRenderer and how layout affects its behavior. In the next section we cover how to use shared graphics across pages.

Shared Graphics with Page Navigation

In this sample I demonstrate how to show XNA Framework graphics in the application background while navigating between pages. This technique would be useful if you wanted to have an animated application background, possibly in 3D, for your application.

We start with a standard Windows Phone project and add two additional pages, Page2.xaml and Page3.xaml. We then edit the pages in Expression Blend so that clicking text on MainPage.xaml navigates to Page2.xaml, and Page2.xaml has a TextBlock that navigates to Page3.xaml. Navigation between pages uses the NavigateToPageAction Behavior configured via Expression Blend.

Background Graphics Infrastructure Classes

For this sample, we need to have the XNA Framework drawing portion exist throughout the application lifetime, surviving page transitions. The application does not have any XNA Framework support, so we will now add support for shared graphics manually to help you see exactly how it works. First add references to these three assemblies:

```
Microsoft.Xna.Framework;
Microsoft.Xna.Framework.Graphics;
Microsoft.Xna.Framework.Interop
```

We need to create two classes for the sample. One will be a base page named RichBackgroundBasePage, and the other will be a class named RichBackgroundRenderer that will enable shared graphics, draw the background, and maintain state / content between page transitions. The application implements the IApplicationService and IApplicationLifetimeAware interfaces in order to maintain state across the application.

Lifetime Aware RichBackgroundRenderer Class

i've covered the IApplicationService and IApplicationLifetimeAware interfaces in Chapter 2 already, but to summarize these interfaces allow you to perform actions when the application loads and when the application exits. In IApplicationLifetimeAware.Started shared graphics are enabled and a ContentManager is created. Update and Draw methods are created as well but not a GameTimer, which we explain in a bit. Listing 8-9 has the full source code of RichBackgroundRenderer.

Listing 8-9. *RichBackgroundRenderer Code File*

```
using System;
using System.Windows;
using Microsoft.Xna.Framework;
using Microsoft.Xna.Framework.Content;
using Microsoft.Xna.Framework.Graphics;

namespace SharedGraphicsBackground.helper
{
    //Be sure to add this class to App.xaml in the <Application.ApplicationLifetimeObjects>
```

```
//element after the graphics adapter is created
public class RichBackgroundRenderer : IApplicationService, IApplicationLifetimeAware
{
  public static RichBackgroundRenderer Current { get; private set; }

  //Constructor
  public RichBackgroundRenderer()
  {
    //There can be only one
    if (null != Current)
      throw new InvalidOperationException();

    Current = this;
  }

  public void Update(TimeSpan elapsedTime, TimeSpan totalTime)
  {
    //Rich background cotent game loop update code goes here
  }

  public void Draw()
  {
    //Rich background content game loop draw code goes here
  }

  #region IApplicationService Implementation
  void IApplicationService.StartService(ApplicationServiceContext context)
  {

  }

  void IApplicationService.StopService()
  {

  }
  #endregion

  #region IApplicationLifetimeAware
  //Implemented
  void IApplicationLifetimeAware.Exited()
  {
    //clean up
    SharedGraphicsDeviceManager.Current.GraphicsDevice.SetSharingMode(false);
  }

  void IApplicationLifetimeAware.Exiting()
  {

  }

  //Implemented
  void IApplicationLifetimeAware.Started()
```

```
    {
      SharedGraphicsDeviceManager.Current.GraphicsDevice.SetSharingMode(true);

      //Load rich background content
      ContentManager content = (Application.Current as App).Content;

    }

    void IApplicationLifetimeAware.Starting()
    {

    }
    #endregion;
}
```

Now that we have our Lifetime aware class, we next create the base page class for our Silverlight pages.

RichBackground Base Page Class

The RichBackgroundBasePage inherits from the PhoneApplicationPage class. Its purpose is to put the XNA Framework shared graphics drawing code in a base class so that the XAML page that inherits from it just has the Silverlight page code.

The base page class manages a GameTimer class instance and a UIElementRenderer class instance. Same as in the previous shared graphics samples, the GameTimer instance is started in the OnNavigateTo method and stopped in the OnNavigateFrom method.

In RichBackgroundBasePage.OnNavigatedTo, the base page's LayoutUpdated event is wired to RichBackgroundBasePage.LayoutUpdated. This allows the base page class to know when to create a new UIElementRenderer if the size changes for the XAML being rendered by the UIElementRenderer.

In the GameTimer's Draw and Update events, the RichBackgroundBasePage obtains a reference to the RichBackgroundRenderer via the static property Current using this code to call Update as an example:

```
RichBackgroundRenderer.Current.Update(e.ElapsedTime, e.TotalTime);
```

In RichBackgroundBasePage.OnDraw the Silverlight UI is rendered using the uiElementRenderer to essentially draw the entire Silverlight page. Listing 8-10 has the code.

Listing 8-10. RichBackgroundBasePage Class File

```
using System;
using System.ComponentModel;
using Microsoft.Phone.Controls;
using Microsoft.Xna.Framework;
using Microsoft.Xna.Framework.Graphics;

namespace SharedGraphicsBackground.helper
{
  public class RichBackgroundBasePage : PhoneApplicationPage
  {
    GameTimer gameTimer;
    SpriteBatch spriteBatch;
```

```csharp
UIElementRenderer uiElementRenderer;
GraphicsDevice graphicsDevice;

public RichBackgroundBasePage()
{
  if (!DesignerProperties.IsInDesignTool)
  {
    graphicsDevice = SharedGraphicsDeviceManager.Current.GraphicsDevice;
    spriteBatch = new SpriteBatch(graphicsDevice);
    // Create a timer for this page
    gameTimer = new GameTimer();
    gameTimer.UpdateInterval = TimeSpan.FromTicks(333333);
    gameTimer.Update += OnUpdate;
    gameTimer.Draw += OnDraw;
  }
}

private void OnUpdate(object sender, GameTimerEventArgs e)
{
  RichBackgroundRenderer.Current.Update(e.ElapsedTime, e.TotalTime);
}

private void OnDraw(object sender, GameTimerEventArgs e)
{
  SharedGraphicsDeviceManager.Current.GraphicsDevice.Clear(
    Microsoft.Xna.Framework.Color.CornflowerBlue);

  // Render the Silverlight page to a texture
  uiElementRenderer.Render();
  RichBackgroundRenderer.Current.Draw();

  // Draw the Silverlight page generated texture
  spriteBatch.Begin();
  spriteBatch.Draw(uiElementRenderer.Texture, Vector2.Zero,
    Microsoft.Xna.Framework.Color.White);
  spriteBatch.End();
}

private void OnLayoutUpdated(object sender, EventArgs e)
{
  // As before, the rendered XAML must have a width and height greater than 0
  if (ActualWidth > 0 && ActualHeight > 0)
  {
    //Check to see if the XAML to be rendered has changed size
    if (uiElementRenderer == null ||
        uiElementRenderer.Texture.Width != (int)ActualWidth ||
        uiElementRenderer.Texture.Height != (int)ActualHeight)
    {
      //Only create a new UIElementRenderer if necessary
      if (uiElementRenderer != null && uiElementRenderer.Texture != null)
        uiElementRenderer.Texture.Dispose();
      uiElementRenderer = new UIElementRenderer(
```

533

```
              this, (int)ActualWidth, (int)ActualHeight);
        }
      }
    }

    protected override void OnNavigatedTo(System.Windows.Navigation.NavigationEventArgs e)
    {
      if (!DesignerProperties.IsInDesignTool)
      {
        // Hook the LayoutUpdated to know when the page has calculated its layout
        LayoutUpdated += OnLayoutUpdated;
        gameTimer.Start();
      }
      base.OnNavigatedTo(e);
    }

    protected override void OnNavigatedFrom(System.Windows.Navigation.NavigationEventArgs e)
    {
      if (!DesignerProperties.IsInDesignTool)
      {
        gameTimer.Stop();
      }
      base.OnNavigatedFrom(e);
    }
  }
}
```

In the next section we wire these classes into our standard Silverlight project manually.

Silverlight Project Modifications

We now have the infrastructure ready to modify the Silverlight application to add shared graphics. We need to create instances of the SharedGraphicsRenderer and RichBackgroundRenderer objects in App.xaml. First bring in the necessary namespaces with this code added to the Application element in App.xaml:

```
xmlns:xna="clr-namespace:Microsoft.Xna.Framework;assembly=Microsoft.Xna.Framework.Interop"
xmlns:sgb="clr-namespace:SharedGraphicsBackground.helper"
```

The instances are created in the ApplicationLifetimeObjects collection:

```
<xna:SharedGraphicsDeviceManager />
<sgb:RichBackgroundRenderer />
```

■ **Caution** If you configure SetSharingMode to True but do not call GameTimer.Start(), your application will hang on the splash screen. Do not enable shared graphics unless you plan on using a GameTimer as well.

A large amount of code must be added to App.xaml.cs to initialize the XNA Framework in Silverlight. The best way to proceed is to simply copy the App class from a Silverlight+XNA Framework project template application. In App.xaml.cs add these using clauses as well:

```
using Microsoft.Xna.Framework;
using Microsoft.Xna.Framework.Content;
using Microsoft.Xna.Framework.Graphics;
```

We next copy over the `AppServiceProvider` class from a Silverlight+XNA Framework project template to the `SharedGraphicsBackground` project as well. As background, the `AppServicesProvider` class is part of the standards shared graphics project template. It provides access to pre-compiled XNA Framework assets to the `ContentManager` instance.

Fix up the namespace if needed to match the target project. Compile the project and no errors should be present. If you try to run it the application will hang on the splash screen. We need to modify the pages to inherit from the `RichBackgroundBasePage` to add a `GameTimer` to the project.

Change the `phone:PhoneApplicationPage` to `sgb:RichBackgroundBasePage` after adding this namespace to each page:

```
xmlns:sgb="clr-namespace:SharedGraphicsBackground.helper"
```

Finally, edit each page's code behind to inherit from `RichBackgroundBasePage` instead of `PhoneApplicationPage` class. With all of these modifications completed, compile and run the application. You will see that the system tray displays and the Silverlight page is drawn correctly and the pages navigate with the plain cornflower-blue background.

Create the Content Projects

You now can modify the `RichBackgroundRenderer` class to load up content, modify the `Update`, and Draw methods to have XNA Framework content render in the background of the application. Since we started with a regular Silverlight application we don't have a separate content project, which is added now.

To add a content project to the solution, right-click the Chapter 8 solution, select Add ➤ New Project, select the XNA Game Studio 4.0 folder and then Empty Content Project (4.0), enter the name `SharedGraphicsBackground` (Content), and click OK. If you try to add a project reference from the `SharedGraphicsBackground` project to the newly created content project, the `SharedGraphicsBackground` (Content) project is not visible in the project list. We must go through an intermediate library project.

Add an intermediary library project to the solution by right-clicking the Chapter 8 solution and selecting Add | New Project. Then select Windows Phone Game Library (4.0), enter the name `SharedGraphicsBackgroundLib`, and click OK. Add a reference to the new library in the `SharedGraphicsBackground` Silverlight project by right-clicking on References, selecting the `SharedGraphicsBackgroundLib` project, and click OK.

The content project has not actually been linked to the `SharedGraphicsBackground` project yet. To do so, right-click on the `SharedGraphicsLib` project, select Add Content Project Reference, choose the `SharedGraphicsBackground` (Content) project, and click OK. Next, add a folder named "textures" and add book.tga texture to it. Load content as before using this line of code in the `RichBackgroundRenderer.IApplicationLifetimeAware.Started` method:

```
bookTexture = content.Load<Texture2D>("textures/book");
```

Modified RichBackgroundRenderer Class

In this section, we modify the RichBackgroundRenderer class to draw an image of the book cover in the background and animate down the screen to demonstrate that the rendering survives page transitions. First we add these fields to the top of the class to support rendering:

```
GraphicsDevice graphicsDevice;
SpriteBatch spriteBatch;

//book graphic fields
Texture2D bookTexture;
Vector2 bookPosition;
Vector2 bookVelocity;
```

Next we modify the Update and Draw methods to perform the rendering and simple animation. Here is the code:

```
public void Update(TimeSpan elapsedTime, TimeSpan totalTime)
{
  //Rich background content game loop update code goes here
  bookPosition += bookVelocity;
  if (bookPosition.Y > 800d)
  {
    bookPosition.X = graphicsDevice.Viewport.Width / 2 - bookTexture.Width / 2;
    bookPosition.Y = -bookTexture.Height;
  }
}

public void Draw()
{
  //Rich background content game loop draw code goes here
  spriteBatch.Begin();
  spriteBatch.Draw(bookTexture, bookPosition, Color.White);
  spriteBatch.End();
}
```

Figure 8-18 shows the animation flowing through after navigating to page 2.

Figure 8-18. Animated background surviving page transitions

While the animation is simple, it demonstrates how you can present unique user interfaces in Silverlight applications that can take advantage of XNA Framework graphics to provide interesting graphic effects that continue between Silverlight page navigation transitions.

Conclusion

This chapter covered extensively the process of building out the game play leveraging existing samples like the Game Screen Game Management and the Sprite Sheet processor samples to build out a 2D game. In the next chapter we focus on making enhancements to this game such as explosions for collisions as well as important housekeeping items such as adding support for saving and loading the game, as well as the very important tombstoning support.

This chapter also covered XNA Framework shared graphics available with Windows Phone OS 7.1. I demonstrated three scenarios, a page dedicated to XNA Framework rendering without any Silverlight rendering. I next demonstrated mixing Silverlight rendering with XNA Framework rendering. Finally I demonstrated XNA Framework rendering in the background that survives Silverlight page navigations.

In the next chapter you will update the AlienShooter game to include a particle system for smoke and explosions as well as other enhancements. Chapter 9 also covers 3D game development, including how it can be combined with augmented reality scenarios.

■ ■ ■

Advanced XNA Framework Development

In this chapter, we continue with our discussion of game development. Chapter 1 provided a basic overview of game development. In Chapter 8, we took the sample code from Chapter 1 and turned it into a structured 2D game, leveraging the AppHub Game Screen Management sample to provide a menu system and a `GameScreen` class to help manage the various screens that users expect to have, such as a main menu, options menu, and the game play screen. We covered 2D animation and encapsulated our game play using a `GameObject` class to represent the enemy alien ships, missiles, and the hero ship.

In this chapter we add a few key enhancements to the AlienShooter game. We take a copy of the code from the Chapter 8 solution and add support for saving and loading the game, as well as tombstoning support. We wrap up with a basic particle system to simulate explosions when the hero ship shoots down an alien enemy ship.

We discussed in Chapter 3 and 4 how developers can call nonvisual APIs across frameworks where Silverlight can call XNA's Gesture API and XNA can call Silverlight Web APIs. In Windows Phone 7.5, Microsoft added the capability to combine rendering technologies as well. In this chapter I cover how to render Silverlight and XNA UI on the same surface, opening up many unique possibilities for application developers.

We then shift gears with an introduction to 3D game development, covering key 3D concepts, a little bit of 3D math, and then the 3D programming model provided by XNA Game Studio. We follow this with an exploration of augmented reality possibilities by combining 3D rendering with the camera sensor and shared graphic rendering.

AlienShooter Enhancements

In this section we add support for functionality you would expect to see if this was a real Windows Phone game. We first implement how to load and save game state. We modify the main menu game screen to have both New Game and Resume Game menu items in the event that previous game state is present.

We next implement tombstoning support so that the user is restored to the main menu screen and has a chance to click Resume to restart game play. The last section covers how to create a basic particle system that simulates explosions when a hero ship missile collides with an alien enemy spaceship.

Load and Save Game State

For our game, we automatically save game state when the user backs out of the GameplayScreen with a game in progress. The main menu screen is modified to include both New Game and Resume Game menu options that will resume an existing game if saved state is present. Automatic save keeps things simple and is a typical state management approach for many game developers.

We set about modifying the `MainMenuScreen` class, renaming the `playGameMenuEntry` object to `newGameMenuEntry` and adding another MenuEntry named `resumeGameMenuEntry`. Here is the modified constructor `MainMenuScreen()`:

```
public MainMenuScreen()
  : base("Main Menu")
{
  // Create our menu entries.
  MenuEntry newGameMenuEntry = new MenuEntry("New Game");
  MenuEntry optionsMenuEntry = new MenuEntry("Game Options");
  // Hook up menu event handlers.
  newGameMenuEntry.Selected += newGameMenuEntrySelected;
  optionsMenuEntry.Selected += OptionsMenuEntrySelected;
  // Add entries to the menu.
  MenuEntries.Add(newGameMenuEntry);
  MenuEntries.Add(optionsMenuEntry);

  // Only display resume game menu option
  //if saved state is present.
  using (IsolatedStorageFile gameStorage = IsolatedStorageFile.GetUserStoreForApplication())
  {
    if (gameStorage.FileExists(AlienShooterStateFileName))
    {
      MenuEntry resumeGameMenuEntry = new MenuEntry("Resume Game");
      resumeGameMenuEntry.Selected += resumeGameMenuEntry_Selected;
      MenuEntries.Add(resumeGameMenuEntry);
    }
  }
}
```

We want to display the Resume Game menu option only when there is game state present, so in the MainMenu there is a `FileExists` check to determine if game state is present. We add a `using System.IO.IsolatedStorage` statement to the top of `MainMenuScreen.cs` as well as a constant declaration of the state filename to wire things up:

```
const string AlienShooterStateFileName = "AlienShooter.dat";
```

We modify the new-game-selected event handler, named `newGameMenuEntrySelected`, to delete any saved game state since a new game is desired:

```
void newGameMenuEntrySelected(object sender, PlayerIndexEventArgs e)
{
  //
  using (IsolatedStorageFile gameStorage = IsolatedStorageFile.GetUserStoreForApplication())
  {
    if (gameStorage.FileExists(AlienShooterStateFileName))
    {
      gameStorage.DeleteFile(AlienShooterStateFileName);
    }
  }
```

```
LoadingScreen.Load(ScreenManager, true, e.PlayerIndex,
                    new GameplayScreen());
}
```

This sets things up for the GameplayScreen to load saved state or start a new game depending on what option is chosen in the MainMenuScreen UI. In the GameplayScreen object we create two new public methods to load and save state. For load state, we do the following:

- Check for saved state; if not present, initialize the variables as before.

- If saved state is present, restore saved state and begin game play.

To save state, we use a System.IO.StreamWriter object. We don't use object serialization, because we need to instantiate the GameObject classes normally, just like when LoadContent is called. Instead, we simply save off the important state values to a text file in Isolated Storage such as the Position and Velocity vector values, the status board game score and remaining lives, and so on. The SaveAlienShooterState method always deletes the file first before saving. Also, the method does not save state if the game is over. Listing 9-1 shows the GameplayScreen.SaveAlienShooterState method.

Listing 9-1. GameplayScreen.SaveAlienShooterState

```
public void SaveAlienShooterState()
{
  //Only save game if not GameOver
  using (IsolatedStorageFile gameStorage =
    IsolatedStorageFile.GetUserStoreForApplication())
  {
    //Overwrite existing saved game state
    if (gameStorage.FileExists(AlienShooterStateFileName))
    {
      gameStorage.DeleteFile(AlienShooterStateFileName);
    }
    if (!statusBoard.GameOver)
    {
      using (IsolatedStorageFileStream fs =
        gameStorage.OpenFile(AlienShooterStateFileName,
                            System.IO.FileMode.Create))
      {
        using (StreamWriter streamWriter = new StreamWriter(fs))
        {
          //Only serialize interesting state
          //Other state MUST be initialized each time
          streamWriter.WriteLine(heroShip.Position.X);
          streamWriter.WriteLine(heroShip.Position.Y);
          streamWriter.WriteLine(heroShip.Velocity.X);
          streamWriter.WriteLine(heroShip.Velocity.Y);
          streamWriter.WriteLine(statusBoard.Score);
          streamWriter.WriteLine(statusBoard.Lives);
          for (int i = 0; i < maxEnemies; i++)
          {
            streamWriter.WriteLine(enemies[i].Alive);
            streamWriter.WriteLine(enemies[i].Position.X);
            streamWriter.WriteLine(enemies[i].Position.Y);
```

```
                    streamWriter.WriteLine(enemies[i].Velocity.X);
                    streamWriter.WriteLine(enemies[i].Velocity.Y);
                }
            streamWriter.Flush();
            streamWriter.Close();
            }
        }
    }
  }
}
```

The `GameplayScreen.LoadAlienShooterState` method instantiates the `GameObjects` and classes, that is, the `heroShip.statusBoard GameStatus` object, and the `enemies` alien ship collection. This code was cut from the `GameplayScreen.LoadContent` method and pasted into the `GameplayScreen.LoadAlienShooterState` method shown in Listing 9-2.

Listing 9-2. *GameplayScreen.LoadAlienShooterState Method*

```
public void LoadAlienShooterState()
{
  using (IsolatedStorageFile gameStorage = IsolatedStorageFile.GetUserStoreForApplication())
  {
    //Initialize all objects as before
    enemies = new List<AlienGameObject>();
    for (int i = 0; i < maxEnemies; i++)
    {
      enemies.Add(new AlienGameObject(alienShooterSpriteSheet, "spaceship", screenRect));
    }

    //Initialize Player Object
    heroShip = new UserGameObject(alienShooterSpriteSheet, "heroship", screenRect,
maxMissiles);
    heroShip.Position = new Vector2(screenRect.Width / 2, 720);
    heroShip.LoadContent(content);
    //Initialize Status Board
    statusBoard = new GameStatusBoard(gameFont);
    statusBoard.LoadContent(content);

    //Set saved state on objects
    if (gameStorage.FileExists(AlienShooterStateFileName))
    {
      using (IsolatedStorageFileStream fs =
      gameStorage.OpenFile(AlienShooterStateFileName, System.IO.FileMode.Open))
      {
        using (StreamReader streamReader = new StreamReader(fs))
        {
          heroShip.Position = new Vector2(
            (float)Convert.ToDouble(streamReader.ReadLine()),
            (float)Convert.ToDouble(streamReader.ReadLine()));
          heroShip.Velocity = new Vector2(
            (float)Convert.ToDouble(streamReader.ReadLine()),
            (float)Convert.ToDouble(streamReader.ReadLine()));
```

```
    statusBoard.Score = Convert.ToInt32(streamReader.ReadLine());
    statusBoard.Lives = Convert.ToInt32(streamReader.ReadLine());
    for (int i = 0; i < maxEnemies; i++)
    {
      enemies[i].Alive = Convert.ToBoolean(streamReader.ReadLine());
      enemies[i].Position = new Vector2(
        (float)Convert.ToDouble(streamReader.ReadLine()),
        (float)Convert.ToDouble(streamReader.ReadLine()));
      enemies[i].Velocity = new Vector2(
        (float)Convert.ToDouble(streamReader.ReadLine()),
        (float)Convert.ToDouble(streamReader.ReadLine()));
    }
    streamReader.Close();
  }
 }
 }
 }
}
```

The Save and Load code isn't the most elegant code you will ever see but it is simple and works fine. With this code in place, when you hit the Back hardware button when playing the game, you get a Resume menu item. Figure 9-1 shows the updated `MainMenuScreen` class UI.

Figure 9-1. *Updated main menu screen with Resume Game menu option*

If you play the game until all of your lives are consumed and then hit the Back button, the Resume Game menu option is not present, because there isn't any saved state.

One issue that remains is, if you are playing the game and then hit the Start button and then the Back button, the game resets to a new game on the GameplayScreen UI. What we want to happen is for state to be saved and the game to resume back on the main menu screen, so that the user has a chance to get ready to play and then tap the Resume Game menu option. We cover how to implement tombstone support in the next section.

Tombstone Support

Adding tombstone support to your XNA Framework game is different from adding tombstone support in Silverlight. In Silverlight, the Deactivated and Activated events only fire when tombstoning and returning from tombstoning respectively. In Silverlight, these events do not fire when launching (the Launching event) nor when closing (the Closing event).

In the XNA Framework, the OnDeactivation (tombstoning) and OnActiviation (returning from tombstone) events also fire when launching and closing the game, making it difficult to distinguish tombstoning events from regular launching/closing events.

To detect tombstoning events, you can use the PhoneApplicationService class available in the Microsoft.Phone.dll assembly. You must also add a reference to System.Windows.dll as well, or a compilation error will occur. Add a using Microsoft.Phone.Shell statement to the top of AlienShooterGame.cs (the default name is game1.cs in a new project). In the AlienShooterGame() constructor (the default name is Game1() in a new project), add this code at the end to hook the Activated and Deactivated events:

```
//Implement tombstoning support globally if managing
//multiple state objects across game gamescreens
PhoneApplicationService.Current.Activated += AlienGame_Activated;
PhoneApplicationService.Current.Deactivated += AlienGame_Deactivated;
```

You can then implement tombstoning for the application in the corresponding event handlers in AlienShooterGame.cs:

```
void AlienGame_Activated(object sender, ActivatedEventArgs e)
{
  //Globally handle return from tombstoning here
}

void AlienGame_Deactivated(object sender, DeactivatedEventArgs e)
{
  //Globally handle tombstoning here
}
```

Where to store game state? As with Silverlight, you can store transitional state in the PhoneApplicationService.Current.State Dictionary object, as in this example:

```
PhoneApplicationService.Current.State[enemies] = enemies;
```

The other bit of information available to you is the PhoneApplicationService.Current.StartupMode property, which can have a value of StartupMode.Launch or StartupMode.Activate. This can be useful if you need to detect whether starting up a new application instance (StartupMode.Launch) or returning from tombstone (StartupMode.Activate) down within the game screens. Note that there isn't a corresponding way to check for deactivation. Only the `PhoneApplicationService.Deactivated` can help there.

For the AlienShooter game, we add code in the `AlienGame_Deactivated` method to find the `GameplayScreen` and call the `SaveAlienShooterState` method. Here is the updated code:

```
void AlienGame_Deactivated(object sender, DeactivatedEventArgs e)
{
  //Globally handle  tombstoning here
  GameScreen[] screens = screenManager.GetScreens();
  foreach (GameScreen screen in screens)
    if (screen is GameplayScreen)
    {
      (screen as GameplayScreen).SaveAlienShooterState();
    }
}
```

We update the `AlienGame_Activated` method to load the MainMenuScreen upon restore from tombstoning, as shown here:

```
void AlienGame_Activated(object sender, ActivatedEventArgs e)
{
  //Globally handle return from tombstoning here
  if (!screenManager.DeserializeState())
  {
    // Activate the first screens.
    // Resume at Main Menu so that user isn't caught off guard
    screenManager.AddScreen(new BackgroundScreen(), null);
    screenManager.AddScreen(new MainMenuScreen(), null);
  }
}
```

There isn't anything else to show for game save/load or tombstoning. Run the code and play around with the functionality, including tombstoning the game. As you will see, the functionally works pretty well and has the feel of a "real" Windows Phone game.

One thing that is missing from the game play is explosions when the missiles collide with the enemy alien space ships. A particle system can assist with implementing "random" looking stuff flying around like you would expect if something is blowing up or smoking from a missile strike.

Particle System

A particle system randomly generates points or small area sprites with a random velocity and rotation, as well as a lifetime, such that the points fly out and then disappear much like you see in Hollywood movie effects. Particle systems can be very simple or extremely sophisticated, capable of generating water effects, fire, smoke, and explosions. AppHub includes a simple particle system that generates smoke and fire for explosions or to show damage. Here is a link to the sample:

`http://create.msdn.com/en-US/education/catalog/sample/particle`

Modifying AlienShooter

In the **AlienShooter** project we add a folder named **ParticleSystem** and copy the following files from the AppHub Particle Sample into the new folder in the **AlienShooter** project, updating the namespace to **AlienShooter.ParticleSystem**:

- ParticleSystem.cs
- Particle.cs
- ExplosionSmokeParticleSystem.cs
- ExplosionParticleSystem.cs
- SmokePlumeParticleSystem.cs

The Particle System classes sample have some ties to the game project so the classes are refactored a bit to fit within the AlienShooter project. The **ParticleSystem** classes are dependent on the **SpriteBatch** being part of the **Game class** instance. In our case, the **Game.Components** collection in the **AlienShooterGame** instance is accessed to grab the **screenManager** object, which then makes **ScreenManager.SpriteBatch** accessible to the particle system classes:

```
((ScreenManager)game.Components[0]).SpriteBatch.Draw
```

Notice that the assumption is that the **ScreenManager** is the first **Component** added with the index of 0 in the **Components** collection, so it is something to be aware of.

Another modification required is to add the **smoke.bmp** and **explosions.png** content files to a new folder named **ParticleSystem** in the **AlienShooter** content project. The path values in the Particle System class files are updated by adding **ParticleSystem/** path info in front of filenames so that the **ContentManager** can find them.

The random number-related helper functions were moved from the game class into the **ParticleSystem** classes directly, helping to encapsulate the functionality better within the classes themselves. Another option is to make the random number helper members a part of the **ScreenManager** object, which could be useful in other situations when a **GameScreen** instance may need a random number for game functionality. Either way, once all of the housekeeping updates to the code are completed, we can now implement explosions and smoke for the AlienShooter game.

Adding Explosions and Smoke to AlienShooter

Once all of the modifications are completed to incorporate the AppHub Particle Sample code into the **AlienShooter** project, it is brain-dead simple to add support for explosions and smoke plume in the game. In **AlienShooterGame.cs**, three additional fields are added:

```
ExplosionSmokeParticleSystem explosionSmokeParticleSystem;
ExplosionParticleSystem explosionParticleSystem;
SmokePlumeParticleSystem smokePlumeParticleSystem;
```

The first two are for the explosion, one for the smoke, the other for the fire. The third field added is for the smoke plume. In the **AlienShooterGame** class constructor, the particle system classes are instantiated and then added to the Game.Components collection:

```
explosionSmokeParticleSystem = new ExplosionSmokeParticleSystem(this, 2);
Components.Add(explosionSmokeParticleSystem);
```

```
explosionParticleSystem = new ExplosionParticleSystem(this, 1);
Components.Add(explosionParticleSystem);
smokePlumeParticleSystem = new SmokePlumeParticleSystem(this, 8);
Components.Add(smokePlumeParticleSystem);
```

The numbers represent the number of particles. Running on a device, you will see that if you set the number too high it will directly affect frame rate and game performance can suffer.

Now that we have our particle system `DrawableComponents` configured, it is time to add explosions and smoke plume support to the `GameplayScreen`. We will add an explosion (both smoke and fire) each time an enemy alien ship is shot down. We will add a smoke plume to the hero ship when a life is lost due to a kamikaze enemy alien ship collision. Since this involves collision detection, you are right to guess that the code to draw the explosions and smoke is added there. Listing 9-3 has the updated `CheckForCollisions` method.

Listing 9-3. *GameplayScreen.LoadAlienShooterState Method*

```
private void CheckForCollisions()
{
  //Checking for two major collisions
  //1 - Has an in flight missile intersected an alien spaceship - score 5 pts
  for (int i = 0; i < heroShip.MaxNumberofMissiles; i++)
    if (heroShip.Missiles[i].Alive)
      for (int j = 0; j < maxEnemies; j++)
        if ((enemies[j].Alive) &&
            (enemies[j].BoundingRect.Intersects(heroShip.Missiles[i].BoundingRect)))
        {
          statusBoard.Score += 5;
          //Display Explosion

((ExplosionSmokeParticleSystem)ScreenManager.Game.Components[1]).AddParticles(enemies[j].Posit
ion);

((ExplosionParticleSystem)ScreenManager.Game.Components[2]).AddParticles(enemies[j].Position);
          enemies[j].ResetGameObject();
          heroShip.Missiles[i].ResetGameObject();
        }
  //2 - Has an alien spaceship intersected the hero ship - deduct a life
  for (int j = 0; j < maxEnemies; j++)
    if ((enemies[j].Alive) && (enemies[j].Position.Y > 600) &&
        (enemies[j].BoundingRect.Intersects(heroShip.BoundingRect)))
    {
      statusBoard.Lives -= 1;

((SmokePlumeParticleSystem)ScreenManager.Game.Components[3]).AddParticles(heroShip.Position);
      for (int i = 0; i < maxEnemies; i++)
        enemies[i].ResetGameObject();
      for (int i = 0; i < heroShip.MaxNumberofMissiles; i++)
        heroShip.Missiles[i].ResetGameObject();
    }
}
```

Essentially, the desired particle system `DrawableComponent` instance is grabbed from the `AlienShooterGame.Components` collection and the correct position Vector2 is passed into the `AddParticles` method. Here is the call to draw a smoke plume at the hero ship's Position property:

```
((SmokePlumeParticleSystem)ScreenManager.Game.Components[3]).AddParticles(heroShip.Position);
```

Note the use of the number index. If the value is incorrect you will get an invalid cast exception at runtime. Figure 9-2 shows an explosion and smoke plume in action.

Figure 9-2. *Explosion and smoke plume*

I won't go into the actual particle system sample code; I'll leave that as an exercise for the reader, but you will see that it isn't terribly complicated code, which is pretty amazing given the robust effects that are provided. If anything, you may want to simplify the code in a real game to minimize performance impact. Try running the game on a device and you will see the frame rate drop occasionally if too many explosions occur at the same time. In the next section we convert the AlienShooter project to use XNA Framework Shared Graphics to render parts of the UI with Silverlight, specifically the menu and the HUD.

AlienShooter with Silverlight

In this section we port AlienShooter to a shared graphics rendering project. Create a new project named AlienShooterSL based on the "Windows Phone Silverlight and XNA Application" template. The

AlienShooter in Chapter 9 leverages the Game Management sample from AppHub. Begin updating it for Silverlight in the AlienShooterSL project by copying over the assets except for the Game Management assets, since Silverlight will be our menu.

We next bring over all of the code into the AlienShooterSL project except for the GameScreen and ScreenManager classes. Bring over the InputState class in the GameManagement folder, as it is a convenient means to handle input. We fix up the namespaces and remove the code specific to game management. One limitation that jumps out is the lack of support for GameObject instances, which is used by the ParticleSystem classes. To work around this, we pass in the main GameTimer object from the game page named AlienShooterGamePage.xaml, located in the screens folder, into the constructor for the base class ParticleSystem:

```
protected ParticleSystem(GameTimer timer, int howManyEffects)
{
  this.gameTimer = timer;
  this.howManyEffects = howManyEffects;
  contentManager = contentManager = (Application.Current as App).Content;

  gameTimer.Update += new EventHandler<GameTimerEventArgs>(gameTimer_Update);
  gameTimer.Draw += new EventHandler<GameTimerEventArgs>(gameTimer_Draw);
  Initialize();
  LoadContent();
}
```

When inheriting from GameObject, descendant classes are automatically plugged in to the Update and Draw loop. In the shared graphics rendering version, event handlers are wired up to the main GameTimer instance in the constructor. This plugs the ParticleSystem class and its descendants into the GameTimer game loop.

The other change is to pass in the GameTimerEventArgs class into the Draw and Update methods for GameObjects instead of the GameTime class. Otherwise, in terms of layout and organization, the code migrates over pretty easily, looking more like the Chapter 8 AlienShooter solution without the Game Management code but with the added Particle System intact. Instead we have Silverlight wrapping the game screen to provide UI for functionality like Settings, Menu, and so on.

We update MainPage.xaml with a space background and three text buttons, New Game, Resume Game, and Settings, as shown in Figure 9-3.

Figure 9-3. *The new Silverlight menu*

Create a fake settings page and put it into the screens folder with AlienShooterGamePage.xaml. We then pass a query parameter with a key value of "start" so that the AlienShooterGamePage page can determine whether to start a new game or resume an existing game by processing the query parameter in the OnNavigatedTo method. The query string value is passed into the LoadAlienShooterState method, which actually handles whether to load state or not.

The next modification is to change the HUD display from XNA graphics to Silverlight graphics. Because of the modular nature of the code, almost all of the changes were in the GameStatusBoard object. The one change in the HUD display is that the parameters passed into the constructor changed from a SpriteFont to a UIElement, Height, and Width values. The rest of the changes are internal. Listing 9-4 shows the code leveraging a UIElement Renderer.

Listing 9-4. *GameStatusBoard Class with Silverlight Rendering*

```
using System;
using Microsoft.Devices;
using Microsoft.Xna.Framework;
using Microsoft.Xna.Framework.Audio;
using Microsoft.Xna.Framework.Content;
using Microsoft.Xna.Framework.Graphics;
using System.Windows;
using System.Windows.Controls;
```

```csharp
using System.Windows.Media;

namespace AlienShooterSL.GameObjects
{
  class GameStatusBoard
  {
    UIElementRenderer HUDRenderer;
    private SoundEffect _alienExplosionSoundEffect;
    private SoundEffect _heroShipDamageSoundEffect;
    private VibrateController _vibrateController = VibrateController.Default;
    private TimeSpan _vibrateTimeSpan = TimeSpan.FromMilliseconds(400);
    //Status Board related fields
    private bool _displayMessage;
    private TextBlock _scoreText;
    private TextBlock _messageText;
    private TextBlock _livesText;

    public GameStatusBoard(UIElement element, int width, int height)
    {
      HUDRenderer = new UIElementRenderer(element, width, height);
      _scoreText = ((Grid)element).FindName("ScoreValueText") as TextBlock;
      _messageText = ((Grid)element).FindName("MessageText") as TextBlock;
      _livesText = ((Grid)element).FindName("LivesValueText") as TextBlock;
      Score = 0;
      Lives = 3;
    }

    #region Properties
    private int _score;
    public int Score
    {
      get { return _score; }
      set
      {
        _score = value;
        _scoreText.Text = Convert.ToString(_score);
        if (_alienExplosionSoundEffect != null)
          _alienExplosionSoundEffect.Play();
      }
    }

    private int _lives;
    public int Lives
    {
      get { return _lives; }
      set
      {
        _lives = value;
        if (_heroShipDamageSoundEffect != null)
        {
          _heroShipDamageSoundEffect.Play();
          _vibrateController.Start(_vibrateTimeSpan);
```

```
      }
    }
  }

  public bool GameOver { get; set; }
  #endregion

  #region Methods
  public void LoadContent(ContentManager content)
  {
    _alienExplosionSoundEffect =
      content.Load<SoundEffect>("SoundEffects/Explosion");
    _heroShipDamageSoundEffect =
      content.Load<SoundEffect>("SoundEffects/HeroShipDamage");
  }

  public void Update(GameTimerEventArgs GameTime)
  {
    switch (Score)
    {
      case 50: _displayMessage = true;
        _messageText.Text = "Nice Start!";
        break;
      case 60: _displayMessage = false;
        break;
      case 100: _displayMessage = true;
        _messageText.Text = "Keep It Up!";
        break;
      case 120: _displayMessage = false;
        break;
      default: break;
    }

    switch (Lives)
    {
      case 3: _livesText.Foreground = new SolidColorBrush(Colors.Green);
        _livesText.Text = "3";
        break;
      case 2: _livesText.Foreground = new SolidColorBrush(Colors.Yellow);
        _displayMessage = true;
        _messageText.Text = "Warning!";
        _livesText.Text = "2";
        break;
      case 1: _livesText.Foreground = new SolidColorBrush(Colors.Red);
        _displayMessage = true;
        _messageText.Text = "Danger!";
        _livesText.Text = "1";
        break;
      case 0: _livesText.Foreground = new SolidColorBrush(Colors.Red);
        _displayMessage = true;
        _messageText.Text = "Game Over!";
        _livesText.Text = "0";
```

```
            GameOver = true;
            break;
        }
    }

    public void Draw(GameTimerEventArgs gameTime, SpriteBatch spriteBatch)
    {
        HUDRenderer.Render();
        spriteBatch.Draw(HUDRenderer.Texture,
            Vector2.Zero, Microsoft.Xna.Framework.Color.White);
    }
    #endregion
    }
}
```

Figure 9-4 shows the new Silverlight-based HUD.

Figure 9-4. *Silverlight-based HUD*

This completes the coverage of the AlienShooter sample. What is great about this sample is that you can simply take it in whole, find and replace namespaces if desired to match your game, and essentially rewrite the GameplayScreen class and GameObject descendants to reflect your game logic. Otherwise, the Game Screen Manager, save and load, tombstoning, and particle system effects are available for use in your game immediately, though you will have to customize the actual code to save and load the correct state for your game.

In the next section we completely shift gears and provide an overview of the 3D game development capabilities available within the XNA Framework. The section won't make you a complete expert, but it will provide you with enough knowledge and understanding to dive into 3D game development if you find you cannot resist the allure of matrix mathematics and 3D model manipulation.

3D Game Development

The rest of this chapter covers 3D game development with XNA Game Studio. The goal is to provide you with the knowledge and understanding of how to develop 3D games, covering the fundamental principles, a little bit of 3D math, and the 3D programming model provided by the XNA Framework. In the next section, we cover the fundamentals of 3D development.

▪ **Note** Many of the 2D concepts I have covered so far still apply in 3D game development as well, such as applying velocity, collision detection, and so on. This section focuses on drawing 3D models and some of the additional considerations related to 3D rendering.

3D Game Concepts

Hopefully by now, if you have read this book straight through—or at the very least have read the XNA Framework-related sections in Chapter 1, Chapter 3, and all of Chapter 8—you have a solid understanding of 2D game development. Programming in 2D is similar in process to hand-drawing a cartoon on paper. You can draw a scene in 2D that makes objects appear near or in the background, providing perspective that models the 3D real world. 3D game development results in the same 2D projection on a flat 2D screen, however, the path to rendering is very different.

▪ **Tip** It is not possible to cover 3D game development in a single chapter, so I recommend *Windows Phone Game Development* (Apress, 2010) by Adam Dawes if you want to explore 3D game development in more detail.

In 3D game development, you create a 3D world using wireframe models with a skin over the wireframe that is a 2D texture. The view into the world is similar to viewing the real world behind a camera, where the front aspect of an object is visible and the back of an object is not; however, the back of an object still exists. As an example, Figure 9-5 shows a sample 3D rendering named Pac Man displayed in Caligari trueSpace with views from different angles.

Figure 9-5. *3D model rendered in Caligari trueSpace*

You can spin, rotate, and zoom in on the model to get a different view of the environment. Just as in the real world, any view you pick is translated into a 2D rendering. However, with 3D game development, as hardware grows more powerful, the 3D model and rendering comes closer and closer to the real world. With the power of matrix mathematics, 3D vectors, and algorithms, a game developer can fly around a 3D model of an imaginary world, resulting in an immersive experience.

Modeling the Real World

For 3D game development, you mathematically create the camera view on the loaded model. As a user manipulates a game controller or tilts a phone in a mobile game experience, the `Accelerometer` readings can be measured and the movement is translated to affect the camera view in the model.

A 3D world can be quite expansive, so much so that trying to render an entire world model will bog down even the most powerful graphics cards. Just like viewing the real world through a camera, developers mathematically create a view that consists of a boxed 3D area that is rendered, called the *frustum*.

The frustum consists of a near plane, a far plane, left and right plane that boxes an area of view, as shown in Figure 9-6.

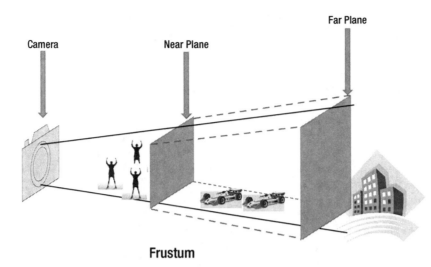

Frustum

Figure 9-6. *Frustum area of a view*

Notice that some objects are shown outside of the frustum; this means that if the scene is rendered, those objects would not be shown. If the user moves the camera closer in, the people would come into view. Likewise, moving the camera toward the cars could begin to bring in the building in the background. Notice in Figure 9-6 that the developer could decide to make the frustum longer, with the near plane in front of the crowd of people and behind the buildings. As mentioned before, this could overload the graphics card, resulting in frame rate loss, especially in a high-speed racing game. This is the essence of 3D game development, building out a model and rendering it in such a way that user movement feels "natural" within the game.

3D Coordinate Systems

The XNA Framework is engineered to work with the modeling techniques discussed in the previous section, modeling the real world via 3D coordinate systems and mathematics to project a view of a 3D experience to a game player. At the heart of 3D is the coordinate system.

Remember in 2D game development that the 2D origin (X,Y) is in the upper left-hand corner of the screen with positive X going left to right and positive Y going top to bottom. In 3D game development, the origin (0,0,0) can be at the center of a car model, or it could be at an arbitrary place in the overall 3D world. In reality, there are multiple 3D origins that are relatively positioned to each other. A model has a 3D origin that runs through the center of the model or could be centered at the bottom of the model, depending on what makes most sense for the game at that time. You can rotate around the model origin, and the model would spin like a top.

Likewise, the overall world will have an origin as well. You can also rotate a model about the 3D world origin like a planet orbiting the sun in our Solar System. These concepts will be explored as we proceed in this chapter, but it is important to break your mind free from the comfort of the rigid 2D coordinate system.

One aspect of coordinate systems that needs to be consistent is how the three axes (X,Y,Z) are oriented. In 3D game development, this is called either a right-handed or a left-handed coordinate system. Figure 9-7 shows the two coordinate systems taken from the DirectX documentation on MSDN.

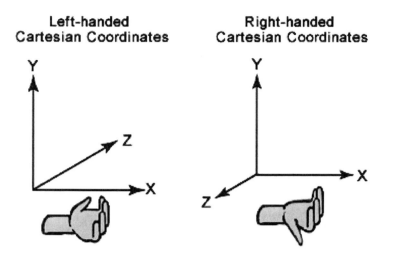

Figure 9-7. *Left-handed and right-handed coordinate systems*

So the idea is you can use your hand to remember the direction of the positive Z access. Point your fingers in the direction of the positive X axis and curl your fingers up toward the positive Y axis, and your thumb points in the direction of the positive Z axis.

The XNA Framework is a right-handed coordinate system, meaning that the Z axis is positive coming out of the screen. There are many programming models including DirectX that are left-handed systems, so be cognizant of the coordinate convention when reviewing sample code and documentation.

Rendering 3D Primitives

Modern graphics hardware is optimized to render triangles. You can take it on to prove it to yourself by reviewing a 3D mathematics text, but any 3D object can be modeled to have smooth edges with enough triangles. Zoom in close enough on a model and the edges can look jagged, but that does not stray too far from reality in this case either. As an example, a golf ball is round with bumps, but if you view it close enough you can see the imperfections, and take comfort in blaming your errant golf swing on the golf ball's imperfections and not your golf skills.

This is another aspect of 3D game development that is art as much as science, managing how many triangles you try to push through the graphics processor unit (GPU) versus rendering quality at different zoom levels. More triangles sounds better, but if the frame rate drops too far over a period of time, a game can become unplayable.

We will work with 3D models in a bit, but let's start out by working with just a few triangles to dip our toe into the water of 3D game development. In the Chapter 9 solution, the **XNA3DPrimitives** project sample demonstrates programming with triangles, which we will walk through now.

Creating 3D Primitives

You don't generally create a 3D game using triangle primitives, but we go through the exercise to define key concepts of 3D development with the XNA Framework. In the end, when you render a 3D model created by a graphics artist, you are rendering bunches of triangles that have been predefined, so the concepts covered in this section translate right over to working with models. To render a 3D scene in the XNA Framework, follow these steps:

- Load your content; in this case, a set of triangles defined as vertex collections where each vertex is one of the three points on a triangle.

- Load any textures that will render over the triangles; in this case, to provide a "skin" that is stretched over the triangle points.

- Pass the content to a vertex buffer containing the triangles that the GPU can render.

- Define the shader effect that will do the rendering.

- Modify the Update method as you did in 2D development to apply translation, rotation, and so on.

- Render the vertex buffer using the shader effect in the Draw method.

In the next section, we go through creating a 3D cube that is rendered to the screen.

From Triangles to Objects

We create a new project named XNA3DPrimitives in the Chapter 9 solution, where we go through the previously covered process in detail. We will draw a 3D cube and apply a color to the cube wireframe. We will then manipulate different aspects of drawing and movement to help you understand how 3D development works.

A cube has six square sides connected at 90 degree angles. Figure 9-8 shows how a cube consists of 12 triangles with two triangles per cube face.

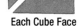

Figure 9-8. *Building a cube with triangles*

Each side has six indices (three per triangle) and four vertices per cube face, representing each corner of the face. When thinking about positioning each cube face, remember that an object can have a coordinate system that goes through the geometric center. In the case of a cube, it is easily to visualize positioning each face on a 3D axis as shown in Figure 9-9.

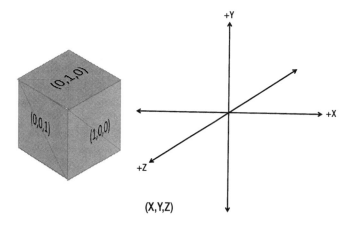

Figure 9-9. Positioning each cube face on a 3D axis

Notice the vector information in Figure 9-9, indicating which axis matches each cube face. Here is a full list of the "normal" vectors for each face, which is a Vector3 that shoots straight out of each cube face at a 90 degree angle (really shooting straight out of the two triangles that make up the cube face):

- (1,0,0): Positive X axis cube face

- (-1,0,0): Negative X axis cube face

- (0,1,0): Positive Y axis cube face

- (0,-1,0): Negative Y axis cube face

- (0,0,1): Positive Z axis cube face

- (0,0,-1): Negative Z axis cube face

3D game developers use normal vectors to figure out positioning between triangles, objects, and so on. As an example, if you want to figure out how to move an object sideways, you figure out the normal to the front and top vectors to give you the "sideways pointing" vector. Mathematically, the cross product can find the normal vector between two vectors. As an example, the Z axis is the normal vector to the Y axis and X axis. The Y axis is the normal to the X axis and Z axis, and the X axis is the normal vector to the Y and Z axes.

Figure 9-9 makes it easy to visualize the normal vector between the X, Y, and Z axes. It is a little bit of math to calculate the normal vector between two vectors. Luckily, the **Vector3.Cross** method takes two vectors and finds the normal vector for the two vectors passed in to the method call. Now we can proceed with building the cube. We add a method call to **CreateCubeObject** in the **Game.LoadContent()** method. We will build up the cube object in the **CreateCubeObject** method.

To render the cube we use two buffers: one that contains the vertex information and the other that contains the index information. Index information allows you to reuse vertex information. For example, when two triangles form a square such as a cube face, two points are shared between the triangles. While you could repeat the vertex information and have duplicates, for a large model this consumes precious memory and should be avoided. One way to avoid duplicates is to store only unique vertices in the vertex buffer and use an index buffer to represent the triangles that are drawn. Figure 9-10 shows how the vertex buffer relates to the index buffer.

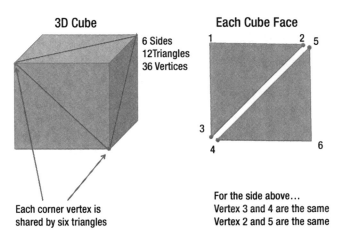

Figure 9-10. *Vertex buffer and index buffer relationship*

In looking at just the side on the top in Figure 9-10, the index buffer would have six slots to represent the two triangles, with three vertices each. However, the vertex buffer would only store four unique vertices. Here is what the vertex and index buffers would look like moving left to right around the side shown on the top in Figure 9-10:

- Vertex buffer: 1,2,3,6 (Vertices 4 and 5 are duplicates and removed)

- Index buffer: 1,2,3,2,6,3 (Always six vertices for two triangles)

The actual drawing is done using the index buffer, because it fully represents each triangle with three vertices per triangle. When the GPU needs the three points to draw the triangle, it looks up the actual vertex in the vertex buffer based on the index buffer with some vertices used multiple times.

In our example, to draw the left / bottom triangle, the GPU uses vertices 1, 2, and 3. To draw the right/top triangle, the GPU uses 2, 6, and 3, reusing two vertices. Although in our example the memory savings may seem trivial, for a large complex model the savings can be significant.

Creating the Cube

Now that you have an understanding of how the vertex buffer relates to the index buffer, we return to the code to use this knowledge to create the cube object. Five new members are added to the Game1 class:

```
VertexBuffer vertexBuffer;
IndexBuffer indexBuffer;

//Lists and variables used to construct vertex and index buffer data
List<VertexPositionNormalTexture> vertices = new List<VertexPositionNormalTexture>();
List<ushort> indices = new List<ushort>();
float size = 3;
```

The vertices and indices List objects are used to construct the primitive cube model. Once the cube is constructed, the data is loaded into the vertexBuffer and indexBuffer members using the SetData method call. Once loaded, the vertexBuffer and indexBuffer objects are passed to the graphics device (the GPU) for rendering using the specified lighting effect. We cover lighting and drawing in a bit.

First let's construct the cube model using the `vertices` and `indices` List objects in the `CreateCubeObject` method, which is called in the `Game1.LoadContent` method after the texture is loaded and shown in Listing 9-5.

Listing 9-5. *The Game1.CreateCubeObject Method*

```
private void CreateCubeObject()
{
  // A cube has six faces, each one pointing in a different direction.
  Vector3[] normals =
      {
          new Vector3(0, 0, 1),
          new Vector3(0, 0, -1),
          new Vector3(1, 0, 0),
          new Vector3(-1, 0, 0),
          new Vector3(0, 1, 0),
          new Vector3(0, -1, 0),
      };

  // Create each face in turn.
  foreach (Vector3 normal in normals)
  {
    // Get two vectors perpendicular to the cube face normal and
    //perpendicular to each other
    Vector3 triangleSide1 = new Vector3(normal.Y, normal.Z, normal.X);
    Vector3 triangleSide2 = Vector3.Cross(normal, triangleSide1);
    // Six indices (two triangles) per face
    indices.Add((ushort)(vertices.Count + 0));
    indices.Add((ushort)(vertices.Count + 1));
    indices.Add((ushort)(vertices.Count + 2));

    indices.Add((ushort)(vertices.Count + 0));
    indices.Add((ushort)(vertices.Count + 2));
    indices.Add((ushort)(vertices.Count + 3));

    // Four vertices per cube face
    vertices.Add(new VertexPositionNormalTexture(
      (normal - triangleSide1 - triangleSide2) * size / 2, normal,Vector2.One));
    vertices.Add(new VertexPositionNormalTexture(
      (normal - triangleSide1 + triangleSide2) * size / 2, normal,Vector2.One));
    vertices.Add(new VertexPositionNormalTexture(
      (normal + triangleSide1 + triangleSide2) * size / 2, normal,Vector2.One));
    vertices.Add(new VertexPositionNormalTexture(
      (normal + triangleSide1 - triangleSide2) * size / 2, normal,Vector2.One));
  }
}
```

The `CreateCubeObject` starts by creating the six vectors that represent each side of the cube. Each vector is normal to a cube face, positioned along a 3D axis as shown in Figure 9-9 earlier.

With each normal vector, two additional normal vectors are created that are perpendicular to the normal vector and to each other. These two new vectors named `triangleSide1` and `triangleSide2` are used to find the four vertices that represent the cube face corner vertices that are added to the **vertices**

List. The indices List is updated to add vertex references in the correct order so that the object can be rendered properly.

Graphics Objects and the Effect Class

We next construct and initialize the graphics objects and buffers to render our cube primitive. We declare an effect object of type BasicEffect at the top of Game1.cs. With XNA 4.0, Microsoft defined several built-in effects classes that draw objects without having to resort to High Level Shader Language (HLSL) coding. Windows Phone does not support HLSL, so we do not dive into HLSL development, but in short the language allows developers to directly program the GPU to create dazzling visual effects.

Not being able to program in HLSL may seem like a major limitation, but the built-in Effect class descendants provide several benefits:

- Cross-platform support is simplified by using the Effect class objects. This is known as the "reach" profile in XNA Game Studio 4.0.

- The Effect class objects are highly configurable, allowing a wide range of visual effects programming in C#.

- Developers do not have to learn yet another language in HLSL.

Table 9-1 has a list of available effect classes in XNA Game Studio 4.0.

Table 9-1. *Configurable Effect Classes in the XNA Framework*

Effect	Description
AlphaTest	Contains a configurable effect that supports alpha testing.
BasicEffect	Contains a basic rendering effect.
DualTextureEffect	Contains a configurable effect that supports two-layer multitexturing.
Effect	Used to set and query effects, and to choose techniques that are applied when rendering.
EnvironmentMapEffect	Contains a configurable effect that supports environment mapping.
SkinnedEffect	Contains a configurable effect for rendering skinned character models.

Each Effect class in Table 9-1 has several configurable "knobs" that provide developers a wide range of control without having to delve into HLSL. This link has more information and samples on the various available Effect classes:

http://create.msdn.com/en-us/education/catalog/?contenttype=0&devarea=14&sort=2

The ConstructGraphicsObjectsForDrawingCube method initializes the graphics objects and the BasicEffect object:

```
private void ConstructGraphicsObjectsForDrawingCube()
{
  // Create a vertex buffer, and copy the cube vertex data into it
  vertexBuffer = new VertexBuffer(graphics.GraphicsDevice,
                                  typeof(VertexPositionNormalTexture),
                                  vertices.Count, BufferUsage.None);
  vertexBuffer.SetData(vertices.ToArray());
  // Create an index buffer, and copy the cube index data into it.
  indexBuffer = new IndexBuffer(graphics.GraphicsDevice, typeof(ushort),
                                indices.Count, BufferUsage.None);
  indexBuffer.SetData(indices.ToArray());
  // Create a BasicEffect, which will be used to render the primitive.
  basicEffect = new BasicEffect(graphics.GraphicsDevice);
  basicEffect.EnableDefaultLighting();
  basicEffect.PreferPerPixelLighting = true;
}
```

The vertex and index data calculated in the CreateCubeObject method are loaded into the vertexBuffer and indexBuffer objects, respectively. The BasicEffect is instantiated next. We discuss effects in more detail later, but essentially the BasicEffect object provides the environmental effects for the scene such as lighting and shading.

Drawing the Cube

To draw the cube we need several additional member variables that are added at the top of Game1.cs.

```
float yaw = .5f;
float pitch = .5f;
float roll = .5f;
Vector3 cameraPosition = new Vector3(0, 0, 10f);
```

The last method related to our cube is the Game1.DrawCubePrimitive method listed here:

```
private void DrawCubePrimitive (Matrix world, Matrix view, Matrix projection, Color color)
{
  // Set BasicEffect parameters.
  basicEffect.World = world;
  basicEffect.View = view;
  basicEffect.Projection = projection;
  basicEffect.DiffuseColor = color.ToVector3();
  basicEffect.Alpha = color.A / 255.0f;

  GraphicsDevice graphicsDevice = basicEffect.GraphicsDevice;
  // Set our vertex declaration, vertex buffer, and index buffer.
  graphicsDevice.SetVertexBuffer(vertexBuffer);
  graphicsDevice.Indices = indexBuffer;

  foreach (EffectPass effectPass in basicEffect.CurrentTechnique.Passes)
  {
```

```
      effectPass.Apply();
      int primitiveCount = indices.Count / 3;
      graphicsDevice.DrawIndexedPrimitives(
        PrimitiveType.TriangleList, 0, 0,vertices.Count, 0, primitiveCount);
  }
}
```

The `DrawCubePrimitive` method is called in the `Game1.Draw` method. This method instantiates the `graphicsDevice` object and passes in the calculated vertex and index information for rendering. Depending on the effect used, one or more passes are executed to create the scene, drawing the triangle primitives using the `graphicsDevice.DrawIndexedPrimitives` method.

The cube is ready for rendering within a 3D scene. We next move to incorporating the cube code into an XNA Framework game.

The Game Class

To draw a 3D scene a developer needs to set up a coordinate system and create a camera to view the rendered scene.

The Camera

We need to create a camera that will be a view into our 3D world of triangles that is rendered by the GPU. Right-click on the `XNA3DPrimitives` project and select Add ➤ New Item ➤ XNA Game Studio 4.0 ➤ Game Component. Name the new game component `Camera` and click Add. Remember from our discussion above that the `Camera` object has a position within the model world, looks in a particular direction, and has a view defined by the frustum. We modify the constructor to take three parameters: `cameraUpVector`, `cameraPosition`, and `cameraDirection` all of type `Vector3`.

The `cameraPosition` and `cameraDirection` parameters orient the `Camera`. As an example, if flying an airplane in the first person, you bank right to turn right, so it would make sense to have the Camera Up Vector oriented 45 degrees to the right through the turn. The camera direction defines the viewing frustum and will be oriented to look toward our triangles when drawn to the screen.

The `Camera` `GameComponent` object will need two public properties: `View` and `Projection`, of type `Matrix`. Don't worry about what it means to define these terms as a `Matrix` type—it isn't critical. It is more important to think of the concepts above as we define them programmatically.

■ **Tip** If you desperately want to understand the math behind 3D game development, and eventually you will need to understand it if you pursue 3D game development, I recommend reading *3D Math Primer for Graphics and Game Development* (Jones & Bartlett Publishers, 2002) by Fletcher Dunn and Ian Parberry.

The `Matrix` class has a static method called `CreatePerspectiveFieldOfView` that defines the frustum for the GPU. This method call takes four parameters:

- `fieldOfView`
- `aspectRatio`
- `nearPlaneDistance`
- `farPlaneDistance`

The `fieldOfView` parameter defines the angle width of the field of view for the frustum in radians, not degrees. Remember from geometry that 360 degrees equals 2pi radians, 180 degrees equals pi radians, and 90 degrees equals pi/2 radians. The `MathHelper` class defines these values for you so you can pass in `MathHelper.PiOver4` to define a field of view of 45 degrees, which is a good starting point for most games.

The `aspectRatio` parameter is defined by the ratio of the screen width divided by screen height. The Game object has these values in this format:
`Game.Window.ClientBounds.Width/Game.Window.ClientBounds.Height`.

The `nearPlaneDistance` parameter defines how far in front of the `Camera` object the near plane from Figure 9-6 is defined. A good starting point is one for our example, but in a real game you may not want the near plane to include every object in front of the `Camera` object. Lastly, the `farPlaneDistance` parameter defines the far plane, that is, the how far into the distance the camera can "see" past the near plane.

Now that we have defined the frustum box, we need to orient the frustrum box in a particular direction to look at the triangles that we are going to draw in just a bit. The handy `Matrix` class defines a static method named `CreateLookAt` that defines the direction that the `Camera` is facing. It takes three parameters:

- Camera Position
- Camera Direction
- Camera Up Vector

The `CreateLookAt` parameters match the three parameters that are passed into the `Camera` `GameComponent` object that we defined above so we pass them into the method call as shown in Listing 9-6.

Listing 9-6. *The Camera GameComponent Class*

```
using Microsoft.Xna.Framework;
namespace XNA3DPrimitives
{
  public class Camera : Microsoft.Xna.Framework.GameComponent
  {
    public Camera(Game game, Vector3 position, Vector3 direction, Vector3 upVector)
      : base(game)
    {
      // Initialize frustum matrix
      Projection = Matrix.CreatePerspectiveFieldOfView(
          MathHelper.PiOver4,
          this.Game.GraphicsDevice.Viewport.AspectRatio,
          1, 20);
```

```
      // Initialize "look at" matrix
      View = Matrix.CreateLookAt(position, direction, upVector);
    }

  public Matrix View { get; private set; }
  public Matrix Projection { get; private set; }

  public override void Initialize()
  {

    base.Initialize();
  }

  public override void Update(GameTime gameTime)
  {

    base.Update(gameTime);
  }
  }
}
```

We next update the Game1 class to include our new Camera object and use it to call the cube-related methods to render the cube in a scene.

Rendering the Cube Scene

To leverage the Camera object we add it to Game1.cs in the Game1.Initialize method:

```
protected override void Initialize()
{ // Initialize camera
  camera = new Camera(this, cameraPosition,
      Vector3.Zero, Vector3.Up);
  Components.Add(camera);
  base.Initialize();
}
```

We update the DrawCubePrimitive method to leverage the Camera object. The method now just takes two parameters. Here is a snippet of the first part of the method where the changes are in effect:

```
private void DrawCubePrimitive (Matrix world,  Color color)
{
  // Set BasicEffect parameters.
  basicEffect.World = world;
  basicEffect.View = camera.View;
  basicEffect.Projection = camera.Projection;
  basicEffect.DiffuseColor = color.ToVector3();
  basicEffect.Alpha = color.A / 255.0f;
  ...
```

The basicEffect object now gets its View and Projection properties from the Camera object in the DrawCubePrimitive method. Here is the Game1.Draw method that renders the cube:

```
protected override void Draw(GameTime gameTime)
{
  GraphicsDevice.Clear(Color.CornflowerBlue);
  // TODO: Add your drawing code here
  Matrix world = Matrix.CreateFromYawPitchRoll(yaw, pitch, roll);
  DrawCubePrimitive (world, Color.Orange);
  // Reset the fill mode renderstate.
  GraphicsDevice.RasterizerState = RasterizerState.CullCounterClockwise;
  base.Draw(gameTime);
}
```

The World coordinate is obtained from configured, yaw, pitch, and role values at the top of Game1.cs, resulting in the rendered cube shown in Figure 9-11.

```
float yaw = .5f;
float pitch = .5f;
float roll = .5f;
```

Figure 9-11. *Rendered cube with configured color*

The scene is static, which is a bit boring. Let's add some movement to the scene in the next section via yaw, pitch, and roll.

Adding Movement

In the previous section, the cube object is positioned using the world Matrix object, which is created using the Matrix.CreateFromYawPitchRoll(yaw, pitch, roll) static method call. The world Matrix object is passed to the DrawCubePrimitive method and assigned to the basicEffect.World property to render the object with the configured yaw, pitch, and roll applied to its coordinates. Figure 9-12 describes these parameters visually.

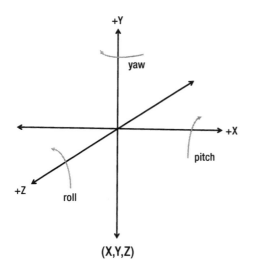

Figure 9-12. Yaw, pitch, and roll

We apply a simple way to manipulate the object by updating the `yaw`, `pitch`, and `roll` members in the Update method shown here:

```
protected override void Update(GameTime gameTime)
{
  // Allows the game to exit
  if (GamePad.GetState(PlayerIndex.One).Buttons.Back == ButtonState.Pressed)
    this.Exit();
  float time = (float)gameTime.TotalGameTime.TotalSeconds;
  yaw = time * 0.5f;
  pitch = time * 0.5f;
  roll = time * 0.5f;

  base.Update(gameTime);
}
```

The `gameTime.TotalGameTime.TotalSeconds` value is fairly small, as it is the elapsed time between frames. Applying the modification on each call to `Update` results in smooth animation. A screenshot doesn't do it justice, so run the sample code to observe the lighting provided by the `BasicEffect` instance when rendering the object as it rotates.

Now that we have covered 3D programming basics and rendering 3D objects generated from triangle primitives in code, we can move on to rendering rich 3D models, building on the 3D game development concepts presented so far.

Rendering 3D Models

A 3D model consists of triangle primitives, but is generally created in a third-party tool, such as Softimage Mod Tool, Daz Studio 3D, blender, or Caligari trueSpace, to name a few of the freely available modeling tools. Paint.NET is a free tool to create 2D textures. Professional modeling tools for purchase are Autodesk's 3ds Max, Autodesk's Maya, and Adobe's Creative Suite for texture creation. XNA Game Studio 4.0 supports importing 3D models in both Autodesk .fbx and DirectX .x formats generated from any of these tools.

Creating 3D models is beyond scope of this book. Instead we leverage models available under the MS-PL license up at AppHub, located at http://create.msdn.com. I've grabbed the spaceship.fbx file from the samples located at AppHub and the background texture from the AlienShooter project, adding them to the content project for a new project named XNA3DModels in the Chapter 9 code solution.

Movable Camera

For the new project named XNA3DModels we need a Camera object to view the 3D scene and model. In the previous sample the Camera was fixed in location. In this sample we create a Camera that can create the appearance of movement based on user input.

■ **Tip** The Camera Projection or field of view does not change; think of that aspect of the Camera as fixed, like looking through a pair of binoculars. The Camera.View property is the direction that the binoculars are pointed and can change based on user input.

For this sample, we demonstrate shifting the View property of the Camera based on Accelerometer input. For more information on the Accelerometer sensor, refer to Chapter 3.

We start with a copy of the Camera class from the XNA3DPrimitives project. Properties for View, Position, and Up are added to the Camera class. We also add a private variable named direction of type Vector3 that is calculated by taking the target Vector3 (the spaceship model) and subtracting the Position Vector3. The Projection property is calculated as before.

The Up Vector3 value is set to Vector3.Up as before and the View property is recalculated each time it is accessed via this read-only property declaration:

```
public Matrix View
{
  get { return Matrix.CreateLookAt(Position, Position+direction, Up); }
}
```

The recalculation is necessary since the Camera Position and direction values will change based on user input in the Camera.Update method. Listing 9-7 has the Camera source code.

Listing 9-7. *Updated Camera Class with Support for User Input*

```
using System;
using Microsoft.Devices.Sensors;
using Microsoft.Xna.Framework;

namespace XNA3DModels
{
  public class Camera : Microsoft.Xna.Framework.GameComponent
  {
    #region private members
    //Camera properties
    Vector3 direction;
    Vector3 Up;

    //Accelerometer input
    Accelerometer accelerometer;
    AccelerometerReading currentReading;

    //Movement parameters
    float speed = 100f;
    //Yaw movement
    float maxLeftRight = MathHelper.PiOver4 / 10;
    float stepLeftRight = MathHelper.PiOver4 / 10000;
    float currentLeftRight = 0;
    #endregion

    public Camera(Game game, Vector3 position, Vector3 target, Vector3 upVector)
      : base(game)
    {
      Position = position;
      direction = target - position;
      direction.Normalize();
      Up = upVector;

      // Initialize frustum matrix, which doesn't change
      Projection = Matrix.CreatePerspectiveFieldOfView(
          MathHelper.PiOver4,
          this.Game.GraphicsDevice.Viewport.AspectRatio,
          1, 20000);
      currentReading = new AccelerometerReading();
    }

    public Matrix View
    {
      get { return Matrix.CreateLookAt(Position, Position + direction, Up); }
    }
    public Matrix Projection { get; private set; }
    public Vector3 Position { get; private set; }
```

```csharp
public void ResetPosition()
{
  Position = new Vector3(0, 1000, 15000);
  direction = Vector3.Zero - Position;
  direction.Normalize();
  Up = Vector3.Up;
}

public override void Initialize()
{
  accelerometer = new Accelerometer();
  accelerometer.ReadingChanged += accelerometer_ReadingChanged;
  accelerometer.Start();
  base.Initialize();
}

public override void Update(GameTime gameTime)
{
  ApplyThrust();
  ApplySteering();
  base.Update(gameTime);
}

private void ApplySteering()
{
  if ((Math.Abs(currentLeftRight) < maxLeftRight) &&
(Math.Abs(currentReading.Y) > .4))
  {
    direction = Vector3.Transform(direction,
              Matrix.CreateFromAxisAngle(Up, currentLeftRight));
    if (currentReading.Y > .2)
    {
      currentLeftRight += stepLeftRight;
      if (currentLeftRight < 0)
        currentLeftRight = currentLeftRight * -1;
    }
    if (currentReading.Y < -.2)
    {
      currentLeftRight -= stepLeftRight;
      if (currentLeftRight > 0)
        currentLeftRight = currentLeftRight * -1;
    }
  }
}

private void ApplyThrust()
{
  //Travel forward or backwards based on tilting
  //device forwards or backwards (Z axis for Accelerometer)
  if (currentReading.Z < -.65)
    Position += direction * speed;
  if (currentReading.Z > -.5)
```

```
            Position -= direction * speed;
                                                    }

      protected override void OnEnabledChanged(object sender, System.EventArgs args)
      {
        if (this.Enabled)
          accelerometer.Start();
        else
          accelerometer.Stop();
        base.OnEnabledChanged(sender, args);
      }

      private void accelerometer_ReadingChanged(
        object sender, AccelerometerReadingEventArgs e)
      {
        currentReading.X = e.X;
        currentReading.Y = e.Y;
        currentReading.Z = e.Z;
        currentReading.Timestamp = e.Timestamp;

#if DEBUG
        System.Diagnostics.Debug.WriteLine("X: " + e.X);
        System.Diagnostics.Debug.WriteLine("Y: " + e.Y);
        System.Diagnostics.Debug.WriteLine("Z: " + e.Z);
#endif

      }
    }

  class AccelerometerReading
  {
    public double X { get; set; }
    public double Y { get; set; }
    public double Z { get; set; }
    public DateTimeOffset Timestamp { get; set; }
  }
}
```

User input is based on **Accelerometer** sensor input. Z axis accelerometer value changes, that is, tilting the phone forward and backward in landscape orientation, will move the **Camera** object closer or further in the direction it is pointed; think of it as thrust. Tilting the phone left or right, that is, changing the Y axis accelerometer, steers the **Camera** left or right. The hard-coded values used to manage user input were derived empirically based on the spaceship model size, projection size, and so on. Finding the right balance based on all the factors in a game are part of the art of providing good game play.

In Listing 9-7 you can find the code to wire up the accelerometer, also covered in Chapter 3. The **OnEnabledChanged** event shown here is overridden to allow starting and stopping the **Accelerometer** object readings based on whether the **GameComponent** is enabled:

```
protected override void OnEnabledChanged(object sender, System.EventArgs args)
{
  if (this.Enabled)
    accelerometer.Start();
```

```
  else
    accelerometer.Stop();

  base.OnEnabledChanged(sender, args);
}
```

This is a good programming practice to do, so that collecting `Accelerometer` input does not needlessly run the battery down. The `Camera` class also contains a `ResetPosition` method for testing purposes in the event that you fly off into 3D space and want to get back to a known good position for the movable `Camera` object.

The `Update` method in Listing 9-7 calls to private methods, `ApplyThrust` and `ApplySteering`. `ApplyThrust` is pretty straightforward. It adjusts the `Position` of the `Camera` along the direction the `Camera` object is pointing, moving the `Camera` backwards and forwards.

The `ApplySteering` method detects changes in the left/right tilt of the phone and applies the change to the `currentLeftRight` float value. This is used to calculate a new value for direction with this line of code:

```
direction = Vector3.Transform(direction,
            Matrix.CreateFromAxisAngle(Up, currentLeftRight));
```

This handy piece of code applies a transform to the direction `Vector3` object. The transform matrix is calculated by taking the `Up` `Vector3` value and an angle in radians that is based on the tilt of the phone. Now that the `Camera` class is updated, we move on to creating a new class for 3D game objects and a 3D game object coordinator class.

3D Game Object Management

In the AlienShooter 2D game, we created a class named `GameObject` to represent the sprite objects in the game. In the `XNA3DModels` project we create a class named `GameObject3D` to represent 3D model objects. We also create a `SceneManager` class that can manage multiple `GameObject3D` instances as part of a 3D game.

GameObject3D Class

The `GameObject3D` class is pretty simple. Just as `GameObject` took a 2D sprite `Texture2D` object, `GameObject3D` takes a `Model` instance loaded from the content project. In our case, that is the `spacehip.fbx` sample spaceship object located in the `XNA3DModelsContent` project `Models` folder. We haven't delved too deeply yet into what a model is, except that it is a computer generated object created by a graphics designer using a tool similar to the tools listed at the beginning of the section titled "3D Game Development" earlier in this chapter. The XNA Game Studio 4.0 documentation covers this in detail at this link:

http://msdn.microsoft.com/en-us/library/dd904249.aspx

Figure 9-13 is taken from the above page and describes the relationships between the Model, Mesh and Bones objects.

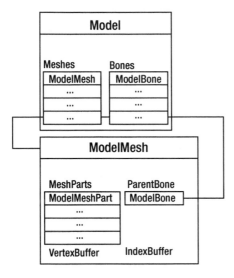

Figure 9-13. *Model internals*

A `Model` object is made up of many vertices and materials organized into a set of meshes. In the XNA Framework, a model is represented by the `Model` class. A model contains one or more meshes, each of which is represented by a `ModelMesh` class. Each mesh is associated with one bone represented by the `ModelBone` class. Notice the familiar `VertextBuffer` and `IndexBuffer` that makes up the `ModelMesh`, which is essentially a collection of triangles under the covers.

The bone structure is set up to be hierarchical to make controlling each mesh (and therefore the entire model) easier. At the top of the hierarchy, the model has a `Root` bone to specify the overall position and orientation of the model. Each `ModelMesh` object contains a `ParentBone` and one or more `ModelBone`. You can transform the entire model using the parent bone as well as transform each individual mesh with its bone.

To animate one or more bones, update the bone transforms during the render loop by calling `Model.CopyAbsoluteBoneTransformsTo` Method, which iterates the individual bone transforms to make them relative to the parent bone. To draw an entire model, loop through a mesh drawing each sub mesh. It is through transforming bones over time that a `Model` can appear to walk, rotate, fly, and so on in a 3D game. With that background out of the way, Listing 9-8 shows how to work with a `Model` in code when rendering.

Listing 9-8. *The GameObject3D class*

```
using Microsoft.Xna.Framework.Graphics;
using Microsoft.Xna.Framework;

namespace XNA3DModels.Models
{
    class GameObject3D
    {
        Matrix[] boneTransforms;
        public GameObject3D(Model m)
        {
```

```
      SpaceshipModel = m;
      boneTransforms = new Matrix[SpaceshipModel.Bones.Count];
    }

    public Matrix World
    {
      get { return Matrix.Identity; }
    }
    public Model SpaceshipModel { get; protected set; }
    public void Update()
    {

    }

    public void Draw(Camera camera)
    {
      SpaceshipModel.CopyAbsoluteBoneTransformsTo(boneTransforms);
      foreach (ModelMesh mesh in SpaceshipModel.Meshes)
      {
        foreach (BasicEffect be in mesh.Effects)
        {
          be.World = World * mesh.ParentBone.Transform;
          be.Projection = camera.Projection;
          be.View = camera.View;
          be.TextureEnabled = true;
          be.EnableDefaultLighting();
          be.PreferPerPixelLighting = true;
        }
        mesh.Draw();
      }
    }
  }
}
```

Notice that we pass the `Camera` object into the `Draw` method to ensure that the `Model` is rendered within the coordinates of the `Camera`. Just like when we rendered primitives in the `XNA3DPrimitives` project, an `Effect` class is used to apply textures and provide lighting. In the next section we cover the `SceneManager` class that manages `GameObject3D` objects.

SceneManager Class

The `SceneManager` class inherits from the `DrawableGameComponent` class. It maintains a collection of `GameObject3D` objects in a `Generic List` collection. As a minimum it loops through each object and calls the `Update` and `Draw` methods for all managed objects as shown in Listing 9-9.

Listing 9-9. *The SceneManager class*

```
using System.Collections.Generic;
using Microsoft.Xna.Framework;
using Microsoft.Xna.Framework.Graphics;
```

```
namespace XNA3DModels.Models
{
  public class SceneManager : DrawableGameComponent
  {
    List<GameObject3D> gameObjects3D = new List<GameObject3D>();
    public SceneManager(Game game)
      : base(game)
    {
    }

    public override void Initialize()
    {
      base.Initialize();
    }

    protected override void LoadContent()
    {
      gameObjects3D.Add(new GameObject3D(Game.Content.Load<Model>("Models/spaceship")));
      base.LoadContent();
    }

    public override void Update(GameTime gameTime)
    {
      for (int i = 0; i < gameObjects3D.Count; ++i)
      {
        gameObjects3D[i].Update();
      }

      base.Update(gameTime);
    }

    public override void Draw(GameTime gameTime)
    {
      for (int i = 0; i < gameObjects3D.Count; i++)
      {
        gameObjects3D[i].Draw(((Game1)Game).Camera);
      }
      base.Draw(gameTime);
    }
  }
}
```

The SceneManager class provides support for managing numerous GameObject3D classes and can be the basis for creating a more complex application in combination with the GameObject3D and Camera classes we have covered so far. We now pull all of the previous pieces together to complete the XNA3DModels project sample in the next section.

XNA3DModels Game Class

The Game class Game1.cs is updated to have three additional private members at the top:

```
SceneManager sceneManager ;
Texture2D backgroundTexture;
GestureSample gestureSample ;
```

A SceneManager instance is added as well as a Texture2D to display a background image. The GestureSample field is used to obtain a touch screen gesture by the user. If a Tap gesture is detected, the Camera.ResetPosition method is called to reposition the Camera in front of the rendered 3D model.

The Camera object is declared as a public property to the Game1 class so that it can be passed into the Draw method of GameObject3D instances. Here is the Camera and SceneManager initialization code in the Game1 class:

```
protected override void Initialize()
{
  // Initialize Camera
  Camera = new Camera(this, new Vector3(0, 1000, 15000),
      Vector3.Zero, Vector3.Up);
  Components.Add(Camera);
  //Initialize SceneManager
  sceneManager = new SceneManager(this);
  Components.Add(sceneManager);

  TouchPanel.EnabledGestures = GestureType.Tap;
  base.Initialize();
}
```

The code also enables the Tap gesture so that the user can reset the Camera position. The Update method is modified to call the HandleInput method shown here:

```
private void HandleInput()
{
  if (TouchPanel.IsGestureAvailable)
  {
    gestureSample = TouchPanel.ReadGesture();
    if (gestureSample.GestureType == GestureType.Tap)
      Camera.ResetPosition();
  }
}
```

The only other code modified in the Game1 class is to load the backgroundTexture and draw the backgroundTexture using a SpriteBatch object as before. Note that you can intermingle 2D code to render textures and screen text with 3D code. Figure 9-14 shows the rendered spaceship model against a space background.

Figure 9-14. *3D Rendered spaceship model*

You should run the sample on a phone to test out the `Accelerometer` input. While this sample isn't super exciting, it demonstrates how to render basic 3D models in the XNA Framework, including a few classes to help you get started with 3D game development.

In the next section we demonstrate how to integrate 3D development with augmented reality in a Silverlight application using Windows Phone OS 7.1 Shared Graphics capabilities, which we cover in depth in Chapter 8 and above. In the next section we add a twist of integrating 3D XNA Framework graphics with augmented reality using the `Camera` sensor covered in Chapter 3.

3D Augmented Reality

In this section I cover how to render a 3D model in space using the Camera sensor as a viewfinder and the Motion sensor for positioning. The idea is that you could geo-reference the model and make it clickable on screen to bring up additional details. Scenarios would be a 3D model representation of a city's downtown area, a theme park, or any other idea that you can come up with.

XAML Code

I cover 3D model rendering above and I covered both the `Camera` and `Motion` sensor in Chapter 3, so this section dives right into the sample code. We add a new project named AR_3D_App to the Chapter 9 solution. Rename `GamePage.xaml` to the more appropriate `ARPage.xaml` and add a `Rectangle` object named `ARViewFinder` in a `Grid` named `layoutRoot` to the XAML. A `VideoBrush` is added to the `Rectangle` as this is where the `Camera` sensor output will display. Also change the supported orientation from `Portrait` to `Landscape`. Here is the XAML from `ARPage.xaml`:

```
<Grid Name="LayoutRoot">
  <Rectangle Name="ARViewFinder" >
    <Rectangle.Fill>
      <VideoBrush x:Name="cameraVideoBrush" />
    </Rectangle.Fill>
  </Rectangle>
</Grid>
```

With the XAML out of the way, we need to bring in the sensors by adding a reference to Microsoft.Devices.Sensors as well as two using clauses:

```
using Microsoft.Devices.Sensors;
using Microsoft.Devices;
```

Add two fields at the top of ARPage.xaml to prepare for the Camera viewfinder rendering:

```
PhotoCamera photoCamera;
UIElementRenderer uierCamera;
```

In the OnNavigatedTo method of ARPage.xaml, we add code to connect the Camera sensor video out with the VideoBrush assigned to the Fill property of the Rectangle and instantiate the UIElementRender:

```
//Set up the Camera Sensor for AR
cameraSensor = new PhotoCamera();
cameraVideoBrush.SetSource(cameraSensor);
//Set width and height for landscape
cameraOutputRenderer = new UIElementRenderer(LayoutRoot,
  SharedGraphicsDeviceManager.Current.GraphicsDevice.Viewport.Width,
  SharedGraphicsDeviceManager.Current.GraphicsDevice.Viewport.Height);
```

We update the OnDraw event handler to render the UIElement named cameraOutputRenderer:

```
private void OnDraw(object sender, GameTimerEventArgs e)
{
  SharedGraphicsDeviceManager.Current.GraphicsDevice.Clear(Color.Black);
  //Render the Camera Output
  cameraOutputRenderer.Render();
  spriteBatch.Begin();
  spriteBatch.Draw(cameraOutputRenderer.Texture, Vector2.Zero, Color.White);
  spriteBatch.End();
}
```

That completes the setup of the Silverlight and Camera Sensor rendering code. Now let's switch to the XNA Framework rendering.

Rendering the 3D Model in Space

To start, we add the 3D model to the AR_3D_AppLibContent project. This is the model we will render in space. Imagine creating an AR shooter game with 3D flying saucers as targets and you get the idea of what is possible. We need to add several fields to ARPage.xaml.cs to lay the groundwork for the XNA rendering:

```
Model flyingSaucerModel;
Motion motionSensor;
Matrix deviceRotation;
Quaternion deviceQuaternion;
Vector3 position = new Vector3(0f, 0f, 3f);
Matrix world, view, projection;
```

You have seen all of these types before except, possibly the Quaternion. The Motion sensor API can return a Quaternion to indicate the position, orientation, and rotation of the device. It is leveraged in the OnUpdate event in ARPage.xaml.cs to get the device position, orientation, and rotation data:

```
private void OnUpdate(object sender, GameTimerEventArgs e)
{
  //Check to ensure Motion Sensor is available
  if (Motion.IsSupported && motionSensor.IsDataValid)
  {
    deviceRotation = motionSensor.CurrentValue.Attitude.RotationMatrix;
    Quaternion q = motionSensor.CurrentValue.Attitude.Quaternion;
    deviceQuaternion = new Quaternion(q.X, q.Z, q.Y, q.W);
  }
}
```

The remaining code is in the OnDraw method, shown in full here:

```
private void OnDraw(object sender, GameTimerEventArgs e)
{
  SharedGraphicsDeviceManager.Current.GraphicsDevice.Clear(
    Microsoft.Xna.Framework.Color.Black);
  Vector3 PhoneForward =
    -new Vector3(deviceRotation.M13, deviceRotation.M23, deviceRotation.M33);
  Vector3 cameraPosition = new Vector3(0, 0, 0);
  // Phone up is always X (in device coordinates)
  // Get it in earth coordinates:
  Vector3 PhoneUp =
    new Vector3(deviceRotation.M11, deviceRotation.M21, deviceRotation.M31);
  // Change of coordinates for XNA:
  Vector3 cameraFront = new Vector3(PhoneForward.X, PhoneForward.Z, -PhoneForward.Y);
  Vector3 cameraUp = new Vector3(PhoneUp.X, PhoneUp.Z, -PhoneUp.Y);
  Matrix viewMatrix =
    Matrix.CreateLookAt(cameraPosition, cameraPosition + cameraFront, cameraUp);
  Matrix worldMatatrix =
    Matrix.CreateWorld(Vector3.Zero, Vector3.Backward, Vector3.Up);
  worldMatatrix *= Matrix.CreateTranslation(position);
  Matrix projMatrix =
    Matrix.CreatePerspectiveFieldOfView((float)(MathHelper.PiOver4 / 1.5f),
    SharedGraphicsDeviceManager.Current.GraphicsDevice.Viewport.AspectRatio,
    0.1f, 10000f);
  //Render the Camera Output
  cameraOutputRenderer.Render();
  spriteBatch.Begin();
  spriteBatch.Draw(cameraOutputRenderer.Texture, Vector2.Zero, Color.White);
  spriteBatch.End();

  Matrix[] transforms = new Matrix[flyingSaucerModel.Bones.Count];
  flyingSaucerModel.CopyAbsoluteBoneTransformsTo(transforms);
  foreach (ModelMesh mesh in flyingSaucerModel.Meshes)
  {
    foreach (BasicEffect effect in mesh.Effects)
    {
      effect.EnableDefaultLighting();
      effect.View = viewMatrix;
      effect.World = worldMatatrix;
      effect.Projection = projMatrix;
```

```
        }
        mesh.Draw();
    }
}
```

As you can see, Windows Phone 7.5 offers near unlimited opportunities to build incredibly rich augmented reality applications. In the next section I provide a quick tour of a very important tool for game development, the Windows Phone Profiler.

Windows Phone Profiler

Windows Phone 7 was a bit of a black box to developers when it shipped in the Fall of 2010. There were APIs to track memory usage but that was about it as far as application profiling was concerned. Luckily with the new Windows Phone Developer Tools for Windows Phone OS 7.1, there is an integrated Profiler available to help you find trouble spots in your application. For most games, resource management is always a challenge, and the Windows Phone Profiler is a great tool to test performance in your games.

Open the Chapter 9 solution if not already open and set the AlienShooter game as the startup project. Go to the Debug menu in Visual Studio and select the Start Windows Phone Performance Analysis menu item. In the window that appears, select Memory as shown in Figure 9-15.

Figure 9-15. Performance Analysis Configuration

Set the deployment to Windows Phone Device, Release configuration, and then click Launch Application. Running performance analysis in the Emulator is not recommended. Play the game for a bit, and the memory analysis looks pretty good as shown in Figure 9-16.

Figure 9–16. Performance analysis results for memory

I am careful to minimize allocations within the game loop and reuse objects. The memory analysis demonstrates the benefits. Go to the Debug menu, and select the Start Windows Phone Performance Analysis option, and this time leave it on Execution. After running the tests there are no warnings, as shown in Figure 9-17.

Figure 9-17. *Performance analysis results for execution*

The UI is encapsulated within the view, so it takes a bit of orientation to understand how to navigate the Windows Phone Profiler. Notice the text Performance Warnings with the arrow to the right. Click on the arrow in the UI to bring up two menu items, titled Frames and CPU Usage, to allow deeper analysis when a warning is shown below in the issues section. You can select the issue and then explore the Performance Warnings menu to drill into the issue to see CPU Time, Frames, Function call tree, and other metrics to identify the problem.

Conclusion

In this chapter, we started off by adding the finishing touches to the 2D AlienShooter project, including support for loading and saving the game as well as support for tombstoning. We also added a basic particle system to the 2D AlienShooter project to have nice explosions when missiles strike enemy alien space ships. Next we converted the AlienShooter to a shared graphics rendering sample, including switching the HUD to Silverlight UI. I then covered some of the issues with this approach, such as the lack of `DrawableGameComponents` and how to work around it.

We switched gears and provided an introduction to 3D game development with extensive coverage of 3D game development concepts. We next moved on to two 3D game sample projects. The first sample demonstrated 3D concepts by rendering triangles to form a cube. The second sample rendered a 3D `Model` that also had a movable `Camera` controlled by the user via the `Accelerometer` sensor. The third 3D sample showed how easy it is to pull in the Camera sensor in a shared graphics application to render an object in 3D space in an augmented reality application.

Finally I covered the Windows Phone Profiler and game development. It is a critical tool to help you understand performance of your code. It also shows the benefits of reusing objects and thoughtful memory allocation to minimize garbage collection and high CPU managing memory.

CHAPTER 10

Building Top-Rated Applications for Windows Phone

In this chapter, I provide a summary of best practices that you should adopt in your Windows Phone applications. I've covered many topics along the way to help guide you on how to build Windows Phone applications. This chapter builds on the previous chapters, highlighting the critical points to help you maximize your opportunity on Windows Phone. The next few sections briefly touch on various topics to provide a quick reference as you consider how to proceed with developing your application through to publishing to AppHub.

I then cover Windows Phone OS 7.1 features that will differentiate your applications and improve your application ratings by end-users. Features like globalization, localization, live tiles, multi-tasking, and push notifications are features that I could have rolled into previous chapters, but I decided to save them for last. Many applications do not go the extra mile to add these features, providing you an opportunity to take your application to the next level. This chapter will help you get started.

Design First

I covered Expression Blend and design in Chapters 1 and 2, but there is much more on the topic that can fill many books by itself. As a developer, you should focus on information architecture, which I covered in Chapter 2. Laying out your screens and mapping the data to display will greatly save you from re-engineering work later.

Remember that a Panorama is not the application. It is the highlights—items like favorites, popular or trending topics, a menu, and content you want to put in front of the user right away. The Panorama is the magazine cover that makes you want to pick up the magazine and dive in more deeply. Keep the Panorama snappy, light, and beautiful.

If the latter is a difficult proposition, that is, if like me you are not artistic, check out the Internet for imagery you can purchase at a reasonable price. I did a quick search and found www.shutterstock.com with images at various price points but many other sites abound. It can make the difference.

For more on Window Phone and design, check out these great tutorials up on .toolbox:

www.microsoft.com/design/toolbox/school/tutorials.aspx

Use the Right Architecture

With Windows Phone 7.5 and Silverlight 4 compatibility, building applications with the right architecture becomes easier with full support for Commanding. I am not one to adopt architecture for its own sake by any means, and I would not make a recommendation to waste your time, but I have seen many developers fail the first time they build an XAML-based application because of a lack of understanding of MVVM and data binding.

With XAML-based development, understanding data binding through and through along with the Model-View-ViewModel architecture is critical. It is the way XAML is designed to work, leveraging data binding for everything from showing data, to determining state, as well as application execution flow. It is why I spend time on the topic in Chapters 2, 6, and 7. Keep researching, experimenting, and studying until MVVM feels as natural to you, as does coding in C#. To put it another way, you'll know MVVM when building applications using MVVM feels right and not like a chore.

Code for the Best User Experience

By coding for the best user experience, I am referring to the nonvisual aspects of user experience. Examples are to use the `Dispatcher` and `BackgroundWorker` classes to do work in the background, taking work off the UI thread. Both are covered in Chapter 2. Another example of coding for UX is to use the `PerformanceProgressBar` class to show activity as data loads.

A key topic in this area is state management through the Application Execution Life Cycle and Fast Application Switching, which I cover in Chapter 4. There are a few scenarios that most developers will need to handle as part of their Windows Phone application development related to tombstoning. However, many developers don't bother, because they either are intimidated by it or think it isn't a big deal. To end users, correctly handling tombstoning data *is* a big deal, and failure to do so may lead to poor end-user ratings.

In this section I cover three key tombstone scenarios that every developer needs to know:

- Panorama

- Pivot

- Listbox

In this section I don't cover how to handle the Application Execution Lifecycle Events in detail, because I covered the topic in Chapter 4 but as a quick refresher, there is an application-wide state dictionary and a page-specific state dictionary where you can save and load state:

- **Application-Wide State:** `PhoneApplicationService.Current.State`

- **Page-Specific State:** `PhoneAppilcationPage.State`

You save state in the `PhoneApplicationPage.OnNavigatedFrom` method and you restore state in the `PhoneApplicationPage.OnNavigatedTo` method.

In this section I focus on how to save and then reposition controls from a UX standpoint.

The code sample is TombstoneUX, which is part of the Chapter 10 solution. It contains four pages, one for each item listed above. Data bound to sample data, the sample demonstrates how to save and restore the UX state so that controls are repositioned.

Panorama Tombstone

For the Panorama control, it is a matter of restoring the position of the control to the PanoramaItem that the user was last viewing. So if the user was on the third Panorama item, visits the Start menu, tombstones, and then returns, the Panorama control should be restored back to the last PanoramaItem that was viewed, in this case the third. There is a SelectedIndex property that you can use to determine the current PanoramaItem in view. To position the Panorama, you set Panorama.DefaultItem to the desired PanoramaItem. Here is the code to save the Panorama position in the OnNavigatedFrom method:

```
protected override void OnNavigatedFrom(System.Windows.Navigation.NavigationEventArgs e)
{
  this.State["Pano"] = Panorama1.SelectedIndex;
  base.OnNavigatedFrom(e);
}
```

Here is the code to restore the position from the OnNavigatedTo method:

```
protected override void OnNavigatedTo(System.Windows.Navigation.NavigationEventArgs e)
{
  if (this.State.Keys.Contains("Pano"))
    Panorama1.DefaultItem = Panorama1.Items[(int)this.State["Pano"]];
  base.OnNavigatedTo(e);
}
```

Run the application, swipe over to a PanoramaItem, and click Start ➤ Back. You will land on the correct PanoramaItem. It is not very mysterious once you see how to handle tombstoning.

Pivot Tombstone

For the Pivot control, saving and restoring the position of the PivotItem in view of the user is aided by the Pivot.SelectedIndex property, which identifies the PivotItem in view. This greatly simplifies the code needed to save and restore the last PivotItem in view prior to tombstoning. Here is the code to save the position from the OnNavigatedFrom method:

```
protected override void OnNavigatedFrom(System.Windows.Navigation.NavigationEventArgs e)
{
  this.State["Pano"] = Pivot1.SelectedIndex;
  base.OnNavigatedFrom(e);
}
```

Here is the code to restore the position from the OnNavigatedTo method:

```
protected override void OnNavigatedTo(System.Windows.Navigation.NavigationEventArgs e)
{
  if (this.State.Keys.Contains("Pano"))
    Pivot1.SelectedIndex = (int)this.State["Pano"];
  base.OnNavigatedTo(e);
}
```

ListBox Tombstone

For the ListBox control, you may be tempted to use the SelectedIndex property, similar to what I just covered with the Pivot control. However, remember that selection in a ListBox is not really a behavior used in Windows Phone; tapping an item is the usual navigation method.

The ListBox requires a similar approach as with the Panorama, accessing the control tree to obtain the ScrollViewer's position to save and restore when tombstoned. Here is the code to save the position from the OnNavigatedFrom method:

```
protected override void OnNavigatedFrom(System.Windows.Navigation.NavigationEventArgs e)
{
  this.State["listBox1"] = ((ScrollViewer)VisualTreeHelper.GetChild(listBox1,
0)).VerticalOffset;
  base.OnNavigatedFrom(e);
}
```

Here is the code to restore the position from the OnNavigatedTo method:

```
protected override void OnNavigatedTo(System.Windows.Navigation.NavigationEventArgs e)
{
  if (this.State.Keys.Contains("listBox1"))
    ((ScrollViewer)VisualTreeHelper.GetChild(listBox1,
0)).ScrollToVerticalOffset((double)this.State["listBox1"]);
  base.OnNavigatedTo(e);
}
```

To test out tombstoning with the ListBox, I created some sample data so that we have something to scroll. Run the app, scroll down the list, and click Start ➤ Back. You should land back down the list where you had scrolled earlier.

Globalization and Localization

At launch, Windows Phone supported the English, French, Italian, and German languages, otherwise known as EFIGs. At Mobile World Congress 2011, Microsoft announced that more languages and markets would be added in 2011. Microsoft has added language support for the following: Brazilian, Portuguese, Chinese (simplified and traditional), Czech, Danish, Dutch, Finnish, Greek, Hungarian, Japanese, Korean, Norwegian, Polish, Portuguese, Russian, and Swedish.

To support East Asian languages, four new fonts have been added that support regular and bold style:

- **DengXian:** Simplified Chinese
- **Microsoft MHei:** Traditional Chinese
- **Yu Gothic:** Japanese
- **Microsoft NeoGothic:** Korean

In addition to rendering text, Windows Phone also supports new keyboard languages, including the following: Brazilian Portuguese, Czech, Danish, Dutch, Finnish, Greek, Hungarian, Indonesian, Japanese, Korean, Malaysian, Norwegian, Polish, Portuguese, Russian, Simplified Chinese, Swedish, Traditional Chinese, Turkish, and Ukrainian.

As an end-user, having an application render in your native language greatly enhances the appeal of the application when published to worldwide marketplaces. Globalizing and localizing your applications increases the usability of your application more than any other feature and will increase your potential market opportunity as well.

The Windows Phone Marketplace allows users to buy apps in the following 35 countries: Australia, Austria, Belgium, Brazil, Canada, Chile, Colombia, Czech Republic, Denmark, Finland, France, Germany, Greece, Hong Kong, Hungary, India, Ireland, Italy, Japan, Korea, Mexico, Netherlands, New Zealand, Norway, Poland, Portugal, Russia, Singapore, South Africa, Spain, Sweden, Switzerland, Taiwan, United Kingdom, and the United States.

■ **Tip** Even if you don't think you will localize your application, I recommend following the process anyway. Once you do decide to localize, it will be much easier to add multi-language support later.

There is money to be had taking the extra mile to at least globalize your application, but I recommend going all the way and localizing your application as much as possible when it makes sense. If you are building a game or application that can be fun and interesting in any language—go for it! Get in early and dominate, say, the Hungarian marketplace. As Windows Phone grows, especially with the recent announcements of two new devices by Nokia targeting the world, your market opportunity and potential profits can grow as well.

■ **Note** The .NET Framework has long supported globalization and localization, so if you are familiar with how these are handled in .NET, then you are already prepared to apply those skills to your Windows Phone application.

Globalization

Globalization is the process of adapting your application to the user's cultural and business environment. Displaying data such as date information and numbers in a way that is familiar to the user and correctly handling user input are two examples of globalization. This link to the MSDN documentation details supported culture codes, such as en-US for USA, formatting and sorting rules, and international phone features as background:

`http://msdn.microsoft.com/en-us/library/hh202918(v=VS.92).aspx`

In the next section I cover how to globalize an application written using the MVVM architecture.

Globalization Steps

Let's now go through the steps to globalize an application using MVVM. I've added a sample called `GlobalizedApp` to the Chapter 10 solution that is based on the MvvmLight (WP71) project template, where we will add globalization features first and then localization.

Remember that globalization is not necessarily about displaying application data in the local language. Rather, it is focused on displaying dates, currency, and calendar information in a format familiar to users.

A *culture code* is a group of settings that apply for a particular group of users based on language and country. A culture code consists of a double-quoted five-character string in the format of a two-letter language code, a dash, and a two-letter country code as described in the previous section.

The CultureInfo class represents a culture code and the related group of settings. Here is an example:

```
CultureInfo cultureInfo = new CultureInfo("fr-FR") ;
Thread.CurrentThread.CurrentCulture = cultureInfo;
```

When you set the culture on the thread, it makes the culture-specific settings available to your application, tailored for the current culture code. The user can also change the Display Language and Region Format for their device by going to Settings ➤ System ➤ Region+Language Option, so you should check the current Culture Info on the main thread upon launching your application so that you can tailor to the culture code automatically.

In the GlobalizedApp project, we update the IDataService to return a list of culture code values via a new method named GetCultureInfo. we also add two methods, SaveCultureSetting and LoadCultureSetting to persist the user's language selection. Listing 10-1 shows the updated DataService class that implements this interface.

Listing 10–1. *The Updated DataService class*

```
using System;
using System.Collections.Generic;
using System.IO.IsolatedStorage;

namespace GlobalizedApp.Model
{
  public class DataService : IDataService
  {
    IsolatedStorageSettings settings;

    public DataService()
    {
      settings = IsolatedStorageSettings.ApplicationSettings;
    }

    public void GetData(Action<DataItem, Exception> callback)
    {
      // Use this to connect to the actual data service

      var item = new DataItem("Welcome to Globalized App.");
      callback(item, null);
    }

    public void GetCultureOptions(Action<List<string>, Exception> callback)
    {
      List<string> cultureList = new List<string>(){
        "cs-CZ", "da-DK","nl-NL","en-GB","en-US","fi-FI",
        "fr-FR","de-DE","el-GR","hu-HU","it-IT", "ja-JP","ko-KR","nb-NO",
```

```
        "pl-PL","pt-BR","pt-PT","ru-RU","es-ES","sv-SE","zh-CN", "zh-TW"
      };
      callback(cultureList, null);
    }

    public void SaveCultureSetting(string cultureCode)
    {
      settings["cultureCode"] = cultureCode;
    }

    public string LoadCultureSetting()
    {
      string cultureCode = string.Empty;
      settings.TryGetValue<string>("cultureCode", out cultureCode);
      return cultureCode;
    }
  }
}
```

In the MainViewModel we add a set of properties that we will use to display data that changes based on the current culture code, named CurrentCulture, PurchaseDate, PurchaseAmount, and ShippingDate using the MVVMLight property code snippet. The CurrentCulture property represents the currently configured culture value. The other properties are fake properties just to show the culture-specific formatting. We also add a property to MainViewModel named CultureCodes listed here:

```
public const string CultureCodesPropertyName = "CultureCodes";
private List<string> _cultureCodes = null;
public List<string> CultureCodes
{
  get
  {
    return _cultureCodes;
  }

  set
  {
    if (_cultureCodes == value)
    {
      return;
    }

    _cultureCodes = value;
    _cultureCodes.Sort();
    RaisePropertyChanged(CultureCodesPropertyName);
  }
}
```

The CultureCodes property will be populated via the DataService.GetCultureOptions method. Note in the setter for the CultureCodes that we call the LINQ Sort method to put the values in alphabetical order, though given that this set of strings doesn't change much, we could have hard-coded the order in the DataService.GetCultureOptions method instead.

Add a folder named View to the project and add a new MvvmView project item named Settings.xaml and point the DataContext for the Settings.xaml page to the MainViewModel class.

Open the project in Blend and switch to the Data tab. Drag the CultureCodes collection from the Data tab onto the Settings.xaml page, and it adds a ListPicker to the page. The MainViewModel has two properties of interest for the Settings page. The first MainViewModel property of interest is CurrentCultureCode, which is the current Culture configured for the application, whether the default or by the user. The other property of interest is CultureCodes, which consists of the available culture codes on the platform.

The ListPicker.ItemsSource property data binds to the CultureCodes collection. This means that when the user taps on the value, it expands out to a full list of available options for easy selection. Where this gets interesting is that we also want the selected value to propagate back to the CurrentCultureCode property so that the MainViewModel can track the user's preferred culture.

The key step is to configure the ListPicker's SelectedItem property to have two-way data binding enabled and data bind it to the CurrentCultureCode property. So, when the user selects a new culture, it updates the SelectedItem property, which then updates the MainViewModel.CurrentCultureCode property. Here is the XAML for the ListPicker on the Settings page:

```
<toolkit:ListPicker ItemsSource="{Binding CultureCodes}"
  SelectedItem="{Binding CurrentCultureCode, Mode=TwoWay}"
  FullModeItemTemplate="{StaticResource CultureInfoDataTemplate}"/>
```

▓ **Tip** Remember that the default data binding is OneWay, so if you need to follow this pattern you must explicitly set TwoWay data binding when your application requires it.

Another feature of the Settings UI is that it displays a message to exit and reload the application to allow the language changes to take effect. The TextBlock that displays the message data binds its Visibility property to the MainViewModel.ShowCultureChangeMessage property of type bool. A simple converter named VisibilityConverter in the Converter folder converts between the Visibility and bool data types, making the TextBlock visible if true, and Collapsed if false. Figure 10-1 shows the Settings view.

Figure 10–1. *Settings View after a Language Change*

Now that we have our Settings UI working properly, let's wire up the MainViewModel to be culture-aware. We add a using System.Globalization statement to the top of the MainViewModel code file and declare a variable of type CultureInfo named cultureInfo. The CutureInfo type provides the formatting needed for dates, calendar, and currency based on the current culture. We use this class to properly format the MainViewModel property values for the current culture.

MainPage.xaml data binds to the MainViewModel class, displaying several MainViewModel properties as shown in Figure 10-2.

Figure 10–2. *MainPage.Xaml View in French Culture Info*

The emulator is configured for the French language and the locale of France. While the UI is not localized, the date of December 6 is displayed correctly for the French language. This was very easy to accomplish via data binding, with the ability to specify a `StringFormat` option for the `TextBlock` `Binding` object and `ValueStringFormat` for the `DatePicker` controls. This property allows you to specify a formatting string directly with the binding that automatically adjusts for the language. Here is the XAML for the "Long Date" DatePicker control:

```
<toolkit:DatePicker HorizontalAlignment="Left" Margin="110,178,0,0"
x:Name="datePicker1" VerticalAlignment="Top" Width="358"
Value="{Binding ShippingDate}" ValueStringFormat="{}{0:D}" />
```

The `ValueStringFormat` value is configured with a capital 'D,' which represents the long date format string formatter object. A capital 'C' `StringFormat` value represents a numerical value as Currency. A lower-case 'd' represents the short date format, and as you would guess, capital 'T' and lowercase 't' represent long and short time string formatting options.

The last bit of code to cover for the `GlobalizedApp` example is the `MainViewModel` `.CurrentCultureCode` property and the `MainViewModel` constructor. Here is the `CurrentCultureCode` property:

```
public string CurrentCultureCode
{
  get
```

```
  {
    return _currentCultureCode;
  }

  set
  {
    if (_currentCultureCode == value)
    {
      return;
    }

    _currentCultureCode = value;
    _dataService.SaveCultureSetting(_currentCultureCode);
    RaisePropertyChanged(CurrentCultureCodePropertyName);
    ShowCultureChangeMessage = true;
    //Update the current thread's culture
    cultureInfo = new CultureInfo(_currentCultureCode);
    Thread.CurrentThread.CurrentCulture = cultureInfo;
    Thread.CurrentThread.CurrentUICulture = cultureInfo;
  }
}
```

The CurrentCultureCode property setter persists the configured culture by calling the _dataService.SaveCultureSetting(currentCultureCode) method. This method is shown in Listing 10-1 earlier, persisting the value using the IsolatedStorageSettings.ApplicationSettings object. The rest of the property switches the culture code for the Thread.Current thread.

The MainViewModel constructor retrieves the CultureInfo setting from IsolatedStorageSettings.ApplicationSettings if present and configures Thread.Current to the user's chosen language and locale:

```
_dataService = dataService;
if (!this.IsInDesignMode)
{
  if (_dataService.LoadCultureSetting() != null)
  {
    cultureInfo = new CultureInfo(_dataService.LoadCultureSetting());
    Thread.CurrentThread.CurrentCulture = cultureInfo;
    Thread.CurrentThread.CurrentUICulture = cultureInfo;
  }
  else
  {
    cultureInfo = Thread.CurrentThread.CurrentCulture;
  }
  CurrentCultureCode = cultureInfo.Name;
}
```

The rest of the code in the MainViewModel constructor loads data values as shown in previous MVVM examples. Now that I have demonstrated how to globalize an application, let's take the next step and localize the app.

Localization

Localization always sounds harder than it is from a development perspective, but it is the process of adapting your application to a specific local market by having all of the text strings, the Application Bar, and the Application Title display in the local language.

Localization takes globalization to the next level. In addition to formatting dates, currency, and calendar info to the correct format, it also includes displaying application text in the local language based on the currently set culture code.

Background

The key to implementing localization is to build your application from the start with localization. It is certainly possible to add it later, but it will be worth the effort and save you time to do it from the start. The critical step is to separate resources, in this case the text string, from your code. Also, when building out a back-end Web API for your application, include a parameter for Culture Code such as en-US. While your application may only support en-US initially, designing for localization up-front will save you time in the long run so that your feeds are ready to provide information in multiple languages You'll just need change the culture code to the desired language.

■ **Tip** When building your user interface, allow for about 40% more characters to display in the visible space. Some languages, like German, can easily exceed space allocated for the same phase in English. The Windows Phone Metro Design Language encourages space, so take advantage of this design guidance for localization as well.

Be careful when parameterizing strings. Localize the entire string, not just the parameter. Also use numerical parameters, like "Each %1 %2" instead of "Each %s %s." This way the order is interchangeable depending each language's needs.

When you place strings in resource files, identify each string using a unique value, which will stay the same regardless of which language is selected. Translating strings correctly is probably the most challenging aspect unless you happen to be multilingual and have lived in each culture to know the nuances of the local language. You can edit the strings directly within Visual Studio by opening the resource files directly. Resource files are in XML format, so they can be more easily edited by nondevelopers.

For applications that have a large number of strings, there are localization tools available for .NET that can take the XML files and present them in a way for nondevelopers to more easily edit them. Another option is to use a localization vendor for applications that contain a large volume of strings in many different languages. This is the easiest but also the more costly option.

Localization Steps

In this section I cover the steps a developer takes to correctly localize an application. I've added a new sample to the Chapter 10 solution named LocalizedApp and copied over the contents of the GlobalizedApp project, fixing up the namespaces and title. This application will serve as the basis for the

LocalizedApp project. In the next two subsections I cover how to localize the application and then how to localize the application title.

App Localization

We first set the neutral language for the application assembly by right-clicking on the LocalizedApp project in the Solution Explorer and selecting Properties. On the Application tab, click the Assembly Info button as shown in Figure 10-3.

Figure 10–3. Configuring en-US as the neutral language for the project

We next need to add fr-FR as a supported culture in the project file by right-clicking the LocalizedApp project and selecting the Unload Project option. Next, right-click the unloaded project and select the Edit LocalizedApp.csproj menu option. Add fr-FR to the SupportedCultures element like this:

`<SupportedCultures>fr-FR</SupportedCultures>`

To add support for multiple cultures in the project file, separate the entries with a semicolon.

The next step is to create the resources themselves. Right-click the `LocalizedApp` project and select Add ➤ New Item to bring up the New Item dialog. Scroll down the list, select Resources File, and give it a name of `AppResources.resx`. Edit the strings for the application UI as shown in Figure 10-4.

Figure 10–4. Default UI Strings in AppResources.resx

I've also set the Access Modifier to Public for the resources as shown in Figure 10-4. Make a copy of `AppResources.resx` and rename the copy `AppResources.fr-FR.resx`, editing the strings using Bing Translator and a little experience with the French language. Figure 10-5 has the updated strings.

Figure 10–5. *Fr-FR UI strings in AppResources.fr-FR.resx*

We next add a new property to the MainViewModel, defined like this:

```
private AppResources _localizedResources = new AppResources();
public AppResources LocalizedResources
{
  get
  {
    return _localizedResources;
  }
}
```

This property creates an instance of the currently loaded resource strings. Next we bind the various TextBlock labels using Expression Blend. Here is an example for the Welcome Message Textblock:

```
<TextBlock Text="{Binding LocalizedResources.WelcomeMessage, Mode=OneWay}"
Style="{StaticResource PhoneTextNormalStyle}" FontSize="40" TextWrapping="Wrap"
TextAlignment="Left" Width="436" Margin="12,0,12,422" />
```

The individual text strings are accessible for data binding via the LocalizedResources properties,— LocalizedResources.LongDate, LocalizedResources.ShortDate, and so on. While it is a bit of extra typing, having all of the resource strings hang off of one property does not clutter up the MainViewModel. Figure 10-6 shows the results when you run the application in the emulator configured for the French language.

Figure 10–6. *Globalized and localized application UI*

Localize the Application Title

The next item to cover is how to localize the application title. To get started, I've added a new project to the Chapter 10 Solution named AppResLib, of type Win32 Project under the Other Languages\Visual C++ folder. In the Project Wizard, click Next to get to the Application Settings step. Choose DLL and check Empty Project, and then click Finish.

■ **Tip** if you don't have access to Visual Studio with C++, check out this blog post for a sample tool to help localize the application title: http://patrickgetzmann.wordpress.com/wp7-localize/

Once the project is added to the Chapter 10 solution, right-click on the AppResLib project and select Properties. Expand the Configuration Properties ➤ Linker ➤ Advanced. For the No Entry Point option, choose Yes /NOENTRY. We are creating a native resource library that contains resource strings for the application Title and Tile Title.

Expand the AppResLib project, right-click the Resource Files folder, select Add, and then choose "Resource" When the Add Resource dialog appears, double-click String Table to create the strings. Figure 10-7 shows how they should look.

Figure 10–7. Native string table configured for French

I created the English version first, compiled the DLL and then copied the DLL, named AppResLib.dll, to the LocalizedApp project folder. This native DLL represents the application Title and Tile Title properties for the neutral language. I then edited the Caption values shown in Figure 10-7 to reflect the French version and compiled the DLL again but this time I renamed it AppResLib.dll.040c.mui for the French version.

■ **Tip** The release and debug folders containing AppResLib.dll are at the same folder level as all of the other folders, so don't be alarmed if you dig into the AppResLib project folder and don't see the DLL file. Instead, navigate one folder up from the AppResLib project folder to find the output folders containing the DLL.

Each language has a unique file name appended to AppResLib.dll. In this case, .040c.mui is appended for the French version. Table 10-1 shows the correct filenames for other languages.

Table 10–1. Native DLL Name for Language-Specific Resources

File	Code	Language
AppResLib.dll.0c0a.mui	3082	Spanish – Spain (Modern Sort)
AppResLib.dll.040B.mui	1035	Finnish
AppResLib.dll.040c.mui	1036	French – France

AppResLib.dll.040E.mui	1038	Hungarian
AppResLib.dll.041D.mui	1053	Swedish
AppResLib.dll.0404.mui	1028	Chinese – Taiwan
AppResLib.dll.0405.mui	1029	Czech
AppResLib.dll.0406.mui	1030	Danish
AppResLib.dll.0407.mui	1031	German – Germany
AppResLib.dll.0408.mui	1032	Greek
AppResLib.dll.0409.mui	1033	English – United States
AppResLib.dll.0410.mui	1040	Italian – Italy
AppResLib.dll.0411.mui	1041	Japanese
AppResLib.dll.0412.mui	1042	Korean
AppResLib.dll.0413.mui	1043	Dutch – Netherlands
AppResLib.dll.0414.mui	1044	Norwegian (Bokmål)
AppResLib.dll.0415.mui	1045	Polish
AppResLib.dll.0416.mui	1046	Portuguese – Brazil
AppResLib.dll.0419.mui	1049	Russian
AppResLib.dll.0804.mui	2052	Chinese – People's Republic of China
AppResLib.dll.0809.mui	2057	English – United Kingdom
AppResLib.dll.0816.mui	2070	Portuguese – Portugal

Go back to the LocalizedApp project, click the button to view hidden files, and add the AppResLib.dll and AppResLib.dll.040c.mui to the project. Make sure that both native DLLs are configured as content in the LocalizedApp project.

The final step is to edit the WMAppManifest.xml file for the LocalizedApp project to obtain the application title and tile title from the native DLL resources. At the top of WMAppManifest.xml, change the <App> <Title> property to this value:

```
Title="@AppResLib.dll, -100"
```

Toward the bottom of the WMMAppManifest.xml file under <Tokens> | <PrimaryToken> | <TemplateType5> <Title> change the value of the Title element to this:

```
<Title>@AppResLib.dll, -200</Title>
```

When you run the application in the emulator and switch between English and French, the application Title and Tile Title switch over as well. Figure 10-8 shows the App Title and Tile Title for French.

Figure 10–8. Localized Application Title and Tile Title for French

This concludes coverage of globalization and localization of Windows Phone applications. Neither is very difficult once you see it demonstrated. Both globalization and localization fit nicely with MVVM and the built-in data binding support, simplifying the effort needed to bring your application to new markets.

Right-to-Left Flow Direction

One topic I should touch on is support for languages that do not flow left-to-right. You can now set the direction of content and layout of each control to flow from right to left. This enables you to develop Windows Phone applications in languages such as Hebrew and Arabic. You set the flow direction via the FlowDirection property on the UI controls.

Live Tiles API

A tile is a link to an application pinned to the Start menu. When you first use a Windows Phone, you see a bunch of tiles pinned to the Start menu. Windows Phone users have an option of pinning additional applications to the Start menu, as well as rearranging how tiles appear. Windows Phone users LOVE live tiles because they present useful information at a glance.

Tile Update Details

Previously with Windows Phone 7, developers could update live tiles via Microsoft Push Notifications Services (MPNS) or via the ShellTileSchedule pull subscription. MPNS allowed developers to update the Application Tile title, background image, and count. ShellTileSchedule allows developers to update the Background image only. Both of these topics are covered later in the chapter, but Windows Phone 7.5 greatly enhances what developers can do when updating tiles.

▪ **Note** The ShellTileSchedule API has not changed much. However, MPNS has been greatly enhanced to take advantage of Windows Phone OS 7.1 features available in Windows Phone 7.5. Both are covered below.

Windows Phone OS 7.1 adds support for Secondary Tiles in addition to the Application Tile. When a user pins an application to the Start menu, it is the Application Tile. From within the application, developers can give the user the ability to pin a Secondary Tile to the Start menu. While the Application Tile always launches a new instance of the application landing on its primary or home screen, a Secondary Tile can have a "deep link" that the app can process and navigate to a specific screen designated by the application developer.

Windows Phone OS 7.1 improvements offer many customizations to Live Tiles, allowing developers to provide a more tailored experience. Developers can update both the front and back of the tile. The Windows Phone OS 7.1 provides a nice "Tile flip" animation to allow the user to see the front and back of the tile without any additional work on your part, though the animation cannot be customized.

On the front-side of the tile you can update the tile title, background image, and count. On the back-side of the tile, developers can update the tile title, background image, and content. Figure 10-9 shows the available customizations.

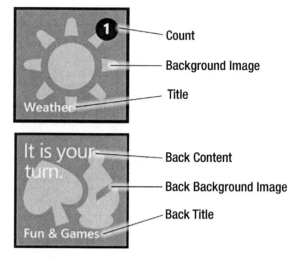

Figure 10–9. Available tile customizations

The top image in Figure 10-9 shows an example front side of a tile. The Title font-size cannot be changed and the text does not wrap, fitting about 15 characters across. The Count can have any value between 1 and 99. A value of zero causes the Count to not show. The BackgroundImage points to an image; details are provided below.

The bottom image in Figure 10-9 shows an example back side of a tile. The Back Title does not word wrap and can display about 15 characters like the Front Title. The Back Background image has the same specs as the front-side Background image, detailed in the next subsection. The BackContent is unique to the back of the tile and can hold approximately 40 characters of text before truncating.

Tile Images

Tile images are a great part of the Live Tile experience for consumers. Tile images can be either .jpg or .png files. If the image is a .png and thus has transparency, the theme color will show through, for an interesting effect. Tiles are 173 × 173 pixels in size. If the image is a different size it will be stretched.

You can retrieve images from a remote server, but the image size must be less than 80 KB or they will not be downloaded. Windows Phone expects tile images to download in 30 seconds or less. If the BackgroundImage or BackBackgroundImage images do not download (because the image is either too large or takes too long to download), none of the other properties will be set on the tile.

■ **Caution** HTTPS cannot be used to download remote images for tiles.

An important consideration for Secondary Tiles is that when creating a Secondary Tile the BackgroundImage and BackBackgroundImage images must be created using a local resource initially. Updates to the Secondary and Application Tile can be done using a local or remote image resource. Local resources can come from the XAP package or from isolated storage. If the URI references an image

603

in isolated storage, the image must be stored in the Shared\ShellContext folder so that the operating system can grab the image.

Coding with Tiles

The relevant API when working with Tiles is the ShellTile API. The ShellTile API allows you to create, delete and update Secondary Tiles. The Primary Tile can only be pinned or removed by the user, but you can use the ShellTile API to update the Application Tile.

To get started, I've created a new project named ShellTileAPISample in the Chapter 10 solution. MainPage.xaml is configured with a short menu, containing one option to update the Application Tile and the other to work with a Secondary Tile. Clicking one of the TextBlock controls navigates to a page in the pages folder, either AppTile.xaml or SecondaryTile.xaml depending on which one you tap.

Application Tile

The AppTile.xaml page allows the user to update the Application Tile (Primary Tile) properties described in the previous section and illustrated in Figure 10-9. Figure 10-10 shows the AppTile.xaml UI in the emulator.

Figure 10–10. *Application Tile update UI*

Update any one of the properties and tap the checkmark in the Application Bar to update the
Application Tile (primary tile). The Application Tile is always the first tile, so this line of code obtains a
reference to the Application Tile, even if not pinned:

```
ShellTile TileToFind = ShellTile.ActiveTiles.First();
```

For any of the data, setting it to an empty string (or zero for count) will clear the property. This code
in AppTile.xaml.cs updates the Application Tile based on the entered data:

```
StandardTileData NewTileData = new StandardTileData
{
  Title = textBoxTitle.Text,
  BackgroundImage = new Uri(textBoxBackgroundImage.Text, UriKind.Relative),
  Count = newCount,
  BackTitle = textBoxBackTitle.Text,
  BackBackgroundImage = new Uri(textBoxBackBackgroundImage.Text, UriKind.Relative),
  BackContent = textBoxBackContent.Text
};
ApplicationTile.Update(NewTileData);
```

That's it for the Application Tile. The Secondary Tile is similar except that it can include a deep link.

Secondary Tiles

The SecondaryTile.xaml page allows the user to create and delete Secondary Tiles as well as update the
properties described in the previous section and illustrated in Figure 10-9. Figure 10-11 shows the
SecondaryTile.xaml UI in the emulator.

Figure 10–11. Secondary Tile update UI

In SecondaryTile.xaml, the OnNavigatedTo override finds the Secondary Tile based on the deep link URI defined by the NavigationUri property. This line of code attempts to find the Secondary Tile:

```
ShellTile SecondaryTile = ShellTile.ActiveTiles.FirstOrDefault(x =>
x.NavigationUri.ToString().Contains("TileKeyData=FromTile"));
```

If the tile is pinned, a reference will be found. The OnNavigatedTo method also checks to see if the QueryString contains the TileKeyData key. If it does, it means that the page was launched from the Secondary Tile:

```
if (NavigationContext.QueryString.ContainsKey("TileKeyData"))
  DeepLinkDataText.Text = this.NavigationContext.QueryString["TileKeyData"];
```

The checkBoxDisplaySecondaryTile_Checked creates the Secondary Tile when checked and deletes the Secondary Tile when unchecked. Note that adding a tile requires that the code be executed within a user-initiated event such as clicking a Button or checking a CheckBox control. Updating and deleting Secondary Tiles can occur on a non-UI initiated event or background process.

While AppTile.xaml.cs updated the Application Tile in one event handler shown above, SecondaryTile.xaml.cs allows you to update individual items on the Secondary Tile. Each event handler is similar to the following, which updates the Count property for the Secondary Tile:

```
private void buttonSetCount_Click(object sender, RoutedEventArgs e)
{
  ShellTile SecondaryTile = ShellTile.ActiveTiles.FirstOrDefault(
    x => x.NavigationUri.ToString().Contains("TileKeyData=FromTile"));
  if (SecondaryTile != null)
  {
    int newCount = 0;
    if (textBoxCount.Text != "")
    {
      newCount = int.Parse(textBoxCount.Text);
    }

    StandardTileData UpdatedTileData = new StandardTileData
    {
      Count = newCount
    };

    SecondaryTile.Update(UpdatedTileData);
  }
}
```

The rest of the event handlers in SecondaryTIle.xaml.cs are similar to this one. As you can see, working with tiles is straightforward and flexible.

Multi-Tasking and Background Processing

In this section I cover the new background processing capabilities introduced in Windows Phone OS 7.1. The Scheduled Tasks and Background Agent APIs allow you to execute application code in the background, even when the application is not running. Leveraging background processing enables your application to do several things to delight users:

- Build more responsive applications in certain scenarios; for example, you can improve load time by updating cached data in the background and loading from cache first.

- Update Live Tiles so that the content remains interesting to users.

- Provide deeper phone integration such as with the Background Audio Agent and integration with the volume control.

Microsoft sat down with developers and asked them to provide feedback on the types of background processing they needed. The product team took the feedback and boiled it down to key scenarios that maximize usefulness to developers without sacrificing performance and battery life for end-users. In the next section I cover the various capabilities available to developers.

Background agent development is straightforward and well-documented on MSDN. This section provides an overview, as I would be remiss if I didn't cover the topic. The subsections point to relevant links into the MSDN documentation so that you can pull down the sample and quickly get started.

Agents

Each application can have one background agent. The agent can be registered as a `PeriodicTask`, a `ResourceIntensiveTask`, or as both types of tasks. An application's Agent runs on a schedule, based on what type of Task is registered, which we cover in a bit, but only one instance of an agent runs at a time.

The base class for an Agent is `BackgroundAgent`. When the agent is launched, the OS calls the OnInvoke method. In this method, the application determines which type of ScheduledTask it is running as and it executes under the constraints for that type of Scheduled Task.

When the Agent completes execution, it calls the `NotifyComplete` or `Abort` event to notify the OS that it has completed. Calling `NotifyComplete` indicates success while calling Abort indicates failure to perform the task. Calling Abort sets `IsScheduled` to false. When the application is launched it can check the `IsScheduled` property to determine whether `Abort` was called.

Types of Scheduled Tasks

While Scheduled Tasks and Background Agents allow an application to execute code in the background even when the application is not running, Windows Phone does not support unconstrained background processing to optimize for performance and battery, learning many valuable lessons from Windows Mobile.

There are several different types of Scheduled Tasks, optimized for different scenarios with different behaviors and constraints. The variability is around scheduling and duration for Scheduled Tasks, described here:

- **PeriodicTask:** Periodic agents run for small amounts of time on a regularly recurring interval. Scenarios include location upload and performing small amounts of data synchronization.

- **ResourceIntensiveTask:** Resource-intensive agents run for a fairly long period of time if the phone meets a certain set of requirements for processor activity, power source, and network connections. This scenario is focused on synchronizing large amounts of data when the device is not actively being used by the user and the phone is plugged in.

Constraints for All Scheduled Tasks

There are a few constraints to understand when working with Scheduled Tasks. Studying the constraints will save you a lot of confusion when something isn't working.

There is a list of unsupported APIs that you cannot call from a Scheduled Task. Calling these APIs will result in an exception and may cause the application to fail certification. The Marketplace Test Kit can help you detect if your Agent is calling unsupported APIs. This link details the unsupported APIs:

`http://msdn.microsoft.com/en-us/library/hh202962(v=VS.92).aspx`

Both PeriodicTask and ResourceIntensiveTask agents cannot use any more than 6 MB of memory. Audio Agents are restricted to 15MB. Agents that exceed these memory limits are terminated.

Your application's Agent expires after two weeks if the user does not launch your application within two weeks since last run. You set the `ExpirationTime` property on the Agent to set it to expire, but again, it cannot be any more than two weeks.

■ **Tip** Any time your application runs, update the schedule for your application's Agent out two more weeks to ensure that the background agent is not removed by the Windows Phone OS 7.1.

Finally, if your agent fails to run successfully two consecutive times due to exceeding the memory quota or any other unhandled exception, the Agent becomes unscheduled. The application can reschedule the Agent when it is run in the foreground.

Periodic Task Constraints

PeriodicTask Agents run every 30 minutes on average, but the time can be anywhere from 20 to 40 minutes as the operating system optimizes execution for battery life. An Agent running as a PeriodicTask can run for 25 seconds, though it could be terminated due to memory limits, and so on.

Windows Phone 7.5 has a Battery Saver option that the user can enable in low battery conditions. A PeriodicTask may not run if battery Saver mode is enabled. This is a good thing for the end-user experience when users are most likely optimizing how they use their phone and not running many applications in low battery mode.

There is another battery-related constraint in that there is a hard limit on the number of PeriodicTask Agents. On some devices it can be as low as six Agents. There is a warning related to this limit where Windows Phone will tell the user that they have multiple background agents running. Also, a user can go to Settings, swipe over to Applications, and select Background Tasks to see a list of applications with background agents available.

Resource Intensive Task Constraints

ResourceIntensiveTask Agents require that the phone is plugged in to a power source to run and the phone must be on a WiFi or Ethernet connection through the PC. The power-level of the phone must be greater than 90% and the device screen must be locked.

ResourceIntensiveTask Agents also do not run if there is an active phone call. If the Agent tries to make a Socket call using the AssociateToNetworkInterface API and force the connection over either MobileBroadbandGSM or MobileBroadbandCDMA network, the call will fail.

One thing to note, if the user unplugs the phone while a ResourceIntensiveTask Agent is running, it is terminated immediately. Also, your ResourceIntensiveTask may never run if the user does not have a WiFi connection when it is being charged up, so you should not rely on this functionality for critical application functions.

Coding with Periodic Agents

Start by creating a new project named PeriodicAgent using the "Windows Phone Scheduled Task Agent" project template in the Chapter 10 solution. This creates the Background Agent. We also need to create a Windows Phone Application to manage the Background Agent. I've added a new Windows Phone project named PeriodicAgentApp to the Chapter 10 solution, which is the application that manages the Background Agent.

Each application can have only one `ScheduledTaskAgent` registered at a time. So as a developer you can create a single background agent instance and register it in `WMAppManifest.xml`. The following example XML registers a background agent:

```
<Tasks>
  <DefaultTask Name="_default" NavigationPage="MainPage.xaml" />
  <ExtendedTask Name="BackgroundTask">
    <BackgroundServiceAgent Specifier="ScheduledTaskAgent" Name="LiveTilesAgent"
Source="LiveTilesAgent" Type="LiveTilesAgent.ScheduledAgent" />
  </ExtendedTask>
</Tasks>
```

You can schedule this background agent as both a resource-intensive agent and a periodic agent. When you call the scheduling APIs from your application, it infers that the background agent you want to schedule is the agent registered in `WMAppManifest.xml` as shown above.

If your application uses both a `ResourceIntensiveTask` and a `PeriodicTask`, you can check the type of the `ScheduledTask` object that is passed into the `OnInvoke` method to determine for which task the agent is being invoked and branch your code execution as necessary.

For a coding sample, please check-out the MSDN sample here:

`http://go.microsoft.com/fwlink/?LinkId=219088`

This code registers both a Periodic and Resource-intensive agent and can serve as a template for your own applications. There isn't much beyond what is in the documentation to cover regarding Background Agent implementation.

Background File Transfer Service

The `BackgroundTransferService` class can transfer, both upload and download, data between your application and the Internet in the background. Transfer requests are created and configured using the `BackgroundTransferService` class.

Each application can have up to five requests queued at any given time. Adding an additional transfer request will result in an exception. Note that you must remove requests manually after they are completed.

To demonstrate how to work with the Background File Transfer Service, check out the MSDN documentation sample available here:

`http://go.microsoft.com/fwlink/?LinkId=219083`

The sample shows you how to use the Background Transfer Service to schedule and manage background file transfers and is based on this walkthrough: How to: Implement Background File Transfers for Windows Phone.

`http://msdn.microsoft.com/en-us/library/hh202959(v=VS.92).aspx`

Background Audio

Beginning in Windows Phone OS 7.1, developers can write applications that play audio even when an application is not running. Audio will play under lock screen where the user can control the audio playback using the Universal Volume Control (UVC), having the same experience as the built-in audio player.

All media on Windows Phone is played through the Zune Media Queue. Background Audio applications send commands to the Zune Media Queue to set the current track as well as play, pause, fast forward, and rewind the audio. This is done via the BackgroundAudioPlayer class with the Instance object communicating with the Zune Media Queue to manage audio playback.

■ **Tip** Check out this link that details the supported media codecs on Windows Phone:

http://msdn.microsoft.com/en-us/library/ff462087(v=VS.92).aspx

---

Mentioned above, the UVC is the built-in audio UI available in the lock screen when audio is playing. The UVC also controls the Zune Media Queue. Your application manages the playlist, while the user can use the UVC to manage playback for seamless integration with Windows Phone.

There are two methods available to play Audio available to developers, the AudioPlayerAgent, and the AudioStreamingAgent, which are covered next.

AudioPlayerAgent

The AudioPlayerAgent allows you to manage a playlist by passing a URI containing the address of the audio file to the Zune Media Queue to set the current track. The URI can be local or remote. To implement a playlist application, your project should contain a Windows Phone application and another project based on the "Windows Phone Audio Playback Agent" project template, which includes a class that inherits from AudioPlayerAgent.

At runtime, the AudioPlayerAgent class implementation runs in the background and makes calls into the BackgroundAudioPlayer, which interfaces with the Zune Media Queue to play the audio. When the playlist completes, call the NotifyComplete event so that the OS can safely shut down the AudioPlayerAgent. For more information on building an Audio playlist application, please check out the source code at this link:

http://msdn.microsoft.com/en-us/library/ff431744(v=VS.92).aspx

AudioStreamingAgent

The other mechanism available to developers to create a background audio application is via the AudioStreamingAgent class. You implement all of the same pieces of the Playlist Application as well as the AudioStreamingAgent, which inherits from MediaStreamSource covered in Chapter 7. For more information on building an Audio streaming application, please check-out the source code at this link:

http://msdn.microsoft.com/en-us/library/ff431744(v=VS.92).aspx

Microsoft Push Notification Services

In this section we cover how Microsoft push notifications work, when to use notifications, and how to add push notifications to your application. First we start with an overview of how Microsoft push notifications work.

Microsoft Push Notification Services (MPNS) provides a facility to connect your Windows Phone application to the server without requiring continuous polling by the application. Polling works and is functional, but if an application is continuously polling and the server response is "nothing to download," the application is potentially consuming battery without any user benefit.

■ **Note** Push notifications are not a new concept in the industry. Other platforms include push notification services as well.

Another challenge with polling is that Windows Phone does not support multitasking for third-party applications running on the device. Therefore, for an application to poll for data it must remain in the foreground as the active application. While not letting any third-party application drain the battery by polling for data in the background helps to enhance the end-user experience, applications still need to be able to react to application data and status changes even when not running.

Raw Push Notification Description

Microsoft Push Notification Services raw push notifications send the actual data to the application but only if the application is running in the foreground. You can use raw notifications in addition to tile and toast notifications to send information directly to your application. It can be up to 1kb in size. The idea is to send a toast that something has happened and then send a raw notification to the application so that it can display the corresponding data when the application is launched.

Toast Push Notification Description

Microsoft Push Notification Services allows an application to receive notifications that data has been updated or application status has changed even when the application is not running. When a toast notification is received, the user receives a "toast," which is a little pop-up across the top of the screen that the user can click on, resulting in launching your application. Figure 10–12 shows a sample toast notification from the MSDN documentation.

Figure 10–12. Example toast notification

The toast notification is system-generated. It displays over any application running, whether the Start screen or running application. If the application that expects to receive the notification is running, the toast notification is not displayed, but because the application is already running, the application simply processes and displays the data directly.

An important user experience consideration is to use toast notifications sparingly and with flexible configuration settings to help the user tune which notifications they are interested in receiving. The reason is that toast notifications are disruptive, appearing over any running application, even an action game.

■ **Note** First-party applications such as the phone dialer and other built-in applications can multitask with a running third-party application, as well as with other first-party applications.

Tile Notification

Another type of notification is a tile notification, which updates the application tile if, and only if, the user decided to pin your application's tile to the Windows Phone Start screen. Tile notifications can consist of a value for the tile Title value, a Count value (between 1 and 99), as well as a 173 × 173 background image for the tile. There are not any additional customizations available but with a little bit of server-side work your application can dynamically generate custom images for the tile background, which we cover later in the chapter.

How Microsoft Push Notifications Work

For MPNS to work by sending important data to the user's phone, there must be some sort of server-side component to the Windows Phone application receiving the notification. Essentially, MPNS is a proxy between the server-side component of your solution and the Windows Phone application component. Figure 10–13 provides a graphical representation of how MPNS works.

Figure 10–13. *Microsoft Push Notification Services process flow*

The user via their Windows Phone initiates the request to MPNS, which receives the request and passes a URI back to the application. The application then passes the URI to the server-side application component along with information on which notifications the user would like to receive, such as scores for their favorite sports team.

The server-side component now has all the information it needs, the "address" to send the notification to via MPNS as well as the criteria the user has chosen for what notifications the user would like to receive.

Getting Started with Push Notifications

Note from Figure 10–13 that there is a server-side component that you must create in order to support push notifications. The server-side component performs the following two primary tasks:

- Receive registration requests and subscription criteria (for example, send me a notification for breaking news regarding my favorite sports team) from the Windows Phone application.

- Perform subscription matching and then send push notification requests to MPNS.

http://msdn.microsoft.com/en-us/library/ff402537(v=VS.92).aspx

Also, there is a full set of Windows Phone labs including labs on push notifications available here:

www.microsoft.com/downloads/en/details.aspx?displaylang=en&FamilyID=ca23285f-bab8-47fa-b364-11553e076a9a

For this section, I want to focus on the Windows Push Notification Server Side Helper Library created by the Microsoft evangelism team to assist developers quickly implement push notification services. The library supports sending all three push notification messages available, specifically Raw, Tile, and Toast. The library abstracts out the complexity of implementing push notifications to just a few lines of code for your application.

To get started, obtain a copy of the Push Notification Server Side Helper for WP7 "Recipe" from this link:

http://create.msdn.com/en-us/education/catalog/article/pnhelp-wp7

The sample code included with the download provides a very powerful example of how to work with the library. It includes a "server" application as a Windows Presentation Foundation client. A real application could be a Windows Service or similar construct on other platforms.

What's great about the sample is that it demonstrates a dialog between the client and the server. For example, the client keeps the server aware of whether the user has pinned the Application Tile. Once the user has pinned the tile, the server-side application is made aware and prepares to send tile updates. Even just switching tabs on the server-side WPF application results in UI updates via RAW notifications on the Windows Phone application. Run the sample to see it in action.

For a more simplified view of Microsoft Push Notification Services, especially if your server-side code is not based on ASP.NET, check out these three samples in the MSDN Documentation:

- Tile Notification Sample: http://go.microsoft.com/fwlink/?LinkId=219079

- Toast Notification Sample: http://go.microsoft.com/fwlink/?LinkId=219080

- Raw Notification Sample: http://go.microsoft.com/fwlink/?LinkId=219081

All the samples include a simple ASP.NET project that demonstrates the message format, which could easily be ported to another back-end technology such as JSP, PHP, and so on.

Updating Application Tile via Web URI Subscription

Microsoft has done research that indicates end-users like applications that support the Live Tiles feature. It promotes "at a glance" information delivery, such as when the Outlook tile indicates the number of unread messages. As mentioned in the previous section, Microsoft Push Notification Services provides fine-grained control over tile updates for maximum personalization.

There are situations where an ISV develops an application that doesn't need full push notification functionality but the ISV would still like to support tile updates. Windows Phone provides a client-side pull API that allows an application to update its pinned tile on a predefined basis of every hour, every day, or every week. No other update schedule is available. Delivery times will vary within the specified schedule; this means that if an application registers for a tile update on a daily basis, the tile update can happen at any time within that time period. Still, this can provide a simple way to add a Live Tile to an application.

The API that provides this functionality is the Microsoft.Phone.Shell.ShellTileSchedule API, which takes a URI to a web service or image located on a web site as well as an interval setting. Listing 6–15 shows the code.

Listing 6–15. ShellTileNotificationSample MainPage.xaml.cs

```
using System;
using Microsoft.Phone.Controls;
using Microsoft.Phone.Shell;

namespace ShellTileNotificationSample
{
  public partial class MainPage : PhoneApplicationPage
  {
    // Constructor
    public MainPage()
    {
      InitializeComponent();
    }
    //store as global variable so that the schedule
    //can be Started and Stopped.
    private ShellTileSchedule shellTileSchedule;
    private void StartShellTileAppBarBtn_Click(object sender, EventArgs e)
    {
      StartShellTileSchedule();
    }

    private void StartShellTileSchedule()
    {
      shellTileSchedule = new ShellTileSchedule();
      shellTileSchedule.Recurrence = UpdateRecurrence.Interval;
      shellTileSchedule.Interval = UpdateInterval.EveryHour;
      shellTileSchedule.StartTime = DateTime.Now;
      shellTileSchedule.RemoteImageUri =
        new Uri(@"http://apress.com/resource/bookcover/9781430232193?size=medium");
      shellTileSchedule.Start();
    }

    private void StopShellTileAppBarBtn_Click(object sender, EventArgs e)
    {
      if (shellTileSchedule != null)
        shellTileSchedule.Stop();
    }
  }
}
```

Create a private variable for the ShellTileSchedule instance so that you can stop it at a later time if the user decides for some reason to turn off Live Tile updates. In this example, two Application Bar buttons, titled start and stop, control the schedule. Once the tile is pinned it can take up the full interval time before it is updated.

Tile updates do not occur if the phone is in an idle state, meaning the screen is off or the lock screen is visible. As soon as the screen is on and unlocked, the tile will update. Figure 10–14 shows the updated tile.

Figure 10–14. *Live tile update*

The image at the URI must be less than 80KB in size with a maximum download time of 15 seconds. If the API cannot download the image within 15 seconds three consecutive times the schedule will be removed.

You can have more than one ShellTileSchedule available in your application, although only one schedule can be active at a time. As an example, let's say you are building an application that provides news coverage for all 32 NFL football teams. You could create 32 URIs that are updated with team-specific content and present a menu to the user that says something like "which team would you like to get live tile updates for?" Once the user selects a team, your app creates the corresponding ShellTileSchedule to that team's URI, and voila! Customized live tile updates with just a few lines of code.

Conclusion

In this chapter I've covered some of the key features that can set your application apart as a top application such as live tiles, background processing, and push notifications. By now you should have a deep understanding of Windows Phone development to tackle these technologies head on.

I've also covered globalization and localization of Windows Phone applications. The samples leverage MVVM in order to demonstrate how localization and globalization fit within this architecture. Once you've gone through these sections, there is no reason not to build applications for the world and expand your market potential.

Index

▓ H

CPSIA information can be obtained at www.ICGtesting.com
Printed in the USA
LVOW050227231211

260829LV00005B/3/P